Individuals and Families
IN A DIVERSE SOCIETY

Senior Author

Maureen Holloway
Social and Global Studies Department Head,
David and Mary Thomson Collegiate Institute
Scarborough, Ontario

Authors

Garth Holloway
Program Team Leader, Social and Global Studies Department,
Earl Haig Secondary School
Toronto, Ontario

Jane Witte
Independent Educational Consultant,
Innerkip, Ontario

Justice Marvin A. Zuker
Ontario Family Court Judge and Associate Professor at OISE
Toronto, Ontario

Toronto Montréal Boston, MA Burr Ridge, IL Dubuque, IA Madison, WI
New York San Francisco St. Louis Bangkok Beijing Bogotá Caracas
Kuala Lumpur Lisbon London Madrid Mexico City Milan New Delhi
Santiago Seoul Singapore Sydney Taipei

McGraw-Hill
Ryerson Limited

A Subsidiary of The **McGraw·Hill** Companies

COPIES OF THIS BOOK
MAY BE OBTAINED BY
CONTACTING:

McGraw-Hill Ryerson Ltd.

WEB SITE:
http://www.mcgrawhill.ca

E-MAIL:
orders@mcgrawhill.ca

TOLL-FREE FAX:
1-800-463-5885

TOLL-FREE CALL:
1-800-565-5758

OR BY MAILING YOUR ORDER TO:
McGraw-Hill Ryerson Ltd.
Order Department
300 Water Street,
Whitby Ontario, L1N 9B6

Please quote the ISBN and
title when placing your order.

Individuals and Families in a Diverse Society

Statistics Canada information is used with the permission of the Minister of Industry, as Minister responsible for Statistics Canada. Information on the availability of the wide range of data from Statistics Canada can be obtained from Statistics Canada's Regional Offices, its World Wide Web site at http://www.statcan.ca, and its toll-free access number 1-800-263-1136.

ISBN: 0-07-090958-X
ISBN-13: 978-0-07-090958-8

http://www.mcgrawhill.ca

5 6 7 8 9 10   TRI   10 9 8 7 6

Printed and bound in Canada

National Library of Canada Cataloguing in Publication

Main entry under title:

 Individuals and families in a diverse society / authors, Maureen Holloway ... [et al.].

Includes index.

For use in grade 12.
ISBN 0-07-090958-X

 1. Family. 2. Marriage. I. Holloway, Maureen

HQ734.I52 2002 306.8 C2002-901691-6

PUBLISHER: Patty Pappas
EDITORIAL DIRECTOR: Melanie Myers
DEVELOPMENTAL EDITOR: Jocelyn Wilson
SUPERVISING EDITOR: Cathy Deak
COPY EDITOR: Kathy Evans
PRODUCTION CO-ORDINATOR: Kelly Selleck
PERMISSIONS EDITOR: Terri Rothman
EDITORIAL ASSISTANT: Erin Parton
INTERIOR/COVER DESIGN: Dave Murphy/ArtPlus Limited
ELECTRONIC PAGE MAKE-UP: Alicia Countryman/ArtPlus Limited
ILLUSTRATIONS: Vesna Krstanovich/ArtPlus Limited

Reviewers

Patricia Cibinal
Fort William Collegiate Institute
Lakehead District School Board

Cheryl Devitt
Crestwood Secondary School
Kawartha Pine Ridge District
School Board

Janet Dryden
Adam Scott Collegiate and
Vocational Institute
Kawartha Pine Ridge District
School Board

Nancy Fitzpatrick
R.S. McLaughlin Collegiate
and Vocational Institute
Durham District School Board

Yvonne Howard
North Park Secondary School
Peel District School Board

Helen Kerr
Oakridge Secondary School
Thames Valley District School
Board

Maria McLellan
Iroquois Ridge High School
Halton District School Board

Nancy Pinder
Eastview Secondary School
Simcoe District #17

Suzanne Robertson
Holy Name of Mary
Secondary School
Dufferin Peel Catholic District
School Board

Family Studies Advisory Group

Patricia Andres
Eden High School
Niagara District School
Board

Penny Ballagh
Ontario Institute for Studies
in Education
University of Toronto

Janet Dryden
Adam Scott Collegiate and
Vocational Institute
Kawartha Pine Ridge District
School Board

Ann Harrison
Social Sciences and Humanities
Toronto District School Board

Maureen Holloway
David and Mary Thompson
Collegiate Institute
Toronto District School Board

Maria McLellan
Iroquois Ridge High School
Halton District School Board

Michelyn Putignano
Delta Secondary School
Hamilton District School Board

Karen Wilson
Westdale Secondary School
Hamilton District School Board

Justice Marvin A. Zuker
Ontario Family Court Judge
and Associate Professor at
Ontario Institute for Studies
in Education

Advisory Group

Jennifer Borda
Appleby College
Oakville Ontario

Colleen Chandler
Mother Teresa Catholic
Secondary School
Toronto Catholic District
School Board

Ilan Danjoux
Markham District High School
York Region District School
Board

Contents

A Tour of Your Textbook

Welcome to *Individuals and Families in a Diverse Society*. This textbook provides you with a solid background in Family Studies. Unit 1 serves as an introduction, including the history of the family in Chapter 1, and, in Chapter 2, the basic theoretical perspectives and developmental theories that will be applied throughout the text. It also provides a guide to conducting research in the social sciences, which you can refer to when completing activities at the end of each chapter.

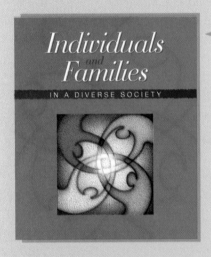

Cover

- Illustrates the central idea of this text and course—that all individuals are unique, but they are connected to families and are also part of local and global communities.

Unit Opener

- **Unit Expectations:** outline the goals of the unit. They are taken from the curriculum guideline for the course and identify what content will be covered in order to fulfill these expectations.

- **Mini Table of Contents:** lists the chapters in the unit.

- A **photograph** that captures the essence of the unit is featured.

- An **Overview** summarizes the unit content and highlights key information.

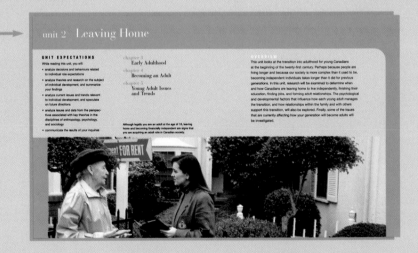

Chapter Opener

- **Chapter Expectations** are your learning goals and include the curriculum expectations covered by the chapter content.

- **Key Terms** lists the words used in the chapter that will become part of your social sciences vocabulary.

- **Research Skills** identify the aspects of research that will be developed in the chapter.

- A **photograph** captures the main theme of the chapter.

- **Chapter Introduction** outlines the content that is explored within the chapter.

Review and Apply

At the end of each chapter are a number of activities that allow you to:

- review chapter content

- perform interviews and conduct surveys and research studies

- research and compile your findings into summaries, abstracts, reports, essays, articles, and/or case studies

DESIGNED AND WRITTEN TO MAKE FAMILY STUDIES UNDERSTANDABLE AND INTERESTING FOR TODAY'S YOUNG PEOPLE

Individuals and Families in a Diverse Society has a number of features that will highlight the content, make family studies relevant to you, and provide interesting and sometimes challenging viewpoints on topics under study.

Abstracts and Research Studies

- Provide you with examples of actual research studies written on a topic under study in the chapter. They are presented in the appropriate format, which you can use as a guide for your own writing.

Developing Your Research Skills

- Will help you to develop inquiry skills, such as formulating questions, developing hypotheses, and designing questionnaires, and research skills, such as using abstracts and citations, selecting reliable academic sources, and evaluating information.

In Focus

- Provide current perspectives on major topics, or highlight the life of a prominent social scientist who has conducted research on the topic under study.

Point of View

- Offer current, and sometimes controversial, perspectives to provide you with alternative ways of looking at a topical issue.

Case Studies

- Provide real-life examples of changes and challenges for various family members of a sample family during different stages of life. In Chapter 1, you are introduced to this sample family, and are given a genogram, to which you can refer as you study this family.

Legal Matters

- Offer legal perspectives and facts about law for some of the definitions or issues studied in the chapter. This feature covers such things as young people's legal rights, marriage and property, divorce, custody and support, violence, and wills.

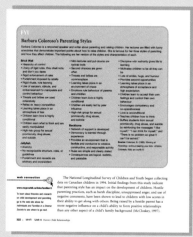

FYI

- Offers interesting information on a topic related to the content under study and appears where relevant.

Web Connections

- Pertinent web sites are provided in every chapter for your use in researching topics under study. These sites can be accessed through the McGraw-Hill Ryerson web site for *Individuals and Families in a Diverse Society* and will be monitored and updated as necessary.

Quotations

- Will appear in the margins of each chapter to provide you with alternative perspectives on the subject matter under study.

unit 1   All in the Family

UNIT EXPECTATIONS

While reading this unit, you will:

- analyze changes that have occurred in family structure and function throughout the history of the family

- use appropriate social science research methods in the investigation of issues affecting individuals and families in a diverse society

- access, analyze, and evaluate information, including opinions, research evidence, and theories, related to individuals and families in a diverse society

- analyze issues and data from the perspectives associated with key theories in the disciplines of anthropology, psychology, and sociology

- communicate the results of your inquiries

Although the form and function of the family have changed throughout time, the family continues to be an important institution in every society in the world.

OVERVIEW

This unit establishes the framework for the study of individuals and families in Canada's diverse society. The purposes of families within all societies will be explained first, and the diversity of families and the roles of individuals within their families throughout history will be described next. Since this is an interdisciplinary and research-based study, the unit presents various theoretical perspectives from which individual and family behaviour can be viewed. Finally, the social science research methods that can be used in the study will be described.

chapter 1

Family Matters

CHAPTER EXPECTATIONS

While reading this chapter, you will:

- explain changing family forms and functions in various societies throughout history, and describe contemporary family forms
- analyze factors influencing the transition of the family from an economic unit to a psychological unit

CHAPTER INTRODUCTION

In this chapter, the rationale for the study of individuals and families in Canada will be determined, by examining the interdependence of individuals, families, and society. What families are and why they exist will be explained, and the evolution of families throughout history will be summarized. A better understanding of the relationships among individuals, families, and societies, and the diversity of families, might enable individuals and families to make wiser choices and enable governments and organizations to make better decisions regarding the social policies in Canada.

Most young Canadians expect to have a family some day. However, with all the changes in family structure that they have observed, they may be unsure about what kind of family it will be.

Connecting Individuals, Families, and Society

I n all societies, individuals live in families. You were likely born and raised in a family, as were your ancestors. When you reach maturity you will probably leave your family and may form a new family and raise children. This cycle of human life has continued for tens of thousands of years and likely will continue in the future. Societies expect the cycle of family life to continue, and in Canada the pattern still applies to most people. However, the choices you make, alone or in collaboration with others, will determine the course of your life. Therefore, to understand families in a diverse society such as Canada's, it is necessary also to understand individuals.

No society can survive unless certain basic functions are carried out. Social scientists call these basic functions **functional requisites** because they are required for a society to work. Individuals are motivated to carry out these functions due to their membership in a smaller group of people, such as a family or household, with whom they share a commitment to co-operate in order to survive. Because of this commitment, families supervise the behaviour of individuals in ways that other institutions cannot. In turn, societies support individuals by providing for the functions of families through such institutions as government, education, and health care. Half a century ago, American sociologist William Goode summarized the important role families play in linking individuals to their societies. His explanation is as valid now as it was then, and will probably be valid in the future.

> It is *through the family* that the society is able to elicit from the *individual* his necessary contribution. The family, in turn, can continue to exist only if it is supported by the larger society. If the society as a larger social system furnishes the family, as a smaller social system, the conditions necessary for its survival, these two types of systems must be interrelated in many important ways (Goode, 1964, p. 3).

Defining the Family

Sound research begins with a definition of terms, so *family* will be defined first. Definitions of family reflect both the *actual* nature of families that exist within the culture and the *desirable* nature of families as described in the social policies of that culture. However, should any single definition become a prescription for what families should be or a standard for evaluating whether the families that people form are "real" families? Individuals define family on the basis of their own personal experience and expectations of what family means to them. For example, in the 1920s, Mrs. Donald Shaw, in a letter explaining why she wanted to adopt an orphan from the Halifax explosion, wrote that the primary role of families is to produce and raise children, that couples should have children, and that a couple without children is not a family (Morton, 1999). Mrs. Shaw obviously had a clear idea of what a family was, but others might not agree. Perhaps you have your own opinion about it.

What definition could you use to determine whether this group of people is a family?

The criteria used in any definition are arbitrary and reflect the purpose of the definition. Definitions of family are used in social policy to determine, for example, who qualifies for the benefits of families, such as who is eligible for orthodontic work under family dental benefits, or who should be responsible for the obligations of families, such as support of children. A definition of family is effective if you can use it to discriminate effectively between families and other groups in a way that suits your purpose for having a definition.

In the social sciences, definitions of family have evolved to reflect our understanding of human society. Anthropologists have provided extensive descriptions of many societies and the ways they have organized themselves to survive and thrive. They have also identified certain basic and universal **functions** as prerequisites for the survival of any society. Each society assigns these functions to individuals or groups to perform. The set of functions that families perform *could* be separated and assigned to various groups in society, but they never have been by any known society (Goode, 1964). Therefore, this set of functions is identified as the universal functions of the family, and anthropologists call the group of people who performs these functional requisites a family.

Sociologists define the family using a variety of criteria. Some definitions are based on who is related to whom. A broad definition was given in 1980 by

web connection

www.mcgrawhill.ca/links/families12

To learn about research on the
family and demographics on the
Canadian family, go to the web site
above for *Individuals and Families
in a Diverse Society* to see where
to go next.

Canadian sociologist Emily Nett, who suggested that a family is "any group of people considered to be related to each other by blood or marriage" (Baker, 1993, p. 4). In a narrower sense, Statistics Canada defines a family as a unit consisting of a married couple living with or without never-married children, or a single parent living with never-married children. This definition, based on residence, is useful for ensuring that each person is only counted once on Census Day in Canada. It reflects the common concept of family as a man-woman-child unit, but it does not include relatives who do not live together. Statistics Canada uses the term **household** for other groups of people who live together, whether or not they are related by birth, adoption, or marriage. None of these definitions consider the behaviour of family members, as anthropologists' definitions do.

A Working Definition of Family

Currently popular are definitions of family based on what they are rather than who comprises them. These definitions are more useful for those who are interested in what families do and how they do it. They reflect a desire to include groups that do not fit the traditional man-woman-child model and a return to the definition that has been used by anthropologists. They are most suited to the study of the interrelationships of individuals and families in this text. The Vanier Institute of the Family, a Canadian organization founded in 1965 to conduct research on the family, uses this broader definition to reflect the diversity of families in Canada:

> Family is defined as any combination of two or more persons who are bound together over time by ties of mutual consent, birth, and/or adoption/placement and who, together, assume responsibilities for variant combinations of some of the following:

- physical maintenance and care of group members;
- addition of new members through procreation or adoption;
- socialization of children;
- social control of members;
- production, consumption, and distribution of goods and services;
- affective nurturance—love.

(The Vanier Institute of the Family, 1994, p. 10)

by Justice Marvin Zuker

Family The legal vision of the family today is one of an important personal and social resource and advantage, whose existence should be fostered and protected. It is a unit of emotional and financial dependency, whether it includes single parents with children, gay or lesbian partners, or unmarried couples. Any legal exclusion for this socially and legally sanctioned state violates human dignity.

The family has taken on a much more public dimension, as legal issues frequently relate to public matters, such as access to benefits, pension benefits, leave policies, and so on.

Extended family While the law has traditionally treated stepfathers as legal strangers and parenthood as an all-or-nothing concept, today courts recognize multiple parents and grandparents and the importance of the children's interest in maintaining family relationships with those who have played significant roles in their lives.

Nuclear family For all practical purposes, the nuclear family and its traditions as people knew them no longer exist to the extent that they used to. Today individuals are dealing with the legal rights of stepparents, grandparents, "persons acting as parents," and so on. It may be that parenthood, rather than marriage, is the central legal issue in family law. However, marriages still remain a cultural symbol of commitment. To some, marriage is important primarily because it is the setting in which most children are raised.

Technological family New technologies make it possible to conceive a baby without having sex. However, evidence suggests that technology itself has played no substantial role in expanding the range of family forms. Families have changed over the past 50 years, but the changes are social, not technological. ■

The Functions of the Family

When social scientists study individuals and families, they examine how persons are organized into families, the specific behaviours family members use to perform their roles within society, and how society motivates individuals and families to carry out these responsibilities. Based on a review of the anthropological research on functional requisites, Shirley Zimmerman, professor of Family Social Science at the University of Minnesota (1988), summarized these basic and universal functions of the family:

1. Families are responsible for the addition of new members through reproduction. A society must maintain a stable population to survive. Population growth provides a competitive advantage that usually enables a society to become wealthier.

2. Families provide physical care for their members, including the adults, their children, and the dependent elderly members. When families are unable to care for their members, hardship will result unless the society is organized to replace the family in this function.

3. Families **socialize** children by teaching them the skills, knowledge, values, and attitudes of their society. Children who learn these are able to work and relate to others within appropriate adult roles.

4. Families are responsible for controlling the behaviour of their members to maintain order within the family and within the society in which they live. Families monitor and evaluate the behaviour of individuals and provide feedback. This social control contributes to the socialization process and protects the reputation of all individuals identified with the family group within the society.

5. Families maintain morale and motivate individuals to participate in society. The commitment to the family may be based on a spiritual sense of duty, or economic necessity. Here in Canada, people assume that **affective nurturance**—that is, meeting the emotional needs of individuals—is the foundation of our commitment to each other. Participation in appropriate social roles contributes to the health of the society as well as providing the means with which families care for their members.

In the modern family, the socialization and discipline of children usually occurs within close, affectionate relationships between parents and children.

6. Finally, families perform the economic function of producing and consuming goods and services. At one time, each family produced all the goods and services it consumed, and used only what it could produce. Now, individuals sell their time and their skills by producing goods and services within a specialized economy, and earn an income with which to purchase goods and services for their families (In Schlesinger, 1998).

In summary, families serve six specific functions that enable societies to survive and to thrive. These six functions, which can be observed in families in all human societies, form a useful framework for comparing the behaviours of families. The formation and organization of family units, how families perform these functions, and how society motivates families have changed throughout history and still vary today. From time to time, attempts have been made to assign some of these functions to other institutions in society, or to create different groups, such as communes, to accept the responsibility. For example, in the early Israeli kibbutzim, children were raised communally in age groups. However, the experiments failed because parents preferred to raise their children in their own homes. As anthropologist Margaret Mead concluded, "No matter how many communes anybody invents, the family always creeps back."

The Family in History

From the time of Canada's Aboriginal Peoples' early ancestors, different cultural groups in Canada have organized their family structures in a variety of ways, influenced by such factors as religious belief, economic activity, geographic location, and relations with other ethnic and cultural groups. However, over time, the modern **nuclear family** form has emerged as more or less the norm in Canada and in most other parts of the world. In this form, the husband and wife live with their children and place more importance on the marital relationship than on relationships with their parents and relatives. Canadian sociologist John F. Conway (1997) suggests using this analogy for putting the change in perspective of time: if the history of the human species is divided into a 24-hour period, the emergence of the modern industrial family form occurred incredibly recently—in fact, only two minutes ago! So, what about the family in the other 23 hours and 58 minutes?

The Origin of the Family

Where and how the human family emerged has been the subject of anthropological speculation and research for the past hundred years. It will never be known for certain where, when, why, and how the human family system originated, since it occurred long before the advent of written history. People can make speculations about the emergence of the human family by studying the fossil evidence that has been uncovered by archaeologists. People can learn from the research of physical anthropologists like Jane Goodall, who have provided us with detailed observations of the living arrangements and social behaviour of other primates. Most useful is the research of cultural anthropologists who have studied isolated human groups that have not been influenced by other human societies prior to those studies. As a result of this research, many theories have been developed to explain the origin of the human family unit and the development of human civilization.

The first grouping of humans into family units may have occurred because of a unique human characteristic—our large brains relative to our body size. It distinguishes us from other animal species and enables us to think, to problem-solve, to use language as a means of communication, to invent, and to feel emotions. So human infants, like other primates, are born with

FYI

The Etymology of *Family*

Etymology is the history of the formation or derivation of a word. The use of the word *family* in the modern context is relatively new. In fact, prior to three hundred years ago, there was no word in any European language that meant a living arrangement based on parents and children living together. The English word *family* is derived from the Latin word *familia*, which was derived from a word that meant *house*. The word *familia* was used to indicate the people who lived in the same house or household, including the slaves and servants and those members of the family that are considered part of the family unit in Canada today. The wife and biological children were undifferentiated from the slaves and servants, perhaps because they also served the master! (Campbell, 1992)

Primate Versus Early Human Social Organization

There is little evidence from either primate researchers like Jane Goodall or from cultural anthropologists of the past hundred years to suggest that non-human primate social organization today is the same as that of the first family structures of our human ancestors. Similar to humans, infants of other primates are dependent on their mothers for a long period of time and live in what can be called troops, with a complex social organization. However, non-human primates do not regulate sexual activity nor do they, as a rule, co-operate in systematic food sharing. There is a vast difference between the social organization of the earliest human societies and that of primates today. Thus, understanding the social life of other primates can provide only a small part of our understanding of the social organization of our earliest human ancestors (Conway, 1997).

large heads to hold their large brains and are helpless and completely dependent on others for at least the first four or five years of life. Thus, it can be argued that humans would not have survived as a species unless some form of family grouping developed to provide the extensive care, protection, and socialization required for our young.

The first family groupings of humans may have been **hordes** or bands much like the troops of our present primate relatives (Conway, 1997). These hordes probably consisted of a loose grouping of males and females and their offspring. They may have had some characteristics in common with the social organization of the chimpanzee group at Gombe, Uganda, studied for more than 40 years by Jane Goodall. However, unlike our primate cousins, our ancestors developed taboos against certain kinds of aggression and sexual activity to ensure the relative peace and co-operation necessary for the survival of the horde. A system of social organization based on kinship had to replace a social hierarchy based on the size and strength of the dominant male. Thus, "the seeds of the human family were thereby sown: the suppression of sexuality within the group, controls on sexual gratification, the prescription to go outside the immediate group for sexual partners, and the subordination of the sexual and aggressive instincts to the tasks of survival and civilization" (Conway, 1997, p. 5).

It is quite likely that the earliest human family form was a kind of group marriage within the horde, in which informal pairing occurred for various lengths of time on the basis of convenience. A simple division of labour probably existed, loosely based on gender and age. Survival of the horde or band was dependent on successful hunting and gathering. The economic activities of the members were based on mutual co-operation. Men and women were likely dependent on one another and of similar status, as the food-gathering activities of the women and children were as essential to survival as the hunting activities of the men (Conway, 1997).

The Hunter-Gatherers

The invention of the family was an innovation of our ancestors that distinguished us as a species from all other primates and ensured our ultimate survival. "With the family came a division of labour, food-sharing, long-term relationships of reciprocity and obligation, the regulation of sexual activity, harmony and co-operation, elaborate kinship relationships binding disparate groups together, and the assurance (more or less) of survival for all members of the family group from birth to death" (Conway, 1997, p. 7).

The earliest human families were hunter-gatherers. It is estimated that for 99 percent of human history, hunting and gathering was the major means of subsistence for our ancestors. Driven by a daily quest for food, both men and women worked full time in search of it (Mandell, 1995). Women were responsible for gathering fruits, nuts, grains, herbs, and small prey. They were also responsible for nurturing young children. In addition, women learned how to use the plants they gathered for medicinal purposes. Men were the hunters and the toolmakers. They often had to leave the family for long periods of time to hunt. They had to pursue larger animals for days to tire the animal, for an easier capture and kill. After a successful hunt, hunter-gatherers ate meat only. In today's hunter-gatherer societies, the women routinely supply two-thirds or more the calories consumed by the group (Kelman, 1998). Because of this and because of their role as childbearers, women in these societies were essential to survival and therefore had relatively high status within the group.

Evidence of descent systems would suggest that an informal group marriage was most prevalent in these societies. Essentially the family consisted of a group of parents and their children (Engels, 1972). This continued as the dominant family system until the development of agriculture. Fifteen thousand years ago, a significant fraction of hunter-gatherer societies were stationary (Diamond, 1999). This probably developed as hunter-gatherer communities were able to stay in one location for long periods of time because of a sustainable and abundant food source nearby, such as a river where they could fish. There was a trend toward couples marrying in stable hunter-gatherer societies so that a man could help to support his own children until they became self-sufficient,

Today, people are able to speculate about the lives of prehistoric families based on the observations of present-day hunter-gatherer people.

The hunter-gatherer lifestyle of the Urueu-Wau-Wau was undisturbed until the development of the interior of Brazil.

The Urueu-Wau-Wau people live in the central highlands of Brazil and are one of several tribes in this region that still live as hunter-gatherers. Their contact with industrialized society occurred when a *National Geographic* researcher made contact with them in 1986. Subsequently, due to the new interest in them, a road was built across part of their land, and it threatened their traditional lifestyle. As a result of both national and international lobbying, the Brazilian government declared their territory off limits to outsiders in order to protect their traditional way of life. Occasionally, rubber tappers who venture into their territory are killed by the poison-tipped arrows of the Urueu-Wau-Wau hunters, who suffer no consequences under Brazilian law.

Members of the tribe do not wear clothes, but use haircuts, tattoos, and makeup to decorate their bodies and to indicate their individual status in the society. They live in small villages of large woven-straw huts surrounding a central meeting place. Among the

Urueu-Wau-Wau, the roles of the men, women, and children are clearly defined and are taught by the community elders, who are of the highest status. The men and women tend to form couples, although strict monogamy is not enforced. The entire community raises the children. As soon as the children are old enough, they perform traditional roles according to their gender. Adolescence as it is known in Canada does not exist in Urueu-Wau-Wau society.

The rainforest environment is essential to their way of life. Women forage and gather food in the surrounding forests, prepare the food, maintain the home, and care for the children of the village. Men make the bows and the poison-tipped arrows that they use for hunting. When they hunt, the men leave the community for days at a time. The entire village celebrates their return with ritual dancing and a large communal feast.

The Urueu-Wau-Wau community has become a living museum of the hunter-gatherer existence, as it has been protected by the Brazilian government from encroachment by outsiders such as international lumbering and drug companies who have an interest in the economic assets of the rainforest in which they live (McIntyre, 1988). ■

---

1. Should the few remaining hunter-gatherer societies in the world today be protected from modern society as the Urueu-Wau-Wau have been?

at about five years of age. Consequently, the men would have figured more in the lives of the children of the group as they started to spend time with individual females. Out of this grew a new social role for men: that of a father to specific children (Kelman, 1998). In effect, a new social role for the family developed: the couple.

The first Canadians, the Aboriginal Peoples, were hunter-gatherers when they came here to stay 13 000–14 000 years ago. Some of them remained hunter-gatherers even into modern times as they continued to forage for food instead of developing agricultural production (Diamond, 1999). Although they became very ethnically diverse as they adapted to quite different physical environments, these hunter-gatherers for the most part lived in small nomadic groups. These bands consisted typically of 5 to 80 people who were related by **consanguinity**, meaning by blood, or by informal relationships that today would be termed "marriage." Bands had no defined hierarchy since they were socially stratified only by gender and age. They were equal in their decision making in that leadership was not inherited but was acquired through personal qualities, such as strength and intelligence. Conflict resolution tended to be informal, since bands lacked formal rules and laws.

Agricultural Families

The earliest known occurrence of agriculture occurred about 11 000 years ago in the Fertile Crescent area of Southwest Asia. Farming developed independently in four other parts of the world: in China by about 7500 B.C.E., in Mesoamerica and South America by 3500 B.C.E., and in the eastern region of North America by 2500 B.C.E. (Diamond, 1999). The change from hunter-gatherer to agricultural societies and the spread of agriculture to other parts of the world changed the fundamental structure of families. Once our ancestors domesticated animals and grew plants for food, their daily quest for it was eliminated, and they were able to live in more permanent settlements. Thus, agricultural communities formed, resembling the agricultural societies that exist throughout the developing world today.

Agriculture ultimately enabled our ancestors to provide much more food, but it also required a great deal of manual labour. These two factors resulted in larger families, because more people were needed to work the land and tend the animals. A family could also acquire more land and become wealthier as a result. Food surpluses also enabled the development of towns and cities and the emergence of new roles, both in the family and in society at large. Once the concept of private property developed, land had to be defended and food surpluses had to be controlled and distributed. Thus, men who chose not to be farmers became artisans, builders, merchants, soldiers, and politicians. Women's economic activity shifted away from the community and became more focused on the increasingly private family household. Women cared for the children and handled domestic work, along with toiling in the family fields.

Families were now highly organized. **Monogamy**, or having one marital partner, became the preferred marital arrangement for women in most parts of the world. Men established a **patriarchy**, in which men were the rulers and decision makers of the family, in an attempt to ensure their fatherhood and the orderly inheritance of their property (Conway, 1997). It was during this period that the relationship between men and women changed, and women became chattels, the property of their husbands, with few legal rights. When agriculture became established, an individual farmer could afford to support several wives, so **polygamy** became more common. **Arranged marriages** with young women ensured that the family would produce more children, who were now viewed as an economic asset because they could work on the land. Since a family needed land for agriculture, young adults continued to live in their parents' household after they married, forming **extended families** that in most areas of the world were patriarchal. As families expanded and acquired more land, or kept larger numbers of animals, they lived in **clans** of many related extended families.

Pre-Industrial Families

Although the majority of people continued to live on family farms, the rapid population increase that an agricultural economy allowed resulted, over a thousand years, in the growth of villages and towns. Commerce, technology, and crafts developed. Merchants and artisans began to work in the family home where their wives and children could help with the work. Today, this economic activity is called *cottage industry*. Families, led by a father who was the head of the household, consisted of his wife and children plus any domestic servants and male apprentices—young men from other families who were learning a trade or craft. These kinds of family enterprises were less able than farms were to sustain a large number of people, so pre-industrial couples were usually monogamous and had fewer children than agricultural families. They continued the tradition of being predominantly patriarchal in their organization.

Until recently, marriage was an economic necessity, not an expression of a couple's love for each other.

European settlers who came to Canada beginning in the seventeenth century brought this pre-industrial family system with them. Government officials, military personnel, merchants, and craftspeople tended to live in villages and towns, but the majority of settlers spread out across the countryside and lived in self-sufficient and sometimes isolated homesteads. Like their European counterparts, these new Canadians had monogamous marriages and most often lived with their extended family. Although not unheard of, romantic love was not usually the basis for marriage. It was an economic necessity for both men and women in the 1600s and 1700s because there was no work for single women and no housekeepers for single men. Life was hard, and there was endless work for everyone.

Children were an economic necessity during a time when less than 50 percent of them reached adulthood. Childhood as a period of innocence and play did not exist. By the age of seven or eight they began to assist in the economic activities of the family, generally in work dictated by their gender. Young adults often left home to live and work in other families. Boys would work on a farm or become an apprentice in a trade or craft. Girls would do household work or labour as domestic servants for other families. Young people married later since their isolated existence often made finding a suitable partner difficult.

Men and women usually worked side by side as they cleared the land and farmed or as they attempted to establish a business. Agricultural and commercial endeavours were family affairs. In the early years of European colonization in Canada, married women enjoyed a relatively high status both because of a shortage of marriageable women and because of their essential economic role. However, once the population grew and stabilized, their roles became more rigidly defined. Men were dominant in public community life, and women were expected to confine their activities to the family household. Because married women and their children were considered the property of their husbands, men could discipline them harshly. Family life could often be violent for women and children, who had little legal protection. Women who physically defended themselves against domestic assault were harshly punished by the legal system, through imprisonment (Mandell, 1995).

Early Canadians had larger families to ensure enough manual labour for clearing the land, planting, and harvesting.

Urban Industrial Families

Like the agricultural revolution, the industrial revolution heralded unprecedented change in the human family system, particularly in the status and roles of women and children. As the economy shifted from one based on agriculture and commerce to one based on factory production in towns and cities, work became something done outside the family home to earn a wage to provide for the family's subsistence. The family unit retained its economic role as a consumer but lost its role as a producer (Conway, 1997). This caused changes in the family system and the development of a new industrial working class, as every family member, including children, began to work in a wage-based labour force in the new factories.

The flexibility of the family as a social institution is apparent in the way it adjusted once again to the new economic reality, and as a new version called the **industrial nuclear family** emerged. In this family, the notion of motherhood as the "sacred" and primary role of women became, if not the norm, then the ideal. Women were nurturers who worked at home and were supported financially by their husbands. Men were money-earners who worked to provide for their wives and children. The role of children changed as well. There was no longer a need for children to work in factories. Compulsory education was instituted in 1871 in Ontario for children under the age of 14 years and in 1905 in all provinces except Québec. Child labour laws were eventually passed in the mid-1880s. It was at this point in our history that the idealized notion of childhood as an "age of innocence" was born. The home was no longer the centre of economic activity, but a place of love and emotional contentment. However, working-class children often left school as soon as they could in order to find work to contribute money to their families. At this time, young people married early and moved away from their parents because they were able to support themselves (Conway, 1997).

After industrialization became established, childhood became an "age of innocence," when children were allowed to play and learn, protected from the harsher reality of the adult world.

For many Canadians in the nineteenth century, this vision of the family was their ideal, but not necessarily their reality. Working-class women and children often had to work in factories along with their husbands and fathers. By the late 1800s, however, the industrial nuclear family was the norm for most Canadians. By the beginning of the twentieth century, it was unusual for married Canadian women to work outside the home. About 5 percent of married Canadian women did so, usually because of economic necessity caused by desertion or widowhood. Women who worked for a wage were believed to threaten the role of men as the sole providers and therefore were demeaned by the general society. Consequently, women workers routinely received one-third less than the "family wage" earned by men for the same work (Mandell, 1995).

In the early twentieth century, the size of families became smaller as birth rates declined. Canadians delayed marriage until they could afford a separate household. More importantly, if there was a good chance that all children would survive, and if they could not work and had to be supported until they finished school, fewer children were wanted. Increasingly, the Canadian family became a **consumer family**. The husband was the exclusive provider, the head of the household, and the link between the family and society. The wife was the homemaker for whom new products were manufactured to assist her in creating a comfortable home for her husband and children.

The roles of men, women, and children changed to reflect the changing perceptions of their natures. A woman's role was to be wife, mother, and housekeeper for the family. Women were thought to be gentler, more patient, and more loving than men, and therefore more suited to the emotional nurturing of children. This mystique of motherhood implied that women reached their potential only if they had children. Men were perceived to possess characteristics like aggressiveness, perseverance, and toughness that made them more suited to the workplace than women were perceived to be. The father, as head of the household, was expected to fund the family, make its most important decisions, and sometimes discipline the children (Mandell, 1995). Children were expected to play under the supervision of their mothers, to attend school, and to remain protected from the hard work of the adult world. Adolescence became a distinct age group because of the extension of schooling into the teen years.

The new medium of television and shows such as *Father Knows Best*, pictured here, supported the ideal of the consumer family in the mid-twentieth century.

By the 1940s and 1950s, Canadians expected and wanted to live as industrial nuclear families. American television programs such as *Leave It to Beaver, The Adventures of Ozzie and Harriet,* and *Father Knows Best* depicted this family organization and were immensely popular in Canada (Conway, 1997). These television programs reflected what was happening in Canadian society during the "baby boom" years from 1946 to 1967. After World War II, the Canadian economy expanded rapidly, and Canadians knew that they could afford to have larger families. Statistics show that Canadian women in that time period averaged four children each (Foot, 1996).

For thousands of years, humans have been fascinated by their personal family histories. In the past, these histories were passed on from one generation to the next through tribal or family storytellers who were, perhaps, the first historians. This interest in family history, or genealogy, has continued to the present day. Most people have some idea who their ancestors were at least two or three generations ago. Some can trace their heritage back even further. Like their ancient ancestors, people have listened to stories of older relatives to understand their roots. Recently, the use of the Internet has made it much easier to trace family lineage through many excellent web sites for genealogical research.

All known societies developed descent patterns, with about 64 percent giving preference to one side of the family or the other in tracing descent (Schaefer et al., 1996). In *patrilineal descent* systems, only relatives on the father's side are important for emotional ties and for the transfer of property or wealth. Conversely, in a society that recognizes *matrilineal descent*, only the mother's family members are significant. Most Canadians follow a *bilateral descent* system, in which both sides of the family are regarded as equally important.

In Canada, *family* and *kinship* are not the same thing. Family implies a common residence and reciprocal relationships on a daily basis. A family's kin group consists of all the uncles, aunts, cousins, grandparents, in-laws, and other relatives, most of whom all family members know about but some of whom they have never met. Often, a family will go for long periods of time without seeing members of their kin group unless weddings, funerals, or family crises bring them together. Nonetheless, a family knows who they are, that they share obligations and responsibilities, and that family members are people who they can turn to for help in an emergency. ■

The Harris—Vidoni Family

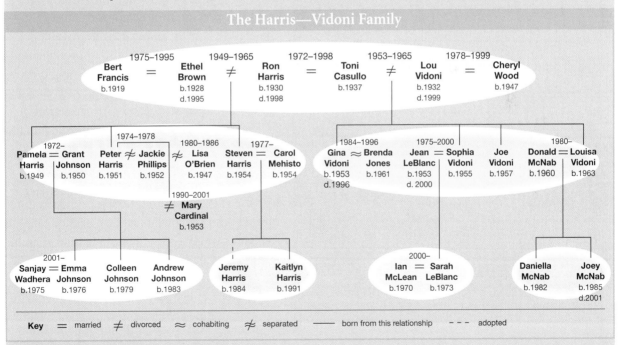

Key   = married   ≠ divorced   ≈ cohabiting   ≉ separated   —— born from this relationship   – – – adopted

This is the family tree of the Harris-Vidoni family, a fictional Canadian family that will be used in examples throughout this book.

The Contemporary Canadian Family

web connection

www.mcgrawhill.ca/links/families12

To learn about tracing a person's family history, go to the web site above for *Individuals and Families in a Diverse Society* to see where to go next.

The past 50 years in Canada have seen significant changes in the family structure as people adapted to new political, economic, and social pressures of life. The ideal family life of the traditional nuclear family in the first half of the twentieth century was dependent on women accepting the role as wife and mother and on a husband's ability to earn enough money to support his family. After the affluence of the post-war decade ended, Canadian families found it increasingly difficult to pay for things that they felt were necessary, on only one wage. By the 1960s and 1970s, women began to work outside the home to supplement family incomes. The birth rate declined again, and the family changed dramatically. For example, in 1966, 27 percent of married women in Canada were working. By 1976, their number increased to 44 percent, including 37 percent of those women with children under the age of six (Conway, 1997). By 1999, 69 percent of all women were employed (Statistics Canada).

Since access to money made women less dependent, the status of women in Canada began to change. A growing women's movement put pressure on the government to change the laws to reflect their new status. The 1968 Divorce Act established more lenient guidelines for divorce, the use and distribution of birth control became legal, and intercourse before marriage became a more acceptable practice. As society changed, new kinds of families emerged and became more common. The nuclear family continues to be the dominant form. However, with the employment of women, the **transitional family**, in which the mother temporarily leaves the work force to look after young children, and the **dual-income family**, in which both spouses work full time, have emerged. Childless couples are more numerous, not because fewer couples are having children, but because couples can have fewer children and live long enough to become "empty nesters" when their children have left

One new and growing category of family is couples that choose not to have children.

home. **Blended families** occur when divorced partners with children remarry. Families with same-sex parents have also become more prevalent (Conway, 1997).

Family formation during the last 25 years in Canada reflects the broader multicultural influences that result from the shift in immigration. In the past most immigrants came from European countries, such as Italy, Germany, and Holland. Now they come from many parts of the world, including the Caribbean, Latin America, Africa, Asia, South Asia, and the Middle East. These immigrant families have brought their diverse family systems, such as arranged marriages and matriarchal families, with them. As they interact with other Canadian families, they will influence the family form, roles, and priorities of the next generation.

The history of the family entails many changes over the millennia, but there is a consistent pattern of men and women co-operating to raise children and to provide for themselves. History supplies valuable pictures of social organization in the past, but there is no way of knowing whether the family patterns described accurately reflect life for all people or whether wide variations existed. You can see, however, the diversity of individual and family lifestyles that exist today. Robert Glossop (2000) of the Vanier Institute of the Family suggests that, "For half a century, our society has valued individual autonomy, achievement, and choice, downplaying the traditional bonds to family, employer, community, and country." On the other hand, American sociologist Valerie Wiener (1997, p. 9), who is currently studying the changing American family, is more optimistic about people's bonds to family:

> Some sociologists say that family life is thriving like never before. How we value our family enhances the lives of each family member. Individuals are no longer locked into traditional roles, including those of marriage and parenting. Of course, these revised roles will influence future generations. Our awareness should prompt us to discover new, improved ways to value our families.

Reflecting on the history of human civilization, eighteenth-century French philosopher Jean Rousseau defined the family as "the oldest institution and the only natural one." Back in the 1960s, William Goode (1964) concluded that, so far, "the family is a rather stable institution." Although some cynics at the end of the twentieth century suggested that change means the family is disappearing (*The Economist*, 1995), the family institution endures because of its ability to change.

Changes in Individual and Family Behaviour

Significant changes have occurred in the organization of individual and family behaviour over the history of human civilization. Although one can never be sure, most experts believe that the diversity of lifestyles is greater now than at any other time. It is no longer essential for a man or a woman to marry to obtain social standing, or for mutual economic support, or even to have intercourse and children. Families in which the relationship between husband and wife is based on love, and in which parents expect to love and be loved by their children, have become the new ideal and, according to many reports, the norm (Bibby, 2001). The family unit is no longer an economic necessity, but has become more of a psychological unit that people choose to form in order to meet their social and emotional needs (Conway, 1997).

You can choose whether to live alone or to cohabit or to marry. Similarly, you can make decisions about children, living arrangements, employment, child care—you have a lifetime of decisions related to your behaviour in your individual and family life. But governments, education systems, and businesses want to know what choices people are making, or how they are behaving, in order to develop social policy or plans for the future that affect individuals and families. Canadians want to know how to achieve their high expectations for the quality of their personal lives. Many people want to understand the meaning of their own existence. Individual and family studies are important branches of the social sciences that seek to understand and explain how people behave in their personal relationships within society, to suggest what they can expect in the future, and to provide some insight into how to manage their lives.

ADAM@HOME ©2001 by UNIVERSAL PRESS SYNDICATE. Reprinted with permission. All rights reserved.

1. Consider and write down how you would define *family*. Compare your definition with the definition used by the Vanier Institute of the Family (see page 6). How would you explain the significance of any differences?

2. Using Shirley Zimmerman's definitions of the functions of a family (see pages 7–8), analyze how the responsibility for performing the six functions is distributed in your family and explain how your family performs each of the functions.

   a) How does each of the functions of a family, as summarized by Zimmerman, benefit Canadian society?

   b) How does the family share these functions with other institutions in Canada, such as the institutions of government, religion, business, law, and education?

   c) Rank the six functions in order of priority from the following points of view: social worker with community services, religious leader, retailer, family court judge, elementary school teacher. Justify your choice of priority for each.

3. Identify five significant changes in the roles of men and women up to the twentieth century and explain the factors that caused them.

4. Suggest what family life might have been like in one of the historical periods summarized in this chapter. Write a critique of family life from the point of view of a young adult during that time and of the opposite gender from you.

5. Describe the Canadian family as you imagine it will be at the beginning of the twenty-second century. Explain the organization of families and society that will perform the functions of the family, and justify your predictions. In your description, use appropriate new terms from this chapter, and define any new terms you need to create.

6. Write a brief rationale for the study of the family at this stage in your life. Explain what you expect to learn and why this learning will be beneficial to you.

Approaches to Studying Individuals and Families

CHAPTER EXPECTATIONS

While reading this chapter, you will:

- formulate research questions and develop hypotheses reflecting specific theoretical frameworks
- demonstrate an understanding of research methodologies, appropriate research ethics, and specific theoretical perspectives for conducting primary research
- evaluate information to determine its validity and to detect bias, stereotyping, ethnocentricity, datedness, and unethical practices, and distinguish among perceptions, beliefs, opinions, and evidence from research
- distinguish between an essay arguing and defending personal opinion and a research paper reporting on an original investigation
- conduct an independent study of an issue concerning individuals or families in a diverse society

RESEARCH SKILLS

- formulating research questions
- developing hypotheses
- understanding research methodologies
- evaluating information
- conducting an independent study

The family is a topic of lively discussion in Canadian society because individuals can choose how their families will fit into their lives.

CHAPTER INTRODUCTION

What concerns do you have about your future life as an individual and as a member of a family? Are they justified? Are they based on knowledge of the facts, or do they reflect perceptions gathered from personal experience or from opinions formed by thinking about incorrect or incomplete information? This chapter outlines how to locate and read research done by others who asked the same questions. It examines the theories that can be used to understand human behaviour. It also describes how to conduct investigations and how to analyze the evidence to determine the facts.

Preconceptions About Individuals and Families in Canada

T he study of individuals and families can be approached with greater prior knowledge than any other subject. The experiences people have had in their own families, the **opinions** they have formed from observing and discussing their friends' families, and the families they have seen portrayed in the media will affect the **perceptions** they have of the subject. Therefore, a study of individuals and families requires that people set out and examine their own beliefs, perceptions, and opinions so that they can approach the subject objectively and with an open mind.

The talk about families reflects widespread concern about the lives of individuals and families in Canada today. In personal conversations and in the media, people discuss how marriage and the family are changing, who is responsible for what is happening to families, what families should be doing, what should be done to support families, and whether governments, charities, or other institutions can do anything to lessen the problems. Some concerns have to do with what is morally right or wrong when there are so many alternatives to choose from. Others ask what is financially sensible when there is competition for limited resources, or what is politically appropriate. The central question is about what choices Canadians should make in their own lives.

What Are Your Preconceptions?

web connection

www.mcgrawhill.ca/links/families12

To learn about Canadian demographics, as well as analyses of trends, go to the web site above for *Individuals and Families in a Diverse Society* to see where to go next.

Concerns about family issues arise because, unlike other current news, they affect us personally. Many young people believe that fewer people are getting married today because of the high divorce rate and that, consequently, they may not marry either for fear of getting divorced. Many Canadians are concerned that because so many marriages end in divorce these days, single parents are raising most of the children. They worry about the emotional consequences of divorce and single parenthood. In addition, some people argue that young women do not have the same educational opportunities as young men and, therefore, single women will not earn as much money to support themselves and their families. Concerns such as these result in anxiety about the future of families in Canada.

Using the Internet, you can locate facts about these concerns.

- Statistics Canada provides an overview of the lives of Canadians and their families. At the end of the twentieth century, trends suggest the following:
  - Canadians are not avoiding marriage, just delaying it until their late twenties, as people did in the 1930s.
  - Prior to marriage, people are cohabiting in larger numbers at all ages.
  - Approximately one-third of marriages will end in divorce at some time.
- The National Longitudinal Study of Children and Youth, begun in 1993 and still continuing, found that almost four out of five young children in Canada are currently living with their two biological parents.
- The report of the Pan-Canadian Education Indicators Program, 1999, reveals that women make up more than 50 percent of the graduates in Canada—from high school, college, or university—and are becoming better educated than men.

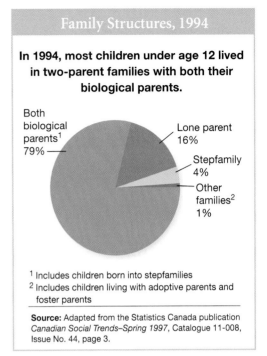

Family Structures, 1994

In 1994, most children under age 12 lived in two-parent families with both their biological parents.

Both biological parents[1] 79%

Lone parent 16%

Stepfamily 4%

Other families[2] 1%

[1] Includes children born into stepfamilies
[2] Includes children living with adoptive parents and foster parents

Source: Adapted from the Statistics Canada publication *Canadian Social Trends–Spring 1997*, Catalogue 11-008, Issue No. 44, page 3.

These facts do not support the common perceptions expressed by many Canadians.

Investigating familiar aspects of life as an academic study within the social sciences can present personal challenges. First, people tend to generalize from their personal experiences and observations. Accurate generalizations require a much larger and more organized set of observations. Second, any objective study in Canadian society will reveal a diversity of experiences that might contrast with one's own. In addition, the fact that individual and family behaviour are such common topics for discussion also makes them popular topics in the media. However, their portrayal of these issues may be entertaining or controversial rather than factual. Finally, setting aside all preconceptions at the beginning can mean abandoning familiar thinking that has provided the criteria for people's decisions in the past. An academic study of individuals and families in Canada, incorporating reliable research methods, will lead to clarification of the issues—a prerequisite for informed and meaningful debate and a stronger basis for decisions.

Smaller. Older. Different. That's not the motto of the Olympic Games, but rather a snapshot of what families will look like in the next century. Robert Glossop, executive director of programs and research for The Vanier Institute of the Family, writes in *Transition* magazine that we are no longer identified by our kinship. "For half a century, our society has valued individual autonomy, achievement, and choice, downplaying the traditional bonds to family, employer, community, and country," says Glossop.

The demand for personal choice is changing the Canadian family. For example, two of the greatest influences in the last half-century were the general use of the birth control pill and the 1986 change in Canada's divorce laws. The result is that we now have many versions of the family. There are married and common-law heterosexual couples with and without children; lone-parent and two-parent families; same-sex couples with and without children; single-earner and dual-earner families; blended families with various configurations of step-relationships; adoptive and foster families.

Indeed, medical science and political legislation will continue having major effects on where the family is going. New human reproductive technologies and the male contraceptive pill will satisfy people who either do or don't want to have children. On the political side, the number of couples having children could be increased by a national day-care program or by tax breaks for stay-at-home parents.

"The immediate future in Canada is that there will probably be a lot more choice and more variety of lifestyles," says Fran Puffer, a tutor in sociology of the family at Athabasca University, Alberta.

Following the uncertainties of life during [World War II], the number of marriages per capita in Canada peaked at nearly 11 per 1000 people in 1946.

Robert Glossop, of the Vanier Institute of the Family

Now there are half as many first-time marriages. Cohabitation and remarriages are on the rise. One American state is even experimenting with marriage contracts that may be renewed every five years.

The number of births per woman in Canada peaked at four in 1961. But due in large part to contraception and rising costs of living, births are now less than the rate of 2.1 it takes to replace our departing population. The result will be more immigration in the new century, bringing cultural changes.

Expensive post-secondary education will keep young people living at home longer. In the twenty-first century, Canadians who do marry and have [children] will do both later in life. The majority of women will spend their twenties going to school and working, rather than raising children.

Delays or downright avoidance of marriage and parenthood will be largely due to personal choice and economics. The average family now needs to work 76.8 weeks a year to pay off all their expenses. That's why a second partner is working at least part time; there are 3.6 million dual-income couples in the country. One hundred years ago, 45 percent of Canadians were employed in farming. Now it's 3 percent. And in the global economy, cheap labour in Vietnam and Mainland China will close Canadian factories, putting Canadian family members out of work.

A major growth industry in the next century will be caregiving. An increase in dual-income families will create enormous child-care demands. And there will be growth in elder care, as the baby boom and modern medicine produce an aging population. The biggest five-year block of population will move from the 30–35 year range in 1996 to the 50–55 year range in 2016.

What will be the political and social will? "We have, in a sense, purchased our individualism at the expense of our family life, our marriages, the safety of our streets, our relationships with neighbours, and, ultimately, at the expense of knowing what purposes we share with others," says Glossop. The price may someday be deemed too high. But not in the immediate future. ■

Source: *Edmonton Journal.* (2000, January 1). p. E2.

1. What does individualism mean?
2. How would individualism and personal choice affect marriage rates and birth rates?
3. What do you think Glossop means when he suggests that the price of our individualism might be too high?

Theoretical Perspectives

This text presents a comprehensive study of the lives of individuals and their families that uses a variety of **theoretical perspectives** from several **disciplines**. Disciplines are specific branches of learning, such as mathematics, physics, or psychology. A theoretical perspective identifies a point of view based on a specific **theory**. A theory is a framework for organizing and explaining observable evidence. Without facts, a theory is just a speculation or a guess. On the other hand, information that has been gathered by observation, experiment, or survey lacks meaning without theory to organize it. Thus, an understanding of individuals and families requires that factual evidence be organized from a specific theoretical perspective (Goode, 1982).

The Disciplines in the Social Sciences

Theories from many disciplines can be used in the study of individuals and families. Social scientists ask four fundamental questions: *What happens? How does it happen? Why does it happen?* and, often, *How can people change what happens?* Each discipline focuses on a specific aspect of human behaviour to answer these questions. It is possible to approach the study of a topic, such as mate selection, using one or more disciplines. The discipline determines what observations a researcher will make and which theoretical perspective will be used to organize and explain the results. The discipline and the theoretical perspective also determine whether the research will be a *macro* (large-scale) study of a society or a *micro* (small-scale) study of individual cases. Finally, the discipline may suggest how the results are applied to predicting what will happen in order to make decisions about the course of human lives within society.

When Colin Turnbull observed the BaMbuti of Africa, he noted the rites of passage that signalled admission into adulthood for Mbuti boys and girls.

"The typical west of Ireland family consists of father, mother, twelve children, and resident Dutch anthropologist."

— Attributed to Flann O'Brien

Anthropology

Anthropology is the study of human behaviour in societies; thus, it is the study of culture—the arts, beliefs, habits, institutions, and other endeavours that are characteristic of a specific community, society, or nation. Anthropologists study culture in various ways. Cultural anthropologists live within a society to observe behaviour in its natural setting and to record anecdotal evidence. For example, English anthropologist Colin Turnbull studied the BaMbuti Pygmies in Zaire by living among them for an extended period, observing their behaviour and questioning them about the meaning of their behaviour (Turnbull, 1984). Cultural anthropologists study contemporary societies to determine cultural patterns and regional or national variations.

Anthropological studies highlight the diversity of behaviours that fulfill the functional requisites of society. An understanding of the diversity is necessary to overcome **ethnocentrism**, the tendency to evaluate behaviour from the point of view of your own culture. For example, when Colin Turnbull compared the initiation rites that marked the transition into adulthood of Mbuti boys with his own experience as an upper-class English boy, he concluded that his private boarding school education did not prepare him for marriage and sex as well as the initiation rites prepared the Mbuti boys (Turnbull, 1984). By reading anthropological studies of other cultures, people will come to understand that all cultural behaviour is "invented" and, as a result, they will develop an ability to observe their own culture objectively.

Sociology

Sociology is the social science that explains the behaviour of individuals in social groups, families, and society. Sociologists investigate social facts, the social sources of behaviour that are used to explain rates of behaviour. For example, Canadian sociologist Reginald Bibby is best known for his studies of adolescence and youth in Canada. The marketing industry has used his analysis of adolescent behaviour and attitudes to plan effective sales strategies targeting the adolescent consumer. Educators have used his conclusions about students to help them design the school curriculum to meet the needs of young Canadians.

Sociological studies are more concerned with the patterns of behaviour observed in large numbers of people or groups rather than with the behaviour of individuals. For example, Statistics Canada uses sociological methods to gather information about Canadians in many aspects of their family, consumer, and business lives. It uses statistical analyses to produce **demographics** of the Canadian population. Governments use demographics for planning social policy, businesses use them for marketing decisions, and you will use them in your academic study of individuals and families. Determining patterns and rates of behaviour of groups facilitates planning and policy decisions within a society, but may not necessarily explain the behaviour of individuals.

in focus | Reginald Bibby, Sociologist

by Brian Bergman

When Reginald Bibby accepted a teaching position at the University of Lethbridge, in 1975, he was concerned he might become just another invisible academic at a relatively small institution. He needn't have worried. From his post in southwestern Alberta, the 58-year-old sociologist has become Canada's foremost tracker of religious trends and an outspoken expert on teen behaviour and attitudes. Two of his earliest books, 1987's *Fragmented Gods* and 1985's *The Emerging Generation* (the latter co-authored by Don Posterski), sold about 30 000 copies each—phenomenal for works centred on academic research. With the publication in April 2001 of *Canada's Teens: Today, Yesterday and Tomorrow*, his eighth book, Bibby returns to one of his favourite topics—the need for teens and their parents to better understand one another. "If you want to talk about two solitudes in this country," says Bibby, "talk about young people and adults."

Bibby comes by his professional passions honestly. The second of seven children, he was born and raised in Edmonton as part of a devout Baptist family. Bibby went on to earn a theology degree and intended at one point to become a minister. But he found himself drawn to sociology, and later earned his Ph.D. from

One of Bibby's favourite topics is the need for teenagers and their parents to understand one another.

Washington State University. While Bibby continues to describe himself as a person for whom faith is important, he is no longer active in any religious group.

Similarly, Bibby's interest in teens stems, in part, from being the father of three grown sons (the boys continued to live with him after their parents' 1979 divorce). Bibby says his experience of the teenage years was very enjoyable, and thinks it can be so for most parents if they strike the right balance between giving teens direction and allowing them to emerge as individuals.

Bibby acknowledges that the very success of his books makes him suspect among some academics, who dismiss him as a "pop sociologist." He is willing to take the knock. "I realized at an early point that, while the work needed to be academically sound, I also wanted it to be enjoyable and widely read." He has succeeded on all counts. ■

Source: *Maclean's.* (2001, April 9). p. 44.

Psychology

Psychology is the study of behaviour based on mental processes. Its focus is how the individual thinks. For example, Swiss psychologist Jean Piaget studied the development of cognition in children by observing them thinking in natural and experimental settings. His theory of the Stages of Cognitive Development (1970) that describes how children think at each age is still the basis of curriculum design in school systems throughout the world. Recent developments in brain imaging technology that enable researchers to observe activity in the brain are helping psychologists to describe the biological and chemical bases for the mental processes that have been described in the past.

Psychologists use an understanding of mental processes and the characteristic patterns of motivation that they call the *personality* to explain individual behaviour. They also examine how individuals interact and influence one another. American psychologist Solomon Asch studied the influence of opinions and social pressure on individuals and concluded that conformity is a major factor in human behaviour that can cause people to doubt their own thinking. Psychology can be used for micro studies of individual behaviour and for macro studies of group behaviour. Psychological research is used to help individuals manage their behaviour. On the other hand, businesses also use the results of psychological research to motivate people to change their productive or consumer behaviour.

Other Disciplines

Other disciplines are useful in the study of individuals and families. Social history can provide facts about life in the past so that people can identify trends. Like anthropology, history will help you develop objectivity. Economics can provide insight into the economic function of families and help to explain how families acquire and use resources. Politics can be used to examine influences on individual power and authority within families. Religion can help you understand the motivation of individuals to participate in society. It is more common now to ask questions that draw on a variety of disciplines when attempting a comprehensive study of an issue concerning individuals and families in a society.

Family Studies is an interdisciplinary study that integrates anthropology, sociology, and psychology. Researchers, often working as teams, can examine individual and family behaviours from several perspectives at once. Psychologist Daniel Levinson worked with a sociologist and a psychiatrist when he analyzed the lives of men and women and determined the predictable developmental stages. David Buss is studying human sexual behaviour as an evolutionary psychologist, a perspective that combines psychology and anthropology, to determine the impact of the evolutionary concept of natural selection on human behaviour. Interdisciplinary studies are efficient ways of using theoretical perspectives as research tools.

In the old story of the blind men and the elephant, five blind men approach an elephant from different angles and reach out to touch the elephant. Obviously, when they compare their perceptions of the elephant, their descriptions do not match, and an argument ensues. The owner of the elephant explains how their five descriptions fit together and invites them to touch the elephant from different perspectives in order to understand the complete animal. He then points out that the most important thing about elephants is how they can be used—you can ride them to get where you want to go (Backstein, 1992). This old story is a useful comparison for social science research. A study of human behaviour, whether of individuals or families, benefits from an interdisciplinary approach that combines theoretical perspective, but what is most important is what people learn from the research.

In the old story, when the blind men examined the elephant, each man had a different understanding of the elephant because each touched a different part.

Basic Theoretical Perspectives

Imagine that you listen in on a discussion about whether parents should spank their children. One person says that, according to the Bible, parents should not "spare the rod." Another argues that all violence is wrong, including spanking. Strict parents counter that spanking teaches children that parents mean what they say. Someone questions whether spanking teaches obedience or fear. Another parent responds that his children, who have never been spanked, are well-behaved. Each person is expressing a point of view about the same subject. Their answers reflect their assumptions about human behaviour and the motivations behind it.

When scientists explain their observations, their answers reflect their theories. Theories are essential tools when conducting research and, like any tool, should be suited to the task and used appropriately. Some theories are durable and have been used to explain human behaviour for many years. Others have fallen into disfavour and have been replaced by newer, more useful theories. In his book *A Brief History of Time: From the Big Bang to Black Holes*, physicist Stephen Hawking (1988, p. 9) tackled a much larger task than explaining individual and family behaviour: he attempted to explain the origins of the universe. Nevertheless, he defined theory in a way that is applicable to all disciplines and explained how to evaluate whether a theory is a good theory:

> I shall take the simple-minded view that a theory is just a model of the universe, or a restricted part of it, and a set of rules that equate qualities in the model to observations that we make. It exists only in our minds and does not have any other reality (whatever that might mean). A theory is a good theory if it satisfies two requirements: It must accurately describe a large class of observations on the basis of a model that contains only a few arbitrary elements, and it must make definite predictions about the results of future observations.

"*It is the theory that determines what we can observe.*"
— Albert Einstein

Theories are not facts, just attempts to explain evidence. In the physical sciences, a valid theory considers all of the evidence and can be used to predict what will happen. Therefore, evidence that does not support the theory would indicate that the theory is inaccurate. On the other hand, theories in the social sciences define patterns and trends, not rules—and probabilities, not absolutes. Therefore, there are many theories that attempt to explain the same set of observations. You will examine two sociological theories, two psychological theories, and several interdisciplinary theories. The purpose of your study will be to suggest which theory is most useful for each investigation and what facts you should gather. Let us return to the analogy of the blind men and the elephant. Although the trunk is an obvious way to explain an elephant, measuring the ears is more useful for determining whether you are observing an African or an Asian elephant.

Functionalism

Functionalism is the sociological theory that attempts to explain how a society is organized to perform its required functions effectively. This theory, also called *structural functionalism* because it focuses on how the structures function within society, is the oldest sociological theory and is also used by anthropologists. These structures, such as the law, the political system, and the family, are called **institutions**. Functionalism assumes that societies are stable when structures function in ways that benefit society. Change can occur if the structures are able to adjust to maintain equilibrium in the society, but change will happen slowly.

Functionalists examine the roles that individuals play within an institution such as the family. As you learned before, the groups within society motivate individuals to act. A **status** is a specific position within a social group. For example, you are a student. A **role** is the set of behaviours that an individual is expected to demonstrate within a status. For example, students are expected to attend class, ask questions, conduct investigations, and complete assignments. As you have noticed, societies run more smoothly when each individual behaves according to his or her specific role. Individuals learn the appropriate behaviour for the many roles they will play in society through the process of socialization.

Stay-at-home dads are becoming more common. Functionalists might ask whether this changing role benefits society, but systems theorists would ask how it affects the roles of wives and children.

Functionalists make observations about role behaviour and determine the rates at which various behaviours occur. They describe the most prevalent behaviours as the **norm**. Behaviours that occur at a lower rate are away from the norm, or abnormal. For example, an analysis of the rates of employment in Canadian families has determined that with most married couples, both husband and wife are employed. In some marriages, the husband is employed and the wife is not, or vice versa. In this case, a functionalist would conclude that it is normal for a husband to be employed, but abnormal for him to stay at home while his wife works. Functionalism uses a macro approach that assumes the organization of society is based on a consensus about what is functional. However, a problem with functionalism is a tendency for functionalists to go beyond explaining how a society is organized to prescribing how individuals within a society should behave.

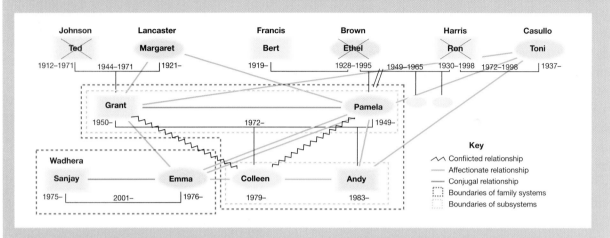

Johnson Ted 1912–1971
Lancaster Margaret 1944–1971 | 1921–
Francis Bert 1919–
Brown Ethel 1928–1995 | 1949–1965
Harris Ron 1930–1998 | 1972–1998
Casullo Toni 1937–

Grant 1950–
Pamela 1972– | 1949–

Wadhera
Sanjay 1975– | 2001–
Emma 1976–
Colleen 1979–
Andy 1983–

Key
- ⋀⋀ Conflicted relationship
- — Affectionate relationship
- — Conjugal relationship
- ⬚ Boundaries of family systems
- ⬚ Boundaries of subsystems

A genogram is a diagram, much like a family tree, that depicts the relationships within a family system. You can use whatever symbols have meaning for you as you identify the members of your family system, describe the subsystems within the family, and analyze the nature of the relationships among individuals in the family.

The Johnson family is an extended family system, part of the larger Harris-Vidoni family that you read about in Chapter 1. Pamela, the oldest Harris child, married Grant Johnson in 1972. They have three children. Emma was born in 1976, Colleen in 1979, and Andy in 1983. Pamela and Grant have been a subsystem within the family system for over 30 years. They share their love of travel, theatre, and politics with their children in the larger family system, but they spend a lot of time together, gardening and discussing their work, without the children. The children, who are now grown up, formed a strong sibling subsystem based on a shared interest in sports leadership. The two girls were especially close, but Colleen and Andy formed a closer relationship, maintaining the sibling subsystem, when Emma went to university.

Emma is now married, forming a new family system with her husband, Sanjay. However, she maintains a close connection with her family of origin, because she and Sanjay live in a basement apartment in Pam and Grant's house.

The family is basically happy, although visitors think they are loud and argue a great deal—the inevitable consequence of living with people with strong opinions! Colleen's relationship with her parents has been conflicted for several years, but it does seem to be improving since Emma got married and Colleen moved away for university. ■

1. What kind of relationships do the children have with their grandparents?
2. What might be the reasons for the conflict between Colleen and her parents?
3. Why is there a boundary around Emma and Sanjay, even though they live in the same house as Pam and Grant?
4. Why is there a boundary around the subsystem of Colleen and Andy?

Systems Theory

Systems theory is the sociological theory that attempts to explain how groups of individuals interact as a system, a set of different parts that work together and influence one another in a relatively stable way over time. Family systems theory applies to the examination of family processes. A basic concept is that family systems have a complex organization. This means that although the organization is not a simple sequential one, it is not chaotic (Kantor & Lehr, 1975).

A basic principle of systems theory is feedback, a process by which the system informs its members how to interact to maintain the stability of the system. Because feedback implies give and take, the individuals within the family system influence one another in a reciprocal way, making it difficult to trace the origins of influence or to describe the organization of the family.

Family systems have special characteristics. They maintain a relatively stable size because members can be added to families only by birth, adoption, or cohabitation or marriage, and can leave only by death. However, some family systems theorists argue that individuals continue to exert an influence on the behaviour of others after they have left the family household, just as they do after divorce (Carter & McGoldrick, 1989). The larger family system contains subsystems:

- the family-unit subsystem of those members sharing a household
- the interpersonal subsystems between individuals, such as husband-wife or mother-son
- the personal subsystem comprised of interaction between the individual as self and as a member of the family

The restricted yet continuous membership, the multi-generational extent, and the hierarchy of subsystems contribute to the complexity of family systems.

Family systems develop strategies for achieving the goals and functions of individuals and of the family, and for interacting with the external society. Strategies are defined as patterns of interaction that are repeated; one could call them *meaningful habits* (Kantor & Lehr, 1975). Strategies require the collaboration of all members to continue. Therefore, all members share responsibility for the patterns of behaviour. For example, people who continually argue about chores share responsibility for this habit. Family systems adapt when a change in one person's behaviour causes the behaviour of others to evolve, resulting in new strategies. For example, when a wife and mother returns to work after having a child, new strategies for doing housework will evolve as her husband and children take on some of the chores. Unlike functionalism, which explains the actions of individuals in groups, systems theory explains the behaviour of individuals as inseparable from the group. A limitation of systems theory is that it can be difficult to determine how others within the family are influencing an individual's behaviour.

Symbolic Interactionism

Symbolic interactionism is a psychological theory that attempts to explain how individuals choose how they will act based on their perceptions of themselves and of others. People experience their social world, and then define and interpret their experiences to give them meaning. It is the perceptions, or the meanings that people give to their experience of the world, that matter, not the social facts. For example, if someone puts a hand on your shoulder, you will interpret the gesture and determine what it means before you respond. Only after the mental process of "giving meaning" do people act. Mental processes are not visible; only the actions that follow them are. Therefore, symbolic interactionists attempt to understand the point of view of the actor to explain the action.

Symbolic interactionism is based on three basic concepts:

1. An individual develops a self that has two parts: the "me" that consists of objective qualities (tall, male, student) and the "I" that is the subjective awareness of self (good student, shy, lonely). According to psychologist Charles Cooley, the "I" is based on how feedback from other people is interpreted.

2. People must also "take the attitude of the other" to be able to anticipate what the other person will do and decide how they should respond. This is what George Mead, a philosopher and psychologist, believed. This role-taking is the basis for human interaction.

3. People are able to interact effectively only if they can communicate using a common language; that is, shared symbols, Mead argued. Language is the means by which individuals interpret and give meaning to their experiences of self and others in order to interact in relationships.

A popular application of symbolic interactionism was used by John Gray in his book *Men Are from Mars, Women Are from Venus* (1992). He explained that men and women have problems in their relationships because they give different meanings to actions and words. Therefore, by acting in ways that reflect their own interpretation of the other sex, they behave in ways that are confusing to the other sex. He generalizes that since men and women do not

Cooley's Looking-Glass Theory

"I am not what I think I am. I am not what you think I am. I am what I think you think I am."

— Charles Cooley

share common symbols, they could improve their relationships by learning what the other sex means by their behaviour.

Symbolic interactionism is a psychological theory because it emphasizes the mental processes of perception and interpretation in determining the behaviour of individuals. It also explains how people present themselves to others using shared symbols. It is useful as a micro theory for analyzing observations of individuals and small groups of people. A limitation of symbolic interactionism is the possibility that because the researcher perceives and interprets the actions of the individuals during the observation, the observations could be influenced by the researcher's self-image and beliefs and could, therefore, be inaccurate.

Symbolic interactionism explains that because men and women might interpret situations differently and use different language to express their ideas, misunderstandings can result.

Social Exchange Theory

Social exchange theory is a psychological theory that attempts to explain the social factors that influence how individuals interact within reciprocal relationships. Social exchange theorists explain that although individuals are constrained by role expectations, they act within each role to maximize the benefits they will receive and to minimize the costs to themselves. Social exchange theory borrows from symbolic interactionism when it says that individuals interpret their experiences of self and others to determine the benefits and costs. Therefore, the benefits and costs of a relationship are not facts, but are perceptions formed by each individual.

Social exchange theory can be used to explain choices of marriage partners. The marriage of Prince Charles and Diana, the late Princess of Wales, illustrates the trade-off in marriage. For the royal family, Diana offered the benefits of youth, fertility, and beauty that would ensure a healthy and attractive heir to the throne and draw favour from the public. She was also of noble blood and had been socialized for public life. Charles offered wealth, a luxurious lifestyle, and the opportunity for his wife to become a queen. Their marriage was successful in that it produced two sons as heirs. However, they separated when it became evident that Charles was unwilling to end his relationship with Camilla Parker-Bowles, and Diana was unable to withstand the restrictions placed on her by the royal family. The costs of the relationship were greater than the rewards.

According to social exchange theory, the benefits of staying in the relationship must outweigh the benefits of an alternative relationship, or it will not last. In the case of Prince Charles and the late Princess Diana, the benefits did not outweigh the costs, and they parted.

Relationships are stable when the benefits that each individual receives balance the costs of the relationship. Benefits are rewarding because they meet a perceived need and can include physical or emotional security, access to goods and services, and social approval. The costs of a relationship are those actions that meet the needs of another, such as providing physical or emotional support, or sharing goods and services. According to this theory, individuals prefer relationships that are cost-effective, those in which the benefits are greater than those of alternative relationships. Social scientists use social exchange theory to explain how individuals make decisions to form and maintain relationships that might appear unacceptable to others. However, the fact that some people are offended by the cost/benefit analysis could be a limitation.

Developmental Theories

Developmental theories use an interdisciplinary approach to attempt to describe patterns of growth and change throughout the human life span. As individuals progress through life, they face role expectations that challenge them to develop. These challenges are called *developmental tasks*. For example, American psychologist Erik Erikson explained that people develop their individual identities separate from their parents to make the transition from adolescence to adulthood. They need to do this before they can form an intimate relationship with another person (Erikson, 1980). Developmental theories describe predictable changes in the behaviour of individuals or families. Because they explain how a personal or a family-unit system adapts in response to internal or external stimuli, they can be combined with systems theory to analyze how the transitions take place.

Developmental theories examine biological, psychological, social, and cultural factors that influence development in an interdisciplinary approach. Developmental theories are attempts to explain the factors that influence differences in behaviour demonstrated by individuals at different ages. Researchers must be careful to determine whether the differences are caused, in fact, by the age-stage of the individuals. Differences in behaviour could reflect factors that are typical only of those born in the same period of time; for example, being a "baby boomer" could result in patterns of behaviour that will not be repeated by adults who were born ten years later. Differences could also reflect social change rather than development (Bee, 1987). Developmental theories based on long-term studies of many **cohorts**, or well-defined groups, can be used cautiously to understand the behaviour of individuals, but are not intended to be used to govern how people should behave or to criticize those whose lives follow a different pattern.

The family life-cycle framework applies the developmental perspective to the life spans of families. It assumes that families, like individuals, have life spans with predictable stages, marked by **normative events** such as marriage, the birth of a child, or a child leaving home. At each stage, the family faces specific developmental tasks that are prerequisites for moving on to the next stage. A newly married couple faces the task of negotiating how they will make decisions and solve problems. Mastering this task prepares them for the challenges of the next stage, if they have children. Of course, not all stages will fit all families, and some families will experience non-normative events, such as the death of a child, that present unique challenges. The identification of stages in the life of families is arbitrary and reflects

The family life-cycle framework predicts that parents of newborn children will have to adjust how they relate to each other to allow for their roles as mother and as father to develop.

the cultural realities of the society. The family life-cycle framework was developed by sociologists after World War II to enable policy makers to determine the needs of American families. Since it assumes that families at a similar stage of their life cycles face similar tasks, it still provides a useful perspective for investigating families in Canada.

Conflict Theory

Conflict theory is an interdisciplinary sociological and political theory that explains how power, not functional interdependence, holds a society together. It states that conflict exists between groups in society because of inequalities in power. It assumes that groups compete with one another to meet their needs. If groups are in competition, then the needs of all will not be met equally. This competition can also result in exploitation by individuals in the group with greater power over others from a group with lesser power. Conflict theory is a macro theory that explains inequalities. Unlike other theories, it is used to criticize, not explain, society. Conflict theorists ask the question

Conflict theory and feminist theories argue that inequalities in power result in social structures that do not work for everyone.

"Functional for whom?" because, unlike functionalists, they question why the structure of society does not work for everyone (Teevan & Hewitt, 1995).

According to conflict theory, society is organized into groups to divide people according to their power and to encourage competition. Karl Marx described the class divisions within capitalist societies in the nineteenth century. He called those who controlled the means of production, the wealthy owners of businesses and factories, the *bourgeoisie*. The bourgeoisie were a small group in society, yet they had tremendous power because they controlled the livelihood of the masses of working people, the *proletariat*. He predicted that the natural evolution would be for the bourgeoisie to become smaller and richer, for the proletariat to become larger and poorer, and the gap between them to become greater. A society would be stable if people perceived the dominant group as being more entitled to the benefits of society than others. Many people believe that this inequality is the natural state of human society. Marx argued that inequalities could and should be eliminated.

German socialist Friedrich Engels suggested that the divisions between the sexes in marriage not only paralleled the divisions between the classes, but also were necessary to maintain the class distinctions of capitalism. Men's labour outside the home was paid, but women's labour inside the home was unpaid. The concept of family wage meant that the salary paid to a man was sufficient to enable him to support a wife and children. Therefore, men of all classes wielded economic power within the household, while women had no alternative but to marry, reproduce, and provide the unpaid labour necessary to maintain the family. However, men could only maintain their power by continuing to sell their labour for wages, and women could not have economic support without maintaining the marriage. Engels argued that the oppression of women was linked to capitalism and would not end until capitalism was eliminated. Therefore, conflict theory describes the relationship of men and women within a family as one of exploitation and oppression, and is used for analyzing power and authority within the family.

Feminist Theories

Feminist theories were developed in the second half of the twentieth century to explain the impact of sex and gender on behaviour, and to consider issues of human behaviour from the specific point of view of women. Feminist theories have their roots in conflict theory, but were developed to separate sex and gender from class. They also developed as a reaction to gender biases in sociology. For example, **androcentricity** is a bias that assumes male experience is human experience and therefore also applies to women. Therefore, it does not consider gender in research. On the other hand, **double standards** are biases that apply different standards for evaluating the behaviour of men and women. Feminist theories, like conflict theory, argue that change is required so that the needs of all people are met.

Feminist theories attempt to explain social inequalities between men and women from a female perspective. *Liberal feminism* argues that discriminatory policies force women into an inferior social class that restricts their rights to participate fully in society according to their individual abilities. Thus, American feminist writer Betty Friedan describes feminism as a theory of human rights (Code, 1993). Liberal feminists try to change social policy through political means. *Socialist feminism* is based on the assumption that the status of women is a social inequality rooted in the sexual division of paid and unpaid labour. It challenges both capitalism and the patriarchal model of the family. *Radical feminism* argues that the differences in power between men and women result in any male-female relationship as being exploitative. It suggests that only the development of a separate female culture can correct this (Code, 1993). The solutions feminists advocate vary because feminist theories differ in how they perceive the causes of the inequity.

The rebirth of feminism in the 1960s resulted in changes in the law to eliminate discrimination against women, but social attitudes adapt more slowly.

Conducting Research in the Social Sciences

The purposes of the social sciences are to describe and explain the behaviour of individuals and families, predict how individuals and families will behave in response to their environments, and suggest ways of managing their behaviour. Social science research methods are used to ask questions, to gather information, and to analyze the information. Knowing the methods used in social science research can help you understand the origins of knowledge presented in this and other books about social science subjects. Developing social science research skills will enable you to evaluate the validity of the information in this book and in other sources. You will also be prepared to conduct your own investigation of issues regarding individuals and the family.

As a social scientist, be systematic in your research. Clarify the topic of study by asking questions. Identify the specific research question to be investigated so that the study has a purpose. Begin the research by finding out what information is already known. Conduct a review of the available literature, including books, periodicals, media, and electronic sources. Select sources that analyze research in answer to your question. These sources are called *secondary sources* because they present someone else's analysis second-hand. Summarize your literature review to help develop a thesis that answers your question. If the answer is not clear after a review of secondary sources, continue your research. State a hypothesis, a possible answer to your question, and design an original investigation to gather additional evidence. The subjects of this kind of investigation are called *primary sources*, because you will get the information first-hand. Analyze the results of your research to form conclusions that indicate whether the hypothesis is true and to determine whether your question has been answered.

Research Papers

Social scientists are expected to write research papers that describe the results of their study for other people. There are two major types of research papers.

- **Research essays** Many research tasks will be complete when the secondary research is finished. The results are presented as a research essay in which evidence from the research is described to support a thesis.

- **Research report** The results of an original investigation of a hypothesis are presented as a research report in which the method and the results are described. A research report enables others to evaluate the methods to determine whether the results are reliable.

Publishing research papers contributes to knowledge about individuals and families in Canada for the benefit of future students and researchers.

web connection

www.mcgrawhill.ca/links/families12

To learn about Canadian studies about families and work, go to the web site above for *Individuals and Families in a Diverse Society* to see where to go next.

Ask these questions to assess whether a source of information is valid.

When was it published?

Consider whether the information still applies or whether legal, economic, or political changes have made the information dated. Recent periodicals and books published within ten years are more reliable unless you require historical information.

Where was it published?

Consider whether information gathered in another country applies to Canada. For example, the United States is ten times the size of Canada, and has significant political, historical, ethnocultural, and economic differences that could affect the validity of applying the information to Canada. Psychological research can be universal, but Canadian sources are more reliable for the study of social behaviour.

Who is the author?

Is the author a qualified expert in the subject study or a professional writer who, like you, has conducted research? As you read, determine whether the author has any biases that affect the reliability of the information.

What is the author's purpose?

Consider the author's motivation for publishing the information. Is the source a report of the results of research, a personal opinion, a persuasive argument, an explanation, or a response to another argument? Although persuasive arguments can be more exciting to read, sources that use evidence from research to support statements are more reliable for your studies.

Who is the intended audience?

Consider who paid for the publication and whether the source presents a biased viewpoint. Material written for a specific audience might rely on shared assumptions or stereotypes to support statements. Look for sources that include all evidence in the presentation of ideas.

What is the author's point of view or theoretical perspective?

Consider how the author's point of view is presented and whether a specific theoretical perspective is identified. In a valid source, the author should discuss all evidence, including that which does not support his or her point of view. ■

Research Questions and Hypotheses

A research question establishes the purpose of the research. Preliminary research will reveal whether the topic is relevant enough for there to be sufficient sources of information and will help clarify which aspect of a topic to investigate. Develop a clearly worded research question about a specific aspect of the topic to guide you in selecting information from secondary sources in your literature review. There are two basic types of questions asked in the social sciences:

- description questions that ask "What happens?"
- explanation questions that ask "Why?" or "How?" (Bee, 1987)

Description and explanation questions form the basis of all research questions.

A *hypothesis* is a possible answer to your research question. You develop it after your review of the literature to explain what happens and why it happens. Sociologists James J. Teevan and W.E. Hewitt of the University of Western Ontario explain *hypothesis* this way:

> An hypothesis is a statement of presumed relationship between two or more variables, usually stated in the form "Other things being equal, if A, then B." If the A variable occurs or goes up or down, then the B variable also occurs or goes up or down. The B variable is usually the one being explained, the A variable the explanation (1995, p. 153).

Variables are qualities, such as gender or birth order, or behaviours, such as marrying or attending university. A is the *independent variable* because it occurs first. B is the *dependent variable* because it depends on A. Thus, A is the cause and B is the effect.

When you study the topic "early adulthood," you could ask the question, "What factors influence an individual's decision about when to leave home?" A review of the literature suggests that the decision is influenced by the make-up of an individual's family. Your hypothesis could be "Children of remarried parents leave home earlier." Notice that although the hypothesis assumes that other things are equal, it usually does not include those words. In this hypothesis, having remarried parents is the independent variable, and leaving home earlier is the dependent variable.

Ethical Research

Any research using human subjects should be conducted in an ethical manner that respects both the well-being and the dignity of people. The procedures outlined by school boards ensure that this happens in the course of studies. Discuss your study proposal and obtain permission from your teacher before you begin to research. Explain the nature of your research to your subjects carefully and obtain their consent to participate, unless you will be observing people in a public setting or conducting an anonymous survey. If your research requires some sort of deception, you could obtain general consent, but then you must explain the deception as soon as possible afterwards. For example, if you wanted to observe how people respond to aggressive behaviour, you could obtain the subjects' consent to participate in a study of behaviour in crowds, and then explain after the observation that you had arranged for a colleague to push them aside so that you could observe their reaction. Finally, you must inform the subjects if the research will cause them any physical or emotional discomfort. When you design your investigation, choose the method that will be most effective while being respectful of the people who are helping you in your research.

There are also ethical issues affecting the reporting of your research. Do not change, omit, or make up evidence in a mistaken attempt to improve your report. Any shortcomings should be discussed as a legitimate part of the discussion in a reliable research report. Use citations and references to give credit to the original authors of any work you have consulted, but ensure that the report reflects your own analysis and conclusions. To submit all or part of someone else's work as your own is plagiarism. You also have an obligation to your subjects to let them know the results of the study as soon as they are available. Since the purpose of research is to answer questions, you are responsible for ensuring that your report presents the evidence accurately.

web connection

www.mcgrawhill.ca/links/families12

To learn the APA citation style, go to the web site above for *Individuals and Families in a Diverse Society* to see where to go next.

Sample Groups

To conduct an original investigation, you need to gather evidence about behaviour from people who represent the topic of your study. Using your hypothesis, define the population who will be the subjects of your study. Remember that your hypothesis assumes "all other things being equal." Define your population so that you eliminate as much as possible other factors that could confuse the effects of the independent variable. For example, if your hypothesis is that "Boys are more likely to write at the top of a chalkboard than girls are," you should set a *parameter* that defines or limits the subjects' height.

While you are a student, your choice of research method might be limited by whether you have access to the population you want to study.

Consider such parameters as age, gender, ethnic group, religion, socio-economic class, and level of education. When there are several related variables, such as height and gender, some studies compare the results for two or more groups within the population.

Conducting research using a *sample group* selected from the people you want to study will ease the constraints of time and money. There are two limits when you select your sample group. First, the sample group must be representative of the population you want to study. For example, if you want to study students at your school and 55 percent of the students are girls, 55 percent of your sample group must be girls. Secondly, you cannot generalize beyond the group from which you draw your sample. For example, if your sample group is selected only within your school, you cannot conclude that the results apply to all students in Canada (Teevan & Hewitt, 1995).

Social Science Research Methods

A hypothesis will suggest the type of information that will be gathered and how the information will be analyzed. *Quantitative methods* are those that gather information from many people, which can be analyzed to describe, explain, and predict patterns of behaviour for groups of people. The results of quantitative research can be analyzed using *statistics* to generalize from the behaviour of the sample group to predict the behaviour of the entire group. *Qualitative methods* are used to gather detailed information from individuals to help the researcher understand their behaviour. It assumes that each subject might behave differently and does not usually predict how others will behave. The evidence gathered by qualitative research can be analyzed to determine the reasons for the subjects' behaviour and can be presented anecdotally as case studies. While you are a student, practical considerations such as whether you have access to the population you want to study or have sufficient knowledge of statistics could limit your choice of research method.

Selecting a Research Method

The theoretical perspective that your hypothesis reflects also suggests the methods of gathering information that are most appropriate for your investigation. Choosing methods that other researchers have used makes it easier to see the connections between your research and the research of others. This overview outlines the methods most commonly associated with each approach.

Functionalism

Functionalists use quantitative methods; that is, they count observable behaviours to determine the *norms* (consistent behaviours) or the *trends* (patterns of change in behaviour). To gather a large body of observations, a functionalist perspective uses survey methods. A statistical analysis is used to identify the norms or trends. For example, Statistics Canada applies functionalism when it conducts a census every five years to produce demographics about Canadian society and publishes reports on the trends in the behaviour of Canadians.

Family Systems Theory

Family systems theory looks for the interactions among family members. It can be used to determine how individuals collaborate to carry out a plan or goal, how a change that affects one individual affects the behaviour of other members of the family, or how a family adapts to internal or external stimuli. Both quantitative and qualitative methods can be used. Observation and interviews are useful research methods that enable researchers to observe the interactions within a family.

Symbolic Interactionism and Social Exchange Theory

Symbolic interactionists and social exchange theorists investigate how people interpret their experiences and how they respond. To understand the mental processes of perception and interpretation, they use participant observation to view real behaviour, including behaviour that people may not be aware of, or may be unable to explain. Symbolic interactionists also use interviews to ask the actors to explain their behaviour as it makes sense to them. Social exchange theorists use survey methods to determine the values and priorities of individuals and experiments to enable them to determine factors that affect the choices people make.

Developmental Theories

Developmental theories describe the patterns in individuals' behaviour over time. Since a large and diverse sample group is necessary for identifying patterns, questionnaires and interviews are used to gather life histories from many people. Experiments can be used to determine cause-and-effect relationships. Some researchers also use content analysis for historical research. The sample group usually includes people of various ages, and the research should be repeated later to determine whether patterns apply to different generations and to ensure that the patterns are reliable for predicting behaviour.

Conflict Theory and Feminist Theories

Conflict theory and feminist theorists argue that objective methods that seek only to describe behaviour support social inequalities. Unlike objective researchers, they assume that the role of research is to facilitate change. Therefore, they gather data using qualitative methods and content analysis to determine the reasons for behaviour. Their analysis results in difficult questions that are designed to point out the inequities.

developing your research skills | Research Methods

Quantitative Research Methods

- **Experiments** In an experiment, the experimenter manipulates an independent variable to observe the effects. *Subjects* in the sample group are assigned randomly to an experimental group, or a control group. The independent variable being studied is applied only to the experimental group and not to the *control group*, and the behaviour of both groups is observed. To be valid, the effects should occur only in the experimental group and not in the control group, and they should be observed when the experiment is repeated.
- **Surveys** In surveys, the researcher asks a sample group questions and records their answers. In *questionnaires*, the questions are written and given to the subject to answer in written form. Usually the questions are *closed questions* that require the subject to select from the answers provided. Questionnaires can be used efficiently with very large sample groups. Interviews are usually conducted orally and *contain open-ended* questions that the subjects can answer freely. Interviews are suitable for smaller sample groups and for studies in which the answers cannot be anticipated.
- **Content Analysis** In content analysis, the researcher examines and classifies the ideas presented in a sample group of communications, such as books, letters, movies, or television commercials. The researcher defines the variables before conducting the research. Although it can be difficult to obtain a reliable sample, content analysis is useful for anthropological and historical research.

Qualitative Research Methods

- **Observations** In observations, the researcher watches and records the subjects' behaviour. Observations might be conducted in a laboratory setting; for example, a child psychologist might observe, from behind a two-way mirror, the interaction between a mother and child. Because the laboratory environment might influence the behaviour, a natural setting is preferred. The researcher can observe from a distance, perhaps using cameras, so that the subjects are unaware that they are being observed. In *participant observation*, the researcher is a participant in the group, and the subjects are aware that they are being observed.
- **Interviews** In interviews, the researcher asks the subject to describe and explain his or her behaviour. As a method of qualitative research, interviews are useful for determining the motivation for the subject's behaviour, which might not be visible to the researcher. To be valid, the interview questions should ask subjects to discuss actions after they occur rather than to speculate about what they might do. Interviews are often combined with participant observation. ∎

A research report is a technical paper that presents research in the social sciences. You will read them as part of your studies, and you will write them after you conduct your own investigations. In a research report, present the topic you investigated, your methods, your results, and the meaning of those results in a chronological order that reflects your research process.

Title

In the title identify the main idea of your paper and include the variables (usually).

Abstract

For the abstract write a summary, in about 100–150 words, of the topic that you investigated, the methods, the results, and the meaning of the results.

Introduction

In the introduction, define the terms, review the literature, relate the study to the review of literature, and state the purpose of the study.

Methods

In the method, describe the hypothesis and the specific research method you used to test the hypothesis.

- **Sample Group** In this section, describe the parameters you used to select the participants for the study and how you selected a representative sample.

- **Instruments** In this section, describe the survey, questionnaire, interview or observation schedule, or experiment used in your investigation.
- **Procedure** In this section, outline, step by step, how you conducted the research. Describe what you said and did in precise action terms.

Results

In the results, state your main findings, supported by detailed descriptions of the evidence and including case studies or statistical analysis.

Discussion

In the discussion, summarize the results of your research, explain how the results relate to the review of literature and the theoretical perspective you used in the analysis, and outline the implications of the results. Briefly state your conclusions in a paragraph that ends the discussion.

References

In a research paper, include citations to tell the reader where you found the information. Use in-text citations, like those used in this text, to refer your reader to the references at the end of the paper that acknowledge all of your sources. Use the American Psychological Association (APA) style in the social sciences. ■

chapter 2 Review and Apply

1. Identify three preconceptions or concerns you have about issues affecting individuals and families in Canada as you start your study. How might each of these concerns affect the choices you make about your life in the future?

2. **a)** What are the four fundamental questions asked by social scientists?

   b) If you apply the four fundamental questions to each of the issues you identified in question 1, what specific questions would you ask?

3. Explain how the disciplines of anthropology, sociology, and psychology differ in their study of individual and family behaviour.

4. Select a topic that interests you about individuals and families in Canada.

   a) What would an anthropologist ask about the topic?

   b) What would a sociologist ask?

   c) What would a psychologist ask?

5. Identify the basic theoretical assumptions of the following theories, and suggest how each would explain what happens in a classroom such as yours.
   - functionalism
   - systems theory
   - symbolic interactionism
   - social exchange theory
   - developmental perspective
   - conflict theory
   - feminist theories

6. Explain how you would choose a representative sample of high school students in your community for a research study concerning the behaviour of high school students.

7. Distinguish between a research essay and a research report. What experience have you had so far in writing, reading, or using each type of research paper?

8. Select an interesting topic concerning individual and family life. Write research questions that could be used as the basis for a research study that reflects as many of the various theoretical perspectives as possible.

9. Select a research study from the Internet. Describe the study under the following headings:

a) Research Question

b) Hypothesis

c) Research Method

d) Sample Group

e) Results

f) Conclusion

10. Identify a topic for a research study concerning individual and family life that you would like to pursue. After some preliminary reading to clarify the issues, formulate a research question that will be the basis of your research.

unit 2 Leaving Home

UNIT EXPECTATIONS

While reading this unit, you will:

- analyze decisions and behaviours related to individual role expectations

- analyze theories and research on the subject of individual development, and summarize your findings

- analyze current issues and trends relevant to individual development, and speculate on future directions

- analyze issues and data from the perspectives associated with key theories in the disciplines of anthropology, psychology, and sociology

- communicate the results of your inquiries

Although legally you are an adult at the age of 18, leaving home and becoming financially independent are signs that you are acquiring an adult role in Canadian society.

OVERVIEW

This unit looks at the transition into adulthood for young Canadians
at the beginning of the twenty-first century. Perhaps because people are
living longer and because our society is more complex than it used to be,
becoming independent individuals takes longer than it did for previous
generations. In this unit, research will be examined to determine when
and how Canadians are leaving home to live independently, finishing their
education, finding jobs, and forming adult relationships. The psychological
and developmental factors that influence how each young adult manages
the transition, and how relationships within the family and with others
support this transition, will also be explored. Finally, some of the issues
that are currently affecting how your generation will become adults will
be investigated.

chapter 3

Early Adulthood

CHAPTER EXPECTATIONS

While reading this chapter, you will:

- describe the diversity in personal and family roles of individuals in various cultures and historical periods
- analyze male and female roles in various societies and historical periods, taking into consideration societal norms and ideals, individuals' perceptions of roles, and actual behaviours
- describe the various roles of individuals in society and the potential for conflict between individual and family roles
- summarize the factors that influence decisions about individual lifestyle in early adulthood, drawing on traditional and current research and theory
- summarize the factors that influence decisions about educational and occupational choices
- select and access secondary sources reflecting a variety of viewpoints
- identify and respond to the theoretical viewpoints, the thesis, and the supporting arguments of materials found in a variety of secondary sources

KEY TERMS

abstract
adolescence
adulthood
age of majority
credentialism
education inflation
mentor
transition

Families help young adults become independent by permitting them to relate to their families as adults and by supporting them in their decisions.

CHAPTER INTRODUCTION

The transition to adulthood is the next step in your life. Some students might consider themselves to be adults already, but most will be focusing on the changes that will occur in the next few years. What are the criteria for defining someone as an adult? Will the transition to adulthood be the same for this generation as it was for your parents' generation or for that of your grandparents? In this chapter, the experiences of earlier generations in completing the transition to adulthood will be examined. When and how the majority of young people separate from their parents to form an independent household will be determined. The changes in educational achievement and employment that enable youth to become financially independent will also be explored. In addition, the important relationships young people need to develop, which provide support for them as they become adults, will be studied.

The Role of Adults in Canada

Adulthood is that period of life that follows childhood and **adolescence** and lasts until death. Therefore, the time that adulthood begins depends on when adolescence ends—a passage that is not clearly defined in Western society. In common use, terms identifying the stages of life are used quite casually. For example, a newspaper item described the death of a Hamilton, Ontario, teenager, aged 18, in a drowning accident, but the headline stated "Police identify Hamilton man." Was the drowning victim an adolescent or an adult? In this textbook it is assumed that you are adolescents until the end of high school. In Canada, you achieve the **age of majority** and become an adult, by law, at 18 years of age. In this chapter, youth, a **transition** that begins during adolescence and continues into early adulthood, will be examined. In research, the boundaries of youth are widely accepted as 15–34 years of age (Meunier, Bernard, & Boisjoly, 1998), but many Canadians feel they are fully adult by their late twenties.

When individuals achieve adult status, they are expected to take on appropriate adult roles in society. In North America, the popular assumption, shared by many researchers, is that to become an adult is to become a self-reliant person. That means that a young adult has formed an identity as an

web connection

www.mcgrawhill.ca/links/families12

To learn about young people's legal rights, go to the web site above for *Individuals and Families in a Diverse Society* to see where to go next.

Expectations of Teenagers			
Do you expect to . . .	**Percent indicating "Yes"**		
	Nationally	**Males**	**Females**
Pursue a career	95%	93%	96%
Get the job you want when you graduate	86	86	86
Stay with the same career for life	62	61	62
Get married	88	87	89
Stay with the same partner for life	88	87	89
Eventually stay home and raise your children	45	47	43
Own your own home	96	97	96
Be more financially comfortable than your parents	79	81	77
Have to work overtime in order to get ahead	44	48	41
Travel extensively outside Canada	72	68	77
Be involved in your community	65	62	68
See the national debt paid off in your lifetime	49	51	47

Source: "Table 4.2: Expectations of Teenagers" from *Canada's Teens: Today, Yesterday, and Tomorrow.* Copyright © 2001 by Reginald W. Bibby. Reproduced by permission of Stoddart Publishing Co. Limited.

There is no single age at which young people are given the rights we normally associate with being an adult. People gain more rights as they grow up, and some rights do not exist until well after legal "adulthood" at age 18. The following is a list of some of some rights that young people acquire at ages ranging from 7 to 19. Some do not come at a specific age, but vary from person to person, depending on the circumstances.

7 and Over

- Consent to be adopted required.

12 and Over

- Can be prosecuted for provincial offences, such as truancy.
- Can be charged with a criminal offence.
- Can consent on one's own to counselling by service provider.
- Consent is required to change name.

14 and Over

- Can reside with a third party or non-custodial parent without criminal repercussion to the parent or third party.
- Can see Adult entertainment movies if with a person 18 years or older.
- Can consent to sexual activity except with a person in a position of authority or trust.

15

- If fifteenth birthday is between first day of school and December 31, can quit school at the end of that school year.

16 and Over

- Is considered an adult under the Provincial Offences Act.
- If sixteenth birthday is between January 1 and the end of August, can quit school on sixteenth birthday.
- Can work during school hours.

- Is entitled to participate in a decision identifying whether one is a special needs student and subsequent placement.
- Can voluntarily withdraw from parental control, but may lose right to parents' financial support.
- Can no longer be apprehended by the Children's Aid Society.
- Can refuse emergency treatment.
- Can be or appoint a substitute decision maker in medical treatment and personal care matters.
- If single, is entitled to social assistance in special circumstances.
- Is protected from discrimination based on age respecting housing.
- Is eligible for novice driver's licence in graduated licensing scheme.
- Has the right to privacy of, and access to, personal information on own behalf.

Under 18

- May be sued on contracts for necessities (such as housing). May be sued on contracts for non-necessities if beneficial to the minor.

18 and Over

- Age of majority—ceases to be a minor.
- Is eligible to vote.
- Adult for the purposes of the Education Act, but if appealing a suspension, parents will still be notified.
- Is protected from age discrimination.
- Can no longer be the subject of custody or access orders.
- Parents' obligation to provide financial support ceases, unless in school full time.
- Is eligible for social assistance, if in need.
- Is entitled to earn full minimum wage.
- Can enter into contracts.

- Can make a will.
- Can change name.
- Can see a restricted movie.
- Can marry without permission.

19 and Over

- Can consume alcohol.
- Can purchase tobacco.

Non Age-Based Milestones

- Pupils of any age can see their school records.

- Consent to medical treatment depends on mental capacity, not age.
- Federal Human Rights Code and Charter protect all ages from age discrimination.
- Single parents of any age are eligible for social assistance, if needed.
- Civil liability of minors depends on maturity, not age (no known case ascribing liability to a child of "tender years," i.e., under 6 years). ■

Source: Justice for Children and Youth

individual, has separated from his or her family of orientation, has started a career, has left the home of origin, and has formed supportive relationships (Bateson, 2000; Côté & Allahar, 1994; Mead, 1935; Shanahan, 2000). Betty Carter and Monica McGoldrick (1989) describe young, single adulthood as the first stage of the family life cycle, since the young adult leaves one family to prepare for the formation of another. Since the transition has changed so much over the last two generations, North Americans question whether adolescents are adequately being prepared for the challenges of adulthood (Bateson, 2000).

Adolescents in Canada are optimistic about their futures as adults. In a study of the attitudes and values of teens aged 15 to 19, Reginald Bibby (2001) found that the majority expect to graduate from school, pursue a career, marry, and be better off than their parents.

This optimism was also found in the answers given by American students in the 1990s (Csikszentmihalyi & Schneider, 2000). However, young people experience some anxiety about making the right decisions and plans to achieve their expectations (Bateson, 2000). Becoming an adult is an important transition in all societies, but the diversity of adult roles available in the twenty-first century makes the nature of this transition more difficult to predict.

In North America, the common assumption is that you will be an adult when you are a self-reliant person.

The Transition to Adulthood in Earlier Times

In the twentieth century, historians started to piece together a *social history*. This section describes the social history of youth in Canada and in Europe.

Later, you will read some observations of this stage in non-Western cultures to remind you that human social behaviours, being inventions and not natural facts, can be very diverse. Social historians, like cultural anthropologists, are limited in their understanding. They tend to examine the observations of other societies to look for examples that are representative. For instance, the common image of youth in the 1960s is the "hippie era of psychedelic drugs and free love." In fact, this behaviour was more prevalent in the early 1970s and was limited to a small segment of the youth population. Therefore, just as you might observe many individual variations in behaviour now, so the conduct of people varies in other societies (Bateson, 2000).

Social historians rely on surviving accounts from the past as their primary sources. Official papers contain information about laws, regulations, and court decisions affecting individual and family matters. Essays advising others about the conduct of people's lives present the ideals of outspoken members of society. Poems and, more recently, novels, reflect the perceptions of their authors. Content analysis of personal papers reveals details of people's lives, including the thoughts and feelings they choose to express. Newspapers document both facts and opinions about day-to-day issues. When analyzing the descriptions of Canadian and other societies, it is useful to consider whether they reflect what actually happened, the opinions of critics, or the ideals of those in power.

The Impact of Industrialization

In pre-industrial societies, there was no adolescence as people know it today. Children were infants until aged seven or eight, when they were considered to be old enough to take on some kind of work. After this age they were called **youth** until they married and lived independently, usually in their mid- to late twenties. Working-class youth often left their families to live in other households in a state of semi-dependence. Their role in that new household depended on their social class. Lower-class children became domestic servants if they were girls and labourers or apprentices learning a trade if they were boys. Upper-class children were educated at home. The father as *pater familias*, father of the household, was expected to treat all who lived in his household—wife, children, servants, apprentices—as family and to be loved by them (Gillis, 1974), but he exerted strict discipline over them regardless of their age.

Functionalists explain that the separation of youth from their parents was a practical solution in pre-industrial societies. The high rates of infant mortality and childhood illnesses resulted in half the children dying before the age of 20.

Families produced many children to improve their chances of having a male heir survive to support them in their old age. Poorer families could not provide enough work for all their children, so they sent them to work for wealthier families until they were old enough to marry. The prevailing advice to parents, to avoid becoming attached to their children, was based more on the fear that their children would probably die soon than on the value of independence (Gillis, 1974). Sending children away achieved the recommended separation of parent and child and also provided youth with some opportunity for social mobility and a choice of occupation.

Industrialization changed all of this. In the nineteenth century, as production moved from the home to the factory, and families migrated to cities to work, it became possible for youth to earn an income without leaving home. Instead of sending them away, fathers took their young sons and daughters to work in factories, where they retained their authority over them and even collected their children's wages until they turned 17. After this age, young people earned an income and became boarders in their parents' homes, still contributing income to the family (Gillis, 1974). The daughters of the new middle class, the factory owners, were educated at home, while the sons were sent away to school. Young men and women with an income enjoyed more freedom when they were finished the long work day, and participated in organized social activities. Although half of them stayed home until they were 24 or older, it is not surprising that they married and left home at a younger age than previous generations did.

In the early twentieth century, middle-class children attended school, but working-class children, such as these newsboys, left school at age 14 or earlier to earn money to help support their families.

The twentieth century was a period of change for the family, as it was for many other institutions. The mechanization of production had reduced the need for labour. Although many parents resisted the change because they felt that they had a right to have their children work (Gillis, 1974), child labour had been abolished, and schooling had been introduced to occupy the children. Early in the century, the age for leaving school was 14, but it was soon raised to 16 as the number of jobs available for young adolescents declined. In 1904, G. Stanley Hall used an old term from the middle ages, *adolescence*, to identify children who had reached puberty but who were still not in the workforce (Allahar & Côté, 1994). With the extension of schooling, adolescence became a time of learning and leisure for the children of the growing middle class. But in the working class, young people continued to leave school to work at menial jobs to help support their families. Those living in urban centres of Canada were able to live at home until they married. Those from rural areas and in regions with depressed economies had to migrate to cities and board with other families as they searched for work there (Brookes, 1982).

Coming of Age in the Twenty-First Century

The major changes in Canadian society that marked the last century have continued into the twenty-first century. Some researchers suggest that the transition from childhood to adulthood has become an extended period of adolescence (Sheehy, 1995). By this they mean that individuals remain emotionally and financially dependent on their parents until their late twenties or later. Youth seem to be leaving school and starting work, leaving home, getting married, and even becoming parents in a more compressed time frame than was the case a hundred years ago (Shanahan, 2000). Young people now spend more years in school but have fewer job opportunities when they leave because there has been another major shift in the economy that has reduced the work available. James Allahar and Anton Côté (1994) argue in their book *Generation on Hold* that youth have lost their voice in adult society because they are held back as consumers of a youth culture rather than allowed to become productive members of society in responsible adult roles.

Do the conditions in Canada make it easy for youth to make a successful transition to adulthood? Allahar and Côté quote Margaret Mead's opinion, based on her observations of the change in various South Sea island cultures, that society should provide two things:

- a set of consistent beliefs about the behaviour of adults
- opportunities for young people to participate in clear adult roles

In Canada, the diversity of roles available for adults presents the challenge of choosing which path to take. Many adult roles are not accessible to youth if, like most, they do not have a stable income, so many young Canadians today do not take on these roles until later than previous generations did. Functionalists explain that delaying the transition into adulthood is necessary to protect young people who are not yet fully socialized for adulthood in our advanced society. On the other hand, conflict theorists such as Côté and Allahar could argue that youth are exploited by a society that does not allow their full participation in the workplace and, therefore, prevents them from achieving independence from their families.

Each of us is a member of a cohort, a grouping of people in society based on age. Cohorts do not correspond exactly to generations but, rather, to fertility patterns. For example, the *baby-boom* cohort was born during a 20-year span from 1947 until 1966, including those who were born in other countries. That 20-year period was marked by a sustained high birth rate in Canada, when women were having an average of just over four children. The Canadian economy was very prosperous in the 1950s and 1960s. Canadians knew they could afford large families because the future appeared very promising. Other cohorts in Canada span shorter periods of time.

Baby boomers are characterized as a special group by the media, particularly because of their influence on Canadian society. This has been the case since they were young adults, has continued to this day, and will continue until most of their cohort has died. There is one simple reason for this: they represent the largest cohort by far—one-third of the Canadian population in 1998. So their influence in Canada, both socially and economically, is tremendous. For instance, when the oldest segment of the baby-boomer cohort reached their thirties in the late 1970s, they were just starting their families and beginning to think about purchasing a house. Consequently, the price of houses increased rapidly because there were far more potential buyers than sellers. This trend continued until the beginning of the 1990s, when demand for homes declined as the last of the baby boomers, known as *Generation X*, reached the house-buying age. The cohort following the baby boomers, called the *baby bust*, is a very small one. It spans only 12 years, from 1967 until 1979, a period of declining fertility in Canada, when women were averaging only 1.7 children each. So you can see why the baby boomers are so influential.

Members of the baby boom echo cohort are the children of the baby boomers.

Your demographic cohort, known as the *baby-boom echo*, was born between 1980 and 1995. You are the children of the baby boomers, who created a mini-boom of their own. Since they started to reproduce late, baby boomers were not as prolific as their parents, averaging just under two children per family. However, the baby-boom echo is still a large cohort because there were 6.5 million by 1998, over 20 percent of the Canadian population. That is why you experienced crowded schools, or why your parents had to line up for hours to sign you up for swimming lessons when you were younger. The size of your cohort explains the success of television programming like MuchMusic or *The Simpsons* and why the minivan was such a success for the North American auto industry—it was built so that this very large cohort could be driven to swimming lessons or hockey practice! The size of the baby-boom echo cohort could mean that you will continue to compete for opportunities throughout your lifetimes. ■

Source: Adapted from Foot, D.K., & Stoffman, D. (1998), *Boom, bust & echo 2000*. Rev. ed. Toronto: Macfarlane Walter & Ross, pp. 24-30.

1. What jobs should be plentiful in the future for your cohort as the baby-boom generation begins to reach retirement age?
2. Why would members of Generation X have found it more difficult to find well-paying jobs that lead to promotion than their parents' generation did, even though they were often better trained and educated?

Leaving Home

In the television program *Friends*, which was popular during the 1990s, six young adults in their mid-twenties lived in several apartments near one another in New York City. They had finished their education and had started to work at their careers, with varying degrees of success. Although they were all sexually active, none of them lived as a married or cohabiting couple until the seventh year of the series. The program was applauded for presenting a realistic image of young adult life. Living independently, either alone or with other non-related people, now seems to be the major event that signals successful transition into adulthood in North America (Vinovskis, 2001).

You will make many decisions as you become an adult. Will you pursue education? Where will you work? Where will you live? With whom will you live?

---

developing your research skills | Using Questionnaires

Using *questionnaires*, you can ask a large sample group of people questions and record their answers. Usually, the questions are *closed*, meaning that the subject must select from the answers provided.

Leaving Home Questionnaire

1. Design a questionnaire to determine whether the adolescents in your school community and their parents have similar expectations concerning adult children leaving home.
   a) Develop a hypothesis stating what you think might be the answer.
   b) Introduce and state the nature of your study.
   c) Include multiple-choice questions to elicit the information needed to test your hypothesis:
      - whether the subject is an adolescent or parent
      - age at which subject expects an adult child to leave home
      - anticipated reason for leaving home (e.g., marriage, work, or to attend school in another location)
   d) Put the results in chart form, using numbers and percentages, and analyze them to formulate conclusions concerning your hypothesis. ■

In other species, the young are expected to leave when they become sexually mature. Anthropologist Robert Sapolsky (1997) describes how male chimpanzees must leave the tribe in which they were raised and join another tribe. To accomplish this, they must survive a fight with an older male of the new tribe. Some human societies have also expected their young to leave the family home early. Among the BaMbuti people of East Africa, adolescent boys leave

web connection

www.mcgrawhill.ca/links/families12

To learn about a service that allows students to exchange homes to reduce the cost of post-secondary education, and a guide to all aspects of post-secondary education, go to the web site above for *Individuals and Families in a Diverse Society* to see where to go next.

their families for *nkumbi*, a challenging initiation that takes place in a small village built specifically for this rite. When the *nkumbi* is finished, the village is burned and the young men return to their original village, but to build their own homes, where they will live until they marry several years later (Turnbull, 1985). In the nineteenth century, puberty occurred at the age of 16 for girls and 18 for boys, and the development of adult size and strength occurred a few years later. Therefore, marriage and leaving home would occur within a few years of physical maturity (Gillis, 1974). Now that improved nutrition has lowered puberty to as early as 10 years of age, sexual maturity occurs five to eight years before individuals achieve their full adult size and strength. In Canadian society, sexual maturity is no longer an appropriate indication that an individual is ready to leave home.

North Americans expect that young adults will leave home before they marry, but it is usually a gradual process rather than an event. Many students have to leave home to attend college or university, where they live in student housing. In some countries, young people leave home for military service and live in communal barracks. For example, in Israel, two years of military service are required of all high school graduates. Young Mormons are expected to perform missionary service away from home for two years. These living arrangements are called *semi-dependent* because it is assumed that parents are still supporting the young adult to some extent and that they will return home frequently. For example, Bateson (2000) tells the story that in Israel they joke that the army doesn't need washing machines—the soldiers take their uniforms home for their mothers to wash! Living independently requires individuals to accept the responsibility for meeting their own needs for food, clothing, shelter, and companionship.

When Adults Leave Home

For many young Canadians, living independently happens later than it used to. The majority are still living at home at 24 years of age (Boyd & Norris, 1999). So are the majority of 24-year-olds in southern Europe, western Europe, and the United States. In their book *Next: Predicting the Near Future*, Ira Matathia and Marian Slazman have dubbed this trend *the Permakid* (1999). They suggest that the family of the near future will have to change to accommodate adult children. Several research questions arise concerning this topic:

- When do young Canadians leave home, and how does the timing compare with earlier generations?

- How do families influence the decision?

- How is the decision to leave home affected by education, employment, and relationships with others?

The American study "High School and Beyond" found that 7 out of 10 high school graduates and 6 out of 10 of their parents expected that they would be living independently by the age of 24 (Goldscheider & Goldscheider, 1993). Therefore, since the average age for marriage is now over 30, both parents and adult children expect that young adults will leave home before marriage. The decision to leave home can be analyzed using the social exchange theory. Young adults have to consider the costs and benefits of staying at home compared with those of leaving. They must weigh a desire for privacy from parental supervision and independence to live a different lifestyle from that of their parents, against the companionship and the financial and emotional support they receive from them. Staying at home allows individuals to invest in further education and to find a good job before having to find affordable housing and pay rent (Boyd & Norris, 1995). Financial costs may tip the balance, but parental expectations concerning the appropriate time are an important factor in determining when adult children will leave home (Goldscheider & Goldscheider, 1993).

"The primary purpose of raising a child is to help that child get out of your life and into a life of its own."

— John Rosemond

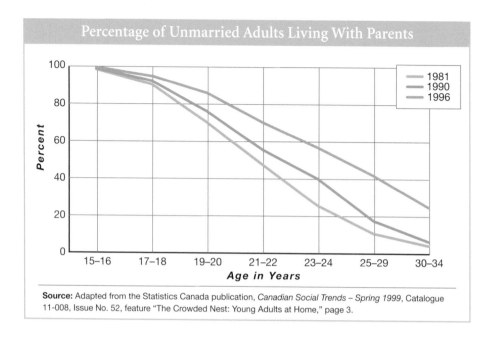

Percentage of Unmarried Adults Living With Parents

Age in Years

Legend: 1981, 1990, 1996

Source: Adapted from the Statistics Canada publication, *Canadian Social Trends – Spring 1999*, Catalogue 11-008, Issue No. 52, feature "The Crowded Nest: Young Adults at Home," page 3.

The age at which young people choose to live independently of their parents is gradually increasing. The Eternal Youth study found that, by 1990, living with parents continued to be almost universal at the ages of 15 and 16 and very rare at the age of 34. Between those ages, however, young people were staying home longer than before. Young women continued to leave home earlier than young men did (Meunier, Bernard, & Boisjoly, 1998). Staying home until older is a trend that has continued. By 1996, 7 out of 10 unmarried adults were living with their parents at the age of 24, and 1 in 4 were still at home between the ages of 30 to 34 (Boyd & Norris, 1999). In a social phenomenon that appears to have spread across the Western world, young adults are choosing to live with their parents longer.

For Better or For Worse®   **by Lynn Johnston**

Source: © Lynn Johnston Productions, Inc./Distributed by United Features Syndicate, Inc.

RESEARCH QUESTION

When do young Canadians leave home, and how does the timing compare with that of earlier generations?

HYPOTHESES

- It is possible that young people now leave the parental home later.
- All forms of cohabitation, other than forming a couple, may be relatively more frequent.
- Gender differences are becoming less of a factor.

RESEARCH METHOD

Using *secondary analysis*, the researchers analyzed data from Statistics Canada's Survey of Consumer Finances on living arrangements and participation in education and employment, sorted by age and gender for 1981 and 1990.

RESULTS

- Between the ages of 15 and 34, young people were leaving home later in 1990 than they were in 1981.

- Although fewer were living as couples in 1990 than in 1981, by the age of 24, more than half of those who had left home were living as couples. Living alone or with a roommate was more common in 1990; however, at the age of 24, it was still in third place behind living with parents or living as a couple.
- Men continue to leave home later than women do at all ages, but the gap was less for those under the age of 20 and greater for those over 20.

CONCLUSION

All of their hypotheses were supported by their investigation. ■

Source: Adapted from Meunier, D., Bernard, P., & Boisjoly, J. (1998). Eternal youth? Changes in the living arragements of young people. In M. Corak (Ed.), *Labour markets, social institutions, and the future of Canada's children*. Ottawa: Statistics Canada.

The Decision to Leave Home

The factors that influence the decision to leave home are complex. It is clear that young adults leave home later than they thought they would, but also later than their parents thought they would (Goldscheider & Goldscheider, 1993). In The Nesting Phenomena Survey, an American study conducted in 1996, many young adults who were living with their parents commented that they enjoyed the security of living at home while they finished their education and were looking for work (Wiener, 1997). On the other hand, some young adults stay because they are responsible for the care of a parent. Parents enjoy the companionship of their adult children if they are able to establish an adult relationship with them (Boyd & Norris, 1995; Wiener, 1997). A comfortable family environment seems to encourage young adults to stay at home.

Leaving home occurs earlier when there is conflict in the family. When young adults feel that their parents demand too much from them without granting them adult status in the family, they may leave home to assert their

Living by yourself requires that you accept responsibility for all the bills and all the housework.

independence (Goldscheider & Goldscheider, 1997). Children of divorced parents are more likely to leave home, especially if one or both parents have remarried. Those who live with a stepparent are most likely to leave home if they feel that it is no longer their home and if they receive less parental support from a stepparent (Boyd & Norris, 1995; Goldscheider & Goldscheider, 1997).

The economics of leaving home is also an important factor. Living at home is usually cheaper than living alone or with roommates. However, some parents are willing to continue to support unmarried children even when they leave home. Choosing to stay at home can be more economical, since most youth pay little or no room and board and continue to do the few chores they took on as adolescents (Goldscheider & Goldscheider, 1997; Allahar & Côté, 1998). There is currently a shortage of housing in many parts of Canada, which results in higher rents and fewer affordable apartments. Young adults with a low personal income, either because they are unemployed or unable to find full-time work or because they are still attending school, are more likely to stay home. The adult children of more affluent parents might be used to a more comfortable lifestyle and more privacy in their parents' home. Therefore, it is not surprising that children of parents with limited incomes are more likely to leave and support themselves, whereas children of higher-income families decide to leave home later (Goldscheider & Goldscheider, 1997; Wiener, 1997).

Women usually decide to leave home earlier than men do. In Canada, the gap between the age when women leave and when men leave is getting narrower for those under 23, but the gap is widening for those over 24 (Meunier, Bernard, & Boisjoly, 1998). The difference might be explained by the rate at which women form couples. Traditionally, women married and left home at an earlier age than men did because they tended to marry men who were two years older. This continues to be the pattern, although marriage is delayed until the late twenties. Perhaps some of the unmarried women who have left home are cohabiting in couple relationships with older men. Another possible reason is that since young women receive more experience in housework as adolescents (Devereaux, 1993; Wiener, 1997), they might be more willing to accept the responsibilities of maintaining a separate household to gain their

Colleen Johnson is a 23-year-old graduate from Trent University who has recently completed her B.A. in Honours History and International Politics. She moved back to Toronto to attend the teacher education program at the University of Toronto. Both of Colleen's parents are high school teachers. Colleen has resisted becoming a teacher, even though it is a career that fits into her life goals, because she doesn't want "to become her parents" and would prefer to do things her own way. This has created a conflict between Colleen and her parents.

Colleen's decision to move back home was necessitated by the fact that she spent her summer travelling in India and Nepal, and because rents in Toronto, even for student accommodations, are very high. She plans to use her qualifications to work as a teacher abroad so that she can continue to travel.

Colleen's transition to living at home again has been very difficult. She has been relatively independent for the past four years at university and has not had to account for herself to others. Her summers have been spent in northern Ontario working as a canoe instructor at a children's camp.

Colleen's older sister, Emma, has recently married and is living in the basement apartment in her parents' house with her husband, Sanjay. Emma is finishing her Ph.D. in International Relations, and Sanjay is working as an economist for an investment firm. Colleen's younger brother, Andy, is a high school student who lives at home, but his part-time job at the local supermarket keeps him busy Friday nights and all day Saturday.

Colleen's parents have enjoyed having her around, but have had to make adjustments to having their middle child living with them again. They had been

Colleen's move back to her parents' home has been difficult after being independent while living on her own throughout university.

used to being alone on the third floor of their house and had been using Colleen's bedroom as a study and sewing room.

Sometimes Colleen wonders whether her parents realize that she has grown up in the past four years. To her, they seem unhappy when she goes out at night and want to know where she is going, whom she is with, and when she will return home. At the age of 23, Colleen feels that they should trust her judgment. Colleen's parents also have asked her to cook the occasional meal and to help tidy up when needed, but because she is busy with her studies, she often does not get around to doing these things even though she intends to. ■

1. What difficulties is Colleen experiencing living in her parents' home again? Why?
2. Are Colleen's difficulties related only to her living arrangement? Explain.
3. What potential conflicts do you think Colleen and her parents may have? Why?
4. Using the social exchange theory, assess the costs and benefits of Colleen's return home for Colleen and for her parents.
5. Systems theory suggests that each household member would have to make adjustments to Colleen's return to the family home. How do you think Colleen's return would affect Emma, Andy, and Sanjay?

independence from protective parents. However, it is possible that the shrinking gap between men and women is a cohort effect that will continue as the baby-bust generation ages, but is not necessarily a change that will continue in future generations.

Although the trend for young adults to leave home later than previous generations did has continued for two decades, it is not known whether it will continue for your generation. There are conflicting viewpoints on the consequences of the current trend. Some suggest that individuals who stay home longer are more likely to acquire the values and behaviour of their parents (Boyd & Pryor, 1990; Meunier, Bernard, & Boisjoly, 1998). Others consider staying at home into the late twenties to be a symptom of immaturity, either in adult children who cannot separate from their parents, or in parents who are unable to let go of their adult children (Goldscheider & Goldscheider, 1997). Valerie Wiener (1997) suggests that Canadians could be observing a gradual redefinition of the family to better meet our needs. When your generation chooses to leave home will reflect the social and economic influences over the next decade.

Completing an Education

The Development of Education

Education is a recent development in human society. In non-literate societies, news and knowledge was spread through storytelling, so young people could begin to know as much as their elders. Youth followed in the footsteps of their parents—girls became mothers, and boys continued the labour or craft of their fathers. Children knew what to do and could work alongside adults, but lacked the experience and, of course, the physical strength to take on adult responsibility (Postman, 1982). By the Middle Ages, wealthy boys were sent to "Latin Schools" to remove them from the company of women. The term *adolescent*, derived from the Latin word *adolescere*, which means *to grow up*, was used briefly by church schools in the fifteenth century to refer to their students. Letters from that time suggest that very little education actually took place, because the boys were undisciplined (Gillis, 1974). Whether the boys and girls were rich or poor, the long period of youth was devoted to maturing and practising the skills needed for their adult roles.

Education for most people became feasible when the development of the printing press in the fifteenth century made it possible to publish written works for a mass audience. Reading gave people access to knowledge that previously had been available only to a few "scribes." Since reading is a solitary activity, it enabled individuals to make their own meaning of the information and to discuss ideas with others. Adults became more knowledgeable than children because reading is a skill that takes time to develop. According to communications theorist Neil Postman, literacy created a division between childhood and adulthood based on access to knowledge (1982). Until the nineteenth century, education for the youth of wealthy families emphasized the classics, Latin, Greek, mathematics, and literature, not job training, but little education was available for the majority of children.

In the late nineteenth century, primary schools were established to educate all children. Since working-class parents knew their children already had the skills required for manual labour, there was widespread resistance to schooling. It was not until the twentieth century that the concept of education for all was widely accepted. Even then, in the first 30 years, most boys and girls left school at the age of 14 to work, and some children from poorer families did not attend school regularly even when they were legally obliged to (Clark, 2000). The assumption was that starting work early was more valuable because they would learn the specific skills required on the job (Côté & Allahar, 1994).

In the 1950s, Canadians believed that providing opportunities for all young people to get a good education would contribute to economic equality.

When the government of Nigeria, West Africa, introduced universal primary education in 1974, rural parents also resisted sending their children to school instead of the fields because they saw no economic advantage to schooling. Although today people accept that education is essential for success in life, there are still many parts of the world where parents do not send their children to school.

In the 50 years since World War II, Canada and other Western countries have continually evaluated whether their education systems were preparing youth adequately. In 1947, fewer than half of students graduated from high school, prompting the Canadian Education Association to call for "the type of training which will enable these young people to assume the full responsibilities of citizenship" (Gaskell, 1993, p. xii). The prosperity of the 1950s led to a new philosophy of education that has continued more or less as policy in Canadian provinces. It was believed that education would contribute to economic growth, as Canadian workers would be more productive. However, it was also believed that education would contribute to economic equality by providing opportunities for all youth to acquire skills that would qualify them for well-paying jobs (Clark, 2000). By the 1960s and 1970s, several "streams" were introduced to high schools so that all students could be educated, regardless of ability. Post-secondary education became more accessible in the 1960s and 1970s, as new universities were built to accommodate the baby-boom children, and community colleges were opened to provide technical and vocational training. In the 1980s, the goal of education was to provide students with the skills that would be required in a changing workplace, but there was also an effort to counsel students to choose an education suited to their interests and abilities (Gaskell, 1993).

Percentage of Young Men and Women Attending School, 1921–1991				
Years	**Ages 15–19**		**Ages 20–24**	
	Men	**Women**	**Men**	**Women**
1921	23%	27%	3%	2%
1931	32	35	4	2
1941	34	37	5	3
1951	41	40	7	3
1961	62	56	12	5
1971	74	56	12	5
1981	66	66	21	16
1991	79	80	32	33

Source: Allahar, A. & Côté, J. (1998). *Richer and poorer: the structure of inequality in Canada.* Toronto: James Lorimer & Company Ltd., Publishers, p. 134.

By the end of the twentieth century, education was viewed as the key to success in life. Assuming that "anyone can get ahead if they do well at school" (Gaskell, 1991), families, schools, and employers encouraged young people to stay in school and to attend post-secondary education to avoid unemployment, get better jobs, and earn a higher income. Youth aspired to high educational goals. In 2000, 62 percent of young people aged 15 to 19 expected to graduate from university, 18 percent expected to graduate from college, and less than 1 percent thought they would not finish high school (Bibby, 2001). Youth talked about having a "career," not a job, and expected to be better off than their parents.

The Value of Education

Most Canadians believe that the best way to prepare for a career is through formal post-secondary education. Students are encouraged to qualify for the jobs they want by learning the necessary skills in a college or university program. In 1999, the Council of Ministers in Education, in their Report on Education (p. 6), emphasized the value of education:

> All jobs, not just new jobs, demand higher levels of education and technical ability. Since 1990, the number of jobs requiring a university degree or post-secondary diploma has increased by 1.3 million. The total number of jobs available for people with less learning has decreased by 800 000. The more learning you have, the more likely it is that you will find a good job.

Increasingly in Canada, education is valued for job training rather than for its intrinsic interest (Gaskell, 1991). Côté and Allahar (1994) refer to this trend as **credentialism**. Students receive career counselling to select courses that provide the prerequisites for further education, and then to choose the post-secondary program that will earn them the credentials for a job. They also tend to select courses in which they expect to achieve higher marks, rather than choose those that are interesting but challenging (Gaskell, 1991). Clearly, Canadian youth expect education to prepare them for work. Ninety percent of post-secondary graduates in 1990 stated that it was important or very important to obtain employment related to their field of study (Little & Lapierre, 1996).

The majority of young Canadians attain some post-secondary education. Canada's secondary graduation rate—the percentage of 18-year-olds outside of Québec and 17-year-olds in Québec, where secondary school ends at grade 11— was 72. However, when students are allowed more years to complete their schooling, 85 percent of 24-year-old Canadians had completed high school

Most high school graduates will go on to post-secondary education to prepare for their careers.

(Clark, 2000). Most of them graduated at the end of their high school years, but others were school leavers who returned to school to complete their high school education. Of those who graduated from high school:

- 80 percent went on to post-secondary education

- 42 percent chose university

- 29 percent chose community college

- the remainder went to other post-secondary programs, such as private business or art schools and apprenticeships

In addition, one in four school leavers—those who had left before graduating—eventually enrolled in post-secondary programs (Clark, 1997). Not all students who enrol will graduate. Universities estimate that 10–20 percent of students will drop out by the end of their first year, and only 58 percent of those who start will graduate within five years. However, Canada now leads the industrial nations of the world in the percentage of the population having post-secondary education (Canadian Education Statistics Council, 2000).

"Jobs demand higher levels of education and technical ability" (Council of Ministers of Education, 1999), but do individuals require the education

web connection

www.mcgrawhill.ca/links/families12

To learn more about school issues of interest to Canadian youth, go to the web site above for *Individuals and Families in a Diverse Society* to see where to go next.

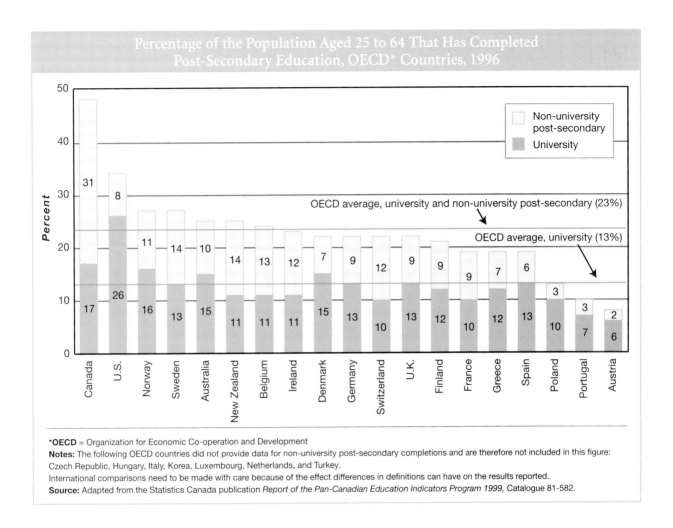

Percentage of the Population Aged 25 to 64 That Has Completed Post-Secondary Education, OECD* Countries, 1996

*OECD = Organization for Economic Co-operation and Development

Notes: The following OECD countries did not provide data for non-university post-secondary completions and are therefore not included in this figure: Czech Republic, Hungary, Italy, Korea, Luxembourg, Netherlands, and Turkey.

International comparisons need to be made with care because of the effect differences in definitions can have on the results reported.

Source: Adapted from the Statistics Canada publication *Report of the Pan-Canadian Education Indicators Program 1999,* Catalogue 81-582.

and technical training demanded to do the job? In their book *A Generation on Hold*, Côté and Allahar argue that **education inflation** has meant that youth today require more education to qualify for some jobs now than was required of the same jobs in the past (1994). Using a conflict theory perspective, they argue that the demand for higher education reflects a desire to gain professional status and wealth, not higher skills. For example, they explain that medicine was not considered to be a respectable occupation until university education became a requirement for doctors in the nineteenth century. They quote the results of an American survey: 40 percent of graduates holding jobs that required a bachelor's degree said they didn't think a degree was necessary to do the job. They conclude by suggesting that "education inflation" is eroding the faith Canadian youth have in education (Côté & Allahar, 1994).

Employment and Education

Whether or not the knowledge and skills acquired in post-secondary education are actually needed to do the job, there is ample evidence that earning a college diploma or university degree will improve your chances of getting a job you enjoy. Many of the jobs that baby boomers did when they started work no longer exist (Clark, 2000). In the 1960s, many young women took "commercial" courses, such as typing and shorthand, to qualify for secretarial work. Now middle management is expected to word process their own letters, and lawyers are required to write documents such as wills using computer software. Employers prefer educated workers with a broad skill base, such as oral and written communication skills and computer literacy. They look for people who can gather information, analyze it, and reach creative solutions. *Symbolic analysts*, people who can manipulate mathematical data and words and identify and solve problems, are in demand for many occupations (Foot & Stoffman, 1998). The skills that enable you to be successful in higher education also make you a more valuable employee, whatever your field of study.

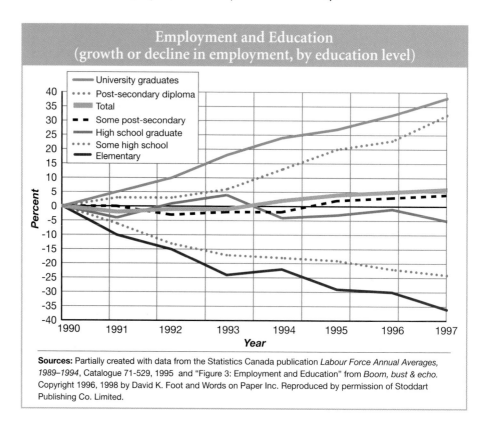

Employment and Education
(growth or decline in employment, by education level)

Sources: Partially created with data from the Statistics Canada publication *Labour Force Annual Averages, 1989–1994*, Catalogue 71-529, 1995 and "Figure 3: Employment and Education" from *Boom, bust & echo.* Copyright 1996, 1998 by David K. Foot and Words on Paper Inc. Reproduced by permission of Stoddart Publishing Co. Limited.

by Robert J. Birgeneau, President, University of Toronto

When I was in Grade 10 at St. Michael's College School in Toronto 45 years ago, I studied history, social science, mathematics, Greek, Latin, German, French, and English. This might seem like an unusual program for a future physicist, but science was dropped from the Grade 10 curriculum that year, and those in the accelerated class studied the humanities almost exclusively. So it is not so surprising that I later came to the University of Toronto on a Classics scholarship.

Others, in high school in the 1960s, had the opposite experience. If they were bright, they quickly got shunted onto the science track and found themselves waving languages, literature, and the social sciences goodbye.

It is no wonder that there is a divide between the sciences and the humanities in our culture. In reality, the divide is an artificial one. The sciences and the humanities are all part of the human continuum. You cannot separate them and understand what it is to be fully human any more than you can remove the colour from a Tom Thomson painting and still call it great art.

Our fundamental purpose at the University of Toronto is to push the frontiers of knowledge on all fronts. Those frontiers are just as noble whether they involve an astrophysicist trying to explain the distribution of matter in the universe, a philosopher probing the meaning of justice in a democratic society, or a playwright illuminating the intricacies of human relationships.

What's more, the humanities play a special role in education for without them, we would merely be training students, not educating them. Typically in our high-tech age, engineers, for example, are no

Robert Birgeneau educates undergraduates for the twenty-first century by combining the sciences with the humanities.

longer practising engineering 10 years after graduating. Therefore, instilling the ability to think about sociological, psychological, and political issues is crucial in preparing them for the leadership roles they will play.

Likewise, it is critical for politicians, writers, and artists to have some understanding from a scientific point of view about the world they inhabit. What are the fundamental constituents of the world? What role is the planet Earth playing in the universe as a whole?

The President's Council on Undergraduate Education, led by Provost Adel Sedra and myself, has been charged with addressing the issue of what constitutes a proper education for our undergraduate students. The twist I am hoping to bring to the University of Toronto, and to undergraduate education in general, is to broaden the armoury of the educated person and incorporate science on an equal basis with the humanities. In my view, in the twenty-first century, if a person does not know what the genetic code is and has no idea what underlies DNA testing, then she cannot call herself an educated person. In the same way, if a person cannot communicate and write fluently, he is not an educated person. Of course, a deep appreciation of music, drama, film, and the arts is also a hallmark of a well-educated person. The University of Toronto offers these experiences fully to its students.

If we widely exploit this scope, our graduates will be able to "read" the natural world. They will be able to navigate the boundary "where art and science meet," as American scientist Stephen Jay Gould put it in a recent work. As Shakespeare expressed it for the ages in *As You Like It*, they will be able to live a life that "finds tongues in trees, books in the running brooks, sermons in stones, and good in everything." ■

Source: *University of Toronto Magazine.* (2001, Spring). p. 5.

1. What is the difference between being an "educated" person and being a graduate?
2. What are the benefits of a broad education?
3. What subjects would you recommend for an "educated" person today?

The Gender Gap in Education

Traditionally, women have received less education than men. Educating a woman was considered to be a waste because she was going to stay home and raise children, and not have a career. However, by the 1970s, more women were working, so there was a need for them to acquire skills to get a good job. For the last 25 years, the education of female students has been a focus of concern in most Western countries. By 1999, Canadian test results showed that 13- and 16-year-old boys and girls perform equally well on mathematics and science tests, and that girls outperform boys in reading and writing (CESC, 2000). Eighty-five percent of all high school students will graduate, but only 78 percent of all boys. At the post-secondary level, in 1997, women earned 58 percent of all university degrees, half of the degrees in medicine and law, and have doubled their enrolment in traditionally male fields like engineering (Clark, 2000; CESC, 2000). At the beginning of the twenty-first century, the widening gap between the educational achievement of men and women suggests that the focus of concern should be on the underachievement of boys.

University Qualifications[1] Granted by Field of Study and by Sex, 1998			
Field of Study	Total	Male	Female
Canada overall	172 076	71 949	100 127
Social sciences	67 019	27 993	39 026
Education	25 956	7 565	18 391
Humanities	20 816	7 589	13 227
Health professions and occupations	12 658	3 514	9 144
Engineering and applied sciences	12 830	10 121	2 709
Agriculture and biological sciences	12 209	4 779	7 430
Mathematics and physical sciences	9 992	6 876	3 116
Fine and applied arts	5 256	1 735	3 521
Arts and sciences	5 340	1 777	3 563

[1] Includes bachelor's and first professional degrees, undergraduate diplomas and certificates, other undergraduate qualifications, master's degrees, doctoral degrees, and graduate diplomas and certificates.

Source: Adapted from the Statistics Canada web site www.statcan.ca/english/Pgdb/People/Health/educ21.htm, extracted September 2001.

Lifelong Learning

Education does not end with graduation. According to the 1998 Adult Education Survey, 39 percent of youth aged 17 to 34 participated in some form of training or education program (Statistics Canada, June 18, 1999). Although adult education could allow those with less education to catch up, that is not the case. Only 11 percent of school leavers, but 48 percent of university graduates, were pursuing training through adult education. It seems that the more education you have, the more you continue to achieve, further widening the gap between graduates and school leavers. Half the people in the sample group were upgrading their skills for their current job, usually acquiring computer skills. Over half the courses were paid for by employers. Other people were paying for courses themselves to enable them to switch careers (Carey, 1996). Since the emphasis has been placed on education as job training, it is interesting that 10 percent of courses were taken out of personal interest (Statistics Canada, June 18, 1999). A goal of education in the Province of Ontario in the 1970s was that everyone would become a self-motivated, lifelong learner. The results of this survey suggest that Canadians have become lifelong learners.

Community College[1] Diplomas in Career Programs, 1994–1995			
Field of Study	**Total**	**Male**	**Female**
Canada overall	**74 548**	30 288	42 260
Business and commerce	**20 979**	6 597	14 382
Engineering and applied sciences	**14 722**	12 150	2 572
Social sciences and services	**14 304**	3 947	10 357
Health sciences	**11 020**	2 043	8 977
Arts	**5 968**	2 518	3 450
Natural sciences and primary industries	**3 708**	2 367	1 341
Humanities	**1 167**	353	814
Arts and sciences	**544**	242	302
Not reported	**136**	71	65

[1] Includes related institutions such as hospital schools, agricultural colleges, arts schools, and other specialized colleges.

Source: Adapted from the Statistics Canada web site www.statcan.ca/english/Pgdb/People/Health/educ19.htm, extracted September 2001.

Entering the Work Force

A successful transition into adulthood depends on acquiring an income. For all but the very wealthy, the major income source is employment. Preparing for an occupation is a process that begins in adolescence, when students are required to choose the program they will study in secondary school and whether they will achieve post-secondary education. This section questions one of the expectations identified by sociologist Margaret Mead as a prerequisite for becoming independent: Does this society provide opportunities for youth to participate in clear adult roles? (In Côté & Allahar, 1994) In this section, these research questions will be investigated:

● What type of work is available for youth?

● When do youth begin working?

● Are youth able to earn enough to become independent?

The Changing Employment Market

As Canada became industrialized, young people migrated to urban centres to work. Employment in the early twentieth century was clearly segregated by gender, age, race, and social class. Women were usually restricted to domestic work: girls from lower classes laboured as servants, and girls from higher classes could become companions. African Canadian men could work as servants or porters but were not allowed in the trade unions. Most Chinese men were labourers. Most Aboriginal men worked in primary industries such as forestry or fishing (Baker, 1993).

Coulter described the effects of industrialization on young workers in Edmonton in the 1920s and 1930s. Those who left school early found themselves limited to menial jobs with no job security and low wages. Employers paid less than minimum wage to apprentices, a status that could last for many years if the practice was abused by shifting young workers to one new job after another within the same business. Wages for all youth were low, so they had to work long hours to afford to pay room and board if they could not live at home (Coulter, 1982). White men had more job opportunities but received lower wages until they were married (Baker, 1993). Because youth were limited to menial work that did not pay enough to allow them to become independent, the benefits of staying in school eventually outweighed the small income that adolescents could add to most families.

In the twentieth century, Canadians expected their children to stay in school long enough to attain the credentials to get a good job. The common belief was that young people would "start at the bottom" and, by working hard and developing their skills, they would eventually move up the "ladder of success" (Allahar & Côté, 1998). In the thriving economy of the 1960s and early 1970s, successful young employees could expect to be promoted fairly rapidly, and they were. Unemployment rates were low and incomes were rising. Youth were able to become independent, leave home, marry, and have children in their early twenties. Parents of the baby-boom generation made the transition into adulthood quickly and with a high degree of success. However, if individuals were promoted to the top early in their careers, they would stay there a long time. So in the 1980s, when Generation X was ready for advancement, there were fewer opportunities for new employees to move up the ladder.

In the later decades of the twentieth century, the Canadian economy changed. There were fewer jobs in the traditional areas of agriculture and manufacturing, and many new jobs in the service economy. Côté and Allahar call this an *advanced industrial economy* (1994). Although young adults aspire to management jobs in the new service economy, those available are in the lower level, require few skills, and are poorly paid. The entry of women into the workforce since the 1970s,

Young adults may have limited opportunities for promotion because there are many older workers in senior positions who have nowhere to advance to, yet they are not ready for retirement.

combined with the fact that there are more older people than younger ones, has created a stagnant employment market. By 1995, this prompted the Canadian Youth Foundation to petition the Canadian government to raise the maximum qualifying age for youth employment programs from 24 to 29 (Allahar & Côté, 1998). Young adults who came of age in the 1990s have started at the bottom but are less able to locate the ladder of success than their parents were.

In 2000, 86 percent of students aged 15 to 19 expected to get the job they wanted when they graduated (Bibby, 2001). All students, male or female, richer or poorer, recent immigrants or those born in Canada, are sure that there will be opportunities for them. Post-secondary graduates, especially those with student loans to repay, are three times more likely to want jobs that pay well than they are to want jobs in their fields of study (Clark, 1999). Their high expectations might be justified. As the baby-boom generation retires earlier than previous generations did, many vacancies must be filled with new workers. There will be a need for well-educated and highly skilled employees to fill the jobs that the baby boomers leave (Carey, 2001). It is possible that the ladder of success will again be there for the next two decades or more.

web connection

www.mcgrawhill.ca/links/families12

To learn about youth employment, go to the web site above for *Individuals and Families in a Diverse Society* to see where to go next.

Some graduates choose to work as volunteers to develop their skills and broaden their experience while helping others, before they settle into a permanent job.

Employment Rates and Income

Higher education improves your job prospects. According to the National Graduates Surveys, most of those who graduated in 1982, 1986, and 1990 found permanent full-time jobs and received reasonably high incomes (Finnie, 2000). Finnie found, however, that the transition into employment was a longer process than individuals anticipated. Employment rates were good after two years, but significantly improved by five years after graduation, at which time 92 percent of males and 82 percent of females were employed full time, and only 5 percent were unemployed (2000). The unemployment rate for high school graduates was 10 percent and for school leavers, 20 percent (CESC, 2000). Youth with less education are more likely to change jobs frequently, so the actual percentage of those who had experienced periods of unemployment was higher than these figures suggest.

The high employment rates for post-secondary graduates mask the concern about underemployment. Krahn and Lowe conducted a longitudinal survey of Canadian students from May 1985 to May 1987 to find out their educational and work experiences. They concluded that the transition to adulthood is prolonged by the difficulty graduates have in finding permanent jobs related to their education. Of greater concern is the fact that many graduates continued to work in the "student work market" in clerical, sales, and service occupations alongside students working part-time (Krahn & Lowe, 1991). By 1999, 50 percent of post-secondary graduates reported being in full-time jobs related to their education two years after graduation (CESC, 2000). Graduates change jobs frequently in the first years, averaging 2.1 jobs in the first two years. Some graduates delay permanent employment in various ways, such as travelling, working at temporary jobs to pay for a year or two of recreation, or participating in volunteer programs. The education-job match might be improved by the end of the longer five-year transition period, which appears to be the pattern (Clark, 1999).

Many post-secondary students believe that it is the degree or diploma that provides the credentials to get a job, not the courses studied (Krahn & Lowe, 1991). Graduates of professional programs, such as medicine, law, nursing, or law enforcement, are most likely to be fully employed. Since these programs place restrictions on enrolment, students have chosen the program with career goals in mind. In stating that one in three graduates felt that their knowledge and skills were not being used, researchers assume that education is "job training," but that is not the expectation of every graduate. Students in undergraduate arts and sciences programs are more likely to have chosen programs that reflect their academic interests without having specific career plans or any expectation that they will eventually use their knowledge in a job. Because graduates may apply their generic communication, information-management, and problem-solving skills in a variety of fields, a graduate in philosophy could become a sales manager in business. The fact that their jobs are unrelated to their fields of study does not necessarily mean that graduates perceive themselves as underemployed.

According to The National Graduates Survey of 1995, graduates discovered that finding a job after completing their education was a challenge. They reported that getting a position that paid enough was the most difficult. They felt well prepared to write résumés and letters of application and to do well in interviews, because most had received career counselling as part of their education. This class of graduates found most of their jobs through networking. One-third got jobs through family or friends, one-sixth by making cold calls to employers, and one-tenth through former employers. Graduates who had co-op experience, previous work experience in the field, or volunteer experiences attained employment more easily. Graduates who started working for an organization part-time before graduation were more likely to stay in that job

Possessing a university degree or a college diploma, regardless of the field of study, can open the door to many careers.

(Clark, 1999). The experiences of the 1995 graduates suggest that while career counselling or courses can help you acquire job-search skills, you can make the transition to work by accumulating experience in your occupational field; talking to family, friends, and former employers about your job search; and making cold calls to potential employers.

The income that young adults earn will determine how easily they can achieve independence from their parents. Although perceptions about the amount of money needed will vary, a sufficient amount is the primary factor in a young adult's decision to leave home. Graduates rank high pay as their first priority when looking for a job, especially if they have accumulated student

How 1995 Graduates Found a Job			
	College	**University**	**Both**
Through family and friends	33%	32%	
Unsolicited calls to employers	17%	18%	
Classified ads			14%
Previous employers			10%
Campus placement office			9%
Employment agencies	3%	4%	
Internet*			1%

[1] The Internet was new at the time.

Source: Adapted from the Statistics Canada publication, *Canadain Social Trends–Autumn 1997*, Catalogue 11-008, Issue No. 46, page 15.

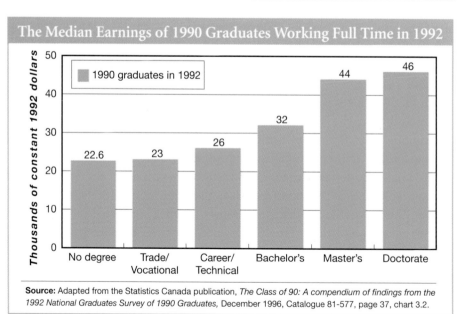

The Median Earnings of 1990 Graduates Working Full Time in 1992

Source: Adapted from the Statistics Canada publication, *The Class of 90: A compendium of findings from the 1992 National Graduates Survey of 1990 Graduates,* December 1996, Catalogue 81-577, page 37, chart 3.2.

loan debts (Clark, 1999). Income levels are affected by the level of education achieved and by the match between the level of education and the job. Very simply, the more diplomas or degrees you achieve, the higher your pay will be. Graduates from professional and vocational programs earn more than graduates from arts and sciences programs (CESC, 2000). The gap between the income of men and women has narrowed, but female graduates still earn less, perhaps because they are more likely to work part-time or to be more constrained in where they can work than men. Over the 20-year period from 1976 to 1996, however, the pay of young men has dropped in terms of actual earnings and relative to the changes in income for older men (Morisette, 1997). Graduates have the potential to earn good salaries, but it will take up to five years to find a well-paying job in your field.

developing your research skills | Using Abstracts

When you do library research, it is important to get to the information that is most useful as quickly as possible. A periodical index or computer database search provides the bibliographical entry for each source related to a topic. This gives only a vague idea of what the study or article is about. University libraries have entire floors designated for journals or periodicals. It would be very time-consuming to find and read each study to determine whether it was useful. Abstracts simplify the search for pertinent research papers. An abstract is a summary of the contents of a document. A well-written abstract includes the research question or hypothesis, the method, and the results of the study. Abstracts of all related studies are collected and bound into volumes each year. They are also available on-line. The abstract also appears on the front page of the research paper. Read the abstract that corresponds to the study you think is important to find out very quickly whether or not you want to read the entire paper. ■

From School to Work: The Evolution of Early Labour Market Outcomes of Canadian Post-Secondary Graduates

by Ross Finnie

This paper reports the results of an empirical analysis of the early labour market outcomes of Canadian post-secondary graduates based on the National Graduates Surveys, representing those who finished their college or university programs in 1982, 1986, and 1990. The major findings include that post-secondary graduates have generally been doing quite well as a group, with most finding full-time and permanent jobs, receiving reasonably high earnings, and otherwise successfully moving into the labour market according to the various outcomes measured here; that the school-to-work transition is clearly a process, rather than an event, with most outcomes improving significantly from two to five years following graduation; that these outcomes vary by level (College, Bachelor's, Master's, Ph.D.) and sex; and that successive cohorts of graduates did not experience any widespread decline in their labour market fortunes over this period.

Relationships

Relationships with others provide support for young people making the transition into adulthood. Parents and teachers are the major supportive relationships in childhood and adolescence. These relationships are provided, not chosen. To become independent, a person will form new relationships with a variety of people who can support the transition. Young adults will also renegotiate their existing relationships with family and friends. Communicating effectively with others in personal, academic, and business relationships is necessary for the individual to take on appropriate adult roles. Research questions that reflect the influence of relationships on this transition are:

- How do young adults and their parents adjust their relationship to reflect the adult status of the children?
- How do young adults form appropriate workplace relationships?

Although working is the most important factor in becoming independent, personal relationships—those with family, friends, and lovers —are the priority for most young adults. People perceive their personal relationships as most important to their happiness (Bibby, 2001). Almost 90 percent of men and women state that friendships enhance their self-esteem. Friends offer emotional support and can provide an objective point of view to help solve problems. They can also lend a hand and provide tangible support when it is needed (Anderson & Hayes, 1996). Most research about relationships focuses on family and on intimate, "romantic" relationships. Less is known about the role of friendships in the lives of young adults, and even less about the functional relationships formed in the workplace. Young adults who develop appropriate behaviour and communication skills suited to their new role and their status within the organization will be more successful in the workplace.

Parent-Child Relationships

Parents know that their children will leave home some day, but neither they nor their sons or daughters can predict when that will occur. Since the 1930s, perhaps following the advice of popular child-care books, North American parents emphasized independence more than obedience when raising their children. Because families no longer send their youth away from home when they become physically mature, young people must become independent while still living in their parents' homes. Individuals who were encouraged to become independent are more likely to have a positive relationship with their parents when they reach young adulthood. This could explain why Goldscheider and Goldscheider found that leaving home appears to have no effect on a young adult's relationship with his or her parents (1997).

From the systems theory perspective, the family has to adjust to allow the adolescent and then the young adult to change. Because systems do not adapt easily, the family will be less stable as the family members attempt to develop new strategies for relating to one another and for completing the work of the family. However, the parents, who have less need to change, will be less motivated to give up the existing strategies that have worked well in the past. Arguments between parents and adolescents during this period of instability break down the old strategies and allow the young person to become more independent by taking on new roles in the family. In some families, the system does not adjust, and parents and adult children continue in the comfortable roles they established in early adolescence, with young adults having very little responsibility until they leave home (Goldscheider & Goldscheider, 1997).

But, as you have seen, young adults seem to be staying home longer than either they or their parents thought they would. When adult children continue to live with their parents, there will often be conflict unless both can change the relationship. The challenge for the young persons will be to balance their responsibility to their family with their need to establish their personal priorities (Wiener, 1997). According to Valerie Wiener, families should negotiate new house rules and routines suited to the lifestyles of all members of the family, but young adults should accept that "the nest is the parents' home, and will still be their home after [the young adults] leave" (p. 92). The challenge for parents is to accept their adult children as responsible people who can make a contribution to the family. The research so far indicates that fewer than 7 percent of young adults living at home contribute any money for their room and board (Allahar & Côté, 1998).

It is possible for adult children and their parents to establish adult-adult relationships if they can establish a more equal footing (Wiener, 1998). The foundation of any relationship is effective communication skills. However, honesty, empathy, and assertiveness, the cornerstones of effective communication, are difficult to achieve in hierarchical relationships in which the parents wield the power. When young adults are financially dependent on their parents, any power they have within the family home is granted to them by their parents. There is some evidence that leaving home temporarily to go to college, university, or the military will change the power structure in the family (Goldscheider & Goldscheider, 1997; Wiener, 1998). Others suggest that families can create their own rituals to replicate the initiation rites of pre-industrial societies (Wall & Ferguson, 1998). Among the BaMbuti people, when male youth return from their initiation rites, they can no longer live with their parents but must build their own hut near them, where they can begin to live an adult lifestyle. Perhaps young Canadians fixing up rooms in the basement so

"Human beings are the only species on the face of the Earth that allow their young to come back home."

— Bill Cosby

web connection

www.mcgrawhill.ca/links/families12

To learn about the relationships between parents and adult children, go to the web site above for *Individuals and Families in a Diverse Society* to see where to go next.

Forming effective relationships with co-workers can help you get the job done well and enable you to demonstrate the skills that can earn you a promotion.

web connection

www.mcgrawhill.ca/links/families12

To learn about workplace relationships, go to the web site above for *Individuals and Families in a Diverse Society* to see where to go next.

that they no longer sleep down the hall from their parents achieves the same purpose. Parental authority gives way to advice and acceptance when young adults are free to accept responsibility for their lives.

Workplace Relationships

Although most young people have worked part-time before they seek their first full-time job, few have experienced the complex relationships of the workplace. Jobs in the "student work market" entail students working alongside other students in temporary positions with few prospects. However, when they enter their first adult jobs, young people enter into relationships in which they must balance the co-operative behaviour required to work as a team to get the job done, with the competitive behaviour necessary to achieve promotion up the career ladder (Gottman, 1999). They will meet people with a wide range of attitudes toward their work. Some will be very ambitious, but others will be content to do the minimum required. For many young people, determining who to align themselves with can be challenging in some workplaces.

Since most friendships in life are formed with those people with whom they associate on a daily basis, individuals navigate through the confusion of workplace relationships to seek connections. As you have seen, most employment opportunities arise from family, friends, and previous employers. Networking by getting to know people who work in the field is an effective way for young adults to prepare for job changes and for promotion. Yet individuals, by nature, are social beings who seek out friendship, even love. It requires a big adjustment in outlook to recognize that the purpose of workplace relationships is primarily to accomplish the goals of the organization and to further individual careers (Yager, 1997).

Mentor Relationships

When young adults begin their careers, they usually start at the bottom and look forward to climbing the ladder of success. When American psychologist Daniel Levinson interviewed young men about their early careers in the early 1970s, they described important relationships with people who helped them up that ladder. Levinson (1978) explained the role of the **mentor**, usually a man several years older than the young man, who assisted him in his transition into a career path. A mentor served several functions. Initially, a mentor helped a young man to understand the people, values, and behaviour in his new environment, and taught the young man to acquire the knowledge and skills he needed. He used his influence to help the young man advance and acted as a role model for him to emulate. He might also have provided advice and support when things went wrong.

Young women are less likely to have mentors, Levinson found in a later study (1996). It could be that there were fewer older women available as mentors for the young women in Levinson's sample group in the 1980s and 1990s. Perhaps young women and older men were reluctant to form mentor relationships out of fear that these relationships might be construed as sexual. Levinson also suggested that women had to compete more for opportunities and, therefore, were less able to assist younger women.

Later research conducted by The National Center for Women and Retirement Research (NCWRR) in 1990 found that women who had graduate and post-graduate degrees and those who saw work as being the core of their lives often identified mentors who played key roles in supporting their dreams. The NCWRR study also found that many women had male mentors (Anderson & Hayes, 1996). Both studies reported that young women have a stronger sense of having achieved success by themselves in a highly competitive work environment. However, because mentors serve an important role in the career success of young adults, perhaps women would benefit from more mentoring.

Successful Transitions

The transition from adolescence to independent adulthood is a process that takes many years. Individuals develop goals in middle adolescence concerning their education and a possible career. Most young Canadians will choose to acquire post-secondary education before they venture into the adult work force. The experience of the last two decades suggests that graduates will spend two to five years, changing jobs several times, to settle into work that matches their education. Although some will choose to marry or cohabit in their early twenties, most young adults will choose to continue to live at home into their mid-twenties. By their late twenties, life finally becomes more stable for young adults. Individuals make many decisions during the transition process. Some lives will follow the life patterns outlined by research, while others will be the exceptions that require researchers to be content with trends, not rules. The next chapter will examine how individuals are motivated to make these important decisions about their lives.

By your late twenties, when, probably, you have finished your education, started your career, and moved out, you might be ready to prepare for the responsibilities of marriage or cohabitation, a home, and children.

Knowledge/Understanding   Thinking/Inquiry

1. When will you and your peers become adults? Explain the criteria you have developed for yourself for defining adulthood.

2. Trace the changes in the transition to adulthood through history as described in this chapter. Identify and explain the factors that encouraged young men and women to take on adult roles at different ages than they do now.

3. a) Using the social exchange theory, identify the costs and benefits of living at home at the following times:
   - while attending high school
   - while attending college or university and working part-time
   - while working at a first job after graduation

   b) When does leaving home become cost-effective, in your opinion?

4. Explain why the following developments in education have occurred.
   - Elementary education was made mandatory until the age of 14.
   - The school-leaving age was raised to 16.
   - Eighty-five percent of high school students now graduate.
   - Eighty percent of high school graduates go on to post-secondary education.
   - More women than men attend college or university.
   - Forty-eight percent of workers with degrees participated in adult education in 1998.

5. Currently, young adults take up to five or six years after graduating to move into jobs that match their education. Summarize the reasons for this.

6. a) Why do you think the men in Levinson's sample group in the 1970s identified mentors, and the women in the 1980s and 90s did not?

   b) What value would mentors have for young women? Suggest whether the situation would be different now than in the 1980s.

7. Based on your experience of working with others in the workplace or in the classroom, describe the challenges people might face in relating to their co-workers.

8. a) Discuss the ways that families must adjust if an adult child lives at home, taking into consideration the potential for conflicting family and individual roles.

   b) Summarize your recommendations in a letter of advice to a graduate who is lmoving home after living with roommates while away at college or university.

9. Do Canadians perceive the purpose of post-secondary schooling to be credentialism or education? Write a brief essay in response to Dr. Birgeneau's article "The Great Divide" (see page 79) in which you defend your thesis based on your experiences in your family, at school, and in Canadian society.

10. a) Design a questionnaire to determine how young adults in your parents' generation left home, completed their education, or found jobs.

   b) Compare the results with the expectations of your generation and with those described in this chapter. What could account for the similarities and the differences?

   c) Suggest the impact of these differences on intergenerational relationships within families and in Canadian society.

11. a) Survey students in your community using a questionnaire to determine their expectations about becoming independent.

   b) Compare their answers with the research results summarized in this chapter.

   c) Analyze the results to determine whether there are variations based on cultural background.

   d) Discuss the implications of these variations in a diverse society.

12. a) Using a questionnaire, investigate the preparation your class has received for choosing a career path and getting a job, and determine the sources of that preparation.

   b) Compare the results to the research evidence.

   c) Suggest improvements to career preparation programs for adolescents.

chapter 4

Becoming an Adult

CHAPTER EXPECTATIONS

While reading this chapter, you will:

- describe the development of individuals in early adulthood, drawing on a variety of developmental theories
- analyze several viewpoints on similarities and differences in male and female development and on the impact of those differences on the roles individuals play
- evaluate emerging research and theories explaining the developmental tasks of individuals in early adulthood
- summarize the factors that influence decisions about educational and occupational choices
- demonstrate an understanding of research methodologies, appropriate research ethics, and specific theoretical perspectives for conducting primary research
- select and access secondary sources reflecting a variety of viewpoints
- identify and respond to the theoretical viewpoints, the thesis, and the supporting arguments of materials found in a variety of secondary sources

KEY TERMS

anticipatory
  socialization
autonomous self
cohort effect
crisis
Dream
ego
identity
individuation
life structure
resocialization
rites of passage
self-esteem

RESEARCH SKILLS

• developing and conducting interviews
• using in-text citations
• selecting reliable academic sources

In early adulthood, you will leave your adolescent life behind and begin to build a unique adult life for yourself.

CHAPTER INTRODUCTION

Becoming an adult is a complex personal process that no longer follows the timetable set by physical maturity. In this chapter, a psychological approach will be used to examine the transition to adulthood using contemporary developmental theories. These will be compared with traditional views of the life span in other societies to determine some life patterns of men and women in Canada's post-industrial society. How individuals interact with families and other groups in society to learn who they will become in adulthood will also be investigated. Finally, the ways that individuals make decisions as they prepare for their roles in early adulthood will be explored.

The Transition to Adulthood

Becoming an adult is a process that begins in childhood and continues until you are an adult in your own eyes, in the eyes of your parents, the law, and the society in which you live. Does becoming an adult occur in predictable stages regardless of the society in which you live? Is the process unique for each individual, or does development occur in patterns for all individuals living at the same time and in the same place? The behavioural norms in early adulthood in Canada have changed, but is the process of becoming an adult changing for individuals living in Canada? To answer these research questions, various developmental theories will be studied first, followed by a study of how individuals change in the transition to adulthood.

Although an individual's development is a very gradual process, it is marked by very distinct and significant turning points, such as puberty, graduation, obtaining a driver's licence, marriage, and parenthood. All known human societies have recognizable stages of life that are distinguished by societal rituals called **rites of passage**. However, stages of development are not exactly alike in all societies, nor are the celebrations of these rites of passage.

In traditional Hindu society, for example, four stages of life are recognized.

- The first stage is youth, or *brahmacharya*, which begins at about the age of ten and lasts for about ten years. Before then, a Hindu child is not considered to be fully formed yet. During this first stage, the primary expectations of the individual are to remain celibate and to become educated, particularly in religious matters.

- The second stage of life, called *grihastha*, is marked by marriage. During this stage, Hindu men and women are expected to raise and care for their family and to do what is economically necessary to ensure that their children prosper.

- Once the children have become established, marked by reaching the second stage themselves, Hindu parents are free to enter the third stage of life, *vanaprastha*. In this stage, they are expected to focus more on religious beliefs and rituals and to begin to separate themselves from their families. During this stage, they gradually give away their material wealth and worldly possessions to prepare for the next stage.

- During *sannyas*, the fourth and final stage of life, some Hindus live as religious mendicants or *sadhus*, dependent on the charity of others in the community and without any personal attachment to family or friends (Turnbull, 1985).

The Pace of Development

It is difficult to define when you will be considered an adult in Canadian society. When you achieve the chronological age of 18, you reach the age of majority and acquire the legal responsibilities and privileges of adulthood. You can vote and sign contracts. You can also get married. When the age of majority was reduced to the age of 18 from 21 years, young adults were leaving school, working, getting married, and having children in their early twenties. By the end of the twentieth century, the usual signs of adulthood—leaving home and becoming self-reliant—appeared to be occurring later. Most 18-year-olds in Canada are still attending school, and many will continue to be dependent on their parents for several years. Marriage and parenthood usually occur six to eight years later. This inconsistency among legal, social, and economic statuses reflects the changing pattern of becoming an adult in Canada.

When young Canadians become 18 years of age, they acquire the right to make their own decisions, including the right to vote for the candidate of their choice.

Progress from one stage of life to another has been described as the interaction of several clocks, each ticking away at its own pace (Kotre & Hall, 1992). The age of majority reflects the chronological clock and defines adulthood precisely in terms of the number of years since birth. The physical changes that result in sexual maturity and the attainment of full adult size and strength are determined by the biological clock. The psychological clock reflects how the brain is developing as individuals acquire new mental processes and more mature ways of understanding the world. The social clock sets the timetable for society's expectations concerning when certain events should occur in the lives of individuals. Since adults are expected to control their sexual and reproductive behaviour within the framework of social constraints, becoming an adult is probably determined more by the social clock than by any other.

In Canada at the beginning of the twenty-first century, the chronological clock continues to tick at a steady pace so that all individuals acquire privileges and responsibilities at the same age. Yet chronological age is not an accurate indication of biological, psychological, or social maturity (Schlossberg, 1987). The biological clock has speeded up, as improved nutrition and health enable bodies to mature sooner. As a result, young Canadians achieve sexual maturity and fertility in their early teen years. The psychological clock is less evident. Since mental processes can be observed only when they are applied, when the nature of the problems that require solutions change, such as the use of a calculator instead of a slide-rule for solving mathematical equations, it is difficult to determine whether individuals are maturing at a faster rate. The social clock changes as social norms determine when events, such as leaving home or marriage, are "on-time" or "off-time" (Bee, 1987). However, the social clock has slowed significantly over the past two decades (Sheehy, 1995). The pattern of life has changed to reflect the interaction of the four clocks.

Developmental Theories

Developmental theories attempt to identify patterns of life and to describe growth or changes in human behaviour as individuals mature. They are created by analyzing the behaviour of large groups of individuals over a long time. The data is gathered by using questionnaires to determine overall patterns of behaviour and interviews to determine how individuals describe their motivation and feelings about their behaviour. Some developmental theories, such as those of Erik Erikson and Jane Loevinger, suggest that growth and improvement occur as individuals progress from one stage to another when they are ready. Other developmental theories, such as the family life cycle and Daniel Levinson's seasons of life, propose that there are age-linked stages in which people change to become different but not necessarily better. Finally, a third group of theories, such as Klaus Riegel's and Leonard Pearlin's, advocate that there are no stages, but that development reflects constant change as individuals respond to environmental influences. Developmental theorists do agree on one basic premise, however: The behaviour of individuals results from inner psychological changes in response to life circumstances (Bee, 1987).

Developmental stage theories describe life as a series of predictable steps, each building and improving on the previous step and progressing toward full maturity.

Erik Erikson's Eight Stages of Life

Erik Erikson was the first psychologist to describe predictable stages of human development from childhood through adulthood. He depicted a series of eight stages in which an individual's **identity** emerges and matures. He suggested that each stage presents a dilemma, in which the person is challenged by new situations and circumstances in life. People are pushed through the stages by their biological clock and by the social clock of the society in which they live. Identity

Using in-text citations, you can inform your readers of the original sources of the ideas included in your research papers. There are many styles of in-text citations. In the social sciences, you will be using reliable academic sources that enlighten your reader about your topic; therefore, the American Psychological Association (APA) style is used. It assumes that ideas are summarized from an entire work, not from single pages. Here are general guidelines for writing in-text citations.

1. The APA style provides the author's last name and the date of the publication from which you have paraphrased or summarized the author's ideas.

2. If you have quoted the author's words directly, then provide the page number.

3. Cite the source that you *actually* used for your research, not a source that the author of the book you are reading has used (but that you have not read). For example, ideas from Erik Erikson's books that were explained in a book written by Helen L. Bee have been used, so the in-text citation credits "Bee, 1987" with the explanation.

4. Cite the edition of the book you have read, not an earlier edition that you have not seen. For example, in this text, a 1980 edition of Erik Erikson's 1959 book *Identity and the Life Cycle* has been used as a source for his ideas on identity. Thus, the in-text citation "Erikson, 1980" has been used, to reflect use of the 1980, not the 1959, edition.

Using In-Text Citations for Research

Using in-text citations, you can locate sources that will provide a more detailed and in-depth discussion of a research topic. Preliminary reading on a subject, such as reading this textbook, will provide an overview based on more in-depth academic books and research publications. Use the author's name and the date of publication to find the title of the publication in the bibliography or reference list at the end of the book, chapter, or article. After a trip to the library, read the original source yourself. Don't stop there. When you have the original source, check its in-text citations and the bibliography. You can also use the author's name from in-text citations to conduct a search on-line for more recent publications by the same researcher on the topic. ■

---

development reflects the progress of the psychological clock. By resolving each dilemma, the individual acquires the basic strength needed to meet the challenges of the next stage in life. Failure to resolve a dilemma suggests that the person might face some difficulties later in life.

Erikson defined the dilemma during adolescence and early adulthood as *identity versus role confusion* (Erikson, 1980). Every individual is challenged to define who he or she is and will be in the future. This problem is demanding because individuals face many decisions at this time in their lives. Adolescents and young adults choose what work to do, how to be a man or a woman, and what to believe in (Bee, 1987), or they remain confused about what role they will play in adulthood. In resolving this dilemma, individuals acquire the basic strength of *fidelity* (Erikson, 1997). It enables individuals to make

Young adults are challenged to find out what they believe as they seek to become their own person in the adult world.

choices that serve the needs, strengths, and interests of themselves, and later, of others. Since Canadian society provides a variety of appropriate adult roles, such as father, mechanic, teacher, wife, making these important choices determines the paths that individuals will take in their adult lives.

The dilemma of early adulthood is *intimacy versus isolation*. Intimacy is being able to merge your identity with someone else's without losing yourself in the process (Erikson, 1980). Since true intimacy is based on the ability to trust a person enough to reveal your personal thoughts and feelings to him or her, it is necessary to have a clear sense of who you are. Erikson suggested that without an identity, formed in the previous stage, relationships would be shallow.

An individual would feel lonely if he or she could not connect with others. The basic strength that is acquired by resolving the dilemma of intimacy versus isolation is *love*, meaning an overall sense of caring and generosity toward others (Erikson, 1997).

Erikson suggested that women might develop identity and intimacy at the same time because they might develop their identities through relationships with others (Erikson, 1980). Thus, they might acquire the enduring strengths of fidelity and love simultaneously. This idea has also been suggested by Carol Gilligan (1982) in her book *In a Different Voice*. Based on her studies of young women, Gilligan concluded that women determine who they are, how to be a woman, and what they believe in terms of relationships, whereas men usually cannot commit to others until they are sure of their own identities.

Adults focus on their contribution to society in the next stage of life, *generativity versus stagnation*. The challenge of this stage is to decide how to make an individual contribution to society and, by doing so, acquire the basic strength of *caring*. Traditionally, most people accomplished this by having children. Some people attained this through "great works." Erikson's theory suggests that this task follows the formation of identity and the development of intimate relationships on the social clock because it requires fidelity and love.

In summary, the tasks of early adulthood are to determine first who you want to be and what you want to do so that you are true to yourself, and then who you want to be with so that you can share yourself with others.

web connection

www.mcgrawhill.ca/links/families12

To learn about Erik Erikson's theory of the stages of life or about other personality theories, go to the web site above for *Individuals and Families in a Diverse Society* to see where to go next.

Erik Erikson was born near Frankfurt, Germany, in 1902 to Karla Abrahamson, a Danish Jew. Karla was abandoned by her partner before Erik was born, and subsequently she married Dr. Theodor Homberger in 1905. The new family moved to Karlsruhe, Germany. After finishing high school, Erikson studied to become an artist and travelled around Europe. While teaching art in Vienna, he learned to become a Montessori teacher and earned a certificate from the Vienna Psychoanalytic Society. By this time, he was more interested in the psychology of child development. While he was in Vienna, Erikson married Joan Serson, a Canadian dance teacher (Boeree, 1997).

Erikson's early life experiences could have resulted in a need to establish his own identity. He had grown up in Germany as a Jewish boy who looked Nordic. He did not learn until he was a young man that Dr. Homberger was not his father. With the rise of Nazism, Erikson and his wife left Vienna and moved first to Copenhagen, from where his mother came, and then to the United States. When he became an American citizen, Erik Abrahamson Homberger established who he was by changing his name (Boeree, 1997). Adapting Nordic tradition, he named himself not after his father but after himself. He became Erik Erikson.

Erikson taught at Harvard Medical School and had a practice in child psychoanalysis. Later he taught at Yale and the University of California at Berkeley. He

In later life, Erik Erikson and his wife, Joan, both wrote about the stages of life.

left teaching during the McCarthy Era, but continued his research and his psychoanalysis practice. He eventually returned to teaching at Harvard (Boeree, 1997).

He wrote *Childhood and Society* in 1950, summarizing his studies of childhood and adolescence among Native Americans and describing his version of Freudian theory. In 1968, he wrote *Identity: Youth and Crisis,* outlining his theory of identity as the focus of human development.

Erik Erikson retired from teaching in 1970, but continued researching and writing, with his wife, about the stages of life, until his death in 1994 at the age of 92. In his revision of his last book, *The Life Cycle Completed,* which was finished and published as an extended version by Joan Erikson in 1997, he stated that his knowledge of the human life cycle was not complete. He suggested that there was, perhaps, a ninth stage of life in very old age yet to be examined (Erikson, 1997). ■

Jane Loevinger's Theory of Ego Development

Jane Loevinger also identified stages toward a higher level of development. She identified ten stages in the formation of the **ego**, a term introduced by Sigmund Freud, meaning the understanding of self. Ego development begins in infancy with the understanding that you are an individual separate from your mother. Loevinger described full ego development as having an

As you move from one period to another, you will face new life experiences and new challenges. Developmental theories suggest that you will change as a result, but you will not necessarily become better or worse than you were before, just different.

autonomous self, a complex concept that includes being a self-reliant person who accepts oneself and others as multi-faceted and unique (Bee, 1987). Like Erikson, she saw the search for an understanding of self as the centre of human development. Loevinger's stages are determined solely by the individual's psychological clock. In fact, she suggested that few adults ever achieve full ego development, but strive toward that goal for a lifetime.

In Loevinger's theory, young adults are at a transitional *self-aware level* between the *conformist stage* and the *conscientious stage*. Adolescents at the conformist stage tend to view life in stereotypical ways and as black and white, in an attempt to classify human experience so that they can see where they belong in society. Young adults at the self-aware level begin to understand and accept individual differences and to distinguish the variations in feelings and opinions that make us unique. Loevinger suggests that in the conscientious stage they are able to appreciate others as individuals in reciprocal relationships. Thus, Loevinger echoes Erikson's theory that individuals require a clear sense of themselves before they can form truly intimate relationships with others. However, Loevinger concluded from her research that because most people spend a lifetime developing this ability, the progress from one stage to the next is determined by an individual's psychological clock, not by chronological age or the social environment.

The Family Life Cycle

The family life-cycle theory describes early adulthood as a stage in which individuals are launched from their families of origin. Parents and children must separate from one another so that young adults can accept emotional responsibility for themselves (Carter & McGoldrick, 1989). According to the family life-cycle theory, three developmental tasks must be mastered for this to happen.

1. Young adults must form an identity separate from that of the family of origin. This process of **individuation** requires young adults to "sort out emotionally what they will take along from the family of origin, what they will leave behind, and what they will create for themselves" (Carter & McGoldrick, p. 13).

2. Young adults must develop new intimate relationships with peers outside the family to provide the social and emotional support they need.

3. Young adults must make their first tentative commitment to a career or workplace role.

These three tasks enable young adults to become self-sufficient adults.

The family of origin, especially the parents, plays an important role in the development of the adult at this stage. The relationship between parent and child must change to become less hierarchical so that a young adult can accept responsibility for making decisions. Parents must be tolerant of differences of opinion as the young adult makes occupational choices. Perhaps most difficult is the need for parents to accept that their child is forming new intimate relationships with others, one of which will become the primary relationship. The family life-cycle theory emphasizes that development involves change in response to a **crisis** so that the family can move on to a different, not necessarily better, stage. Separation from the family of origin is best accomplished when the family can let go, so that the young adult and the parents can begin the next stage of life.

For a young adult to separate successfully from his or her parents and become an independent adult, the parents must be willing to tolerate differences of opinion.

Daniel Levinson's Theory of the Seasons of Life

Daniel Levinson has proposed that the era of early adulthood lasts 25 years, beginning near the end of high school at about 17 years of age and ending with the transition to middle age in the early forties. During the *early adult transition*, from the ages of 17 to 22 years, his research suggests, an individual must leave behind adolescent life and begin to prepare an adult **life structure**. Like the family life-cycle theory, Levinson wrote of separation from the family of origin. However, he emphasized changes in the attachment between adult child and parents—not necessarily physical separation—to allow the individual to participate in the adult world. The young adult will also modify or end relationships associated with an adolescent life to make way for new adult relationships. By completing education and starting work, individuals make some preliminary plans for adult life.

During the period from the age of 22 to about 28 years, the individual is *entering the adult world*. Early adulthood is a time for building the structure of one's life. According to Levinson "the life structure is the pattern or design of life, a meshing of self-in-world" (1978, p. 278). He identified four major tasks of this period (1978, p. 90):

1. Forming a Dream and giving it a place in the life structure

2. Forming mentor relationships

3. Forming an occupation

4. Forming love relationships, marriage, and family

> "Experience is not what happens to a man. It is what a man does with what happens to him."
>
> — Aldous Huxley

The **Dream** is the individual's sense of self in the adult world and is the core of the life structure (Levinson, 1978). The nature of the Dream will vary, but most describe some combination of occupational, family, and community roles. Men are more likely to describe Dreams involving occupational accomplishments, but some men and many women described Dreams related to community and family (Levinson, 1996). A Dream might be as precise as "I want to have my own business in the graphic arts industry by the time I am 30 so that I can control the type of work I do," or more mythical, such as, "I am going to be a leader." Initial choices of occupation, love relationships, and peer relationships may support the Dream. Many individuals develop relationships with mentors who support their Dreams and facilitate their progress. From the ages of 22 to 28, young adults build and test a preliminary life structure that integrates work, love, and community to attain their Dreams.

The challenge for young adults is to balance the creative exploration of various options for their life structure with a pragmatic desire to make a commitment to a life structure that supports their Dream. The dilemma is that until individuals begin to live out the life structure, all of the possibilities are not known, yet without some commitment to the choices they have made, it is not possible to determine whether the life structure might be realistic or satisfying.

For many young men and women, a successful career is at the core of their Dream.

The *age 30 transition* occurs between the ages of 28 to 33 years. Individuals re-evaluate the life structures that they formed in their early twenties to determine whether they are living out their dreams. Levinson (1976, p. 58) described this re-evaluation as an inner voice that says, "If I am to change my life—if there are things in it that I want to modify or exclude, or things missing I want to add—I must now make a start, for soon it will be too late." Individuals might choose to marry or to get a divorce, to have children, or to change jobs at this time as they adjust their life structures. Many of Levinson's subjects described this as a time to "get real" after testing their early choices for a few years before *settling down* in their thirties.

Daniel Levinson, a Yale psychologist, led a major study of adult life to determine and describe developmental patterns in early adulthood. The results of his study were published as an academic paper in 1977 and as the book *The Seasons of a Man's Life* in 1978. The initial study was limited to men. A follow-up study of women was conducted from 1979 to 1982 to determine whether the pattern of development for women was the same or different as that for men.

RESEARCH QUESTION

What is the pattern of life for middle-aged men?

HYPOTHESES

- Diverse biological, psychological, and social changes occur in adult life.
- These changes occur between the ages of 35 and 45.

RESEARCH METHOD

Using interviews, a team of researchers surveyed 40 men between the ages of 35 and 45 years who were selected from a group who had volunteered as college students for an earlier study. Subjects included ten workers paid hourly, ten executives, ten Ph.D. biologists, and ten novelists. Each man was interviewed five to ten times for a total of ten to twenty hours by one researcher. A follow-up interview was conducted two years later. The interviews were based on key questions designed to cover certain topics, but subjects were encouraged to give open-ended and wide-ranging answers to tell their life histories. This method is called *biographical interview*. In preparing and analyzing the biographies, a pattern emerged that was formed into a developmental theory.

RESULTS

- The life cycle evolves through a sequence of eras, each lasting approximately 25 years.

- The eras overlap in transitional periods lasting four to five years.
- In early adulthood, a young man develops an identity and makes decisions concerning work and love as he develops a life structure.

CONCLUSION

As the result of his research, Levinson concluded that there is a common series of age-linked periods in adult life for men that he called *eras* or *seasons*. The conclusion of the follow-up study of women is that the age-linked seasons are the same as those for men, but that gender differences exist because of the different roles of men and women in North America. ◼

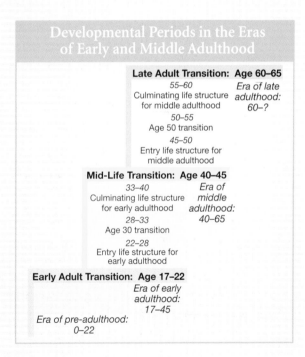

Developmental Periods in the Eras of Early and Middle Adulthood

Late Adult Transition: Age 60–65
55–60 — Culminating life structure for middle adulthood — *Era of late adulthood: 60–?*
50–55 Age 50 transition
45–50 Entry life structure for middle adulthood

Mid-Life Transition: Age 40–45
33–40 Culminating life structure for early adulthood — *Era of middle adulthood: 40–65*
28–33 Age 30 transition
22–28 Entry life structure for early adulthood

Early Adult Transition: Age 17–22
Era of early adulthood: 17–45
Era of pre-adulthood: 0–22

Source: From *The Seasons of a Man's Life* by Daniel J. Levinson, copyright © 1978 by Daniel J. Levinson. Used by permission of Alfred A. Knopf, a division of Random House, Inc. and from *The Seasons of a Woman's Life* by Daniel J. Levinson, copyright © 1966 by Daniel J. Levinson. Used by permission of Alfred A. Knopf, a division of Random House, Inc.

Klaus Riegel's Interpretation of Development

American psychologist Klaus Riegel suggests that development in adulthood occurs not in predictable stages but as individuals adjust in response to the interaction of both internal and external changes. His theory accepts an internal biological clock and a changing external social clock. He identified four interrelated internal and external dimensions of development:

1. The *individual psychological dimension* describes emotional maturity and independence, and the maturity of mental processes.

2. The *individual biological dimension* describes physical and sexual maturity.

3. The *cultural-sociological dimension* describes the expectations and opportunities that each society defines for individuals.

4. The *environmental dimension* describes the physical, economic, and political environment in which the individual lives. (Kimmel, 1990)

According to Riegel, development occurs when a change in one dimension requires an adjustment in one or more of the other dimensions. In this respect, his theory reflects systems theory. For example, when individuals are physically mature and emotionally ready for marriage, they will marry, if they are old enough according to the culture and the society in which they live, and if they can afford to live independently within the economic environment. However, if individuals are unable to earn enough money to become financially independent, they might continue to live with parents, forgo marriage, and have to adjust their sense of their own maturity. Since Riegel's theory integrates internal physical and psychological dimensions with external social and environmental dimensions, it explains how the pace of adult development reflects the changing social clock.

Leonard Pearlin's Theory of Psychological Distress

"I think somehow we learn who we really are and then live with that decision."

— Eleanor Roosevelt

American sociologist Leonard Pearlin attempted to rationalize how development can be unique to each individual yet appear to occur in a common pattern. He disagreed with stage theories, suggesting that adulthood is not a series of transitions from one period of stability to another, but rather a lifetime of continuous change in which individuals might experience occasional periods of stability. According to Pearlin, four elements determine the path that individual lives will take:

1. Individual characteristics, such as gender, race, intelligence, family background, personality, and education

2. The range of skills individuals have for coping with stress or change

3. The availability of social support networks

4. The nature and timing of stress that requires response (Bee, 1987)

He agreed that early adulthood might be the time for acting on the dreams of adolescence. However, he believed that people are able to change the life structure at any time (Smesler & Erikson, 1980).

Pearlin suggested that there are similarities in life flow because individuals change in response to similar external circumstances and stresses that affect their lives. Many stresses, such as leaving school, starting work, even getting married, are scheduled by the social clock of society and are predictable. Therefore, individuals can anticipate role changes. Societies support individuals in their development by socializing them for these scheduled events (Bee, 1987). In effect, Pearlin is suggesting that the patterns that Erikson, Levinson, and other developmental theorists have observed are a **cohort effect**, that the changes in behaviour result from socialized responses to a common social clock rather than from age-linked inner changes.

web connection

www.mcgrawhill.ca/links/families12

To learn about the predictable stages of adult life according to Gail Sheehy, go to the web site above for *Individuals and Families in a Diverse Society* to see where to go next.

in focus | Gail Sheehy's *Passages*

Gail Sheehy's *Passages: The Predictable Crises of Adult Life*, a book that was named in a Library of Congress survey as "one of the ten most influential books of our time," was published in 1976. Using case studies, Sheehy described the life transitions of adulthood. She outlined the stages of adulthood in several other books published in the 1990s. Yet Sheehy's name seldom appears on the reference lists of academic studies, and she is often dismissed as a "pop psychologist." How can people distinguish between reliable academic research and "pop" psychology?

"Pop" is short for popular, and Gail Sheehy was certainly popular. *Passages* remained on *The New York Times* bestseller list for more than three years and was widely discussed in the media. She is credited with encouraging millions of people to re-examine their lives to see opportunities for growth in adulthood. She wrote for the general public, not an academic

Even though Gail Sheehy's research is sound, her work is not referred to in academic studies because she is a journalist and not a social scientist.

audience. Gail Sheehy is not a professional psychologist; she is a journalist. In writing her books, she uses the methodology of psychological research to serve a journalistic purpose.

When she started to write *Passages*, Sheehy set three objectives:

1. To locate the inner changes common to each stage of life

2. To compare the developmental rhythms of men and women

3. To examine the crises that couples can anticipate (Sheehy, 1976)

She conducted her secondary research by studying the research of psychologists Else Frankel-Brunswick, Erik Erikson, Daniel Levinson, and Robert Gould. Extensive notes are included in her book. Her primary research consisted of 115 biographical interviews of men, women, and couples, aged 18 to 55. Her analysis of these interviews became the predictable crises she outlined in her book.

Gail Sheehy's predictable crises match the periods that Daniel Levinson outlined, but the names are more creative. She describes early adult transition as *Pulling Up Roots*, entering the adult world as *The Trying Twenties*, and age 30 transition as *Catch-30* (Sheehy, 1976). Unlike Levinson's early work, she examined the lives of both men and women and their lives together. She also used the experiences of her case studies as a springboard for providing advice to her readers on managing the transitions in their own lives.

When researchers like Levinson and his team publish their results, they do so first in academic journals for peer review. Their methodology and results are examined by other professionals to determine whether they have been responsible in their research and whether the results can be replicated by further research. When journalists like Gail Sheehy publish their work in magazines or books, they are reviewed by critics and by the public, who base their judgments on a wide variety of criteria. Gail Sheehy has been accused of changing the evidence from her interviews to suit her purpose as a journalist. However, critics who dismiss Sheehy reject her thesis by presenting their own view of adulthood, not by criticizing her methodology.

Since Sheehy published *Passages* in 1976, interest in psychology and the social sciences has grown. Sheehy herself has written four more books about adult life. Now, many researchers publish two versions of their research—an academic version for peer review and research, and a popular version for the interested public, as Daniel Levinson did with *The Seasons of a Man's Life* in 1978 and *The Seasons of a Woman's Life* in 1996. ■

---

1. Using the criteria outlined in Chapter 2, page 45, is Gail Sheehy's *Passages* a valid academic source?
2. Will your research resemble that of Gail Sheehy or Daniel Levinson?
3. Will your research be valid?

Socialization for Adulthood

Becoming an adult requires that individuals alter their behaviour as they take on new adult roles in life. Psychologist Nancy K. Schlossberg explains that individuals making a transition change their relationships, perform new work, establish new routines, and develop new assumptions (1987). Socialization is the process by which people learn appropriate social role behaviours in order to participate in a new society. It also includes learning values, attitudes, and expectations. When an individual makes a transition to a new role, **resocialization** enables the person to discard old behaviour and to change his or her behaviour. For example, new employees will learn appropriate attitudes toward the organization that has hired them as they assume their new roles in full-time career positions rather than from their previous temporary or part-time jobs. In preparation for major role changes, **anticipatory socialization** allows people to learn and practise role behaviour before actually taking on a new role. For example, being a shift manager in a part-time job prepares a person for the management skills that may be required in a future career. If transitions are anticipated, individuals can view the changes in a positive way, consider various options, and develop strategies for managing their lives. The social clock, which outlines when certain events should happen in society, enables young adults and those who support them to anticipate the changes in their lives and to be socialized for their new roles.

What happens when the social clock changes? Functionalists explain that the roles of individuals within a society change as necessary to enable the society to continue to perform its functions when other social conditions change. The norms concerning leaving home and becoming self-reliant, the traditional markers of adulthood, have changed in the past few decades. Functionalists would suggest that the changes in the expectations of young adult behaviour reflect a new economic and social organization in Canada. How young men and women are socialized for contemporary adult roles will be examined, focusing on two research questions:

- How do individuals form an identity?
- How do individuals choose an occupation?

Identity and Self-Esteem

When Erikson first wrote about the importance of identity in 1959, he explained that it was the foundation on which individuals would build their lives. Identity appears to include three aspects: a consistent sense of self, a realistic perception of the world, and a sense of control over one's own life (Erikson, 1968). Earlier, Freud had described a mature ego as the ability to modify one's ideas and actions to fit the real world in culturally appropriate ways (Teevan & Hewitt, 1995). This definition of identity is similar to the Dream, the sense of self in the adult world described by the subjects in Levinson's studies of men and of women (1978, 1996), and to the idea

Role models can help young adults foresee roles for themselves in the adult world.

of **self-esteem**. If identity includes not only "who I am" but also "who I will be," then it is necessary for an individual forming an identity to be able to foresee himself or herself playing realistic adult roles in the future (Côté & Allahar, 1994).

The development of a sense of self can be explained by the theory of symbolic interactionism. Individuals form a sense of themselves based on their interpretations of how others act toward them. In his looking glass theory, Charles Cooley compared the significant people in one's life to looking glasses or mirrors. When you present yourself to others by your words and actions, you interpret others' reactions as reflections of their evaluation of you, and form your self-identity as a result of their interpretations (Schaefer et al., 1996). Erikson (1980) explained that forming a true identity required that one's self-image matches the image he or she thinks others have of him or her. Just as the quality of a mirror affects the accuracy of one's body image, so others can affect the accuracy of an individual's identity. Erikson (1968, p. 128) described the importance of choosing reliable significant others as role models:

> If the earliest stage bequeathed to the identity crisis is an important need to
> trust in oneself and in others, then clearly the adolescent looks most fervently
> for men and ideas to have *faith* in, which also means men and ideas in
> whose service it would seem worthwhile to prove oneself trustworthy.

Anticipatory socialization provides opportunities for youth to learn and to practise the new behaviours, skills, and attitudes required for future roles from role models (Teevan & Hewitt, 1995). Identity develops as a result of the individual's personal and symbolic interpretation of their performance in these experiences (Anderson & Hayes, 1996).

Both men and women achieve their identities by assessing their accomplishments (Anderson & Hayes, 1996). Self-control, people's sense that they can make choices about what they will do and what can happen to them, is therefore an important aspect of identity. For individuals to have a sense of self-control, they must be aware of their personal resources and be able to assess situations realistically. They must also develop the skills necessary for making choices and have opportunities to make decisions for themselves about challenges that really matter (Owens, Mortimer, & Finch, 1996). Individuals' family backgrounds, school experiences, and social networks are important factors in how they are socialized to become self-aware, to acquire skills, and to make choices.

"There is time for work. And time for love. That leaves no other time."

— Coco Chanel

Socialization Within the Family

Family homes are the first environment in which people are socialized. Individuals acquire personal qualities from their family members that might affect their socialization. Family members are the primary role models for children and play a major role in identity formation. Adolescents whose families both support them and encourage them to participate in challenging activities develop a sense of control and self-esteem (Csikszentmihalyi & Schneider, 2000). Family background also determines the extent to which children can benefit from the opportunities available to participate in society.

When parents choose activities in which to participate, they determine which basic values, interests, and skills they will transmit to their children.

Family background is a significant factor in identity formation. Children acquire the status of their family of origin, so individuals usually identify with the race, religion, and ethnicity of their parents. Individuals often acquire the same expectations of life as their parents by participating in various activities, such as attending a religious service, doing their own home repairs, marching in political demonstrations, or volunteering on the weekend. Parents are role models for their children, and they provide feedback concerning their behaviour. In Reginald Bibby's study of adolescent attitudes in Canada, the most common source of influence, mentioned by 91 percent of adolescents, was "the way you were brought up" (2000). Values and beliefs are clarified by reflecting on one's actions and experiences. Bibby (2001) found that most adolescents prefer their parents to discipline them through discussion, a method that would encourage them to reflect on the reasons for their behaviour (Teevan & Hewitt, 1995). People acquire a sense of who they are, what they can do, and what they believe from their families.

Family background can also determine the paths that individuals take in adolescence and early adulthood. How much independence families allow their children depends on how parents perceive their own autonomy. Parents who feel they have little control over their lives are more likely to raise their children to be obedient, not self-reliant (Erikson, 1968). Family background can act as a filter that selects which environmental factors will influence their children. Filtering explains why some individuals play the piano or speak three languages or have no interest in sports. In a diverse society such as Canada's, families socialize their children to identify with one another on the basis of shared interests and culture, and to appreciate the need to behave appropriately in order to live and work co-operatively within that culture (Teevan & Hewitt, 1995).

The family system must adjust to allow the young adult child to become independent. Carter and McGoldrick (1989) suggest that families must withdraw financial support, establish residential boundaries, and encourage their young adult to make decisions independently. For example, families might provide furniture, food, and financial support for their young adult living with roommates in student housing, but withdraw the support when he or she leaves home to live independently. As with all adjustments in a family system, if the young adult signals a need for parents to let go, how parents respond will depend on the experiences they had in their own separation from their parents when they pursued a career, got married, or made other transitions.

The Role of School in Socialization

According to Erikson, school challenges individuals to develop competence, a sense of being capable of doing things that are worthwhile. This is accomplished by working and learning, but also by evaluating one's own accomplishments against those of others (Erikson, 1980). The organization of the school system requires students to participate in various tasks to acquire the knowledge and develop the skills that are deemed essential for taking on appropriate adult

Assessment of performance of school tasks helps individuals develop realistic expectations of themselves.

roles. Schools give students feedback about their competence through formal assessment. In high school, adolescents have greater opportunity to explore their competence by choosing the subjects they will study. Students who are encouraged to take a variety of demanding courses develop a sense of self-control and a more consistent sense of what they can do (Csikszentmihalyi & Schneider, 2000).

Going to school is the first step a child takes in separating from the family (Turnbull, 1985). When children enter the school system, they acquire two distinct sets of significant others outside the family who will give them feedback on their behaviour: teachers and peers. The socialization role of the school is defined in the form of the curriculum. Teachers are expected to transmit the knowledge and skills required by society and to assess the students' perfor-mance so they can acquire a realistic perception of what they can do. During adolescence, the peer group exerts a stronger influence than teachers (Csikszentmihalyi & Schneider, 2000). Since the social behaviour and expecta-tions within the peer group can be negotiated, or alternative peer groups can be chosen, adolescents have an opportunity to decide who they want to be. Symbolic interactionism suggests that school experiences challenge individuals to develop a consistent identity by interpreting feedback from a wider range of role models among their peers.

by E. Kaye Fulton

In the 1980s, the decade of indulgence, pop psychologists urged men and women to search for the "inner child" that cowered within. Lighten up, they said, and reap the rewards of innocence, either lost or never nurtured in its proper time. Thus prompted, a generation of adults armed with credit cards romped its way to decadence, deficits, and defaulted car payments. In the sobering 1990s, and—mercifully for those whose childish inner self proved to be more obnoxious than carefree—there was sensible Toronto psychiatrist David Leibow. In a timely how-to guide, *Love, Pain and the Whole Damn Thing*, Leibow argues that it is fine to be, or at least strive to be, an adult—to solve those problems, to act your age. "There's an easy way to do it, and a hard way," he writes. "Being an adult—and feeling like one—is the easy way."

A tantalizing concept, adulthood. To many embattled post-pubescents, the natural inclination is to scuttle by bookstore shelves littered with a shocking array of self-help tomes encouraging childlike self-indulgence. But the middle-aged, Hamilton-born psychiatrist has latched onto a somewhat novel idea. Although experts have produced a deluge of material on childhood and adolescence, the transition to adulthood—that awkward phase that begins with physical maturity and can linger on into the forties, the fifties, and perhaps beyond—is largely unexplored. According to Leibow, adulthood is much maligned as a joyless, predictable plateau that often ends in stunned senility. Quite the opposite is true, he maintains. And it need not be approached with a grim sense of responsibility. "When we get old enough to have sexual intercourse, we don't stop kissing," he writes. "When we get serious about life, we don't lose our sense of humour."

Psychiatrist David Leibow wrote about the transition to adulthood.

The quality of adulthood depends on how much childish baggage is cast away. A graduate of McMaster University Medical School, Leibow cites many of the troubled characters who have trudged through his private practice in Toronto since his return to Canada in 1985 after a six-year teaching stint at Columbia University in New York City. Most of his patients have shared the same affliction—depression. And to Leibow's growing interest, many have recounted the same frustrations. "To a degree, it was a reflection of a more sober, realistic zeitgeist," Leibow said. In their jobs, homes, and social milieus, patients struggled with the pressures, even the freedoms and the privileges, of adulthood. They were also quick to blame their mothers, fathers, bosses, or spouses—anyone but themselves—for their predicaments. "The problem is that we want it both ways," writes Leibow. "We want to enjoy the perks and prerogatives of adulthood, yet retain access to the excuses and freedoms of childhood."

The first, and central, step in becoming an adult is renouncing the old parent-child relationship and its tired catalogue of beefs, dependencies, and hostilities. "One of the subtlest and most persistent forms of dependency is the hoarding of old complaints," writes Leibow. "By keeping track of the ways our parents have failed us, we hope that we'll be able to invoice them for it sometime in the future. Then, if they can't make us happy when we present them with the bill, they will at least feel properly remorseful." Another must: abandon the romantic notion of ultimate happiness. "We will never recapture the state of bliss that we felt, or imagine we felt, when we were very, very young," Leibow contends. "It is this painful realization—the collision of fantasy and reality—that precipitates the crisis of pre-adulthood."

These are hardly revolutionary thoughts. The spectre of Oedipal fixations reaches further back than Freud. And much of Leibow's thesis—the sanctity of monogamy, marriage, and work—reflects conservative family values to a fault. Meanwhile, the author seems to have been unsure whether to target the book at his psychiatric peers or at the general public. That dilemma is evident as *Love, Pain* veers from dry clinical observation to colourful anecdotes and, occasionally, sly wit. But the thread of Leibow's argument rarely unravels. The wiser people become, he argues, the less likely they are to be blown about, like a raft on the ocean, by impulses and emotions. "Contrary to popular belief," he writes, "being stable does not make life boring; it makes life manageable."

The reward is apparently worth the effort. Adulthood is not bestowed. To Leibow, it is a magical dawning—when a person goes from feeling like a kid to feeling like an adult. "Then, just as when you learned to ride a bicycle, the unpleasant feelings of turbulence and uncertainty you felt beforehand give way to exhilarating feelings of pleasure and competence," he writes. Leibow's own moment came about in 1985 after an exhausting week of treating 60 patients. "I was out to dinner and I felt elated about putting in a full week, of doing what I trained for," he says. "I knew right away that I had turned a corner." And once there, Leibow concludes, no self-respecting adult can ever go back. ▪

Source: *Maclean's.* (1995, July 17). p. 49.

1. Why does Dr. Leibow suggest that people have resisted growing up?
2. Why is it necessary to separate from parents in order to become an adult?
3. What are the rewards of becoming an adult?

Preparing for an Occupation

Some people live to work; others work to live, but all young Canadians are expected to prepare for an adult life that includes a job as its major component. Work is an economic necessity for those who want to become independent, but it also enables individuals to pursue their dreams. For some people, performing a certain kind of job is their dream. For others, work provides the income to pursue a dream in other aspects of life (Avard, 1999; Levinson, 1978). In an American study on gender, identity, and self-esteem, 88 percent of women and 91 percent of men identified work as a major contributor to their self-esteem (Anderson & Hayes, 1996). Here is how American social commentator Studs Terkel explained the meaning of work (in Anderson & Hayes, 1996, p. 245):

Work—it is about a search for daily meaning as well as daily bread, for

The occupation that you choose determines many aspects of your lifestyle, such as income, working hours, and flexibility, for balancing other aspects of life.

recognition as well as cash, for astonishment rather than torpor; in short, for a sort of life rather than a Monday through Friday sort of dying.

Since work contributes to self-esteem, a satisfying job is an important part of a life structure. Choosing an occupation determines how much individuals can earn, how they can use their time, how challenging their work will be, and with whom they will interact. It can also affect how much flexibility they will have for changing their life in the future. In an Angus Reid survey conducted in 1996, only 37 percent of young adults reported that they were very satisfied with their jobs (Chamberlain, 1996). How gratifying a job will be day to day depends on finding work that meets one's expectations. Satisfaction in the workplace is linked to better health, lower stress levels, and an ability to balance home and work. The choice of an occupation is really a lifestyle preference (Avard, 1999).

Until the last century, people were not required to choose an occupation, usually because young people would simply follow in their parents' footsteps. The knowledge and skills required to work were learned throughout childhood. The transition from youth to adulthood would have required no change in attitudes or values. Now that work is separated from home and there are so many new occupations to consider, parents no longer have the diversity of knowledge and skills, nor the time, to prepare their children for employment. The transition from school to work appears to depend on several factors. Families provide the inherited intellectual potential and the social and cultural attitudes and skills that enable young people to succeed. School and the community provide opportunities for anticipatory socialization. Society determines the job opportunities (Csikszentmihalyi & Schneider, 2000).

The Role of the Family in Forming an Occupation

Families seldom teach the skills and knowledge required for work, but they play a major role in transmitting the basic values and attitudes that determine the likelihood of success in adulthood. There has been extensive evidence for many years that the parents' level of education, the family income, and the parents' employment history are linked to their children's level of education and their income as adults (Lewis, Ross, & Mirowski, 1999). The Sloan Study

By conducting interviews, you can ask a small sample group of people questions to gather information to test a hypothesis. Usually, the questions are open-ended to encourage the subject to provide detailed information, because interviews are useful tools for gathering data when you do not know what information the subjects have. Additional closed questions can be used to prompt subjects to continue speaking in more detail about a topic. Information gathered through interviewing several people can be compared to determine general patterns of behaviour. Interviews can also be used to develop case studies for analysis using a symbolic interactionism approach.

Anticipatory Socialization Interview

Working with a group of classmates, design an interview to determine whether young adults believe they have been adequately prepared for the role behaviours expected in their occupations.

1. Develop a hypothesis stating what you think might be the answer.

2. Introduce and state the nature of your study.

3. Begin with factual questions to identify your subject and to allow participants to become comfortable answering your questions. For example:

    Describe your current job.

4. Include open-ended questions to elicit the information needed to test your hypothesis. Include secondary questions that can be used, if necessary, to prompt answers on specific topics. For example:

    What experiences did you have before you started to work full time that prepared you for your occupation?

    Did you work part-time during high school?

    Were any of the skills you learned in that job useful in your full-time job?

5. Conduct interviews. Arrange to interview young adults who have been employed full time for at least one year. Record the answers in notes or use a tape recorder.

6. Analyze the results of your interview and compare them with those of your classmates. Formulate conclusions concerning your hypothesis.

7. Write a brief report of your results, using quotations from your interview results to support your statements. ■

of Youth and Development stated that these factors in the parents' work experience determine the values and attitudes toward work that they teach their children (Csikszentmihalyi & Schneider, 2000).

Finding work rewarding is an attitude that is essential to success and satisfaction in adulthood. Work is rewarding when challenges match abilities and when the job requires enough concentration for people to feel in control of their time yet find it passes quickly (Csikszentmihalyi & Schneider, 2000). In an Angus Reid survey of 850 Canadians, 75 percent reported that they enjoyed the type of work they do, and 71 percent found their work challenging

web connection

www.mcgrawhill.ca/links/families12

To learn about occupational choices
and to explore related careers, go to
the web site above for *Individuals
and Families in a Diverse Society* to
see where to go next.

and interesting. Pay is not a factor for satisfaction for most working people
(Chamberlain, 1996). Families teach young people that work is rewarding by
expecting them to complete challenging tasks at home and at school. Facing
appropriate challenges, such as doing laundry, washing the car, caring for
younger children, or studying physics, allows young people to experience the
intrinsic rewards of a job well done whether in the workplace, at home, or in
the community (Csikszentmihalyi & Schneider, 2000).

Young people learn self-reliance and responsibility from authoritative
parents. Authoritative parents set high expectations and encourage adolescents
to make decisions. Parents discipline their children by discussing the results
of those decisions. Authoritative parents encourage exploration and tolerate
mistakes, but they expect adolescents to accept responsibility for "cleaning up
their own messes" (Jarman, 1992). By making and evaluating their choices,
adolescents develop a sense of control and clarify their values, interests, and
goals (Owens, Mortimer, & Finch, 1996). Parents with higher education and a
higher level of control at work are more likely to perceive self-reliance and
responsibility as essential attitudes in the workplace and, therefore, to transmit
these values to their children by adopting an authoritative parenting style
(Erikson, 1968). Authoritative families are better prepared to allow young
adults to separate from the family and to explore a variety of occupational
and lifestyle alternatives (Carter & McGoldrick, 1989).

Between Friends

Reprinted with special permission of King Features Syndicate.

The Role of School in Occupations

Schools and post-secondary institutions have assumed the major responsibility
for socializing young people for occupational choices. The courses that students
take enable them to explore real-world applications of their interests and
skills and to investigate occupations in those fields. The tasks and the working

conditions are role expectations that require students to develop the values and attitudes that are necessary for success in adult life. Students develop concentration by persevering at a task that is challenging. They develop self-control by working at a clearly defined task. They also learn to adjust their social behaviour and communication skills to suit the role expectations of the classroom. In addition, extracurricular involvement helps students develop teamwork and management skills. Anticipatory socialization for adult work roles at school affects whether students are successful, and prepares them for the transition to adult roles in the workplace (Csikszentmihalyi, 2000).

Students often have unrealistic career expectations. The Sloan Study of Youth and Development asked male and female high school students what occupation they expected to enter when they left school. The ten most popular jobs (shown in the following chart) accounted for 55 percent of all students, and were consistent for gender, race, and social class. All were professions requiring university education, except businessperson and professional athlete.

Frequently Mentioned Occupations in Study of Youths' Career Expectations				
Occupation	Expect to Have		Would Like to Have	
	Rank	Percent of Sample	Rank	Percent of Sample
N (number in the sample group)		3 891		4 281
Doctor	1	10	2	11
Businessperson	2	7	5	6
Lawyer	3	7	3	9
Teacher	4	7	6	4
Professional Athlete	5	6	1	15
Engineer	6	5	8	3
Nurse	7	4	9	3
Accountant, CPA	8	3	—	2
Psychologist	9	3	10	3
Architect	10	3	—	2
Musician, Composer	—	2	7	4
Actor, Director	—	2	4	6

Source: From *Becoming an Adult* by Mihaly Csikszentmihalyi and Barbara Schneider, Copyright © 2000 by Mihaly Csikszentmihalyi and Barbara Schneider. Reprinted by permission of Basic Books, a member of Perseus Books, L.L.C.

case study | Ian Enters the Adult World

Ian McLean is a 31-year-old firefighter living in Barrie, Ontario, who has just recently married his girlfriend, Sarah. He has been a member of the Barrie Fire Department for the past year. Although he always told his guidance counsellors at school that he was interested in firefighting as a career, Ian has had a number of different jobs since he graduated from high school. After working in construction with a friend and then at a brief job in sales and carpet laying, he worked for his father for several years in the printing business. In fact, for most of his twenties, Ian worked only to make enough money to pay for some of what he calls his "expensive habits," such as golf and snowboarding, and occasional trips to attend Leafs, Raptors, or Blue Jays games.

Ian grew up in Barrie and has five brothers and sisters, all of whom still live in the Barrie area. He was an average student and he enjoyed the extracurricular sports and the social life of school. He worked part-time at a sporting goods store throughout high school and considered opening his own store at one time, but decided that the hours were inconvenient for family and social activities. After graduation, he accepted a job with an older friend's company rather than going to college because he wasn't sure of what he wanted to do, and felt that he was ready for an adult job. Since Ian has a warm relationship with his parents, brothers, and sisters, he has always expected that he would enjoy being a good husband and father someday.

Ian has known Sarah since he was about 15. Sarah is best friends with his younger sister, Annie, who is the mother of two-year-old twin girls. Sarah and Ian had been dating off and on for almost ten years before they decided to get married. They have been socializing for several years with a large group of common friends from their high school days, playing softball in the

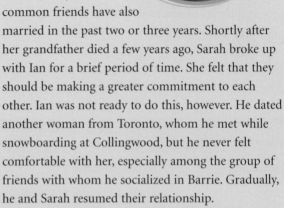

Ian took a step into the adult world by becoming a firefighter.

summer months and bowling in the winter. Many of their common friends have also married in the past two or three years. Shortly after her grandfather died a few years ago, Sarah broke up with Ian for a brief period of time. She felt that they should be making a greater commitment to each other. Ian was not ready to do this, however. He dated another woman from Toronto, whom he met while snowboarding at Collingwood, but he never felt comfortable with her, especially among the group of friends with whom he socialized in Barrie. Gradually, he and Sarah resumed their relationship.

Beginning three years ago, Ian gradually made some changes in his life. He decided that he would stop working for his father and become a firefighter. While Ian was away from home training to become a firefighter, he realized that he did not want to be apart from Sarah. They decided together to continue to live with their respective parents while they saved money to buy a house. A year ago, when he was 30, Ian began to work as a firefighter, and he moved out of his parents' home to live with Sarah in the house they bought together. ■

1. What characteristics of Ian's identity are revealed in this case study?
2. How did Ian choose his occupation?
3. Analyze Ian's life as a young adult using developmental theories. Do any of the patterns described by the developmental theorists fit Ian's life?

The study also found that students did not know the educational requirements for these occupations (Csikszentmihalyi & Schneider, 2000). Career-planning courses can encourage male and female students to explore a variety of occupations and investigate the preparation required for those occupations. Job-shadowing, work experience, and co-operative education provide opportunities to combine academic learning and anticipatory socialization for the tasks and skills required at the job. Flexible career decisions based on matching an individual's identity to realistic occupation preparation ready young adults for work (Borgen & Amundson, 1995).

The Role of Part-Time Work in Forming an Occupation

Part-time employment and volunteer work provide opportunities for young people to take on responsible roles in the community. Since adolescents report that they work to earn money to spend on activities or to save for post-secondary education, they appear to be motivated by an extrinsic value: money. Studies have found that part-time work had very little effect on young people's work values, although girls were more likely to value the intrinsic rewards, perhaps because they have been socialized to do work that they like. However, when adolescents felt that they were able to accept responsibility, work with others, and manage their time, studies suggest that both males and females view the intrinsic rewards of work as more important. That is, they value their autonomy and the social culture of work more than the money (Mortimer et al., 1996).

Adulthood at Last

Becoming an adult is a lengthy process. Although individuals are often asked as children what they want to be "when they grow up," the transition really begins in adolescence, when they become aware of the expectations of their families, their schools, and the broader society, concerning when and how they should really grow up, and when they are required to make decisions that determine the direction their transition will take. The diversity of family backgrounds and the variety of adult roles that Canadians can choose from require that the development process is an individual one. The developmental theories are useful for understanding how the transition occurs in a fairly consistent pattern, and the influences of families, school, work, and peers have been summarized from recent research. However, the cohort effect suggests that the social environment of the time will result in each generation becoming adult on its own terms. What issues will influence your generation, and how will you become an adult?

chapter 4   Review and Apply

Knowledge/Understanding   Thinking/Inquiry

1. Summarize and compare the developmental theories of Erikson, Loevinger, Levinson, and Riegel. Identify the criteria you will use for your comparison; for example, you could compare how each reflects the four clocks or the developmental tasks described by the family life-cycle theory. Create a chart to organize your point-form summaries.

2. Which of the developmental theories best fits your perceptions of early adult life? Explain your choice using evidence from your observations of adults you know.

3. Summarize the influence of the following on the development of identity in early adulthood:
   - family
   - school
   - work

4. Explain how family, school, and part-time work prepare young adults for an adult occupation, according to research. Choose examples from your own experience to support the explanation.

Knowledge/Understanding   Thinking/Inquiry   Communication

5. Write a reaction paper in which you respond to one of the ideas presented in this chapter. Include at least one direct quotation. Use in-text citations in APA style to credit the original source.

6. Gail Sheehy revised her "map of adult life" in 1995 to suggest a ten-year shift. She defines adolescence as ending at 30. What markers would you use to define adulthood? Discuss the markers and determine the age that signifies the end of adolescence and the beginning of adulthood. Draw a "map" to portray your conclusions.

7. Is the transition to adulthood the same for men and women in Canada today, or are there clear gender differences? Discuss this question with your classmates, using evidence from this chapter and from personal experiences.

8. Conduct a survey of your classmates to determine how they have been prepared to choose an occupation. Compile the results. Design a flow chart to illustrate the steps in deciding on an occupation, including suggestions for steps not yet completed.

9. Design questions for a biographical interview for an adult aged 32 to 35 within a specific community (e.g., Canadian-born women of parents born in the Caribbean). Analyze the results to determine which theory best explains the pattern of development in early adulthood and the stresses that influenced its development. Write a report for members of that community.

10. Using interviews and a symbolic interactionist approach, investigate how students perceive their socialization for adulthood. Working in small groups, compare the results for males and for females to determine whether there are gender differences, and form conclusions. Write a report for parents of high school students summarizing the results and making recommendations.

chapter 5

Young Adult Issues and Trends

CHAPTER EXPECTATIONS

While reading this chapter, you will:

- analyze changes in labour-force participation, taking into consideration male and female participation rates and the impact of work on socialization
- explain the impact on individual development and decision making of social changes and challenges and life events
- demonstrate an understanding of the effect of various aspects of social systems on individual development
- demonstrate an understanding of research methodologies, appropriate research ethics, and specific theoretical perspectives for conducting primary research
- use appropriate current information technology to access or transmit information
- use current information technology to compile quantitative data and present statistical analyses of data or to develop databases
- identify and respond to the theoretical viewpoints, the thesis, and the supporting arguments of materials found in a variety of secondary sources
- distinguish among, and produce examples of, the following: an essay arguing and defending personal opinion; a reaction paper responding to another person's argument; a research paper reporting on an original investigation
- conduct an independent study of an issue concerning individuals or families in a diverse society, and report the results, using a social science format and documenting sources accurately, using appropriate forms of citation
- produce examples of a research paper reporting on an original investigation

Becoming an adult can be great when all your expectations are met, but it can be challenging when family circumstances and social conditions do not always support the changes that you must make in your life.

CHAPTER INTRODUCTION

In this chapter, some of the issues in Canadian society that affect an individual's transition into adulthood will be examined. The current perceptions, opinions, and demographic trends in Canada will be studied, focusing on a few specific changes, challenges, and life events. Various theoretical perspectives will be applied in an attempt to understand how each issue might affect individuals and their families during early adulthood. How the social systems and structures of Canadian society can influence the effects of each issue and provide support for individuals will also be explored. The topics in this chapter might provide interesting opportunities for further independent study.

Early Adulthood

E arly adulthood is a period of life that requires individuals to make major changes in role behaviours as they leave youth behind and take on the responsibilities of full participation in society. You have learned that the pattern of adjustment is determined by the interaction of individuals, their families, and the society in which they live. How individuals cope with the challenges of early adulthood depends on several factors. Leonard Pearlin suggested that personal factors, such as personality, family background, and the extent of an individual's coping skills, will determine how an individual faces difficulties. He stressed that whether an individual anticipated a problem was a key factor in the ability to cope with it. He also explained that how a society is organized to provide social support would contribute to how well an individual adjusts (Bee, 1987).

Many of the challenges faced by young adults can be anticipated. Leaving home, forming new relationships, completing post-secondary education, and finding work are part of the normal pattern of life for Canadian men and women. As a result, there are expectations concerning how and when these events will occur. You have learned that these events are happening later than they did in previous generations, but most young Canadians look forward to developing new life structures in their twenties.

However, there have been many changes in Canadian society that have altered the transition to adulthood for the generations that came of age in the late twentieth century. Perhaps the most pervasive is the change in gender roles that has affected the lifestyle decisions of both men and women. Many new Canadians face resocialization into Canadian society at the same time as they are attempting to develop independent life structures as young adults. Economic changes influencing education and employment continue to affect the lifestyle expectations that individuals have and their chances of achieving them.

Some individuals do not make the transition to independent adulthood successfully. For those who delay independence, living at home and continuing to be financially dependent on their parents might be a manageable alternative. However, there are currently two developments that reflect problems that are not being managed. A growing number of young adults in many industrialized countries, including Canada, are homeless, and since 1970, there has been an unprecedented increase in Canada in the number of suicides among youth aged 15 to 29. These issues may reflect how individuals are unable to cope with transitions. However, they also reflect the structure of Canadian society and the social supports available.

by Derek Chezzi
"Over to You" column contributor, *Maclean's*

Despite what you've been told, it's easy to be a kid these days. It's much tougher to be considered an adult. In the 1960s, baby boomers used to say "Don't trust anyone over 30." Today, many boomers, now in their fifties, have a new mantra: "Don't trust anyone *under* 30." At 26, I feel like I'm going on 16, because, at every turn, my generation is treated as too young for serious consideration. How did this happen? And why are you so afraid of us?

Younger generations have always been looked on with suspicion. Today's media coverage offers a few immediate images: either we're making millions building Web sites (or hacking into them), dying from drug overdoses at raves, beating on each other, or threatening drivers with squeegees. Through it all, endless explanations are trotted out: violent video games, the absence of family values, the lack of emotional support. . . . Parents throw their hands up, unable to protect their children from a dangerous world. Lawmakers and enforcers claim young people are out of control. The hand-wringing often ends with attempts to legislate youth culture.

Squeegee "kids" are hardly that: most are in their twenties and some in their thirties. With education costs on the rise and no guarantee of a job that will let you pay back your loan upon graduation, squeegeeing becomes a necessary alternative. But this type of enterprise doesn't wash with some people. In Ontario, squeegee kids are now outlawed.

Much has been made over the alleged dangers of raves—all-night parties attended by teens, twentysomethings, and fortysomething journalists wanting a scoop. If you've never been to one, they sound scary—rife with stories of drug use. Some people want to ban the party. Reality check: in 1995, the Canadian Centre on Substance Abuse and the Centre for Addiction and Mental Health said there were 804 illicit-drug-related deaths in Canada. In the same year, just over 6500 died from alcohol-related causes and more than 34 000 died of tobacco-related consequences. But no one wants to close down wine and oyster bars, or fully ban smoking.

Many young people in their twenties take temporary jobs while waiting for baby-boomers to retire and free up jobs.

Consider this. Few of us are rich. Many of my graduate friends work in call centres or dispense coffee at the local Starbucks. Those who work in new media take a second job to pay the bills and wind up floating from contract to contract with no security. In another era, we'd be married with a full-time job, a first home, and a child on the way. Today, we wait for people more than twice our age to retire, wiping tables after them in the meantime.

The youth of the 1960s still change the world. Now, forced retirement is a hot-button item because some people don't want to quit work at 65. Health issues, such as geriatric care and housing, top the nation's agenda. We're left out of the discussion, then told pension and health-care programs won't be around for us when we hit retirement age. Surprise! Boomers will take it all to the grave with them.

I don't want to deny boomers their attempts at feeling young. They're welcome to wear denim and go to a Rolling Stones concert. Considering themselves "hip" is harmless, but it's demeaning to dismiss anyone younger as too immature to shoulder a decent job or take care of ourselves without draconian laws.

You reap what you sow. Treat us like young punks and that's what you get. Given the chance, we're as capable of handling responsibility as previous generations at our age. In the words of geezer rockers The Who: the kids are all right—but we're not kids anymore. ■

Source: *Maclean's* (2000, February 28). p. 8.

1. What is the thesis of Derek Chezzi's essay?
2. What supporting arguments does he present to support his thesis?
3. Does your experience of Canadian society support or refute Chezzi's arguments? Give two or three arguments to support your answer.

Gender Roles

Although the role of women has been changing in North America for over a hundred years, there have been major changes in the last thirty years that have affected how young women and young men prepare for adulthood. The most significant role change is that women are now employed, even when they have children. This role change requires that young women be socialized for employment just as young men have been. It also suggests that a young woman's Dream might incorporate her occupational role in addition to family and community roles (Levinson, 1996). Systems theory suggests that a change in one part of a system will require other parts of the system to adjust in order to maintain **homeostasis**, a state of equilibrium; therefore, as the roles of women change, the roles of men must adjust also. To what extent does Canadian society support the altered roles of women and the resulting changes in the roles of men?

Women now work at paid employment at almost the same rate as men. As a result, the work and family roles have changed for both women and men (Ghalam, 1997). The 1995 General Social Survey found that 86 percent of men and 64 percent of women responded that paid work was important to their personal happiness. Those figures rose to 91 percent of men and 83 percent of women among those aged 15 to 24 (Ghalam, 1997). That same survey found that almost half of both men and women agreed that what women want most

Now that it is recognized that women are as productive as men in the workplace, more women are entering non-traditional occupations.

is a home and children. Although it has always been assumed that men could work and be fathers, 55 percent of those surveyed felt that young children would suffer if both parents worked. Many young women are socialized for employment, but role segregation in the workplace continues despite the evidence that there are few differences between men and women that affect their productivity (Côté & Allahar, 1994).

Occupational segregation by sex is almost universal, but the classification of jobs as male or female and the wage differential vary (Wilson, 1991). A hundred years ago, any jobs that required the use of machines were men's jobs, including those requiring the use of the typewriter! By the 1950s, job classification reflected the roles of men and women as defined by functionalists. As a result, women worked in the so-called helping jobs, such as clerical, nursing, and teaching occupations. Legislation dating back to the 1960s in Canada requires that men and women doing the same job for the same employer must be paid the same wages. The 1977 Human Rights Act forbids **discrimination** in hiring; for example, by defining the gender, race, or religion of suitable employees. However, since men continue to outnumber women in all of the highly paid occupations and women dominate the poorly paid occupations, the rate of pay for an occupation, regardless of the qualifications required, appears to reflect the ratio of men to women (Phillips & Phillips, 1993). **Pay equity** laws, which require employers to assess the relative value of work so that work of equal value is paid the same, might eliminate any discrimination on the basis of gender. Since pay equity laws have not been enacted in Canada because employers believe that the costs would not be feasible, the solution has been to encourage young women to enter the so-called non-traditional but better-paying occupations.

web connection

www.mcgrawhill.ca/links/families12

To learn about changing roles of women and men in Canada, go to the web site above for *Individuals and Families in a Diverse Society* to see where to go next.

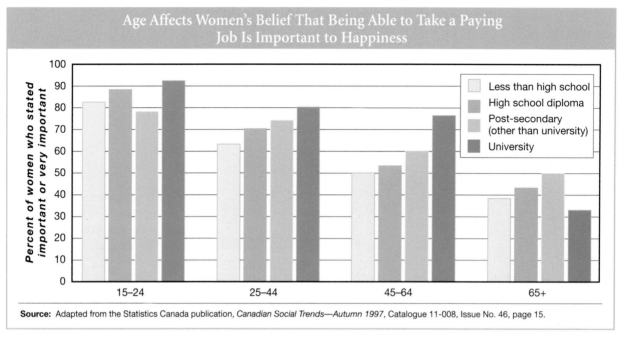

Age Affects Women's Belief That Being Able to Take a Paying Job Is Important to Happiness

Source: Adapted from the Statistics Canada publication, *Canadian Social Trends—Autumn 1997*, Catalogue 11-008, Issue No. 46, page 15.

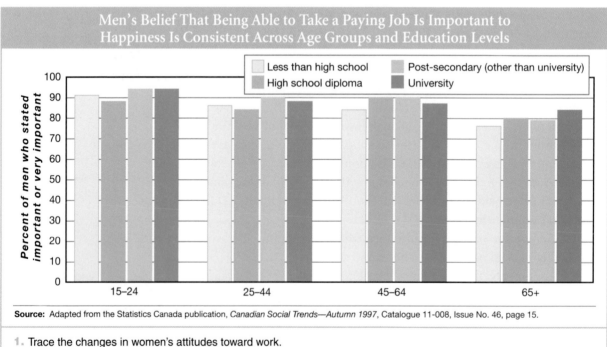

Men's Belief That Being Able to Take a Paying Job Is Important to Happiness Is Consistent Across Age Groups and Education Levels

Source: Adapted from the Statistics Canada publication, *Canadian Social Trends—Autumn 1997*, Catalogue 11-008, Issue No. 46, page 15.

1. Trace the changes in women's attitudes toward work.
2. Develop a hypothesis that could be investigated concerning the changes in women's attitudes toward work. Explain how you could test the hypothesis.
3. How has the power balance changed in relationships now that more women are working?
4. How have men's and women's roles changed?

by John Pitchko
"Minus 20" column contributor, *Regina Leader Post*

It is a known fact that Canadian women earn less than Canadian men do. This reality, which naturally seems unfair to women, has been a fact for many years. In the last few decades, the women's movement has fought against injustices in salaries. Currently, it is illegal to pay a woman less than a man if they are doing substantially the same work for the same organization, firm, or company. However, the new trend enveloped by the women's movement is "equal pay for work of equal value," which is also known as pay equity.

The current argument by women's groups is that equalization of salaries should not be restricted just to men and women doing the same job in the same company. Instead, they say it should extend among companies in the international market. Pay equity means that if a man and a woman are essentially doing the same job, they should earn the same wage.

In order for pay equity to occur, occupations and jobs need to be compared, so an evaluation takes place—usually through a job-to-job comparison or a proportional value comparison. External companies or government agencies given this task use a point system for job evaluation. Some factors are further broken down to identify specific qualities, such as labour separated into physical and mental effort. The points are tabulated and used to compare different jobs in the market. Using the points system, equivalent jobs are compared and solutions are hopefully found. If two jobs have a similar point value, duties, and responsibilities, they are usually said to be of equal value. In such a case, the arbitrator or employer solves any discrepancies in the salary or wage. Although this practice is becoming increasingly common in the market, women's groups are pushing to back pay equity with laws.

There are several flaws, however, to the pay equity system. The points system used to evaluate jobs does not assess every aspect of a job. Some aspects, such as risk, popularity, and employer, are not factored into the point system. Certainly, a job with higher risk would pay more than a safer job. An unpopular job would likely pay more than a popular job because of the smaller number of workers interested in it. And finally, a person employed by a private company would likely earn more than a civil servant because of the strict budgets imposed by public employers. As a result, many differences in pay are the result of factors not considered by a normal evaluation.

A second fault with pay equity is the increased spending an employer must allocate to wage increases. If pay equity were made into law, businesses all across Canada would be suddenly forced to increase the salaries of some employees. A salary increase for many workers could cause a company to have financial problems or maybe even go out of business. It becomes especially worrisome when employers are forced to pay an average additional $10 000 per qualified employee.

On the other hand, there are several positive reasons to have pay equity. First, women who earn more money have more disposable income. They are thus able to make a better contribution to the economy. Perhaps more importantly, single mothers could provide a better lifestyle for themselves and their children. They would be able to pay for childcare, extended education, and extracurricular activities for themselves or their children. They could also benefit from being able to make long-term financial investments, such as retirement plans and personal savings.

Pay equity also benefits employers as well as employees. Companies that adhere to pay equity guidelines and laws have better employee policies and public representation. Because these companies are trying to create equality in the workplace, their employment policies are superior to other companies not incorporating pay equity. As a result, companies with pay equity can expect to attract and keep the most qualified and diverse employees. In addition, these companies have higher employee morale and a positive working environment.

In my personal opinion, however, forced pay equity is currently not a sensible economic idea. If companies throughout Canada were forced to incorporate a pay equity system, unnecessary chaos would be created and firms in both the private and public sectors would have to divert millions of dollars into restructuring their individual pay systems. Enormous and inefficient bureaucracies would need to be created and maintained in order to ensure that pay equality is established. Not only do such bureaucracies cost money, but if an unresolvable conflict ever arose among an employee, employer, and a pay equity commission, an intense, lengthy, and costly legal struggle might take place. In addition, the sheer cost of balancing wages and salaries could destroy companies. Smaller companies and companies struggling to survive would be hard hit by sudden and expansive

wage increases. Consequently, these businesses might be forced to go out of business, possibly crippling local, national, and/or international economies. Organizations in the public sector would face rising costs with already-dwindling budgets. By creating more money for wage increases, government and public sector corporations would need to either slash their budgets and expenditures or raise taxes, both causing public outcry.

Currently, pay equity does not appear to be a beneficial economic policy. Even though the benefits of improved morale and public relations would result from pay equity, the cost of disrupting an entire economy is far too great. In the future, after more consideration and revision has been given to current pay equity beliefs and practices, a more sensible form of pay equilibrium may be produced which would better integrate with the economy. At present, however, no matter how noble the idea of pay equity is, it is not feasible economically. ■

Source: *Regina Leader Post.* (2001, September 10). p. A7.

---

1. What is John Pitchko's thesis?
2. Identify the theoretical perspective(s) that he used in his analysis.
3. How successful has he been in supporting his thesis?
4. How has he dealt with the arguments that are counter to his thesis?
5. What further evidence is required to determine whether pay equity should be implemented, in your opinion?

Average Earnings

Number and average earnings of full-year, full-time workers in the 25 highest-paying occupations, by sex, Canada, 1995

	Number of Earners			Average Earnings ($)		
	Both Sexes	**Men**	**Women**	**Both Sexes**	**Men**	**Women**
Total—25 highest-paying occupations[1]	368 325	287 955	80 365	80 206	86 139	58 943
Judges	1 765	1 360	405	126 246	128 791	117 707
Specialist physicians	12 560	9 345	3 220	123 976	137 019	86 086
General practitioners and family physicians	21 670	16 055	5 615	107 620	116 750	81 512
Dentists	8 530	6 995	1 535	102 433	109 187	71 587
Senior managers—goods production, utilities, transportation and construction	35 510	32 625	2 880	99 360	102 971	58 463
Senior managers—financial, communications carriers, and other business services	23 055	19 190	3 860	99 117	104 715	71 270
Lawyers and Québec notaries	44 385	32 305	12 080	81 617	89 353	60 930
Senior managers—trade, broadcasting and other services	28 665	24 610	4 060	79 200	84 237	48 651
Primary production managers (except agriculture)	7 075	6 670	405	76 701	78 421	48 479
Securities agents, investment dealers, and traders	14 520	9 640	4 880	75 911	90 391	47 323
Petroleum engineers	2 765	2 585	180	72 543	73 657	56 506
Chiropractors	2 370	2 000	370	68 808	71 032	56 764
Engineering, science, and architecture managers	17 835	16 165	1 665	68 235	69 792	53 138
University professors	31 395	23 210	8 190	68 195	72 532	55 909
Senior managers—health, education, social and community services, and membership organizations	8 025	4 410	3 615	68 187	78 012	56 190
Air pilots, flight engineers, and flying instructors	7 490	7 290	195	67 581	68 219	43 991
Geologists, geochemists, and geophysicists	4 935	4 375	555	66 210	68 116	51 151
Utilities managers	6 645	5 955	690	64 816	66 239	52 564
School principals and administrators of elementary and secondary education	23 000	14 700	8 300	64 513	66 837	60 394
Optometrists	2 045	1 285	760	64 419	73 920	48 337
Insurance, real estate, and financial brokerage managers	22 835	15 135	7 700	64 197	73 419	46 070
Commissioned police officers	3 680	3 345	335	63 518	64 865	50 011
Senior government managers and officials	15 655	10 690	4 965	63 195	69 477	49 667
Supervisors, mining and quarrying	4 425	4 375	0	62 537	62 768	0
Information systems and data processing managers	17 490	13 640	3 855	62 387	64 999	53 140

[1]Although athletes were in the 25 highest-paying occupations, their very small numbers rendered their income statistics unreliable. Hence the individuals in these occupations were excluded from this table.

Average Earnings

Number and average earnings of full-year, full-time workers in the 25 lowest-paying occupations, by sex, Canada, 1995

	Number of Earners			Average Earnings ($)		
	Both Sexes	**Men**	**Women**	**Both Sexes**	**Men**	**Women**
Total—25 lowest-paying occupations[1]	**567 765**	**179 950**	**387 810**	**17 729**	**20 238**	**16 564**
Inspectors and testers, fabric, fur, leather products manufacturing	1 860	400	1 455	20 001	25 396	18 507
Light duty cleaners	46 875	15 330	31 535	19 991	23 829	18 125
Early childhood educators and assistants	32 480	1 105	31 375	19 772	25 074	19 586
Pet groomers and animal care workers	4 175	1 370	2 805	19 716	24 467	17 398
Taxi and limousine drivers and chauffeurs	16 695	15 720	980	19 664	19 845	16 756
Visiting homemakers, housekeepers, and related occupations	22 775	2 175	20 600	19 607	24 751	19 063
Hotel front desk clerks	7 660	2 760	4 900	19 220	20 364	18 575
Cooks	68 775	38 025	30 755	19 054	20 224	17 607
Maitres d'hôtel and hosts/hostesses	4 590	965	3 620	18 873	24 649	17 336
Kitchen and food service helpers	24 825	9 385	15 440	18 799	17 320	19 697
Hairstylists and barbers	43 120	10 835	32 280	18 292	22 867	16 755
Painters, sculptors, and other visual artists	4 405	2 595	1 810	18 188	20 421	14 982
Tailors, dressmakers, furriers, and milliners	8 855	1 865	6 990	17 850	24 686	16 025
General farm workers	42 925	27 365	15 560	17 756	19 990	13 825
Estheticians, electrologists, and related occupations	6 845	245	6 600	17 658	22 889	17 462
Sewing machine operators	30 235	2 490	27 750	17 613	20 664	17 340
Cashiers	56 140	9 025	47 110	17 553	20 557	16 977
Ironing, pressing, and finishing occupations	3 370	990	2 375	17 322	19 297	16 499
Artisans and craftspersons	5 880	2 840	3 040	16 943	20 555	13 565
Bartenders	15 570	7 080	8 495	16 740	18 899	14 940
Harvesting labourers	1 130	525	605	16 426	18 683	14 465
Service station attendants	10 800	8 630	2 175	16 203	16 520	14 947
Food service counter attendants and food preparers	22 225	5 550	16 680	15 487	17 912	14 681
Food and beverage servers	50 190	11 940	38 250	14 891	18 192	13 861
Babysitters, nannies, and parents' helpers	35 365	740	34 625	12 713	15 106	12 662

[1]Although trappers and hunters were in the 25 lowest-paying occupations, their very small numbers rendered their income statistics unreliable. Hence the individuals in these occupations were excluded from this table.

Source: Adapted from the Statistics Canada publication, *The Daily*, May 12, 1998, Catalogue 11-001, page 13.

1. In which occupations do men outnumber women, and women outnumber men?
2. In which occupations do women earn more on average than men?
3. How can the difference in earnings between men and women in the same occupations be explained?

Women now graduate from high school, college, and university at higher rates than men do, but they are still underrepresented in careers that are well paid. Educational programs across Canada that have focused on encouraging girls to study math and science have had some success. However, studies show that although they can do well in these subjects, girls are not as interested in them as boys are. Women also have different expectations of work than men do. Although both men and women place great importance on their jobs being interesting, women place more value on the implicit rewards of competence and people-oriented goals, whereas men place higher value on extrinsic rewards such as high pay and status (Bibby, 2001; Morgan, 2001). These results suggest that men outnumber women in math and science careers because women do not find them as interesting as careers in education and social services, for example. These differences correspond to the research on female development that suggests that women are more likely to form an identity through their relationships with others rather than through their individual accomplishments (Gilligan, 1993).

Characteristics of "a Good Job"

Percent Indicating "Very Important"	Nationally	Males	Females
The work is interesting.	86%	84%	87%
It gives me a feeling of accomplishment.	76	70	81
There is a chance for advancement.	68	70	66
It pays well.	66	72	60
Other people are friendly and helpful.	63	59	67
It adds something to other people's lives.	59	53	64
There is little chance of being laid off.	57	60	55
It allows me to make most of the decisions myself.	49	53	45

Source: From *Canada's Teens: Today, Yesterday, and Tomorrow.* Copyright © 2001 by Reginald W. Bibby. Reproduced by permission of Stoddart Publishing Co. Limited.

1. Compare the expectations of males and females.
2. This survey gathered the opinions of 15- to 19-year-old Canadians. How might the results differ for those aged 19–24 years?

Despite the changes in education and career planning, men and women are choosing different paths in early adulthood because they have different interests. It is not clear why girls and boys grow up with different expectations in life. Some people suggest that differences are innate; that is, girls are biologically programmed to reason differently from boys, so women have different motivation from men (Gilligan, 1993). Functionalists suggest that the differences in interests and motivation are formed through socialization so that men and women can perform appropriate gender roles in society (Mandell, 1993). Symbolic interactionists explain that children are influenced by the role models they observe in the media and in daily experience more than by the guidance they receive from their parents and teachers. Consequently, children see themselves in traditional gender roles even when they have been taught that they have broader options (Wilson, 1991). During adolescence, there is an intensification of gender identification as individuals seek an identity, so feedback from peers also contributes to narrow gender identity and the gender-based aspirations of young men and women (Côté & Allahar, 1994). Since the 1970s, educational developments have focused on encouraging girls to consider non-traditional subjects leading to wider career and family options. The work patterns evident in the late 1990s suggest that these programs have been quite successful, but that women still earn less than men.

point of view | Where Are the Boys?

by Garth Holloway
Social and Global Studies Department Head
Earl Haig Secondary School, Toronto

You have seen the statistics for the academic success of girls in Canada's high schools, colleges, and universities compared to those of boys. Are there other areas in which girls show more involvement and success that contribute to their achievement at university? Let's look at one high school's leadership development programs to see if there was a gender difference as well.

Earl Haig Secondary School in Toronto is a large academic school of approximately 2500 students. It is

The Yearbook Committee for Earl Haig Secondary School, 2001–2002.

known across the city for the students' enthusiastic involvement in the school's extensive extracurricular program. Like most secondary schools, Earl Haig has an elected Student Council. Although more girls run for election to the 14 positions, students usually elect a balance of boys and girls.

Because of its large size, Earl Haig also has a Leadership Council that organizes and runs events and programs for students both within the school and in the larger community. For example, this council is responsible for a peer-helping program, a school-wide tutoring service, a reading program in local elementary schools, an orientation program in the Fall for Grade 9 students, and for helping out at Parents' Nights and special events throughout the year. Involvement in this leadership program is voluntary, but candidates who apply for executive positions are interviewed by a combination of out-going executive members and teachers.

The Leadership Council is divided into four key committees headed by co-chairs. In the academic year 2001–2002, only two of the eight co-chairs were boys. Of the approximately 125 active members of these four committees, only 40 are boys.

Similar gender differences are found in other organizations at Earl Haig. The yearbook committee at the school, which annually produces a 216-page yearbook called *The Delphian*, has a staff of three senior editors and 24 sectional editors. Of the 27 positions, 19 are held by girls. A large part of the leadership development program at the school is an annual school trip, primarily for Grade 11 students, to Greece and Italy, which has run for 18 years. In the past few years, school employees have noticed more and more girls and fewer boys are participating. The March 2002 trip had 83 girls and only 27 boys!

Finally, a look at the school's sports programs yields similar results. There are as many girls' teams as boys' teams with about equal involvement of both genders. However, the Athletic Council of 15 members has only three boys.

Extensive research tells us that involvement in a school's extracurricular program will more likely lead to future academic success as well as professional and social happiness (Csikszentmihalyi & Schneider, 2000). Parents know this, as do high school students. So, where are the boys? ∎

1. Think about the extracurricular and leadership development programs at your school. Is the gender involvement similar to that of Earl Haig?
2. Why do you think boys are less involved at Earl Haig? What do you think the boys are doing while the girls participate in extracurricular activities and voluntary work?
3. Should something be done to re-involve the boys? What action would you suggest?
4. Do you believe this is a positive or a negative trend? Why?

Cultural Conflict

The major challenges of early adulthood identified by researchers are to form an identity, a tentative adult life structure, and intimate relationships. You have seen that for Canadians and Americans, an identity is an image of self as an independent individual. Young adults expect to live out their "Dream" by

web connection

www.mcgrawhill.ca/links/families12

To learn about cultural variations in socialization for adulthood, go to the web site above for *Individuals and Families in a Diverse Society* to see where to go next.

pursuing their occupational goals, leaving home, and, perhaps, finding a partner. Perhaps this should be called the North American Dream, because young adults in other cultures might not have the same expectations.

Identity, as defined by Erikson, is founded on **individualism**, a social philosophy that emphasizes independence and self-reliance and that favours the free action of individuals. During the second half of the twentieth century, individualism changed the way that people perceived their lifestyles and their roles in the family and in society (Glossop, 1999). However, in Eastern cultures, identity is based on duty and obligation, first to family, and then to society. A **duty-based moral code** encourages individuals to consider the expectations of family more than personal considerations when making important decisions.

Romola Dugsin's (2001) study of young adults living in immigrant East Indian families found that conflict arose when children approached adulthood. Using a symbolic interactionist perspective, she asked the participants to describe their experience. Both men and women felt pressure from their parents to excel at school and in an occupation, but they were expected to assume traditional gender roles within the family. They perceived their families as closely intertwined, with an emphasis on duty and obligation to parents, family, and extended family. The expectation that they would respect the wishes of their elders limited their ability to communicate openly about their individual goals. Dugsin concluded that these East Indian immigrants were most likely to develop a life structure that was consistent with their East Indian values if they were first able to develop self-esteem inside the family by feeling accepted, nurtured, and respected as an individual.

When children attend school and are socialized into new cultures, seeds of conflict with the traditional family culture may be sown.

The children of immigrants are more likely to become assimilated into Canadian culture than their parents are because they go to school, where the major activity is socialization. Canadian-born and immigrant children participate in the same reflective activities and observe the same role models as they form their individual identities and acquire their values. Canadian schools emphasize independence, individual accomplishment, co-operation, the expression of personal opinions, and responsible decision making. These qualities form the basis of identity and an adult life structure as expected in Canada, but they might not reflect the expectations of some families from other countries.

| Conflict and Healing in Family Experience of Second-Generation Emigrants from India Living in North America

by Romola Dugsin, Ph.D. Candidate,

Center for Humanistic Studies, Detroit, Michigan

RESEARCH QUESTION

What causes conflict in East Indian families with young adult children living in North America, and how can the families be healed?

HYPOTHESIS

There was no hypothesis because the Grounded Theory Method was used, a specific analytical approach in which no hypothesis is stated prior to the researcher's development of an explanation from the data.

RESEARCH METHOD

Using qualitative analysis, the researcher, Romola Dugsin, analyzed the results of six open-ended interviews with second-generation East Indian immigrants. The subjects were between the ages of 24 and 36, three were male, three were female, two lived in the United States, and four lived in Canada.

RESULTS

- Cultural conflict results from expectations concerning being East Indian, education and success, family ties, parental control, and dating and marriage.
- Subjects reported loneliness, pain, lying or rebellion, or acceptance in response to the conflict.
- Family healing methods include communicating openly with parents, seeking therapy in areas of anger and self-esteem, and finding support outside of the family.

CONCLUSION

The strong sense of obligation to family ties and traditional East Indian values can present conflict in the process of individuation and separation from the family of origin for second-generation immigrants. ■

Source: *Family Process*. (2001, Summer). 233–241.

The emphasis on duty and obligation to the family of origin is found in many cultures in Canada, and could result in some difficulty for young adults attempting to develop an individualistic life structure. Leonard Pearlin suggested that specific characteristics, such as race and family background, influence the direction that individuals take in life. He also suggested that the availability of social support networks, such as school, could assist youth in making the transition (Bee, 1987). Immigrant families and their adult children, as well as the children of families in religious groups such as the Mennonites and the Hutterites, with their values, face additional challenges in the transition to adulthood if there are conflicting cultural values. However, some people question whether the individualism that has become the dominant philosophy in North America is beneficial to individuals, their families, or Canadian society (Glossop, 1999).

by Dr. Arnold Rincover
Psychologist and Associate Professor of Psychology,
University of Toronto

Many immigrant families are torn apart when children embrace the new Western culture while parents cling to the old culture. It doesn't matter whether you are of Asian, Spanish, Indian, African, Italian, Russian, Arabic, or any other descent, you need to prepare yourself for some tough times down the road. Problems may begin to crop up virtually anywhere—a child doesn't want to wear the turban or the sari, wants to date, celebrate Christmas, sleep over at a friend's house, speak English at home, use slang expressions that parents find offensive.

Mai Lee was 16 years old and she was walking on air—the "man of her dreams" just asked her out on her first date. Her parents, however, were Asian immigrants and they didn't feel she should be dating until she was 19. They wanted her to focus solely on school. So, Mai Lee started to see her prince on the sly. Her parents found out and it almost destroyed the family. The parents were devastated that she would lie and defy them. They threatened to throw her out of the house if she ever talked to this boy or disobeyed them again. There were daily eruptions at home until they learned to avoid each other. Both Mai Lee and her parents thought they were right, that the other was rigid. Neither even considered the possibility that they were wrong, that the other person's argument had some merit (or was even rational), that there was a compromise to be made.

Sometimes the upheaval in immigrant families is not from the kids. Perhaps women didn't work outside the home in the "old country" and now Mom has to work for the family to survive. Dad feels incompetent. Mom may even make more money than him, which

Many immigrant families experience conflict when the children go against the parents' wishes.

further destroys his self-esteem. In these cases, fathers often resort to alcohol or withdraw from the family.

Many children of immigrant families are eventually referred to a psychologist because the child is showing behavioural problems or depression. Yet, there is no way to treat those behavioural problems or that depression unless the family problem is addressed. Enter family therapy.

The brokering of two cultures means that both the child and the parents must learn to appreciate each other's point of view . . . and compromise. It must heighten the child's understanding of the family's roots. This may mean the child attends religious services, celebrates holidays, conforms to dress and other rituals at certain times that are important to the parents. The child may take religious classes, attend social functions which have an ethnic flavour. It may also mean that the child cannot do everything that his or her (Western) friends do.

For the parents, there is often much to be done. We [family therapists] must first encourage them to take English courses, so they can participate in their new culture—without some command of English, they'll miss out on their own children's development. We encourage the parents to negotiate with their children. They must understand that it would be quite cruel to tell a child he or she can't date when all his or her friends are dating. It will destroy the parents' relationship with that child. If the concern is schoolwork or safety, then those should be conditions upon which dating will be allowed. If parents think the child is too immature, then the child should be told how to demonstrate more maturity. If parents wish to chaperone the young person until the age of 18, so be it. They shouldn't say "NO," but "when" or "how."

For families who have immigrated to Canada, it is important to understand that such conflicts are inevitable. It is often essential to get an outside professional to help. ■

Source: *Regina Leader Post*. (2001, July 14). p. G7.

1. What is Dr. Rincover's thesis, and what arguments does he present to support it?
2. What are the benefits and/or drawbacks for young adults of abandoning the values of their traditional families?
3. What might be the consequences of following Dr. Rincover's advice?
4. Should schools support youth in rebelling against their parents' traditional values? Why or why not?

case study | Sanjay's Quest for Independence

Sanjay Wadhera is a 26-year-old Canadian whose family emigrated to Canada from India the year before he was born. He has an older sister, Geeta, and an older brother, Ameet, who were five and two respectively when the family arrived in Canada. His father, a professional engineer, and his mother, a secondary school teacher, both left good jobs with secure futures to move to Canada, where they felt their children would have more opportunities and more freedom. His family settled originally in Winnipeg, where an uncle and his family were already living. Sanjay's father soon started a research job with a large international electronics firm. Sanjay was born the next year.

When Sanjay was four, his father was transferred to the Toronto area, a move that pleased his parents because of the much larger Hindu community that lived there and because of the less extreme winters of southern Ontario. The family settled in Mississauga, where houses were more affordable and within easy commuting distance to his father's job.

Things went very well for the Wadhera family, and they were able to purchase a larger home in a new subdivision in Burlington. To help pay for the home,

Sanjay and his parents had conflicting values and goals.

and because the children were now much older and less dependent, Sanjay's mother opened a small day care, which she has operated out of the basement of her home ever since. Unfortunately, Sanjay's father lost his engineering job in 1990 when his firm downsized as a result of an economic recession. After spending 18 months unsuccessfully looking for jobs in his field, Sanjay's father eventually bought a convenience store in a new plaza in Burlington. Sanjay's parents have expected that both he and his brother work in the family store on weekends and during the summers to save the family from having to hire part-time employees. The store has provided the Wadheras with a steady family income.

Sanjay is very proud of his parents' accomplishments and hard work, and he particularly respects the strength and commitment that they have shown for the family. However, he has found himself in continual conflict with them over the past few years about his future career and the kind of life that he wants to live as an adult. This conflict started while he was in high school, where he played football and baseball for the school teams. His parents wanted him to help out at the store after school. In his final year of high school, Sanjay argued with his parents over his choice of university. Ameet attended McMaster University and continued to live in his parents' home and work part-time in the family business. Most of Sanjay's friends were applying to Queen's, Western, and Waterloo universities and were anticipating the next year of living in residence and being "out on their own." Sanjay's choice of majoring in Economics at Queen's University did not make his parents happy, since they could not understand why he would want to be so far away from home.

Paying for university was another source of conflict for Sanjay and his parents. Because most of the Wadheras' financial resources were tied up in the convenience store, Sanjay was dependent on government assistance. He knew that he would have a substantial student debt at the end of his undergraduate program and wanted to work at a summer job that would reduce the size of his student loan each year. However, his parents needed him to work in the store in the summers and argued that if he was so concerned about his debt, then he could transfer to a closer university to which he could commute from their Burlington home.

Another problem between Sanjay and his parents was his choice of friends. The family's entire social life revolved around the activities of the temple that they attended and the large Hindu community to which they belonged. They expected Sanjay to participate in these activities, just as Geeta and Ameet had done. Sanjay preferred the company and activities of his more culturally diverse high school friends. When Sanjay met Emma Johnson during his first year at Queen's, she was initially welcomed into his parents' home. However, when his parents realized that Sanjay and Emma's relationship went beyond friendship, they told him that he was no longer allowed to see her. Sanjay continued to date Emma, deceiving his parents, often with the help of Ameet and Geeta.

During his third year at Queen's, Sanjay began to realize that his chances of employment at graduation would be greater if he acquired some related summer work experience. A number of Toronto companies visited Queen's to interview for summer positions, and Sanjay and many of his classmates applied. He was interviewed by several companies and was offered positions with two of them. However, he was unable to accept either position because his father was planning to travel to India in the spring to visit family and to help expedite the move of Sanjay's grandmother to Burlington. By this time Ameet had graduated from McMaster and had started a full-time job in the accounting department of a small company in Oakville, so Sanjay was needed to run the store while his father was away. ■

1. What factors in Sanjay's family background are influencing his individuation?
2. Suggest how Sanjay's socialization has resulted in a conflict between Canadian and East Indian values.
3. Compare Sanjay's transition to adulthood with that of Colleen's in Chapter 3, page 71, and Ian's in Chapter 4, page 120.
4. What life structure does Sanjay appear to be attempting to build for himself?
5. Using social exchange theory, assess the costs and benefits of the decisions that Sanjay faced. What choices do you think he should have made?

The Costs of Education

Most young Canadians expect to attend post-secondary education when they complete high school to prepare for a career, but also to experience the particular extension of youth culture that attending college or university can provide (Moffat, 1993). For many high school students, going to college or university is the goal, not acquiring the education, because their occupational plans are not yet formed. Unlike high school in Canada, post-secondary education is subsidized, but not free. Students must pay tuition, purchase books, pay for their activities, and, unless they live near a college or university, pay for room and board. At the beginning of the twenty-first century, many families are concerned about the increasing costs of tuition.

The belief that the costs are too high might discourage some young people from pursuing the education they need to achieve their goals. A 2001 survey of high school graduates in Alberta revealed that 70 percent agreed that the total cost could serve as a barrier to pursuing post-secondary education, and 66 percent thought that the tuition cost would be a barrier. In the same survey, the respondents overestimated the tuition cost by $2000, an error of over 50 percent (Holubitsky, 2001). However, tuition costs in Canada did double between 1988 and 1999, during a decade in which family incomes did not increase, so families have reasons to be concerned about paying for education.

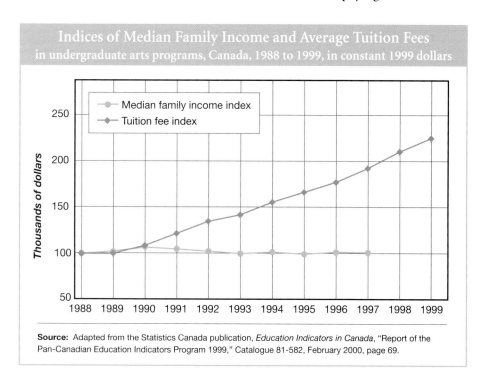

Indices of Median Family Income and Average Tuition Fees in undergraduate arts programs, Canada, 1988 to 1999, in constant 1999 dollars

Source: Adapted from the Statistics Canada publication, *Education Indicators in Canada*, "Report of the Pan-Canadian Education Indicators Program 1999," Catalogue 81-582, February 2000, page 69.

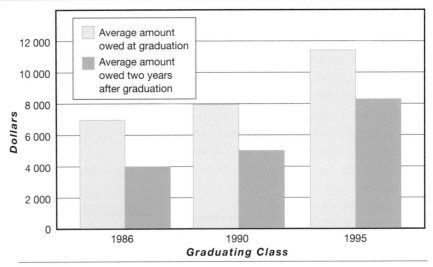

Average amount owed to student loan programs, by college and university graduates who borrowed from student loan programs, Canada, 1986, 1990, and 1995, in constant 1995 dollars

Legend:
- Average amount owed at graduation
- Average amount owed two years after graduation

Y-axis (Dollars): 0, 2 000, 4 000, 6 000, 8 000, 10 000, 12 000

X-axis (Graduating Class): 1986, 1990, 1995

Source: Adapted from the Statistics Canada publication, *Education Indicators in Canada*, "Report of the Pan-Canadian Education Indicators Program 1999," Catalogue 81-582, February 2000, page 68.

1. What does constant dollars mean, and why are they used for comparison?
2. What factors would influence the impact that rising tuition costs would have on families of students entering post-secondary education?

Many parents have high expectations that their children will attend post-secondary education when they finish high school, but few anticipate the real costs.

Although 87 percent of Canadian parents hope that their children will attend post-secondary education (Statistics Canada, 2001), they wonder if they will be able to afford to pay for it. The results of the 1999 Survey of Approaches to Educational Planning found that 41 percent of families were saving for their children's education. However, the amount of money saved, a median amount of $3000 for all children under 18, fell very short of the actual costs of tuition. Almost all parents expected that their children would work while at college or university, and 70 percent expected that their children would work part-time during high school to save for their education. Many parents also expected that their children would require a student loan.

Parents have high expectations for their children's education, but students wonder whether the increased earning potential when they graduate will justify the expense. They fear that they will graduate with large debts that might affect their flexibility to search for jobs that suit their interests, or their freedom to consider other options when they graduate. In 1998, the average student who had taken loans graduated with a $12 000 debt that they were able to reduce by 25 percent within two years (Statistics Canada, 1999). David Stager, a professor of economics at the University of Toronto, used a costs and benefits analysis to study the effects of education on income. He calculated that the costs of education, including tuition fees, room and board, and the forgone income, earn an after-tax return of 13.8 percent for men and 17.6 percent for women in additional income after graduation (Theobald, 1997). Although the debt might be unsettling for graduates just starting out in their occupation, as the wage gap between high school graduates and college and university graduates widens, the cost of education becomes a better investment.

Rates of Return

Annual after-tax rate of return for a university education, Ontario, 1990

Bachelor Degree Programs	Males	Females
Humanities, Fine Arts	7.3%	14.8%
Social Sciences	12.8	17.0
Commerce	16.2	21.8
Biological Sciences	6.8	15.0
Maths, Physical Sciences	15.1	21.2
Health Professions	14.9	21.0
Engineering	16.0	19.8
Law	15.0	16.0
Medicine	20.8	19.7
All Bachelor and First Professional Degree Programs	**13.8%**	**17.6%**

Note: Social Sciences excludes Commerce, Social Work, and Law. Health Professions include Nursing, Pharmacy, and Rehabilitation Medicine.

Source: David Stager, Retired Professor of Economics, University of Toronto.

1. Which programs provide the best return on financial investment for men and for women?
2. What factors would affect the rate of return?
3. Why is the rate of return higher for women than for men?

Family income can influence the career expectations of young people. Although students identify similar career aspirations regardless of gender, race, or family background, family income can affect whether students expect

web connection

www.mcgrawhill.ca/links/families12

To learn about the costs of post-secondary education and employment opportunities for graduates, go to the web site above for *Individuals and Families in a Diverse Society* to see where to go next.

to achieve their goals. Individuals from lower-income families can qualify for student loans, which can mean that they will graduate with a much larger debt than individuals from higher-income families will. Some people argue that a well-educated population benefits a society so it should pay for education through taxation. In some industrialized countries, such as the United Kingdom, post-secondary education at public institutions is free for students because it is completely subsidized by the government in the same way that public elementary and secondary education is in Canada. Others argue that educated people benefit from an increased income and should, therefore, pay for their own education. In Canada, students pay tuition fees that, in some provinces, vary according to the earning potential of graduates. The tuition is government-subsidized, but a higher family income increases the chances of students attending college or, to a greater extent, university, so that they can achieve a higher future income also. However, in the future, if tuition continues to increase, post-secondary education may be affordable only to the upper-middle class of Canadian society.

point of view | Levelling the Playing Field

by Robert J. Birgeneau
President, University of Toronto

In the summer of 2001 the presidents of 28 leading universities and colleges in the United States, including such august institutions as Yale, Stanford, Notre Dame, Massachusetts Institute of Technology (MIT), and the University of Chicago, recommitted their institutions to providing need-based financial assistance alone. They also endorsed a set of common standards for assessing a family's ability to pay for undergraduate education. In so doing, they in effect created a common front against the practice of competitive bidding for students. Most important, they guaranteed that qualified students from the poorest families could have access to the very best in undergraduate education. This continuing commitment to need-based, as opposed to merit-based, aid is both courageous and admirably idealistic.

You might ask what the situation is in Ontario, and at the University of Toronto. In fact, we are proud that U of T has made a significant commitment to need-based financial student aid. In 1998 the university made a bold guarantee that no student would be prevented from coming to our university, or from finishing a degree, for want of financial assistance.

About three-quarters of the financial support we offer undergraduates, about $23 million annually, is awarded primarily on the basis of need, and this figure has more than doubled since 1997–1998. What's more, the university gives entering students an assurance that they will not be met with unanticipated tuition hikes. When there is a gap between an undergraduate's assessed need and the maximum loan allowed under the Ontario Student Aid Program (OSAP), U of T will cover the shortfall through a non-repayable grant. All of this is possible only because of our own major investment in student aid, the support of government, and the continuing generosity of our friends—especially our alumni and alumnae.

Nevertheless, there are still inequities. On the one hand, it is very important that OSAP loans make it possible for even the poorest students to attend university. However, these same students then may graduate with quite large debts. Fortunately, their numbers are small. Still, it is unfair that students from well-off families graduate debt-free while those whose families struggle financially graduate with OSAP debts as large as $28 000.

I should emphasize that the issue here is not tuition. Our tuitions in Ontario are modest when compared with expected income gains due to a university education, or with university tuitions in many other countries, including our neighbour to the south. Further, our tuition in undergraduate arts and science, corrected for inflation, has actually been decreasing over the past several years.

How do we level the playing field? I believe that the entire Ontario university system needs to move toward a predominantly need-based undergraduate financial-aid system. Further, to the extent that we retain merit-based aid, the size of the scholarship should be based on financial need. This is already the case for several programs including the province's Aiming for the Top Scholarships and our own

University of Toronto National Scholarship Program, including the Bank of Montreal scholarships. The current practice by some Ontario universities of "bidding" for the students with the top high school grades is, at best, wasteful of our limited resources for financial aid.

It would be difficult for any university in Ontario to make the transition to need-based aid unilaterally. It must happen system-wide. Students should attend the university that best meets their educational goals, rather than the one that appears to be most advantageous financially. I call on my fellow Ontario university presidents to join me in emulating the 28 U.S. presidents who have taken a huge step toward levelling the playing field for all students. ■

Source: *Uni5versity of Toronto Magazine.* (2001, Autumn). p. 5.

1. What is Dr. Birgeneau's thesis and theoretical perspective?
2. What arguments does he present to support his thesis?
3. What conflicting viewpoints does he counter?
4. Would you like to see the proposals suggested by Dr. Birgeneau implemented at all Canadian universities and colleges? Why or why not?

Homeless Youth

The picture of **homelessness** is changing in Canada, reflecting differences in the economy and the social support networks since the 1980s. Homelessness is defined as having no fixed place to sleep at night. The homeless include people staying in motels until their money runs out, those staying with friends, those staying in shelters, and those sleeping outside or in whatever space they can find to protect them from the weather. There have always been homeless people, but the number has been growing in industrialized nations to an extent that The Toronto Disaster Relief Committee calls homelessness a national disaster (TDRC, 2001).

It is difficult to determine the number of people who are homeless. Estimates are based on the number of people who stay in shelters and who use soup kitchens. The Mayor's Homelessness Action Task Force determined that almost 26 000 people used the shelter system in Toronto in 1996, and estimated that the number of homeless youth had increased by 80 percent to 28 percent of hostel users between 1992 and 1998 (City of Toronto, 2001). The Montréal Public Health Department estimates that there are 4000 to 5000 homeless youth in Montréal (Ward, 1999). Authorities estimate that there are 100 homeless youth in Halifax (McLaughlin, 2001). Homeless people migrate to the larger cities—47 percent of shelter-users in Toronto came from outside the city (City of Toronto, 2001). Clearly, homeless young adults who beg for change on street corners are the tip of the iceberg.

The homeless are those who sleep in shelters, doorways, and stairwells, but also include those who stay with friends and in motels because they have nowhere else to go.

point of view | Notion of Homeless Youth Raises Some Questions

by Ross Nightingale
"Letters to the Editor" Contributor,
The London Free Press

I suffer from a generation gap when I read the word "homeless." I picture elderly people who haven't the education or health to hold a job. The men are unshaven, poorly dressed, sleep on the street, or live in wooded areas. The women are poorly dressed and push all their belongings in a shopping cart.

The pictures I see today depict the homeless as well-educated, well-dressed, articulate young people between the ages of 19 and 25. This brings many questions to mind:

- Where do they obtain money? They cannot draw welfare as they have no address. Do they work, but don't have a starting salary to afford the lifestyle to which they would like to be accustomed? Are they lobbying for subsidized housing so they will have an address and be able to apply for welfare?

- Why can't they use existing facilities we provide? Is it that they do not like the surroundings or the rules and regulations?

- My generation started on small salaries (34 cents an hour) and improved our standard of living over the years as our income increased. Do the homeless regard this as foolish and suggest we should have been lobbying for government assistance?

- Do these homeless not have parents or relatives who would gladly supply accommodation? Or would there be rules and regulations to such an arrangement?

If unemployment is the problem, I suggest activists and civic bodies spend their time placing these young people in jobs, instead of concentrating on government subsidies. I also suggest the activists, civic bodies, and the newspaper profile the people involved to provide answers to these questions so we "oldies" can get hep to the modern thinking. ■

Source: *London Free Press* (2001, October 6). p. H2.

1. What is Ross Nightingale's thesis?
2. How does he support his point of view?
3. What further information would you require to determine whether Nightingale's thesis is accurate? How could you acquire that information?

The causes of homelessness fall into three broad categories (NCH, 1999). The first category for youth leaving home stems from disruptive family conditions that make living on the street seem like a better alternative. These may range from physical, psychological, or sexual abuse to neglect or abandonment. A 1992 study in Ottawa-Carleton found that 75 percent of street youth reported being victims of abuse (Casavant, 1999). Some youths leave home when neither parent wants custody of them after a marriage breakdown. Others leave to escape parental restrictions that they consider to be too harsh (Deziel, 1999). The second category for homelessness is residential instability. An American study estimates that 20 percent of homeless youth had been in foster care before they moved to the streets. Over 50 000 young Canadians run away from home each year. Police report that 90 percent of runaways return home within 60 days, but most of the remaining 10 percent become homeless. The third category of homeless youth are those who leave home to work and live independently but become homeless when they are unable to move back home after suffering a financial crisis. For most homeless youth, returning to their parents is not a realistic option.

Being homeless presents so many challenges for youth that they generally live day-to-day, unable to develop plans for forming a productive life structure. Although some homeless youth are employed, most depend on begging or illegal means, such as selling drugs or sex, to earn enough money to cover their basic needs. The health of homeless youth is compromised by their high-risk lifestyle. They are more likely to suffer from infections, malnutrition, and sexually transmitted diseases (Casavant, 1999). Since an estimated 40 percent are users of intravenous drugs, and many are working in the sex trade, the rate of HIV-related health problems is higher. The rates of psychological and psychiatric disorders are also very high. Doctors in Montréal report that street youth have a mortality rate 13 times higher than other youth, and that the high rate of drug use is a coping strategy for dealing with the pain in their lives (Ward, 1999).

web connection

www.mcgrawhill.ca/links/families12

To learn about the support available for homeless youth in Canada, go to the web site above for *Individuals and Families in a Diverse Society* to see where to go next.

"The mark of a great society is how well they care for their most disadvantaged."
— Samuel Johnson

Services such as food and emergency medical treatment are available to help individuals cope with the symptoms of homelessness, but long-term assistance is needed to resocialize them for a productive life.

The consequences of homelessness for those who should be making a transition to adulthood are extreme. Most homeless youth left a family life that was disrupted. Some of them were moved by child protection authorities to live in foster care, but most chose to leave abusive home environments themselves. Their education has been disrupted, and the prospects of returning to school while they live on the streets are negligible. About 45 percent are working, but at low-paying, transient jobs (Casavant, 1999). Most homeless youth have limited knowledge and skills and report low self-esteem. The lack of competence and control over their life circumstances probably results in role confusion because they have not formed an identity. Although many street youth describe lofty goals of getting good jobs and leading happy family lives rather than the hopelessness of their real lives, their dreams do not reflect their limited resources.

The problem of homelessness is as difficult to solve as it is to define. The long-term solution is more challenging because there is no consensus on the social conditions that allow homelessness to increase. Some people accuse the homeless of creating their own problems by abusing drugs or alcohol and consequently squandering their money so they cannot afford housing. Others assume that homeless youth have chosen street life because they are unable to conform to the rules of their families or other accommodations. These arguments reflect a functionalist perspective, because they suggest that homelessness is a failure of socialization.

Social activists use a conflict perspective to argue that a decline in stable employment opportunities for those with few skills has reduced the ability of many people to afford housing. They also suggest that the increasing cost of housing forces people down the housing chain into cheaper housing so that those with the lowest incomes are squeezed out onto the streets. They propose that homelessness is an indicator of the growing gap between rich and poor in Canada. Until programs that respond to any of these theories are established to prevent homelessness, many governmental and non-profit organizations are working to alleviate the immediate needs of the homeless, especially for youth, so that they can begin to become self-reliant.

Suicide

When individuals choose to end their lives, family and friends are left to grieve. Family and friends feel saddened by their loss, but also confused and angry as they seek reasons for the suicide. Many feel guilty about whether they could have prevented the death. However, the causes of suicide remain a mystery. Suicide occurs in all societies, but the rates differ significantly from country to country. Percentages for males are higher than those for females in all countries. Suicide raises both ethical and practical questions: Is suicide normal? Is suicide wrong? Can suicide be prevented?

Suicide is a relatively rare cause of death, but it has increased in Canada in the past few decades. Approximately 3500 Canadians die from suicide each year, accounting for 2 percent of all deaths (Ungar, 2001). The actual number of suicides and attempted suicides is difficult to determine because many suspicious accidents, such as vehicle collisions, drug overdoses, and falls are reported as accidents, not as suicides. However, it is estimated that there are 20 to 40 attempts for every successful suicide (Conway, 1997). Men are four times more likely to commit suicide, but the lower rate for women could reflect the fact that they choose less lethal methods, such as drugs and poisons, so there is a greater chance of being saved. According to the World Health Organization, Canada's suicide rate is in the lower third of those for 20 Western industrialized nations, but higher than that of the United States.

web connection

www.mcgrawhill.ca/links/families12

To learn about suicide prevention, go to the web site above for *Individuals and Families in a Diverse Society* to see where to go next.

Suicide Rates Per 100 000 in Canada and the United States in 1990								
	5–14	15–24	25–34	35–44	45–54	55–64	65–74	75+
Canada								
Men	1.2	24.6	29.6	26.7	23.4	22.6	20.7	32.4
Women	0.4	3.9	6.4	9.0	6.9	5.4	5.9	4.2
United States								
Men	1.1	22.0	24.8	23.9	23.2	25.7	32.2	57.9
Women	0.4	3.9	5.6	6.8	6.9	7.3	6.7	6.0

Source: Hollinger, Paul C. et al. (1994). *Suicide and Homicide Among Adolescents.* New York: The Guilford Press, pp. 88–89.

1. Compare the suicide rates for men and for women in Canada and the United States.
2. Suggest reasons for the differences in the suicide rates for women and for men.
3. What social conditions might account for the differences in the suicide rates of young men, aged 15 to 24, between Canada and the United States?

The grief that people feel over the loss of a friend or family member who has chosen suicide is complicated by feelings of guilt that the death might have been prevented, and anger toward the person for causing such hurt.

The reasons why individuals choose to end their lives by committing suicide remain unclear. Those who attempt suicide say that they suffer unbearable psychological pain and feel a sense of hopelessness. Factors that are associated with suicide include psychological problems, the suicide of a friend or family member, breaking up with a boyfriend or girlfriend, drug and alcohol abuse, separation from a parent because of death or divorce, and physical or sexual abuse (Conway, 1997). These are events that occur in the lives of many people, yet most can cope with them and do not take their own lives. The difference for people who commit suicide appears to be the hopelessness that arises from perceiving a lack of control (Sakinofsky, 1998).

Emile Durkheim, who is considered to be one of the fathers of sociology, published *Suicide: A Study in Sociology* in 1897, and sociologists still consider it to be the classic study of suicide. Durkheim explained that the fact that suicide rates vary from society to society and that the rates are higher for men than for women suggests that suicide has a social cause. His idea was that suicides increase when expectations, not needs, are not met. The factors that are associated with suicide are fairly common, yet it is not the people who suffer the worst hardships that choose to die. Therefore, Durkheim explained, those who expected more will experience a greater lack of control in a crisis (Durkheim, 1951). Since identity, as described by Erikson, includes the ability to realistically assess one's place in society and to feel a sense of control, suicide results, perhaps, from a failure to form an identity. Durkheim (1951) explained the lower suicide rate for women with the reason that women have had lower expectations for their roles in society, so they are less likely to feel that these have not been met. Since women form their identity through relationships with others, they are more likely to seek support from others, so the suicide rate for women will be lower (Conway, 1997). Durkheim (1951) wrote that social causes, such as economic loss, depend on the extent to which the society encourages individuals to have realistic expectations and provides opportunities for them to have control over whether their expectations are met.

Because suicide results from a decision, there have been various civil and religious attempts to prevent individuals from making that decision. Some societies, such as those based on traditional Roman Catholic beliefs, treat suicide as a sin in a religious context. Others treat suicide as a criminal act. Until

Section 213 was removed from the Criminal Code of Canada in 1972, attempted suicide was punishable by imprisonment for six months or by a fine (Leenars et al., 1998). Another reason for suicide is a mental illness that prevents an individual from making a rational decision. These explanations reflect a functionalist perspective, because they all describe suicide as abnormal behaviour that destabilizes the society.

point of view | Aboriginal Groups Warn of Suicide Crisis

by Louise Elliott
Canadian Press

A youth suicide epidemic in Ontario's North has spread to reserves formerly unaffected by the crisis, as this year's toll threatens to become the worst on record. With 16 suicides on 49 northern reserves as of July 30, 2001, this year's toll could end above the record 26 suicides across Northern Ontario last year, leaders and experts warned yesterday.

"It's been the worst year to date in a six-month period," said Arnold Devlin, mental health supervisor at Dilico, an Aboriginal peoples mental health agency in Thunder Bay. "It speaks to the need for a region-wide suicide protocol." Such a protocol, which would include programs for crisis response, counselling, media strategies, and prevention, is even more critical after suicides this year in areas previously untouched by the crisis, Devlin said. "People weren't prepared for it," he said of a suicide in Pelican Falls High School in Sioux Lookout, which is attended by Aboriginal children from across the North. "That spurned a whole series of resignations."

Media attention has focused recently on Pikangikum First Nation, where seven young people have died since January. There were eight suicides in total at Pikangikum last year, mainly by young girls. But the problem is region-wide, and it's also worse than statistics suggest, said Stan Beardy, grand chief of

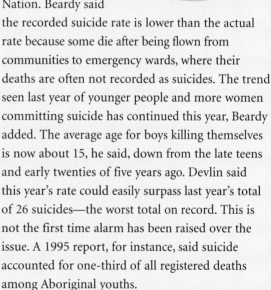

A suicide epidemic in Ontario's North highlighted the need for suicide prevention and education strategies.

the Nishnawbe-Aski Nation. Beardy said the recorded suicide rate is lower than the actual rate because some die after being flown from communities to emergency wards, where their deaths are often not recorded as suicides. The trend seen last year of younger people and more women committing suicide has continued this year, Beardy added. The average age for boys killing themselves is now about 15, he said, down from the late teens and early twenties of five years ago. Devlin said this year's rate could easily surpass last year's total of 26 suicides—the worst total on record. This is not the first time alarm has been raised over the issue. A 1995 report, for instance, said suicide accounted for one-third of all registered deaths among Aboriginal youths.

Beardy accused Indian Affairs Minister Robert Nault of contributing little assistance while fanning the flames of the crisis with talk about opening up the Indian Act whether Aboriginal peoples want to or not. "Nault is going around the country telling people how much money is being wasted on Native people" while there were 28 suicides in Nault's riding last year, he said. Nault recently handed Pikangikum's finances over to a third-party manager, even though the community has never run a deficit. Nault has said one reason for handing over the reserve's finances is concern about the high suicide rate. Pikangikum's leaders accused Nault last week of pressuring them to drop their constitutional challenge against his department, to stop talking to the media, and to hire only Indian Affairs workers. Renewed talks with the federal and provincial governments about resource development in the North offer the only long-term hope for battling the suicide epidemic, Beardy said, because jobs and a land base will give young people a sense of purpose now lacking in a region with 80 percent unemployment. "That's one of the problems with Nault's plan (to open up the Indian Act): There is no mention regarding financing our own activities," he said.

Suicide prevention and education strategies are also essential, he added. "It would provide more awareness to help people deal with their everyday frustrations."

But an intergovernmental committee on youth suicide is now making progress toward better management of the crisis, committee members say. Federal, provincial, and Aboriginal government ministries are now trying to improve interdepartmental communication and service co-ordination, said Carol Rowlands, a spokesperson for Nishnawbe-Aski Nation. But Beardy said adequate funding is still required. A mental health policy was submitted to Health Canada about a year ago, but has received no official ratification, he said. ■

Source: *Toronto Star*. (2001, July 31).

---

1. What factors in Ontario's northern communities might act as social causes for suicide?
2. How might a symbolic interactionist explain the high suicide rate on northern reserves?
3. In addition to suicide prevention and education strategies, what actions would you recommend?
4. What might account for the higher suicide rate among girls in this community, a trend that is different from the national statistics?

web connection

www.mcgrawhill.ca/links/families12

To learn about services and resources for suicide prevention, go to the web site above for *Individuals and Families in a Diverse Society* to see where to go next.

Symbolic interactionists would describe suicide as resulting from individuals' perceptions of their situation and their ability to control their lives. This perspective would help to explain why some individuals choose suicide when most individuals in the same situation do not. A century after Durkheim completed his extensive sociological study, the causes of suicide are no clearer. Menno Boldt, a Canadian psychologist who worked in suicide prevention in Alberta, reached this conclusion (1998, p. 17):

> People kill themselves because they find their life intolerable, and because they believe their future holds no hope for improvement. If we want to be effective in suicide-prevention, we must do more than merely prevent people from killing themselves. We must act to make every life tolerable. We must act to change the coercive circumstances in the lives of individuals that impel them to seek an escape from life. In short, we must treat suicide prevention as a cause— the cause of enhancing human lives. This implies a need for a deep personal commitment to the promotion of the values of humanity and human dignity in our society.

developing your research skills | Writing a Research Essay

A research essay is a paper that presents an argument based on research in the social sciences. You will read them frequently in the media and as part of your studies, and you will write them after conducting your own investigations. In a research essay, the results of an investigation are presented in a thesis that proposes the key understanding of the topic from a theoretical perspective. The thesis would then be supported with selected arguments that relate the evidence to the thesis.

Title

In the title, identify the main idea of your paper and suggest your theoretical perspective.

Introduction

In the introduction, state your thesis, define your terms and your theoretical perspective, and introduce your supporting arguments.

Discussion

In the discussion, present the arguments derived from analyzing the results of your research from your theoretical perspective, and outline the implications of the results.

Conclusion

In the conclusion, briefly restate your thesis and your strongest arguments.

References

In a research essay, include citations to inform the reader where you found the information. In a formal essay, use in-text citations, like those used in this text, to refer the reader to the references at the end of the paper, which acknowledge all the sources. Use the American Psychological Association (APA) style in the social sciences. However, when writing a personal research essay—for example, for publication in magazines or newspapers—omit formal citations and consider using quotations instead. ■

1. Identify the arguments that have been used to explain why women earn less than men, and suggest what evidence exists to support each argument.

2. Distinguish between individualism and a duty-based moral code. Explain which philosophy most resembles the expectations of your parents.

3. According to the research, how do Canadian parents expect the costs of post-secondary education to be paid? Compare the results with the expectations of your family.

4. List the major causes of homelessness and suggest how each would affect the formation of an identity for a young person.

5. What social conditions might be a factor in suicide? Why do they only affect some people?

6. Select one of the essays from this chapter and write a personal essay in which you respond to the author using the same theoretical perspective that he or she did. Identify the perspective, state your response as a thesis, and include additional information from the text to support your arguments.

7. Select an essay from this chapter and write a response in the form of a letter to the editor, using a different theoretical perspective than in the essay. Identify the essayist's and your theoretical perspective.

8. Select an issue examined in this chapter and develop a hypothesis concerning a possible action for Canadian society to take. Use the Web Connections to conduct research about the current situation, and form an opinion about what steps should be taken. Present and support your opinion orally as part of a town hall debate about the role of your community.

9. For one of the issues examined in this chapter, develop a hypothesis explaining the impact of it on one aspect of the transition to adulthood. Conduct an investigation using the Web Connections and other secondary sources. Present the results of your investigation as a formal research essay.

10. Identify another issue that is currently affecting the transition to adulthood. Conduct an information search to find a variety of viewpoints on the impact of the issue.

unit 3　Couples

UNIT EXPECTATIONS

While reading this unit, you will:

- analyze changes that have occurred in family structure and function throughout the history of the family

- analyze theories and research on the subject of the development of, and the psychological tasks connected with, intimate relationships, and summarize your findings

- analyze current issues and trends affecting the dynamics of intimate relationships, and speculate on future directions for individuals and families

- use appropriate social science research methods in the investigation of issues affecting individuals and families in a diverse society

- access, analyze, and evaluate information, including opinions, research evidence, and theories, related to individuals and families in a diverse society

- analyze issues and data from the perspectives associated with key theories in the disciplines of anthropology, psychology, and sociology

- communicate the results of your inquiries

In this unit, the conjugal relationships of Canadians, including marriage and alternative intimate relationships, will be examined. To determine the role that intimate relationships and marriage play in Canadian society, the diversity of conjugal relationships will be reviewed first. Then the history of marriage and intimate relationships will be traced. Next, the psychology of attraction, courtship, mate selection, and the factors that contribute to satisfying relationships for men and women will be examined. Finally, the specific issues and trends that are influencing the formation and development of marriage and other intimate relationships today will be explored.

People form intimate relationships for biological, social, and psychological reasons.

Marriage, Intimate Relationships, and Society

CHAPTER EXPECTATIONS

While reading this chapter, you will:

- explain changing marital forms in various societies throughout history, and describe contemporary marital forms
- analyze factors influencing the transition of the family from an economic unit to a psychological unit
- analyze the historical and ethnocultural factors affecting variations in mate selection, marriage customs, and marital roles
- demonstrate an understanding of the role of intimate relationships in the lives of individuals and families, considering the similarities and differences for males and females, and traditional and non-traditional relationships
- describe current perceptions, opinions, and demographic trends relating to intimate relationships, and speculate on the significance of these trends for individual and family development
- select and access secondary sources reflecting a variety of viewpoints
- identify and respond to the theoretical viewpoints, the thesis, and the supporting arguments of materials found in a variety of secondary sources
- distinguish among, and produce examples of, the following: an essay arguing and defending personal opinion; a reaction paper responding to another person's argument; a research paper reporting on an original investigation

- accessing information from academic journals
- identifying theoretical perspective, thesis, and supporting arguments
- writing an argument using a specific theoretical perspective

Although fewer Canadians are getting married, couples continue to be the basic human bond and the focus of our social organization.

CHAPTER INTRODUCTION

In this chapter, intimate relationships and marriage will be studied from a sociological perspective. Marriage will be defined and its history will be examined to understand its cultural diversity and that of other intimate relationships. Marital norms will be determined, and the role of marriage for men and women in Canada in a post-industrial society will be discussed. The controversies surrounding marriage and cohabitation in a changing society will be explored so that you will be better prepared for the decisions you will soon face concerning the intimate relationships in your life.

The Purpose of Marriage

Marriage can be defined broadly as "a socially legitimate sexual union, begun with a public announcement and with some idea of permanence, and assumed with a more or less explicit contract" (Schlesinger, 1984, p. 78). In Canada, most individuals today form their first sexual union, or **conjugal relationship**, by cohabiting, not marrying. Some have a relationship with someone of the same sex. Since the practice of marriage varies widely, it is necessary to examine its diversity to fully understand how Canadians form couples. Despite the predictions of cynics for hundreds of years, marriage in all its forms has survived as the primary relationship and the rite of passage that signifies transition into adulthood, in almost all societies.

Helen Fisher, an American anthropologist, suggests that the durability of the **pair-bond** is essential to the survival of humans. She explains that the only way people can ensure their continued existence is by reproducing and then protecting their children. She also proposes that both men and women have a biological urge to produce children. Fisher concludes that the desire to form an enduring pair-bond between a man and a woman is a basic biological drive (Fisher, 1992, p. 72):

> Human beings almost never have to be cajoled into pairing. Instead, we do this naturally. We flirt. We feel infatuation. We fall in love. We marry. And the vast majority of us marry only one person at a time.
>
> Pair-bonding is the trademark of the human animal.

Marriage is the primary social group and the foundation of the family. However, people who are in love marry for personal reasons, not to fulfill a role in society.

The pairing of men and women may be the result of a natural biological desire, but marriage is a social invention. Functionalists describe marriage as a social institution that developed as an important part of the organization of society to meet humans' basic needs. The diversity of marriage reflects the various ways that societies organize to meet the functional requisites of sexual reproduction, socialization of children, and division of labour. Individuals are socialized into the appropriate roles for men and women in their societies and are expected to marry into complementary roles. Moreover, because men and women serve useful purposes for society when they are married, functionalists argue that people are happiest if they marry. Therefore, sociologists are interested in the norms that regulate the institution of marriage and the stability of the social group formed by marriage (Whyte, 2001).

Most people, however, choose to marry for more personal reasons. Many individuals feel that getting married confers upon them adult status within their society and, more importantly, within their families. Until recently, marriage provided and limited access to sexual partners and ensured the bearing and raising of children. Today, people might have sex before marriage, but they might marry because they want to have children. On a more practical level, marriage allows individuals to share resources to improve their standard of living. Marriage may also help form an individual's identity by providing a sense of purpose. For most Canadians, marrying is a cultural expectation that they will fulfill at least once in their lives simply because it allows them to commit their unfailing love and support to the person they love (Ward, 1994).

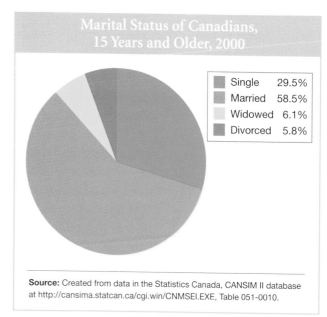

Marital Status of Canadians, 15 Years and Older, 2000

Single	29.5%
Married	58.5%
Widowed	6.1%
Divorced	5.8%

Source: Created from data in the Statistics Canada, CANSIM II database at http://cansima.statcan.ca/cgi.win/CNMSEI.EXE, Table 051-0010.

People marry for both social and psychological reasons. Contemporary social life is based on couples, so marriage continues to be a convenient primary relationship, offering friendship and companionship for men and women. The ideal of marriage conveyed in many cultures and contemporary media suggests that it is a happy state in which one can love and be loved, even for those individuals in arranged marriages. From the perspective of the social exchange theory, the desire to marry reflects a belief that being married will be better than being single. Monica McGoldrick suggested that men and women marry because it is just the natural thing to do (McGoldrick, 1989, p. 210):

> In most societies to talk of the choice to marry or not would be almost as relevant as to talk of the choice to grow old or not: it has been considered the only route to full adult status. To marry has simply been part of the "natural" progression through life, part of the inevitable, unless catastrophe intervened.

At the beginning of the twenty-first century, it is evident that many people are not marrying. The marriage rate has declined, yet men and women continue to form conjugal relationships. Consequently, it is necessary to expand the study of marriage to include other intimate relationships, such as **common-law** marriages or **cohabitation**, in which a male and female live together as husband and wife without legally marrying, and to consider the choice of being sexually active singles.

The History of Marriage

Marriage as a binding relationship between a man and a woman was probably one of the earliest developments when human societies began to organize themselves. It regulates sexual activity so that the biological father can identify his offspring. Consequently, adults become mutually responsible for nurturing and socializing their children. Since marriage unites men, women, and children into a family unit that can share resources and own property, it has been viewed primarily as an economic unit. In fact, for most of history, love was seldom a consideration in the decision to marry, and most women had little to say in their choice of partner (Yalom, 2001). **Polygyny**, the practice of a man having more than one wife, appears to have been the preferred form of marriage in most societies historically, since 84 percent of recorded cultures have allowed it (Kelman, 1998). However, monogamy has been and continues to be the most common custom. Some anthropologists suggest that in the societies that permit polygyny, monogamy occurs only when it is not feasible for men to support more than one wife. **Polyandry** occurs, on the other hand, when a culture, such as rural Nepal, is so poor that several men are required to support a wife and children (Kelman, 1999).

The historical roots of marriage traditions and legal practices in Canada can be traced back to the Ancient Romans, Greeks, and Hebrews. To understand the diversity of intimate relationships in Canada, the historical roots of Canadian Aboriginal Peoples and immigrants from non-European cultures also need to be considered. The study of history allows people to determine marriage expectations as described in recorded rules, but it does not always provide insight into married couples' personal relationships. For better or for worse, there is no way to legislate the feelings of individuals (Yalom, 2001). There is usually a gap between the ideals of those in power and the common practice of various social classes within any society (Kelman, 1999).

An analysis of marriage in history or in contemporary Canada focuses on several questions:

- How are marriages formed?
- What are the obligations of spouses?
- What are the expectations of the marriage relationship?
- How can an unsatisfactory marriage be ended?

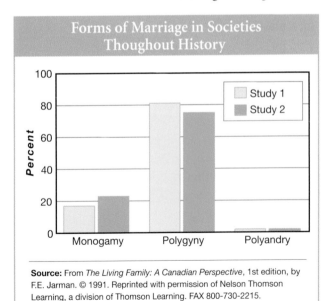

Forms of Marriage in Societies Thoughout History

Source: From *The Living Family: A Canadian Perspective*, 1st edition, by F.E. Jarman. © 1991. Reprinted with permission of Nelson Thomson Learning, a division of Thomson Learning. FAX 800-730-2215.

Marriage in Ancient Times

The marriages of the ancient Hebrew people over 4000 years ago were usually arranged between patriarchal extended families for the purpose of producing sons. A **betrothal**, or promise to marry, might have been agreed upon when a boy and a girl were quite young, but the marriage might not occur until many years later. Although marriages were arranged, the views of the young man and woman were probably considered. The bride's value as a potential mother was symbolized by the payment of a **bride price** by the groom's family to the bride's family. The bride's family gave her a **dowry** in the form of money, household items, or land, so that she was able to establish a home for her new family. She also gained **dower rights** to property from her husband for her support. The mutual obligations of husband and wife were recorded in a **marriage contract**. A wife was expected to obey her husband, and she could be divorced if she could not bear sons (Yalom, 2001). The Old Testament marriage records suggest that the relationships between partners were usually very affectionate, although love was seldom a consideration during the initial betrothal.

Roman marriages were monogamous and equal partnerships for the wealthy, as shown in this painting "Roman Wedding" by J. Saint Saveur.

Marriages in Ancient Rome during the Early Roman period resembled Hebrew marriages in that they were the basis for a household or kinship group that was patrilineal, patriarchal, and **patrilocal**, or located near the husband's family. One major difference, however, was that Roman society was strictly monogamous (Queen & Habenstein, 1974). Later, as Rome became larger and the Roman Empire expanded and became wealthier, the Roman family system changed. Men were away for long periods of time, leaving women to run the households. This resulted in a less patriarchal and more equal society. As patrician, or prominent, families acquired wealth, marriage was seen less as an enduring union and more as an opportunity to attain riches and political advantage. Divorce, initiated by men and women, became widespread, which led to an increase in family disorganization and instability. It was common for a member of the patrician class to marry several times over a lifetime. The historic figures Cleopatra and Anthony were married four times each (Queen, Quadagno, & Habenstein, 1974). This family and marriage system was the norm in Rome at the time of the early Christian apostles, who regarded it as degenerate and destabilizing. The early Christian movement, upon which the Western family value system is primarily based, looked to the early Roman and the ancient Hebrew patriarchal system as the standard for the Christian system of marriage.

The marriage system of the early Middle Ages was informal, loosely organized, and casually enforced. Common-law marriages were widespread and were as legal as church marriages. The Catholic Church did not attempt to regulate marriage until the twelfth century. By then the feudal system, its economic and social influence on the organization of medieval society, and the importance that it placed on inheritance laws, necessitated the regulation of marriage for social stability. It was during this period that marriage became a witnessed public event and a sacrament in the Catholic Church. The reading of marriage **banns**, a public announcement three weeks prior to the marriage ceremony that a couple are to be married, and the priest's question as to whether anyone has good reason to object to the marriage, were also initiated (Carroll-Clark, 1994). This was done to ensure that both the man and the woman were entering the contract willingly and that there were no reasons to invalidate the marriage, such as consanguinity or other existing betrothals, both of which created problems for inheritance and disposal of property.

Marriage in Canada

When Europeans began to colonize Canada in the sixteenth and seventeenth centuries, they encountered Aboriginal Peoples who were still primarily living a hunter-gatherer existence. Since the men were away from home for long periods of time and the women remained in their temporary settlements looking after the children, most Aboriginal tribes were matrilineal and **matrilocal**. Families lived at or near the home of the woman's family because it was the women who provided stability to the social organization of the society. In traditional Huron society, marriages occurred only when a couple had a child. In both Ojibwa and Iroquois social organization, marriages were usually arranged and were expected to be enduring. Men and women in these hunter-gatherer societies had a clear division of labour, with complementary roles that were both highly valued. The matrilineal organization of their societies was changed to a patrilineal one long after the nineteenth century conquest, when husbands and fathers were given legal authority over their wives and children (Baker, 1993).

The marriage system brought to Canada by both French and British colonists was the patriarchal, patrilineal system of the Christian church. The first colonizers were mostly men from France and England who came to make their fortunes as fur traders for the Hudson Bay Company or as soldiers, and whose stay was temporary. Since European women were in short supply, they turned to Aboriginal women for what became known as *marriage á la façon du pays*, a temporary marriage arrangement. By 1821, the Hudson Bay Company introduced marriage contracts between their employees and Aboriginal women that declared the husband had a binding responsibility to support his wife and children, even if he returned to Europe. This marriage practice declined with the arrival and influence of the Jesuits and the increase in eligible European women in Canada, so that Aboriginal women who formed relationships with European men were regarded more as prostitutes or, at best, mistresses, not wives (Eichler, 1997).

Most Aboriginal families were matrilineal and matrilocal to maintain stability while the men were away hunting.

During the history of Canada since the European conquest, men have often outnumbered women during times of high immigration as well as in frontier communities. Records from New France indicate that prior to 1700, male colonists outnumbered females by two to one. The average age of a first marriage for women was 20 and for men, 28 (Kelman, 1998). By the nineteenth century, most immigrants were from northern and western Europe. One of their traditions was that children who were not heirs to the family estate would leave the family homes. Consequently, these immigrants brought with them the custom of living in primarily nuclear households. Since these families were the primary unit of economic production in the nineteenth century, a large financial investment was needed to establish an independent home. To

A shortage of marriageable women in early Canada resulted in women marrying young and men marrying later, when they could afford to set up a home.

afford marriage, young people often had to save for several years. As a result, most people were older when they first got married or, in some cases, they remained single. Although many nineteenth-century marriages were arranged, most were free-choice marriages. Couples who were exploring the possibility of

www.mcgrawhill.ca/links/families12

To learn about marriage in Canada, go to the web site above for *Individuals and Families in a Diverse Society* to see where to go next.

marriage tended to socialize in their family homes under the supervision of the parents. This gave parents some control over the marriage choices of their offspring. A young woman's selection of a **spouse**, or marriage partner, was especially subject to the approval of her parents, since marrying against their will risked estrangement from the family (Ward, 1990). After the emancipation movement of the 1880s and 1890s, women began to enjoy the same relative freedom as men over their choice of marriage partner.

The timing for marriage ceremonies tended to correspond to the agricultural cycle. June was a popular month because it was after spring planting; another popular time was after the fall harvest. Census records reveal that among those born in colonial Canada between 1821 and 1830, the average age for a first marriage was 26 for men and 23 for women. Forty years later, the average age for a first marriage had risen to 29 for men and 26 for women. By the second half of the nineteenth century, the percentage of unmarried men in Canada fluctuated between 13 and 15 percent, while that for unmarried women was about 11 or 12 percent (Kelman, 1998). By the middle of the twentieth century, this percentage dropped to 10 percent for both men and women.

Generally, divorce was rare in nineteenth-century Canada. Marriage was seen as a sacrament by Catholics and as a sacred institution by Protestants. In Québec, divorce was illegal, since the province maintained a different civil code from the English civil law of the rest of the country. Even after the British North America Act was passed in 1867, in which the issuing of a divorce became a provincial jurisdiction, divorce was illegal in Ontario until 1930 and in Québec until 1968 (Kelman, 1998). In fact, historically, Canada has had one of the lowest divorce rates in the Western world. Access to divorce was extremely limited in Canada until the change in divorce laws enacted by the federal government in 1968 (Ward, 1994). Prior to 1968, divorce was granted for few reasons, with proof of adultery being the most usual.

Prior to the Divorce Act of 1968, which allowed divorce for irreconcilable differences after a three-year separation, Canada had one of the lowest divorce rates in the world.

Canadians who were born in the early twentieth century tended to marry at a later age, like their nineteenth-century counterparts. During the economic hardship of the Depression in the 1930s, most young Canadians postponed marriage. According to census data, among those born between 1906 and 1914, the average age of a first marriage was 28 for men and 25 for women. World War II changed this. The generation of Canadians who married from the mid-1940s until the 1960s were younger at their first marriage than previous generations were, as young as 25 for men and 22 for women. Less than 5 percent

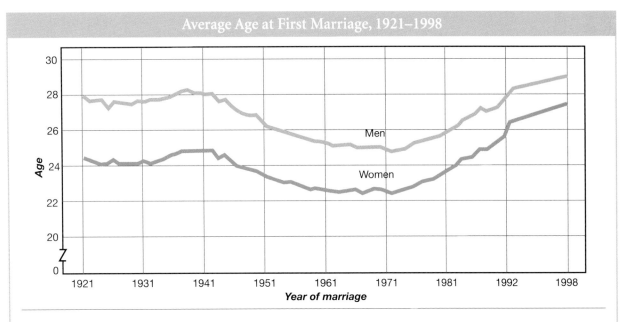

Average Age at First Marriage, 1921–1998

Age (y-axis): 0, 20, 22, 24, 26, 28, 30

Men

Women

Year of marriage (x-axis): 1921, 1931, 1941, 1951, 1961, 1971, 1981, 1992, 1998

Source: Created from data published in the Statistics Canada publications *Marriage and Conjugal Life in Canada*, Catalogue 91-534, April 1992 and *Canadian Social Trends*, Catalogue 11-008, Spring 2000.

of Canadians born in the 1930s and the 1940s had not been married by the time they had reached the age of 50 (Kelman, 1998). These Canadians reached marriageable age during a time of economic prosperity, when they felt very optimistic about their financial future.

Contemporary Marriage and Intimate Relationships

Almost all Canadians form marriage or other conjugal relationships at some point in their lives. A study by Statistics Canada using the 1995 General Social Survey found that 94 percent of women aged 30 to 69 had formed at least one union. The proportion of women who had married was highest for those aged 40 to 69. The proportion of women aged 20 to 29 who had married was lower, but it is assumed that some would still marry. Few women reported no conjugal unions at all, but an increasing number had formed a second union after a separation or a divorce, if they had been married. Although this study focused on the behaviour of women, men and women, by definition, marry at almost the same rate (Le Bourdais, Neill, & Turcotte, 2000). Since

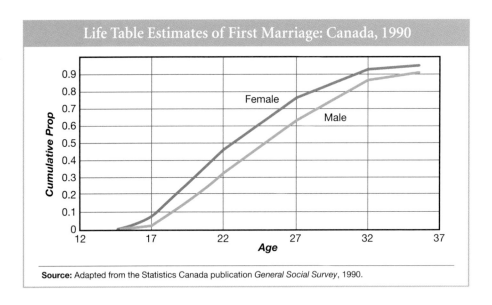

Life Table Estimates of First Marriage: Canada, 1990

Source: Adapted from the Statistics Canada publication *General Social Survey*, 1990.

FYI

Statscan Would Sooner Count Marriages Than Complaints

by Michael Jenkinson

Faced with mounting public opposition, Statistics Canada decided the agency would continue to compile annual statistics on marriage and divorce. The agency announced early in 1996 it would drop the tally to save $150 000 annually; it argued these statistics were no longer useful given the number of common-law unions. Critics maintained Statscan was trying to undermine the importance of marriage. Statscan was inundated by so many complaints it had to hire a part-time secretary to keep up with the mail volume. "It was one of those things that seemed like a good idea at the time," said Janet Hagey, director of the agency's health statistics division.

Source: *Alberta Report/Western Report*. (1996, December 2). (23), 43.

Bibby (2001) found that 88 percent of adolescents aged 15 to 19 expect to marry and stay with the same partner for life, either the number of young women that marry will increase, or some young men and women will change their minds about whether to marry. There are several research questions that arise concerning marriage and intimate relationships in Canada:

- At what age and rate do Canadians marry or form other intimate relationships?

- What is the purpose of marriage?

- How has the changing role of women affected marriage?

- What role does cohabitation have in Canadian society?

Despite the popularity of marriage, Canada's marriage rate was at an all-time low of 5.1 per 1000 population in 1998. This rate is similar to the marriage rates of Germany and the United Kingdom; higher than that of France, Italy, and Sweden; and substantially lower than the U.S. rate. Both men and women seem to be rejecting marriage, but it is difficult to gather data about choices that do not have to be registered, such as remaining single or living together. Some sociologists argue that people want to marry but they are unable to; others suggest that people are less willing to marry (Goldscheider & Waite, 1991). For example, an increasing divorce rate is often cited as a deterrent to marriage. The lifetime risk of divorce for

Canadians is about 31 percent, compared to the rate of 44 percent in the United States (Ambert, 1998). However, the divorce rate has declined at the same pace as the marriage rate in Canada during the 1990s.

In the past, almost all men and women married; now, many are choosing to live in common-law relationships. Fewer women aged 20 to 29 are married, but the decline is almost offset by the greater number of younger women who reported at least one common-law union. The proportion of women who had married was highest for those aged 40 to 69, but more than 1 in 4 women in this age group had cohabited at least once. Common-law relationships have become so widespread that they were the first conjugal relationship for 52 percent of women under 30. Although cohabitation begins less formally than marriage, the spouses are still subject to some legal obligations, as the term "common law" implies, and they are more likely to separate than if they were married (Le Bourdais, Neill, & Turcotte, 2000).

The Conjugal Relationships of Canadian Women					
Age in 1995	60–69	50–59	40–49	30–39	20–29
Proportion of all women experiencing	Born in				
	1926–1935	1936–1945	1946–1955	1956–1965	1966–1975
At least one union	96	97	96	94	87
At least one marriage	96	95	92	84	66
First union starts with marriage	95	91	78	56	35
At least one common-law union	8	22	35	49	59
First union starts with common-law union	1	6	18	38	52
At least one separation	25	32	40	43	—*
At least two unions	14	27	34	39	—
At least two separations	8	13	16	—	—

* — Sample too small to produce reliable estimate.

Source: Adapted from the Statistics Canada publication *Canadian Social Survey*, Catalogue 11-008, Spring 2000.

The Time for Marrying

The timing of significant developments in life is determined by a culture's social clock and by an individual's readiness to make the change. When asked for their opinions about the appropriate time for starting a family, Canadians believe the best age to marry is 24 and the best age to have the first child is 25

(Gee, 1995). However, according to Statistics Canada, Canadians are now waiting until their late twenties to get married. The average age of first-time brides in 1998 was 27.6 years; the average age for grooms was 29.6 years. Three-quarters of all marriages in 1998 were first marriages for both bride and groom (Statistics Canada's *The Daily*, 2001, November 15). Young adults are delaying marriage, but they are not postponing sexual activity. Most cohabit before they marry, but it is not clear whether cohabitation is a cause or an effect of delayed marriage (Gee, 1995).

Marriage is no longer the significant rite of passage into adulthood that it once was. Several adjustments in the social clock accommodate these changes. Marriage has been delayed to allow for post-secondary education for men and women, and to give young people time to find jobs in their chosen careers. Marriage might also be delayed until the man's employment is secure and he feels that he can afford to marry, which might take several years after the completion of post-secondary education (Goldscheider & Waite, 1991). Those who do not have a stable job or who do not think they can afford to marry are likely to cohabit instead (Clarkberg, 1999). Since many young couples are living together before marriage, they might delay marriage until they are ready to have a child. Women today expect to establish a career for themselves before taking time out from the labour force to have a baby (White, 1992). Currently in Canada, most young people plan to complete their education and become financially independent before they marry and have children.

Why People Marry

In Canada, the romantic dream is that individuals will fall in love and marry some day. Even many people whose marriages are arranged believe they will fall in love after the ceremony. Spouses are expected to be close friends and companions and to love and support each other (Broderick, 2002). In the National Fertility Study of Canadian women conducted in 1984, 75 percent of women considered "love strongly" as absolutely necessary for marriage, and 55 percent believed that love should become at least "deep affection" for the marriage to last. The women were almost unanimous in feeling that "having a lasting relationship as a couple" was necessary for happiness (Balakrishnan, Lapierre-Adamczyk, & Krotki, 1993). In Russell Wild's 1998 survey in which "150 Guys Reveal What Prompted Them to Pop the Question," two-thirds of the men married for love and companionship. Generally, marriage in Canada is assumed to be a relationship based on an enduring romantic attraction.

Why Men Marry			
Friendship/companionship	66%	Escape loneliness	12%
Children	32%	Sex and romance	12%
It was just the thing to do	16%	Cooking/housekeeping	8%
To avoid dating	16%	She gave me an ultimatum	8%
Gain respectability/ social acceptability	15%	Fear of growing old/ dying alone	6%
Personal growth	14%		

Husbands and wives are expected to express their love for each other in an exclusive sexual relationship. That a marriage must be consummated by sexual intercourse to be valid emphasizes the role that sexual activity should play in a marriage, and husbands and wives assume they will enjoy an active sex life (Ward, 1994). In the National Fertility Study, 40 percent of women stated that sexual attraction was absolutely necessary for marriage, but 75 percent said that sexual fidelity was necessary for a marriage to last (Balakrishnan et al., 1993). Since extramarital sex is widespread, a double standard exists in many cultures: because children are clearly linked to their mother, a woman should be a virgin at marriage and faithful once married, but these restrictions are not placed on a man. An exclusive sexual relationship is central to the purpose of marriage; therefore, refusing to have sex with a spouse was grounds for divorce, as was **adultery**, or sex with a partner other than a spouse, until no-fault divorce was instituted in Canada in 1968. Marriage continues to define the legitimate sexual partners of individuals.

For Better or For Worse   by Lynn Johnston

© Lynn Johnston Productions, Inc./Distributed by United Feature Syndicate, Inc.

abstract | The Significance of Romantic Love for Marriage

by Jürg Willi, M.D., University Hospital, Zurich

In this study, 605 subjects were asked about romantic love and marriage. Married people differentiated themselves from single people with stable partners and divorced people with new partners by more frequently living together with their great love, more reciprocity in that love, and fewer disappointments in love relationships prior to the current relationship; but they also described themselves as less happy and satisfied than the single and divorced respondents, particularly with regard to tenderness, sex, and conversation with their partners. Independent of marital status, those who were greatly in love with their partners describe themselves as happier. Love at first sight, relative to a gradually developing love, nevertheless, did not have a worse prognosis for happiness in marriage. Being in love seems to be of greater importance for the prognosis of the marriage than marital happiness and satisfaction. ■

Source: *Family Process.* (1997). (36), 171–182. © 1997 by Family Process Inc. Reproduced with permission of Family Process Inc. via Copyright Clearance Center.

Couples who choose to get married are announcing their commitment to their family, friends, and community.

Identity

When individuals marry they acquire the status of husband or wife. Marriage changes how other people see them, but it also changes how individuals see themselves. Symbolic interactionism explains that by interacting with others who see them as a husband or a wife, individuals take on the appropriate marital role (Mackie, 1995). From a developmental perspective, the choice to marry requires that individuals adjust their identity so that they can share themselves with others in intimate relationships (Erikson, 1968). Although men no longer receive a wage bonus upon marriage as they did in early twentieth-century Canada, the assumption that they will be more reliable, stable, and productive encourages them to marry before they become middle-aged (Wild, 1999). This desire suggests that men have formed a Dream that includes marriage as an essential part of their life structure (Levinson, 1978). Being married continues to be the default setting in identity for adults.

People seem to desire commitment, despite the acceptance of cohabitation and the availability of sex before marriage (White, 1992). In the National Fertility Study, an overwhelming 93 percent of married women aged 18 to 49 said that "Marriage adds something positive to a relationship" (Balakrishnan et al., 1993). Men and women are socialized to have children; however, smaller families require less emphasis on parenting and a greater emphasis on marriage as a rewarding relationship for husband and wife (Broderick, 2002; Ward, 1994; White, 1992). The **companionate marriage** is based on shared lifestyle. Rather than marrying to acquire status, as was the case in the past, individuals who want to achieve a higher status are likely to choose a partner who has similar goals and the financial means to afford a shared status (Balakrishnan, 1993; Ward, 1994).

Some people are more willing than others to make the commitment to marriage. Individuals often make the decision following a family or societal crisis, such as the death of a parent, or a war, that emphasizes the importance of family ties (McGoldrick, 1989). On the other hand, people who have experienced their parents' divorce are less likely to marry (Goldscheider & Waite, 1991). Canadians whose parents divorced also appear to be delaying marriage: 40 percent of men and 54 percent of women married by their late twenties and early thirties compared to 50 percent of men and over 60 percent of women whose parents were not divorced (Statistics Canada, 2000, March 16). Finally, women who are cohabiting are more likely to separate than to marry their partners (Le Bourdais et al., 2000). Family background affects whether individuals perceive marriage as a desirable step, and if and when they are willing to take the chance.

The Economics of Marriage

Marriage provides physical and economic survival benefits for a couple (Ward, 1994). From the functionalist perspective, the division of labour provides for the well-being of spouses and children and benefits the society in which they live. Talcott Parsons, an American sociologist who used the functionalist perspective, described clearly differentiated roles for men and women. Men had a goal-oriented **instrumental role** of providing for the family by working and earning an income. Women had an emotional **expressive role** of providing a supportive home for their husbands and their children (Jarman, 1992). Parsons was describing the distinct roles of middle-class American families in the 1950s and 1960s. Although his ideal became the model for young couples for several decades, such a distinct division of roles has never been an achievable norm for most couples.

Many men and women associate marriage with negative gender roles. Men with traditional views still feel pressured to accept full financial responsibility for supporting a wife and children. On the other hand, many women feel that they are expected to accept responsibility for housework and child care and to maintain a career, too (Goldscheider & Waite, 1991). Traditionally, when women married men who were older, they lost power because they were female and younger, and lost potential income because they stopped work before they could achieve the increased income gained by experience

"Here I am, here you are, and here we are. Marriage is the commitment to that which we are."

— Joseph Campbell

(Gee, 1995). In two-thirds of the marriages in Canada in 1998, the groom was older than the bride, but one-quarter of brides were older by an average of 3.7 years (Statistics Canada, 2001, November 15). This could indicate a willingness to break with tradition, but it is more likely that there are not enough younger women because of the declining birth rate. However, if women have a

developing your research skills | Accessing Information From Academic Journals

Academic journals publish research articles so that research results can be reviewed by others who work in the same academic field. This process, called *peer review*, ensures that the results are reliable. Some research is also reported in the popular media. Newspaper and magazine articles can be located easily in the clipping files of libraries or on the Internet to help you locate academic articles that describe the research methods and results in greater detail.

- When you are looking for research articles, look for the names of the researchers, the title of the original publications, or the names of the organizations who sponsored the study.
- Using the library catalogue and the Internet, conduct a search to locate the original reports. You might also be able to find more current research by the same researchers. Journals are available for reference on the Internet (usually), at public libraries, and at college and university libraries.

Example

The newspaper article "Want the good life? Get married," written by Elaine Carey, demographics reporter, and published on January 24, 1996, in *The Toronto Star*, summarizes the results of two research articles published in the November 1995 academic journal *Demography* and reports the number of marriages for 1994.

To follow the leads to access valid secondary sources, especially academic journals:

- Locate the November 1995 issue of *Demography*, Vol. 32, No. 4, the journal of the Population Association of America, in public or university libraries or on the Internet. There you would find:
  - On page 483, "Does Marriage Matter?", a research essay by Linda J. Waite, in which she argues the thesis that, because individuals weigh the costs and benefits of marrying to themselves, not to society, demographers have an obligation to inform people about the costs and benefits of marriage that have been determined through research. She provides a thorough review of previous studies of marriage illustrated with graphs to support her thesis (Waite, 1995).
  - On page 521, "Dissolution of Premarital Cohabitation in Canada," a research report by Zheng Wu and T.R. Balakrishnan in which they present the results of a Canadian study to determine whether cohabiting couples are more likely to marry or to separate and the factors that affect the outcome. They conclude that although they are transient relationships, cohabitation appears to be emerging as a new form of family living (Wu & Balakrishnan, 1997).
- Search Statistics Canada's web site to locate the most recent marriage rates in Canada and to check for publications on the topic.
- Using the Internet, locate more recent studies by the researchers Zheng Wu, T.R. Balakrishnan, and Linda Waite. ■

similar earning potential to men, men are less likely to accept full financial responsibility for their families. Likewise, women who are educated and earning comparable incomes to their husbands are less likely to accept traditional marriage roles. As the dual-income marriage becomes the norm, **egalitarian relationships**, in which men and women share the responsibilities rather than adhere to fixed gender roles, are more common (Goldscheider & Waite, 1991).

Marriages are no longer essential for economic survival now that women are employed and self-supporting (Conway, 1997). From a social exchange perspective, there must be benefits to marriage that outweigh the advantages of the alternatives—cohabitation or remaining single—for individuals to choose to marry. Men and women with traditional views of marriage roles are more likely to marry. In addition, the more education men have, the more likely they are to approve of women working and the more likely they are to marry. However, more education for women decreases their opportunity to choose marriage (Goldscheider & Waite, 1991). Since the persistence of traditional functional roles results in an unequal power balance within marriage, and men and women have nearly equal power outside of marriage, men are assumed to benefit from marriage more than women do (McGoldrick, 1989).

"I have yet to hear a man ask advice on how to combine marriage and a career."
—Gloria Steinem

legal matters | Marriage and Cohabitation

by Justice Marvin Zuker

Marriage

When individuals enter into marriage, they enter into a contract and, as such, are subject to the rules that govern other contracts. The action for breach of promise to marry has been repealed in Ontario, and no action can be brought for any damages that result from a failure to marry.

The Constitution of Canada, Constitution Act, 1867 (see s. 91 (12), (13), (26)), provides that legislative jurisdiction with respect to marriage is shared between the federal and provincial governments. Parliament has exclusive jurisdiction concerning marriage and divorce, and the provincial legislatures have exclusive jurisdiction concerning solemnization of marriage, property, and civil rights in the province. The Constitution provides for overlapping legislative authority. Parliament has legislative authority with respect to who can or cannot marry and has enacted legislation prohibiting certain persons who are related by blood or adoption from marrying in the Marriage (Prohibited Degrees) Act, Statutes of Canada, 1990, Chapter 46, s. 4.

Degrees of Consanguinity Which, Under the Marriage (Prohibited Degrees) Act, 1990 (Canada), Bar the Lawful Solemnization of Marriage	
A man may not marry his	**A woman may not marry her**
1. Grandmother	Grandfather
2. Mother	Father
3. Daughter	Son
4. Sister	Brother
5. Granddaughter	Grandson

The relationships set forth in this table include all such relationships, whether by whole or half-blood or by order of adoption.

In Ontario the Marriage Act sets out who may perform marriages, when a licence is required, where and from whom that licence may be obtained, and who may obtain one.

- A marriage licence cannot be issued to a minor without the written consent of both parents. Obtaining the consent of parents is regarded as a matter of the formalities requisite for marriage. It is, accordingly, a matter regulated by the law of the place where the marriage is celebrated. A marriage that has been celebrated is valid and not void or voidable if performed without the requisite parental consent.

- If a marriage has been entered into in a country where no formalities are required other than an agreement to marry followed by cohabitation, that marriage will be, with respect to formalities, regarded as valid in Ontario.

- Marriage is a relationship of heterosexual monogamy. The case law definition of marriage may be stated "...as the voluntary union for life of one man and one woman, to the exclusion of all others." No person is entitled to undergo a second form of marriage while the first marriage remains valid and subsisting.

- A marriage will be void if one of the parties does not have the capacity to understand the basic nature of a marriage and its obligations. An operative lack of understanding may result from a lack of mental capacity or such non-inherent factors as being under the influence of drugs or alcohol. Duress of such a kind as to negate consent also invalidates a marriage.

- A decree of nullity must be distinguished from a divorce. A divorce puts an end to a valid marriage. Nullity rectifies the status of the parties as a result of some defect or disability at the time of the marriage ceremony.

- A marriage can be voided or annulled if one of the parties was unable to consummate the marriage at the time of the ceremony. A marriage is consummated when ordinary and complete sexual intercourse takes place between the spouses after the marriage ceremony. Accordingly, the use of contraceptives, sterility, or capricious refusal to engage in sexual intercourse does not amount to an inability to consummate.

In Ontario, the Family Law Act has several definitions of "spouse." For the purposes of Part I (family property) and Part II (matrimonial home), "spouse" refers to a man and a woman who have entered into a valid marriage, and extends to void and voidable marriages if the marriage was entered into in good faith on the part of the person asserting a right under the Act. Part III of the Family Law Act imposes mutual obligations of "spouses" to support each other. There is a duty on parents to support their children, and no distinction is drawn between children born in void, voidable, or valid marriages. In defining the rights of children, the law in Ontario no longer distinguishes between children born within or outside of marriage unless paternity is an issue.

Cohabitation

The term "cohabit" is defined in the Family Law Act as "to live together in a conjugal relationship, whether within or outside marriage." In Ontario, there are few remaining legal differences between married and cohabiting couples. Perhaps the most important distinction is that, under Part I of the Family Law Act, equal contributions are assumed, entitling a married spouse to a share of a wide range of assets acquired during the relevant period, whereas it is certainly more difficult for a cohabitant to access "non-family type" assets acquired during the relationship. In Ontario, the right of possession to the matrimonial home arises under Part II of the Family Law Act. However, that right is currently restricted to married persons, as the definition of "spouse" is the same in Part I and Part II.

In Ontario, although common-law and same-sex couples are still excluded from the property division scheme set out in Parts I and II of the Family Law Act, since the passage of the Ontario Family Law Act, 1978, cohabitants have been covered under the provincial statutory support provisions under Part III.

Section 29 of the Family Law Act defines a "spouse" for the purposes of Part III of the Act as including "either of a man and woman who are not married to each other and have cohabited,

a) continuously for a period of no less than three years, or

b) in a relationship of some permanence, if they are the natural or adoptive parents of a child."

Cohabitants cannot inherit under the intestacy provisions (when a person dies without a valid will) in the Succession Law Reform Act. However, a cohabitant may apply for support under Part V of that Act if he or she was a "dependant." Cohabitants can, of course, provide for each other by will.

Since the 1970s, cohabitation agreements have been expressly provided for in provincial legislation dealing with domestic contracts (s. 53-54). The couple may provide for the custody of children (subject always to the overriding jurisdiction of the court. Since cohabitants are not covered under Part II of the Family Law Act, they are not subject to the restrictions dealing with the family home that are imposed on married spouses in the context of marriage contracts.

The Canada Pension Plan, Revised Statutes of Canada, 1985, extends spousal benefits to cohabitants who have cohabited for at least one year. In Ontario the Pension Benefits Act includes cohabitants as defined in Part III of the Family Law Act. In Ontario, following the Charter of Rights and Freedoms in April 1985, a large number of statutes were amended to include heterosexual cohabitants within the definition of spouse because it was assumed that marital status would be found to be an analogous ground of discrimination. (See The Equality Rights Amendment Act, 1986, Statutes of Ontario, 1986, Chapter 64.) ■

Cohabitation

Cohabitation has become so common in Canada that almost 60 percent of young Canadians live together in their first conjugal relationship (Turcotte & Belanger, 1997). Most people assume that cohabitation means living together *before* marriage; that is, it is a prelude to marriage, not an alternative. In the National Fertility Study, 70 percent of married women and 82 percent of women who were separated or divorced said that "cohabitation was acceptable as insurance that marriage will last," but less acceptable if the couple "do not want to make a long term commitment" (Balakrishnan et al., 1993, p. 156). In Canada, 63 percent of cohabiting couples eventually marry after living together for an average of 2.3 years (Conway, 1997). Cohabitation is gaining greater acceptance as a trial run at marriage.

Many young couples are reluctant to marry without living together first. Both men and women might want to determine whether they are compatible when they are not on their best behaviour, as they would be during traditional dating. The high divorce rate makes some people feel a need to test their relationship before making a firm commitment and exposing themselves to the risk of divorce (Gee, 1995). Some individuals feel that marriage would not change their relationship. This argument is used in Québec, for example, where women do not change their name at marriage. Since the roles of men and women are changing, women might want to determine whether their partners can accept their independence, and men might be looking for more egalitarian divisions of labour and responsibility (Conway, 1997).

Views on How Being Married Would Change Their Life: Cohabitors Under Age 35						
	Better		Same		Worse	
Aspect of Life	Male	Female	Male	Female	Male	Female
a. Standard of living	19	18	74	76	7	6
b. Economic security	24	32	67	61	9	7
c. Overall happiness	30	36	57	57	13	7
d. Freedom to do what you want	11	9	59	74	30	17
e. Economic independence	11	10	75	78	14	12
f. Sex life	22	14	68	81	10	5
g. Friendships with others	14	12	73	80	13	6
h. Relations with parents	22	24	71	72	7	4
i. Emotional security	28	38	63	57	9	5

Note: Cohabiting respondents age 35 and younger were asked: "How do you think your life might be different if you were married now?" A 5-point scale was used for responses. The "better" category above includes "somewhat better" and "much better." "Worse" includes "somewhat worse" and "much worse."

Source: Adapted from Ferguson, S. J. (2001), *Shifting the center: understanding contemporary families.* (2nd ed.) Mountain View, CA: Mayfield Publishing Company. p. 166. Reproduced with the permission of The McGraw-Hill Companies.

Although cohabitation is perceived to be insurance for a lasting marriage, it is not effective. Common-law couples are more likely to separate than married couples. This would suggest that it is a good thing they did not marry. However,

Views on Reasons For and Against Cohabitation: Cohabitors Under Age 35

Reasons why a person might WANT to live with someone of the opposite sex without being married. How important is each reason to YOU?

Response	Important		Not Important	
	Male	Female	Male	Female
a. It requires less personal commitment than marriage.	14%	18%	46%	48%
b. It is more sexually satisfying than dating.	17	18	49	59
c. It makes it possible to share living expenses.	28	26	32	29
d. It requires less sexual faithfulness than marriage.	12	10	64	69
e. Couples can be sure they are compatible before marriage.	51	56	18	16
f. It allows each partner to be more independent than marriage.	17	19	36	41

Source: Adapted from Ferguson, S. J. (2001), *Shifting the center: understanding contemporary families.* (2nd ed.) Mountain View, CA: Mayfield Publishing Company. p. 167. Reproduced with the permission of The McGraw-Hill Companies.

couples that marry after cohabiting are also more likely to get divorced. The reasons for this are unclear. People who cohabit might do so because they have characteristics that do not make them good marriage partners. Perhaps living together without a commitment changes people's idea of marriage and family and reduces the importance of commitment so that they are more likely to separate when problems arise (Baker, 1993). In some cases, the problems that prevented marriage in the first place might continue to cause difficulties after the marriage (Bumpass, 2001).

Cohabitation is an alternative to marriage for some Canadians. Traditionally, men or women who were not able to divorce their first spouse would choose to cohabit in subsequent relationships. Young men and women in romantic relationships who are not fully employed, who are students, or who are not yet earning enough to afford the lifestyle they want as a married person are likely to cohabit (Clarkberg, 1999). Living together can also be more economical than living apart (Bumpass, 2001). Cohabitation might enable couples to maintain greater personal freedom and avoid commitment. The second relationship after divorce is likely to be a common-law relationship. However, cohabiting couples will acquire some legal rights and responsibilities for each other eventually as common-law partners.

research study | Economic Circumstance and the Stability of Non-Marital Cohabitation

by Zheng Wu, Associate Sociology Professor, and Michael Pollard, Ph.D. Student, University of Victoria

RESEARCH QUESTION

What is the role of economic circumstances in the process of non-marital union dissolution?

HYPOTHESES

- Cohabiting couples who experience difficult economic circumstances are less likely to marry and more likely to separate.
- Improved economic circumstances and social assistance for women may increase union instability.
- An increase in men's economic position should elevate the likelihood that cohabiting couples will marry.

RESEARCH METHOD

Using secondary analysis, the researchers analyzed data from the ongoing Survey of Labour and Income Dynamics, Statistics Canada, to trace a cohort of individuals who were cohabiting for a period of two years. The dependent variable was married, cohabiting, or separated. The independent variable was the economic circumstance of the individuals. Other factors that affect stability, such as age, education, or motherhood, were controlled.

RESULTS

- Canadian cohabitations were more stable than American ones, and more stable than before,

Zheng Wu of the University of Victoria has conducted extensive research on cohabitation in Canada.

perhaps because they are more accepted or, alternatively, because newer relationships that are more stable were in the sample group.
- The probability of separation decreased when household earnings increased.
- When women's earnings increased, the couple was more likely to separate than marry.
- Men's increased personal earnings contributed to the probability of separation.
- Increased total household earnings contributed to the stability of the cohabitation.
- Increased social status increased the probability of marriage.

CONCLUSION

The first two hypotheses are proven by the evidence. However, men's increased earnings improved the probability of marriage only when matched with better social status, such as a professional position (Wu & Pollard, 1998). ■

Source: Statistics Canada. The Income and Labour Dynamics Working Paper series. Catalogue No. 98-10. July 1998.

Sarah LeBlanc is a 28-year-old insurance adjuster who recently married her boyfriend, Ian. She is the only child of a French Canadian father and an Italian Canadian mother. Sarah lived with her parents in her maternal grandparents' home for the first two years of her life, until her parents could finish high school and get established in secure employment. Sarah's maternal grandmother, Toni, had just recently remarried and was living with her new partner, Ron, with his two teenage sons and three of her children from her first marriage.

In many ways, Sarah was as much a daughter as a granddaughter to grandparents Toni and her husband, Ron. Her Nana Toni babysat Sarah during the day while her parents worked until she was school-aged, and her grandparents always took her with them on their holidays. With two sets of parents, Sarah was well-loved as a child, and she grew up in a very happy and stable family.

Sarah has known her husband, Ian, since grade 7, when she changed schools and met her best friend, Annie, Ian's younger sister. She started to date Ian after she graduated from high school and started to work as a cashier at the local Canadian Tire store. Ian played softball on a mixed team, and he asked his sister to help him find another girl to play on the team. Sarah and Ian dated casually over the next three or four years but continued to see others as well. It was Sarah who kept the relationship at that level, because she felt that Ian too often treated her as his kid sister's friend. Also, when she went to Ian's home, she always felt uncomfortable in such a large family, since Ian's four brothers teased her mercilessly.

Sarah's mother and her grandmother had married as teenagers, and she had grown up hearing their stories about how difficult it was financially and emotionally

those first few years. Sarah was determined that she would not get married until she was older and became more independent, if at all. Sarah's attitude toward marriage changed when she was 25 and her beloved grandfather died suddenly of a heart attack. She and Ian were still in a comfortable relationship and continued to live in their respective parents' homes. Sarah was working for an insurance company and had been recently promoted to the position of claims adjuster. She liked her job and was taking night-school courses at a nearby community college so that she could qualify as an insurance agent. Ian was working for a carpet laying company but did not really like the work. When Sarah's best friend, Annie, got engaged, Sarah talked to Ian about living together. He was not ready to make a commitment, so they decided to break up.

During the next year, Sarah focused on her job and completed her insurance qualifications. She dated occasionally but was not really interested in a serious relationship. Her father was diagnosed with cancer, and Sarah was preoccupied with helping her mom and dad with his recovery. Often, she drove her dad to Toronto for his chemotherapy sessions. As Annie's wedding day drew nearer, Sarah and Ian found themselves together at various pre-wedding social events, since Sarah was the maid of honour and Ian was the best man. Ian was now training to be a firefighter, something that he had been talking about doing for a long time. Gradually, Ian and Sarah got back together and resumed their relationship. This pleased Sarah's mom and dad, who really liked Ian and thought he was good for Sarah.

With many of their friends getting married, Sarah and Ian naturally began to talk about the possibility themselves. They knew that they loved each other, but were very comfortable with their lives the way they were, and both were afraid to change things. They reached an understanding that they wanted to marry in the future, and they began to save money to put into a mortgage for a house when they finally decided to move in together. Then Sarah's father was diagnosed with cancer again. However, this time he did not recover and he died shortly after. Sarah was very close to her dad, and his death was difficult for her. Ian was very supportive, and the crisis in Sarah's life brought them closer together.

When Sarah's mom sold her house a few months later and moved into a small condominium in the same building as Sarah's Nana, Ian and Sarah bought a house and moved in together. Ian worked for the Barrie Fire Department, and Sarah's career at the insurance company was progressing rapidly. One year later, they were married. A few months later, they announced to their immediate families that they were expecting a baby. ■

Sarah and Ian were married.

1. What factors affected Sarah's choice not to marry earlier?
2. What reasons explain why Sarah and Ian married when they did?
3. Speculate on the likelihood that this example of the marriage process will become the norm in Canada.

The Future of Marriage

Marriage continues to be typical for individuals in Canada and in all parts of the world. Despite the common assumption that men and women will meet, fall in love, marry in their early twenties, and stay married to the same partner, in fact there has been constant change in the pattern of marriage. The current ideal of romantic marriage might be threatened by the increasing divorce rate, or it might be strengthened by an understanding that couples who no longer love one another need not stay together. Cohabitation could also threaten the stability of marriage, or it might raise questions about the purpose of marriage. Current challenges to the definition of marriage as an exclusively heterosexual union raise questions about the meaning of love and the reason for marriage. Each couple makes a decision according to their own evaluation of the benefits of marriage and the alternatives. From a social exchange perspective, perhaps the various controversies concerning the choice to marry will require a redefinition and clarification of marriage and intimate relationships for future generations.

chapter 6   Review and Apply

1. The definition of marriage used by Benjamin Schlesinger calls marriage a "socially legitimate relationship." What does "socially legitimate" mean? Identify the variety of intimate relationships that exist in Canada today. Classify them as socially legitimate or not socially legitimate.

2. Explain the purposes of marriage from the point of view of:

   a) anthropologists

   b) sociologists

3. Using a comparison chart, show the different ways marriages are formed, the obligations of spouses, the expectations concerning the marriage relationship, and how marriages can be ended, throughout the historical periods described.

4. Using data available from Statistics Canada, summarize the demographic changes that have occurred in the formation of marriages in Canada since Confederation.

5. Summarize the evidence from the chapter that supports procreation, love and companionship, identity, and economics as the purposes of marriage. Explain which purpose appears to be the most relevant today.

Knowledge/Understanding   Thinking/Inquiry   Communication

6. What are the legal requirements of marriage in Ontario? Conduct an Internet search to see how these requirements may differ from other provinces in Canada.

7. Whether it is relevant to continue gathering data on marriage and divorce might depend on your theoretical point of view.

   a) In the article "Statscan Would Sooner Count Marriages Than Complaints" on page 170, what theoretical perspective did the original decision by Statistics Canada reflect?

   b) What theoretical perspective does the criticism reflect?

   c) Write a response to the newspaper report about Statistics Canada's decision in which you state an opinion based on your theoretical perspective and support your opinion on the controversy.

8. Should cohabitation have the same legal standing as marriage, or should cohabitation be an alternative relationship for those couples who want none of the legal rights or responsibilities of marriage? Choose an appropriate theoretical perspective and explain the two sides of the controversy.

Knowledge/Understanding Thinking/Inquiry Communication Application

9. Develop a hypothesis regarding the purpose of marriage for young men and young women. Conduct an investigation using a survey and analyze the results. Speculate on the impact of the results on marriage for that cohort.

10. Using the Internet, conduct an investigation to determine whether the controversies concerning marriage and intimate relationships in Canada are being experienced in countries from which Canada's immigrants have come. Write a report summarizing various cultural viewpoints on the controversies.

11. Select one current trend in marriage and intimate relationships. Conduct research using the Internet to locate research articles and summarize the results. Organize and conduct a debate that presents conflicting theoretical viewpoints.

Intimate Relationships and Marriage

CHAPTER EXPECTATIONS

While reading this chapter, you will:

- describe research findings on attraction and the development of intimate and love relationships in contemporary Canadian society
- explain initial role expectations in intimate relationships on the basis of theories of attraction
- summarize current research on factors influencing satisfaction within enduring couple relationships
- explain the role negotiation required for effective relationships at various stages of life, drawing on a variety of theoretical perspectives
- identify factors that are detrimental to maintaining satisfying relationships and explain strategies for communicating and negotiating to maintain satisfying relationships
- summarize research on the causes and nature of conflict, and evaluate strategies for managing and resolving conflict in intimate relationships
- demonstrate an understanding of research methodologies, appropriate research ethics, and specific theoretical perspectives for conducting primary research
- identify and respond to the theoretical viewpoints, the thesis, and the supporting arguments of materials found in a variety of secondary sources
- describe and produce an example of an essay arguing and supporting an opinion

RESEARCH SKILLS

- using experiments
- developing case studies
- writing anecdotal summaries

For many Canadians, getting married is the beginning of a relationship that will last a lifetime.

CHAPTER INTRODUCTION

In this chapter, marriage and intimate relationships will be examined at several levels, starting with the personal level, using a psychological approach. To understand how couples develop, various theories of attraction, love, and mate selection will be examined. Next, the formation of committed relationships, including the negotiation of roles and the diversity of marriage relationships, will be explored. Factors that are harmful to marriage are also identified by research about factors that influence satisfaction in marriage. Finally, strategies for maintaining relationships and managing conflict will be discussed.

Forming Intimate Relationships

Intimate relationships are a common topic of movies, novels, television programs, poems, and songs, and these media often seek to portray them as pleasurable and to comment on their role in contemporary society. The romantic couple has become the dominant media icon (Dym & Glenn, 1999), and as such is assumed to be a desirable and natural relationship. In the 1954 Alfred Hitchcock movie *Rear Window*, Stella, the nurse, commented on the relationship between the main characters, Jeff and Lisa:

> When a man and woman see each other, they ought to come together—wham!—like a couple of taxis on Broadway, not be analyzing each other like two specimens in a bottle. . . . Once it was see somebody, get excited, get married. Now it's read a lot of books, fence with a lot of four-syllable words, psychoanalyze each other, until you can't tell the difference between a petting party and a civil service exam.

The decisions that Jeff and Lisa were having difficulty making about their relationship reflect the challenges for men and women in Canada today. Faced with the diversity of roles that they can play, individuals must decide whether to marry, who they *should* marry and who they *want* to marry, what their marriage will be like, or, increasingly, what other form of relationship would better meet their needs. Many Canadians still worry about whether they will be able to form a satisfying relationship that will last a lifetime without having to give up who they are and who they want to be.

The eternal question in romantic relationships is "How do I know if this is the right person for me?"

Marriage is assumed to be a binding and enduring relationship between a man and a woman, but that is not the case for many people. Some sociologists estimate that only about 10 percent of contemporary marriages are truly monogamous relationships, in which one man marries one woman for a lifelong relationship. Polygyny, marriage between one man and two or more women, and polyandry, marriage between one woman and two or more men, are considered more desirable by many people in the world, although few today can afford polygamous marriages—more than one husband or wife (Barrett, 1992). In Western countries and in many other parts of the world, **serial monogamy**, marriage to several spouses one after the other, is a logical result of divorce. The arrival of immigrants from countries where the social norms concerning marriage include various forms of arranged marriage challenges Westerners to consider whether their dating and courtship customs are a better way. The increase in cohabitation and divorce rates also suggests concern about whether marriages are meeting individuals' needs. However, newlyweds in most societies expect that their marriage will be for life, regardless of the prevailing divorce rate, and choose their partners accordingly.

Despite Stella's advice in *Rear Window*, Canadians analyze their relationships on an ongoing basis. A psychological study of the interaction of individuals as they form and attempt to maintain their relationships will examine the role that these relationships play in individuals' lives. Given the diversity of intimate relationships, this chapter will focus on marriage and cohabiting relationships that are like marriages. Several research questions that will be explored are:

- What is the nature of sexual attraction, mate selection, and romantic love?
- What is the relationship between attraction and marriage roles?
- How do couples negotiate satisfying roles in their relationships?
- What are the factors that are detrimental to forming enduring relationships?
- How do couples manage conflict in their relationships?

Attraction, Mate Selection, and Romance

Many Canadians believe that lasting intimate relationships are based on romantic love and sexual attraction between two people. Many marriages in Canada result from **free-choice mate selection**, in which individuals are attracted to each other, fall in love, and decide to marry. It is not yet clear whether romantic love is a fairly recent social development or whether love has a basis in human biology (Wilson, 2001). Marriage probably had its roots in the biological urge to reproduce, but it has evolved as the basic social and economic unit in human societies. Although historically and in many cultures today romantic love has been considered a hindrance to marital stability (Kelman, 1999), in 87 percent of all cultures the relationships between men and women exhibit romantic love (Nadeau, 1997). In *The History of the Wife*, Marilyn Yalom of Stanford University suggests that a man and a woman who lived and worked together, shared a bed, and raised children together would probably grow to love each other regardless of how their marriage came about (2001). The attraction of men and women has evolved also to reflect the increasing complexity of their relationships.

Theories of Attraction and Mate Selection

The new discipline of evolutionary psychology suggests that the origins of the human characteristics that people find attractive today can be traced back to our prehistoric ancestors. Using anthropological evidence, evolutionary psychologists explain that the mate-selection preferences that were most likely to ensure that children were born and survived to adulthood to reproduce most likely would be passed on to the next generation through the process of **natural selection** (Small, 1995). Women preferred to mate with men who would be good fathers and who would stay around to be good providers for themselves and their children because women were unable to both care for infants and gather enough food. Men preferred to mate with women who could bear healthy babies, who could feed their children, and who had the intelligence and temperament to raise them well. Prehistoric men formed lasting relationships because women could withhold sex until they got the qualities they wanted or needed in evolutionary terms. Children raised without a father were poorer and could not compete well in prehistoric society because they did not learn the necessary skills (Fisher, 1992). Men and women who made successful choices would have more children to inherit or be taught their mate selection preferences. Two processes were at work for men and

At social events, men and women seek out partners who are attractive to them but who also appear to come from similar socio-economic backgrounds.

women to exchange their valuable reproductive resources: individual preferences for an attractive mate and competition with others for a mate (Buss, 1994; Fisher, 1992).

In his book *The Evolution of Desire*, David Buss, an American anthropologist and evolutionary psychologist, summarizes the results of extensive studies on sexual attraction today (1994). His research around the world suggests that people's behaviour as they interact with potential partners is still patterned to enable them to select the person with whom they can raise the most successful children.

Buss has determined that in all societies women seek to "marry up." They are twice as likely to seek financial resources in a man than men are in women, even when women have substantial financial resources of their own. Buss also determined that women are attracted to men who are healthy, intelligent, well-educated, hard-working, and ambitious because these qualities enable men to be successful providers for their families in the long term. Men, on the other hand, are attracted to physically appealing, young, and healthy women. Shiny hair, clear skin, full lips, and a shapely figure are recognized as the common characteristics of female beauty in all societies. For example, a figure with hips that are wider that the waist is considered attractive in all societies, regardless of the current fashionably thin body size, even in remote societies that have not been influenced by media. This may be because this ratio indicates a pelvis that is wide enough to allow for an easy birth and sufficient body fat to sustain a pregnancy (Buss, 1994). In summary, anthropology explains that women are attracted to good providers, and men are attracted to women who appear to be fertile (Fisher, 1992; Buss, 1994; Small, 1995).

In the competition for a desirable partner who will meet one's social and economic expectations and will result in a stable and rewarding family life, it is fortunate that not all people find the same individuals attractive. Using the functionalist perspective, sociologists suggest that the variations in attraction can be explained using the theory of **social homogamy**. This describes how individuals are attracted to people from a similar social background (Wilson, 2001). Tests in which individuals rated the attractiveness of others have shown a mathematical correlation for social homogamy. The highest correlations were found for age, race, ethnic background, religion, socio-economic status, and political views. Correlations were also found for physical characteristics, such as length of fingers and space between eyes, suggesting that people find others with a similar appearance attractive (Buss, 1994). In a diverse society like Canada's, social homogamy can be used to explain the attraction of two individuals who are of different races or ethnic groups but who, because they were born and socialized within the same environment, are similar in other aspects of their social and economic background.

The contemporary image of a companionate marriage assumes that the relationship is based on romantic love. The *ideal mate theory* attempts to explain attraction from a symbolic interactionist perspective. Psychologists suggest that attraction is based on an individual's unconscious image of the ideal mate formed from his or her perceptions of the meaning of certain characteristics. The ideal mate theory supports the concept of "love at first sight," because everyone has an unconscious ideal with which they compare a person to find him or her attractive or to make the immediate judgment of the person as lovable. This theory also supports the evidence for social homogamy by explaining that perceptions of an ideal mate are formed from

Social homogamy theory explains that people usually look for someone with a similar appearance and background as their own.

pleasant experiences with other individuals in childhood, usually from a person's family, from people within the community, and from media personalities who are similar to one's self. Individuals also react to negative experiences by identifying unattractive characteristics that they perceive will be unacceptable for a successful marriage. The ideal mate image sets the standards that influence a person's judgment of potential mates without the person being aware of them (Nadeau, 1997).

Individual preferences determine who is attractive as a potential mate, but finding someone appealing does not guarantee that the feeling is mutual. In most societies individuals must compete with others to win the hand of the man or woman of their dreams. As many individuals have discovered in arranged marriages or on blind dates, having qualities that suggest an ideal match for marriage does not necessarily mean that someone is that person's counterpart (Kingston, 1999). The social exchange perspective suggests that attraction is based more on reality than fantasy, and explains that almost everyone finds a mate in his or her society because individuals are attracted to different people. People assess the resources they have to offer, such as physical attractiveness, wealth, pleasant personality, or social status, and look for the best possible mate who will be attracted by these resources (Small, 1995). In arranged marriages, the relative social values of the boy and girl are negotiated by the families or by the matchmakers on the basis of social homogamy, although in traditional societies a dowry may have increased the marriageability of a girl. That individuals are attracted to and fall in love with those who are equally appealing has been demonstrated in research studies, but this can also be observed by looking at the people who are attracted to each other within your own community (Buss, 1994).

In today's complex human societies, the social and psychological roles of couples determine the success of the marriage more than the biological role of reproduction does. Proximity is a major factor in mate selection. Individuals are attracted to, fall in love with, and marry those who live and work nearby, belong to the same religious community, or attend the same cultural events (Broderick, 2000). Social homogamy helps to ensure that couples are compatible. Similarity of backgrounds makes it more likely that couples will share common expectations for their relationship and their lifestyle, will manage their shared resources more efficiently and with less conflict, and will

"As a general thing, people marry most happily with their own kind. The trouble lies generally in the fact that people usually marry at an age when they do not really know what their own kind is."

—Robertson Davies

be able to raise children more easily. Couples who have similar backgrounds are more likely to raise their children according to their cultural expectations (Buss, 1994; Small, 1995). Two people who have similar beliefs about the roles of husband and wife and who share similar expectations for their family life will enjoy each other's company and will be more likely to fall in love. Since most parents wish their sons and daughters to have happy and lasting marriages and to pass on their cultural heritage to their children, social homogamy is also the basis of mate selection in societies that practise arranged marriages.

Intimacy in relationships requires a full appreciation of each other's uniqueness and separateness. The developmental perspective suggests that individuals are not able to relate to someone else without understanding first who they are and what their roles in life are. A lasting relationship based on companionship requires an understanding of what one has to offer another and what one needs from another in return. Therefore, individuals are not capable of a fully intimate relationship until the identity crisis of the transition to adulthood is resolved. Committing to intimate relationships earlier would result in defining identity through the relationship (Kimmel, 1990). However, as Levinson and Erikson suggested, women are more likely to define themselves through their connections with others, and so might develop a committed relationship as part of forming their identity. Men prefer to retain more independence in their relationships and, therefore, might delay forming committed relationships until their life structures are established (Levinson, 1976). Thus, as Stella argues in *Rear Window*, when a man is ready to marry, he will marry the woman he is with. The challenge of intimate relationships is gaining intimacy without losing self (McGoldrick, 1989).

The differences between what men and women want might explain why women usually marry older men. The age difference between men and women averages three and one-half years worldwide. The average age difference for Canadian men and women is two years—the lowest in the world. Iranians' average age difference—husbands are, on average, five years older than their wives—is the highest. Perhaps women are more likely to marry during the identity transition and are ready to marry earlier, but the age difference can also be explained in evolutionary terms. Older men, who are stronger, wiser, more stable, but not so old that they will not be around when the children grow up, are considered more desirable by women in all societies. Younger women are considered more sexually desirable, although few Canadian men are likely to describe the attraction in terms of fertility (Buss, 1994). The social exchange perspective suggests that younger, more attractive women have greater resources to offer older, successful men (Fisher, 1992). The conflict and feminist perspectives, on the other hand, suggest that a match between an

web connection

www.mcgrawhill.ca/links/families12

To learn about research studies on romance and attraction, go to the web site above for *Individuals and Families in a Diverse Society* to see where to go next.

older man and a younger woman ensures that the man has greater resources, and that the younger woman will need his resources to acquire an improved lifestyle. Therefore, the age difference is necessary for men to maintain a dominant status in a patriarchal marriage (Burggraf, 1997). Although women now have increased financial potential and extended fertility, the age differential between bride and groom continues to be the social norm.

Romantic Love

Despite the stereotypes perpetuated by cartoons and stand-up comedians, love and commitment are desired by both men and women for marriage (Balakrishnan, 1993; Wild, 1999). David Buss determined that a woman would not marry a man with all the qualities she desired unless she loved him or thought she could love him (1994). Although love has been described for thousands of years, it became the subject of social science research only recently. To determine the qualities of romantic love and to distinguish between romantic love and friendship, American psychologist Robert Sternberg interviewed hundreds of men and women who said they were in love. He determined that romantic love has three "faces": passion, intimacy, and commitment (Trotter, 1986). He also determined the following:

- Passion, a strong feeling of sexual desire for another, develops the most quickly of the three.

- The intense friendship of intimacy develops more slowly, as each individual shares himself or herself with another and becomes willing to meet the other's psychological needs.

- Commitment to maintaining the relationship grows as the rewards of this relationship over others become evident, and individuals accept reciprocal roles.

Sternberg chose to represent love as a triangle so that relationships with various proportions of passion, intimacy, and commitment could be depicted by varying the length of the sides. Because these characteristics develop at different rates, the nature of romantic love changes with time.

The passage of romantic love has been measured and explained in biological terms. The sudden and dramatic feelings of passion when lovers fall "head over heels in love" result from high levels of

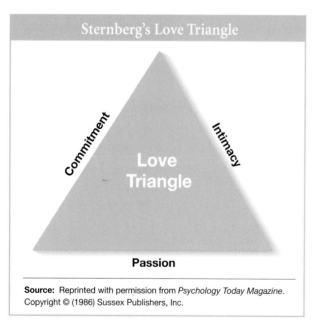

Sternberg's Love Triangle

Commitment · Intimacy · Passion

Love Triangle

Source: Reprinted with permission from *Psychology Today Magazine*. Copyright © (1986) Sussex Publishers, Inc.

The balance of passion, intimacy, and commitment may differ, but all three are found in romantic and companionate love in North America.

amphetamines, such as phenylethylamine (PEA), released by the hypothalamus gland. These amphetamines make lovers feel alert, a sensation that is accompanied by an increased heart rate, flushed face, and rapid breathing. Psychobiologists, such as Michael Liebowitz, who study the physiological basis of human behaviour, call this blissful emotional state **limerance**. Liebowitz, author of *The Chemistry of Love*, explains that limerance is similar to fear in its physical aspects and is distinguished from it only by the mind being focused on the loved one. This fact could explain why passion usually includes a feeling of anxiety about losing the other. After several years as a couple, amphetamine levels drop and are replaced by the hormone oxytocin. The highly aroused but exhausting state of limerance gives way to a state of calm and satisfaction that may be less exciting but is more enduring (Alaton, 1995). From an evolutionary perspective, love is advantageous: passion draws individuals together with a desire to reproduce, but the intimacy and commitment that follow allow them to maintain their relationship over the long term, to support each other, and to nurture and raise children.

"Love consists in this, that two solitudes protect and touch and greet each other."
—Rainer Maria Rilke

FYI

Romantic Love

Helen Harris of the University of California describes the psychological motivation for romantic love as "a desperate need to connect and a fear of being alone." Based on a metastudy in which she compiled the results of the various research studies on love, Harris identified the following attributes of romantic love:

1. A desire for a physical and an emotional merger: "Sexual desire and a desire for emotional intimacy are different but flip sides of the same thing."

2. Idealization of the love object: "Putting a positive spin on neutral and even negative traits."

3. Emotional dependency: "If there is some interruption of the progress to intimacy, people get very upset."

4. Desire for exclusivity.

5. Reordering of motivational priorities: "What used to be on the top of the heap— job, other relationships—moves down."

6. Intrusive thinking: Thoughts of the other person burst into everything, perhaps due to self-esteem problems in the obsessed lover.

7. Concern for the beloved. "This is seen as altruistic, although it can be an expression of self-interest. The flip side of this is how often love can turn to hate."

Source: Alaton, S. What is this thing called love? *The Globe and Mail* (1995, February 11).

By giving gifts of luxury items, such as flowers, men demonstrate that they can afford to support a family.

Romantic love provides the psychological motivation for individuals to want to marry or to form enduring intimate relationships in societies in which marriage is not a social, economic, or familial obligation. Since there is a biological basis for attraction and a psychological desire to be loved, individuals have a desire to connect with another and to follow the social norm of being a couple.

Courtship

In societies that permit free-choice mate selection, **courtship** allows individuals to win the affection of those to whom they are attracted. Whether you believe that evolutionary drives or social homogamy determine who would be appropriate marriage partners, individuals marry the person they love and who loves them in return. In courtship rituals in all societies, men display their resources to prove they have the potential to be good providers, and women display the qualities that make them desirable and nurturing (Buss, 1994). Diverse courtship customs and restrictions on courting can be described for each culture, historical period, and social class. However, many people are not conscious of the specific rituals of their society. In Canada, courtship is viewed as a quaint term from the past that no longer applies to relationships between men and women in the twenty-first century. Individuals may not be aware that their behaviour in a romantic relationship conforms to the traditional courtship rituals of their society, but the similarity in the choice of partners and the timing of marriage suggests that unspoken rules govern the choice of a desirable life partner.

The Evolution of Courtship

Courtship rituals in North America have evolved over the last century and have varied according to social class. In early Canada, following the formal customs established in Britain, young, middle-class women might invite men to call on them when they were "at home." A young man would leave his calling card if the young woman was not seeing visitors, in the hope that he would be invited back. Families would make discreet inquiries about the social and economic suitability of the callers. A young woman, with her mother, might receive several visitors, who would understand that they were expected to compete for her affection. Later, as a sign that she had made her choice, the young woman might receive only one man. Not until then would her mother leave the couple alone to get to know each other. A New England custom in rural families with fewer rooms in their homes was called **bundling**. The young couple would be tucked into bed with a "bundling board" between them so that they could have private conversations without getting cold. The privacy allowed by both of these customs enabled men and women to get to know each other. During the 1700s in the United States, these customs resulted in one-third of brides being pregnant on their wedding day (White, 1992).

During the twentieth century, courtship evolved into the informal North American social invention of **dating**. Early in the century, young people met at church or community events and went out together to socials in groups. By the 1920s, however, when men began to take the

When teenagers gained disposable income and cars, dating became more of a recreational activity than a courtship ritual.

initiative by asking women out and by organizing and paying for the activity, dating became common. Since women could accept or reject the invitations, the choice of activity and the amount of money spent indicated to them, not to their parents, the social and economic resources the men had to offer. In the 1930s "going steady" meant a couple had an exclusive relationship but were not necessarily discussing marriage (White, 1992). With the advent of the consumer society and the growing affluence of young people, couples were able to buy entertainment, and dating became an opportunity to spend time together for pleasure and romance. Teenagers began dating earlier, and there was less aware-ness that it was a process of choosing a suitable marriage partner (Whyte, 2001).

By the 1950s the Western ideal was that dating would lead to falling in love and becoming a couple. The *market experience perspective* suggested that dating was effective because it enabled individuals to learn to relate to the opposite sex and to judge character so that they would be able to determine what personal qualities they desired in a marriage partner (Whyte, 2001). Bernard Murstein explained the relationships among dating, social homogamy, and social exchange as a multistep process. He used the analogy of sifting to suggest that individuals pass their dates through a series of "filters" to screen out unacceptable marriage partners and to select those who are similar to themselves. As the relationship becomes more serious and the individuals get to know each other, the filters become finer until only one person passes through it for readiness to marry (Stevens-Long & Commons, 1992). The social rituals of dating, shared informally among young people, describe the expectations for spending time together, for exclusivity or "cheating," and for when it is appropriate to hold hands, kiss, and progress through subsequent stages of sexual intimacy. Traditional dating norms enable sexual passion to be suppressed until the couple knows each other well enough for an intimate relationship, has invested enough time and energy into it to feel a commitment to it, and has fallen in love and chosen to marry.

Murstein's Filter Theory

Field of Eligibles

Propinquity Filter

Attraction Filter
Physical attraction   Personality

Homogamy Filter
Age, race, education, socio-economic class, religion

Compatibility Filter
Temperament, attitudes and values, needs, roles, habit systems

Trial Filter
Cohabitation, engagement

Decision Filter

Marriage

Bernard Murstein suggests that dating enables individuals to sift through potential partners with finer and finer filters to select compatible partners and the one person they are ready to marry.
Source: From Rice, P.R. (1990). *Intimate relationships, marriages, and families*. Mountain View, CA: Mayfield, p. 181. Reproduced with permission of The McGraw-Hill Companies.

Dating and Marital Success

"Dating is just a job interview that lasts all night."

—Jerry Seinfeld

The preference for free-choice marriage in North America suggests that dating experience leads to greater marital success, and that arranged marriages may be less successful because the partners would not know each other. Conventional wisdom suggests that marrying your first love is not a good idea because you do not have enough understanding of what you want (Whyte, 2001, p. 135):

The rationale of our dating culture was that having had a variety of dating partners and then getting to know one or more serious prospects over a longer period of time and on fairly intimate terms were experiences more likely to lead to marital success.

In addition, an understanding that sex is very important in marriage, combined with a greater acceptance of premarital sex by the end of the twentieth century, has led many people to believe that they should test their sexual compatibility before marriage (Whyte, 2001). On the other hand, although dating reflects the pattern of competitive mate selection based on a "display of resources" that is found in all societies, it could be argued that dating encourages individuals to make their most critical judgment about others on the basis of people's best behaviour in artificial circumstances on "dates."

Martin King Whyte tested the hypothesis that dating experiences lead to successful marriages by conducting extensive interviews about dating with couples in Detroit. The results of his study found no correlation between dating experience, length of dating, engagement, degree of premarital intimacy, and marital success. Whyte argues against the market experience perspective by explaining that mate selection is not like buying a car, since you cannot "test drive" various partners at the same time. Also, if you decide on one you tried before, he or she might have moved on to someone else and not be available. Therefore, in free-choice mate selection as it is practised through dating, you have to decide "yes" or "no" to one person at a time. Paradoxically, the current practice in arranged marriages in Canada is more likely to allow young men or women to meet and consider a number of potential partners at the same time before choosing one. The fact that marriages are slightly less successful with more dating experience could also suggest that it increases an individual's expectations and, therefore, makes it more difficult for the person to make a choice or to feel satisfied in a relationship (Whyte, 2001).

Dating is not an indicator of marital success, but love is. The second conclusion of Whyte's Detroit study is that being in love when you marry is the best indicator of marital success. In practice, the process of getting to know someone to determine degree of compatibility is combined with increasing sexual expression. However, greater permissiveness about non-marital sex may mean that the expression of passion through sexual activity precedes the development of intimacy and **commitment**, or devotion, to the relationship (Wilson, 2001). Robert Sternberg's research found

Being deeply in love with a partner is more important than dating experience for predicting the success of a marriage.

that couples who reported they had a strong sexual desire for each other, who knew each other well to enjoy each other's company, and who had made the relationship a priority in their lives defined themselves as being deeply in love (Trotter, 1986). Couples who remember being deeply in love when they married have the happiest marriages, regardless of dating experience (Whyte, 2001).

At the beginning of the twenty-first century, when couples cohabit before marriage and delay marriage perhaps until they are ready to have children, the courtship behaviour of Canadians has changed. Many young couples no longer date in the formalized way of their parents' generation. The use of expressions such as "being with" or "seeing someone" to describe a relationship suggests a more casual approach to forming an intimate relationship, yet the rules have become more restrictive. For example, "seeing someone" implies an exclusivity that was not required until a couple was "going steady" in the past. In addition, the expectations that men and women have of their intimate relationships also may have changed. Now that women have the same financial potential as men, women, like men, may be concerned about pursuing their individual goals as well as marrying. There appears to have been a shift from competing to win someone's affection to being very selective about what the other has to offer (Dym & Glenn, 1993). A less formal pattern of courtship today masks a much more challenging process now that marriage, as well as mate selection, is a matter of free choice.

in focus | When Marriage Is a Family Affair

by Salem Alaton

The day Salma and Saleem Ataullahjan first met, they were at a special occasion—their wedding. That was 19 years ago in Pakistan. Today, they appear to have what most people seek in marriage, a loving, intimate, mutually respectful relationship.

Saleem, an electrical engineer in his mid-50s, first came to Canada in 1968 to study at the University of Windsor. He ended up staying and reaching his 30s as a bachelor. But one day he returned to visit his family, knowing the time had come. "I said, 'Here I am, get me married,'" he recounts.

Following a long tradition of family-arranged marriages in Muslim culture, Saleem's parents knew

Islam taught Salma and Saleem Ataullahjan about each other before they met at their wedding 19 years ago.

the kind of social compatibilities their son would need in a partner. In this case, Saleem's father and Salma's grandfather had been friends. Salma's family was wealthier, but both families were considered highly respectable; both belonged to the Pukhtun-speaking tribe in Pakistan's frontier region. And so the prospective couple didn't even bother with the chaperoned meetings they were entitled to before committing to be wed. "I'm starting an arranged marriage, I don't want to meet the guy," says Salma, now a real estate agent. Despite her somewhat Westernized upbringing at British private schools in Pakistan, Salma, now in her mid-40s, felt confident in Muslim custom.

As incongruous as these attitudes may seem in a North American culture obsessed with romance and sex, they hold sway among countless Muslims, Hindus, and people of other religions, even among Jews and Christians. Indeed, throughout history and around the globe today, the West's romance model of marriage tends to be the exception. In most places where tribal identity is strong and people live in extended families, such as Asia, Africa, and parts of South America, marriages are either arranged or partners must at least be chosen with closely determined lines of family approval.

Since marriage governs sexual behaviour, guides family formation, and determines lineage, much rides on it, and its contractual overtones—such as each spouse's responsibilities, the role of the in-laws, and the material commitments of both families—are particularly strong in Muslim and Hindu customs.

"Marriages are arranged in many cultures because marriage is seen as something too important to be left to chance," explains Leslie Orr, a Hinduism specialist at Concordia University in Montréal. Moreover, arranged marriages often have a good track record. The three arranged marriages among Salma's siblings have held firm, while the two "love matches" ended in separation.

"The encouragement of the family is very highly recommended (for marriage) because the family structure in Islam is so strong," says Raheel Raza, who does some matchmaking on behalf of Muslim parents in the Muslim community here. "It has been the practice for many centuries, and very successfully, too, I might add."

Some marital customs abroad have led to abuses of women, such as the sometimes appalling experiences of dowry brides in India, but Hindus and Muslims here insist these are aberrations and contrary to religious law. "Especially the Western media seems to confuse arranged marriages with forced marriages or child marriages," Raza says. "It is the acceptable norm in Islam that the woman has the right to refuse a partner."

Even back in Pakistan and India, there is greater aspect of choice now and the parental decision isn't as rigid. "It's what I call 'influenced' marriage now," says Liyakat Takim, who teaches Islamic culture at McMaster University in Hamilton. "We tend to polarize between love marriage and arranged marriage, but there is something in between. It's a kind of parental guidance." Islam doesn't compel but strongly encourages marriage, Takim notes, adding that "even under strictly arranged marriages, people were not forced."

R.K. Moorthy, 60, and his wife Suganthan, 54, were brought together by their families in India before coming to Canada in 1977. They were introduced at a Hindu religious festival and met once again at a family function before their wedding 30 years ago. But they don't expect their own grown children, who have spent most of their lives in Canada, to follow suit. The most important factors in Hindu culture for marriage, says Moorthy, director of compensation for Ontario Hydro and a trustee for the Richmond Hill-based Hindu Temple society of Canada, are the reliability of the partner's family, the compatibility of the couple, and "the belief that marriage is a long-lasting institution."

A traditional view of compatibility means religious and ethnic sameness and similar socio-economic standing of both families. Issues of marrying within one's "class" are hardly unfamiliar in the West, but India's marital customs have been criticized for enforcing a caste system. Orr says this is changing even to the extent of on-line searches. "It may have been in the past that young people felt they had no choice but to agree to their parents' arrangements for them." And despite an old custom of children being symbolically married as a way to designate their adult partner in advance, "In India the average age of marriage has been going up steadily," she says.

It is sometimes said that the West believes in love before marriage and the East in love after marriage. In Canada, the path the Ataullahjans took may be hard to imagine. Yet neither of them concedes to having had any doubt or anxiety at their wedding. What they needed to know about their unseen life partner that day, Islamic tradition had already taught them. ■

Source: *The Toronto Star* (1999, May 1). p. L14.

1. What are the benefits of arranged marriages, according to the couples in this article?
2. How can the various theories of attraction, mate selection, and love be used to explain arranged marriage?
3. If your parents were arranging a marriage for you, what qualities would they consider to be desirable in a spouse for you? What qualities of yours would they emphasize to suggest that you are a desirable spouse?

Negotiating Satisfying Roles in Relationships

Although marriage is no longer required for social status, financial well-being, or reproduction, it remains a major life transition for both men and women. Marriage can appear to be the happiest and the easiest transition in life because it is ritualized, highly organized, and supported by family and friends. Getting married signifies stability in the relationship with another. However, because Canadians romanticize marriage and focus on the wedding day, it is possible to view the wedding as the end of a process, not the beginning of a lifelong commitment to building a marriage. The couple might not realize that because their status has changed, they must negotiate the relationship they want to have and the compatible roles each will play (McGoldrick, 1989). Erik Erikson explained that individuals have to resolve the dilemma of intimacy versus isolation to develop the enduring strength of love within the relationship (Erikson, 1980). The challenge for two people who marry is how to grow both independently and as a partner within a couple (Carter & McGoldrick, 1989; Kingston, 1999).

Role Expectations in Marriage

In the late twentieth century, the purpose of marriage changed, and the traditional roles of husband and wife have become less attractive. Contemporary men and women seek friendship, caring, and support from their partner, in enduring intimate relationships based on companionship, not parenthood. In the traditional marriage, women maintained the marriage, and men pursued independence; however, now that women bring financial and educational resources to the marriage, they may be looking for personal fulfillment and independence also (Dym & Glenn, 1993). Companionate relationships identify marriages or committed cohabiting couple relationships that are based on the principle of equality. The focus of these relationships is intimacy and commitment (Helgerson, 1997). Establishing a companionate relationship is a process, not an event, that occurs over the first years of the relationship. The couple may have tested their compatibility during the dating period, but negotiating the relationship really begins with the change in status that occurs with the transformation to becoming married or committed cohabiting partners.

According to systems theory, couples must discuss the structures, or the hidden rules, of their new marital system. **Negotiation** is a process of conferring with others in order to reach an agreement. The issues of daily living that must be agreed upon by the couple, such as when, where, and how to eat, talk, have sex, argue, work, and relax, might not seem important compared to decisions made outside the family, but they are not trivial simply because they are so personal (McGoldrick, 1989). In negotiating the details of their personal lives, couples are determining the rules for division of labour and decision making for the marital system (Nett, 1993). Marriage is not just the joining of two individuals but also the joining and overlapping of two family systems to create a third; therefore, couples need to adapt the structures that each brings from the family of origin (Carter & McGoldrick, 1989). Since the partners' expectations originate primarily in their families of origin, they take the details for granted and may not be aware of the collaboration involved in committing to **shared roles** in marriage.

Couples who commit to a lasting relationship will be establishing it within a social environment that presents competing demands. The expectation that people marry to have children and stay together for the purpose of raising them has given way to the expectation that marriage will be emotionally close and personally rewarding. A stable marriage can provide support to individuals as they attempt to meet the many demands of personal development and careers. However, the social environment may restrict individuals' freedom to establish the type of relationship they would like to have. For example, family law in Canada assumes that both spouses are making an equal contribution to both financial and household responsibilities, yet media stereotypes continue

Today, women and men share household tasks based on personal preference rather than role expectations.

to present financial matters as a man's responsibility and housework as primarily a woman's. The progress of cohabiting relationships differs from marriage's, because cohabiting couples are less likely to recognize the change in status and the necessity of negotiating their roles. Conflicting demands between personal needs and social and economic responsibilities create tensions for those in traditional patriarchal relationships and for those attempting to establish modern companionate relationships (Goldscheider & Waite, 1991).

FYI

Nine "Psychological Tasks" Needed for a Good Marriage

by Judith Wallerstein

Psychologists have long studied the factors that contribute to troubled marriages, but have devoted relatively little time to finding out what makes good marriages succeed. Judith S. Wallerstein, Ph.D., co-author of the book *The Good Marriage: How and Why Love Lasts*, listed nine "psychological tasks" as the pillars on which a marital relationship rests. Wallerstein identified the nine tasks after conducting separate and joint interviews with 50 San Francisco Bay-area couples who had been legally married at least nine years; had children together; and independently regarded their marriages as happy. She also conducted follow-up interviews two years later. The nine psychological tasks required for a happy marriage, as outlined by Wallerstein, are:

1. Separating emotionally from the family of one's childhood so as to invest fully in the marriage and, at the same time, redefining the lines of connection with both families of origin.

2. Building togetherness based on mutual identification, shared intimacy, and an expanded conscience that includes both partners, while at the same time setting boundaries to protect each partner's autonomy.

3. Establishing a rich and pleasurable sexual relationship and protecting it from the incursions of the workplace and family obligations.

4. (For couples with children) Embracing the daunting roles of parenthood and absorbing the impact of a baby's entrance into the marriage. The couple must learn to continue the work of protecting their own privacy.

5. Confronting and mastering the inevitable crises of life.

6. Maintaining the strength of the marital bond in the face of adversity. The marriage should be a safe haven in which partners are able to express their differences, anger, and conflict.

7. Using humour and laughter to keep things in perspective and to avoid boredom and isolation.

8. Nurturing and comforting each other, satisfying each partner's needs for dependency, and offering continuing encouragement and support.

9. Keeping alive the early, romantic, idealized images of falling in love, while facing the sober realities of the changes wrought by time.

Wallerstein emphasized that these nine tasks are not assigned from outside of the marital relationship, but are inherent in the marriage. They do not represent a chart to be hung on the kitchen wall and checked off daily.

Source: © 1995-1996 by the American Psychological Association. Adapted with permission <http://helping.apa.org/family/marriage.html> and from *The Good Marriage* by Judith S. Wallerstein and Sandra Blakeslee. Copyright © 1995 by Judith S. Wallerstein and Sandra Blakeslee. Reprinted by permission of Houghton Mifflin Company. All rights reserved.

Stages in a Marriage

What is the normal pattern in the development of a marriage? Although early marriages usually live up to peoples' expectations, many couples become disappointed, because marriage gets more difficult during the first five years (Lawlor, 2001). In the 1970s, when couples were beginning to challenge traditional role expectations and negotiate their own roles in their marriages, Daniel Goldstine, Shirley Zucherman, and Hilary Goldstine (1976) tracked the changes in marriage over time. They identified three predictable stages of a relationship:

- **Stage 1:** Relationships are romantic, warm, and respectful, focusing on exploration, sexual attraction, and the idealization of the partner. Individuals also build self-esteem as they try to develop the relationship they want.

- **Stage 2:** Conflict arises as individuals become more demanding to meet their own needs. This results in instability in the relationship and requires both partners to change their behaviour. Individuals feel let down because the relationship is less rewarding.

- **Stage 3:** Couples compromise and negotiate a relationship that meets their needs as well as possible. The relationship becomes more realistic, mature, and stable.

The key to surviving stage 2 is to recognize that intimacy means being honest about one's own needs and conferring with one's partner to solve problems. At each stage, individuals are transformed as they respond to their partner and adjust to the more flexible roles they play in the developing relationship. Goldstein et al. determined that the changes reflected development in that the relationships were improved if they were able to achieve stage 3.

In 1993, Barry Dym and Michael Glenn described a new understanding that goes beyond the three stages of relationships identified by Goldstein et al. Their studies of enduring relationships suggest that crises, many of which are normal and predictable, cause the instability of stage 2 to recur and require that the couple renegotiate their relationship repeatedly. The *family life cycle framework* explains that there are many predictable developmental crises in a relationship. They are:

- adjustment to marriage
- birth of a child
- teenage years
- children leaving home
- retirement
- growing old together

> "*The meeting of two personalities is like the contact of two chemical substances: if there is any reaction, both are transformed.*"
>
> —Carl Jung

Some couple relationships will also be challenged by **non-normative crises**, such as unemployment, infertility, illness, or infidelity (Carter & Peters, 1996). Couples who achieve a resolution to their problems in the first stage establish their **marital system**, the characteristic structures that they will rely on when they need to resolve problems in the future. Although the initial starry-eyed romance may not appear again, the pessimism of the second stage gives way to perspective and enduring love, founded on the knowledge that the individuals can resolve their differences (Dym & Glenn, 1993).

in focus | Matrimony as the Ultimate Adventure

by Judith Timson

It is the month of love, and the dark of winter. Approaching Valentine's Day, I find myself meditating on my marriage but interrupted by the ringing telephone. It is yet another woman friend calling to say, "How can I off-load this jerk?" I wonder, Am I the complaints department of modern life? Or maybe a secular domestic priest(ess) whose confessional box is the telephone? Those complaints hover in the air, infecting me (who actually was feeling [positive] about love) with their [bitterness], and their truth: *He promised me he would organize our daughter's birthday party—did he not see me angrily stuffing 12 loot bags while he channel-surfed in the living room? . . . I worked all day, made dinner, cleaned up, and then he has the nerve to comment on my lack of a sex drive? . . . She comes in at night, saying she wants to spend time with us, gives the kids and me an absent-minded hug, and then sits down to read a report!*

Ah, modern marriage. That continual search, against all odds, for connection, for intimacy, for a moment the soul can revel in. When it is bad, it is so very bad. You long for a connection, you think you are the only one without it, you imagine everywhere happy women whose partners are standing in the kitchen looking a little like Hugh Grant (well, maybe not Hugh Grant, that creep), but anyway looking tousled and

Judith Timson, a Toronto-based writer, considers marriage as an adventure to discover "who we are."

handsome, drinking a glass of wine, and wittily recounting their day as you recount your own. Instead, whimpers one woman, "I just want a husband who comes in and doesn't fan the mail before he acknowledges me." Instead, moans one man, "She is always at me. No matter what I do, it is never enough."

I take cover from all this domestic disharmony in the words of Joseph Campbell. Campbell is the late American mythology professor who, during a series of interviews he gave in the 1980s (later collected in a book, *The Power of Myth*), rivetingly discussed the nature of love and marriage.

Modern marriage as a concept, says Campbell, began in the twelfth century with the troubadours, who went in search of the perfect love, describing it as "perfect kindness." Before the troubadours, love was simply regarded as Eros—the god who excites you to sexual desire, a biological urge. Then, love was transformed into the highest spiritual existence, and the courage to love—to choose one's life partner—became the courage to affirm one's own experience against tradition.

In a committed marriage, says Campbell, love "is the high point of life," and the only point: "If marriage is not the prime concern, you're not married." Campbell does call marriage "an ordeal—the submission of the individual to something superior to itself," which is exactly how I see it on a morning when I am having trouble even with the sound of my partner chewing his cornflakes.

But Campbell's words urge all of us on to higher ground. "The real life of a marriage or of a true love affair," he says, "is in the relationship . . . here I am, and here she is, and here we are. Now when I have to make a sacrifice, I'm not sacrificing to her, I'm sacrificing to the relationship."

No friend I've ever talked to imagined that marriage would be as hard as it really is. To many, the terror of thinking you're with the wrong person is surpassed only by the terror of thinking you're with the right person—and it's still this difficult.

But Campbell manages to transform marriage into a romantic, even a heroic, struggle. What he celebrates is the sharing of pain—and destiny—with another human being. Most love affairs, says Campbell, last only as long as they benefit both parties. But a marriage? "A marriage is a commitment to that which you are."

Why do these words seem so thrilling to me? Lately, I confess, I have been regarding my own husband with renewed astonishment. His good qualities, were they there all along? His smile, for instance. His grace and equanimity on family excursions when I have lost it. His day-to-day resilience. His ability to master on the piano, after much practice, a Chopin sonata. His tremendous civility. His arms around me at night.

Isn't perfect kindness that morning cup of coffee he brings me after I stay up most of the night agonizing over a child's problem? Of course, if we were in a down phase, I would point out he chose to snore while I worried.

But I have just finished reading words that seem to me more powerful—and certainly more sexy—than any trumped-up message on a card could ever be. Sexier still because he gave them to me to read. Here I am, here he is, and here we are. ■

Source: *Chatelaine*. (1996, February). Courtesy of Chatelaine © Rogers Publishing Ltd.

1. Apply systems theory to explain "Here I am, and here he is, and here we are."
2. Why does Timson suggest that the relationship takes priority over the individuals?

Defining Success

Martin Whyte's (2001) final conclusion of his Detroit study of dating and marriage suggests that marital success can be predicted. He found that although dating experience was not a predictor of success, enduring married couples had several characteristics in common. They are:

- having similar values
- enjoying similar leisure time activities
- pooling their incomes
- sharing in power and decision making in their relationship
- having friends in common
- having an active social life together

These characteristics suggest that social homogamy was a factor in their selection of a marriage partner, and that the couples have made their marital relationship a priority in their lives. The couples also suggest that they have settled the issues of power and influence in their relationships. These results echo the results of other studies on lasting marriages.

research study | Why Marriages Succeed or Fail

by Dr. John Gottman, Professor of Psychology at University of Washington

Dr. John Gottman, psychology professor and director of The Gottman Research Institute.

RESEARCH QUESTION

What are the differences between happy and unhappy couples?

HYPOTHESIS

The quality of the interaction between partners is a predictor of marital success.

RESEARCH METHOD

Using experiments in the laboratory, John Gottman observed what happens when couples interact. Couples were observed as they spent weekends living in the Family Research Laboratory. They were also given specific tasks to perform, such as discussing an issue that caused conflict in their relationship. Their behaviour and responses were recorded using video cameras, heart monitors, blood and saliva tests for hormones, even sensors under the chairs to determine whether they were squirming. Couples also completed extensive questionnaires and were interviewed apart and together.

RESULTS

- Couples who stay together maintain a 5:1 ratio of positive to negative interactions in their relationship. They put a positive spin on the events of their relationship.
- There are three types of stable marriages based on how couples handle disagreements: emotionally stable or "validating"; emotionally intense or "volatile"; and emotionally inexpressive or "conflict avoiding." Couples do not benefit by changing their style, but couples who have different styles have to negotiate which style or combination of styles to use.
- Fighting and getting angry early in the relationship suggests a more successful relationship than not fighting at the beginning. Fighting seems to strengthen a relationship against later troubles by establishing a compatible fighting style.
- Men who do housework have happier marriages, better health, and more satisfying sex lives.
- There are no discernible gender differences in the quality and quantity of emotional expression in happy marriages.
- There are four destructive communication behaviours that can threaten the stability of a relationship—criticism, contempt, defensiveness, and stonewalling—but couples can head them off with "repair attempts" to minimize the negative effect.

CONCLUSIONS

Marriages based on affection, humour, appreciation, and respect, in which partners have a positive attitude to the relationship and to their mate, and respond to destructive behaviours with "repair attempts," are more stable and enduring. ■

Source: Gottman, J., & Silver. N. (1999). *The seven principles for making marriage work*. New York: Crown Publishers, Inc.

Benjamin Schlesinger, Professor Emeritus of the Faculty of Social Work, University of Toronto, asked Canadian couples to identify the most important factors for a lasting marriage. His study, conducted in 1981 in the Toronto area at a time when the role expectations of marriage were being transformed, determined the perceptions of educated, middle-class men and women. The results suggested that both men and women believed that companionship was more important in a marriage than parenting, and that it was based on love, mutual respect, trust, and open communication (Schlesinger, 1984). More recently, John Gottman's experiments to determine the nature of the interactions between married couples found that if the positive moments are to outweigh the negative ones by 5:1, mutual commitment to the relationship and effective communication are critical (Gottman & Silver, 1996).

"For those who have long-term, happy marriages, 'till death do us part' is not a binding clause but a gratifying reality."

—Jeanette and Robert Lauer, *Marriages Made to Last*

Every marriage is unique. Couples measure the success of their relationship in their own terms.

The definition of a successful marriage is very subjective. In his study, Schlesinger defined a stable marriage as one lasting 15 years and having one child. He asked participants about lasting marriage, with some questions about satisfying relationships, but he did not ask about happiness. Some people might say that any couple that lasts five years has been successful in a time of easy divorce. Individuals decide whether or not the marriage is successful based on the expectations they had when entering the relationship and on their willingness to adjust as the relationship matured. The criteria are also determined by the social context in which the couple lives. From a social exchange perspective, people stay in relationships when they perceive the balance of give and take to be fair, and when the benefits of staying in the relationship outweigh those of leaving. Since each individual uses subjective criteria to decide whether a relationship is satisfying, the nature of lasting relationships differs widely.

David Olson, a psychologist and professor of family social science at the University of Minnesota, and Yoav Lavee, of the University of Haifa, asked couples in lasting relationships to measure the level of satisfaction in their marriages. For most couples, the level of satisfaction was found to be affected by personal factors within the relationship itself, such as their sexual relationship. Couples were also influenced positively or negatively by factors outside their relationship, such as money, religion, family, and friends. The results of their study outline the diversity of lasting relationships. One in ten couples reported that they were very satisfied with every dimension of their marriage, but four in ten could not identify any satisfying dimension at all! In between were five different types of marriage with varying strengths and priorities. The variations in the different relationships reflected many common problems in marriage, but all couples had made the decision to stay in the relationship— for the time being (Kay, 1994).

Achieving a Satisfying Relationship

Familiarity breeds intimacy in a relationship. Knowing who you are, where you came from, and where you are going prepares you to know your partner well. Sharing values and activities must be based on honesty. Monica McGoldrick suggests that individuals who have not become independent from their parents may enter into an intimate relationship hoping to earn the love of another by pleasing that person at the cost of denying who they really are (1989). Forming an identity enables individuals to be honest in their self-talk and to self-disclose, or reveal things about themselves to their partner. John Gottman's research demonstrated that the communication skills of self-disclosure and listening enable enduring couples to have clear "love maps" of each other's interests, values, feelings, and dreams (Gottman & Silver, 1999). Honest communication nurtures trust and shows respect for the other by allowing each partner to maintain his or her differences. A couple who knows each other well can develop a deep love and respect for each other and enjoy each other's company.

"Let there be spaces in your togetherness."
—Kahlil Gibran, *The Prophet*

As evolutionary psychologists have pointed out, the "natural" basis for couple relationships is reproduction. Functionalists also advise people that marriage serves an important economic and social purpose in society. The psychological needs of individuals in companionate relationships are a fairly recent social invention, and therefore are not natural behaviour. People have to learn how to give and take in a loving relationship to meet each other's social and emotional needs (Naiman, 2001). They must learn how to communicate their needs and concerns to their partners (Goldscheider & Waite, 1991). For many people, especially men, this conflicts with the assumption that strength of character means being able to handle emotions and solve problems independently (Johnson & Marano, 1994). Betty Carter, family therapist and author of *Love, Honor and Negotiate: Making Your Marriage Work*, tells couples to each accept responsibility for themselves and their own needs and to take an assertive "I" position by stating what they want in terms that the other person can understand. Individuals who are assertive respect their own and others' needs, and trust that their partner will respond in a positive way (Carter & Peters, 1996).

Couples in satisfying relationships are able to make decisions jointly and to agree on solutions to their problems. Couples develop their strategies by negotiating the everyday details and establishing a shared meaning, or a mutual understanding of what their relationship means, in the early stage. From a systems perspective, they are developing a couple "mythology," an understanding of "who we are," and a set of strategies that will provide a framework for resolving bigger problems when they arise. Successful negotiation requires that each individual accepts the influence of the other by respecting and honouring his or her opinion. Sharing power in this way, putting "us" ahead of "me," results in solutions that are satisfying for both, and makes the relationship more stable. John Gottman found that successful couples turn *to*, not away from, each other when problems arise, and invest time and energy in maintaining the relationship. Couples who have experienced positive solutions in the past are more likely to survive the occasional negative experience (Gottman & Silver, 1999).

"Rituals are the glue that hold a family together."
—Pierre Berton

Zits

© Zits Partnership. Reprinted with special permission of King Features Syndicate.

Few couples are truly **egalitarian,** or equal partners. However, the actual balance of power in a relationship does not matter as much as the couple's shared perception that they negotiate the solutions together (Peplau & Campbell, 2001). During childhood, boys are less likely to accept others' influence than girls are, perhaps because of a biological drive to compete to achieve an evolutionary advantage, so they become men who probably want to solve problems alone. Girls are more likely to accept others' influence because their play tends to be more co-operative, so they become women who want to solve problems together. Gottman found that a husband's acceptance of a wife's influence in decisions was beneficial to the marriage, even in traditional patriarchal relationships (Gottman & Silver, 1999). Dr. Ted Waring, retired professor of psychiatry at Queen's University, believes that a relationship is doomed if one of the pair cannot adjust his or her role in the relationship as a result of the other's influence (Helgerson, 1997).

FYI

Claude Guldner's Six Rs of Marriage

Claude Guldner, Professor Emeritus of Family Studies at the University of Guelph and a family therapist, uses "the 6 Rs" to summarize the systems perspective on the negotiations required in early marriage.

Roots
Roots are the boundaries and strategies learned in your family of origin. They are the "default setting" for your interactions in your new relationship. It is a good idea to check out each other's roots to understand how you have learned to relate to others.

Rhythms
Rhythms regulate the sharing of space, time, and emotional energy within the relationship. Couples need to negotiate the rhythms of separateness and togetherness in a new relationship.

Rules

Rules are the strategies for maintaining the system on a daily basis, but also for dealing with stress and conflict. Couples need to negotiate the mundane routines of their shared lives.

Roles

Roles are the fluctuating power levels in the relationship. The "Power Dance" allows couples to change power levels appropriate to the situation. Couples have to negotiate how they will share power so that they can manage their lives efficiently and avoid power struggles.

Relationships

Relationships pass through a series of stages of development and change in response to the needs of the individuals and the crises in their lives. Couples need to allow time for the relationship to mature, but also be open to change.

Rituals

Rituals are the unique patterns of behaviour that make up a couple or family culture. Creating unique patterns for companionship, affection, and sexuality holds the relationship together as a special place that outsiders do not share.

Problems, Conflict, and Power in Marriage

Problems that require a solution occur in all marriages, but few couples can anticipate what they will be. Potential problems might exist prior to marriage, but they have been difficult for researchers to identify, perhaps because rather than asking for help, couples split up (McGoldrick, 1989). However, when asked, young people in a Montréal study anticipated several problems if they married. Communication was the most frequently mentioned, but they thought that jealousy would probably be a bigger issue in their relationships. The authors, Jean-Marie Boisvert et al., suggested that fear of jealousy results from uncertainty related to today's liberal attitudes toward relationships and greater flexibility in roles. Only one in five of those questioned said they would take premarriage courses, and their concerns were more about adaptation to parenthood. Since the current trend in Canada appears to be for couples to delay marriage until they want to have children, but to cohabit for several years before marriage, perhaps they

Many young people believe that jealousy will be one of the big issues in their relationships.

think they have negotiated their roles already and know how to solve problems (Boisvert, Ladouceur, Beaudry, Freeston, Turgeon, Hardif, & Roussy, 1995).

Conflict, or the opposition of incompatible needs and principles, is natural in marriage because of the problems that individuals face in their lives together. Conflict theory suggests that the nature of intimate relationships and the changing roles of men and women in a diverse post-industrial society such as Canada's result in three related dilemmas for couple relationships:

- individual versus collective interest
- women's rights versus male entitlement
- "mine" versus "yours"

These dilemmas exist in society, but each couple has to deal with them within their own relationship (Dym & Glenn, 1993). On a personal level, the common conflicts resulting from these dilemmas concern two issues:

- division of labour
- expressive quality of the relationship (Dempsey, 2001)

In companionate relationships, the goal is neither sex for reproduction, nor economic efficiency, but maintaining intimacy, so fighting tends to be about how issues affect the balance of individuals versus couple (Johnson & Marano, 1994).

Power is the ability to influence the behaviour of someone else. In personal relationships, the person who has resources that the other needs has the power. In prehistoric times, the women's reproductive and nurturing resources balanced the men's support and physical protection. In industrial society, men who worked to earn the money that was needed to buy the goods and services the family required had greater power than women, because housework was less valued since it was seen as unskilled (Eichler, 1997). In contemporary companionate relationships, the ability to meet the social and emotional needs of another is a source of power that motivates individuals to reciprocate in meeting each other's needs. The **principle of least interest** explains that the person with the least commitment to the relationship actually has the greatest power, since the person with the greater commitment is more likely to give in to maintain harmony (Peplau & Campbell, 2001).

In a recent study to determine what problems couples are likely to experience in contemporary North American marriages, men and women in the United States who had taken a premarriage course offered by the Roman

"No matter how much love you feel, relationships in our money-driven society tend to be governed by the Golden Rule: Whoever has the gold, makes the rules."

—Betty Carter, *Love, Honor and Negotiate*

Catholic Church were asked to rate problems during the first five years of their marriage. The problems they identified related to time, sex, and money:

- balancing job and family
- frequency of sexual relations
- debt brought into marriage
- husband's employment
- financial situation
- household tasks

In general, men and women identified the same issues. They felt that there was a conflict between each person's individual performance in the workplace and their collective responsibility as a couple for the relationship (Lawlor, 2001). Having enough money to afford the lifestyle they want is a problem that many couples face together. However, sharing incomes that may not be equal and managing individual debts are problems likely to arise from the conflict of "mine" versus "yours" over money. Sex becomes a problem when there is conflict about emotional expression, but also from differing demands that cause physical and emotional fatigue. Problems related to household tasks reflect the conflict of traditional male entitlement and women's rights. The problems that arise during the first five years of marriage reflect the challenges of managing underlying conflict in marital roles (Kingston, 1999).

In general, men and women perceive conflict differently. Symbolic interactionism explains that men and women perceive the problems in their relationships differently because they express emotions differently. For example, men might complain that they do not get enough sex, but women might say they have insufficient time with their partner or not enough emotional support. The fact that women have also taken on the man's role of supporting the family but men have not equally taken on the female role of housework creates a different conflict from a woman's point of view than from a man's (Dempsey, 2001). Evolutionary psychologist David Buss explains that women's bodies evolved to recover from stressful events so that they could maintain breastfeeding, or children would not survive. Men evolved to recover slowly and become angry, perhaps so that they were able to fight off danger. Consequently, women are more willing to make complaints and raise conflict in a relationship (Buss, 1994). In general, women expect more than they get in a marriage, and men feel pressured to give more (Gottman & Silver, 1999). Women are more likely to define themselves in terms of their relationships and how they are loved, and consequently feel more responsibility for dealing with issues to maintain the marriage (Cancian, 1987).

web connection

www.mcgrawhill.ca/links/families12

To learn about couple relationships, go to the web site above for *Individuals and Families in a Diverse Society* to see where to go next.

Conflicts can arise in marriages if men and women communicate following conventions suited to their traditional gender roles. Deborah Tannen (1994) explains that male communication is competitive and based on the power of outdoing an opponent, whereas females relate to others on an equal footing. Therefore, when a man talks to a woman, she may be seen as slightly beneath the man, in his terms. Men like talking to women for this very reason. However, these conventions cause difficulty when negotiating solutions to problems. Women soften their complaints, but men are straightforward. Men make strong arguments and expect to be challenged, but women make tentative arguments to seek support, and view challenge as a personal attack. Women complain and expect their partner to commiserate with them, but men respond with a challenge or a suggestion. Men complain and women express sympathy but do not offer a solution (Tannen, 1994). From a symbolic interactionist perspective, gendered communication patterns can interfere with solving problems.

According to John Gottman, most marital conflict cannot be solved, but conflicts do not necessarily ruin a marriage (Gottman, 1999). Based on his observations of couples in a laboratory study, he contends that successful conflict resolution is rarely seen; couples can resolve each problem as it occurs, but the underlying conflicts recur. For example, a couple can negotiate how they will spend their vacation this year, but if one partner prefers quiet relaxation and the other craves adventure, the conflict will arise again next year. Some couples overcome conflict by avoiding arguments about areas of disagreement; others have explosive arguments over the same battles; and others calmly focus on the problems at hand (Gottman & Silver, 1999). Individuals with the basic strength of fidelity realize that they cannot change their partners (Erikson, 1997). However, systems theory explains that if they are willing to change their own behaviour, their partners will have to adjust their behaviour to maintain stability in the relationship (Naiman, 2001). Whatever their style, Gottman found that enduring couples manage conflict by tackling the specific problems that arise in a positive way, allowing themselves to be influenced by their partner, and giving in to the relationship when necessary (Gottman & Silver, 1999).

Money, Housework, and Power

Symbolic interactionism suggests that what is *perceived* as fair in a relationship, rather than an objective measure, affects the satisfaction in a marriage. In traditional marriages, the division of labour, including the paid and unpaid work, is usually perceived by both partners as being fair. Since a man earns the family income by pursuing his individual interests, "his" interests are

"If you're thinking of splitting, remember, you're going to have to take yourself with you."

—David Rubinstein

abstract | Gender Ideology and Perceptions of the Fairness of the Division of Household Labor: Effects on Marital Quality

by Theodore N. Greenstein, Professor, North Carolina State University

Under what circumstances will married women perceive inequalities in the division of household labor as unfair? This research develops and tests a model based on relative deprivation theory that suggests that gender ideology functions as a moderator variable in a process through which inequalities in the division of household labor come to be seen as inequities. Using data from the National Survey of Families and Households, three empirical tests of

the model provide evidence that inequalities in the division of household labor are more strongly related to perceptions of inequity for egalitarian than traditional wives, and that perceptions of inequity are more strongly related to the quality of the marital relationship for egalitarian than for traditional wives. The findings suggest that researchers studying the division of household labor need to shift their focus away from analyses of objective inequalities and toward the study of perceived inequity. ■

Source: *Social forces.* (1996 March). 74 (3), pp. 1029–1042.

assumed to be "theirs." According to symbolic interactionism, men have greater power because they may have more money and may be considered stronger and smarter than women; therefore, men are entitled to make the decisions. Traditional roles are clearly defined for men and women. Dual-income couples expect their relationship to be based on egalitarian decision making and division of labour, but the evidence so far shows that the division of labour has not changed. Change is not occurring because it is not in men's best interests to do more housework, and women are not pressuring them enough to change, perhaps because the social norms reflect the traditional power balance (Dempsey, 2001). Barry Dym and Michael Glenn found that both men and women overestimate the power that the other wields because they both feel they have had to change (1993). Those who expect their relationship to be egalitarian are more likely to see differences as inequitable than those in traditional relationships (Goldscheider & Waite, 1991; Greenstein, 1996).

A comparison of housework over 30 years suggests how couples are negotiating the responsibility for it. Housework was defined as cooking meals, meal clean-up, house cleaning, laundry and ironing, outdoor chores, home repairs, garden and animal care, bills and accounts, but not child care. The results indicate that from 1965 to 1995, the average number of hours of housework done by women declined from 30 to 17.5 hours per week. The average number of hours done by men doubled from 4.9 to 10 hours per week. This result supports the belief that men are doing much more.

Although the ratio of work done by women to that done by men dropped from 6:1 in 1965 to 2:1 in 1995, women still do more than men. The total amount of housework done also declined, despite the fact that homes are an average of 39 percent larger than 30 years ago. Educated men do more housework than those who are less educated, perhaps because they have a greater sense of equity, the study concludes (Dubin, 1999).

What kind of relationships will Canadian couples negotiate in the future? Feminist sociologist Pepper Schwartz described the characteristics of **peer marriage**, a truly egalitarian companionate relationship. She was not able to find many. In these relationships there is no more than a 60:40 traditional division of household and child-care roles. Peer couples have negotiated gender roles so that each is equally responsible for financial and household duties and each partner's work is given equal importance, regardless of the income each receives. When peer couples assess their own relationships, both partners perceive that they have an equal influence over each other and equal control of their shared money. From a social exchange perspective, peer couples identify that their relationship is the most important aspect of their lives and that intimacy and commitment were benefits, but that placing a marriage ahead of careers might mean sacrificing opportunities. Couples reported that it is hard work being fair, especially when there are so few role models, and that their new roles, which were negotiated by agreement over values and flexibility to compromise, found little support from a society that is still organized on traditional roles. The costs of egalitarian marriages might explain why they are so uncommon (Schwartz, 2001).

case study | Emma and Sanjay's Marriage

Sanjay Wadhera and Emma Johnson are in their second year of marriage. They met while they were students at Queen's University and married a year after they both graduated. Sanjay, an Economics graduate, is working for a small investment firm in Toronto that specializes in investment opportunities in the e-business sector of the economy. Emma attends graduate school at the University of Toronto and is presently working on her Ph.D. in International Relations. She is hoping to have a teaching position at either U. of T. or at York University upon graduation. Since apartment rents are so high in Toronto, they have been living in a basement apartment in Emma's parents' home. It is conveniently located, close to both the downtown financial district where Sanjay works and to the university Emma attends. They both hope to be able to move into their own apartment as soon as Emma is employed full time and to eventually buy a small house where they can raise a family.

Although Sanjay and Emma have been happy in their marriage, their financial situation occasionally puts some strains on their relationship. Sanjay had a student loan debt of over $45 000 from his five years at university, and much of his salary is being used to pay down that debt. Emma, on the other hand, came into the marriage debt-free, as her parents contributed toward her education to supplement the money she had earned as a student working part-time and during the summers. Now, part of Sanjay's earnings is being used to pay some of Emma's education costs, since the tuition for graduate programs has tripled in the last four years. Emma's parents have indirectly helped out as well by not charging rent for the basement apartment.

Sanjay and Emma share household responsibilities. Emma grew up in a family in which both finances and household chores were shared as equally as possible. Part of the Johnson's "family lore" is how her father had always done the laundry and had washed and folded all the children's diapers! So Emma came into the marriage with the expectation that Sanjay would also contribute equally. Sanjay, on the other hand, grew up in a more traditional family, in which his mother and older sister primarily looked after the household chores, so his adjustment to living with Emma was a little more difficult. His experience of sharing an apartment with three others while at Queen's University helped in this adjustment, however. Emma and Sanjay have developed a rotating work schedule for the housework that neither of them likes doing. They both feel that it is working fairly well. When they first started living together, Sanjay requested that he not do the laundry. That was fine with Emma, as long as Sanjay looked after cleaning the bathroom. Emma does a lot of her schoolwork at home. When Sanjay returns home from work late, even though it is his responsibility, he is often surprised to find that Emma has not prepared dinner.

Sanjay and Emma both like to cook, so they often entertain by inviting their friends over for dinner. Often, these friends are people they met while attending university or working. Sometimes, Emma will also get together with old high school and neighbourhood friends who are living in the city. Sanjay would like to do this as well, but since he grew up in Burlington, many of his old friends do not live in Toronto. As Emma and Sanjay have chosen not to own a car, visiting Sanjay's friends or family in Burlington is always difficult. When they do go, they generally borrow Emma's parents' car.

Emma and Sanjay's relationship with his parents remains strained. Although they finally have accepted Emma as a daughter-in-law, Sanjay's parents have never felt totally at ease with her, primarily because she is not a daughter of the local Hindu community. They also feel that Emma and Sanjay should be living with them in Burlington. Emma still feels that Sanjay's parents resent her because she "took their son away." Ironically, it is usually Emma who keeps in touch and who arranges the social engagements between them. They do, however, see Sanjay's brother Ameet regularly, since he works as an insurance firm accountant in Toronto and will often stop by before heading home to Burlington. ■

1. Analyze Emma and Sanjay's marriage using Wallerstein's "Psychological Tasks" of marriage. (See page 206.)
2. What problems do you expect Emma and Sanjay will face in the next few years? What factors in their relationship might prevent resolving those problems?
3. Based on the research, what advice would you give them for ensuring that their marriage is successful?

chapter 7 Review and Apply

1. a) What are the various theories of mate selection, what discipline does each reflect, and what characteristics does each explain?

b) Which of the theories do you think is the most effective for explaining mate selection in your community? Justify your choice.

2. The article on arranged marriage, "When Marriage Is a Family Affair," suggests that it and free-choice "love" marriages are simply two places on a continuum. Where would you place personal ads and dating services on the continuum between free-choice and arranged marriages? What other forms of mate selection practised in Canada would you place on the continuum?

3. Based on the research reported in this chapter, summarize the factors that might cause problems in a marriage. Discuss whether these problems could be prevented by making a better choice of marriage partner.

4. a) What are your expectations concerning the division of labour in your potential marriage?

b) How did you acquire these expectations?

c) What challenges will these expectations present if/when you marry?

5. a) Interview couples you know, perhaps neighbours, or friends of your parents, to determine how they met, how they "courted," and how they decided to get married.

b) Record the results as anecdotal summaries—brief descriptions of their experiences written as case studies.

c) Write a research paper in which you analyze their choices using various mate selection theories.

6. Do you agree with Judith Timson's viewpoint in her article, "Matrimony as the Ultimate Adventure"? Write a response expressing and supporting your opinion with evidence from the research done in question 5.

7. a) What are the criteria for social homogamy today? Conduct an observation to determine whether social homogamy determines whom boys and girls in your school community find attractive as dating partners.

b) Analyze the results and design a questionnaire that could be used for a computer dating activity.

c) Why do you think computer dating and matchmaking organizations develop? Do they support a particular theory, or is the idea based in history? Defend your answer.

8. Does television present an accurate picture of marriage, according to the research on marital success? Using the research, develop criteria for assessing an effective marriage relationship and analyze one of your favourite family programs portraying a marriage. Present your analysis as a letter to the producer of your favourite family program. Support your evaluation with anecdotal evidence from recent episodes.

9. Couples who cohabit, and those who cohabit before marriage, are less likely to have a satisfying and lasting relationship than couples that marry. Based on marriage research, design a course for cohabiting couples that might improve their chances of success. Identify the topics you would include and a rationale for each.

Relationship Issues and Trends

CHAPTER EXPECTATIONS

While reading this chapter, you will:

- describe current perceptions, opinions, and demographic trends relating to intimate relationships, and speculate on the significance of these trends for individual and family development
- analyze current issues relating to intimate relationships
- identify the role of various social institutions as they relate to intimate relationships
- demonstrate an understanding of the cycle of violence in intimate relationships and of strategies for avoiding and responding to violence in relationships
- formulate research questions and develop hypotheses reflecting specific theoretical frameworks
- demonstrate an understanding of research methodologies, appropriate research ethics, and specific theoretical perspectives for conducting primary research
- use appropriate, current information technology to access or transmit information
- evaluate information to determine its validity and to detect bias, stereotyping, ethnocentricity, datedness, and unethical practices, and distinguish among perceptions, beliefs, opinions, and research evidence
- use current information technology effectively to compile quantitative data and present statistical analyses of data, or to develop databases
- distinguish among, and produce examples of, the following: an essay arguing and defending personal opinion; a reaction paper responding to another person's argument

Sooner or later, most Canadians form committed couple relationships. Current issues will affect whether they live "happily ever after."

CHAPTER INTRODUCTION

This chapter will examine issues that are affecting intimate relationships and marriages in Canada today. Current perceptions and opinions concerning intermarriage, same-sex relationships, infidelity, spousal violence, and divorce will be examined. Demographic trends will be presented to illustrate the changes in couple behaviour in Canada. Social, economic, religious, and legal aspects will be considered. Various theoretical perspectives will be used to investigate the impact of specific issues on couple relationships, families, and Canadian society.

Relationship Issues

Men and women undertake marriage with the hope of having a meaningful and enduring relationship that meets their needs with someone they love. The motivation to marry is partly a biological desire to form a sexual relationship, perhaps to have children. The married couple is also the primary social group in most societies, as people enjoy their social lives and interact with others as couples. The acceptance of romantic love as a basis for marriage underlines the expectation that marriage meets individuals' need to be loved and desired and the reciprocal need to be exclusively with the one they desire. However, the focus on romantic love clouds the importance of marriage as a social, legal, and religious institution in Canadian society.

Whether couples have the enduring happiness they aspire to when they marry depends on their abilities to negotiate and maintain the relationship within the circumstances that surround them. Relationships that are outside the accepted norms of family or society appear to be less stable on the whole. Marriages between individuals from different social or cultural backgrounds are more likely to end in **divorce**, the legal dissolution of a marriage. It may be that the couples have to negotiate many more aspects of their daily lives because they have come from different lifestyles, or perhaps they have conflicting expectations concerning the roles of husband and wife. Similarly, relationships between partners of the same sex may face difficulties. The expectations and gender roles acquired in their families of origin, Claude Guldner's "roots" (examined in Chapter 7) are confusing when they are clearly linked to gender. Couples who join forces against the opposition of those outside the relationship might gain strength from this alliance, but may lose sight of the challenges of negotiating their own relationship.

Serious problems in negotiating mutually satisfying roles within a relationship might threaten the relationship's stability. Violence and extramarital sexual relationships are problems involving one individual betraying the trust and respect that are the basis of committed relationships. Whether couples will be able to maintain their relationship under these circumstances depends on their ability to change their behaviour. When problems in the relationship seem to be overwhelming, couples may seek counselling, or the help of a third party, in negotiating solutions to their problems. However, divorce has become the solution to a failed marriage for about one-third of married couples in Canada (Ambert, 1998). The various factors affecting the stability of relationships will be examined in this chapter, and the impact of social policy, religious and moral considerations, and legal rights and responsibilities will be considered.

Discussion of issues related to individual lives, family and intimate relationships, and the role of social policy, religion, and law in human lives often elicits strong feelings that are often based on personal experiences. Scholars and researchers conducting investigations into these issues attempt to deal with them objectively by focusing on facts and theories and setting aside their emotions. However, individuals may present their ideas in a more subjective way, allowing their personal beliefs, emotions, and opinions to affect their interpretation of the issues. Others present a biased viewpoint in an attempt to influence the behaviour of others. The Academic Skills Centre at Trent University recommends that you identify bias by asking whether the author uses the following errors in reasoning.

- Does the author **avoid the question** by arguing around the issue without ever actually dealing with it?
- Do the arguments **beg the question** by assuming the thesis is true rather than providing evidence to prove it?
- Does the author **assume something is true** because there is no evidence to prove it false?

- Does the author use **special pleading** to apply the evidence to some cases but not others?
- Does the author resort to **name-calling** and stereotypes to discredit an argument?
- Does the author present **black-and-white thinking** and ignore possibilities between the extremes?
- Does the author present **superstitious thinking** by suggesting a cause-and-effect relationship when there is no evidence to support it?
- Does the author use **non sequiturs** by making conclusions that do not follow logically from the evidence?

Biased sources may be useful for your research if you are careful to gather those that present alternative viewpoints. Understanding individuals' biases concerning issues that affect their personal lives can provide insight into the decisions that people make about their own lives and those concerning social policies and legal rights and responsibilities as citizens of a democratic country. ■

Source: *Thinking it through: a practical guide to academic essay writing. (1989).* Peterborough, ON: Academic Skills Centre, Trent University, 66–68.

Intermarriage

Intermarriage, or **heterogamy**, means marriage between partners who are from different social, racial, religious, ethnic, or cultural backgrounds. It is the opposite of homogamy. Those who advocate marriage between partners who are similar are often quite specific in defining intermarriage, because they identify certain characteristics as the focus of concern. Although interracial marriages, for example, between an African American person and a white person might be controversial in parts of the United States and Canada, interfaith marriages between a Catholic and a Protestant are of greater concern in Northern Ireland, and a marriage between an Aboriginal woman and a white man has some legal implications, involving status, in Canada.

by Ted and Virginia Byfield

Given Canada's multi-ethnic history, marriages of people from different cultures can hardly be considered novel. Yet in the first great wave of immigration to western Canada, between 1900 and 1913, the religious background of the newcomers was Christian, as was the religion of nearly everyone already here. Cultures differed, but religious origins did not. All three versions of Christianity—Catholic, Protestant, and Eastern Orthodox—share much the same Bible, and a common history up to the eleventh century. The same is true of the wave of immigrants from post-World War II Europe who, if not Christian, were from a culture with Christian origins. Even in the third wave, from the 1970s onward, many (perhaps most) of the newcomers are practicing Christians, be they Catholic Filipinos, Anglican blacks from Caribbean and African countries, evangelical Chinese, or Orthodox Lebanese and Egyptians. However, the third wave has also introduced tens of thousands from Muslim or Sikh backgrounds, and the case in point at Prince George concerned one of these. The Sikh girl's wedding to someone from another cultural heritage attracted much local attention.

We personally have been acquainted with probably a dozen interracial marriages—about ten of them marriages of Caucasians with Asians, and two of blacks with whites. All of these survived and, so far as such things can be externally assessed, eminently succeeded. But in nearly all, the parties were both Christians, and would no doubt declare that theirs was indeed a three-way marriage—of husband, wife, and Jesus Christ.

Parents may become understandably concerned, however, when a couple decides that neither cultural nor religious background matters because they love

Mixed culture marriages may still be hindered by cultural differences.

each other and "love conquers all." Whether this idea is valid depends on what they mean by the word "love," and few ever try to define it. It is a dangerous omission, because "love" has become one of the most overworked and under-defined words in the English language. Chances are they share the sensation of being "in love," a kind of wildly emotional interest each has in the other, an obsession that occupies the mind, body, nerves, and imagination in every available waking moment. Never has this condition been more extolled than in the present century. It was the subject of almost every popular song written in North America between roughly 1920 and 1960, and probably half of them since. It was the fuel upon which Hollywood ran from the beginning. It usually involves declarations of lifetime "commitment" and promises an undying passion.

But [it] doesn't deliver on this promise. It never has. Interest in the other party may survive; enjoyment of one another's company may actually increase; but the obsession, the heated passion with which the relationship began, the state of "being in love," rapidly fades. Christian writers regard this as natural and intended. They see the phenomenon of "being in love" as a sort of starter motor whose function is to get the main engine going. But the couple, indoctrinated by the prevailing social attitude, too often regard the starter motor as the whole thing. When it sputters out, they see their marriage as no longer viable. "I don't love her (or him) anymore," they say, as if that ended the commitment.

The parents, knowing all this because they themselves have experienced it, wonder what will sustain the marriage when this condition of infatuation ends. It is here that a cultural and religious tradition should come into play to hold it together. If those factors are absent, they fear the marriage will break up, leaving any children who may meanwhile have arrived minus one parent or the other. And they know their fears of such a failure are valid because they are surrounded by countless instances of it.

In the current circumstances, therefore, you'd wonder why religious schools—whether Christian, Muslim, Jewish, or Sikh—many of which teach endlessly of the wonders wrought by God's "love," don't address themselves more diligently to explaining what they mean by this word. Maybe their students have something quite different in mind. ■

Source: *Alberta Report/Western Report.* (1996, August 5). 23, p. 35.

1. What is Ted and Virginia Byfield's thesis?
2. Explain how the thesis echoes Robert Sternberg's "Triangle Theory" of love. (See Chapter 7, page 196.)
3. What arguments do they present to argue their thesis?
4. What evidence do they use to support their arguments?
5. What further information is required to determine whether their opinion is valid? How could you gather that information?

Intermarriage, whether the difference is racial, religious, or ethnic, appears to be more common, particularly in Canada's urban communities. There are currently no restrictions on intermarriage. There has been very little research on intermarriage in Canada, yet it may be a factor that will affect a couple's satisfaction with their relationship and the durability of that relationship (Wu & Penning, 1997).

In a diverse society such as Canada's, children of all races, religions, and ethnic groups attend school together and grow up together. In many ways, they are socialized at school, in community activities such as Scouts or sports, and through increasing exposure to television and other media, into a similar mass culture. The more successful people become as a society in raising children to be "colour blind," to see others who are of a different race, religion, or ethnicity as equal and similar in culture, the more likely it is that young people will meet, be attracted to, and fall in love with someone from a different background.

Problems in interracial marriages are more likely to arise because of the racist attitudes of others than from differences between the partners.

The differences, if there are any, between individuals of different races, religions, or ethnic backgrounds exist in their personal family lives. Claude Guldner describes the different expectations, customs, roles, and rituals of family life as the "roots" of a family because they nurture and support individuals and families, yet they are invisible (1982). Intermarriage brings together two individuals who share a similar contemporary culture but discover that they have different "roots" when they begin to negotiate the roles, rules, and rituals of their marriage.

Interracial marriages are the most visible forms of intermarriage. Research on interracial marriage reflects the concerns of the societies. In the United States, prejudices about race have resulted in assumptions that individuals who marry someone of another race are motivated by rebellion against their families or by a desire to marry up by choosing someone of a more "desirable" race. Clayton Majete, an American sociologist and anthropologist, negates those assumptions in his research (1997). When individuals have similar socio-economic backgrounds, racial differences have little impact on the aspirations of individuals, on their reasons for marrying, or on the daily routines of their married life, but the couple may have to identify more with one racial community than the other. Interracial couples adjust to marriage as well as any couple does. The real challenge of interracial marriage is raising a biracial child, because it requires that both partners reflect on their individual identities. To help their child develop a positive identity, the couple must first reflect on the role that race plays in determining their own identities (Majete, 1997).

Couples in interfaith marriages in Canada face a different set of problems because faith, unlike race, is a chosen attribute, as it is possible to convert to another faith. Partners in interfaith relationships may appear to be very similar and usually have a similar economic and educational background, but their family and social experiences might have been quite different. Unlike interracial couples who face the challenges of racism in society together, couples of different faiths face difficulties within their families and relationships. Of course, they will have to decide how they will recognize holidays and festivals, but on a deeper level, they also have to examine their personal and cultural value systems to negotiate the daily lifestyle they will share with each other. Studies of lasting marriages suggest that common values, similar leisure

web connection

www.mcgrawhill.ca/links/families12

To learn more about intermarriage in Canada, go to the web site above for *Individuals and Families in a Diverse Society* to see where to go next.

by Clayton Majete, Professor of Sociology and Anthropology, City University of New York

RESEARCH QUESTIONS

1. Why do Blacks and Whites marry each other?
2. How are their marriages different from or the same as same-race marriages?
3. How do they overcome the overt racial prejudices in society to function in their relationship?

HYPOTHESIS

Interracial marriage is misunderstood because it is distorted by myth and bias based on the racial divisions in society.

RESEARCH METHOD

Using *survey method*, during the 1990s, Majete interviewed over 200 American, interracial middle-class couples who volunteered to participate. The couples were well-educated, with 25 percent of the partners having post-graduate degrees. Although 6 out of 10 women worked outside the home, 90 percent of the couples reported a traditional patriarchal marriage structure.

RESULTS

- These are love relationships. Couples met at school, at work, or at social events, and in most cases the White partner initiated the relationship. Partners have similar socio-economic backgrounds. There is no evidence that the marriages were motivated by a desire to improve the social status of either partner.
- Over 75 percent of families are accepting of interracial marriage, although Black families are more accepting than White families. Three-quarters

of Black families have no problem with their son's or daughter's choice to marry a White person, but three out of ten White families were concerned. The responses of families ranged from acceptance to hesitation to outright hostility, but most couples were eventually accepted and supported by their families. Those couples whose families were hostile were distressed by their reaction. This indicates that the marriage is not motivated by rebellion against the family of origin.

- As anticipated, the major concerns were about racial identity, the values that society places on race, and raising biracial children in a country that requires a racial identification. Although couples had struggled with racism, parents developed strategies such as adding "biracial" to the list; however, by historical precedent in America, biracial means "Black." Most reported that their children had adjusted well and had no more problems than middle-class Black children.

CONCLUSIONS

Majete concludes that the hypothesis is proven. Couples in his study perceive themselves to be ordinary middle-class couples with the same concerns about their personal aspirations and their shared relationships as same-race couples. He suggests that the assumption that there are more problems than actually exist creates stress for interracial couples. Couples have responded by communicating openly about racial issues and by choosing to live in interracial communities. ■

Source: Majete, C. (1997, July 1). "What you may not know about interracial marriages." *The World & I.* 12, p. 300.

Decisions about the daily rituals of their faiths require that individuals in an interfaith marriage consider the roles that religious faith and culture play in their lives.

interests, and an active social life are important (Whyte, 2001). Couples who respect each other and are willing to compromise can find ways to share their lives. However, individuals from different faith backgrounds have to choose whether to compromise some of their beliefs and customs or to accept their spouse's beliefs and customs as well as their own. The couple must also decide what faith identity to provide for their children. Unlike race, faith is a chosen attribute that determines membership in a faith community. It is not surprising that interfaith marriages are more likely to succeed if at least one partner does not practise his or her religion or is willing to convert.

Marriage between individuals of different ethnic backgrounds is perhaps the most complex form of heterogamy. Ethnicity can be a complex mixture of national and racial heritage, religion, and culture. In Canada, where many people are "hyphenated Canadians" or have two cultures—for example, Japanese-Canadian—self-identification as a member of an ethnic group suggests that an individual adheres to the specific value system, family structure, and role expectations that are associated with that ethnic group. The major variations among ethnic groups involve gender roles within marriage and in the workplace, the independence and responsibilities of children, and the relationship between the conjugal and the extended family. Each of these affects how a couple will negotiate their relationship at each stage (Baker, 2001). However, now that most women are working outside the home, that children are staying in school longer, and that social programs are providing some support for families, differences among ethnic groups are decreasing.

Same-Sex Relationships

Over the past several decades, there has been increasing acceptance of heterosexual cohabitation, but there has been great resistance to the recognition of same-sex relationships. However, in recent years, there has been a tremendous acceleration in the acknowledgment of such relationships. A survey released in April 2001 showed that 55 percent of Canadians supported same-sex marriages, and another in June 2001 concluded that 65 percent supported them (Environics Research Group, 2001). The 2001 Canada Census for the first time asked people whether they lived with a common-law partner of the same sex and explicitly stated that children of a person's common-law, same-sex partner should be considered that person's children as well. Some argue that continuing discrimination against lesbians and gay men will result in under-reporting of lesbian and gay families. Kathleen Lahey, who studies gay, lesbian, bisexual, transgender, and transsexual people, summarized their feelings (1988, pp. 262–263):

> Because I have now gone through the emotional process of realizing how much of myself I have had to shut down in order to function as a lesbian woman in Canadian society, I know that other doors must still lock important parts of my heart. And now that I am a member of a family, I know that important parts of my children's hearts are under lock and key as well. They know, as do I, that many areas of concrete discrimination and social disapproval still affect all of us. They know, as do I, that our entire family is still legally incapacitated in many ways that would never even occur to other people.

The existence of couple relationships between individuals of the same sex challenged our understanding of love and marriage long before the contemporary debate concerning whether they should have the right to marry. Same-sex relationships have always existed. In his discussion of the meaning of love, the ancient Greek philosopher Plato suggested that early humans were essentially two people combined, and that there were three sexes: those with two male halves, those with two female halves, and those with one of each. As punishment for their misbehaviour, the god Zeus cut all humans into two people, each of them doomed to wander the Earth in search of his or her other half. Since then, there have been homosexual men, lesbians, and heterosexuals, all seeking their other half, the one person with whom they can share themselves and their lives (Sullivan, 1997). In Plato's Greece, homosexual relationships were commonplace and were considered to be normal. Today, the legal debate concerning same-sex relationships challenges society to examine the purpose of marriage and the role of intimate relationships in the lives of individuals. At the root of the debate is whether homosexuality is normal and, therefore, acceptable (Sullivan, 1997).

In Canada, intimate relationships are usually based on the romantic attraction of partners, not on the traditional responsibilities that are defined in the law or by religious beliefs. Few heterosexual couples would identify their legal entitlement to spousal benefits as their reason to marry. Gays and lesbians, on the other hand, are not allowed to marry legally, but they acquired many of the economic benefits of heterosexual spouses in Canada in 2000 and are free to enter into financial contracts with each other.

by Rachel Giese

With a crowded press gallery, a protester claiming to be a messenger from Jesus, and a notice asking for money for the legal fund (in lieu of gifts), it wasn't exactly a romantic wedding. But that wasn't the point. Anne and Elaine Vautour, Joe Varnell, and Kevin Bourassa have already been married, spiritually at least, in holy union ceremonies. Sunday's double wedding was about politics, not romance. About calling the provincial and federal governments' bluff and forcing their hand on gay marriage.

It's a testament to the durability of the mythology of marriage that people of both sides of the debate remain so passionate. After all, giving same-sex couples the right to legally marry wouldn't considerably alter the status quo. Gay couples already live together, raise children together, and receive almost all the benefits (health insurance, pensions, etc.) that "straight" married and common-law couples receive.

What's at stake here is something far less tangible, but arguably even more important: Winning the legal right to marry may not matter much materially to gay couples, but for some it would be a critical psychological victory. Because, at its heart, this is about seeking approval and acceptance. For people who have suffered daily indignities and hurts of parental rejection, not having a partner included at an office event, or being stared at disapprovingly for an innocent act of public affection, receiving approval is no mean feat.

Of course, the psychology runs both ways. There is something pathological about straight people erecting barriers around an institution they've so thoroughly mangled. Not to mention something pathetic about those who went to the Metropolitan Community Church on Sunday to voice their disapproval of the union of two couples whom they've never even met.

Anne Vautour, left, places a ring on the finger of her partner, Elaine Vautour, as Reverend Brent Hawkes looks on during their wedding ceremony at the Metropolitan Community Church in Toronto.

It's fair to say that marriage is in crisis or, at least, in a time of tremendous revolution: 50 percent of straight unions end in divorce and a woman and man who have never met can legally wed on television as a game show finale. And people think that gay marriage mocks this heterosexual institution? The only place to put blame for the erosion of traditional families is squarely on traditional families themselves.

Yesterday I received an e-mail from a frustrated television producer: "Look," she wrote, "we really want to do something on gay marriage, but aside from pointing out the two sides of this, what can we talk about? Is there any new angle on this debate?" To answer her question, I'd say that I'm fascinated by how such a private and intimate matter is being battled over in such a public way.

There isn't anything more personal than deciding how one chooses, acknowledges, and lives with a companion. So, to me, it's odd that there should be rules at all about how those unions should be celebrated, or whether some deserve more merit and respect than others. No one—gay or straight—should have to seek permission or approval of their relationship. People should not feel compelled to marry if it isn't meaningful to them, just as they should not be denied the right to marry if, for them, it's a valuable ritual.

The government shouldn't be involved in recognizing or validating relationships at all. There's no compelling reason. The way forward isn't to legalize gay marriage, but to delegalize marriage, making it strictly a private arrangement, with no automatic benefits, privileges, or responsibilities conferred at all. Which isn't to say that there couldn't be legal frameworks to relationships, just not one standard, Grade-A, government-approved one.

To protect themselves and their interests, people entering into a domestic arrangement could draw up contracts, wills, powers-of-attorney, and so on, to suit their own needs and situations, to make provisions for the joint ownership of property, occasions of financial dependence, and the raising of children.

Marriage, then, would strictly be a private and personal matter, with weddings, celebrated according to one's own spiritual, religious, and aesthetic values. Individual churches and congregations could decide their own criteria for who they would and wouldn't marry. People could create whatever kind of ceremony they want and use whatever terms—husband, wife, spouse, partner—they feel suited them.

It sounds radical, even heretical, but separating the legal and financial components of marriage from its emotional and spiritual ones would actually restore the deepest and most profound purpose of marriage—to celebrate the free choice of two people to make a home and life together. And that, I think, is the very thing needed to revive and rejuvenate this battered and fought-over institution. ■

Source: *The Toronto Star*. (2001, January 18). p. A31.

1. What thesis is Rachel Giese arguing in this essay?
2. What arguments does she use to support her thesis?
3. What appears to be the theoretical perspective behind her arguments?
4. Giese admits that this is a radical idea. What are the arguments against her thesis? What evidence can you offer to support these arguments?

Canadian law, reflecting the dominant Judeo-Christian heritage of early Canadians, assumes that couples are heterosexual, although often this fact is not stated. Religious opponents of homosexual relationships quote from the Bible to argue that God condemns them, whereas other religious scholars within Judaism and Christianity argue that the literal interpretation of the Bible no longer governs most sexual behaviour (John, 1997). Some Christian and Jewish religious scholars believe that God created homosexuality as normal behaviour for a minority of human beings, and therefore same-sex couples who wish to enter a relationship based on love and commitment should be able to have their relationship blessed within their faith (Spong, 1997; Kahn, 1997).

Those who argue for legalizing same-sex relationships suggest that marriage would provide the same protection to partners and their children in existing gay and lesbian families that it provides to heterosexual couples (Stacey, 2001).

In the midst of the public debate about whether their relationships are acceptable, gay and lesbian couples are more concerned about the roles their relationship plays in their own lives. Gays and lesbians want stable love relationships based on affection and companionship (Peplau, 1988). Contrary to the stereotypes, same-sex relationships do not mimic heterosexual gender roles, with partners playing complementary male-female roles. An individual's gender identity as male or female is not affected by his or her homosexuality. Therefore, gay and lesbian couples who have few role models as they negotiate their relationships are more likely to choose roles on the basis of interests and personal strengths (Marecek, Finn, & Cardell, 1988). Satisfaction with same-sex relationships seems to depend on the same variables as heterosexual relationships: mutual respect, shared values and goals, and the ability to manage conflict (Jones & Bates, 1988). During the last decades of the twentieth century, as sociologists and psychologists began to study homosexual relationships as alternative, rather than deviant, lifestyles, it has become evident that, regardless of their sexual orientation, individuals have the same expectations of their intimate relationships.

The debate about same-sex relationships can be viewed from several theoretical perspectives. Questions concerning whether same sex-relationships are normal and whether they benefit society reflect the functionalist view of male and female roles in society. These often focus on procreation as the foundation of the family (Arkes, 1997). Symbolic interactionism can be used to investigate how being gay or lesbian affects individual identity and the nature of homosexual relationships (DeCecco & Shively, 1988). Systems theory can be used to explain how couples establish their lives together. Developmental theory can be used to illustrate how enduring same-sex relationships progress through a series of stages as couples adjust their relationships through the inevitable crises presented in the lifespan (McWhirter & Mattison, 1988). Each point of view on same-sex relationships requires that people clarify their values, beliefs, and expectations concerning sexuality and intimate relationships.

Infidelity

Sexual fidelity remains an important value in intimate relationships in Canada (Nett, 1993). Although evolutionary psychologists' studies suggest that it is inherent in the nature of humans to be unfaithful, the norms of

legal matters | Same-Sex Relationships

by Justice Marvin Zuker

In Canada, gays and lesbians are recognized in a variety of legislative schemes as spouses or quasi-spouses but they cannot choose marriage. The most significant developments in the recognition of same-sex unions have occurred in employment and benefits concerns because sexual orientation is a prohibited ground of discrimination under many human rights statutes, including the Ontario Human Rights Code. In 2001, eight couples from Ontario, one couple from Québec, and five couples from British Columbia began legal actions to end what they feel is discrimination. They are seeking a court order that they be granted licences to marry, and a declaration that any law, practice, or policy of government that restricts otherwise lawful marriages between two persons of the same sex is contrary to the Charter of Rights and is, therefore, unenforceable.

Although the federal government has jurisdiction over capacity to marry, the provinces have jurisdiction over the solemnization of marriage. Except in Québec, provincial legislation does not require that a couple be of the opposite sex in order to marry, although the statutes do contain language that presumes the parties are heterosexual (the vows must include the words "husband" and "wife," for example). However, when Parliament enacted the Modernization of Benefits and Obligations Act, S.C. 2000, c. 12, it included in section 1.1 of that Act, under the title "interpretation," the following:

> For greater certainty, the amendments made by this Act do not affect the meaning of the word "marriage"; that is, the lawful union of one man and one woman to the exclusion of all others.

It is important to distinguish religious marriage from civil marriage. Only the latter is in issue in the same-sex marriage claims currently before the courts. Legally extending civil marriage to same-sex partners would not require religious congregations, contrary to their beliefs, to marry same-sex partners. The Charter's guarantee of freedom of religion would presumably protect religious congregations from any legislative attempt to compel them to perform same-sex marriages. While human rights legislation prohibits discrimination on the basis of sexual orientation with respect to access to services customarily available to the public, it is doubtful whether marriage in any particular religious congregation would ever be held to be a service customarily available to the public. Therefore, same-sex partners could not legally compel a religious organization to marry them. ■

Western societies define extramarital sexual relationships as unacceptable behaviour. According to Helen Fisher (1992) and David Buss (1994), early man was motivated to have many sexual partners to enhance his chance of having offspring, whereas woman tended to be very selective about her sexual partners to improve the chances of having the man stay to support their offspring. There is no evidence that the sexual activity of humans is still motivated by these biological drives. Limiting sexual partners benefits a society because it strengthens the conjugal family, ensuring the greatest population growth and the support and socialization of offspring (Conway, 1997).

Functionalists explain that all societies define role behaviours for individuals to ensure that the functions of society are met and that the social norms defining role behaviours are passed on through the process of socialization. Adultery does not work to the benefit of society, so people are taught that it is wrong.

web connection

www.mcgrawhill.ca/links/families12

To learn more about the topic of infidelity, go to the web site above for *Individuals and Families in a Diverse Society* to see where to go next.

Many Canadians do not approve of extramarital affairs. When Reginald Bibby asked Canadians in the early 1980s whether they approved of sex outside marriage, three out of four Canadian men and women considered extramarital sex to be wrong under any circumstances (1983). In 1998, a poll conducted by *Maclean's* magazine and the Canadian Broadcasting Corporation (CBC) found that attitudes had not changed: 89 percent said that it was "unacceptable" to have an extramarital affair, and 72 percent found it "very unacceptable" (Clark, 1998). Family therapist Betty Carter writes that in all her years of counselling married couples, she has never seen a situation in which partners accepted an extramarital affair (Carter & Peters, 1996). The actual rate of sexual **infidelity** is more difficult to determine. Some popular sources, such as *The Monogamy Myth* (Vaughan, 1998), suggest that, based on informal surveys,

An affair can be an exciting sexual adventure, but it has a short life. Although infidelity usually results in divorce, few individuals marry their extramarital lovers.

60 percent of men and 40 percent of women have had extramarital sex. When the General Social Survey, conducted by the National Opinion Research Center at the University of Chicago, asked a representative sample of Americans, "Have you ever had extramarital sex?" 23 percent of men and 12 percent of women said they had (Wiederman, 1999). Considering the results of the *Maclean's*/CBC poll, if the statistics are the same in Canada, many people have extramarital sex despite their opinion that it is unacceptable behaviour.

Contrary to the excuses that evolutionary psychology might suggest, extramarital affairs do not appear to be about sex. Psychologists and marriage counsellors have found that individuals have affairs when their needs are not met in their marriages (Carter & Peters, 1996; Anderson, 2001). Just as the first stage of a marriage relationship is passionate and exciting (Goldstine, Larner, Zucherman, & Goldstine, 1977), so infidelity is more exciting than marriage, not because the sex is better but because of the initial passion of a secret relationship, apart from the routine of everyday life (Leibow, 1995). Research on moral development suggests that individuals act initially out of self-interest, then learn to consider the needs of others, before becoming mature enough to conform to social norms of right and wrong and to accept the rules of society. David Leibow explains that an individual who has an affair when the opportunity arises is acting out of self-interest because affairs are "narcissistically gratifying" (Leibow, 1995, p. 73), and so affairs represent immature moral behaviour in an adult.

The behaviour of men and women differs when it comes to illicit sex. Perhaps because of the original biological motivation, men are more likely to have an extramarital relationship that is primarily sexual, whereas women are more likely to seek an "affair" based on romance and affection and to have sex only when they are "in love" (Nannini, 2000). The fact that intimate friendships would not be counted as extramarital sex might account for the gender difference in infidelity rates. This same motivation explains why women are more tolerant of sexual infidelity than emotional infidelity in their partners, but men are more threatened by their partner's sexual infidelity than by their emotionally intimate relationships (Nannini, 2000). That men have greater opportunity for affairs and seek younger women for extramarital affairs could explain why one-third of men aged 60 to 69 reported one or more affairs, but the peak rate for women was 19 percent, of those aged 40 to 49. Another possible explanation is the "double standard" that tolerates and even expects more sexual activity for men than for women (Wiederman, 1999).

Infidelity results in divorce 65 percent of the time (Anderson, 2001). Prior to the legalization of divorce in Canada, extramarital affairs were tolerated as a solution to unsuccessful marriages as they have been in most societies for thousands of years (Kelman, 1998). Now that couples can divorce when they have irreconcilable differences, infidelity is the most common reason given for divorce. When an unfaithful partner leaves careless clues about an affair, the infidelity might be a "cry for help" that the relationship is in trouble and can be salvaged with effort from both partners (Carter & Peters, 1996). In these cases, Betty Carter suggests that counselling can help the couple recover from the affair and negotiate a better relationship. John Gottman (1999) counters that, although affairs don't cause a marriage breakdown, few can recover from infidelity, because it destroys the trust in a relationship. The "wronged party" feels betrayed and humiliated, especially if others know about the affair. Marriage and enduring relationships cannot compete with an illicit affair for excitement. When a secret affair is maintained for a long time, the marriage is probably over, but very few people go on to marry their lovers (Carter & Peters, 1996).

by Norma Fitzpatrick

One recent Friday night, my husband and I sat around our kitchen table with Robert, a close mutual friend. We mentioned to him that we had recently come to an agreement regarding certain guidelines concerning my husband's behaviour. The guidelines included: not drinking alone socially with another woman, not dancing with a female when I am not present, and not physically touching a woman in a way he would not do to a male, such as rubbing her back in a supportive manner. In short, anything that could lead to being misconstrued as flirting.

I looked at Robert's eyes widen as his mouth opened just enough to let a quietly controlled gasp of disbelief escape. I felt an explanation was needed to restore his usually sedate exterior. "I expect my husband to be attracted to other women throughout our married lives, just as I may be to other men," I told him. "What I don't expect is for him to put himself in a position where he has the opportunity to act on these attractions. Flirting presents this opportunity. I will do the same for him and avoid placing myself in these situations where men are concerned."

Robert contemplated my explanation as he looked off momentarily to the right corner of the ceiling. He was silent. He prided himself on being diplomatic and I knew he was trying to temper his reaction and his words. He failed. "You must be worried that your husband will cheat on you. You, of all people, are feeling insecure? A woman who could model for Victoria's Secret?" His eyes pierced mine as he looked for a hint of the insecurity he felt he heard in my words.

Although I was flattered, our friend was missing the point. I feel comfortable with the manner in which my husband conducts himself socially. He is

This woman (background right) feels comfortable about her husband socializing with other women because, as a couple, they have established behaviour guidelines for their interactions with the opposite sex.

the life of the party and feels at ease in my presence to talk and dance with any woman without fear of hurting my feelings or suffering repercussions from me later on, in private. He also enjoys the occasional weekend trip and night out with his male friends. In 14 years, he has never given me cause to doubt his fidelity. And I know he never will.

Not in 14 years have I ever curtailed his social activities. He has a strong personality, being both assertive and, when need be, aggressive in his personal and professional lives. Even if I wished to, he would not allow me to control him. I, however, don't want to make the arrogant mistake of assuming my husband and I are immune to the human fallibility of being tempted, even fleetingly, to act on our impulses at least once in our lives. I have faith our marriage is perfect in every way—we are each other's best friends and supportive partners in all that we do. I have faith we will remain loyal to each other. But it is not a blind faith, rather an educated, deliberated one.

Failed marriages, not unlike successful ones, usually start with a promise to love each other forever and remain monogamous—not the intention to seize the opportunity to act on attractions to others. According to Statistics Canada, more than one in every three Canadian marriages end in divorce. Nearly one in five divorce applicants cite infidelity as the reason for their marital break-up.

Stating aloud guidelines assures husband and wife are of one mind and know what is and is not acceptable to each other. What may be friendliness to one may be a flirtation to another. To state the obvious is good. It leaves no room for misinterpretation or misunderstanding by either partner.

I have personally seen the powerful threat that seemingly innocent flirtations can be to a marriage: my boss's endearing smiles and excessive compliments to his assistant culminated in a five-year affair; and my married neighbour ran away with another's husband after countless flirtations flowed unchecked between them at different neighbourhood parties.

I admit, for the time being, my husband will be the one who will have to exercise the code more than me. He is an entrepreneur in the beauty industry—an industry dominated by young, attractive women, where socializing and working with women is a part of daily business. He also regularly attends week-long conferences in other countries to which he must bring some of his employees—again, predominantly young, attractive, and often single ladies.

I, on the other hand, have temporarily put my career on hold and am proud to be a stay-at-home mother. My closest encounter with the opposite sex is usually an inadvertent brush of the hand with some 17-year-old, acne-prone boy as he passes me my grocery bags. Not exactly an adrenaline rush.

I also admit that although we both collaborated on these guidelines and my husband is happy with the outcome because he, too, places our marriage above all else, I was the one who initiated the conversation. Unlike our friend, Robert, I see this initiation as a sign of security, not insecurity. I am not afraid to discuss what could be seen as an unpleasant issue for fear it may end up opening a Pandora's box and become a self-fulfilling prophecy. I am also secure enough to know that even though I see myself as attractive, intelligent, and kind, my husband may still occasionally be attracted to other women. He is, like me, a human—not a saint. To him, however, I am worth showing respect by not acting in ways that would make me feel uncomfortable.

Regardless of which spouse opens up the discussion or has more interactions with the opposite sex, protecting a marriage from opportunities to be unfaithful is not a frivolity born from insecurity, rather a wisdom born from a mixture of realism and a wish to create and maintain the best marriage possible. ■

Source: Fitzpatrick, N. (2000, October 5). "Fear Pandora's box? not me." *The Globe and Mail*.

1. What thesis does Norma Fitzpatrick argue in her essay?
2. What arguments does she present to support her thesis?
3. What assumptions does she make about human behaviour? What theoretical perspective do these assumptions reflect?
4. What data would you need to determine whether the assumptions are valid? How could you gather the data?
5. Would you accept for yourself the agreement that Norma and her husband have negotiated for their relationship?

Spousal Violence

In 1999, 8 percent of women and 7 percent of men in marriage or common-law relationships in Canada reported that they had been the **victim** of violence, or the person mistreated, by their partner in the past five years. The rate for women was down from 12 percent in 1993, but this was the first time that a rate had been determined for men (Johnson & Hotton, 2001). The North American ideal of a happy marriage based on enduring romantic love is tarnished by the reality that marriage can be dangerous, especially for women. Since **spousal violence** was first defined as a problem in the 1970s, research has resulted in a better understanding of the nature of violence, and the differences between ineffective conflict resolution skills or "arguments that get out of hand" and systematic violence (Browne, 1997). Using various theoretical approaches, researchers have attempted to explain the causes of spousal violence and to determine how it can be prevented.

Violence is any action that is intended to physically hurt someone, but it is only defined as a problem by the context. For example, just as a fistfight in a hockey game is defended as "just part of the game," hitting a wife or a child was considered acceptable, even necessary, discipline in the past. The expression "rule of thumb" dates back to nineteenth-century common law, which gave a man the right to use a stick no thicker than his thumb to chastise his chattels; that is, his wife, children, and servants. In the early and mid-twentieth century, **domestic violence** was assumed to be a private matter. Police could lay charges only if they actually witnessed the assault themselves. Family and neighbours minded their own business. Women who sought help from their clergy were advised to return home and to work out the problem with their husbands. Early in the twentieth century, women who left their husbands were guilty of desertion. They lost custody of their children and were entitled to no support. When divorce was legalized early in the twentieth century, cruelty was grounds for divorce, but was difficult to prove. Until recently, men who beat their wives were protected from the justice system, and women had no choice but to stay in an abusive home. However, by the 1970s, public opinion about violence changed. Violence within intimate relationships is now legally defined as **assault**. Recent legal changes require that police respond to domestic violence calls and lay charges when there is evidence of assault (Conway, 1997; Ward, 1994).

In the 1970s, spousal violence was regarded as ineffective conflict resolution and the power struggle between husbands and wives. This viewpoint was supported by evidence that spousal violence occurred in relationships of all socio-economic, religious, and ethnic backgrounds. Some people developed

web connection

www.mcgrawhill.ca/links/families12

To learn about marital violence, go to the web site above for *Individuals and Families in a Diverse Society* to see where to go next.

"When we do evil
We and our victims
Are equally
bewildered."

—W. H. Auden

Types of Violence in Marital Unions

| | Violence by Previous Spouse | | | | Violence by Current Spouse | | | |
| | Total | | Violence Ended at Separation | | Total | | Violence Occurred After Separation | |
	No. (000s)	%	No. (000s)	%	No. (000s)	%	No. (000s)	%
Total Violence								
Female Victims	**437**	**100**	**264**	**100**	**259**	**110**	**172**	**100**
Threatened to hit	307	70	168	64	145	56	137	80
Threw something	211	48	122	46	90	35	88	51
Pushed, grabbed	378	87	228	87	187	72	150	87
Slapped	203	46	113	43	77	30	89	52
Kicked, bit, or hit	177	41	102	39	50	19	75	44
Hit with something	127	29	65	25	28*	11*	61	35
Beat	139	32	71	27	33*	13*	68	40
Choked	114	26	56	21	26*	10*	58	34
Used or threatened to use a gun or knife	86	20	40	15	—	—	46	27
Sexual assault	117	27	57	22	21*	8*	60	35
Total Violence								
Male Victims	**259**	**100**	**173**	**100**	**303**	**100**	**83**	**100**
Threatened to hit	173	67	107	62	162	53	66	79
Threw something	147	57	99	57	163	54	46	55
Pushed, grabbed	135	52	84	48	103	34	51	61
Slapped	162	63	109	63	153	51	53	64
Kicked, bit, or hit	161	62	102	59	124	41	59	71
Hit with something	93	36	60	35	53	17	33	0
Beat	41	16	25*	14*	13*	4*	16*	20*
Choked	18*	7*	—	—	—	—	—	—
Used or threatened to use a gun or knife	35*	14*	20	12	—	—	15	19
Sexual assault	—	—	—	—	—	—	—	—

— Amount too small to be expressed.
* Coefficient of variation is high (16.6% to 33.3%).
Percentages may not total 100% due to rounding.

Source: Adapted from the Statistics Canada publication, *Family Violence in Canada: A Statistical Profile 2001*, Catalogue 85-224, June 2001, Table 4.6, pg. 39.

1. What is the male/female ratio for victims of violence?
2. What are the most common types of violence experienced by male victims and by female victims?
3. Compare the incidence and types of violence during a marital union, ending at separation and continuing after separation, for male and female victims.
4. Does the data in this table provide evidence for Conway's argument that the violence experienced by female victims is more serious than the violence experienced by male victims?
5. What additional data would be required to complete your understanding of spousal violence? How could this data be gathered?

effective ways of settling their conflict amicably, and a minority of people used violent tactics. The **intergenerational cycle of violence** describes the evidence that individuals who experienced violence or abuse as a child, or who observed the assault or abuse of their mothers, are more likely to become either victims or perpetrators of violence in their intimate relationships (Nett, 1993). Social role theory suggests that individuals learn how to behave in a role such as "wife" or "husband" by observing and imitating significant role models. If violence is learned behaviour, and spousal violence results from arguments that get out of hand, social role theorists suggest that both victims and perpetrators of violence can learn more effective ways of dealing with anger and resolving conflict to break the **cycle of violence** (Lynn & O'Neill, 1995). The solutions put forth by social role theorists include counselling those who use violence and counselling children and youth who have experienced or witnessed violence. Domestic violence could be prevented by ensuring that individuals learn anger management, communication, and conflict resolution skills.

The focus on spousal violence in the 1970s and 1980s revolved around why women stayed in violent or abusive relationships. This focus reflected the systems theory perspective that views all participants as part of the problem and suggested that if the woman left, then the violence would stop. The cycle of violence, described by Lenore E. Walker in 1979, explained that the violent phase of the cycle was followed by a period in which the perpetrator was apologetic and remorseful or, at worst, acting as if nothing had happened. For couples with a commitment to a relationship, it was possible for both partners to believe that the violence would not happen again. Systems theory explains that the couples had established a pattern of interaction that is difficult to change. The social exchange perspective, on the other hand, suggested that women stayed because the consequences of leaving the relationship were worse than tolerating occasional assaults. Women usually experienced many bouts of violence before eventually leaving a violent spouse. Women's shelters, transition houses, and counselling programs have been established in communities across Canada to help women break out of the cycle of violence and begin to establish a new life for themselves and their children.

The conventional understanding that spousal violence was a universal problem that affected couples of all walks of life was challenged by an analysis of the 1993 Violence Against Women Study. The evidence in this Canadian study suggested that poor men were twice as likely to beat their wives as well-off men, and half the perpetrators were under 29 years of age. The following key risk factors were identified, and the presence of each of these factors increased

The Cycle of Violence

TENSION BUILDING

CALM-AND-PENANCE

ABUSIVE INCIDENT

- **The tension-building phase** The victim attempts to maintain equilibrium by carefully acquiescing to her partner's demands. As the tension builds with any stress or conflict, the victim rationalizes minor violent outbursts and often accepts responsibility for them. This phase can last a long time.
- **The abusive incident or acute battering phase** One or more serious assaults occur, triggered by an event that is usually unpredictable. Medical treatment might be required. The victim might report the assault to the police or seek help, but she is more likely to conceal the fact that she was assaulted. As the cycle is repeated, the victim responds with anger and disbelief that the perpetrator has not kept his promise, or with relief that what she had feared would happen was finally over. This phase lasts 2 to 24 hours.
- **The calm-and-penance phase** The perpetrator becomes remorseful and apologetic and attempts to make up for the violence by affectionate or romantic acts, and promises never to do it again. The victim might withdraw her threats to leave, or refuse to give evidence against her partner. This phase may last a day or a few months, until the tension begins to build again.

Source: Timothy Jackson and Jeff Olson, *When Violence Comes Home.* Copyright 1995 by RBC Ministries, Grand Rapids, MI. Reprinted by permission. The cycle of violence was first identified by Lenore E. Walker (*The Battered Woman*, Harper Perennial, 1979).

1. Systems theory suggests that both victim and perpetrator are caught within the cycle of violence. What would motivate each of them to stay in a relationship during the tension-building phase?
2. Why might the victim stay in the relationship after the acute battering or abusive phase? What theoretical perspectives support your answer?
3. What could be done to break the cycle of violence?

the likelihood that a man would assault his wife (Conway, 1997, p. 169):

- unemployment for more than one month
- personal bankruptcy
- a drop in wage or salary
- taking an additional job to make ends meet
- child support or alimony payments that he did not have before
- a move to less-expensive accommodations

- taking in a boarder to make ends meet
- one or more demotions
- loss of income due to a return to school
- some other important career setback
- some other significant negative change in economic circumstances

The rate of assault for men experiencing none or only one of these events was 8 in 100 men. For men experiencing six or seven of these events, the rate rose to 33 in 100 men—over four times the lowest rate. Women were most at risk of violence if they were in newer marriages, young, living in a low-income household, living with an unemployed man, pregnant, disabled, or ending or thinking about ending the relationship (Conway, 1997). These factors suggest a correlation between economic instability and domestic violence, but not causality. That is, there is no proof that financial hardship causes people to become violent, but individuals in difficult financial circumstances are more likely to experience spousal violence.

Feminist theorists argue that spousal violence is the misuse of power and control. They prefer the terms "violence against women" or "wife battering," arguing that most violence is perpetrated by men, women are most at risk of violence from their intimate partners, and this violence is tolerated by a patriarchal society. They emphasize that although most men are not violent, a significant minority of men choose to be violent (Lynn & O'Neill, 1995). They suggest that as men lose control of their jobs in the workplace and become economically vulnerable, they lose power and seek to regain a sense of power by exerting control in their family. In a patriarchal marriage, men acquire power by their gender, their age, but also by their greater physical size and strength. What begins as controlling, possessive behaviour escalates into violence for some men, and the violence becomes most serious when the man believes he is losing control of the woman because she threatens to leave the relationship (Browne, 1997). The risk factors cited in the 1993 Violence Against Women Study and the pattern of violence in the 1999 study offer support for this theory. Feminist theorists suggest that the solution is to change the social structure so that there is greater equality between men and women, and to ensure that domestic assaults are treated as serious offences by the legal system.

The evidence of the Violence Against Women Study of 1993 and The General Social Survey of 1999 demonstrates that even separation does not always break the cycle of violence. Kathleen Ferraro (1997) argues that the cycle of violence does not sufficiently explain the progression of violence. She identified **stages of engagement** that include two additional stages that might occur after the cycle is broken. The first of these stages is "terror." Some women stay in violent relationships because their lives or the lives of their children have been

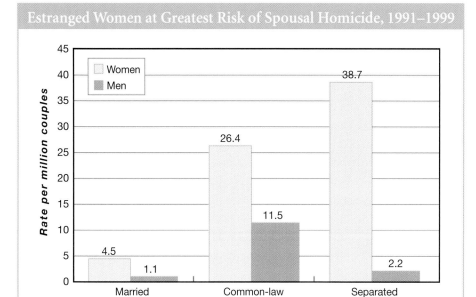

Estranged Women at Greatest Risk of Spousal Homicide, 1991–1999

The 1991 and 1996 Census were used to estimate the number of women and men aged 15 and older who were married, in a common-law union, and separated from legal marital partners during the reference period. Spousal homicide rates were not calculated for those separated from common-law partners, as there are no reliable estimates for this sub-population available from the Census. All known cases of homicide perpetrated by an ex-common law partner (as identified from police narratives) have been omitted from the separated rates. The denominators used for inter-censal years were estimated by averaging the difference from the known population figures in 1991 and 1996.

Source: Adapted from the Statistics Canada publication, *Family Violence in Canada: A Statistical Profile 2001*, Catalogue 85-224, June 2001, pg. 33.

1. What is the ratio of female homicides to male homicides in each category?
2. In what type of marital situation is a woman most likely to be killed?
3. In what type of marital situation is a man most likely to be killed?
   What are possible explanations for the different rates for men and women?

threatened, but others leave and attempt to hide from their ex-partner. Leaving or threatening to leave can make the violence worse for some women. In some cases, the final stage is homicide. Some women are killed by their partners or ex-partners and some women kill their partners. Thirty-nine percent of ex-partners who kill their wives commit suicide after the homicide, and six percent attempt it. According to police records, the motivation most often identified by men for killing an ex-partner is jealousy—the belief that if he can't have her, then no one will. In 74 percent of cases, the men have police records of previous violence. Women are much less likely to kill their partners and are most likely to act in defence during or following a violent assault (Johnson & Hotton, 2001).

In Canada, social and legal systems provide support for victims of domestic violence. The percentage of female victims who reported assaults to the police increased from 29 to 37 percent between 1993 and 1999, suggesting that there is greater faith that the criminal justice system will protect women. The policy of mandatory arrest for spousal violence reflects the attitude that domestic violence will not be tolerated. Shelters and counselling services offer support for abused women and assist them in starting a new life. In cases that indicate a clear threat of future violence, courts issue restraining orders forbidding contact between the perpetrator and the victim. Eight percent of men who murder their ex-partners had restraining orders against them. Spousal violence is a complex issue that requires careful consideration by men and women, but more importantly by governments that provide funding for social services. The decline in the spousal assault rate for women since 1993 raises hope that the solutions have been effective in Canada.

point of view | With Friends Like Feminists . . .

by Chris Champion

Kimberlee Blair is raising five kids on her own in Leduc, Alberta, while her husband, Carl, serves a six-month minimum security sentence. Blair was convicted last month of beating up his wife while severely intoxicated. He'd been acquitted at an earlier trial in October 1994 on the basis of alcohol-induced automatism—that he was too drunk to know what he was doing. Mrs. Blair opposed the second trial. "There was never any need for all this," she told the judge. Later, she added, "We were doing fine, working it through, and then those yakking do-gooders stuck their noses in our business."

The 37-year-old woman was referring to feminist lobbies who have taken a loud interest in the couple's case. Mrs. Blair admits she was hit "with an open hand" by her husband, grabbed by the throat, and rammed against the wall. She testified that Carl only slapped her once in 12 years of marriage. A neighbour, Lucas Malic, contradicted her; he'd seen Blair slapping his wife before. Mr. Malic also said his neighbour had

Feminists' "support" has not helped.

telephoned him during the rampage and accused him of having an affair with his wife—testimony that undermined the automatism defence.

After the retrial, Mrs. Blair's remarks became the subject of feminist analysis in the media. Dorothy Mandy of the Alberta Status of Women Action Committee (ASWAC) told the *Edmonton Journal*, "I used to work in a women's shelter so I'm quite familiar with such reactions. . . . One day she'll realize she's a victim." In the same article Edmonton Sexual Assault Centre director Catherine Hedlin said, "My role is to advocate for all women, for all people who might be victims." As a battered wife, she feels Mrs. Blair was fair game for comment.

But Kimberlee Blair doesn't think she's been battered beyond common sense. "I'm not stupid," she insists. "I wouldn't be here if it [the abuse] had been an ongoing thing." Mrs. Blair says what Mr. Malic thought he saw was in reality a minor squabble, very different than the incident that triggered Blair's arrest. On that occasion, after a 30-hour binge, he went "berserk—I'd never seen that side of him before." The 42-year-old welder and backhoe operator, whose Nisku job awaits his release, had downed 80 ounces of liquor and 12 beers on top of heart and thyroid medications. "I don't condone it," Mrs. Blair adds, "but it was a one-time thing and we've worked it through."

Moreover, the activists who were so quick to analyze have offered no practical help in caring for and feeding Mrs. Blair's children. "I've never heard from them," she says. "Never had anything to do with them before the trial or since. They just go off on their [political] rampages." As for their diagnosis of alleged battered-wife syndrome, Mrs. Blair says, "They should wait for someone to ask for their help. These are women who have nothing to do with their time."

ASWAC's Mandy wondered aloud why Mrs. Blair feels her marriage somehow changes the situation. Assault is a crime and, in her view, drunkenness should never be a defence. "I don't see why this issue of her raising her kids alone is even coming up." But to Mrs. Blair, the children are one powerful reason why she and her husband should have been given the option of working out their own destiny if she, the injured party, wished to do so. ■

Source: *Alberta Report/Western Report.* (1996, February 12). 23, p. 22.

1. What evidence is presented for the case against Mr. Blair?
2. Why was he convicted, although Mrs. Blair opposed the trial?
3. Battered-wife syndrome refers to the behaviour of women in the cycle of violence. Based on the facts provided, was there a cycle of violence?
4. Evaluate the response of each of the individuals named in the article.
5. What point of view is Chris Champion expressing in this article? What perspective does this opinion reflect?

Divorce

Divorce results from the failure of a marriage to meet the expectations of one or both marriage partners (Ahrons, 2001). The common perception is that there are more divorces now than ever before, and that people should be very worried by this. However, divorce rates have fluctuated in Western societies to reflect the current social and moral values concerning marriage and the levels of control held by religion and state. The changes in the pattern of divorce in Canada can be explained by examining the changes in divorce law and in values related to marriage.

In the early twentieth century, divorce was rare in Canada. The functionalist perspective on divorce is based on the prevailing attitude toward marriage at that time. Emile Durkheim, called the first sociologist, argued that the division of labour along traditional gender lines is the basis of stability in marriage and of parental authority (Sev'er, 1992). In traditional marriages, the emphasis was on the economic, childrearing, and household responsibilities of marriage partners, and the happiness of husband and wife was not considered. Divorce was only granted when one partner sued the other for the "matrimonial offences" of adultery or cruelty, so being divorced resulted in social embarrassment. However, at that time many Canadians went to the United States for divorces, and there is no way of determining how many couples were living separate lives within their homes (Ahrons, 2001).

Divorce Through the Years in Canada			
Year	Number of Divorces	Rates Per 100 000 Population	Rates Per 100 000 Married Couples
1921	558	6.4	N/A
1941	2 462	21.4	N/A
1961	6 563	36.0	N/A
1968*	11 343	54.8	N/A
1969	26 093	124.2	N/A
1981	67 671	271.8	1 174.4
1985**	61 980	253.6	1 103.3
1986	78 304	298.8	1 301.6
1987***	96 200	362.3	1 585.5
1990	80 998	295.8	1 311.5
1994	78 880	269.7	1 246.3
1995	77 636	262.2	1 221.9

*Reform of Divorce Laws
**Divorce Act ("no fault")
***Peak year

Source: Ambert, Dr. A.M. (1998). *Divorce: facts, figures and consequences*. Toronto: York University. From The Vanier Institute of the Family web site: www.vfamily.ca/cft/divorce/divorce.htm.

1. What happened to the divorce rates after the Reform of Divorce Laws in 1968?
2. What happened to the divorce rates after "no-fault" divorce was instituted by the Divorce Act of 1986?
3. Why is it more accurate to consider the rate per 100 000 married couples?
4. The highest rate of divorce occurs at five years after marriage. Does the passage of the baby-boom cohort through this peak time appear to have affected the divorce rate?
5. What other demographic factors might affect the divorce rate?

The development of romantic love as the basis for marriage and the changing economic role of women altered the criteria with which partners assessed their satisfaction with their relationship. The Divorce Act of 1968 reflected the expectation that marriage should be based on love and companionship and allowed divorce for "marriage breakdown" after a separation of three years. Subsequently, the divorce rate in Canada increased dramatically, perhaps because many who had been separated prior to 1968 rushed to divorce at this time, contributing to the large numbers of divorces. In 1986, the Divorce Act of Canada reduced the period of separation to one year and introduced "no-fault" divorce. Again, the divorce rate increased before beginning a steady decline. It is currently estimated that about one in three marriages will end in divorce. However, because those who have divorced are more likely to divorce a second or third time, most individuals have less than a one in three chance of ever divorcing (Ambert, 1998).

legal matters | Divorce

by Justice Marvin Zuker

The Divorce Act of 1985 replaced the earlier Divorce Act that had been law since 1968 and changed both the grounds for a court of taking jurisdiction and the grounds for the recognition of foreign divorces. The 1985 Act expanded the court's jurisdiction by requiring that only one spouse be ordinarily resident in the province for at least one year before the commencement of divorce proceedings.

The Divorce Act of Canada became law on June 1, 1986. The Act is federal in nature and applies throughout Canada. Matters of property are local, with each province or territory having its own legislation and sometimes its own approach to principle or details. A proceeding for divorce is brought to the Superior Court of Justice in Ontario or the Unified Family Court in Ontario.

There is a single ground for divorce, called "breakdown of marriage," that must be established by showing one or more of three conditions:

1. The spouses were living separate and apart for at least one year immediately preceding the determination of the divorce proceeding and were living separate and apart at the commencement of the proceeding.

2. The other spouse has committed adultery.

3. The other spouse has been guilty of cruelty.

A separation entails the mental element of an intention to separate. The decision may be made by one spouse against the will of the other spouse. In other words, a valid separation may be created by one spouse "deserting" the other. As long as the separation persists for one year after the desertion, it qualifies to prove the breakdown of marriage ground.

The intention to live separate and apart may be made by one person (unilateral) or by both partners (mutual), but must be present in one of these forms. A mere physical absence of one spouse is not necessarily a separation. There must be a withdrawal from the matrimonial relationship with the intent of destroying the matrimonial union. Spouses are not living separate and apart unless both conditions are met.

The separation need not be in terms of place, but may exist solely in terms of attitude toward each other. A physical separation evident to persons in the community is not required. A separation under the same roof, where it can be said that there are two households or that the spouses are living separate lives, is sufficient. The evidence that a couple under the same roof are living separate and apart must be clear and convincing, but such evidence is not impossible to produce at law.

Adultery or cruelty as evidence of a marriage breakdown goes back to the old theory of matrimonial offence. The first characteristic is that the offence must be committed by the other spouse. It is the "wronged" spouse who sues the "guilty" party. A spouse cannot petition for a divorce on the ground that his or her own adultery produced the breakdown. This means, for instance, that a spouse cohabiting with another person and wishing a divorce so that he or she can marry that person cannot use his or her obvious adultery as proof of breakdown of marriage to obtain an immediate divorce. Instead, he or she must prove the breakdown through a separation, which requires obtaining the divorce no earlier than one year from when the separation in the marriage began, or must prove the adultery or cruelty of the other spouse.

Another characteristic of the offence theory is that acts of adultery or cruelty can be wiped out as actionable offences for divorce purposes. Subject to an important exception in the statute, if the offence is condoned or forgiven (a substantial period of cohabitation after knowledge of the offence usually implies forgiveness) or connived at (encouraged or promoted by the suing spouse), the offence is rendered inoperable and cannot be used to support a divorce proceeding. The standard of proof in a divorce case is the ordinary civil standard of establishing the allegations to meet the balance of probabilities, and not the higher criminal standard of showing proof beyond reasonable doubt. Direct evidence of adultery is rarely available. What is required is proof of opportunity and proof of facts from which it can be reasonably inferred that the opportunity was used.

Cruelty is physical or mental treatment "of such a kind as to render intolerable the continued cohabitation of the spouses." A spouse may be guilty of cruelty if, in the marriage relationship, the conduct causes wanton, malicious, or unnecessary infliction of pain or suffering upon the body, the feelings, or the emotions of the other, and is of such a kind as to render intolerable the continued cohabitation of the spouses. Only conduct that is of a "grave and weighty" nature can reach this standard. Conduct that is "trivial," or that could be characterized as little more than a demonstration of incompatibility of temperament, does not qualify. Cruelty occurring after separation is within the scope of the Divorce Act and may be relied on in support of a claim for divorce. Whether or not grave and weighty conduct amounts to cruelty in a particular case is measured against a subjective rather than an objective standard. It is not what the effect would be on any reasonably minded spouse that matters; it is the effect upon the petitioner with regard to his or her own particular temperament, sensibility, and state of health. ■

Divorce occurs for many reasons. Canadian sociologist Emily Nett (1993) identifies two categories of divorce: marriage "mistakes" and marriage "failures." She suggests that the 17 percent of divorces that occur in the first five years of marriage reflect the basic incompatibility of couples that made the wrong choice of partner, whereas those couples who divorce later have failed to adjust their relationship through critical transitions in their marriage. A greater risk of divorce is associated with factors that could affect compatibility, such as dissimilar backgrounds, a teenage marriage, a brief courtship, or a pregnant bride. Low socio-economic status, limited education, or the presence of stepchildren can lead to more difficult adjustment problems for couples. Most divorces occur between five and fifteen years of marriage, although some couples choose to divorce much later, even in their retirement years.

The social exchange perspective suggests that when the costs of the relationship are high, or the alternatives become more attractive than the marriage, individuals may choose to divorce. Divorced people identify many "costs" as the reasons for divorce. Citing personal reasons, such as incompatibility, irresponsibility, or immaturity, suggests that a couple was unable to adjust to their married status. Other factors, such as infidelity, sexual deprivation, and cruelty, result from a deterioration of commitment to the relationship and to the partner (Sev'er, 1992; Nett, 1993). More women initiate the action for divorce, but it is possible that men act to encourage them to in order to avoid guilt (Nett, 1993). Since the consequences of divorce are complex, getting divorced is a process that most couples undertake with great difficulty.

The decision to divorce occurs in a three-phase process over a two- to three-year period. The adjustment occurs on both an emotional level, as the individuals separate from each other, and on a practical level, as they move into separate households (Peck & Manocherian, 1989).

- In the **Awareness Phase**, one individual decides to initiate a divorce, often after recognizing ongoing problems and a period of denial. The partner may eventually know what is happening but deny knowledge until confronted with a request for a divorce. During the first phase the partners begin to withdraw from the relationship by shifting their energies to other roles.

- In the **Separation Phase**, the couple plan the break-up of their marital system, settle child custody and financial issues, notify friends and family, and create separate households. At this time the two partners must accept the economic realities of divorce.

"One of the reasons it feels so good to be engaged and newly married is the rewarding sensation that out of the whole world, you have been selected. One of the reasons that divorce feels so awful is that you have been deselected."

—Paul Bohannan

web connection

www.mcgrawhill.ca/links/families12

To learn about divorce in Canada, go to the web site above for *Individuals and Families in a Diverse Society* to see where to go next.

by Mary Beth Faller

In divorce, it's not only the marriage that's put asunder—often, it's the friendships, too. In some cases, long-time pals are cast into "his" and "her" alliances. Other times, a person can't handle the trauma of a friend's divorce. "Ultimately, a friend of a couple has to align with one person," says Donna Rogg, a counsellor with Family and Children's Agency Inc. of Norwalk. "They can't maintain a level of friendship with both people. What I've seen, typically, is that they will align with the person who has been left or the one who was hurt."

That's what happened with the friends of Bill Boccuzzi of Norwalk, Conn., who was divorced 3 1/2 years ago. "I hung on to them and she didn't," he says of his former wife. "My friends don't hate her, but they don't respect her as much." Sometimes, Rogg says, the friends can't decide what to do. "Frequently, they feel very torn and they disappear over time." But even friendships between two women or two men can be shaky during a divorce, Rogg says. "Maybe the friend felt threatened by the divorce because their own relationship (with a spouse) is at risk. Or they idealized (the friend's) marriage and it fell apart."

As searing as divorce is, the process can forge new friendships. "There's this whole new world of friends I never would have made," says Diane, who didn't want to use her last name. Five years ago, she found new friends at a divorce support group at a church. "They were wonderful. They understand the ups and downs, the court process, the feelings of losing your self-worth, the parenting issues," says Diane of Stamford, Conn. Rogg says that women who married young, submerged themselves in family life and later divorced are amazed at the new friends they make as they re-enter the world of work and socializing.

Losing friends during divorce is hard. Venturing out to make new ones is hard, too. But maybe the hardest part is thinking of a former spouse as a friend. "In our culture, we don't have much permission to divorce as friends," says Bill Ferguson, a former divorce lawyer in Houston. Ferguson runs a counselling service and Web site called www.divorceasfriends.com, and has appeared on *Oprah* to discuss his work. He's also written three books on the subject. While Ferguson doesn't pretend to make bitter enemies into best buds, he says that becoming friendly with an ex is important for the welfare of any children and for the couple themselves. "When someobody carries resentment, a part of them dies inside, and they carry that in every relationship," he says. "It destroys the quality of life."

Easier said than done.

"I was with her since high school," Boccuzzi says of his ex-wife. "I can talk with her. I am friends with her. But I can't trust her." ■

Source: *The Toronto Star*, (2001, November 24). p. M14. Reprinted by permission of *The Stamford Advocate*.

1. What theoretical perspective does this article reflect?
2. Why does divorce cause disruptions in friendships?
3. How do recently divorced people form new relationships?
4. Research in the United States revealed that 50 percent of divorced couples eventually become co-operative, even friendly (Peck & Manocherian, 1989). Why does Bill Ferguson encourage divorced couples to become friendly with each other?

- In the **Reorganization Phase**, the two individuals establish their separate lives and negotiate their new parental roles if they have children (Peck & Manocherian, 1989; Ward, 1994).

Divorce is a non-normative event that presents individual developmental tasks similar to those experienced at a spouse's death. Individuals have to accept the loss and mourn the end of the relationship. However, the emotional adjustment is often complicated by feelings of guilt, anger, hurt, and a sense of failure. Individuals also have to redefine their identity as a single person and adjust their life structure. Finally, they have to adjust their social relationships with family, with friends, and at work, and form a new social network (Ward, 1994; Carter & Peters, 1996). The immediate emotional consequences include loneliness, sadness, and depression (Nett, 1993). Most divorced people make a satisfactory adjustment within a few years and many remarry, but the effects of the stress can last a lifetime. In the long term, divorced individuals have twice the rate of suicides, car accidents, and physical illness and six times the rate of psychological disorders compared to married people (Peck & Manocherian, 1989).

The economic consequences of divorce differ for men and women. Both will experience a reduced household income and a lower standard of living. The division of property leaves each former partner with half of what they had, but partners may also lose spousal insurance or pension benefits. The reduction in lifestyle is usually temporary for men because they have a greater earning potential, and most remarry to form a joint household again (Ward, 1994). Women, on the other hand, usually have a lower earning potential and are less likely to remarry, especially if they are older. Women who have custody of children suffer the greatest financial difficulties. The results of a study that traced the effects of divorce for 10 years found that while 10 percent of divorced people reported that their quality of life was greatly improved, 20 percent reported that it was significantly worse (Nett, 1993).

"A divorce is like an amputation: you survive but there is less of you."

—Margaret Atwood

Peter Harris was married when he was 23 to Jackie Phillips, whom he met while working as a staff member of an adolescent group home in Thunder Bay, Ontario. Peter was the middle child of an English family who had emigrated to Canada in the late 1950s and settled in a subdivision in Richmond Hill, Ontario. His parents divorced in 1965, when Peter was 14. Shortly after, his father moved in with a woman whom he had met at work and whom he eventually married. Peter's mother, Ethel, had never been happy in Canada. In fact, she only agreed to emigrate here with the hope that a new home and a new life might improve her marriage to her husband. Peter missed her presence in the family when she returned to England a few months after her separation.

Jackie had migrated to Ontario from her home in rural Alberta toward the end of her teenage years, which she acknowledged were turbulent. After Peter dropped out of first year at the University of Waterloo, he moved to Thunder Bay looking for a new start and worked at various jobs before becoming a youth worker in a group home. He liked this job very much and felt that he related to the home's residents successfully. This job provided him with a strong sense that he was "making a difference," and the group home environment provided him with a family atmosphere that he had been missing for a long time.

When Jackie was hired, Peter immediately felt strongly attracted to her. Both of them were seeking companionship and intimacy, and the fact that they were both from outside the Thunder Bay area naturally drew them together. Being a couple gave them a sense of family that neither of them had experienced for a long time. They became inseparable and within three months were married. Soon after, Peter and Jackie moved to Sudbury, where Peter began an

In 1974, Peter and Jackie were eager to marry and enjoy their lives together.

undergraduate program at Laurentian University. His positive experience of working at the group home resulted in a Dream of getting a degree in social work and becoming a professional family counsellor. Peter was also motivated by his desire to have a successful marriage and to help others have happier family lives than he and Jackie had. Jackie supported Peter by working as a nurse's aide in a seniors' home, and Peter supplemented the family income by working as a taxi dispatcher on weekends.

The stress of going to school and trying to manage financially created problems in their relationship. Although the first three years of their marriage were not as happy as they had both imagined they would be, they thought that once Peter was established as a family counsellor, things would work out. When Peter graduated from Laurentian, they moved to Brampton and rented a small apartment. Peter had been accepted at the School of Social Work at Laurier University, and Jackie began taking courses in nursing at Humber College. They chose Brampton because they wanted to settle down in southern Ontario and because it was situated between their respective schools. Also, Jackie wanted to be closer to Peter's extended family since, by then, she had completely cut herself off from her own family of origin. Commuting so far to school and working long hours at part-time jobs put an additional strain on their relationship, however, and eventually Jackie ended up in the hospital with a nervous breakdown.

From that point on, their relationship changed irreversibly. Jackie no longer seemed interested in making the marriage work and she began to spend more and more time with a girlfriend whom she met at Humber College. Peter and Jackie continued to live together in the Brampton apartment, but argued constantly, particularly about the amount of time that Jackie spent with her new friend. Eventually, Jackie revealed to Peter that she had been having an affair with her girlfriend and that she thought she was a lesbian. She left Peter and moved to Toronto to live with her girlfriend. A year later, Peter and Jackie were divorced.

It took Peter a long time to recover from his stormy relationship with Jackie and the subsequent end of his marriage. He had worked hard to make the marriage successful, and when it ended, he felt he had failed as a husband. He did complete his social work degree, however, and settled in Kitchener, where he worked for the local Children's Aid Society. He eventually had long-term common-law relationships with Lisa O'Brien and then Mary Cardinal, but was unable to make the final commitment of marriage to either of them. Today, he still lives in the Kitchener area, where he has built a successful family counselling practice. At present, he is not in a relationship. ◾

1. What factors in Peter's and Jackie's family backgrounds increased the risk of divorce?
2. Why do you think Jackie married Peter?
3. In your opinion, would it have been better for Jackie to have ended her lesbian relationship and to have stayed married to Peter? Why?
4. How might Peter's relationship with Jackie have affected his subsequent relationships?
5. Examine the Harris-Vidoni family tree (see Chapter 1, page 19). Suggest reasons why Peter's history of intimate relationships with Lisa and Mary differs from that of his siblings.

chapter 8 Review and Apply

Knowledge/Understanding   Thinking/Inquiry

1. **a)** According to the research, what are the difficulties of intermarriages?

   b) How do the challenges faced by couples in interfaith marriages differ from those in interracial marriages?

2. Compare heterosexual and homosexual relationships using the following criteria:
   - purpose
   - attraction
   - negotiation of roles
   - conditions for satisfaction

3. Based on the research on infidelity, develop a profile of someone who is likely to have an affair.

4. **a)** Distinguish between violent arguments and the cycle of violence.

   b) Summarize the evidence supporting the argument that women are more likely than men to be victims of the cycle of violence.

5. Summarize the reasons why couples divorce and explain whether the reasons reflect a change in expectations about marriage in the twentieth century.

Knowledge/Understanding   Thinking/Inquiry   Communication

6. Write an essay defending your point of view on one form of intermarriage. Support your opinion with arguments reflecting at least two theoretical perspectives.

7. Select a newspaper or magazine article expressing an opinion about same-sex relationships.

   a) Identify the thesis and the theoretical perspective.

   b) Write a response to the article from another theoretical perspective.

8. Write an essay analyzing a character in a book, a television program, or a movie who has admitted to an extramarital affair. Include your moral belief about infidelity.

9. Write a case study that distinguishes between couple violence and a pattern of violence in a couple relationship.

10. Write a brief article that outlines risk factors for divorce. Direct the article at unmarried adult readers of a local newspaper.

Knowledge/Understanding Thinking/Inquiry Communication Application

11. a) Suggest reasons why there has been so little research on intermarriage in Canada.

b) Write a proposal for a research study of a form of intermarriage that is common in your community. In the proposal, identify the research questions and suggest the hypotheses.

12. a) Conduct a survey of young adults to investigate how they define infidelity, whether it is acceptable, and how they think they would respond to infidelity in an intimate sexual relationship.

b) Compare males' and females' responses and compare both to current research.

13. Explain which theory of spousal violence provides the best explanation of the evidence. Evaluate whether the laws concerning spousal violence and the social services available in your community reflect that theory.

unit 4 Parent-Child Relationships

UNIT EXPECTATIONS

While reading this unit, you will:

- analyze theories and research on the subject of parent-child relationships and their role in individual and family development, and summarize your findings

- analyze decisions and behaviours related to parental and caregiver role expectations, including the division of responsibilities for childrearing and socialization

- analyze socialization patterns and the roles of children and parents in various historical periods and ethnocultural contexts

- analyze current issues and trends affecting childrearing and socialization, and speculate on the changing role of children

- demonstrate an understanding of the cycle of violence and the consequences of abuse and violence in interpersonal and family relationships

- use appropriate social science research methods in the investigation of issues affecting individuals and families in a diverse society

- access, analyze, and evaluate information, including opinions, research evidence, and theories, related to individuals and families in a diverse society

- analyze issues and data from the perspectives associated with key theories in the disciplines of anthropology, psychology, and sociology

- communicate the results of your inquiries effectively

Parenting can be one of the most rewarding experiences adults will have in their lifetime.

OVERVIEW

In this unit, parent-child relationships will be explored through an analysis of related theories and research. The roles of children and parents will be examined, with a focus on the diversity of these roles. The history of socialization patterns, parent-child relationships, and the roles of children and parents in Canada will be traced. The trends in Canada today will be evaluated. Next, the role of parent-child relationships in individual and family development will be examined. The parental and caregiver role expectations will be explored, including the division of responsibility for childbearing and socialization. Finally, specific issues and trends that have had an impact on Canadian parent-child relationships will be discussed.

chapter 9

Parenthood Today

CHAPTER EXPECTATIONS

While reading this chapter, you will:

- describe patterns and practices in childbearing in various cultures and historical periods
- analyze the roles of children in the family and society in various cultures and historical periods, taking into consideration expectations for pace of development, rites of passage, participation in education or labour, and the nature of parent-child relationships
- describe current perceptions, opinions, and demographic trends related to childbearing and childrearing and speculate on the significance of these trends for parent-child relationships
- explain the factors that influence decisions relating to childbearing
- demonstrate an understanding of research methodologies, appropriate research ethics, and specific theoretical perspectives for conducting primary research
- use current information technology effectively to compile quantitative data and present statistical analyses of data or to develop databases
- identify and respond to the theoretical viewpoints, the thesis, and the supporting arguments of materials found in a variety of secondary sources

KEY TERMS

biological clock
childhood
delayed
  parenthood
family wages
female infanticide
fertility
fertility rate
genetic diseases
infant mortality
  rate
infertile
lineage
parenthood
parenting styles
stereotypes
sterilization
voluntary
  childlessness

RESEARCH SKILLS
• creating charts and graphs using information
  gained from primary research

Although the family
is ever-changing, it
continues to survive.
In Canada today, the
majority of couples,
whether married
or cohabiting,
have children.

CHAPTER INTRODUCTION

In this chapter, parent-child relationships will be studied and the role of parenthood
in Canada will be examined. Insight into parenthood, parent-child relationships, and
the role expectations of parents and children will be developed, from both a historical
and a cultural perspective. Childbearing will be explored, and demographics will
provide a foundation for determining such factors as the changes in the reasons for
having children and the size of families. The theoretical perspectives in this chapter
will be based on sociology.

Families in Canada

The Vanier Institute of the Family has analyzed the composition of Canadian families based on the information from the 1996 census. According to the pie graph on this page, the majority of Canadian families have children living at home. It should be noted that some of the families listed may have children who do not live at home, as the designation "without children" includes never-married children who do not live at home. Having children is still seen as a natural and desirable part of a committed relationship.

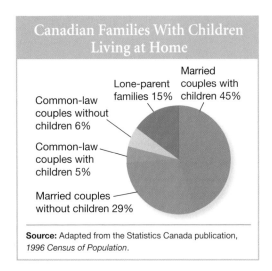

Canadian Families With Children Living at Home

Married couples with children 45%
Lone-parent families 15%
Common-law couples without children 6%
Common-law couples with children 5%
Married couples without children 29%

Source: Adapted from the Statistics Canada publication, *1996 Census of Population*.

Looking Back at Family Life

To fully understand families with children today, people need to examine the ways couples in the past have moved beyond the couple relationship and made the transition into **parenthood**. There are several myths about the typical family of the past. Suanne Kelman (1998) discusses the three great myths of the history of family life:

1. Until the twentieth century, family groupings consisted of large extended families with at least three generations in one home.

2. The nuclear family is a form unique to the industrialized world.

3. For most of history, the family was merely an economic unit until the West invented romantic love.

Kelman states that the belief that the nuclear family is a recent development is false, and that household size has been relatively small in much of Europe and North America for centuries (Kelman, 1998). In fact, homes filled with many generations of the same family were the exception, not the rule. "Despite what some radical critics believe, the nuclear, monogamous family is not a recent innovation. It's been present in some societies from the dawn of history" (Kelman, 1998, p. 2).

In other societies prior to the twentieth century, large families were the norm. In Asia and Africa, the paternal grandmother would reside with the family (Kelman, 1998). In other areas of the world, a large communal family was the norm. In parts of Nepal, India, and Tibet, the family consisted of a couple, their sons, and a communal wife whom the sons shared and who bore all the children for the next generation. This arrangement was used to keep the population growth small, since one woman cannot have as many children as a number of women can. Also, there were few natural resources in this area for sustenance, so keeping the family population growth to a minimum was essential. In these areas, this family type was considered the norm. This family type shows that the meaning of natural behaviour in human families is debatable, and that instinct does not guide human behaviour in the same way it guides other animals (Kelman, 1998). This family arrangement, viewed from a functionalist perspective, suggests that the society cannot afford to have large numbers of children, and thus has devised a system that places very restrictive limits on population growth.

In Europe during the Middle Ages, people had children for reasons that depended more on a family's social class than anything else. An upper-class family took great care to ensure that their child married someone who was suitable for carrying on the family line. People had children in order to con-tinue this family line. Lower-class families needed children to contribute their labour to the family unit. As both classes had children for particular reasons, they also valued children differently (Mandell, 1995). The upper classes often sent their children away until they were ready to join the adult world. Children spent their infancy with a woman who was hired to breast-feed another's baby, their early childhood with a governess, and their school years at boarding schools. They would return home as young adults to take their place in society (Kelman, 1998).

In contrast, women in the lower classes breast-fed their own infants. From the time they could walk, the children would accompany an adult of the same gender during the day to learn his or her chores. The children's labour contributed to the family from an early age, so their membership in the family was valued. Children of lower-class families left home in their early teens to work. Some would work in the community and still reside with their family, while others would be sent to a distant commu-nity to live and work. Most were expected to contribute at least part of their wages to the family income (Mandell, 1995).

Even though people think that nuclear families are a modern "invention," they have been in existence for quite some time.

The history of parenting is often remembered with a nostalgic view and an assumption that it was better than it is now. A close look into history helps put today's parenting into perspective. If you look far enough back, you can see a wide variety of **parenting styles**. In Europe between 1500 and 1700, fathers had absolute rule over the household. Women and children were considered his property, to do with as he pleased. Children often suffered brutal treatment at the hands of their parents and could be sold as property (Mandell, 1995). From a modern perspective, many past customs exhibited brutality toward children that would be horrifying by today's standards. Customs such as wrapping infants tightly in cloth for extended periods of time (swaddling), or beating a child are no longer acceptable, and would be subject to child abuse investigations if they were practised today. In contrast, during the later years of the Roman Empire, children might be considered spoiled by today's standards. Children were indulged, and fathers made sacrifices to keep them happy (Kelman, 1999).

Family History in Canada

To gain a better understanding of Canadian families today, it is necessary to study the changes they have undergone throughout history. The goal of most parents then was not to raise happy, well-adjusted children, but to have someone to pass on the family name and its traditions, as well as to provide the necessary labour to maintain the family unit (Kelman, 1999).

Aboriginal Families

Family history in Canada begins with the hunter-gatherer societies of the Aboriginal Peoples. These families lived in groups and travelled together. They were egalitarian, since the contributions of all members of the family were valued by the entire band (Ishwaran, 1983). The division of labour was based primarily on sex. The men and older boys went out to hunt in the forests, while the women, older girls, and young children worked in the clearings, tending to plants and the few animals they kept. The labour performed by the children was an important part of the family's success. These hunter-gatherer societies existed in Canada from the beginning of its history, well over 13 000 years ago (Mandell, 1995) and in various areas of the country. Some Inuit of the Canadian North still practise a hunter-gatherer lifestyle.

After 1500 B.C.E, many groups of Aboriginals began to give up their nomadic way of life. They started cultivating the land and planting and harvesting crops. This was the beginning of agriculture in North America. By the 1500s there were two types of Aboriginal communities in Ontario: hunter-gatherers in the north, and those that relied on agriculture in the south. Families worked together in a co-operative manner and shared most duties, including child care (Ishwaran, 1983). Women and younger children took primary responsibility for agriculture, while men and older boys hunted locally. Families within the large group were nuclear in nature (Mandell, 1995).

In hunter-gatherer societies, all family members, including children, were an important part of the team. Children were valued and cherished.

The arrival of the Europeans in North America between 1500 and 1700 meant the end of their former way of life for many Aboriginal groups. The European involvement in Aboriginal ways was to change their culture forever. Before the Europeans' arrival, Aboriginal societies hunted only what they needed. As a result of the Europeans' demand for fur, they began to hunt more, taking the men away from their families for longer periods of time. The Europeans introduced diseases into Aboriginal communities, which killed many of them. They also introduced alcohol to the Aboriginal Peoples, trading it for furs. As there were few European women in North America at that time, many European men lived with or married Aboriginal women, thus blending two cultures that differed greatly in their family values and customs. The children born of these unions were raised by parents of two different cultures that had very different views on children's roles.

The marriages were considered temporary, and when the fur traders returned to Europe, their Aboriginal wives and children would often return to their original families. In the mid- to late- 1700s, the Hudson's Bay Company forbade their employees from bringing their Aboriginal families back to Europe with them. The traders often retired to Eastern Canada or Britain, leaving behind their Aboriginal wives and children, and often married a European woman in their retirement. Many of the traders did make provisions for their Aboriginal families to receive support in the form of supplies from the trading company. Other traders would pass their Aboriginal wives and children on to an incoming trader. Aboriginal husbands readily accepted the wives and children from marriages to fur traders. This reflects the strong kinship ties and the great love of children that is characteristic of Aboriginal society (Van Kirk, 1992).

The Aboriginal Peoples had a very different sense of family than the Europeans, whose society was very male-dominated.

> [Aboriginal] family relationships baffled Europeans [because of their] personal autonomy; lack of hierarchy; spousal interdependence; abundant love for their children; abhorrence of inflicting corporal punishment, fear, or humiliation on children (Mandell, 1995, p. 22).

They placed a high value on their children and raised them with care. Corporal punishment of children was not accepted. When French missionaries first arrived in Canada, they could not understand the democratic parenting practices of the Aboriginal Peoples (Kelman, 1999). The missionaries made it their goal to correct what they thought were poor parenting practices. They felt that the Aboriginal Peoples allowed their children too much freedom and that the lack of corporal punishment would "spoil" them (Mandell, 1995).

Looking at the changes in the Aboriginal Peoples' family life from the arrival of the Europeans to the present time, from a systems perspective there is dramatic evidence of how a change in one part of the system can affect the entire system. The Europeans changed the Aboriginal Peoples' way of life and the roles of Aboriginal adults and children from equality, caring, and understanding to the European way of male dominance and control. Prior to the coming of the Europeans, Aboriginal men and women shared an equal partnership with each other and a great love of their children. This was seen as improper by European religious leaders. Their devaluing of women and children caused conflict and role confusion in the Aboriginal community. The change in status and role for women and children altered the entire social fabric of Aboriginal communities.

European Families

In the 1600s and 1700s, marriage and family patterns in Canada varied greatly. In Québec, romantic love was not usually the basis of marriage. In the middle and upper classes, marriages were arranged based on the size of the bride's dowry as well as her potential to bear children (Mandell, 1995). Men were concerned with maintaining biological ties to their families, continuing their good **lineage**, and protecting the family wealth through inheritance. Children were an important part of continuing the family legacy, and they were valued as a means of passing on family traditions and wealth (Daly, 1995). In farming and peasant families during this time, marriage and children were viewed as economic necessities. Women were valued for their ability to work and contribute to the family enterprise. They shared a fairly equal role with their husbands, and their marriages were like partnerships. Children were necessary for the labour they provided, and often farmers had large families to provide enough labour to run the farm. Children were allowed to be consumers only when they were very young. As they grew up, they were expected to be producers for the good of the entire family. Family tasks were differentiated by sex, with the boys working farther from the home and the girls working closer, modelling the roles of their parents. The home was the centre of all domestic, economic, and social activity (Gaffield, 1992). Children were raised and educated by both of their parents as well as their older siblings, other relatives, and unrelated members of the household, usually servants (Hareven, 2000). Many families cared for elderly relatives, and children were valued for their future contributions to the family for this purpose.

Schooling was not compulsory for children during this time. It was supplied through religious groups. Upper-class boys were more likely to be given formal instruction than any other group. However, among farmers and peasants, girls were much more likely than boys to be taught basic literacy skills. Children were often sent away from home to serve as apprentices. Girls apprenticed in household tasks, and usually left home around the age of 10 and stayed with their employer's family until they married (Mandell, 1995). Boys apprenticed for a wider variety of occupations, including carpenters, coopers, accountants, doctors, lawyers, and blacksmiths. They usually left home between the ages of 9 and 10. In many working-class families, older brothers and sisters acted as role models and were responsible for helping their siblings move into the work force (Hareven, 2000). Children were only allowed to marry when their parents could afford to do without their incomes (Mandell, 1995).

Difficult conditions that existed at the time, such as poor sanitation, disease, inadequate housing, and a lack of medical knowledge, led to high infant mortality rates as well as shorter life spans for adults. As a result of this, many children were orphaned at a young age. Often, children who still had one living parent were sent to live with relatives or stepfamilies, or they were sent away as servants (Mandell, 1995). Older children

Children went out to work at a young age, since families needed their wages in order to survive.

frequently played a role in raising the younger children, since they had more contact with them than their parents did. This happened for many reasons, such as the early death of parents, the age range and number of children in a family, and the fact that older children taught younger ones how to do their family chores and other tasks outside the family. Families had more children, and the spread in ages was quite large. Often, only the oldest children knew their parents as young people, while the younger children knew their parents when they were middle-aged or older (Hareven, 2000).

Families tended to live closer together, and grandparents, aunts, uncles, and cousins would reside in the same community. This gave children an extended kin group in the neighbourhood, but not in the same house. Due to the shorter life spans of adults, most grandparents did not live to see all their grandchildren grow up (Hareven, 2000).

Since women and children were considered the property of their husbands, they had no legal rights of their own. Many became victims of a violent husband or father. Those who acted in self-defence were tried in public and often put to death, to warn others not to follow the same path. One such example is Marie-Josephte Corriveau of Québec, who in 1783 admitted to killing her husband with an axe while he slept. Her body was hung in a public place for more than a month by the British authorities as a lesson to other women (Mandell, 1995). When viewed from a structural functionalist perspective, this is an example of the ways societies have tried to control its members. The harsh structure of the laws of the time functioned in a manner to keep women in their "proper" place, under the control of men.

Until the beginning of the 1800s, Canada's economy was based mainly on farming, fishing, lumbering, and some fur trading. Homes were still the centres for production, and the labour of all family members was still highly valued and necessary. However, two major changes occurred that forever altered Canadian family life.

1. Small-scale farms, which simply met the needs of the farm family, began to be replaced by large-scale commercial farms, which produced excess goods to be sold at market.

2. Employment moved from being home-based to factories and shops.

The economy changed from an agricultural base to an industrial base. As people moved from small farms to the city to find work, cities grew at a rapid pace. The West was opened up, and immigrants were brought into Canada to settle the land. Many changes in the family were brought about by these shifts in Canadian society. Families changed from self-sufficient economic units on the farm with each member of the family contributing to the overall well-being of the family by working on the farm. When families moved to urban areas, every family member was sent out to work, and children turned over their wages to their parents in order for the family to survive economically. Women and children were often exploited in the workplace, labouring for long hours in poor conditions (Larson, Goltz, & Munro, 2000).

Later in the 1800s, men in unions fought for **family wages**, which was enough money to support a wife and children. Labour laws changed, and children were no longer sent out to work. Consequently, at this time, only about 5 percent of married women worked at a paid job, while the rest stayed at home and provided a nurturing environment for their growing children (Mandell, 1995). During the early 1900s, especially for the middle classes, few women were involved in the work force, because men were considered to be responsible for earning the family income. Women supported men by maintaining the household and raising the children (Mandell, 1995). Families became consumer units, and their lives depended on the male's income.

These changes influenced the roles of men, women, and children in families. Men's contribution to the family unit was the wages that he earned from his employment outside the home. His contribution to the running of the household was diminished and his parenting role changed from one of high involvement to one of provider of leisure activities and money (Hareven, 2000). Women gained sole responsibility for the functioning of the household and assumed primary responsibility for caregiving. They were seen to possess the characteristics more suited to childrearing, such as being gentle, patient, sweet, and comforting. Men were considered to have the characteristics of what was thought to be ideal workers, such as being aggressive, tough, and competitive. This increased emphasis on the differences between men and women led to a clear division of family roles based on gender. Children raised during the early 1900s had strong sex-role **stereotypes** (Mandell, 1995). Girls were socialized to be like their mothers and boys to be like their fathers. This division lasted until the early 1970s. From a systems perspective, the changes in the family system that made it the norm for men to be the sole provider had long-lasting effects on the contemporary family.

The roles of children also changed with this move to a consumer family. Children were no longer needed for their labour. They lost their economic value and became cherished for sentimental reasons. Compulsory schooling and restrictive child labour laws took children out of the labour force. In 1891, 13.8 percent of all children between the ages of 11 and 14 were employed; by 1921, the percentage was reduced to 3.2. Since children no

During the 1950s, very few women worked outside the home. Those who did, did so out of necessity, and were seen as incompetent mothers since they spent less time with their children than the average woman did.

longer went out to work, it became the mother's responsibility to ensure that her children were raised properly. The mother in the middle-class family was now valued for her contribution to the social and moral upbringing of the children. Her economic contribution to the family was no longer valued. Working-class women employed outside the home were considered to be economically productive as wives, but incompetent as mothers, since they were not at home providing proper guidance for their children (Mandell, 1995).

Families became smaller, as there was no longer the need for women to bear many children for the labour the children could provide. Homes evolved from a place for performing social, economic, and domestic activities to a private retreat, away from the rest of the world. Households became smaller, more specialized, and more isolated from the outside world (Larson, Goltz, & Munro, 2000). Many middle-class families moved farther away from relatives to seek work, so although grandparents were living longer, the children did not get to spend extended time with them, because of distance between residences (Hareven, 2000).

The experience of the lower classes was different from that of the middle classes. The lower classes were dependent on kinship groups for the social and economic support of the family unit. Children of working parents were often cared for by the extended family (Mandell, 2000).

As the roles of husband and wife changed with this trend toward domesticity in the first half of the nineteenth century, the role of children changed also. Children were gradually removed from interaction with adults when they moved from the workplace and home into schools, as **childhood** became to be recognized as a distinct stage in development. As families became smaller, the age difference between parents and children lessened, as did the age difference between children. This, in turn, changed the nature of the sibling relationships. Children who were close in age were not expected to care for one another; consequently, the childrearing responsibilities of older children diminished (Hareven, 2000).

Before the 1950s, Canadian **fertility rates** had been in a century-long decline. After World War II, there was an unanticipated increase in the birth rate. In the 1960s, married couples who did not have children were considered selfish (Carter & McGoldrick, 1989). Most women did not work outside of the home after they were married. They had a social support system in the community, since the majority of them were at home with their children during the day. Mothers of baby-boom children were expected to stay at home and care for them (Haraven, 2000). From a social exchange perspective, the exchange of services between the male breadwinner, earning the income for the family, and the female homemaker, maintaining the family home and caring for the children, was considered fair. Therefore, this became the norm for the majority of couples during this time.

Families in Other Cultures

Examining the role of children in other cultures results in an understanding of the many differences in childrearing practices throughout the world. Children were raised in different ways, and there are differences in how they were valued. What one culture considers the norm today may have been the norm centuries ago in another culture.

The Classical Chinese Family System

The classical Chinese family existed for 2500 years prior to the beginning of the twentieth century. Social organization and customs remained relatively stable during this time, and thus the family structure that existed then is referred to as "the classical Chinese family." In the classical Chinese family, pregnant women were said to have happiness in their bodies. They were pleased at the birth of a son, who could carry on family traditions, but the birth of a daughter was not usually celebrated. Large, wealthy families were not as concerned about the sex of the infant as peasant families were. Peasant families had few resources to share with "unnecessary" children. Female infanticide was an accepted practice. Poor families did not value female children, because they would marry and leave the family just when they were old enough to make an economic contribution to the family through their labour (Queen, Habenstein, & Quadagno, 1985). Functionalists would view this undervaluing of females in terms of females' contribution to the economic well-being of the family. Since female children were not able to contribute much to their family of origin, they

Looking at the differences in the way boys and girls were treated in the past and in a variety of cultures enables us to appreciate the advances in gender equality that exist in North America and other countries today.

were not highly valued by them. From the functionalist perspective, the system that supported female infanticide served a purpose.

During the first two years of life, the Chinese child was kept close to the mother, usually sleeping with her during this time. The father maintained a distance from infants. Children were not trained or disciplined during infancy, and their mothers or servants met all of their needs. After the age of three, children were expected to have control over their bodily functions. At this time, another child was often born into the family. The new infant slept with the mother, while the older child slept with the father. After the age of four, children began training for adult life. Boys were sent to live in the male section of the household, while girls remained with their mothers to learn the duties of wife and mother. Boys were either tutored or were sent to school. Schools were places of strict discipline, and adults were respected without question. Boys who questioned authority were severely punished. Girls, however, were spared the harsh discipline that boys received at the hands of the schoolmaster and their fathers. As children became teenagers, boys were well trained to take on the role of head of the household. Girls learned to accept the fact that they would soon leave their families forever, since after marriage they became a low-status person in their husband's family (Queen, Habenstein, & Quadagno, 1985).

It is often difficult for Westerners to understand the values of different cultures. The custom of female infanticide practised by the Todas is one example.

The Toda Family

At the end of the nineteenth and the beginning of the twentieth centuries, the Toda family of the Nilgiri Hills in South India practised childbearing rituals in a very different manner than the Western family. The culture was polyandrous, meaning there were many husbands to one wife. From the fifth month of pregnancy, the expectant mother was sent off to a mud hut on the edge of the village. After the birth, she lived in seclusion for another month, until the father came and his legal parenthood was established, after which she could return to her home. The Todas practised **female infanticide** for a number of years, meaning the female children were killed immediately after birth. If twins were born, one would be killed. The practice of female infanticide has been banned in the Toda culture.

Toda females were seen as inferior to males, and families could not support large numbers of female children. The role of females in the Toda society was severely limited, and they were seen as impure and unclean because of bodily functions, such as menstruation and childbearing. The value of females to their family of origin was short-lived, as they were usually married off by adolescence. Male children were highly valued in the Toda culture (Queen, Habenstein, & Quadagno, 1985).

Buffalo were sacred to the Toda. Men maintained the dairy, and only dairy priests could tend to the herds and perform sacred tasks of churning and clarifying butter. Women were not allowed to tend the dairy, they could not walk on the same path as buffalo, and they could not cook foods that contained milk or products made from milk (Queen, Habenstein, & Quadagno, 1985).

Infants were kept in seclusion after birth. Babies' faces were kept covered from view until they were three months old. The sex of the baby determined how his or her face would be uncovered. The male child was brought to the front of a dairy and his head was touched to the threshold. He was then carried to a place where buffalo grazed. Then his face was turned toward the sun and uncovered. The female child was taken to the place where women received buttermilk from the dairy. There, her face was uncovered. This was an important ceremony for the Todas, since it demonstrated that, from birth, the male members of the society were given much higher status than the females.

The Todas were very fond of their children, and all adults felt a responsibility toward them. Toda mothers formed strong bonds with their infants and nursed them for two years. Children spent most of their time playing. Some of the games were imitations of the real-life roles they would assume in their adolescent years. Toda male children participated in caring for the buffalo as soon as they were able. Toda female children learned the domestic arts and were usually married by the time they reached adolescence (Queen, Habenstein, & Quadagno, 1985).

Developing an understanding of the role of children in other cultures allows people to compare the childrearing practices of their own culture today with those of other cultures in the past. The differences in how children were valued within their own families and the culture, as well as how they were raised, offer a different perspective on how children are valued and raised in a person's own time and culture.

Childbearing in Canada Today

Canadian couples in the twenty-first century who are considering having children have many more choices and face more complex issues than couples did in the past. The Canadian social system has changed. Institutions such as marriage have undergone significant adjustments. The transformation of

"The thing about having a baby is that thereafter, you have it."
—Jean Kerr

social norms in regard to sex roles, conception, and the equality of women are said to be contributing to the decline in Canadian fertility rates. Since the 1970s, marriage rates have fallen and rates of cohabitation have increased. Divorce rates have stabilized, but at a high level. It is estimated that 30 percent of all marriages since 1965 will end in divorce. People are postponing both marriage and babies. Contraception is widespread and very efficient. Couples who have had their desired number of children now perform permanent forms of birth control through tubal ligation or vasectomy (Balakrishnan, Lapierre-Adamczyk, & Krotki, 1993).

New attitudes toward marriage and childbearing have developed since the 1970s. In the past, lack of reliable birth control measures made children an inevitable part of married life. Now, couples choose when and if to have children. Children are no longer valued economically, but rather for their emotional fulfillment. They are seen as the entity that completes the married couple's relationship (Balakrishnan, Lapierre-Adamczyk, & Krotki, 1993).

Changing attitudes toward childbearing can be explained using the social exchange theory. Couples are looking to receive something back from their children in exchange for the time, energy, and money that they put into raising them. In this case, the parents are looking for emotional fulfillment and love from the child in exchange for the caregiving they provide.

Women and Work-Force Participation

Women are participating in the work force at a much greater rate than ever before. Their employment outside the home is an important variable in fertility rates. Traditionally, women worked until they married. This pattern is changing, since women are continuing to work after marriage and after the birth of children (Balakrishnan, Lapierre-Adamczyk, & Krotki, 1993). In the 1970s, one-third of couples were dual-earners. Today the number has risen to seven out of ten couples with children under the age of seven (Vanier Institute of the Family, 2002). There are many reasons why women stay employed outside the home. Many need to provide an income for their families, either as the primary earner in a lone-parent family or as a primary or secondary earner in a dual-income family (Vanier Institute of the Family, 2002). The contribution of women's wages is essential for many families to balance the family budget. In nearly half of all families, women's income contributes between 25 and 40 percent of the family income. In 25 percent of all families, women contribute half or more of the total family income (Vanier Institute of the Family, 2002). From a systems perspective, the work pattern of women has had an impact on all members of their families and on their families' lives.

web connection

www.mcgrawhill.ca/links/families12

To learn about mothers employed outside the home, go to the web site above for *Individuals and Families in a Diverse Society* to see where to go next.

Over the 1990 to 1999 period, the low-income rate among single-earner families, with or without children, increased. Among dual-earner families during the same time period, the low-income rate decreased. The second income gained from the work of women is a key factor to a family's climb from poverty (Sauvé, 2002).

Many women have invested much time and energy in building their careers. They gain satisfaction from pursuing their career goals and, for this reason, continue to work. Unplanned pregnancies are seen as disruptive to their career path (Daly, 1995). Work patterns outside the home and the social and psychological satisfaction gained from work are reasons why women are waiting to have children, and why they are having fewer when they do (Balakrishnan, Lapierre-Adamczyk, & Krotki, 1993). The majority of women are no longer at home caring for their children for long periods of time. Those who do take time off from work to care for their children do not have a large network of other stay-at-home parents to rely on.

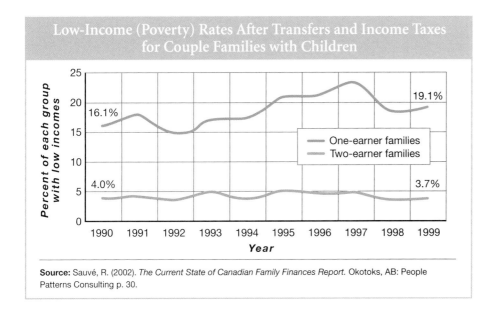

Low-Income (Poverty) Rates After Transfers and Income Taxes for Couple Families with Children

Source: Sauvé, R. (2002). *The Current State of Canadian Family Finances Report.* Okotoks, AB: People Patterns Consulting p. 30.

Advances in Medical Science

Medical developments have changed the way couples approach family planning. There are now safe and convenient methods of reliable contraception that allow couples some control over the timing of and years between children. A major shift in birth control practice is that younger women and men who have attained their desired family size can choose **sterilization** to maintain that family size. Canadian sterilization rates have increased dramatically in recent times. In the Canadian Fertility Survey, 65 percent of couples in which the wife was over 35 had chosen sterilization as a method of birth control. Across all groups of Canadian women, the extensive and effective use of birth control means that unwanted pregnancies are likely to decrease (Balakrishnan, Lapierre-Adamczyk, & Krotki, 1993). The changes in the means of controlling **fertility** have had an impact on the timing and number of children born to Canadian couples.

Advances in reproductive technology now allow otherwise **infertile** couples to have children. Until the past few decades, couples who could not have their own children relied on adoption to become parents. There are now many alternatives for these couples. Artificial insemination of the husband's sperm, artificial insemination of a donor's sperm, and in vitro fertilization are just a few options available (Eshleman & Wilson, 2001).

People now know much more about prenatal care—such as the importance of a pregnant woman's nutrition, and the dangers of smoking, drinking alcohol, and taking drugs during pregnancy—resulting in healthier babies. Developments

Infant Mortality Rates					
	1993	1994	1995	1996	1997
Canada	**6.3**	**6.3**	**6.1**	**5.6**	**5.5**
Newfoundland	7.8	8.2	7.9	6.6	5.2
Prince Edward Island	9.1	6.4	4.6	4.7	4.4
Nova Scotia	7.1	6.0	4.9	5.6	4.4
New Brunswick	7.2	5.4	4.8	4.9	5.7
Québec	5.7	5.6	5.5	4.7	5.6
Ontario	6.2	6.0	6.0	5.7	5.5
Manitoba	7.1	7.0	7.6	6.7	7.5
Saskatchewan	8.1	8.9	9.1	8.4	8.9
Alberta	6.7	7.4	7.0	6.2	4.8
British Columbia	5.7	6.3	6.0	5.1	4.7
Yukon	7.9	2.3	12.8	0.0	8.4
Northwest Territories	9.6	14.6	13.0	12.2	10.9

Note: The infant mortality rate is calculated as the number of deaths of children less than one year of age per 1000 births.

Source: Adapted from the Statistics Canada web site
http://www.statcan.ca/english/Pgdb/People/health/health21.htm.

1. How could you account for the differences in infant mortality rates in different provinces?
2. Why do the Northwest Territories continue to have high infant mortality rates?
3. What do the provinces with lower rates have in common?

in genetic testing enable couples to determine the risk of inherited problems, and to choose whether to terminate an unhealthy pregnancy. The **infant mortality rate** in Canada has been declining steadily over the past century. In just four years, from 1993 to 1997, it decreased almost 1 percent, a significant amount, considering the time frame. This has had an impact on the number of children Canadians are having (Balakrishnan, Lapierre-Adamczyk, & Krotki, 1993).

Divorce

Increased divorce rates in Canada have caused young people to question the certainty of a long-lasting marriage. The stability of marriage is no longer guaranteed by the strength of the institution. Many young Canadians today who are considering having children have experienced their parents' divorce or the divorce of someone with whom they were close. This has caused them to consider carefully the addition of a child to their family. Young couples are re-assessing marriage and the relationship between men and women. This re-assessment is one of the factors being attributed to lower fertility rates (Balakrishnan, Lapierre-Adamczyk, & Krotki, 1993).

Lack of Support for Parents

Canadian society as a whole is not seen as supportive of children and families. Evelyne Lapierre-Adamczyk, a demography professor at L'Université de Montréal, claims that young couples see families "struggle to balance careers and children" (Campbell, October 2000, p. 6). Workplaces that do not allow enough flexibility for parents and that have inadequate child-care programs are just two of the concerns young couples have when considering having children. Lapierre-Adamczyk feels that society should support families, and that workplaces need to be more accommodating of parents in terms of the hours they work, the opportunity to work from home, and the ability to take time off to care for ill children, for example. Governments need to develop social programs that will assist them. According to Dr. Benjamin Schlesinger, University of Toronto, and Rachel Aber Schlesinger, York University, society needs to do more to help parents who are assuming the costs of bearing and rearing children. Better-quality day care and more day-care spaces are important steps in supporting working parents. The Schlesingers question just how much Canadian society values children, when so little is done to support caregivers in the important task of raising children (1992).

Even with all the reasons Canadians should be cautious about having children, 90 percent of couples today have, or would like to have, children. In a 1999 Angus Reid survey, Canadians between 20 and 39 years of age were asked about the total number of children they intended to have. Ninety-six percent of women between 20 and 29 years of age reported that they planned on having at least two children. Men of the same age group reported similar results. Whether or not all of these people actually do have children remains to be seen, but at least it is known that the majority of young Canadians intend to have children (Avard & Harmsen, 2000).

"Babies are such a nice way of starting people."

—Don Herold

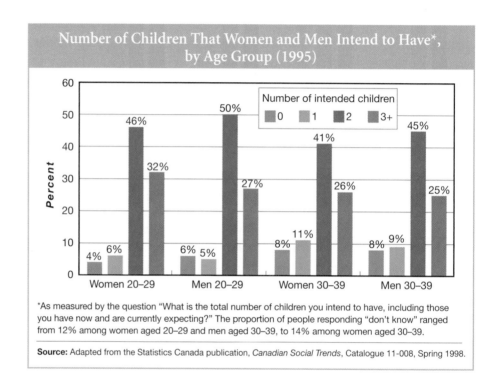

Number of Children That Women and Men Intend to Have*, by Age Group (1995)

*As measured by the question "What is the total number of children you intend to have, including those you have now and are currently expecting?" The proportion of people responding "don't know" ranged from 12% among women aged 20–29 and men aged 30–39, to 14% among women aged 30–39.

Source: Adapted from the Statistics Canada publication, *Canadian Social Trends*, Catalogue 11-008, Spring 1998.

Factors for Would-Be Parents to Consider

Young couples planning to have children must weigh all of the considerations carefully to come to a decision that is best for them and their future children. These factors (Campbell, October 2000) include:

- society and social values
- religion
- economic conditions and personal finances
- feelings about children
- psychological readiness

- genetic diseases that could be passed on to children

- pressure from peers, parents, and other family members

Canadian society encourages young couples to have children, since it needs to replace itself. Most faiths also encourage childbearing. Couples who attend faith services tend to have more children than couples who do not. Campbell notes that even though government and businesses do not seem to do enough to support families, they still assume that most people will become parents (October 2000). Peer pressure is another factor that influences a couple's decisions about when to start a family. Often when friends begin to have children, couples feel pressured to have children of their own. They feel left out of conversations and events that revolve around children. Parents and other family members also put pressure on young couples to have children. Often parents expect grandchildren soon after a couple is married. Siblings can also put pressure on a couple if they want to become aunts or uncles (Balakrishnan, Lapierre-Adamczyk, & Krotki, 1993).

Economics play a role in the decision and timing of childbearing. Many couples are delaying the birth of their first child until they have some measure of financial security, whether this is owning a home or having savings. Other couples feel it is important to establish themselves in a career prior to becoming parents. When the job market is good, it is easier for a member of a couple to take time away from work, since there are probably some jobs waiting upon his or her return. In tough economic times, when there are very few jobs available, this is not the case (Balakrishnan, Lapierre-Adamczyk, & Krotki, 1993).

Some couples avoid having children of their own because of the fear of passing on genetic diseases to their child. **Genetic diseases** include diabetes, anemia, hemophilia, sickle-cell anemia, cystic fibrosis, and Tay-Sachs disease, among others. Now, there are tests available to couples to determine if either partner is predisposed to passing on a genetic disease. From the results of these tests, couples can make informed decisions about whether or not they want to risk having a child with a genetic disease (Sasse, 2000).

When to Have Children

Once couples have decided to have children, they need to decide when they will have them. In the 1960s and 1970s, women had their first child when they were in their early twenties. Now, the average age at a first birth is when women are in their mid-twenties (Vanier Institute of the Family, 2000). Fertility rates between 1986 and 1997 show that most children are born to women who are between 20 and 34 years of age. Trends demonstrate that a

"Death and taxes and childbirth! There's never any convenient time for any of them."

—Margaret Mitchell

shift took place between 1986 and 1997. There was an overall decrease in the number of women having children in their twenties, but at the same time there was an increase in women having children in their thirties. This **delayed parenthood** will have an impact on Canadian birth rates, as women who begin childbearing later in life will have a shorter time in which to have children.

Women's Fertility Rates, 1986–1997					
Rate per 1000 women					
Age of woman	1986	1991	1995	1996	1997
15–19 years (includes births to women under 15)	23.01	25.98	24.49	22.34	20.19
20–24 years	78.74	77.50	70.53	67.28	64.07
25–29 years	119.01	120.33	109.69	105.82	103.88
30–34 years	72.52	83.63	86.77	85.51	84.44
35–39 years	22.30	28.27	31.26	32.22	32.52
40–44 years	3.15	3.88	4.83	5.06	5.19
45–49 years (includes births to women over 50)	.13	.17	.19	.20	.20

Note: The rate is determined by dividing the number of live births in each age group by the total female population in each age group.

Source: Adapted from the Statistics Canada web site
http://www.statcan.ca/english/Pgdb/People/health/health08.htm.

Delayed Parenting

The average age of a first birth has been increasing since the 1970s, and now sits at 27.1 years of age (Eshleman & Wilson, 2001). The greatest increase in first-time parents occurred among women who were between 30 and 34 years of age. That percentage rose from 14 percent in 1970 to 25.8 percent in 1982 to 30 percent in 1990. Couples who delay parenting tend to be well-educated, middle-class, and work-oriented (Schlesinger & Schlesinger, 1992).

Both women and men are staying in school longer. This longer period of education has had an impact on when they are starting their career, when they are getting married, and when they are starting to have children. Canadian couples are getting married later now than they did earlier in the twentieth century. The later couples get married, the later they start their family, and the fewer children they will have. The family size of those who delay will be smaller, since the woman's **biological clock**, or the length of time that a woman's body is able to conceive and carry a child, limits the number of children she can bear. For couples who are career-oriented, a small family is more practical than a large one; consequently, a small family is the norm for couples who delay parenthood (Schlesinger & Schlesinger, 1992). From the symbolic interactionism perspective, couples who delay parenting are choosing to control their own destiny. Their fertility behaviour is controlled more by themselves than by older societal norms. In the past, these couples may have been considered too old to become parents, but now they have created new norms through their behaviour.

There is more support for delayed parenting now than in the past. Young couples are no longer rushed into parenthood and are often cautioned to wait until they are ready and established before having children. As medical technology develops, it is possible for women well into their forties to give birth to healthy babies. Many couples delay parenthood until they are psychologically and financially ready. Many dual-income couples delay parenting until they can afford the cost of caring for a child. They must be able to afford for one spouse to take an extended leave of absence from employment or to pay for child care. Often couples will save up for and purchase a home prior to starting a family (Baker, 1998). Delayed parenting is also reflected in the media. Older mothers are seen in advertisements, in movies, and on television shows. Books and magazine articles support bringing up a baby later in life. Growing up with your children is no longer the norm (Schlesinger & Schlesinger, 1992).

Between Friends

Some women delay parenting, then find that they cannot have children. They may attempt to have children through the use of reproductive technologies, but the success rate is still quite low, and many women end up being denied the parenting experience. Elizabeth Bartholet, an American professor, claims that many of these women who are unsuccessful with assisted reproduction could have enjoyed the parenting experience through adoption. She feels that Canadian society encourages women to expose themselves to the disappointment of unsuccessful fertility treatment by placing more value on childbearing than on the actual experience of parenting (1994). Another issue to consider is the emotional health of the women who cannot conceive, even with assisted reproductive technologies. A study conducted by Harvard University in 1993 found that anxiety and depression among infertile women was similar to that of women who were dealing with cancer, heart disease, or were HIV-positive (Kershner, 1996).

research study | Family and Childbearing in Canada: A Demographic Analysis

by T. R. Balakrishnan, Sociology Professor, University of Western Ontario; Evelyne Lapierre-Adamczyk, Professor and Director of the Departement de demographie, Université de Montréal; and Karol J. Krotki, Sociology Professor, University of Alberta

RESEARCH QUESTIONS

1. What are Canadians' attitudes regarding family size, timing of births, and family planning?
2. How do expectations within marriage, value of children, and satisfaction or utility from work outside the home affect childbearing?
3. How do religion, ethnicity, education, income, place of residence, and female labour-force participation affect fertility and marriage?
4. How do separation and divorce affect fertility behaviour?
5. What are the patterns of contraceptive use?
6. What are the implications of reproductive behaviour for population and aging?

HYPOTHESIS

The change in the institution of the family is the primary determinant of recent reproductive behaviour.

RESEARCH METHOD

The researchers used the *survey method*. They collected information from women in the reproductive years between 18 and 49. Random household telephone numbers from across Canada were sampled. A total of 22 169 households were called and 5315 interviews were conducted.

RESULTS

- Most Canadian couples expect to have 1 to 3 children. Couples use various forms of birth control to manage family size and timing of births.
- In the past, couples had children because it was the norm for all married couples to complete their union by seeking happiness through the birth of children. Couples are now more interested in a personally fulfilling life. They are deciding to have children for their own personal satisfaction, not because of societal expectations and traditional values. Couples are delaying childbearing because of work outside the home. More women work outside the home before and after childbirth.

- Many factors that influenced fertility in the past no longer have as great an impact. Higher rates of fertility used to be related to religion, ethnicity, and language of origin. Important determinants are education, place of residence, religiosity, and female labour-force participation. They still lead to lower fertility rates; however, the strength of their impact has narrowed. The impact of income has almost disappeared. Delayed childbearing is influenced by education, urban residence, and work delay. It is important to note that this does not have a significant effect on family size, since couples who started childbearing earlier in life tend to use sterilization as a means of contraception in order to limit family size. Religiosity, or religious attendance, is an overwhelming factor. Those who attend church regularly are less likely to cohabit, less likely to divorce, and have larger families.
- Couples who divorce are more likely to have married young, below the age of twenty; are less religious; and are more likely to have had premarital births and conceptions.
- Canadians start using contraceptives early. Many use them before pregnancy and between first and second pregnancies. Canadian women want to control the number and timing of births. After they have reached the desired family size, many Canadians resort to sterilization as a permanent means to control fertility.
- Very few of the respondents expected to depend on their children in old age, and thus this was not a motivating factor in childbearing. Most would not want to live with their children in their old age, and would prefer to live independently or in a seniors' home.

CONCLUSIONS

Canadians are taking more control over their fertility by controlling the timing, spacing, and number of children they have. Some Canadian women are delaying childbearing until they are older in order to complete their education and begin careers. Canadian women are working before and after the birth of their children. Factors that historically led to increased fertility, such as ethnicity and religion, no longer have as strong an influence as in the past. The fertility patterns of Canadians are more consistent now than in the past. Couples who divorce tend to have married younger and had premarital conception or births. Few Canadians expect their children to care for them in old age. As a country we need to heed these changes in our social planning for day-care facilities, schools, and seniors' services. Fertility rates are now below replacement and should be considered when forming immig ration policies. ■

Source: Balakrishnan, T. R., Lapierre-Adamczyk, E., & Krotki, K. (1993). *Family and childbearing in Canada: A demographic analysis*. Toronto: University of Toronto Press.

Births Outside of Marriage

Although the Canadian birth rate has been steadily declining, births by women outside of marriage have increased. In 1971, 9 percent of births were to unmarried women. This number increased to 14 percent in 1981 (Eshleman & Wilson, 2001). Another significant change in births outside of marriage is the age of women who are giving birth. In the past, births outside of marriage were primarily to women in their teens. Now, more than half of all unmarried mothers are over the age of 25. Many of these women are cohabitating at the time of birth. The birth rate for unmarried women is highest in Québec, where cohabitation is more common than in any other province in Canada (Eshleman & Wilson, 2001). The symbolic interactionist perspective suggests that this change reflects individual women having an impact on the norms of society and changing how unmarried mothers view themselves, and an increasing acceptance.

Proportion of Births to Unmarried Women, 1961–91

*Excludes Newfoundland   Year

Proportion of All Couples with Children Living Common Law

Québec	Canada outside Québec
4%	3%

Québec	Canada outside Québec
14%	6%

Source: Adapted from the Statistics Canada publication, *Canadian Social Trends,* Catalogue 11-008, Spring 1994.

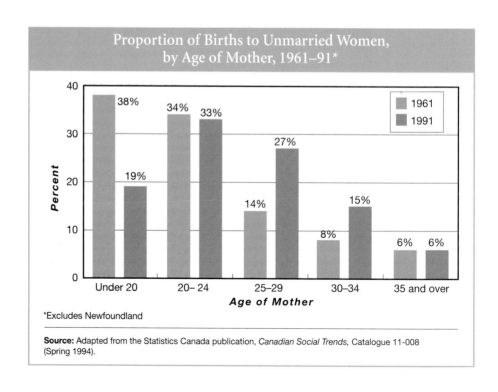

Proportion of Births to Unmarried Women, by Age of Mother, 1961–91*

Age of Mother	1961	1991
Under 20	38%	19%
20–24	34%	33%
25–29	14%	27%
30–34	8%	15%
35 and over	6%	6%

*Excludes Newfoundland

Source: Adapted from the Statistics Canada publication, *Canadian Social Trends,* Catalogue 11-008 (Spring 1994).

Teenaged Births

Teenaged births have always been a concern in Canada, since there is considerable evidence of the negative long-term effects of teen childbearing (Eshleman & Wilson, 2001). In 1994, the rate and number of births by teenaged women were lower than they were in 1974. Now, almost as many teenagers have abortions as live births. Canadian teenagers have lower pregnancy rates than their American counterparts. One reason cited for this difference is that Canadian teens have more education about contraception and more access to contraceptive products. Other reasons cited were that American teens are more willing to take risks and that they are more ambivalent about sex.

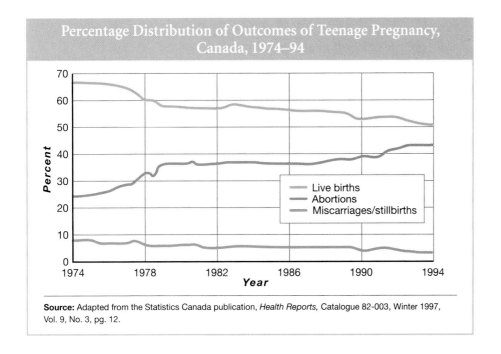

Percentage Distribution of Outcomes of Teenage Pregnancy, Canada, 1974–94

Source: Adapted from the Statistics Canada publication, *Health Reports,* Catalogue 82-003, Winter 1997, Vol. 9, No. 3, pg. 12.

Number of Children

The birth rate in Canada has been declining steadily since the last half of the twentieth century. According to Lapierre-Adamczyk, in 1960 the birth rate in Canada was 3.8 children per family. Now it has declined to 1.5 children per family (Campbell, October 2000). A small family of two to three children is now the norm (Balakrishnan, Lapierre-Adamczyk, & Krotki, 1993).

web connection

www.mcgrawhill.ca/links/families12

To learn about family statistics, go to the web site above for *Individuals and Families in a Diverse Society* to see where to go next.

Factors Influencing Fertility

Year of Birth	Risk Ratio for Having a Third Child*
Before 1945	**1.76**
1945–1954	1.06**
1955–1964	1.07**
After 1965	1.00
Age of woman at birth of first child	
Under 25	2.53
25–29	1.60
30 or over	1.00
Interval between first two births	
Less than 30 months	1.00
30–53 months	0.66
More than 53 months	0.31
Marital status	
Not in union	0.63**
Common-law union	1.05
Married	1.00
Employment status after second birth	
Working	0.65
Not working	1.00
Education	
No secondary completion	1.31
Secondary completion	1.00
Post-secondary completion	1.02**
Province of residence	
High fertility rate	1.17
(Prince Edward Island, Manitoba, Saskatchewan and Alberta)	
Average fertility rate	1.00
Religious attendance	
Weekly	1.46
Other	1.00
Number of siblings	
None	0.96**
One	1.00
More than one	1.11**
Place of birth	
Canada	1.00
Europe and North America	0.80
Other countries	1.48

* Numbers greater than 1.0 indicate a high correlation between the factor and the chances of the woman having three or more children. A ratio of less than 1.0 indicates that the factor is negative. A factor of 1.0 indicates that there is no influence by that factor.
** Not statistically significant

Source: Adapted from the Statistics Canada publication, *Canadian Social Trends*, Catalogue 11-008, Summer 1999.

Ann Walmsley

I have two wonderful children, but I've mused about having a third ever since a couple of attempts ended in miscarriages some years ago. I tend to pine at the most subliminal suggestion of larger families. In fact, any family-life scene can get me started—a magazine car ad that portrays three children in the back seat, a television commercial showing sisters phoning each other long distance, my brother's young children, even the bags of toys in our basement.

I suppose for some people, the question of how big the family should be remains unresolved throughout adult life. Longing wrestles with logic and it becomes hard to know when you have finally put the decision behind you. Other couples seem enviably sure of the magic number of children for them—even before they are married. They tend to talk about "a nice round number" or "an even number so one will not be left out" or "the same number of siblings as I had growing up." A few leave it to fate. But most of the parents interviewed for this story wanted to control the outcome in some way, and ended up weighing everything from finances and health risks to the number of bedrooms in the house and the desire to have both boys and girls.

Regardless, life has a way of scuttling such plans. Fertility problems, accidental pregnancies, and luck of the draw in terms of gender often factor in. Those who elect to have a small family when their kids are young and needy may find themselves revisiting the issue as their children become more independent. And sometimes when parents divorce and then remarry, they decide they want more children with their new spouse.

Conversely, a few regret having as many children as they did. Baby lust gives way to reality and the

Deciding how many children to have is often a difficult decision for a couple.

enormous responsibility of caring for each child. Said one mother frankly of her marriage and eventual separation: "Three children brought us together; four put us over the edge." The whole subject evokes some very raw emotions, and parents' candor seems to stem from their search for the right answer. "It's the only decision we ever make that we can't go back on," says Margaret Fisher Brillinger, a Toronto marriage and family therapist with a background in parent education. "If you marry and it doesn't work out, you can get a divorce. If you buy a house you don't like, you can move to another house. But once you become a parent, you can't become an unparent."

Despite the very personal nature of the decision, Brillinger says that a third party can help couples sort through the issues and identify the unconscious feelings or needs that may be influencing their judgment. Brillinger herself is deft at separating reasons that are based in fantasy from those grounded in reality (see "Myth Conceptions" on page 292). "There is no ideal number of children in general," she says. "You have to think about each parent's own developmental stage or timing in her career path, the strength of the marriage relationship, how tasks are divided, whether or not stepchildren are involved, and the parents' time and energy. Adding another child is not just adding a person, it is adding a whole new set of complex interactions."

Although anecdotally there appear to be plenty of three-children families these days, statistically, Canadians are having fewer kids than they did 20 years ago. According to Statistics Canada, the total fertility rate was 1.66 births per woman in 1994, down from 1.83 in 1974. Women born in 1930 had the largest families this century: 3.39 children.

An unspoken reason for large families earlier in the century was to compensate for lower child survival rates. Even today, some parents are willing to voice that fundamental fear of losing a child, explaining that it can have bearing on their thoughts about family size. "I decided that if I only had two and something happened to one of them, then there would be an 'only child' to deal with me in my old age, so three was the number we thought would be good," says Sheri Grant of Port Coquitlam, British Columbia. But the growing number of older first-time mothers, the greater participation of women in the work force, and the rising cost of childrearing have combined to drive fertility rates down. The cost of raising a child in Canada from birth to age 18 is about $160 000, according to 1998 statistics from the Manitoba government. Add to that Statistics Canada's figure of $32 000 for a four-year university education (including campus room and board), and you're talking big bucks.

Some parents who have opted for large families say that the determining factor for happiness is the parents' ability to enjoy chaos. "Once you go beyond two, you enter a different level of parenting because you don't have time for them all," says Roy MacGregor of Kanata, Ontario, an adoring father of four children aged 15 to 21, and author of the popular children's book series *The Screech Owl Mysteries*. But MacGregor claims that he loves noise and turmoil and is now aching for a younger child. His solution? "I've created my own fictional 11- and 12-year-olds in the series. They exist in my head."

In addition to concerns about giving enough time to each child, parents worry that having more children will limit the extras they can offer them, such as music lessons and travel. But according to Dave Wright, who has seven children ranging in age from six to 24 (five of whom were delivered by C-section), this should not be the deciding factor when discussing how many children to have. "People who are 'just waiting until we can better afford it' should raise goldfish instead," says Wright from his home near Rodney, Ontario. "If you have the capacity for the love that it takes, don't let anything or anyone stop you." Wright, a banker who works from home, and his wife, Raina, a stay-at-home mom, say they can afford only one activity a year per child, and the kids accept that. But they do have ample time for each child. "I still manage to go to almost all of the school recitals and we play together and read together every day," says Dave. "I even know the names of the girls my teenage son likes. And they all give you challenges, but they don't compound because one child may be struggling with toilet training and another is worried about boyfriends."

The Wrights had intended to stop at three children, but changed their minds after a surprise fourth pregnancy. The pregnancy was medically precarious for months but ultimately successful, despite doctors' predictions. The couple, who are devout United Church members, took it as a sign that more children were preordained. So they took no birth-control measures and had another three, stopping only when Raina reached the age of 40.

There is a certain exhilaration in letting nature take its course, but more often than not, parents seem to form their idea of what constitutes a whole family from a grab bag of psychological and personal impulses. Loree Burnham of Merritt, British Columbia, says that she can't explain why the number three sticks in her head. "We know how smoothly things ran when we had two roaming around," she says. "Oddly enough, though, I felt that I needed more children to feel like a whole family." Charlotte Pepin, a mother of three in North Bay, Ontario, says that having a crop of kids close together is her way of fulfilling a missed opportunity in her own childhood. Because her three siblings were much older, she grew up feeling like an only child. Pepin, whose children now range from nine months to seven years, always said that she wanted five or six children, but settled on the idea of four as more realistic. In her mind is a dream moment, probably seven years down the road, when her current three and an as-yet-unconceived fourth will be old enough to play board games together and go camping. "All the things I never got to do," she says.

In contrast to the boisterous atmosphere that the Pepins enjoy, the Smith family of Yarmouth, Nova Scotia, has found a sense of completion with only one child. Lisa and her husband, Darrin, made the decision to stop at one when their son Avery was only four months old. Lisa suffered from postpartum depression and has concluded that she does not want to endure it again, while Darrin, an only child himself, had always expressed his wish for a one-child family.

According to Brillinger, this desire to follow the model of the family you grew up in is a common, albeit unconscious, factor. Still, Lisa Smith claims that negative comments from others in the community have led her to believe that "this choice isn't widely accepted in today's society—at least not in the small town where we live. People say that we will have a bad child, a spoiled child. One person said, 'But what would happen if something happened to this child?' As if having two or 20 more children could ever replace that life. Imagine!" Despite these pressures, the Smiths are ardent about their choice and delighted to offer their son undivided attention.

The most difficult realization for some parents is that their choices may be limited by external factors such as disagreement with a partner about the desired number of children. Another hard reality: Raising kids can be tougher than imagined, and may change your outlook. Francise Turcotte-Boucher of Kapuskasing, Ontario, says she and her husband are having second thoughts about their original plan to have three kids because of their trouble coping with a challenging second child. "The personality and temperament of your children are important factors in deciding whether to expand the family," says Turcotte-Boucher. Their two-year-old son bites and hits his older sister and parents, screams to provoke reactions, and thwarts any attention paid to his sister. "We wouldn't want to deny our oldest more attention by having a third child when she has already missed so much attention because of her brother."

Health risks to the mother can also complicate the decision. Edwina Mills's experience with hypertension during pregnancy was a key reason why the Maxville, Ontario, teacher and her husband, Stephen, decided to stop after two children. Doctor-ordered bed rest and hospital stays were a routine part of her pregnancies and restricted Stephen, an archaeologist, from doing field work. But like many parents who are forced to make this decision, Edwina revisited the issue frequently. "My heart still ached when I saw mothers with their new babies," she says. "I had not thought of our younger son as our last and I was somehow left wanting. Never again would I feel the warm snuggle of a child burrowing his face into my shoulder looking for that perfect comfort zone." It was only when her period was overdue some months later and she panicked at confronting another high-risk pregnancy that she was able to put the decision behind her. "My period finally did arrive one week and three pregnancy tests later, and our decision to be content with two children came with it."

There was a time when my daughter made fairly regular requests for a baby brother, which is a factor that many parents don't anticipate: a sibling's own yearnings. In our case, a kitten and two fire-bellied newts seemed to fulfill her desire to some extent. But I often look at my daughter and son walking together down the sidewalk and wonder if their lives would be fuller with another sibling tagging along. Then I see them laughing over a shared joke and I realize that it isn't the number of children that counts, but the quality of family interaction: the intimacy, the humour, and the desire to spend time together. In that sense I know we are fortunate—and complete. ■

Source: *Today's Parent*. (1999, February 1). 16, pp. 54–57.

1. What are the factors to take into consideration when deciding on the number of children to have?
2. According to Brillinger, why is the parenting decision so important?
3. What are some of the factors that are lowering fertility rates in Canada?
4. What are the concerns of parents of larger families?
5. What are some of the reasons couples had more than two children?

Myth Conceptions

Toronto marriage and family therapist Margaret Fisher Brillinger points out that a variety of myths tend to influence couples' decisions about family size. Here she exposes some of the most common ones:

1. Just because children are close in age does not mean they will be friends.
2. Having four children does not settle the concern that one child will be routinely left out of a three-child family. The key to solving this problem is to encourage children to mix with their siblings in different ways at various times, sometimes dividing in terms of age, sometimes by interests, etc.
3. Remarried couples with stepchildren should not immediately have their own baby to knit the family together. The first task is to integrate the existing children into the blended family.
4. Having more children will not compensate for emptiness left from a lack of intimacy or love in your own childhood.
5. The model of your own childhood might not apply in 1998. It may be that five-kid families were fine a generation ago, but there can be several reasons why five won't work for you now.
6. The idea that the bigger the family, the happier is a Hollywood concoction. Many are, of course. (Brillinger herself has four children.) But big families are also hectic and involve balancing many demands.
7. A baby does not bring a couple together when they are experiencing difficulties in their relationship.
8. The idea that a child of a certain gender will offer a different or specific type of parent-child bond may be illusory. Those bonds have more to do with personality than gender.

Childlessness

Recent studies have surveyed childless couples to determine their attitude toward children in their future. The Canadian Fertility Survey results, by T.R. Balakrishnan, Evelyne Lapierre-Adamczyk, and Karol Krotki, showed that even though at the time of the survey 35.2 percent of the women were childless, only 9.6 percent expected to remain childless (1993). When discussing childlessness it is necessary to consider whether a couple remains childless by choice or naturally.

	Percentage of Women Childless at Time of Interview and Expecting to Remain Childless by Marital Status							
	All Women		Ever-Married		Currently Married		Never-Married	
Age at	Childless at survey	Expect to be childless	Childless at survey	Expect to be childless	Childless at survey	Expect to be childless	Expect to be childless	
18–19	94.3	15.0	56.2	4.0	59.4	4.5	16.0	
20–24	74.5	9.0	45.2	3.1	47.2	2.9	11.9	
25–29	39.9	7.9	25.6	3.7	23.9	3.1	20.6	
30–34	21.6	10.5	12.6	6.3	11.0	5.2	39.8	
35–39	14.5	10.9	11.2	8.6	10.0	7.4	47.1	
40–44	10.1	9.3	6.8	6.4	6.6	6.2	77.1	
45–49	7.9	7.9	4.3	4.3	4.5	4.5	92.1	
Total	35.2	9.6	15.7	5.7	15.4	5.1	20.4	
Number of women	5315		3884		3283		1431	

Source: Balakrishnan, T.R., Lapierre–Adamczyk, E., & Krotki, K. (1993). *Family and Childbearing in Canada: A demographic analysis.* Toronto: University of Toronto Press.

Childless by Choice

Even though 90 percent of the population wants to be parents, not all couples feel that way. Couples who choose to remain childless challenge the traditionally held belief that children are a natural and desired part of marriage (Ishwaran, 1992). The term **voluntary childlessness** is given to couples who deliberately decide not to become parents, either biologically through childbearing or socially through adoption (Schlesinger & Schlesinger, 1992).

Not all couples choose to remain childless for the same reasons. Some couples decide very early on in their relationship that they do not want to have children, while others make the decision gradually during the course of their marriage. For some couples the decision to remain childless is mutual, while for others one member convinces the other to remain childless. In some marriages one member of the couple would have had children if he or she had been married to someone else, while other childless couples would not have had children regardless of who they married. Reasons for not having children vary from a rejection of a child-centred lifestyle, in which life revolves around the child's needs and wants, to the attraction of an adult-centred lifestyle, in which the needs and wants of the adults are of foremost importance (Larson, Goltz, & Hobart, 1994). The social exchange theory provides a rationale for childlessness. These adults do not see the benefits of childbearing as a fair exchange for the time, energy, and money they have to contribute to raising a child.

The lifestyle of the childless couple is very different than the lifestyle of parents. Couples without children can pursue personal interests and hobbies without having to worry about child care or scheduling their interests around those of their children (Ishwaran, 1992). Studies have shown that marital "satisfaction among couples who remain childless is higher than among parents (Eshleman & Wilson, 2001).

Natural Childlessness

Couples who cannot bear children of their own are called infertile. Many infertile couples desperately want to have children who share the same genetic history. Often they spend years being tested and treated and trying a variety of reproductive technologies. Infertile couples want to have blood-related children in order to carry on and preserve the family tree. They do not want to miss out on the parenting experience. Some do not want to disappoint their parents by not making them grandparents. By remaining infertile the couples interrupt the life cycle of both themselves and their parents. Consequently, much social pressure to have children is put on them (Daly, 1995). Studies have shown that couples who experience natural childlessness also experience a great deal of stress in their lives. Frustrations over childlessness often have an impact on other aspects of their lives, including work, finances, and social life. This can cause strain in relationships with family, friends, and coworkers (Eshleman & Wilson, 2001).

Adoption

The number of Canadian children placed for adoption has decreased in the past two decades. In 1980, 5376 children were placed for adoption compared to 2836 in 1990. There are fewer adoptions of children under the age of one since there are fewer infants available. Most children who are up for adoption are older and, therefore, harder to place. The number of private adoptions, in which the mother puts the child up for adoption through a means other than the Children's Aid Society, has increased in recent years. The decline in the number of children available for adoption is not due to an increase in the number of abortions but an increase in the number of mothers raising their children on their own. Of the women who give their child up for adoption, 51 percent do so because they feel they are too young to be a parent. Other considerations are the inability to care for a child financially, and the disruption the addition of a child would cause to education or career plans (Eshleman & Wilson, 2001).

Adoption provides for the social continuation of the family, since it allows families to pass on their patterns, customs, and values. It does not provide for the biological continuation of the family. The biological ties and histories of adoptive children are often ignored. Consequently, they are often unaware of important genetic factors that may be helpful for them to know about in the future (Daly, 1995).

Attitudes Toward Childbearing

In the past, the value of children was different than it is today. In the seventeenth century, children were seen as objects of affection and discipline and as a valuable source of labour in the eighteenth and nineteenth centuries. Now, children are viewed as a source of developmental satisfaction that is accompanied by a set of monetary costs (Daly, 1995). Couples having children in Canada today are doing so because they feel that it will fulfill them and add to their relationship. They question whether or not having children will make them happier. If the answer is yes, then they have children. Canadian women place considerable importance on personal relationships and love as being necessary for happiness. Couples today do not look to traditional institutions and values in the same way that couples did in the past. They need to see parenthood as having emotional benefits (Balakrishnan, Lapierre-Adamczyk, & Krotki, 1993).

Childbearing and Intergenerational Concerns

Reduced fertility has an impact on the older generation. As parents age, there are fewer children to care for them in their senior years. However, it appears that Canadians are not relying on their children to support them financially in the future. Parents surveyed expected emotional support and personal care from their children rather than money. Today's parents do not anticipate that they will have to live with their children. Couples are not having children to have someone to support them financially or to live with when they are older (Balakrishnan, Lapierre-Adamczyk, & Krotki, 1993).

Role of Society in Childrearing

In today's society, the family has handed over many of the functions it performed in the past to other institutions and agencies. Families once educated their children. Today, children are socialized, taught, and raised in schools for approximately 20 hours every week (Schlesinger & Schlesinger, 1992). Families used to provide most of the recreational opportunities for their members. Now, they seek recreation in places like hockey rinks, soccer fields, movie theatres, play groups, parks and other recreational programs, drop-in centres, and various other places. Children are coached and socialized by a number of non-family members when they participate in different recreational activities.

case study | Deciding to Have a Child

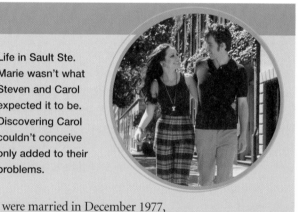

Life in Sault Ste. Marie wasn't what Steven and Carol expected it to be. Discovering Carol couldn't conceive only added to their problems.

Steven Harris and Carol Mehisto met in 1972 during their first year at Laurentian University and have been together ever since. Both Steven and Carol came from large families. Carol was born in Thunder Bay, Ontario, and is the oldest of five children. She spent her high school years in Toronto living with her aunt, while the rest of her family lived in Ghana. Steven, along with his sister and brother, was born in England. His family emigrated to Canada when he was four, and he grew up and went to school in a small town north of Toronto.

Like some of their generation, Steven and Carol lived together for a period of time before getting married. They rented a tiny basement apartment near Kensington Market in Toronto. Steven attended classes at the School of Social Work, and Carol enrolled in an education program at the University of Toronto. Soon after, Carol decided that she didn't want to be a teacher and got a job in a local library, where she worked while Steven attended classes. They were married in December 1977, five months before Steven completed his master's degree in social work. Upon graduation, Steven was hired by the City of Toronto, where he worked in the Welfare Department. However, his real interest was in public housing, so when a job opening became available in the Ontario Ministry of Housing in Sault Ste. Marie, Steven applied for it and got it.

Life in Sault Ste. Marie wasn't what Steven and Carol expected. After the initial excitement of buying a house and "settling down" in a community, they ran into some problems. Carol was unable to get a job of any kind, let alone one that interested her. Although the people in the community were friendly, Steven and Carol found that, as outsiders, they had a great deal of difficulty making new friends. They joined the local curling club and began to attend church services in the hope of meeting other young couples, but that didn't work. As well, Steven's job did not turn out to be as interesting and as challenging as he thought it would be. He discovered that he was only managing housing issues and was not involved in policy and decision making, which was being done at the Ministry offices in Toronto. His job also took him away from home for long periods of time, since his office administered public housing across Northern Ontario. Carol began to feel very lonely and isolated and yearned for something more fulfilling in her life.

Carol began to raise the issue of having children. They both loved children and had enjoyed spending time with Steven's older sister, Pam, who had a daughter. Both of them knew that raising a family was part of their dream, but they hadn't planned to have children until later, when they were both established in their careers. As Carol was not working, and felt emotionally and intellectually unfulfilled, they eventually decided to start a family. Unfortunately, she did not become pregnant over the next few months. This added to their dissatisfaction and frustration.

Soon after, they made the decision to move back to the Toronto area, where many of their friends and family lived. Steven was able to secure a transfer to the Ministry of Housing office and Carol began to work again in the library system, although she could only get part-time work. They bought a three-bedroom house in a quiet east-end neighbourhood, just up the street from the local elementary school. Carol and Steven settled into an active social life with their family and friends. At this point, Steven had been promoted into a more interesting position in the policy department at the

Ministry and was making more than enough money to support Carol and a family. Carol really didn't like her job, and yearned to be a mother. Eventually, they went to a fertility clinic for advice, but continued to be unsuccessful. Their infertility began to put a strain on their relationship. Tired of being teased by family members, they began to withdraw from family social activities, since Carol found it hard being around her three young nieces. The fact that most of their married friends had begun families made them more frustrated and unhappy, since conversation and social activities with them inevitably began to centre around children.

Although adoption was not something that they had previously considered, they began to apply at various adoption agencies. This led to contact with other couples in the same situation, and they soon organized a support group for infertile couples that continues to this day. Their activity in this organization provided both of them with tremendous satisfaction, particularly since they were able to mentor other couples who were experiencing the same frustrations they had been feeling. Finally, in the spring of 1984, through a private agency, they adopted a son, Jeremy, and their family became complete. Much to their surprise, Carol became pregnant six years later, and in 1991, their daughter Kaitlyn was born. ■

1. What factors motivated Steven and Carol to have children?
2. What effects did their fertility problem have on their relationships with each other and with their extended families?
3. Using the perspective of symbolic interactionism, suggest the effects on Carol of not being able to have a child, of adopting a child, and of having a biological child.
4. What adjustments would having children require in Steven and Carol's relationship?

Places of worship provide for the religious needs of families. The state and other agencies provide for families' security and safety (Ishwaran, 1992).

There are many ways that the larger society influences children outside the local community. One such influence outside the family is television and the mass media. Children spend up to 31 hours a week watching television. The mass media, including television, movies, music, and video and computer games, has become a large part of their lives. Consequently, children receive many messages from the mass media, and its influence on them has become a source of concern. Sometimes the messages transmitted by the mass media are not those that parents want their children to receive. Now, parents have to compete with the media in the socialization of their children (Schlesinger & Schlesinger, 1992).

Other influences outside the family are the people who provide care for children. While parents are at work, many of their children spend part of their day in the care of someone else. Some children are cared for by licensed child-care providers, day-care centres, nursery schools, and licensed home care. Other children spend time with unlicensed providers in private homes. These non-family caregivers also have an impact on the socialization of children (Ishwaran, 1992).

With this change in the way outside agencies interact with families and children, one function of parents has become co-ordinating the use and effects of the agencies. Parents are now responsible to ensure that the outside agencies have a positive impact on the everyday life of their children (Ishwaran, 1992).

Charts and graphs can be used to display the information gained through primary research, thus adding a different dimension to the reporting of your results. Using a visual presentation to convey your information will enable you to clearly and concisely illustrate the material to be presented.

Most word processing packages include a spreadsheet program. Use the following steps with the spreadsheet program to create charts to present research findings.

1. Organize the data you have collected from your survey. Make sure that you have tallied your answers by category.

2. Open the spreadsheet program.

3. Type in the answers to the question across the top row of cells.

4. Type in the results across the next rows of cells, using as many rows as there are possible types of answers. See the example below.

5. Use the mouse to select all the cells into which you have entered information.

6. Look in the menu bar for the chart function. Depending on the software program, it could be listed as a chart wizard, as an insert, or under options.

7. The chart function will allow you to choose the type of chart or graph you wish to make with your data. It will prompt you to add a title to the chart or graph as well as label the axes.

Charts and graphs are best used for closed questions. ■

Example: Survey results from the question "How many children do you expect to have?" done with a class of 31 students.

	A	B	C	D	E
No. of children desired	1	2	3	4	5 or more
Total	4	15	7	4	3
Female	1	8	4	2	1
Male	3	7	3	2	2

Knowledge/Understanding Thinking/Inquiry

1. Summarize the changes that have taken place in childbearing and childrearing practices in North America since the time of hunter-gatherer tribes. Describe characteristics of the past that you still see in existence in current childbearing and childrearing practices.

2. Discuss the childbearing practices of your grandparents and how they differ from that of your parents. Was there a difference in practices between your maternal and your paternal grandparents?

3. Look at the fertility rates chart on page 282. Make note of the changes occurring between 1986 and 1997. Explain why these changes took place. Predict what changes you think will occur between 1997 and 2007.

4. a) How many children are in your family? Ask your parents or guardians, grandparents, or other older parents you know what factors they considered when determining the number of children to have.

   b) How many children do you think you will have? What factors will you consider?

5. Summarize the impact of the following on childbearing in Canada.

   a) decline of family wage

   b) increased divorce rate

   c) developments in contraception

   d) female employment

   e) genetic testing

Knowledge/Understanding Thinking/Inquiry Communication

6. Research the childrearing practices of another culture, past or present. Present your information in a chart format. Consider the following:
   - time period
   - value of children in general
   - value of male and female children
   - attitudes toward children
   - discipline

7. Using the social exchange perspective, analyze the costs and benefits of delayed childbearing. Write an essay arguing an opinion about the trend of delayed childbearing, and support it with arguments based on your analysis.

8. Choose a genetic disease to study. Study a web site for that disease and find out if there is genetic testing available to determine if a couple is liable to pass on the disease. Investigate the following:
   - known interventions
   - risk factors
   - numbers of children and pregnancies affected each year in Canada

Present your information to the rest of the class in the form of an electronic presentation.

Knowledge/Understanding Thinking/Inquiry Communication Application

9. Investigate infant mortality rates in Canada from the early 1900s to the present. Use a computer program to create a graph to show how rates have declined over the past century.

10. Are the intentions of the students in your school toward childbearing consistent with those of adults? Develop a research question and design a short survey of students in each grade in your school. Write a brief report, using graphs to present your results.

chapter 10

Parents and Childrearing

CHAPTER EXPECTATIONS

While reading this chapter, you will:

- describe the development of parent-child relationships, drawing on a variety of theories
- explain several theoretical perspectives on the role of the parent in the development and socialization of children, and describe supporting evidence from published research
- evaluate parenting styles and strategies for achieving developmental and socialization goals, using socialization theories as criteria
- evaluate opinions and research on the subject of working mothers and related issues
- identify the role that different types of social institutions and systems have in the rearing and socialization of children
- analyze the division of responsibility for childrearing and socialization, and the interaction of caregivers
- select and access secondary sources reflecting a variety of viewpoints
- demonstrate an understanding of research methodologies, appropriate research ethics, and specific theoretical perspectives for conducting primary research

RESEARCH SKILLS

- conducting observations and experiments
- compiling and summarizing results using theories of socialization
- writing an anecdotal summary

Being a parent is a lifelong commitment that offers many rewards.

CHAPTER INTRODUCTION

This chapter focuses on the development of parent-child relationships. The parents' role in the socialization of children will be investigated using socialization and developmental theories. The nature and impact of the following parent-child relationships will be explored: the parents' marital relationship, parenting styles, the perspectives of both parents, and the parents' work situations. A discussion of adult-child relationships would not be complete without examining the influences that other caregivers have on a child's development. The research used throughout this chapter will reflect psychological perspectives.

The Transition to Parenthood

Many social scientists, including Carter, McGoldrick, and Erikson, consider the transition to parenthood to be one of the most significant events in life. Some people do not consider that couples are a family until they become parents, while others view becoming parents as the final step of reaching adulthood. There are many adjustments couples have to make, both individually and as a couple, to successfully complete the transition to parenthood. "There is no stage that brings about more profound change or challenge to the nuclear and extended family than the addition of a new child to the family system" (Bradt, 1989, p. 235).

The family life-cycle theory sees the transition to parenthood as a major **normative event**, one that occurs naturally in the course of a person's life. During the transition, the family unit has several developmental tasks to complete. They need to adjust and accept a new member, a child, into the system. The couple must alter their relationship as a couple to make room for children. When a couple adds a child to their family unit, they move up a generation by becoming parents (Carter & McGoldrick, 1989). This brings with it a change in self-image; the new parents have to make changes in the way they organize their personal, family, and work routines to fit in the new demands of child care. They also need to work through issues related to how they will raise the child, how the child will be cared for, what roles they will play as **primary caregivers**, and who else will be included in child care. The additional tasks that come with the birth of a child also change the division of household jobs that the couple had established during earlier stages in their relationship (Carter & McGoldrick, 1989).

Many couples experience some decrease in marital satisfaction after the birth of a child (Eshleman & Wilson, 2001). Couple time is diminished, because caring for a child, especially in the first year, is very time-consuming. New parents surveyed by Ralph LaRossa reported that the change that bothered them most was the lack of time—personal time, couple time, time with extended family, time with friends, and time commitments at work. They complained of lack of time for such activities as watching television, sleeping, communicating with each other, having sex, and even going to the bathroom! It takes a while to adjust to the additional time required to care for a child (Eshleman & Wilson, 2001).

The couple's financial situation also changes, since the addition of a new member to the family brings additional costs. Some of these expenses are incurred immediately, such as the cost of the food, clothing, and equipment for the infant. Others occur in the near future, such as day-care costs. Still others occur in the distant future, such as funding post-secondary education.

During parental leave from the work force to care for a new baby, employment insurance does not compensate for the entire wage that is lost. The Canadian Employment Insurance program provides a basic benefit rate of 55 percent of the person's average insured earnings up to a maximum amount, which was $413 per week in 2002. This amount is subject to income tax, as is any other income. The decline in the income of young men since 1980 means that they are no longer earning "a family wage," meaning enough money to support a family (Morisette, 1997). It is often difficult for some couples to make up the income lost during the first few years of a child's life (Schlesinger & Schlesinger, 1992).

Many couples make the parenting decision without fully considering the cost of having a child. The following tables show a breakdown of the costs of raising a girl and a boy to age 18 in Canada.

The Cost of Raising a Child

Cost of Raising a Girl to Age 18*									
Age	$ Food	$ Clothing	$ Health Care	$ Personal Care	$ Recreation, Reading, Gifts, School Needs	$ Trans- portation	$ Child Care	$ Shelter Furnishings, Household Operation	$ Total
Infant	1 406	1 695	149	0	0	0	4 568	1 855	9 673
1	687	512	149	93	456	0	6 200	1 940	10 037
2	724	507	149	93	456	0	5 200	1 906	9 035
3	724	507	227	93	456	0	5 200	1 872	9 079
4	964	544	227	93	456	0	5 200	1 872	9 355
5	964	678	227	93	517	68	5 200	1 872	9 483
6	964	678	227	89	627	68	3 805	1 872	8 329
7	1 103	678	227	89	883	68	3 805	1 872	8 724
8	1 103	678	227	89	883	68	3 805	1 872	8 724
9	1 103	709	227	89	883	68	3 805	1 872	8 756
10	1 316	709	227	89	883	68	3 805	1 872	8 968
11	1 316	709	227	89	883	68	3 805	1 872	8 968
12	1 316	1 106	261	271	965	439	0	1 872	6 230
13	1 403	1 106	261	271	965	439	0	1 872	6 316
14	1 403	1 106	261	271	1 105	439	0	1 872	6 457
15	1 403	1 138	261	341	1 333	439	0	1 872	6 786
16	1 324	1 138	261	341	1 333	439	0	1 872	6 707
17	1 324	1 138	261	341	1 333	439	0	1 872	6 707
18	1 324	1 138	261	341	1 287	439	0	1 872	6 661
Total	$21 869	$16 339	$4 315	$3 172	$15 706	$3 548	$54 397	$35 649	$154 993

Source: Manitoba Agriculture and Food. August 2001. www.gov.mb.ca/agriculture/homeec/cba28so2.html.

Cost of Raising a Boy to Age 18*

Age	$ Food	$ Clothing	$ Health Care	$ Personal Care	$ Recreation, Reading, Gifts, School Needs	$ Trans- portation	$ Child Care	$ Shelter Furnishings, Household Operation	$ Total
Infant	1 406	1 695	149	0	0	0	4 568	1 855	9 673
1	687	438	149	93	456	0	6 200	1 940	9 963
2	724	449	149	93	456	0	5 200	1 906	8 976
3	724	449	227	93	456	0	5 200	1 872	9 021
4	964	474	227	93	456	0	5 200	1 872	9 875
5	964	474	227	93	517	68	5 200	1 872	9 414
6	964	551	227	93	627	68	3 805	1 872	8 205
7	1 141	551	227	89	883	68	3 805	1 872	8 635
8	1 141	551	227	89	883	68	3 805	1 872	8 635
9	1 141	592	227	89	883	68	3 805	1 872	8 676
10	1 419	592	227	89	883	68	3 805	1 872	8 954
11	1 419	592	227	89	883	68	3 805	1 872	8 954
12	1 419	1 064	261	165	965	439	0	1 872	6 185
13	1 663	1 064	261	165	965	439	0	1 872	6 429
14	1 663	1 064	261	165	1 105	439	0	1 872	6 569
15	1 663	1 020	261	241	1 333	439	0	1 872	6 829
16	1 920	1 020	261	241	1 333	439	0	1 872	7 085
17	1 920	1 020	261	241	1 333	439	0	1 872	7 085
18	1 920	1 020	261	241	1 287	439	0	1 872	7 039
Total	$24 863	$14 675	$4 315	$2 459	$15 706	$3 548	$54 397	$35 649	$155 611

* These projections are based on Budget Guides 2001 data and do not include inflation.

Source: Manitoba Agriculture and Food. August 2001. www.gov.mb.ca/agriculture/homeec/cba28so2.html.

1. Why would the costs to raise a boy and a girl be different?
2. Who is more expensive to raise?
3. In which categories are the expenses the same? Why?
4. In what areas are there differences? How can these be explained?
5. What are the factors that could change this? Explain.

Relationships undergo a major change at this stage of the life cycle. The transition to parenthood changes the couple's relationship with others in their family. When a couple becomes parents, their parents become grandparents, and their siblings become aunts and uncles. Systems theory looks at this change in the system as a major shift in the family unit. The addition of a child changes the system because it requires the development of new strategies for caring for and relating to the child and the adjustment of existing strategies to allow for new responsibilities. Relationships within the extended family must be rebuilt to allow for the couple's parents to develop as grandparents, and a clear hierarchy must be established to avoid conflict over the child's care. The couple's new emphasis on family will affect their relationships with friends as well. Some relationships will be slow or resistant to change. One of the parents' tasks is to work through these changes in the best possible manner for themselves and their child. This can be one of the most challenging developmental tasks of new parents (Carter & McGoldrick, 1989).

A baby's arrival affects everyone and everything in the larger family.

Relationships will also change if one member of the couple decides to leave the work force for an extended period of time to provide child care. An individual's identity is related to the work role as well as the family role, because a job provides people with opportunities to feel competent. The couple will have to realign their roles within the home to adjust to both the new baby as well as one person's absence from the workplace. The lack of anticipatory socialization can mean that new parents will not feel as competent in their new roles as parents as they do in their workplace roles. Usually, it is the mother who takes time out from her career to care for children. This change in role can be either positive or negative, and seems to depend on the amount of caregiving performed by the father after the birth of a child. Situations in which the father spent more time caring for the child were deemed to have higher marital satisfaction than in those in which the father was less involved (Demo & Cox, 2000).

Past research on the transition to parenthood has focused on the negative adjustments couples have had to make when they became parents. As a result, a great deal of research has shown the marital satisfaction of new parents to be lower than that of couples without children. During the 1990s, more research has been done on the long-term satisfaction of couples. New studies have focused on understanding the diverse ways in which different couples adjust to parenthood, and the factors that are associated with the various degrees of marital satisfaction that exist between couples. David Demo and Martha Cox, family studies professors at the University of North Carolina, report that after an initial disruption in marital satisfaction, most couples seem to be happy and enjoy life as parents. According to recent research, the best predictor of marital satisfaction during the transition to parenthood is marital satisfaction before it. The better adjusted couples are prior to becoming parents, the better they are able to cope with the demands of parenthood (Demo & Cox, 2000).

Social scientists use the technique of observation to learn many things about people's behaviour. There are several techniques and methods of reporting observations.

- **Observing frequency of a response** Researchers use this method of observation to quantify the number of times a behaviour occurs. This type of research can be used to study anyone who performs repetitive behaviours; for example, an autistic child. Researchers specify a time period and count the number of times a behaviour occurs. This method is useful for a functionalist perspective on role behaviour.

- **Observing family interaction patterns** Researchers observe family members interacting and make anecdotal comments. They note negative and positive interactions. They look for patterns in the interactions and try to assess the patterns' impact on individual members of the family. This type of observation is used in family counselling sessions that try to determine the roots of family problems using a systems perspective.

- **Observing behaviour in an experimental setting** Researchers first observe individuals in a setting in which there is no intervention. They observe both an experimental group and a control group. After they have observed the initial behaviour, they will intervene in some manner with the experimental group to introduce an *independent variable*. They will then observe the individuals again to see if the independent variable caused a change in behaviour, or the *dependent variable*. An example of this is the observation of a mother-child interaction while the child is performing a task. The researcher would note the ways the mother interacted with the child. An independent variable would be to suggest that the task be done within a certain time frame not suggested the first time to the experimental group. As the child repeated the task after this intervention, researchers would look for changes in the behaviour of the mother. ■

Parent-Child Relationships

"Parents: A peculiar group who first try to get their children to walk and talk, and then try to get them to sit down and shut up."

—Wagster's Dictionary of Humor and Wit

A great deal of research has been done on the **attachment** relationship between mother and infant. Attachment is defined as the behaviours that represent the need of the infant to attain and maintain proximity and protection with an available and responsive caregiver. In his psychoanalytic theory, Sigmund Freud emphasized this relationship. Freud saw the infant-mother relationship as the foundation for personality growth, since the mother was the infant's first love relationship and the model for all future ones. If the relationship with the mother was a good one, then the foundation for future positive relationships was laid. In Freud's theory, the quality of the bond between mother and child is the foundation for personality growth and determines how well the child adjusts later in life (Demo & Cox, 2000).

Infant attachment to the primary caregiver, usually the mother, is seen to be essential for normal child development (Larson, Goltz, & Munro, 2000). Erik Erikson, one of Freud's students and also a psychoanalyst, saw socialization as a process that lasts a lifetime, beginning at birth and continuing into old age. He identified eight stages of human development, with each involving a crisis brought on by the changing social situation. During the period of infancy, the crisis faced by the developing child is *trust versus mistrust.* Trust is developed when the infant's needs are met. How well the sense of trust is developed depends on the quality of care the infant receives (Gale Research, 1998).

A great deal of the research has focused on infants between the ages of 6 months and 24 months. This research used *observation in the stranger situation* to assess the degree of infants' psychological and biological attachment to their parents. In these situations, a stranger enters a room where an infant and the parents are at play. The infant's reaction determines the degree of attachment. **Securely attached infants** head for their mothers, rather than their fathers, in a stressful situation such as the entrance of a stranger. If the mother is not there, the infant will go to the father. An **insecurely attached infant** who experiences the same stress from the appearance of a stranger will either avoid or resist the parents. Most of this observational research has been done in laboratories. However, in a Canadian study done in 1995 by David Pederson and Greg Moran, observations were made in the family home, and the research findings were consistent with those done in the laboratory (Larson, Goltz, & Munro, 2000).

Attachment research has tended to focus on the mother-infant bond and has almost completely ignored the father-infant bond. As fathers' involvement in their children's lives has become more apparent, the research has shifted (Larson, Goltz, & Munro, 2000). Studies have found that fathers of secure infants were more extroverted and agreeable, had higher levels of self-esteem, and had marriages that were more positive. These fathers had positive work and family boundaries, with work demands that did not override family commitments (Demo & Cox, 2000; Larson, Goltz, & Munro, 2000). Fathers who developed a commitment to their infants during pregnancy maintained it after birth, and were more likely to be involved in infant care. These fathers tended to be more caring, nurturing, child-oriented, and affectionate than non-involved fathers (Larson, Goltz, & Munro, 2000).

Securely attached infants and toddlers will seek out their primary caregiver when confronted by strangers, or their secondary caregiver if that person is not present.

"*If a child is to keep alive his inborn sense of wonder, he needs the companionship of at least one adult who can share it, rediscovering with him the joy, excitement, and mystery of the world we live in.*"

—Rachel Carson

If you asked this man if he is babysitting his child, he would probably answer, "No, I am parenting. I am the father."

FYI

Two Views on the Education of Children

John Locke and Jean-Jacques Rousseau, two philosophers of the seventeenth and eighteenth centuries, respectively, developed opposite views on the education of children. Locke believed that, at birth, a child was an unformed person whose mind was a blank slate, which he termed a *tabula rasa*. He felt that it was the parents' responsibility to fill the child's mind through education, reason, and self-control and, by doing so, create a civilized adult. Rousseau believed that a child was born with an innate capacity for understanding, curiosity, and creativity that was often deadened by the education, literacy, reason, and self-control imposed by the adults around him or her.

Source: Adapted from Postman, Neil. *The disappearance of childhood*. New York: Vintage Books, 1994.

Recent research on attachment has focused on the stability of attachment over time and how secure attachment affects social adaptation later in life. Demo and Cox found that secure attachment patterns are far more stable than insecure ones, and adults who had secure attachments are better adjusted socially later in life. Children coming from higher-income homes show more stability and better social adaptation later in life than those who come from lower-income homes do. In 1996, Teti, Wolfe, Sakin, Kucera, and Corns looked at the security patterns of first-born children after the arrival of a new sibling and found that their attachments were less secure after this arrival (Demo & Cox, 2000). Children who do not have a secure attachment may remain socially and emotionally underdeveloped into adulthood, and may have difficulty with trust, empathy, self-esteem, and successful relationships for the rest of their lives. Insensitivity to children's needs may cause some areas of the brain to overdevelop, which leads to intense rage, anxiety, impulsiveness, and a predisposition to violence (Steinhauer, 1997).

Attachment is often viewed as love between parents and their children. Love develops over a period of time. In the beginning, parents touch their children, make soothing sounds, and look at them with affection. Babies respond to this attention, and love develops. As babies grow, they begin to reach out to touch their parents, make responsive sounds, and look affectionately at their parents. This pattern is seen in securely attached infants. As children grow and mature, the knowledge of their parents' love gives them self-confidence and self-esteem. Children who feel secure in their parents' love are better able to meet the challenges of the outside world. Children who are secure in their parents' love are more likely to be socially competent and better able to make the transition from dependence on their parents to autonomy. Older children who do not feel secure in their parents' love are more likely to experience feelings of separation, hostility, aggression, low self-confidence, and have poor peer relations (Bodman & Peterson, 2000).

Research from the Canadian National Longitudinal Survey of Children and Youth, as well as the Early Years Study in Ontario, leaves no doubt about the important role

abstract | Links Between Perceived Parent Characteristics and Attachment Variables for Young Women From Intact Families

by Laura V. Carranza,
University of California, San Diego

This study examined links between perceived parent characteristics and attachment variables for young women from intact families (biological parents still married to each other). One hundred and fifty-four female college students served as subjects. They rated both parents using items derived from Secunda's (1992) descriptions of father characteristics, and also were assessed on measures of adult attachment, self-esteem, and interpersonal trust. Positive correlations were found between secure attachment and self-concept, good father characteristics, and doting mother characteristics. An insecure attachment pattern was associated with lower self-worth, less interpersonal trust, distant and demanding father characteristics, and absent mother characteristics. A fearful attachment pattern was associated with distant father and absent mother characteristics. A preoccupied attachment pattern was linked to absent, seductive, and demanding father characteristics, and demanding mother characteristics. A dismissive attachment pattern was associated with distant father characteristics. Collectively, father characteristics related more strongly to an insecure attachment pattern, while mother characteristics related more strongly to a secure attachment pattern. ■

Source: *Adolescence.* (2000, Summer).

parents play in child development. Brain development research has shown a connection between good parenting and optimal brain development. Children who receive language stimulation from their parents develop better language skills than those who do not. The emotional development of children during the first six years of life is dependent on strong parenting skills. Canadian psychiatrist Paul Steinhauer believes that children who do not receive proper stimulation during the early years will suffer from a deficit that is difficult to make up. Steinhauer thinks that the quality of this development is very dependent on family environment. He strongly feels that "it is so much better, in human and economic terms, to improve the quality of parenting while the windows of opportunity are open, than to try to change a child's established but destructive behaviour patterns after the windows have been closed" (Steinhauer, 1997, p. 2). John Bruer, an American researcher, also believes that the earlier parents improve the lives of their children, the better, but that people should not think that the windows of opportunity close forever. Later intervention with good parenting skills can help improve the lives of all children. He reminds parents that there are a wide variety of ways to enrich the lives of children, and that it is important to provide enrichment throughout the life of the child (Bruer, 1999).

by Margaret McCain, Former Lieutenant-Governor of New Brunswick, and Fraser Mustard, Founding President of the Canadian Institute for Advanced Research

RESEARCH QUESTION

What impact does the new research on brain development have on child development?

METHOD

This metastudy synthesized new research on child development from various fields of study. The authors established a framework for understanding the early years of child development and the effects on learning based on existing research. Then, discussions were held with a wide range of people and organizations concerned with early child development and learning. From these discussions, the authors outlined the future directions for the province in order to optimize the brain development of Ontario's children.

RESULTS

- New knowledge has changed the understanding of brain development. Early experiences and stimulating, positive interactions with adults and other children are far more important for brain development than previously realized.
- Experiences in the early years, from conception to age 6, have significant influence on brain development and subsequent learning, behaviour, and health. During the first six years, critical periods of neural development include binocular vision (use of both eyes), emotional control, habitual ways of responding, language and literacy, symbols, and relative quantity.
- The brain develops through the stimulation of sensing pathways. Proper care and nutrition provide the optimal conditions for child development.

Children who do not receive good nutrition and positive stimulation during this critical time may never overcome this poor start to life, and thus may never achieve their full potential.

- In the early years, nurturing by parents provides essential emotional experiences that affect brain development. It influences all parts of the developing brain, including the neural cross connections that influence arousal, emotional regulation, and behaviour, and improves the outcomes for the children's learning, behaviour, and physical and mental health throughout life.
- Children who receive inadequate or disruptive stimulation will be more likely to develop learning, behavioural, or emotional problems in later stages of life. They will also have an increased risk of health problems.

CONCLUSIONS

The authors feel strongly that the issue of brain development is of major importance to the children and citizens of Ontario. They suggest that society should give as much attention to the early years as they do to the years for school and post-secondary education. They would like to see early childhood development programs that involve parents and other primary caregivers of young children from all socio-economic groups in society. They feel that these programs can influence how they relate to children in the home and can vastly improve the outcomes for children's behaviour, learning, and health in later life. Programs need to be based on high-quality, developmentally attuned interactions with primary caregivers, and opportunities for play-based problem solving with other children that stimulates brain development. ■

Source: McCain, M., & Mustard, F. (1999, April). *Reversing the real brain drain: The early years study, final report.* Toronto: Children's Secretariat.

In the Early Years report (see the Research Study on the opposite page), Margaret McCain and Fraser Mustard emphasize the importance of parental support in early learning. They state that new evidence on brain development research supports what "good mothering" has done for centuries: "Babies and young children need good nutrition, stimulation, love, and responsive care" (1999, p. 6). They use "mothering" as an inclusive term, since they believe that both parents have a critical role to play in the optimal development of their children (McCain & Mustard, 1999).

web connection

www.mcgrawhill.ca/links/families12

To learn about the Ontario Early Years Initiative and brain development, go to the web site above for *Individuals and Families in a Diverse Society* to see where to go next.

in focus | Dr. Fraser Mustard

J. Fraser Mustard was born in Toronto and attended the University of Toronto. A physician by training, he has worked in a variety of careers, including scientist, educator, thinker, and policy maker. Early in his career, he helped found the McMaster University Medical School, known across Canada for the past generation for its progressive curriculum. In 1982, he established The Canadian Institute for Advanced Research (CIAR), which he ran for 14 years. This large research organization has helped to influence government policy in science, technology, economic growth, health, and human development.

Dr. Mustard's primary interest over the past ten years has been in early childhood development and, in particular, how early childhood development has an impact on the health and happiness of people during their adult years. As a result of his extensive research, he has been a strong advocate for increasing

Dr. Fraser Mustard is an advocate of the importance of early childhood education.

government resources to help parents nurture children in their first six years of life. He strongly believes that stimulation is critical for the best brain development of children and that without it, children will not realize their intellectual potential and will be more likely to have serious health problems in later life.

Dr. Mustard is the father of six children and the grandfather of nine. He has received numerous awards during his long and distinguished career, including the Companion of the Order of Canada. ■

Bruer refers to the current discussions about brain development and the impact of childrearing as "strangely reassuring. . . . [They] capture the essence of our cultural beliefs about infants, mothers, and the early years of life" (1999, p. 183). He claims that these beliefs have been incorporated into theories of child development. He cautions, however, that people do not get so caught up in the very early years that they forget that good parenting needs to continue throughout children's lives to make a significant impact on their overall development. Children who have a difficult start in life are not doomed forever, and good parenting can improve their circumstances later in life (Bruer, 1999).

Parental Roles

In the past the role of the parent was different from what it is today. Parents of previous generations relied on firm disciplinary practices and unquestioning obedience from their children due to the difficult times in which they lived. Parents and children faced many hardships, including ill health, high infant and childhood mortality rates, and short life spans for adults. Adults worked long and difficult hours to provide for their families. It was important for children to develop self-discipline from an early age, as they contributed to the family's economic well-being as soon as they were able. The style of parenting practised in the past was seen as critical to provide children with the self-discipline required by societies in which strict obedience to authority was expected from citizens. Some of the forms of discipline widely accepted then are currently considered to be child abuse. Today, parents use more democratic strategies in their parenting. A combination of rational control, strong communication between parent and child, and high levels of affection are the norm (Bodman & Peterson, 1995). Recent research has looked at the parent's role from a systems perspective, with the understanding that parents and their children do not live in a vacuum but within a larger family grouping and society in general. Researchers have looked at the role of parents and children within this broader context, and it has an impact on the parent-child relationship (Bodman & Peterson, 1995). Parents take their parenting cues from the society in which they live. In the past, society expected parents to exert firm discipline over their children, while today it views corporal punishment as unnecessary and excessive and accepts a more democratic parenting model. Parents are responsible for socializing their children so they can function in the society in which they live.

Socializing children is one of the most important tasks parents have. Socialization is the process of learning one's culture and acquiring one's personality and personal values throughout life. There are three important aspects of socialization:

1. How it affects the attitudes and behaviour of the individual being socialized to social institutions and cultural norms.

2. How the people who are doing the socialization affect the individual.

3. The way in which the socialization takes place. In most societies, it is the function of the family (Eshleman & Wilson, 2001).

Although much of the research has focused on the socialization of young children, people are always in the process of developing the self and learning how to function in society and the world around them. Parents socialize their children by influencing and shaping their behaviour, and children socialize their parents in a similar manner (Eshleman & Wilson, 2001). There are two preconditions for socialization:

1. The child must have the physical capacity to learn.

2. The child lives in a society that has values, norms, statuses, role, institutions, and a variety of social structures.

If a child is missing any of these preconditions, then socialization is not possible. The infant is exposed to agents of socialization, which parents and others pass on the patterns of thinking, feeling, and acting in their society (Eshleman & Wilson, 2001).

In every culture in the world, women are the primary caregivers to children, and consequently, for many, parenting and mothering are one and the same. However, as more and more North American women stay in the work force after the birth of their children, they are no longer at home to be the sole caregiver (Eshleman & Wilson, 2001).

As the mother's role has changed, so has the father's. In the past, especially in the 1950s and early 1960s, the father's roles were that of breadwinner and head of the household. Many of the television shows of the time, such as *Father Knows Best*, portrayed that image. Today, couples have a more equal role to play in the family, and the head of the household is both parents. Michael Adams, a researcher with Environics in Toronto, discusses a statement that Environics used in a poll of Canadians since 1983: "The father of the family must be the master in his own house" (2001, p. A11). In 1983, 42 percent of Canadians agreed with this statement. By 1992, this number was reduced to 26 percent, in 1996, to 20 percent, and in 2000, to 5 percent. The results were consistent across gender, age groups, marital status, size of community lived in, and the region of the country, with very little variation across the varying groups (Adams, 2001). As the research shows, Canadians no longer agree that the father is the "master." This change is reflected in many aspects of our culture, from advertising to television shows.

"Most times, after my mother made dinner, my father would put the apron on and do the dishes, and this was never beneath him.... It didn't even occur to him that it might make him look wimpy or henpecked. I definitely picked up that attitude from my dad. And the way I've used it in my own life is by treating women, men, and children— with respect."

—Robert Pastorelli

Changing ways of life in North America have changed fathers' involvement with their children. Most participate in prenatal classes with their wives and are present for the birth of their children. More divorced fathers now have joint or sole custody of their children. However, many men still only "help" with household chores and the care of their children, instead of sharing full responsibility with their partners (Eshleman & Wilson, 2001). Even though fathers are more involved with their children, mothers still perform many of the more mundane tasks associated with parenting, and parental roles still follow more traditional gender roles. Fathers tend to do the more skilled jobs, like awakening, playing with, and educating their children, while mothers tend to do less skilled jobs, like laundry, dishes, and feeding their children (Dulac, 1994; Glossop & Theilheimer, 1994).

Reasons for fathers' more traditional roles in the family include the fact that male and female roles are not considered to be interchangeable, since society sees the mother as the principal parent responsible for the family's care. Also, men often wait to be asked to help. The concept of reciprocity, in which each spouse gives and expects something in return, allows for the couple to define who is giving what in terms of parenting (Dulac, 1994). Functionalists would see this role division as consistent with the homemaker-breadwinner ideology. They believe that the function of the nuclear family is to raise children, and the structure of the male and female roles within that family supports that function. Conflict theorists would maintain that men reject female roles in parenting as a way of maintaining their power position within the family and society. Childrearing is seen as a job with less status and, therefore, less power (Tanfer & Mott, 1997).

Research focused on single-parent families headed by females has given the impression that, in many families, there is no father figure. In fact, there is a father present in 78 percent of Canadian families. In the United States, the percentage of homes with a father present is less than in Canada, which may account for the misconception. Many Canadian children benefit from the involvement of their fathers in their lives (Campbell, 1999). Studies by Paul Amato and John Snarey have documented the importance of the father in the life of the child. Being close to their father has an

Children gain emotional and intellectual benefits from playing with their father.

by Elaine Carey, Demographics Reporter

Dads still aren't pulling their weight. When both parents are working, mothers are spending an average of two more hours a day with their young children than fathers do, Statistics Canada said. They're also doing most of the housework, spending about an hour more a day on tasks other than child care, it says. At the end of the day, mothers of young children have a full hour less leisure time than fathers do and they spend proportionately more of it with their kids.

The study is the first to look at the time working parents spend with their children at different ages and what they actually do, says author Cynthia Silver, a senior StatsCan analyst. And most of it isn't quality time. In fact, the harried working parents of pre-schoolers are managing to find only about half an hour a day each to play with them. The rest of the time they're doing other things, like shopping, cleaning, and the laundry, while they keep an eye on the kids.

The study confirms that the gap between men and women is getting smaller when it comes to housework and child care. "And that's good news," said Kerry Daly, a University of Guelph professor and author of *Families and Time: Keeping Pace in a Hurried Culture.* "But it's clear to me there is still a disparity, a very continual asymmetry, that continues to exist between men and women," he said.

And nobody is very happy about that, says the study of working couples with children, which is based on the 1998 General Social Survey of about 11 000 adults. Two-thirds of full-time working parents were dissatisfied with the balance between their job and home life. When the children are asked for their views, "one of the things they say they want is more time with their parents, hanging around doing nothing in particular—quality time that seems to be missing here," said Alan Mirabelli, Executive Director

Children say that the one thing they want is more time with their parents doing nothing in particular.

of the Vanier Institute of the Family.

"Parents feel guilty and stressed for time, asking, 'How can I show up at home without the stress of work in my head and show up at work without the stress of home?'"

About two-thirds of the 1.5 million Canadian women with children under six are in the workforce. That jumps to 75 percent of those with children aged six to 15. Working mothers spend more time with young children than fathers, partly because mothers spend about an hour-and-a-half less a day at their jobs.

But as the kids get older, they spend less time with the kids and more time at work. By the time children are young teens, fathers and mothers are each spending about two hours and 40 minutes a day with them, a large part of it chauffeuring them to various activities. Family meal time may be a vanishing art but still happens, the study says. After child care, it was the most common activity shared by parents and their children. ■

Source: *The Toronto Star.* (2000, June 14). p. A24.

1. According to this article, how are the roles of mother and father becoming similar?
2. What disparities still exist between the father's role and the mother's role?
3. What do children want from their parents, according to this article?
4. How would additional time for the activities desired by children improve the parent-child relationship?

impact on children's happiness, life satisfaction, psychological well-being, intellectual development, and educational and occupational success. Children with absent fathers have lower levels of academic achievement, are more likely to be delinquent or deviant, and more likely to drop out of school (Eshleman & Wilson, 2001).

Fathers and mothers interact differently with their children. Fathers tend to be more physically engaged and less emotional with their children than mothers are. Play with fathers involves more teamwork and games, with fathers stressing healthy competition, risk taking, and independence. This type of play is said to help children develop the ability to manage their emotions and to improve their intelligence and academic achievement (McClelland, 2001).

People are reconstructing the social image of fatherhood (Dulac, 1994). Men are starting to realize what they did not get from their own fathers and want a different type of relationship with their children. They are not willing to pay the same price for their careers as their fathers did (Glossop & Theilheimer, 1994). Many fathers today understand that "a family is a mother and father working together as a team" (Campbell, 2000, p. 7). The new image is based on a father's feelings, experiences, and relationships with his children. Some of this change comes from necessity, as most women with young children are now working and fathers have to spend more time parenting than before.

One of the problems facing today's new fathers is the lack of role models. Their fathers were raised in a time when fathers were primarily the breadwinners. They therefore cannot provide role models for fathers in a dual-income family (McClelland, 2001). Social learning theorists would argue that men learn to be fathers by watching their fathers. The lack of role modelling makes it difficult for today's fathers to make the transition to a different time and social reality. Erikson's theories of development would explain that involved fathers are experiencing parental generativity by promoting children's ability to develop to their full potential (Tanfer & Mott, 1997).

Many authors argue that Canadian society needs to change the ways that fathers are treated in order to better reflect fathers' views of themselves as parents. Society is more accommodating of mothers as parents, and not of fathers. People assume that when fathers are caring for children they are babysitting, not parenting. We maintain a culture of jokes that show fathers as incompetent parents. Many families find that the wife's workplace is more accommodating of the responsibilities that come with parenting than the husband's workplace (McClelland, 2001). Research by Linda Druxbury, an associate professor of business at Carleton University in Ottawa, determined that women's increased labour force participation has not made them more like men, but men are becoming more like women in that they now face the competing demands of work and family. Men are more stressed and overloaded from juggling the obligations of work and family, but this is what working women have been experiencing for years (Glossop & Theilheimer, 1994). Canadian society needs to support men who become more involved in parenting. There are many provisions for women, but few for men. Society needs to develop programs for men to share with men their feelings and concerns about their parenting roles (Mann, 1995).

Parents are the main agents of socialization for their children's gender roles. Babies are socialized from the moment they enter this world to be masculine or feminine. Many hospitals provide blue accessories for male babies and pink for female babies. Children see definitions of what it means to be male and female all around them—in books, on television, in their neighbourhoods, and in their own families. Children view the tasks performed by their parents in the home and come to gender-based conclusions about who should perform which jobs (Eshleman & Wilson, 2001). Parents encourage certain sex-role stereotyped behaviour through something as simple as buying toys, disciplining their children, and responding to them when they are sick.

Individuals' attitudes toward gender roles may be changing, but it is taking a while for all aspects of society to catch up.

The National Longitudinal Survey of Children and Youth is studying gender issues related to Canada's children to determine how growing up as a boy or a girl in Canada influences a child's long-term physical and emotional health. Girls are more likely to experience sexual violence, exploitation and harassment, mental health problems, smoking, attempted suicide, and sexually transmitted diseases. Boys are more likely to be hospitalized for, or die from, injuries, commit suicide, use alcohol, and engage in early sexual activity. Understanding the unique needs of boys and girls can assist politicians and other policy makers to develop strategies that will address such issues as systematic discrimination and gender inequality in Canadian society (Rogers & Caputo, 2000).

Parenting Styles

During the twentieth century the majority of North Americans have increasingly come to value individualism, competition, and independence. This has led to parents raising their children to be more independent and self-reliant, rather than focusing on family ties and commitments to the larger family. In comparison, children from some cultures are raised to value co-operation, sharing, reciprocity, obligation, and interdependence of the larger family and kinship network (Demo & Cox, 2000). Families develop a shared view of the world, and this shared view has an impact on parent-child relationships. Shared views consist of assumptions that families hold on the following:

● how the world inside and outside of family boundaries is organized

● how members relate to one another

● how the family treats the environment surrounding them

Shared views provide a sense of meaning and order for families, establishing a rationale for many of their functions, such as setting goals, making decisions, governing behaviour, and managing their resources. Each family constructs its unique view to suit its needs. This view influences the parent-child relationship and represents the belief system under which the parents operate. Views change over time as outside forces come to influence the family's thinking. Factors such as education, differing social or work experiences, or a family crisis can change a family's shared view. In this way, shared views are representative of the systems theory, according to which influences in the system affect the entire system (Bodman & Peterson, 1995).

The commonly held views of the family have a direct impact on parenting and parent-child relationships. Parents who value career and work success highly will place a different value on family time and time with their individual children than those who place less value on work success. Parents who value the goals and needs of individuals over the family will have a difficult time putting their personal needs on hold to care for family members. Parents who are busy fulfilling their individual needs may not take the time to parent in a democratic and nurturing manner. Instead, they may use punishment or coercion to get their children to behave. Parents who spend a great deal of time with their children get to know them better and become more sensitive to their needs. Children who spend a great deal of time with their parents may also become more sensitive to their parents' needs (Bodman & Peterson, 1995).

Parenting style and its impact on the development of the child has been another subject of much research. Three basic styles of parenting have been

"Loving a child doesn't mean giving in to all his whims; to love him is to bring out the best in him, to teach him to love what is difficult."

—Nadia Boulanger

considered: **authoritative**, **authoritarian**, and **permissive**. There has been a focus on authoritative parenting, which is characterized by warmth, support, acceptance, and indirect positive control of the children. It is compared to authoritarian parenting, which is distinguished by more parental control and use of punishment, as well as to permissive parenting, which is typified by few rules and by the children controlling family situations.

Recent studies have contrasted the qualities of authoritative parenting and authoritarian parenting in relation to a child's psychological development and well-being. Children raised by authoritative parents are better adjusted psychologically and have a better self-concept. In contrast, authoritarian parents use more physical punishment, which has been shown to negatively affect the child's adjustment, especially if it is severe and frequent. Children who experience this type of parenting feel rejected by their parents. Children raised by authoritarian parents tend to have more problems with psychological adjustment (Demo & Cox, 2000). Children raised by permissive parents who offer much warmth and encouragement tend to be more irresponsible, impulsive, and immature,

Positive parenting practices lead to a child who is better adjusted psychologically, emotionally, and socially.

while children raised by permissive parents who are hostile and rejecting tend to be flighty, anxious, and emotionally impoverished. Permissive parenting is not the best for the child. Optimum parenting provides a balance between over-control and permissiveness (Larson, Goltz, & Hobart, 1994). Factors that inhibit parents from showing the consistent warmth, support, and effective discipline of an authoritative parenting style are economic hardship, marital conflict, conflict between spouses regarding parenting style, maternal antisocial behaviour, and neighbourhood poverty (Demo & Cox, 2000). Risk factors such as these contribute to the parent's inability to parent effectively. Using positive parenting techniques despite these risk factors can, however, reduce the impact of the risk factors. No matter what situation the parent and child are living in, good parenting is crucial to a child's development (McCloskey, 1997). Many parents find that one of the greatest challenges of parenting is to come to terms with issues related to discipline, punishment, and guidance of their children. Developing their own parenting style is a challenge for most parents.

FYI

Barbara Coloroso's Parenting Styles

Barbara Coloroso is a renowned speaker and writer about parenting and raising children. Her lectures are filled with funny anecdotes that demonstrate important points about how to raise children. She is famous for her three styles of parenting and how they affect children. The following are her version of the styles and characteristics of each.

Brick Wall
- Hierarchy of control
- Litany of rigid rules, thou shalt nots, and don't you dares
- Rigid enforcement of rules
- Punishment imposed by adults
- Rigid rituals, rote learning
- Use of sarcasm, ridicule, and embarrassment to manipulate and control behaviour
- Threats and bribes are used extensively
- Relies on heavy competition
- Learning takes place in an atmosphere of fear
- Children learn love is highly conditional
- Children learn what to think and are easily manipulated
- High-risk group for sexual promiscuity, drug abuse, and suicide

Jellyfish
- Anarchy
- No recognizable structure, rules, or guidelines
- Punishment and rewards are arbitrary and inconsistent

- Mini-lectures and put-downs are typical tools
- Second chances are given often
- Threats and bribes are commonplace
- Learning takes place in an environment of chaos
- Emotions rule behaviour of parents and children
- Children learn love is highly conditional
- Children are easily led by peer influence
- High-risk group for sexual promiscuity, drug abuse, and suicide

Backbone
- Network of support is developed
- Democracy is learned through experience
- Provides an environment that is flexible and conducive to creative, constructive, and responsible activity
- Rules are simple and clearly stated
- Consequences are logical, realistic, and palatable

- Discipline with authority gives life to learning
- Motivates children to be all they can be
- Lots of smiles, hugs, and humour
- Provides second opportunities
- Learning takes place in an atmosphere of acceptance and high expectation
- Children learn to accept their own feelings and control their own behaviour
- Encourages competency and co-operativeness
- Love is unconditional
- Teaches children how to think
- Buffers students from sexual promiscuity, drug abuse, and suicide by reinforcing the messages "I like myself," "I can think for myself," and "There is no problem so great it can't be solved."

Source: Coloroso, B. (1989). *Winning at Parenting—without beating your kids*. Littleton, Colorado: Kids are worth it!

web connection

www.mcgrawhill.ca/links/families12

To learn about theories and research on child development and parenting, go to the web site above for *Individuals and Families in a Diverse Society* to see where to go next.

The National Longitudinal Survey of Children and Youth began collecting data on Canadian children in 1994. Initial findings from this study indicate that parenting style has an impact on the development of children. Hostile parenting practices, such as harsh discipline, unsuppressed anger, and use of negative comments, have been shown to lead to children with low scores in their ability to get along with others. Being raised by a hostile parent has a more negative influence on a child's ability to form positive relationships than any other aspect of a child's family background (McCloskey, 1997).

Positive parenting practices result in positive scores in social relationships, helping behaviour, and motor and social development, while negative parenting styles lead to negative scores. Further research into children who are living in an at-risk situation—such as in lone-parent families, teen-parent families, low-income families, low social-support families, parents with little educational attainment, and dysfunctional families—shows that if the style of parenting is positive, they score at least as well as children who are not at risk but who are exposed to negative parenting styles (Eshleman & Wilson, 2001).

web connection

www.mcgrawhill.ca/links/families12

To learn about challenges to section 43 of the *Criminal Code*, go to the web site above for *Individuals and Families in a Diverse Society* to see where to go next.

legal matters | Parental Authority

by Justice Marvin Zuker

One of the driving concepts in law is that of the "best interest of the child" rather than parental rights. In a case decided in 1995, Jehovah's Witness parents had refused consent to a blood transfusion for their newborn daughter who had been born prematurely. Their refusal was on religious grounds, and the medical evidence indicated that transfusions would be necessary to protect the child's life. After the child was treated, the girl was returned to parental custody, but the parents appealed the original decision on the grounds that it had violated their constitutional rights.

A judge of the Supreme Court of Canada maintained that the liberty interest in section 7 did not include the right of parents to make medical decisions or to raise their children without undue state interference. A majority of the court believed that the parents' rights to rear their children according to their religious beliefs was a fundamental part of freedom of religion and that, accordingly, their section 2(a) rights had been infringed. They went on to state that the careful legislative scheme implemented by the state was saved by section 1, which states, in part:

The common law has always, in the absence of demonstrated neglect or unsuitability, presumed that parents should make all significant choices

affecting their children, and has afforded them a general liberty to do as they choose.

This liberty interest is not a parental right tantamount to a right of property in children. . . . Parents should make important decisions affecting their children both because parents are more likely to appreciate the best interests of their children and because the state is ill-equipped to make such decisions itself. . . . This is not to say that the state cannot intervene when it considers it necessary to safeguard the child's autonomy or health. But such intervention must be justified.

This case underlines reluctance to allow a doctrine of a parent's rights to be set up in opposition to the interests or health of a child. But that does not mean that it is not willing to protect the procedural interests of parents. This is consistent with the view of the family as a central social unit whose integrity should be encouraged and protected.

Section 43 of the *Criminal Code* states:

Every school teacher, parent, or person standing in the place of a parent is justified in using force by way of correction toward a pupil or child as the case may be who is under his care if the force does not exceed what is reasonable under the circumstances.

The case of David Peterson was brought before an Ontario judge in 1997 amid a storm of controversy. Peterson, an Illinois family man, was vacationing in London, Ontario, when he was arrested and charged with assault. An eyewitness report indicated that Peterson had spanked his five-year-old daughter on her bare bottom. Peterson testified that he had spanked his daughter to punish her for intentionally slamming the car door on her brother. Ironically, Peterson wanted to teach his daughter that wilfully hurting her brother was not acceptable. The judge ruled that in the eyes of the law, a father has the right to physically discipline his children.

A Québec judge ruled that a teacher who grabbed a 15-year-old boy by the hair and banged his head onto his desk had not committed an offence since Section 43 of the *Criminal Code* prohibited the "excessive" use of force, not the "disgraceful" use of it.

In Manitoba, a father who removed his shoe before kicking his son down the stairs was exonerated by the application of Section 43. The judge ruled that the father had exercised restraint and reason by removing his shoe before he began kicking.

Section 43 of the *Criminal Code* became a focal point in the debate about corporal punishment in childrearing. It does not expressly outline the nature or limits of the force that is justified other than to require that it be "reasonable in the circumstances" and be for the purposes of "correction." Because the notion of reasonableness varies with the beholder, it is perhaps not surprising that some of the judicial decisions applying section 43 to excuse otherwise criminal assault appear to some to be inconsistent and unreasonable.

As recently as January 15, 2002, the Ontario Court of Appeal upheld an earlier decision that Section 43 does not violate subsection 7, 12, or 15, of the Canadian Charter of Rights and Freedoms. It may ultimately be for the Supreme Court of Canada to strike down Section 43, if appropriate.

There is a growing consensus that corporal punishment of children does more harm than good. It has been banned in virtually all Canadian school systems, and the federal Ministry of Health has mounted an educational campaign teaching that hitting children is wrong. Canadian attitudes toward corporal punishment are changing. An increasing number of Canadian adults believe that many forms of corporal punishment, at one time considered acceptable, are no longer acceptable. ∎

Family Structure and Parent-Child Relationships

Over 30 years ago, family structure was fairly consistent across Canada. Most families were **intact,** meaning both parents were in their first marriage and they had biological or adopted children. Most single-parent families existed because of the death of one spouse. Family breakdowns occurred, but they were not as widespread as they are today. Currently, children live in different family structures, which have been arrived at in a variety of ways. In the past, over 90 percent of children were born into a two-parent family. Now, for several reasons, an increasing number of children are born to single parents. Children are living in lone-parent families at younger and younger ages. For children born in the early 1960s, 25 percent were living in lone-parent families by the time they were 20 years old. This increased dramatically through the 1980s, when 22 percent of children had lived in lone-parent families by the time they were 6. For children born in 1989–1990, 37 percent had lived in lone-parent families by the time they were 4. It is clear that the percentages of children living in lone-parent families are increasing, while the age at which they do so is decreasing (Marcil-Gratton, 1998).

Distribution of Canadian Children According to Their Age and the Types of Family in Which They Reside at the Time of the Survey, 1994–1995

| | Type of Family[1] | | | | | | | |
Age (birth cohort[2])	Intact	Step (not blended)	Step Blended	Lone-Parent (mother)	Lone-Parent (father)	Lone-Parent (other)	Total	N[3]
0–1 year (1993–94)	80.3	0.4**	7.0	12.1	0.2**	0.0**	100.0	3661
2–3 years (1991–92)	76.8	1.1*	5.4	15.9	0.8**	0.1**	100.0	3858
4–5 years (1989–90)	74.8	2.6	6.7	14.5	1.2*	0.1**	100.0	3903
6–7 years (1987–88)	74.2	2.8	5.5	16.4	0.9*	0.1**	100.0	3729
8–9 years (1985–86)	75.2	4.1	5.7	13.0	1.7*	0.3**	100.0	3815
10–11 years (1983–84)	72.9	3.9	6.2	14.8	1.8*	0.3**	100.0	3820
All ages 0–11 years	75.7	2.5	6.1	14.5	1.1	0.1*	100.0	22 786[4]

* Estimate to be interpreted with caution because of sampling variability.
** Estimate does not meet Statistics Canada quality standards. Conclusions and interpretations based on   this estimate cannot be considered reliable.
[1] Intact: All children are biological or adopted children of both members of the couple.
Step: Two-parent family in which one parent is not the biological parent of the children.
Blended: Two-parent family in which at least one of the children does not have the same biological or adoptive parents as the others.
Lone-parent (other): Non-biological mother or father.
[2] As indicated, children's years of birth are those of the majority of cohorts. Thus, the 0–1 year cohort (1993–94) was born between November 1992 and March 1995.
[3] Numbers of cases weighted, brought back to sample size.
[4] Forty-five cases had missing information.

Source: Adapted from the Statistics Canada publication, *Growing up with Mom and Dad? The intricate family life courses of Canadian children.* Catalogue 89-566, August 1998.

Most research considers the intact family to be the guideline against which to measure other family forms. A great deal of important information has come from this research; however, it is limited, because it creates broad categories of families, whereas more defined ones would provide more valuable information. For example, single-parent families tend to be put into one category rather than sorted by type of single-parent family, such as male-headed, female-headed, or by reason for being single, such as never married, divorced, or widowed. This type of research ignores many important variables, such as the amount and type of resources available (for example, money, time, support from family and/or friends) and differing outcomes in various family forms (Demo & Cox, 2000).

A parent's gender plays a more important role in parental involvement than living arrangement does. Fathers, regardless of where they live, tend to be less involved with their children than mothers are. Divorced fathers tend to see their children infrequently, and their contact with their children usually decreases over time. Recent research contradicts past research, showing that many non-residential fathers maintain frequent contact with their children. Further studies demonstrate a difference between what the mother reports as father contact and what the father reports. It has been suggested that past research has relied on the mothers' reports to determine fathers' contact, and this may have led to unbalanced views of father involvement (Demo & Cox, 2000).

abstract | Family Structure and Children's Success: A Comparison of Widowed and Divorced Single-Mother Families

by Timothy J. Biblarz and Greg Gottainer, University of Southern California

Compared with children raised in single-mother families created by the death of the father, children raised in divorced single-mother families have significantly lower levels of education, occupational status, and happiness in adulthood. Yet divorced single mothers are not significantly different than their widowed counterparts in childrearing, gender role, family values, religiosity, health-related behaviors, and other dimensions of lifestyle. However, relative to widowed single mothers, divorced single mothers hold lower occupational positions, are more financially stressed, and have a higher rate of participation in the paid labour force. We speculate that the contrasting positions in the social structure of different types of single-mother families may account for observed differences in child outcomes. ■

Source: Copyrighted 2002 by the National Council on Family Relations, 3989 Central Ave. NE, Suite 550, Minneapolis, MN 55421. Reprinted by permission.

The National Longitudinal Survey of Children and Youth found that more fathers of children who are born to single mothers are acknowledging their paternity by putting their name on the child's birth certificate, compared to any time in the past, when paternity was seldom acknowledged. This same research shows that fathers who are not married to the mothers are often living with them at the time of the child's birth. However, children born to common-law unions are three times more likely to have to deal with the break-up of their parents' relationship than children born to married couples (Marcil-Gratton, 1998). Systems theory suggests that removing the father from the home, or not having a father in the home, affects the family dynamics of the entire household. The relationship between the children and the father changes as the rest of the system does. Children who have been accustomed to frequent contact with their father may have difficulty in other areas of their lives due to their father's absence.

The dynamics of a couple's relationship has an impact on their children's development. Marital conflict is more strongly related to disrupted parenting and child adjustment than is parents' overall marital satisfaction or the quality of a marriage. When a child is old enough to understand intense marital conflict that is child-related and is not resolved in a constructive manner, there are direct negative effects on the child. David Demo and Martha Cox found that children who are exposed to conflict that is resolved in a constructive, non-aggressive, and productive manner do not suffer the same negative effects (Demo & Cox, 2000; Larson, Goltz, & Munro, 2000). Couples who engage in **constructive conflicts** may be able to parent better, since they are able to solve problems as a couple and provide good role models for their children. Parents who engage in hostile and angry conflicts with each other are more likely to use this same method of solving conflicts with their children. This can have long-lasting, negative consequences for their children. Parents who engage in this type of **destructive conflict** in their marital relationship may not have the energy left to be available to their child emotionally and, consequently, may experience more tension in the parent-child relationship. Parents' anger from a destructive marital conflict may cause them to reject their children and be hostile or physically abusive toward them. This may hold true for fathers more than for mothers (Demo & Cox, 2000).

Witnessing destructive parental conflict has long-lasting negative repercussions on children, while witnessing constructive conflict can help develop their problem-solving skills.

Marital conflict has negative effects on children, but conflict between parent and child has a greater negative effect, especially when the child is an adolescent. Another factor that influences how conflict affects the child is how the child interprets the conflict. Children who spend much of their time living in a conflicted household tend to become sensitized to it and view it as more negative than children who spend less time living with conflict would. The strategies a child uses to cope with parental conflict determine the effect of the conflict on the child. Children who become involved in the conflict suffer more maladjustment than those who distance themselves or seek support outside of the family (Demo & Cox, 2000).

Parents, Work, and Child Development

Most mothers of young children in Canada today work at least part-time. The Canadian National Child-Care Study, using data from the 1988 census, looked at working families and the age of their children. They found that as children get older, it was more likely that both parents were working full time. In 33 percent of families with children aged 0–17 months, both parents worked full time. However, when they included either full or part-time employment of the mother, the percentage increased to 56 (Larson, Goltz, & Munro, 2000). More often, mothers are working before and after the birth of their children. In the 1950s, only 8 percent of mothers went back to work within two years after the birth of a child. In the 1990s, that figure increased to 57 percent. In Canada, there is a nationally funded maternity- and parental-leave system that allows parents access to employment insurance to support staying home to care for infants. The system provides for mothers, primarily, but also for fathers, to spend time with the infant and meet the needs of themselves and their families after childbirth. At the end of the leave, 45 to 50 percent of women return to work, while others are more likely to return at the end of two years (Larson, Goltz, & Munro, 2000).

According to the Canada Census results between 1971 to 1991 for where people work, the percentage of people working from home has remained steady at between 7 and 8 percent over the past three decades. The General Social Survey, done in 2000, questioned if respondents usually work at home, and found that 17 percent of the population did. Men do more work from home than women do, with 10.8 percent of men working from home, while 9.8 percent of women do. Working from home is more prevalent among families with young children: 14.8 percent of employees with families compared to 11.3 percent of employees without children. Much of the increase of home-based

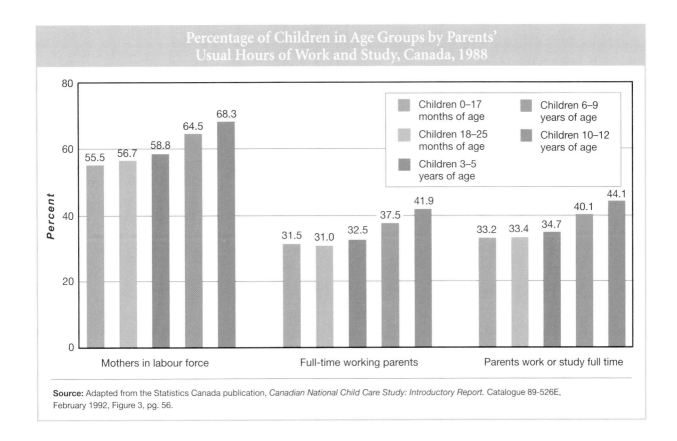

Percentage of Children in Age Groups by Parents' Usual Hours of Work and Study, Canada, 1988

Legend:
- Children 0–17 months of age
- Children 18–25 months of age
- Children 3–5 years of age
- Children 6–9 years of age
- Children 10–12 years of age

Mothers in labour force: 55.5, 56.7, 58.8, 64.5, 68.3

Full-time working parents: 31.5, 31.0, 32.5, 37.5, 41.9

Parents work or study full time: 33.2, 33.4, 34.7, 40.1, 44.1

Y-axis: Percent (0, 20, 40, 60, 80)

Source: Adapted from the Statistics Canada publication, *Canadian National Child Care Study: Introductory Report*. Catalogue 89-526E, February 1992, Figure 3, pg. 56.

work has been linked to the use of computers and related technologies. There are advantages to working at home, especially for families with young children: different child-care arrangements, less time spent commuting, more time with children, and more flexibility. There are also disadvantages, such as a decreased social network, isolation from colleagues, interrupted work, and inconsistent hours (Akyeampong & Nadwodny, 2001).

Working full or part-time has an impact on the parents' level of satisfaction concerning the amount of time they get to spend with their children. The State of the Family in Canada, a national survey taken in 1994, showed that mothers who worked 20 hours per week were more satisfied than those who worked more. The more hours parents worked, the

Parents who are overloaded by work have less time to give to their children, which may affect the children's development in a negative way.

less satisfied they were with the amount of time they had with their children. This pattern holds true for their satisfaction with work and family balance (Larson, Goltz, & Munro, 2000). Parents who work in stressful environments may bring that tension home with them, which can have an influence on the family. Parents who work in situations in which they see children at risk—for example, a police officer, or a child and youth worker—may become overprotective of their children, or they may perceive "abnormal" situations as normal. There are many ways that the parents' work situations can affect the parent-child relationship (Bodman & Peterson, 1995).

Family time is an essential part of the optimal development of a child, but Canadian families are facing a time crunch. Parents are having a hard time balancing work and family demands. Thirty-six percent of working fathers and 50 percent of working mothers report having difficulty managing their time (McCloskey, 1997). The National Longitudinal Survey showed that 26 percent of all Canadian children and 41 percent of children in single-parent families are experiencing emotional, behavioural, academic, and/or social problems. Statistics show that today's parents spend less time with their children than any family surveyed by Statistics Canada since the survey began 60 years ago. Parents who have little free time devote less time to parenting their children. They cannot provide as much sensitive nurturing, intellectual stimulation, and firm, consistent discipline to enable their children to reach their full potential.

"Some families are aware of the work addict's effect on them, yet feel very conflicted. Their conflict arises because the workaholic provides them with luxuries they would not ordinarily have. This is a typical bind for upwardly mobile workaholic families."

—Diane Fassel

Parenthood Within the Larger Society

The parent-child relationship exists within a larger society. Systems theory looks at the ways the larger system affects this relationship. Some of the many outside influences on the family include neighbourhood and community, extended family and ethnic background, work situations, social networks, and socio-economic status. Each of these factors provides a different influence on the relationship between parent and child (Bodman & Peterson, 1995). These same influences on the family can also be viewed from a functionalist perspective. The structure of a society has an impact on the ways families function.

Significant others are the people who make an important contribution to the developing child's life. For infants and young children, parents are the most significant others. Individuals who come to be important are siblings, aunts and uncles, grandparents, peers, teachers, athletes, celebrities, and so on. People want to please and receive approval from these individuals. Significant others affect children by what they do and say, and the manner in which they do and say it. They influence developing children and their view of their future role in life, and thus become children's role models.

Reference groups are groups of people with whom one identifies. Children may see themselves as a member of a team or club. They may wish to become part of a team or club they admire, such as a travelling hockey team. In a symbolic interactionist perspective these reference groups act as standards against which the child measures himself or herself. For most adolescents, peer groups become the main reference group in their lives (Eshleman & Wilson, 2001).

Socio-economic status has an impact in many ways. The higher the socio-economic status of the family, the more control they have over many other influences on their lives. Parents can choose to live in safer communities or provide activities for their children, while parents who are struggling to survive economically have few choices and worry about the negative effects of their socio-economic status on their children (Bodman & Peterson, 1995). Parents who consider their neighbourhood safe will be more likely to allow their children to move about in the community more freely, thus encouraging their children's autonomy. These parents will practise more democratic parenting than those who do not consider their neighbourhood safe. Parents who live in unsafe communities may place more restrictions on their children, expect more obedience from them, and use a more authoritarian form of parenting to protect their children from the community itself (Bodman & Peterson, 1995).

Many recent immigrants experience conflict between parenting styles and values in the system of the country they have left and those in Canada. Children tend to take on the values of a new country sooner than adults do, and this can be a source of conflict in the parent-child relationships of these families. The greater the difference between cultures, the more impact this will have on the family system and the relationships between the parents and their children (Bodman & Peterson, 1995). The functioning of the family is changed by the structure of the new society. The greater the difference between the two cultures, the more problematic the change is for families.

The parents' social network also influences their parenting. Parents tend to spend time with other parents to share common interests and concerns. They can gain insights into parenting by

Parents associate with other parents because they have more in common with them than with childless couples. Indirectly, they may also observe parenting techniques that they may want to adopt.

viewing other parents with their children and incorporating into their style techniques that they view as positive. When parents spend time with childless people, it has a different type of influence. For example, a young mother whose friends are single and free to do as they please may come to resent the time demands of caring for a young child (Bodman & Peterson, 1995).

The National Longitudinal Survey on Children and Youth in Canada studied the impact of poverty on children. The survey showed that children in poor families have twice as many negative outcomes, such as chronic health problems, hyperactivity, school issues, and emotional disorders as children who are raised in families with sufficient income. The researchers also found that these children had triple the rate of conduct disorders, including aggressive and antisocial behaviours. An important finding of this survey was that poor children who have parents with good parenting skills adjust as well as, and sometimes better than, children with sufficient income whose parents have poor parenting behaviours (Steinhauer, 1997).

Care of Children by Others

There has been a great deal of research on the effects of non-parental care on young children. Several ongoing research projects have shown that infants under the age of 12 months in day care for more than 20 hours a week are more likely to develop insecure attachments with their mothers. These children are also more likely to develop heightened aggressiveness and non-compliance during their preschool and early school years (McCain & Mustard, 1999). Michael Lamb reported in the *Canadian Journal of Psychiatry* that even though regular exposure to non-parental care can have negative effects on a child, this is not always the case. He states that the quality of the parent-child relationship is the key factor in determining how the child develops. Children who spend substantial amounts of time with non-parental caregivers and who have good relationships with their parents do not suffer the ill effects seen in some research. Parents who are moderate- to high-risk in terms of their parenting behaviour are more likely to have problems with children who spend more time in day care than parents who are not high risk (Larson, Goltz, & Munro, 2000).

The National Longitudinal Survey of Children and Youth also studied the impact of parents' work on Canadian children. Findings show that the vocabulary development of preschoolers is affected by the amount of time a mother reads to the child rather than whether or not she chooses to work or stay at home. The behavioural, math, and reading scores of older children demonstrate the same results. Good parenting is seen to be a more significant factor than work. Researchers suggest that society should invest in more resources and child-friendly workplace policies. They believe this would allow parents to spend more time with their children and, thus, encourage child development. They also encourage good-quality day care as a means of supporting child development for working parents (Human Resources Development Canada, 1999).

Most families do not use public day-care centres to tend their children. Most use sitters, licensed in-home child care, or relatives. Many parents consider relatives to be more trustworthy than other caregivers. Grandparents are the most commonly used relative, followed by aunts or uncles (Larson, Goltz, & Munro, 2000). Research suggests that child care by family members is part of an exchange of services between these individuals. Parents who seek child care from their kin usually do so out of economic necessity. When the cost of family care becomes too great, they seek other forms of child care. Parents with higher incomes are less likely to use kin care. Researchers suggest that government policy makers consider providing subsidies and other incentives for kin care of children (Brandon, 2000).

Many Canadian families live too far from their extended family to be able to rely on them for child care (Steinhauer, 1997). Day-care centres are used by only 8 percent of families. Those who advocate for day care argue that the availability of high-quality day care is a critical support for parents of young children. Licensed day cares must have trained staff, low staff-child ratios, flexible hours, high-quality facilities, low turnover rates, and parental involvement. Advocates claim that licensed day care must be available and accessible for all families. This is called **universal day care** (Larson, Goltz, & Munro, 2000).

In Canada, there are not enough licensed day-care spaces available. In 1990 there were 1.3 million preschoolers whose mothers were in the paid labour force and only 321 000 licensed spaces available. The benefit of high-quality day care for high-risk and disadvantaged children and for children in single-parent families has been proven in the research (Larson, Goltz, & Munro, 2000). As a nation, Canada needs to provide a variety of child-care situations for working parents to ensure that children have good-quality care, no matter what the parents' work situation is. Providing flexible options that meet various situations is an important part of the future of child care in Canada. Providing effective support for parents has been shown in the research to also improve children's chances for a successful future (Steinhauer, 1997).

web connection

www.mcgrawhill.ca/links/families12

To learn about work and day care in Canada, go to the web site above for *Individuals and Families in a Diverse Society* to see where to go next.

"The most important thing is not so much that every child should be taught, as that every child should be given the wish to learn."

—John Lubbock

Grant Johnson always knew that he wanted to be a father, although when he first started to date his wife, Pamela, in 1970, he often spoke out about the so-called "irresponsibility of bringing a child into an overpopulated world of poverty, ethnic conflict, war, and environmental destruction." Despite his idealistic leanings, Grant prepared himself in his youth for being a father. He worked part time at the YMCA through high school and university, and spent his summers until he was 21 as a staff member of various Y summer camps. He loved children, enjoyed being with them, and was a positive role model for them. It was no surprise to his family and friends that he eventually chose teaching as a career after trying many other jobs.

Grant and Pamela had been married for four years before deciding to start their family. When Emma was born in 1976, Grant was already working as a high school teacher and was ready to start this new period in his and Pamela's life together. Grant had expected to be actively involved in raising his children. Both he and Pamela had come from families in which both parents had worked, and they had agreed early in their relationship that Pamela would continue with her career after having children. They had also decided they would utilize home child care and community day care when their children were young. Grant's father had taken a very active role in raising him and his older brother, and Grant naturally expected to follow his example.

Having Grant present at Emma's birth was a joy for both Grant and Pamela, and the first few weeks of the baby's life were emotionally satisfying for both of them. He liked being home with the baby and did not even mind changing her dirty diapers. The only conflict that arose was arguing about who got to carry Emma in her "Snuggly" when they went out as a family!

Once Emma was born and Pamela went back to work, Grant had to contribute more to the housework.

Things changed, of course, when Pamela went back to work when Emma was three months old. Grant liked having a stay-at-home wife and was spoiled by Pamela, who had taken over many of the household chores that Grant was used to doing. He resumed responsibility for the household tasks that he had handled before, including the laundry and housecleaning, but these jobs became even more time-consuming now that they had Emma. He dropped off and picked up Emma from a day care that was close to his school, but had to give up his regular squash games after work with his friend Richard, since he no longer had the time. His regular Friday evening out with the guys from work also became a problem, since it meant less time with Emma and because Pamela was really tired at the end of the week and especially appreciated Grant's company and help then. However, they eventually adjusted to the rhythm of their life as a family. They began to spend more time with other couples who had children and less time with their single friends.

Money became more of a concern for Grant and Pamela. No matter what anyone had advised them, they found that they were not prepared for the amount that was required to raise a family. They were unable to afford many of the things that they could before, such as travelling during their vacation time, renovating their house, and driving new cars. To ensure that their day-care costs remained affordable and to have some control over the quality of care that Emma was getting during the day, Grant and Pamela helped start up a co-operative day care in the local elementary school. Grant took on the position of treasurer and performed those duties for the next nine years.

By the time that Colleen, and later Andrew, were born, the Johnsons were a family fixture in their community. They were part of the endless series of car pools and child-centred recreational activities. Grant enjoyed taking his children to the local community centre for "gym and swim," playing with them at the local park, and teaching them to play soccer and baseball. Although his life had changed dramatically, in that the majority of his leisure time was now spent with his family, he felt tremendously fulfilled. He loved everything about being a dad, and looked forward to seeing his children grow up and mature and to experiencing the change in his role as a father as he aged with them. ■

1. How did the transition to parenthood affect Grant and Pamela's lifestyle?
2. In what way did Grant's role within the family change when he became a father? Explain the changes from a systems perspective.
3. From a social exchange perspective, what are the benefits of fatherhood for Grant?
4. Using the perspective of symbolic interactionism, explain how Grant's identity changed to include himself as father.
5. How might things have happened differently when considering the division of labour, finances, and going out with friends?

chapter 10   Review and Apply

1. What do you remember about your child-care situation as a child? Check with your parent(s) or guardian(s) to see who cared for you when you were young. Compare your child-care situation with that of your classmates.

2. Discuss the various roles of parents in the development of children. How do the roles of mother and father differ? How are they similar? Give specific examples to support your statements. What roles do your parents assume? What roles do you plan on assuming in your future?

3. Use the theory of symbolic interactionism to discuss marital conflict and its impact on child development.

4. The systems perspective assumes that the system is influenced by outside forces. Using systems theory, explain how the work situation of the following parents might affect their relationships with their children. At what age of the children will each of these jobs have the most effect on the parents' relationship with them?

   a) A mother who works in the young offenders unit of a large urban police force

   b) A father who manages a trendy restaurant and employs many people in their late teens and early twenties

   c) A father who works in the emergency department of the local hospital

   d) A mother who is an elementary school teacher

5. Discuss the issue of child care by extended family from a structural functionalist perspective.

6. Significant others and peer groups have a larger influence on school-aged children than society realizes. Write a reaction paper supporting your opinion on this statement. Give three reactions and evidence and/or research from this chapter to support your opinion.

7. One of the main causes of social problems in Canada today has to do with the fact that the majority of mothers with young children are working outside the home. Discuss whether this statement can be proven.

8. Write a letter stating the need for good-quality child care in your community. Choose an appropriate audience—newspaper editor, city hall, or MP—to address the letter to. Use research on child development from this chapter and other sources.

9. Investigate the number of local companies and organizations that assist parents in caring for children. What types of programs do they offer? How flexible are they? As a future parent, which company do you feel would best meet your needs?

10. Canadian society does not support involved fathers. Choose one of the following tasks related to this statement:

   a) Write an essay expressing and supporting your point of view on this topic.

   b) Interview an involved father about the support, or lack of support, for fathers.

Knowledge/Understanding   Thinking/Inquiry   Communication   Application

11. Write and conduct a survey to determine the changes couples encountered upon becoming parents. Consider the factors discussed in this chapter. Tabulate the results and present them in the form of a graph or chart.

12. Conduct an observation of a parent and child interacting with each other. Record anecdotal notes as you observe their behaviours. Write a summary of your observations.

13. Interview a couple who are parenting in a non-traditional manner (for example, the father stays home while the mother works; the parents work alternate shifts to enable their children to be with a parent at all times; the parents work from home). Write a case study describing their parenting roles.

Parent-Child Issues and Trends

CHAPTER EXPECTATIONS

While reading this chapter, you will:

- describe current perceptions, opinions, and demographic trends relating to childbearing and childrearing, and speculate on the significance of these trends for parent-child relationships
- explain the impact that current issues relating to parents and children have on the bearing and rearing of children
- demonstrate an understanding of the nature, prevalence, and consequences of child abuse, and describe strategies and programs that would facilitate its prevention and remediation
- summarize current research on the effects of divorce on child development and socialization
- summarize the impact of economic and political instability and migration on child development and socialization
- formulate research questions and develop hypotheses reflecting specific theoretical frameworks
- identify and respond to the theoretical viewpoints, the thesis, and the supporting arguments of materials found in a variety of secondary sources
- use current information technology effectively to compile quantitative data and present statistical analyses of data or to develop databases

Parenting is a challenging job, especially when other factors enter into it to make it even more difficult.

CHAPTER INTRODUCTION

There are many changes and challenges facing parents and their children in Canada today. In this chapter, significant issues that affect parent-child relationships will be explored. Topics surrounding reproductive technologies will be discussed, then the impact of divorce on the development and adjustment of children will be considered. Following that, some of the difficulties that immigrant families encounter when adapting to a new culture will be examined. The long-lasting effects of poverty on children will be explored. Also in this chapter, the causes and effects of child abuse will be discussed. Finally, parents' and siblings' reactions to the death of a child in the family will be considered.

Issues Affecting Parent-Child Relationships

Most Canadians plan to become parents at some point in their lives. Canadian couples are marrying and starting families later. The motivation for most couples to have children is to seek fulfillment as both individuals and as a couple. Most couples practise birth control measures when they are young, to plan when they will begin their family. Unfortunately, infertility is a problem many couples do not consider. Realizing that they may never be able to have children because of the delay can be devastating for some couples. Others may find that their marriage cannot withstand the added stress of parenthood. The high divorce rate in Canada has sparked much debate on the effects of divorce on the overall social, emotional, intellectual, and physical development of children who experience their parents' divorce. When couples plan to become parents, they do not consider that they may outlive their children. Dealing with the death of a child is a very difficult experience for parents. Many issues can affect a couple's expectations of parenthood.

Canadians in general enjoy a good standard of living, often failing to recognize that others may not have the same benefits that they have. Many Canadian children are suffering from the effects of poverty. Others have suffered from the effects of war and migration. Child abuse is an issue that most people find difficult to comprehend. It is difficult to understand how a child can be severely beaten or killed by the person who is responsible for loving and caring for them—the parent. As governments at all levels are cutting programs to deal with deficit budgets, the long-term effects of the loss of a social safety net will be felt by children.

"There is always one moment in childhood that the door opens and lets the future in."
—Graham Greene

Reproductive Technologies

For some Canadian couples, having children is not easy, and they turn to **assisted reproductive technologies (ART)** to fulfill their dream of becoming parents. These couples undergo in-depth fertility investigations, and may use drug therapies and technologies, such as **artificial insemination**, **in vitro fertilization**, and **embryo implants**, to achieve their goal of having a child (Larson, Goltz, & Munro, 2000). Medical science has been working on assisted reproduction for a number of years and, as a result, many couples who could not have borne their own children before are now becoming parents. This raises questions about the impact of assisted reproductive technologies on families, such as:

- How will older parents cope with the demands of parenting?

- What will be the long-term consequences of the increasing numbers of multiple births that have resulted from assisted reproductive technologies?

- How does the use of donated sperm or eggs affect the definition of parenthood? (Golden & Murphy Paul, 1999)

- What right do children conceived through in vitro fertilization have to accessing identifying information about the egg or sperm donor and their health records?

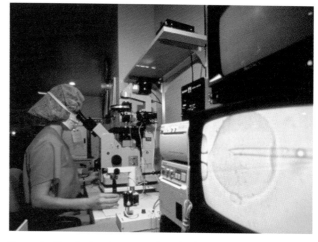

Reproductive technologies such as in vitro fertilization help parents to conceive when otherwise they would not have been able to do so.

The whole issue of assisted reproductive technologies has caused much debate in the 1900s and 2000s. For couples who have had success, there is no debate—assisted reproductive technology was the miracle they were seeking. For those who do not conceive, ARTs are one of life's greater disappointments. Often, couples spend considerable time and energy attempting to conceive a child using ARTs, only to be disappointed (Kershner, 1996).

Much debate has occurred in Canada over the past two decades regarding reproductive and genetic technologies. Canadians are coming to some consensus about which technologies they approve of and which ones they have difficulties with. Most Canadians support placing limits on, or prohibiting, technologies that they do not see as reflective of human dignity and equality (Health Canada, 1999).

The first child conceived through in vitro fertilization is now in her twenties. Since her birth, there have been many children born who were conceived through assisted reproductive technologies. How are these children and their parents faring? Does waiting so long to become a parent affect parenting? Frederic Golden and Annie Murphy Paul claim that mothers who had their children with the use of ART tend to show more warmth toward their children, are more emotionally involved, interact more with their children, experience less stress related to parenting, and feel more competent in their parenting skills. Golden and Murphy Paul attribute these findings to the fact that these mothers desperately wanted to become parents and were very committed to parenthood. Other factors that may influence the parenting styles of mothers

"Any parent who has ever found a rusted toy automobile buried in the grass or a bent sand bucket on the beach knows that objects like these can be among the most powerful things in the world."

—Sports Illustrated

who used ART are that they tend to be older, as they usually attempt to conceive a child on their own first. They usually have more wealth than the general population and therefore can give their children advantages other mothers cannot. Dr. Dorothy Greenfield of Yale University states that couples who undergo ART have faced issues in their marriage that most couples do not have to confront, and therefore they have a stronger marriage (Golden & Murphy Paul, 1999).

Assisted reproductive technology has allowed many women, including lesbian mothers, to conceive a child with donated sperm. In the past, most lesbian mothers were involved in a heterosexual relationship when they had their children, and later declared that they were lesbian. Lesbian couples can now raise children from birth. Golden and Murphy Paul state that research has found that lesbian and heterosexual mothers raise their children equally well. Dr. Nanette Gartrell, of the University of California in San Francisco, studied discrimination against lesbian mothers and their children. Gartrell found that recently divorced lesbian mothers experienced a double psychological burden, that of divorce and of coming out. Gartrell found that the mothers' struggle affected their children. However, they tend to have a more equal division of household chores and duties (Golden & Murphy Paul, 1999).

Fertility drugs and assisted reproductive technologies have resulted in a dramatic increase in multiple births.

The number of multiple births has risen dramatically over the past decade, due to the number of older women having babies, fertility drugs, and ART, which place more than one fertilized egg at a time in a woman's uterus. Golden and Murphy Paul report research that shows multiple-birth mothers as tired and more likely to be depressed. The stresses of caring for an infant are increased as the number of infants increase. Mothers of multiples face stresses that mothers of single infants do not (Golden & Murphy Paul, 1999). Twins are more likely to be born premature and at low birth weights. As a result, they have an increased risk of neurological disabilities.

An Australian study found that babies born from in vitro fertilization are four times more likely to die in the first month (Kershner, 1996). Other concerns raised regarding ART are related to the costs—to governments, to health care, and to the individuals attempting to become parents. Drugs for aiding fertility are very expensive and are not covered by drug plans. Couples often spend great amounts of money attempting to have a baby. Wealthy couples can afford the technologies, but the average couple can risk losing all they own in an effort to have their own child. The chances of success vary by method of intervention, but overall the success rate is not high. The Canadian Royal Commission on Reproductive Technologies concluded that the only effective method of assisted reproduction is the treatment of blocked Fallopian tubes, to remove blockage. Considering the costs to both the health care system and the couples, some say that the money would be better spent improving the overall health of women and children (Kershner, 1996).

There has been a great deal of debate and controversy over the regulation of ART in Canada. Dr. Patricia Baird headed the Royal Commission on Reproductive Technologies, which filed its report in December 1993. Over a four-year period, the Royal Commission heard from 40 000 Canadians and made 293 recommendations. The government tabled Bill C-47, which dealt with reproductive technologies, in June 1996. In 2001, Health Minister Allan Rock unveiled a draft proposal before the House of Commons Health Committee. In the proposal, Rock is calling for a ban on some research techniques, while protecting couples who want to use assisted reproductive technologies to have children. His main concern regarding the technologies that allow couples to have children is with the safety of the procedure for both the mothers and the infants. New issues have arisen since the Royal Commission and the introduction of Bill C-47. Human cloning, once thought to be science fiction, is now becoming a reality (Pole, 2001).

Feminists have opposing views on assisted reproductive technologies and their impact on women. Some say that any interference in a woman's body, for example, removing eggs from the womb, is wrong. Others feel that if reproduction can take place outside a woman's body, then she is freed from the biological necessity of bearing children and thus becomes equal with men. **Ecofeminists**, who believe that the domination of women is directly connected to the environmental destruction of nature, and who promote the interconnected web of life, dislike intervention in the uterus because they say such intervention is essentially masculine and anti-woman. They claim that women's life-giving ability makes them different from men and gives them power over them (Lublin, 1998). The debate will continue for years to come. For many infertile couples, the chance to gaze into the eyes of their newborn infant is a risk worth taking.

web connection

www.mcgrawhill.ca/links/families12

To learn about assisted reproductive technologies, go to the web site above for *Individuals and Families in a Diverse Society* to see where to go next.

**by Preston Manning, Former Leader
of the Opposition, House of Commons, Canada**

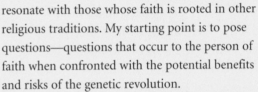

Preston Manning is concerned with many of the ethical issues raised by reproductive technologies.

Some time soon, Health Minister Anne McLellan will introduce a bill to regulate assisted human reproduction and related science. The regulatory body to be created by this statute will likely become the principal regulator of "the genetic revolution" in Canada—a revolution created by breakthroughs in the life sciences, with enormous potential for both good and harm. I was a member of the standing committee on health that reviewed an earlier draft of this legislation. In presenting it, Allan Rock (then health minister) recognized the potential conflict between what was scientifically possible and ethically acceptable, saying: "There must be a higher notion than science alone . . . that can guide scientific research and endeavour. Simply because we can do something does not mean that we should do it." But what might that "higher notion" be?

One of the candidates is "faith"—religious faith; faith in the existence of God; faith that the universe, including human life and the genome, is His handiwork; faith that we are somehow made in His image and subject to His providential care; and faith that there are universal and transcendent moral principles that ought to govern us in addition to the principles of physics, chemistry, and biology to which we are all subject. The pollsters tell us that although only a minority of our political, media, and scientific elites share this "faith perspective," more than 65 percent of Canadians share various elements of it. The health committee recommended to the minister that, in addition to scientific and medical perspectives, the faith perspective should also be given "standing" before any tribunal charged with regulating the genetic revolution. The "faith perspective" that I bring to this question is that of historic Christianity. But most of the points I want to raise will also resonate with those whose faith is rooted in other religious traditions. My starting point is to pose questions—questions that occur to the person of faith when confronted with the potential benefits and risks of the genetic revolution.

First, relationships. My faith tells me that our relationships—with each other and with God—are the most important dimension of life, and that love is the supreme ethic that ought to govern those relationships. What does the genetic revolution do to our relationships? To the extent that it helps infertile couples to have children or prevents parents from passing on inheritable diseases to their children, surely it is to be supported and encouraged. But if it encourages man to play God or reduces human reproduction to a technological process to be carried out in a laboratory or a factory—surely those dimensions of the genetic revolution should be constrained. If you are a child of the twenty-first century, with five names on your birth certificate—those of the sperm donor, egg donor, surrogate mother, adoptive mother, and adoptive father—can love still be at the centre of that network of relationships? And, if not, what ethic will govern those relationships?

Second, the moral obligation to respect life. My faith teaches me that life is precious, not just for its own sake, but because it originates from God. More and more Canadians of all persuasions are acknowledging our need to be more respectful of life—all life. There is growing acceptance of an "environmental ethic" that insists that we protect plants, trees, and animals from destruction and extinction. But what about greater respect for human life, dignity, and personhood? Particularly as science pushes back the definitions of when life and the distinguishing characteristics of personhood begin—from the newborn, to the fetus, to the embryo, to the pre-embryonic. To the extent that the genetic revolution is respectful of life and increases our understanding of its preciousness, it will be a great boon to humanity. But to the extent that it reduces our conception of life to the mere product of some biochemical reaction, it needs to be constrained and redirected. Will legislative efforts to regulate assisted human reproduction and related science reopen and inflame the old pro-life, pro-choice controversy over abortion? I am hopeful that the genetic revolution will put that conflict into a new context more conducive to resolution.

Over the past 20 years, the pro-choice movement has promoted women's reproductive rights to the point where they are now well established in law and practice. At the same time, responsible pro-life advocates urge a parallel development of legal protection for the unborn—in particular, for human fetuses and embryos—and this new law about to be brought forward by the government will take several steps down that road. Then the issue will become, what to do when the legal rights of the unborn and the mother conflict? This is the issue that legislators and the courts should have been wrestling with all along, instead of avoiding it by embracing the now unscientific legal fiction that human personhood does not begin until birth. Parliament might well decide that where there is such a conflict, the rights of the mother should prevail, which in effect is the current state of the law. Or Parliament might at least start to address

possible exceptions, as when the activities of the mother (drug abuse or excessive alcohol consumption, for example) predestine the child to death or crippling disabilities.

Third, the moral obligation to heal. The Christian faith has long taught that we have a moral obligation to heal and care for the sick. I have been greatly encouraged by the numbers of scientists and medical people I have met in Canada's hospitals and laboratories who are deeply committed to this objective. Of course, there are other motivations—scientific curiosity, profit, competitiveness—for participating in the genetic revolution. But to the extent that our scientists and medical people are motivated by a moral obligation to heal, surely they deserve our wholehearted encouragement and support. This, of course, brings us to a cruel dilemma. What do we do when the moral obligation to respect life and the moral obligation to heal conflict? For example, when our scientists seek permission to destroy human embryos in order to obtain embryonic stem cells that may be used to treat juvenile diabetes or some other degenerative disease.

Are there limits to our moral obligation to respect life? Are there limits to our moral obligation to heal? Are there any circumstances where it is morally justifiable to take life in order to save life? Are there other options—such as focusing on adult stem cell research—that may help us to avoid choosing between the lesser of two evils? My own faith perspective tells me that we should not destroy life to save life—even at the embryonic level—and should increase our efforts to find better ways to achieve the objective of saving life.

Fourth, the search for universal and transcendent moral principles to guide the genetic revolution. This is the "higher notion" of which the former health minister spoke. Do such principles exist? People of faith believe they do, even though we may disagree on what they are, and all of us "see as through a glass darkly" when it comes to understanding them. What this means is that we must rededicate ourselves to the search for such principles, rather than abandoning it and settling for some inconclusive moral relativism that says, "You believe what you believe, and I'll believe what I believe, and somehow everything will work out."

Five thousand years ago, a man of faith came down from a mountain with two tablets of stone in his hands. Written on those tablets was a code—a code for governing human life at the individual and societal level by honouring the source of life and prohibiting activities that diminish or destroy life. In our day, men and women of science have also come down from the mountain with a code in their hands—a code written not on tablets of stone but in strands of DNA woven into double helixes. It, too, is a code for governing human life—at the most elemental level.

People of faith believe that the author of these two codes is one and the same, and that each sheds light on the other. The regulatory regime to be established by Canada's new legislation will serve us well if it brings both science and faith to bear on the governance of the genetic revolution. ■

Source: *The Globe and Mail*. (2002, April 5). p. A15. Reprinted with permission of Preston Manning.

1. What is Manning's thesis?
2. What is Manning's concern with reproductive technologies?
3. For what purpose do you think reproductive technologies should be allowed?
4. What limits, if any, do you think the government should place on reproductive technologies? Support your argument.
5. What role do you see for other social systems, for example, religion, in this debate?

Divorce

Divorce is affecting an increasing number of Canadian families. The number of families with children under the age of 12 in which the parents are separated or divorced has tripled in the last 20 years (Voices for Children, 2002). Canadian statistics predict that 31 percent, or almost one in three marriages, will end in divorce. In 1995, there were 1222 divorces per 100 000 marriages, or 1.2 percent of all married couples (Ambert, 1998). This leaves many questions as to how parents' separation and divorce affects their children. This has been the topic of much research in recent years in Canada and around the world. Originally, a great deal of the research focused on the negative aspects of divorce, such as looking for lack of adjustment in children. Recent research has tended to look at the factors that help some children adjust to their parents' separation or divorce better than other children do.

There are several risk factors that have an impact on children's development after the divorce of their parents:

● Parental conflict frightens children and does not show them how to solve problems in a healthy manner.

- The economic resources available for parenting are often reduced after divorce. Divorced women and their children are the fastest-growing group of poor people in Canada. Inadequate resources affect parents' ability to supply children with all of their needs.

- Parents adjust to divorce differently. Those who suffer from stress may not be able to parent as well as usual.

- Parents who rely on their children for support are putting undue pressure on them, which has a negative impact on their adjustment.

- Parent-child relationships change with divorce and must be renegotiated. Children need to be free to develop relationships with both parents after the divorce.

- A number of parents disappear from their children's lives. These children feel abandoned and have a difficult time adjusting (Freeman, 1999).

Questions are being raised about the underlying reasons for the negative consequences of divorce. Are they the result of divorce itself, or are they the result of the decreased standard of living most single divorced mothers and their children face? Mothers who are under severe economic strain find it difficult to parent. Carolyne Gorlick, Associate Professor of Sociology at the University of Western Ontario, cites studies indicating that children suffer from parental conflict, whether it is in divorce or an unhappy marriage. She suggests that children's ability to adjust to their parents' divorce has to do with a number of influences, including family relationships, income decline, and change in residence. The ages and gender of the children must be considered when looking at these factors, since each adjusts differently. The parents' ability to co-operate for the sake of the children also has an impact on their adjustment (Gorlick, 1995).

There is much debate on how children cope with their parents' divorce. Two well-known American authors have conflicting views on the subject. Judith Wallerstein, a researcher and psychologist, claims that half of all children suffer serious long-term consequences from their parents' divorce (Freeman, 1999). Long-term effects include poor social and emotional development, poor school results, substance abuse, and having their own marriages end in divorce. She claims that children of divorce lack the model of a healthy marriage, and thus have difficulties in their own marriages. Children of divorce often have long-term problems with trusting others, and show a reluctance to

When parents divorce, children are often caught in the process.

commit to a relationship (Peterson, 2002). Mavis Hetherington, a researcher and professor of psychology, disagrees and suggests that children of divorce can be divided into three groups: winners, survivors, and losers, with losers being a smaller group than shown in previous research (Freeman, 1999). Hetherington claims that much of the previous research has focused on the negative and ignored the possible positive effects of divorce, which may include taking children out of a hostile environment. Hetherington's long-term research shows that after two years, the majority of children of divorce are functioning reasonably well. Her studies reveal that for every young adult from a divorced family who is experiencing problems, there are four who are not. Twenty-five percent of children of divorce have serious social, emotional, or psychological problems, compared to ten percent of children from intact homes. Hetherington claims that most single mothers are providing good homes for their children and should be considered heroes. She points out that it is essential for children's success to have a competent, caring parent (Peterson, 2002).

"As we read the school reports on our children, we realize a sense of relief that can rise to delight that— thank heaven— nobody is reporting in this fashion on us."

—J. B. Priestley

FYI

The Consequences of Divorce on Children

Short Term

Children of divorced parents

- suffer from anxiety, depression, and emotional disorders
- show behavioural problems including aggressiveness, hyperactivity, and hostility
- are more likely to become young offenders
- are more likely to do poorly in school and to drop out of school
- experience social problems, have few friends, and are less involved in extracurricular activities

Long Term

Children of divorced parents

- are more likely to have children out of wedlock
- are more likely to experience teen pregnancy
- have lower overall levels of education
- experience more unemployment
- experience more marital problems
- are more likely to divorce when they are adults
- are more likely to be poor

Ambert, Anne-Marie. (1998). *Divorce: Facts, figures and consequences.* Ottawa: Vanier Institute of the Family.

The general assumption has been that divorce has long-term negative consequences for children. Carolyne Gorlick reports on findings that show that children of divorce are more likely to experience emotional and physical trauma, which is then blamed on the missing father and the overwrought mother. She states that children of divorce are more likely to be sick than those in two-parent families. It is assumed that children in two-parent families have a safer and more comfortable environment in which to grow up. Children in single-parent and stepparent families are at greater risk in general for adjustment problems. These problems are not due to family structure; rather, they seem to be caused by other factors, such as social stresses, economic insecurity, living in poverty, and the time pressures of balancing work and family, especially in single-parent families (Gorlick, 1995).

The household income level of Canadian women after divorce is reduced by 50 percent, while men's income is reduced by only 25 percent. The poverty level of women before divorce is 16 percent, and it rises to 43 percent after divorce. Therefore, poverty and all of the stresses associated with it seriously affect children's adjustment after divorce (Voices for Children, 2002; Ambert, 1998). Dr. Anne-Marie Ambert, from York University in Toronto, claims that as well as poverty, **diminished parenting** and continued parental conflict after divorce are detrimental to children of divorce. Diminished parenting refers to the lessened ability to parent for people who are suffering the stress that comes with divorce and a newly single life. Parents who are facing increased emotional and financial burdens as a result of divorce cannot cope easily with the pressures of parenting. Continued parental conflict after divorce is very stressful and provides children with a dysfunctional model to follow (1998).

Many factors affect the development of children after divorce. Stresses on single mothers affect their ability to parent.

abstract | Parental Predivorce Relations and Offspring Postdivorce Well-Being

by Alan Booth and Paul Amato,
Pennsylvania State University

This two-part study uses national longitudinal interview data from parents and their adult children to examine the way in which predivorce marital conflict influences the impact of divorce on children. In the first study, we find that the dissolution of low-conflict marriages appears to have negative effects on offspring's lives, whereas the dissolution of high-conflict marriages appears to have beneficial effects. The dissolution of low-conflict marriages is associated with the quality of children's intimate relationships, social support from friends and relatives, and general psychological well-being. The second study considers how parents in low-conflict marriages that end in divorce differ from other parents before divorce. We find that low-conflict parents who divorce are less integrated into the community, have fewer impediments to divorce, have more favorable attitudes toward divorce, are more predisposed to engage in risky behaviour, and are less likely to have experienced a parental divorce. ■

Source: *Journal of Marriage and Family 63* (2001, February). pp. 197–212. Copyright 2002 by the National Council on Family Relations, 3989 Central Ave. NE, Suite 550, Minneapolis, MN 55421. Reprinted by permission.

There is no such thing as a traditional divorce. Each family goes through its own process. Some families find divorce very trying, while others consider it a new beginning. Rhonda Freeman, a Canadian social worker and researcher, believes that divorce is a developmental process that unfolds over time. The process begins when the parents begin to think about separating and continues through the divorce until the creation of a post-divorce family. Divorce is a way for adults to resolve their problems, not for children to (Freeman, 1999). No matter what the family structure, a child's overall adjustment in life has more to do with the quality of parenting the child receives than the structure of the family. Children who have at least one positive, warm, and authoritative parent, regardless of the status of the parents' marriage, are likely to be competent and well-adjusted during childhood and later in life. Children adapt better in a harmonious single-parent household than in a two-parent household that is full of conflict (Voices for Children, 2002).

point of view | Chretien to Hear Calgary Youth's Divorce Concerns

by Chris Cob
Ottawa Citizen

Calgary teenager Clayton Giles handed a petition to Prime Minister Jean Chretien on September 18, 2001, and asked for changes to the federal Divorce Act that will give children the automatic legal right to have equal access to both parents. Fourteen-year-old Clayton, who told reporters that he contemplated suicide during a three-year separation from his father, has cycled 5000 kilometres across Canada and into the United States, collecting thousands of signatures in his campaign for custody and access reform in both countries.

Canada's Divorce Act is expected to be reformed next year [2003] but pro-father and grandparent groups fear that current recommendations from a joint Senate-Commons committee will be ignored by the Chretien government in favour of measures that stick to the existing regime of custody and access. The cornerstone of the parliamentary committee's recommendations tabled more than two years ago was a new system of

Clayton Giles cycled across Canada and the United States collecting signatures for a petition to gain children equal access to both parents after divorce.

automatic shared parenting in which both parents would have access to their children and input into their children's lives.

Clayton Giles, accompanied on his cycling trek by his father, Eric, told reporters on Parliament Hill that when a Calgary court separated him and his younger sister from their father in 1995, he sank into a depression. "When I lost my father," he said, "I also lost my grandmother, the most wonderful, loving person you will ever meet. Grandparents are special people and no child should ever be deprived of their love and attention."

In January 2001, Clayton went on a 19-day hunger strike to protest the court ruling and was eventually allowed to live with his father. "I had accomplished as much as I could accomplish," he said, "but I have not stopped fighting. Divorce harms most children most of the time, but when children are used as pawns by warring parents and adversarial lawyers, the children are destroyed that much faster."

In a self-assured presentation at his news conference, Clayton told reporters that the children of divorce are in a numerical minority, but comprise the majority of Canada's problem children. "Although children of divorce make up only one-sixth of the child population," he said, quoting from federal statistics, "they account for 91 percent of child suicides, 78 percent of young offenders, 65 percent of teen pregnancies, 90 percent of runaways, and 71 percent of school dropouts. They make up 85 percent of children with behavioural problems, 75 percent of the occupants of chemical abuse centers, and 80 percent of the adolescents in psychiatric facilities."

Eric Giles, a contractor who lived 15 minutes from his children during the separation, owed $10 000 in legal fees to his wife, which he said are now paid.

There were no other unpaid bills or allegations against him, he said. "I think I was punished because I represented myself in court," he said.

Clayton said he has a "neutral" relationship with his mother but hopes to see more of her when he gets back to Calgary. His 12-year-old sister lives with their mother but visits her father regularly.

The father and son were at the end of their trek and on their way back home when they received a call saying the prime minister would meet with Clayton. ■

Source: *Edmonton Journal.* (2001, September 18). p. A17.

1. What rights do you think children should have when issues of custody and access are being discussed?
2. At what age should the courts consult the children?
3. How can the courts deal more effectively with custody and access?
4. What factors help children deal more effectively with their parents' divorce?
5. What responsibilities do parents have toward their children when going through a divorce?
6. What responsibility does society have to protect the children of divorce?

Immigration

Fifteen to twenty percent of Canada's children are either immigrants or refugees (Morton, Hou, Hyman, & Tousignant, 1998). Canada is an increasingly ethnically diverse country. In the early 1970s, the majority of children living in Canada were of British or French ancestry, with German, Italian, and Ukrainian being the next largest ethnic groups (Ross, Scott, & Kelly, 1996). The linguistic diversity in Canada is a reflection of the ethnic diversity due, for the most part, to immigration. Almost 80 percent of immigrants who came to Canada between 1991 and 1996 reported a first language other than French or English. During that time, the majority of immigrants came from Asia and the Middle East. In contrast, between 1961 and 1970, 54 percent of all immigrants could not speak French or English, and two-thirds of immigrants came from Europe. Ontario, British Columbia, and Québec receive almost 90 percent of all immigrants to Canada, with most of them settling in large urban areas (Harmsen, 2000).

The way new arrivals adjust to life in Canada has much to do with the reason they came. Immigrants generally choose to come to Canada to build a better life for themselves and their families. Refugees, on the other hand, come to get out of a situation that is dangerous to either themselves or their families. Leaving home is often not their first choice. Both groups usually leave behind family members. When they arrive in Canada, immigrants have to adapt to a new culture and a new way of life. Culture is an important part of who we are. It is reflected in many ways—through art, music, as well as food and clothing. It is based on a shared language, values, attitudes, and customs. Culture provides emotional stability, self-esteem, and influences a person's behaviour. When immigrants come to Canada, Canadian ways may seem strange to them, and their ways may seem strange to Canadians. Children from immigrant families who maintain a strong identity with their culture do better than children who were forced to assimilate (Avard & Harmsen, 2000).

Many immigrant families experience poverty when they first arrive. Unlike Canadian families who experience poverty, immigrant families see it as a necessary and temporary part of resettling in a new country. They do not believe it will be long-term, and work to build the better life for which they came to Canada. It has been shown that even though many new immigrant families struggle in the first decade they are in Canada, after 10 to 12 years, they have caught up to or exceeded the national average wage. Poverty in the general population may be seen as part of a downward mobility and be associated with many other problems. Even though immigrant children experience more poverty than children born in Canada (30 percent compared to 13.2 percent), they experience lower rates of mental health problems. In school, immigrant children often out-perform children born in Canada (Morton, Hou, Hyman, & Tousignant, 1998).

Children and teens, especially, are faced with the challenge of balancing two cultures. Almost one-third of all new immigrants coming into Canada each year are children and youth under the age of 25. Most come as dependants of their parents, some come to study at colleges or universities, and others come to work. The biggest adjustments immigrant children and youth face are getting used to a new school system and balancing the expectations for children and youth in their new country with those from their country of

by Cathy Campbell

In the former Yugoslavia, Ahmed was a well-respected medical doctor. In Canada, he delivers pizza. His wife works full time in a bakery to help support the family. It's a story heard in immigrant and refugee families across Canada. A story of fading hopes and dreams. A story of fathers and their families.

"New immigrant fathers face a whole series of challenges as they attempt to adapt" to Canadian society, says David Este, associate professor in the Faculty of Social Work at the University of Calgary. According to Professor Este, immigrant and refugee fathers confront under-employment, racism, language barriers, role reversal, and sometimes declining self-esteem. The whole family feels the impact.

In 1999, Professor Este and two colleagues at Calgary's Mount Royal College—Dr. Rena Shimoni, associate dean of the Faculty of Health and Community Studies, and Dr. Dawne Clark, chair of the Department of Child and Youth Studies—began to interview immigrant fathers about their experiences. Their findings were presented at a national symposium on fathering held in Montreal. Professors Este, Shimoni, and Clark, whose work was sponsored by the Calgary Immigrant Aid Society and funded by Health Canada, have also developed a manual for social service agencies. The manual provides information to increase awareness of the issues facing immigrant fathers and help agencies develop culturally appropriate materials for immigrant and refugee men "in the context that these men are part of a family," Professor Este says.

Issues include the problem of under-employment. According to the Burnaby, B.C.-based Opening Learning Agency, employment is a basic necessity for survival in a new country. Not only because the new immigrant depends on an income to be able to sustain a home and

Many fathers lose their sense of self in a new country where their skills are not recognized.

a family, but also as it relates to self-esteem and a sense of settling in a new country. In Canada, "we don't do a very good job recognizing qualifications obtained in other countries," Professor Este says. When immigrant and refugee men can't get work in their chosen professions, "it really damages their sense of self-worth," says Professor Este, who is also the director of research for the Cultural Diversity Institute at the University of Calgary. "There's a psychological let-down. People come to Canada because it's a rich country and they think they will have no difficulty getting jobs. Professor Este says that Canadians need to look at new immigrants and refugees from the perspective of the strengths and assets they bring. "We're dealing with some very talented individuals."

Racism and discrimination in the workplace are other issues facing recent immigrants, Professor Este says. Many men struggle because they can't speak either of Canada's official languages. Immigrant families "may experience severe role reversals," says Professor Este. "Immigrant and refugee women tend to be more flexible in what kind of work they're willing to take on," he says. As a result, women often find jobs more easily than men. Fathers who can't find work begin to take on greater responsibility in the home. "It's hard for some of these men to take," Professor Este says. On the other hand, fathers who work shifts or hold more than one job complain that they spend too little time with their children.

Until now, there has been little research done to examine the role of immigrant fathers in Canada, Professor Este says. About 30 men from Latin America, China, South Asia, and the former Yugoslavia were included in the Calgary study. ■

Source: *Families & Health*. (2000, October). Vol. 14, p. 1–3. Published by the Vanier Institute of the Family.

1. What does Campbell say are the concerns for immigrant fathers?

2. How does the lack of recognition for the knowledge and skills immigrant men bring to Canada affect their self-concept?
3. Why would some men find it difficult if he were at home while his wife were working?
4. How does the underemployment of immigrant men affect the economic and social well-being of their families?

Moving is difficult enough for children, but when it is from one country and culture to a completely different one, it can be challenging.

origin. Recent immigrants do not have as large an extended social and kin group as people born in Canada do, and thus lack the support system of other youth. They tend to spend more time in religious activities than do Canadian-born youth in the beginning. However, the longer they stay in Canada, the less time they are involved in them.

Many recent immigrant children and youth experience social isolation, because of language barriers that exist when they first immigrate. Many immigrant children and youth enjoy the new freedoms they experience in Canada; however, this can cause conflict with their parents, who have different cultural and behavioural expectations of them. Many immigrant children and youth report experiencing racism. Younger children report it at school, while youth experience it while looking for work. Many immigrant young people said they found it difficult to feel totally accepted in Canadian society because their accents and their physical features set them apart. They believed that their parents experienced more difficulties than they did, especially in finding a job. Many immigrant youth use services geared to them only for social functions and to go on organized outings (Hanvey & Lock Kunz, 2000).

Another important issue facing immigrant children and their families is health care. Different cultures have different attitudes and beliefs about health care issues. For some immigrants, Canadian medicine is an unknown and is therefore feared. Dr. Ben Tan, editor of a Canadian Pediatric Society book on health care for immigrants and refugees, advises physicians to get to know their patients and to gain some understanding of their cultural beliefs around health care to better treat them. Many immigrants come to Canada having lived in difficult conditions that had inadequate health care. Ben Tan claims that physicians need to be aware of where immigrants come from in order to understand their needs and level of health. Some immigrants coming to Canada from developing countries bring with them a different set of health issues, such as intestinal parasites, dental problems, nutritional deficiencies, and irregular immunization, than those coming from developed countries. Canadian health care professionals must take this into consideration to help immigrant children develop to their full potential (Vanier Institute of the Family, 2000).

web connection

www.mcgrawhill.ca/links/families12

To learn about issues that immigrant families in Canada face, go to the web site above for *Individuals and Families in a Diverse Society* to see where to go next.

Poverty

Poverty is a serious issue that Canadian society must deal with. Brian Wharf, from the University of Victoria, claims that "the most significant crises which affect families arise from the absence of an adequate income" (1994, p. 55). Professionals who work with troubled families observe that poverty is a major issue underlying social problems. In Victoria, B.C., it is the most significant factor in the caseload of the Ministry of Social Services. This problem exists across the country. While the percentage of children living in poverty has been increasing, Canada's social safety net has been eroded through deficit reduction at both the federal and provincial levels (Vanier Institute of the Family, November, 2000). Canadians are being told that they can no longer afford their generous social programs because they are too costly and take away the incentive to work from Canada's poor. Often

Children raised in conditions of severe economic stress rarely reach their full potential.

Canadians feel overtaxed, especially when compared to Americans, whose taxes are lower but whose social programs are less generous and whose poverty rates are higher. It has been shown that poverty rates are lower when social programs are universal, yet the Canadian federal government has made no move to provide universal support for families. Social assistance varies by province and is being cut in favour of deficit reduction by provincial governments (Baker, 1996).

There are many web sites that have information on parent-child relationships. If you check the web connections in this text, you will be guided to many of them. Two of the main web sites for this course are for Statistics Canada and the Vanier Institute of the Family. Both of these sites have search engines.

Searching the "Statistics Canada" Web Site

1. On the Internet, go to www.statcan.ca. This will take you to the Statistics Canada home page.

2. Click on the appropriate language for your search. The information is available in both of Canada's official languages, French and English.

3. There are a number of options when you reach the next frame (see example below).

4. You can view *The Daily*, a daily news release with information relating to the latest census data released by Statistics Canada. It contains:

   a) The **Census**, where you can obtain specific data related to the most recent census taken in Canada. You can also see the release dates for further information.

   b) **Canadian Statistics**, where you can access information from previous censuses. There are several categories to choose from, depending on your research topic. Some examples are: The Economy, The Land, The People, and The State. (The People is where you will find much information for this course under subject headings like Population, Education, Health, Families, Households, and Housing.)

   c) **Community Profiles**, where you can find information about specific communities in Canada.

   d) A **search engine**, which allows you to search the entire site for information on a topic. Some of the information is available free, while other information is available at a cost. You can choose to view only free information or both. Most of the information that is available at cost can be found in libraries.

   e) An **Other Links page**, which will direct you to other web sites.

Searching the "The Vanier Institute of the Family" Web Site

1. Go to www.vifamily.ca. This will take you to the home page.

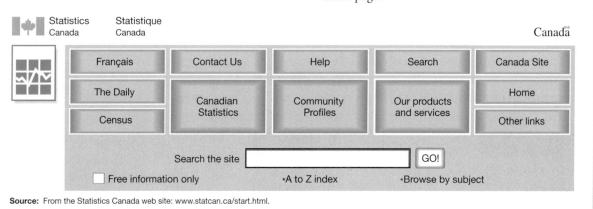

Statistics Canada   Statistique Canada

Canada

Français	Contact Us	Help	Search	Canada Site
The Daily	Canadian Statistics	Community Profiles	Our products and services	Home
Census				Other links

Search the site [   ] GO!

☐ Free information only   •A to Z index   •Browse by subject

Source: From the Statistics Canada web site: www.statcan.ca/start.html.

2. At the bottom of the page, the areas you can explore are listed (see below). If you click on any one of the topics, you will be directed to that page.

Example

Family Facts	What's NEW
Did You Know?	Speeches & Press Releases
Publications	Transition Magazine
Essays on Contemporary Family Trends	Families and Health Newsletter
Work and Family	Wealth & Family
About the Vanier Institute of the Family	Links
Contacts	Become a Member

a) You can view **Family Facts**, which provides updated facts on families in Canada. Some of the topics covered here are: What is a family? How many families are there? How many families have children? How big are families? How many are married? How many are living common-law?

b) You can view **Did You Know**? which offers information on questions about Canadian families, such as, How many hours do Canadians watch TV? How frequent is cohabitation?

c) You can view **Publications**, which supplies a list of recent publications by the Vanier Institute, many of which are available free as a download. Topics of publications varies.

d) You can view **Families and Health Newsletter**, which was published from 1999 to 2000, and has many topics of interest to those studying the Canadian family.

e) You can view **Transition Magazine**, the official magazine of the Vanier Institute. It is published four times a year and contains information on families. You can see which topics are in current and back issues, as well as those in upcoming issues. Back issues are available on-line for free, while current issues are available for purchase or in most public, college, or university libraries.

f) You can use a **search engine**, which allows you to input a topic and search the entire web site for information. Some of the information is available for free, while some is available at a cost. You can choose to view only free information or both. Much of the information that is available at cost can be found in libraries.

g) You can view the **Links** page, which will direct you to other web sites containing information on families. ■

Between 1989 and 1995, the number of children living in poverty in Canada has increased by 58 percent, to approximately 1 million, or 21 percent of all children (Voices for Children, 2002). The percentage fell to 19.8 percent in 1997, when the economy improved, but has not been reduced since then. This translates to approximately 1.5 million Canadian children living in poverty (Vanier Institute of the Family, 2000). Families living in poverty are those defined by Statistics Canada as living below the **low income cut-off (LICO)** point. Another significant factor is that the majority of Canadian families living in poverty are single-parent families headed by women. One child in five grows up in a family headed by one parent, usually the mother, and more than half of single parents raise their families on incomes below the low income cut-off point (Voices for Children, 2002; Vanier Institute of the Family, November, 2000). Research from the National Longitudinal Survey of Children and Youth (NLSCY) reveals that family type has a major influence on poverty rates in children, as shown in the table below (Ross, Scott, & Kelly, 1996).

Distribution of Poor* Children Aged 0 to 11 Years by Family Type, 1		
Family Type	**Poor* (%)**	**Non-Poor (%)**
Two-parent family	16.5	83.5
Single-parent family	68.0	32.0
Female single parent	70.9	29.1
Male single parent	30.7**	69.3

*Poverty is measured using Statistics Canada's low income cut-offs (LICO).

**Estimate less reliable due to high sampling variability.

Source: Adapted from the Statistics Canada publication, *Growing Up in Canada (National Longitudinal Survey of Children and Youth Series)*, Catalogue 89-550, November 1996, p. 34.

1. Account for the large difference between poor and non-poor children in two-parent families.
2. Why are children of single-parent families headed by women more likely to be poor?

One of the issues under study using the NLSCY results from all families living in poverty in a certain year is hunger among Canadian children. They studied the families that reported that their children had gone hungry because they had run out of money to buy food, or run out of food altogether. They found that 1.2 percent of the families in the sample had experienced this problem. Translated into numbers representing the Canadian population, that would mean approximately 57 000 families have experienced hunger. Some characteristics of families experiencing hunger are as follows (Vanier Institute of the Family, November 2000):

- They are eight times more likely to be led by a single parent.
- They are four times more likely to be of Aboriginal descent and living off the reserve.
- They are thirteen times more likely to report their income as coming from social assistance or welfare.
- Mothers had less education than those in families who were not experiencing hunger.

- The primary caregivers in these families suffered more chronic health problems.

- The children reported poorer health than those who had not gone hungry.

- Cigarette smoking was higher among the mothers in families who experienced hunger. Cigarette use among disadvantaged women is said to reduce stress and suppress their appetite.

- Parents report skipping meals and cutting down on their personal food intake when food supplies were low.

- Families reported visiting food banks and seeking assistance from families and friends.

For children, the consequence of being poor is that their families have insufficient income, time, and energy, due to the pressures of poverty, to make sure they grow up in safe neighbourhoods, receive a good education, participate in sporting and cultural activities, or nourish them well enough to make them healthy (Wharf, 1994). Children living in poverty are twice as likely to be born prematurely and with low birth weights, have shorter life expectancies, and face twice the risk of chronic health problems. In the Early Years Study, McCain and Mustard explain the crucial impact of early environment on all aspects of childhood development (1999). Families' financial insecurity should not deprive Canadian children of an environment with appropriate and adequate stimulation (Voices for Children, 2002).

Why do so many Canadian children and their families experience hunger?

The NLSCY raises many other questions about the effects of poverty on children. Although early results of the study find that poverty has less effect than researchers expected, there are many reasons for these results and many factors yet to be explored. One of the concerns is the use of cross-sectional data to investigate the issue, which, in this case, means all families living in poverty in a certain year only. Within that group of families, some may only have been living in poverty for one year, while others may have been living in poverty for several years. The NLSCY plans to explore the differences between short-term and **persistent poverty**, which lasts for a long time, with the results of long-term research. Persistent poverty is more of a problem for lone parents than for two-parent families. When studying lone-parent families from 1982 to 1993, the Applied Research Branch of the Canadian government found that 75 percent were living in poverty during this entire period. The researchers involved in the NLSCY believe that as the long-term patterns emerge in their research, people's understanding of the impact of poverty will increase significantly. They see it increasing with the age of the child (Human Resources Development Canada, 1999).

Canadians need to be concerned about the child poverty rate in Canada, not only from a human perspective, but also from an economic perspective. Child poverty rates reflect how well the Canadian economy is doing and how well it will do in the future. Living with a close, stable, and supportive family provides children with important protective factors that reduce the possible negative effects of living in a low-income environment (Voices for Children, 2002). The National Longitudinal Survey of Children and Youth and the Early Years Study support findings that good parenting can reduce the negative effects of poverty on children (Human Resources Development Canada, 1999; McCain & Mustard, 1999). All Canadians will eventually suffer the consequences of child poverty in terms of the future health of communities and the nation. Canada must be willing to invest in its children through such programs as Employment Insurance, social assistance, the Child Tax Benefit, and the taxation system in general (Vanier Institute of the Family, 2000).

web connection

www.mcgrawhill.ca/links/families12

To learn about Canadian children and poverty, go to the web site above for *Individuals and Families in a Diverse Society* to see where to go next.

point of view | Child Poverty

by Susan McClelland, Journalist

It was supposed to be Ed Broadbent's swan song, and his legacy to Canadian families. On November 24, 1989, in his final resolution in the House of Commons, the retiring leader of the federal New Democratic Party proposed to eliminate child poverty by 2000. Broadbent called the plight of poor children in Canada "a national shame, a national horror," adding: "Our obligation is to ensure that every kid in this country has full opportunity to become all he or she can become." The resolution passed unanimously.

Flip ahead a year, when Prime Minister Brian Mulroney co-chaired the United Nations World Summit for Children in New York. The high point of the event was the adoption of the Declaration on the Survival, Protection, and Development of Children. World leaders, including Mulroney, promised that in good economic times or bad, children's interests would come first. Delegates made firm commitments to reduce malnutrition, expand early-childhood development and education programs, and improve

When will our government fulfill its promise to end child poverty in Canada?

the living conditions of poor kids by, again, 2000. So what happened?

In 2001, at a United Nations' Special Session on Children, in September, child poverty in Canada is observed to be worse, not better. All levels of government in Canada have failed to provide for their most helpless constituents. More than a million children in Canada—an increase of about 28 percent since 1989—now live in households with incomes below what Statistics Canada calls the low income cut-off. Facing long waiting lists for subsidized housing, more families with young kids are ending up homeless. The number of people using food banks is up 92 percent over the past decade, and studies suggest about 40 percent of users are under the age of 18.

It's not just that governments failed to fulfill their noble goals. They did it knowingly. According to a 67-page report that Prime Minister Jean Chretien took to a United Nations' session in New York, Canada is a First World country struggling with inequality, and children of single parents and those of Aboriginal descent have been hit the hardest. Good intentions were derailed by the early 1990s' recession and deficit-reduction mania, and funding for social programs was not restored once the deficits were reined in. Meagre incomes were frozen or even reduced, widening an already gaping divide between rich and poor. Bridging that gap, says Senator Landon Pearson, Chretien's personal representative to the United Nations' session, is "a concern to our delegation. It doesn't seem to be something that worries some of our provincial leaders," she adds. "If we hadn't had the right-wing pressure accusing Liberals of spending, there might have been more programs in place."

There ought to be. For many families, the grip of poverty seems impossible to break. The federal report calculates that it now takes 75.4 weeks of work—the equivalent of one-and-a-half full-time jobs at an average wage—to cover basic expenses for the Canadian family each year. That's a dispiriting reality for single parents, of whom there were nearly 1.3 million in 2000 compared with 950 000 in 1991. According to Statistics Canada, more than a million of these families were headed by women, and their average annual household earnings were the lowest of any family type—$25 000 after taxes. "One always wants a better record," Pearson concedes. "If we hadn't dealt with the deficit, we would have had more capacity to respond."

The Canadian report to the United Nations did cite several promising initiatives. In the early 1990s, Chretien's Liberals launched the Canada Prenatal Nutrition Program and the Community Action Program for Children for kids up to six years of age. They provided such things as food, counselling, and education for at-risk families, including those in isolated communities and in situations of abuse. The Liberals also established Aboriginal Head Start to improve health, education, and nutrition for Aboriginal kids on and off reserves. In 1998, a new child tax benefit was put in place, which, by 2004, will give back to Canada's lowest-income families up to $2500 a child. And in 2000, the federal government agreed to transfer $2.2 billion over five years to the provinces for programs such as early-childhood development. Among other things, the funds are to be used to strengthen child care, a breaking point for working families.

All good, say some child-poverty experts, but not nearly enough. "What we need is an ongoing commitment," says Marvyn Novick, a professor of social work at Toronto's Ryerson Polytechnic University. "Not 'Here is your money for three years, five years.'" Novick points out that the objectives of two of the programs are compromised anyway because some provinces are unwilling to play their part. When a family on social assistance in all of the provinces except Manitoba, New Brunswick, and Newfoundland receives its child tax benefit, those provinces claw back that amount from the welfare cheque. And Ontario refuses to implement a child-care system with its portion of Ottawa's early-childhood development funds. "We've let Conservative governments led by Ontario and Alberta sabotage the national agenda," concludes Novick.

There's support for that hard-line approach beyond a few provincial capitals. Many critics claim that efforts to help poor kids by boosting their parents' income too often fail because the cash can be spent on non-essentials. And some Conservatives have a different measure for what constitutes poverty. Unlike some other countries, Canada has no official "poverty line," so most researchers rely on Statistics Canada's low income cut-off measurements, which are based on a complicated formula using family expenditure and income surveys.

But Christopher Sarlo, a professor of economics

at Nipissing University in North Bay, ON, whose work has been published by the Fraser Institute in Vancouver, challenges the rationale behind using the low income cut-off. Sarlo has created a series of poverty lines by calculating how much money a household requires for basic necessities. By Sarlo's reckoning, households that don't have these funds are considered poor. For instance, a single person in Halifax is living in poverty if he or she earns less than $8946 a year; a family of four in Calgary, $18 299. Using these rates, Sarlo places the prevalence of child poverty at closer to 10 percent, not the frequently quoted 17 percent that's based on Statistics Canada figures. "I'm not saying there is no problem," says Sarlo. "But if we want to measure poverty properly, we need to have better information, including the numbers of people who don't have enough money to meet their basic needs."

A 1999 study, however, suggests Sarlo's point is moot. In the report, Ottawa's Canadian Council on Social Development concluded that children in families whose incomes are below the Statistics Canada cut-off suffer poorer health, more behavioural problems, and worse grades in school than children from higher-income families. "The research isn't saying that all rich kids will be immune to these outcomes," says Paul Roberts, a research associate with the council and co-author of the report. "What it does say is that children with lower incomes are at greater risk."

Canada isn't the only developed country grappling with the issue. A 2000 report, Child Poverty in Rich Nations, published by the United Nations' Children's Fund, concluded that 47 million children in 23 of the wealthiest countries live in poverty. In Canada, there are a number of explanations for this, says economist Armine Yalnizyan: corporate downsizing, the growth of part-time and contract employment, and the

decline of stable positions. The situation has been exacerbated, she adds, by cuts to employment insurance, welfare, and social-housing programs that coincided with increases in private housing prices. "In the great economic boom of the 1960s, we had public investments, people's wages increased, and we expanded income-support programs," she says. "We have just gone through the biggest economic boom in 30 years, but we did the complete opposite."

That's evident in the United Nations' Children's Fund report. Canada ranked near the bottom among developed nations in the percentage of public dollars spent on social programs, and in the percentage of households with single and/or unemployed parents. The report calculated Canada's child-poverty rate at 15.5 percent—more than 10 percentage points higher than Sweden, Norway, and Finland. Rent De Grace, president and Chief Executive Officer of UNICEF Canada, says Canada has the equivalent resources of the Northern European countries, but doesn't use them as well. "It's our hope," De Grace says, "that all nations will be reminded that children are our best investment for human development." A lofty goal, and one, it is hoped, Canadian politicians act on. ■

Source: *Maclean's*. (2001, September 17). p. 18.

1. a) What is the author's thesis?
   b) What evidence does she suggest to prove it?
   c) Is she successful in proving it? Why or why not?
2. a) What factors contribute to children living in poverty in Canada?
   b) How do the statistics of children living in poverty in Canada compare with those in other countries?
3. What effects of poverty are described in this article?
4. What impact would a wider gap between rich and poor have on poor families?
5. What additional information would be useful for examining the issue of poverty?

Child Abuse

Child abuse is a growing concern in Canadian society. People are gaining a better understanding of the long-term negative consequences of abuse, as well as the need to break abusive cycles. There are many stressors that can affect a parent's ability to raise children well. Understanding these, as well as teaching parenting skills, are important ways to deal with the issue of abuse. As Canadian society has changed over the past few decades, definitions of child abuse have changed as well. In the past, spanking children was considered to be an acceptable, if not favoured, form of punishing children who misbehaved, since it quickly showed them the error of their ways and who was in control. Recently, there are citizens who call the police and file complaints of child abuse against parents who spank their children. Redefining punishment and abuse, and deciding when society has the right to intervene on behalf of a child, are some of the challenges faced by Canadian society today.

"Children can stand vast amounts of sternness. They rather expect to be wrong, and are quite used to being punished. It is injustice, inequity, and inconsistency that kills them."

—Robert F. Capon

In abusive families, the abuser tends to victimize the weakest member, and thus women and children are the most vulnerable. According to research, the youngest children, under the age of six, suffer the most physical abuse. Some children suffer from neglect, emotional abuse, and sexual abuse by family and non-family members. Children who witness their parents' abusive relationships are also considered victims. They are more likely to suffer from physical abuse and neglect (Larson, Goltz, & Munro, 2000). The Canadian Incidence Study of Reported Child Abuse and Neglect detailed cases that were being investigated by Canadian child welfare agencies. They differentiate cases into the following categories:

- substantiated—the balance of the evidence indicates that abuse has occurred

- suspected—there is not enough evidence; however there is a strong suspicion that abuse occurred

- unsubstantiated—the evidence does not lead to a conclusion of abuse

In 1998, the year of the study, there were 21.52 investigations of child abuse and neglect for every 1000 Canadian children (Trocmé, 2001).

Child Maltreatment Investigations by Level of Substantiation in Canada in 1998 (Weighted Estimates)

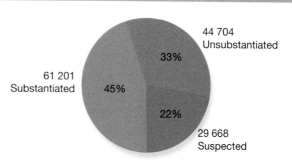

44 704 Unsubstantiated — 33%

61 201 Substantiated — 45%

22% — 29 668 Suspected

Source: Trocmé, N., et al. *Canadian Incidence Study of Reported Child Abuse and Neglect: Final Report.* Ottawa: Minister of Public Works and Government Services Canada, 2001, Cat. H49-151/2000E.

1. How can one account for the number of unsubstantiated cases of abuse or neglect?
2. What is the total number of cases that are either suspected or substantiated?

Reading each day about the horrors visited on a seven-year-old Toronto boy named Randal Dooley, whose father and stepmother were found guilty in April 2002 of second-degree murder after a gruesome three-month trial, was almost too painful. A little boy beaten so badly and so often—with belts, fists and feet, a bungee cord—that, in his fear of his step-mother, he became incontinent. His dying body placed in a cold bath in the dark. His eight-year-old brother, Tego, setting him gently in bed, where he expired from massive brain injuries. His father boiling hot dogs as firefighters arrived after his 911 call.

Randal's murder sends a clear and disturbing mes-sage. Too often, Canada is failing to protect its children from abuse. This death should not be treated as simply another wake-up call—there have been plenty enough of those over the years in every province—but as a cry for a complete overhaul of child protection.

As every child's life is unique, so, too, is each pre-ventable death. But a common theme is now clear. At countless stages, the child-protection system, and the people who make their living in it, are forsaking chil-dren, inexplicably so at times. This was the message from the 2001 inquest into the death by starvation of 35-day-old Jordan Heikamp, who was living with his mother in a Toronto women's shelter, under the super-vision of the Catholic Children's Aid Society. It was the message in 1995 from B.C. Judge Thomas Gove, who investigated the death of five-year-old Matthew Vaudreuil, suffocated by his mother despite the exten-sive involvement of social workers and physicians.

Randal Dooley could have been saved. His Grade 1 teacher discovered that his back and arms were criss-crossed with welts. This brought him to the attention of Toronto's Children's Aid Society (CAS) and police. The CAS made a cursory check and accepted the

Too many Canadian children, like Randal Dooley, die at the hands of their parents or guardians.

stepmother's story that his cousin had whipped him in a game. Police wanted to interview Randal alone, but his stepmother insisted on being present. Five months later, he was dead.

Randal's death should be as much a watershed as that of 19-month-old Kim Anne Popen of Sarnia, who died of horrific abuse at the hands of her mother in 1976. County Court Judge H. Ward Allen spent four years on an inquiry into that death and his findings came to 1826 pages. Out of that came more effective protocols for responding to suspicions of abuse.

But the system has become fatally flawed. Bureaucratic interests have overtaken children's interests. Social workers are now spending 85 percent of their time on paperwork, and 15 percent on families and children, according to a study of Ontario's 55 child-protection agencies. Budget restraints during the first half of the 1990s led to higher caseloads and lower salaries. So burdened is the system—the Toronto CAS receives more than 54 000 reports of abuse a year, or

150 a day, seven days a week—that only the rare, witnessed act of violence against a child tends to receive much scrutiny. And recruiting and keeping workers across Canada is a major challenge.

From 1991 to 1999, there were 363 children 11 and under who were homicide victims in this country—roughly the number in a typical elementary school. Four out of every five were killed by their parents. The number of deaths, which fluctuate wildly from year to year, were roughly the same in 1997 as they were two decades earlier.

Astonishingly, the B.C. government is now dismantling some of the very improvements that Judge Gove had fought for. It is losing an independent children's advocate. It is time for another look at the protection of children. Ontario should take the lead after Randal Dooley's needless death in setting up an inquiry. Randal belongs to all of us. We must not look away. ■

Source: *The Globe and Mail.* (2002, April 20). p. A20. Reprinted with permission from *The Globe and Mail.*

1. What is the thesis of this article?
2. What are some of the issues that are stopping Children's Aid Societies from protecting children?
3. a) What role does the rest of society have in protecting children from abusers?
   b) Who should carry out those roles? How?
   c) What role do you have?

Child Neglect

Child neglect covers a wide range of parental behaviours, from failure to provide the necessities of life, to inadequate supervision, to emotional neglect, when the parent withdraws emotionally from the child, providing little love or emotional support. Neglectful families tend to have a number of problems. They are characteristically led by a single parent, are poor, and have large numbers of children. Often, very young parents do not have the skills or emotional maturity to deal with raising a child, and their children are at high risk for neglect. Usually, the parents in this family do not have the time, energy, or resources to deal effectively with their children. Children of alcoholic parents suffer from neglect and are often left to fend for themselves. These children suffer lasting psychological, social, and emotional consequences (Larson, Goltz, & Munro, 2000). Results from

Neglect means failing to provide a child with the basic necessities of life.

the Canadian Incidence Study of Reported Child Abuse and Neglect show that neglect was the most often reported form of abuse to be considered substantiated and suspected. In 1998, in 40 percent of investigations, neglect was the primary reason for the investigation (Trocmé, 2001).

Children often suffer both **physical** and **verbal abuse** at the same time. Verbal abuse, which can also be referred to as **emotional abuse**, is emotionally damaging, because it hurts children's emerging vision of who they are and how they define themselves. If children receive only negative messages of who they are, they believe them to be true and will be scarred for life. This is called a **self-fulfilling prophecy**. Physical abuse is defined as non-accidental physical injury to a child resulting from actions of a parent or guardian. The message children receive when they are physically abused is that they are so bad, they deserve to be mistreated. This message also damages children's self-image. Severe physical abuse of children may lead to trauma, increased aggressiveness, nightmares, depression, neuroses, or an inability to express emotions. Children who do not suffer from physical abuse but who witness it have a tendency to be more aggressive, have difficulty in school, withdraw from social situations, oppose parental authority, and have sleep-related problems. The most disturbing characteristic of abused children is that they often become abusers in adulthood—they repeat the parenting behaviours they learned as children—or they become passive, willing victims, and are likely to be abused. As with neglect, abusive families are characterized as poor, large, with parents who do not have the resources and skills to deal effectively with their children. There is a higher incidence of abuse among parents who abuse alcohol or other substances (Larson, Goltz, & Munro, 2000). The age and sex of a child has an impact on whether or not they will be victims of abuse (Trocmé, 2001).

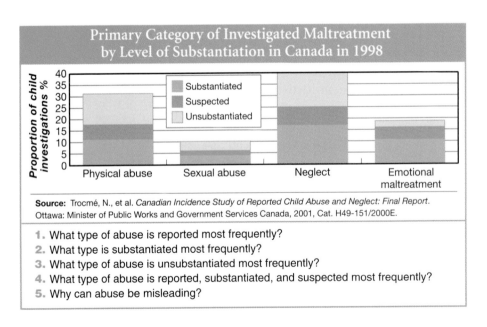

Primary Category of Investigated Maltreatment by Level of Substantiation in Canada in 1998

Source: Trocmé, N., et al. *Canadian Incidence Study of Reported Child Abuse and Neglect: Final Report.* Ottawa: Minister of Public Works and Government Services Canada, 2001, Cat. H49-151/2000E.

1. What type of abuse is reported most frequently?
2. What type is substantiated most frequently?
3. What type of abuse is unsubstantiated most frequently?
4. What type of abuse is reported, substantiated, and suspected most frequently?
5. Why can abuse be misleading?

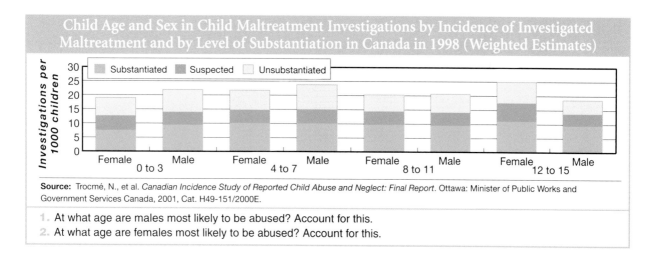

Child Age and Sex in Child Maltreatment Investigations by Incidence of Investigated Maltreatment and by Level of Substantiation in Canada in 1998 (Weighted Estimates)

Source: Trocmé, N., et al. *Canadian Incidence Study of Reported Child Abuse and Neglect: Final Report*. Ottawa: Minister of Public Works and Government Services Canada, 2001, Cat. H49-151/2000E.

1. At what age are males most likely to be abused? Account for this.
2. At what age are females most likely to be abused? Account for this.

Sexually abused children suffer from incest, intercourse with a blood relative, sexual assault, intercourse with a non-blood relative, abusive sexual touching either by the child being forced to touch the adult or the adult forcing the child to touch himself or herself, and sexual exposure of either the adult or the child. Girls are more often victims than boys are, since they tend to be more passive, and the abuser tends to be a heterosexual male, usually the father, stepfather, or a male cohabitor. Daughters of actively dating single mothers who bring their dates home are at highest risk for sexual abuse. These families tend to function poorly, be less stable, have poor interpersonal relationships, and experience less personal growth. Parents tend to be younger and less educated, have more children living at home, have few friends, and have above average levels of depression (Larson, Goltz, & Munro, 2000).

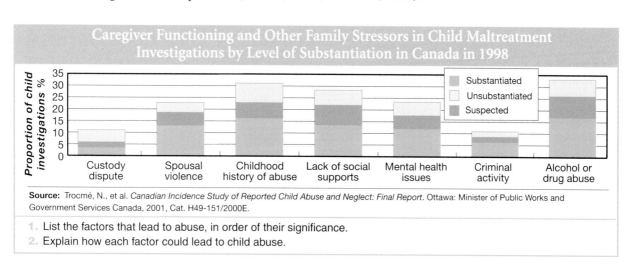

Caregiver Functioning and Other Family Stressors in Child Maltreatment Investigations by Level of Substantiation in Canada in 1998

Source: Trocmé, N., et al. *Canadian Incidence Study of Reported Child Abuse and Neglect: Final Report*. Ottawa: Minister of Public Works and Government Services Canada, 2001, Cat. H49-151/2000E.

1. List the factors that lead to abuse, in order of their significance.
2. Explain how each factor could lead to child abuse.

by Justice Marvin Zuker

Section 43 of the Criminal Code is an exception to the general rule that it is criminal assault to use force against another without consent. This section allows a parent, a person in the place of a parent, or a teacher to use force to correct a child in his or her care, where the force used is "reasonable under the circumstances." Section 43 has been part of the Criminal Code since 1892.

Section 43 became a focal point in the debate about corporal punishment in childrearing because it does not define the nature or limits of the force that is justified other than to require that it be "reasonable in the circumstances" and be for the purposes of "correction." Because of growing concern that physical punishment of children does more harm than good, it has been banned in Canadian schools, and the federal ministry of health has mounted an educational campaign teaching that hitting children is wrong. Canadian attitudes toward corporal punishment are changing, and many forms of it, at one time considered acceptable, are no longer so.

The Canadian Foundation for Children, Youth and the Law challenged Section 43 of the Criminal Code as unconstitutional, but the court dismissed the claim. The trial judge concluded:

> Having regard to the history of the legislation, that Parliament's purpose in maintaining Section 43 is to recognize that parents and teachers require reasonable latitude in carrying out the responsibility imposed by law to provide for their children, to nurture them, and to educate them. That responsibility, Parliament has decided, cannot be carried out unless parents and teachers have a protected sphere of authority within which to fulfill their responsibilities. That sphere of authority is intended to allow a defence to assault within a limited domain of physical discipline, while at the same time ensuring that children are protected from child abuse....

The judge did summarize certain agreements of social scientists concerning corporal punishment. These included:

- Spanking is defined as "the administration of one or two mild to moderate 'smacks' with an open hand on the buttocks or extremities that do not cause physical harm."
- Corporal punishment of very young children has no value, is wrong and is harmful.
- Corporal punishment of teenagers is not helpful and is potentially harmful.
- Use of objects, such as belts, rulers, etc., is potentially harmful and should not be tolerated.
- Corporal punishment should never involve a slap or blow to the head.

This decision was later appealed in the Ontario Court of Appeal and was denied. The appeal judge concluded that the best interests of the child were served by allowing Section 43 to remain, and that concerns about the misuse of corporal punishment were best addressed by educational programs. ■

Abuse and neglect of children has short- and long-term effects. Short-term effects are those that occur within two years of the incident. These include fear and anxiety; feelings of anger, hostility, guilt, and shame; depression; low self-esteem coupled with a poor self-image; physical illness and sleep disorders; disturbances in sexual behaviour and overall poor social functioning. In general, long-term effects of abuse or neglect are measured in young adults who were victims as children. These include depression, anxiety, psychiatric problems, post-traumatic stress, emotional and behavioural problems, and thoughts of, or attempts at, suicide. Adult victims of physical abuse also tend to be less tolerant, distrustful, suspicious, fault-finding, and resentful. They have difficulty forming relationships, experience more conflict in their relationships, and suffer from low self-esteem. Victims of sexual abuse suffer from high levels

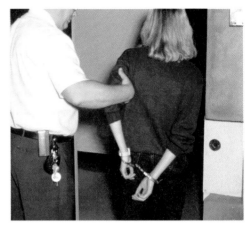

One of the long-term consequences of abuse is the young person having excessive anger.

of addiction and neuroticism, sexual dysfunction, as well as the effects previously mentioned. All victims of abuse and neglect are at high risk for becoming abusers themselves as parents. When the other risk factors of abuse are combined with being a victim oneself, the danger increases. How well adults deal with childhood abuse and neglect depends on their coping strategies, the level of social support they receive, and the functioning of their family during childhood (Larson, Goltz, & Munro, 2000).

web connection

www.mcgrawhill.ca/links/families12

To learn about child abuse, go to the web site above for *Individuals and Families in a Diverse Society* to see where to go next.

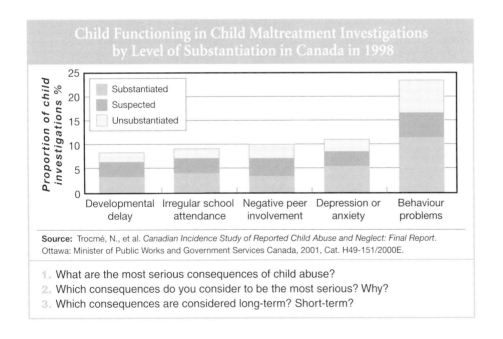

Child Functioning in Child Maltreatment Investigations by Level of Substantiation in Canada in 1998

Legend: Substantiated, Suspected, Unsubstantiated

Y-axis: Proportion of child investigations %

X-axis: Developmental delay, Irregular school attendance, Negative peer involvement, Depression or anxiety, Behaviour problems

Source: Trocmé, N., et al. *Canadian Incidence Study of Reported Child Abuse and Neglect: Final Report.* Ottawa: Minister of Public Works and Government Services Canada, 2001, Cat. H49-151/2000E.

1. What are the most serious consequences of child abuse?
2. Which consequences do you consider to be the most serious? Why?
3. Which consequences are considered long-term? Short-term?

by Rory Leishman, Freelance Writer

Is it always wrong to spank a child? Health Canada thinks so. In Nobody's Perfect, a program that teaches parenting skills to parents with children under five, this agency of the federal government states: "No matter how angry you are, it's never OK to spank children. It's a bad idea and it doesn't work." Millions of Canadian parents disagree. While they would never condone the use of excessive force to discipline a child, they would not rebuke a loving mother who mildly spanks her youngster for chasing a ball into the street.

Perhaps some parents have managed to raise well-disciplined children without ever spanking them. But is the achievement of a few parents reason for the state to invoke criminal sanctions as a means of forcing all parents to try to do the same? Surely not. Yet such drastic state interference in the autonomy of the family is a real threat. With the support of the Ontario Association of Children's Aid Societies and $69 000 in funding provided by the Jean Chretien government through the Court Challenges Program, a fringe group of child's rights extremists —the National Foundation for Children, Youth and the Law (NFCYL) —is seeking a judicial ruling that would make it a criminal offence for any parent to spank his or her own child.

In the days when Canada was still a functioning democracy and judges were bound to uphold the law, the courts could have been counted upon to reject out of hand such a ludicrous lawsuit. Today, that is no longer the case. Under the pretence of upholding the Canadian Charter of Rights and Freedoms, our judicial masters on the Supreme Court of Canada have arrogated to themselves the right to strike down or amend any law that has been duly enacted by elected representatives of the people.

In our revamped criminal courts, it's often not so much the accused as the law that is on trial. In the anti-spanking case brought by the NFCYL, there was no accused before the court at all. This travesty of a trial focused entirely on the abstract merits of Section 43 of the Criminal Code: "Every schoolteacher, parent, or person standing in the place of a parent is justified in using force by way of correction toward a pupil or child, as the case may be, who is under his care, if the force does not exceed what is reasonable under the circumstances." In the end, the trial judge, Mr. Justice David McCombs of the Ontario Superior Court of Justice, upheld the law.

Among other considerations, he pointed out more than spanking is at issue. "Without Section 43," he wrote, "other forms of restraint would be criminal, such as putting an unwilling child to bed, removing a reluctant child from the dinner table, removing a child from a classroom who refused to go, or placing an unwilling child in a car seat." On January 25, 2002, the Ontario Court of Appeal unanimously agreed with McCombs. Whether our nine arbitrary rulers on the Supreme Court will condescend to concur is anyone's guess.

Meanwhile, do the Chretien Liberals have no qualms about using taxpayers' money to help finance this litigious attack on loving parents? And what about the role of the Ontario Association of Children's Aid Societies in this fiasco? This agency should concentrate upon preventing the kind of horrendous child abuse that killed Jordan Heikamp, the five-week-old baby who died of starvation while supposedly under the care of his mother and Toronto's Catholic Children's Aid Society.

Instead, the Ontario Association of Children's Aid Societies is trying to persuade the courts to make Canada the first country in the world to criminalize the behaviour of every loving parent who spanks his or her own child. This is outrageous. Who can have any reasonable confidence in an agency that has mounted such a totalitarian attack on the rights of parents to decide for themselves what reasonable measures to take for the discipline and instruction of their children? ▪

Source: *London Free Press*. (2002, February 5). p A7.

1. What thesis does Rory Leishman argue in this article?

2. What arguments does he present to support his point of view?

3. Do you agree with the author? What are your reasons?

4. To what extent should the question of parental discipline be decided by law? Justify or support your answer.

5. The Ontario Court of Appeal ruling suggested that clearer guidelines defining spanking should be developed. What would you suggest they be? Why?

Katherine Covell, Associate Professor of Psychology, and Brian Howe, Associate Professor of Political Science, of the Children's Rights Centre at University College of Cape Breton, argue that the only way to solve the issue of child abuse is to force couples to get a licence to parent. They believe this would satisfy the demands for children's rights made by the United Nations. They claim the laws that exist in Canada today are merely reactive to the problem. Covell and Howe believe that people must become proactive to protect future generations of Canadian children from abuse. They cite three main reasons for their demand for licensing:

1. The number of children whose development is compromised by abusive situations.

2. The difficulties faced by child welfare agencies in protecting children from abusive situations.

3. The costs to individuals, and society as a whole, of abuse.

Covell and Howe advocate parent licensing to help adults better perform their role of raising children. They claim that parenting is a privilege, not a right (1998).

In recent years, there has been a great deal of controversy over the right to spank a child. Children's Aid Societies have filed charges against parents who spank their children. Many say that spanking is an unacceptable form of discipline and leads to abuse. Others argue that it is a quick and effective means to stop unwanted behaviour in children. In a poll conducted by *The Toronto Star*, 70 percent of Canadians opposed having the federal government pass a law that

"Remember, when children have a tantrum, don't have one of your own."

—Judith Kuriansky

would stop parents from spanking their children. In the same survey, respondents were evenly split on whether or not they thought that a light slap was an effective way to make a child think. Children's Aid Societies feel that spanking is seldom done in a cool, objective manner and often leads to corporal punishment (McKenzie, 2002).

The Death of a Child

No parents are ever prepared to deal with the death of their child.

When a child is born, a parent looks into the future and sees him or her going to school, becoming a teenager, going on a first date, leaving home to go to work or to continue their education, getting married, and providing grandchildren. Parents do not consider the fact that their child could die before them. A child's death upsets the "natural order" of life. Dealing with it is a challenge parents fear and hope they never have to face. The death is not anticipated, because it is out of place in the life cycle (Herz Brown, 1989). At the beginning of the twentieth century, 1 in 7 children died between the ages of 1 and 14 years, so death was a common occurrence in families (Statistics Canada, 1999). Functionalism suggests that because a child has few responsibilities in a family and in society, a child's death would leave fewer gaps to be filled by others than an adult's death would. In the twenty-first century, when the death of a child is rare, systems and social exchange theories recognize that children are an important emotional focus in a family, and are the extension of their parents' hopes and dreams for the future. Therefore, Fredda Herz Brown, Director of Training for the Family Institute of Westchester, concludes from her clinical work with bereaved families in the late twentieth century that "the death of a child is certainly viewed by most people as life's greatest tragedy" (1989, p. 446).

In Canada, few children die, but when they do, it is a devastating event for parents and families. The causes of death in children differ by age and sex. Most children's deaths occur as the result of illness. The greatest causes are **congenital anomalies**, or problems with which the children are born, that often cause death within the first few years of life, and **perinatal** problems, which are related to the birth, and that cause death shortly after the child is born. Other children develop cancer, or respiratory or cardiovascular diseases. Older children are more likely to die as the result of accidents, especially males aged 15 to 19, but the accident rate has dropped. Boys in this age group also die from suicide and murder more than any other age group (Statistics Canada, 1997). Death from all external causes has declined so that child mortality is "exceptionally rare in Canada" (Statistics Canada, 1999, p. 31). The impact of a child's death on the

| Number of Deaths of Children by Selected Causes, Age, and Sex, Canada 1997 | | | | | | | | | | | |
| Ages | Total | Less Than 1 | | 1–4 | | 5–9 | | 10–14 | | 15–19 | |
		Male	Female	Male	Female	Male	Female	Male	Female	Male	Female
All Causes	4253	1076	852	250	205	176	140	246	154	824	331
Diseases	714	74	72	76	75	60	56	66	53	115	67
Congenital and Perinatal Causes	1531	783	620	28	32	14	8	10	11	21	4
Accidents	632	6	8	35	19	38	22	53	32	288	131
Suicide	312	—	—	—	—	—	—	39	12	207	54
Homicide	76	3	2	11	8	6	6	6	4	23	7
Other	988	210	150	100	71	58	48	72	42	170	68

Source: Adapted from the Statistics Canada publication, *Mortality, summary list of causes, 1997–Shelf Tables*, Catalogue 84F0209, April 2001.

1. Account for the differences in the numbers of accidental deaths between male and female children.
2. Account for the differences in the numbers of deaths from homicide between male and female children aged 15–19.
3. What factors could contribute to the fact that the total number of deaths for males is greater than for females?

family depends on the child's age and the degree to which the family perceives the death to have been preventable (Herz Brown, 1989).

A child's death from a serious illness has different effects on family members than a sudden death does. When a child is seriously ill, it is important to let the child and siblings know that the child is dying. Research by Elisabeth Kübler-Ross has determined that even young children anticipate their own deaths when they are very sick, and want to talk about their fears. Children may ask to prepare their own funeral. Other children in the family may feel guilty for wanting attention. Knowing that their child is dying has a profound effect on parents because they have to deal with their own sorrow at the same time as they provide support for the dying child and their other children. However, when the death is sudden, parents may feel guilty for having to inform others of the sad news. A sudden death does not allow parents and siblings time to prepare for the abrupt ending to their lives as they have known them (Kübler-Ross, 1983).

Mortality Rates, Children Aged 1 to 14, Canada 1970–1972 to 1995–1997

Source: Adapted from the Statistics Canada publication, *Health Reports*, Catalogue 82-003, Winter 1999, Vol. II, No. 3.

After a child's death, parents, siblings, and the extended family have to let go of the child and cope with their sadness in individual ways. The ritual of a funeral allows individuals to say goodbye to the child and enables others to provide much-needed support. Young children should be allowed to attend if they wish, but they will express their feelings when they are ready. Siblings may experience difficulties at school, behaviour problems, or depression as they deal with their feelings of sadness, fear that they could die too, and perhaps a need to fill the place of the dead child in their parents' lives (Herz Brown, 1989). Parents may be haunted by thoughts of "What if?" and feelings of guilt that they did not prevent the death (Kübler-Ross, 1983). The more important parenthood is to an individual's sense of identity, the greater the sense of loss will be. The support of caring professionals before and after the child's death can help couples avoid the high divorce rate associated with this tragedy (Herz Brown, 1989).

case study | Donald and Louisa

Donald and Louisa met in high school when Donald was in Grade 12 and Louisa was in Grade 9. They were inseparable from the moment they met, and they married just before her eighteenth birthday. They had both left high school before graduating and had settled into jobs at a local factory, where Louisa's older sister, Sophia, was already working. They received a great deal of support during their first few years together, particularly from Louisa's family, since many of them lived nearby. Louisa was the youngest of her mother's children and was only two years old when her mother, Toni, started to live with Ron, whom she later married. Of the seven children in Toni and Ron's blended family, Louisa was the one whom they had raised together and, for that reason, was special to them both.

Daniella, Donald and Louisa's first child, was born in 1982. Louisa quit work to look after her and supplemented Donald's factory wages by starting a home day care in their rented house, taking in three local children. Donald was able to work overtime occasionally,

Donald and Louisa's son Joey died in a skateboarding accident.

and eventually they had enough money to purchase a small home.

Life for their young family became difficult when Donald lost his job while Louisa was expecting their second child, Joey. The American-owned factory suddenly shut down with only a few weeks' warning and gave only a small severance package. Donald was forced to look immediately for other work. He was unable to find a job that paid as much as he had earned at the leather factory, so for the next few years he worked at a variety of jobs. Eventually Donald found a position at a local production facility of a large Canadian brewery. When he started working there, he felt that their economic future was finally secure.

Daniella and Joey prospered in the small Ontario community where they lived, near Barrie. Both children were popular at the local elementary school and in the larger community, and many of their best friends were other children who had grown up in the day care that their mother operated. Louisa decided to close the day care when a friend said that a nursing home in Barrie was looking for staff. There were fewer young children requiring care in the village, and Louisa was ready for a change. The new job involved shift work, but it paid more. The family was already accustomed to Donald's different shifts, and Daniella and Joey were getting to be independent by then. Because Donald and Louisa were both working in Barrie and Joey and Daniella were being bused to a high school there, Louisa suggested that they move there, because she felt that it would give their two teenagers more opportunities. Donald resisted the change, however, as he liked living in a village. Over the next few years, the couple continued to discuss the possibility of moving, and they finally put their house up for sale around the time Daniella graduated from high school.

Tragedy struck the family about a month before the move. Joey was an avid skateboarder and could always be found at the town's skateboard park. One summer evening after his parents had gone to bed, Joey was skateboarding with a few of his friends when he fell and was hit by a passing car. The accident occurred just down the road from his house, and he died in the ambulance with his distraught parents at his side.

For Donald and Louisa, there could be no greater grief than losing a child. Like all parents, they blamed themselves, because children are not supposed to die before their parents. They had warned Joey thousands of times about the dangers of skateboarding on the busy road where he was killed, especially at night

when it was more difficult to be seen by passing drivers. But, like all parents, they knew that teenagers take risks and this was part of growing up and becoming independent. They wondered whether they should have banned their son from skateboarding altogether, as some of the neighbours had done with their children. Donald especially regretted not making the move to Barrie earlier, and felt that if he had only listened to Louisa, their son's death might have been avoided. They also were troubled by the opportunities they had missed when Joey was growing up—the camping trips and outings that were postponed because of chances to work overtime.

During the year after his death, the family usually stayed at home, and Donald especially has been reluctant to participate in social activities with friends and family. Daniella has found it very difficult to work and has chosen to spend her time with her boyfriend and his family or with her grandmother. Some time has passed now since Joey's death, and the family still struggles to rebuild their lives without him. Donald and Louisa know that only time will heal the horrendous loss that they feel, but they also believe that their strong commitment to each other will ease them through the next few years, just as it helped them get through those terrible weeks after Joey's death. ■

---

1. What hopes and dreams might Donald and Louisa have had for Joey?
2. What conflicted feelings might Donald and Louisa have experienced after Joey's death?
3. How has Joey's death affected Donald, Louisa, and Daniella?
4. How has Daniella's relationship with her parents changed since Joey's death?
5. Suggest how Joey's death would affect others in his extended family.

chapter 11 Review and Apply

1. Identify the arguments that have been used to propose that society should not explore reproductive technologies. Support each argument with evidence.

2. Find out how much it would cost a Canadian couple to undergo fertility treatments in Canada. Does the cost vary by province? Is any part covered by provincial health care plans? Do all Canadian couples have access to this type of treatment?

3. How does the way our society is structured have an impact on child poverty? Discuss the issues of child poverty from a structural functionalist approach.

4. What is the low income cut-off point? How has it changed in the last ten years?

5. Explain the various factors that influence how well children adjust to their parents' divorce.

6. Using research on abuse, develop a profile of someone who is likely to abuse a child.

7. What are some of the issues faced by immigrant children?

Knowledge/Understanding Thinking/Inquiry Communication

8. Write a personal essay about the death of a child from the perspective of a parent, caregiver, sibling, grandparent, aunt, or uncle. Describe the impact of the death on the family.

9. Write an essay defending your point of view on the use of a reproductive technology.

10. List the major problems that children living in poverty face. Write a brief article for a local newspaper that outlines the risks.

11. Arrange for a panel to speak to your class about the challenges facing immigrant parents and children when they come to Canada.

12. Create a documentary describing the ways our society can support parents to reduce the negative effects of divorce on children. Videotape your documentary to show to the rest of your class.

13. Write a case study that shows the cyclical pattern of child abuse. Make this case study into a play that could be presented to others in your school or community.

14. Debate the following topic: All prospective parents must pass a parenting test to receive their parenting licence prior to having children.

15. Select an article from this chapter and write a response in the form of a letter to the editor, using a different theoretical perspective than the article's. Identify both the author's theoretical perspective and yours.

Knowledge/Understanding **Thinking/Inquiry** **Communication** **Application**

16. Use the web connections in this chapter to access information on poverty rates in your province. Compare them to the rest of Canada. Make charts or graphs to show the difference. Write a brief explanation of the reason for the variations in different regions of the country.

17. Select an issue examined in this chapter and develop a hypothesis concerning a possible action for Canadian society to take. Use the web connections to conduct research about the current situation, and form an opinion about what steps need to be taken. Present and support your opinion orally as part of a town-hall debate about the role of your community regarding the issue.

18. Identify another issue that is currently affecting parent-child relationships. Do a web search to discover a variety of viewpoints on the impact of the issue.

unit 5 Later Life

UNIT EXPECTATIONS

While reading this unit, you will:

- explain the historical and ethnocultural origins of contemporary individual lifestyles, socialization patterns, and family roles

- analyze changes that have occurred in family structure and function throughout the history of the family

- analyze decisions and behaviours related to individual role expectations

- analyze current issues and trends relevant to individual development, and speculate on future directions

- analyze current issues and trends affecting the dynamics of intimate relationships, and speculate on future directions for individuals and families

- analyze decisions and behaviours related to parental and caregiver role expectations, including the division of responsibilities for childrearing and socialization

- access, analyze, and evaluate information, including opinions, research evidence, and theories, related to individuals and families in a diverse society

- analyze issues and data from the perspectives associated with key theories in the disciplines of anthropology, psychology, and sociology

Older Canadians can now enjoy a more active lifestyle than any generation before, thanks to their increased life expectancy and improved health.

In this unit, the lives of individuals in middle and late adulthood, and their
families, will be examined. To determine the role that adults of all ages play
in Canadian society, the age transitions of adulthood, midlife, retirement,
and old age will be outlined. Then the history of adulthood and aging will be
traced. Next, the psychology of aging, and the factors that contribute to
satisfaction at each stage of life for men and for women, will be examined.
Finally, the specific issues and trends that are influencing the transitions
from adulthood to midlife and to senior years today will be explored.

chapter 12

Adults and Their Families

CHAPTER EXPECTATIONS

While reading this chapter, you will:

- describe the various roles of individuals in society and the potential for conflict between individual and family roles
- explain changing family forms and functions in various societies throughout history, and describe contemporary family forms
- describe the diversity in personal and family roles of individuals in various cultures and historical periods
- analyze male and female roles in various societies and historical periods, taking into consideration societal norms and ideals, individuals' perceptions of roles, and actual behaviours
- describe current perceptions, opinions, and demographic trends relating to the life patterns of individuals, and speculate on the significance of these trends for individual development
- describe current perceptions, opinions, and demographic trends relating to intimate relationships, and speculate on the significance of these trends for individual and family development
- identify and respond to the theoretical viewpoints, thesis, and supporting arguments of materials found in a variety of secondary sources
- summarize the factors that influence decisions about individual lifestyle at various stages of life, drawing on traditional and current research and theory
- summarize the factors that influence decisions about educational and occupational choices at various stages of life
- demonstrate an understanding of the role of intimate relationships in the lives of individuals and families, considering the similarities and differences for males and females, and traditional and non-traditional relationships
- analyze the division of responsibility for childrearing and socialization, and the interaction of caregivers

Grandparents are playing a more active role in their families' lives than in the past, partly due to an increase in dual-earner parents.

CHAPTER INTRODUCTION

In this chapter, individuals and their families in adulthood will be studied from a sociological perspective. Adulthood, midlife, and aging will be defined, and their history will be examined to understand the cultural diversity of adult life. The interrelationship of individual, family, and work roles for men and women in Canada in a post-industrial society will also be explored. The impact of an increasing life expectancy, a declining birth rate, and the increase in the employment of women will be presented, so that you will be better prepared for making decisions concerning the later years of life.

Adult Life in Canada

Canadians are living longer lives than ever before. The increase in life expectancy over the last hundred years means that when young people become adults in their early thirties, they can look forward to almost fifty more years of adulthood. If midlife is calculated as the middle of the normal life expectancy, midlife for men begins at 39, and at 41 for women. The lack of any common rite of passage suggests that adulthood is one long stage, but, according to the family life-cycle perspective, the normative events of marriage, childbearing, grandparenting, and retirement are transition points in the lives of most Canadian adults (McPherson, 1990). Significant trends in Canadian society are affecting the transitions in adult life (Veevers, 1991, p. 25):

- individuals are marrying later
- divorce and remarriage are more common
- working spouses face conflicting family and work roles
- the retirement age is declining
- the proportion of seniors in the population is increasing

The definitions of adulthood, midlife, and old age are usually determined by the chronological clock, which is based on age norms. Traditionally, sociologists identified middle age as the time in life when children left home, but now that childbearing is often being delayed and children do not always leave home until their late twenties, that significant rite of passage occurs long after the midpoint of the life span (Baker, 2001; McDaniel, 2001). In practice, however, there are cultural variations in the chronological clock that might limit opportunities for some individuals. For example, a compulsory retirement age could lead to the false assumption that individuals become less productive as they approach that age. However, the age of retirement in various countries ranges from the mid-50s to 70. Every society assigns its own meaning to age. In Japan, where age is valued, aging has a different meaning than in North America, where youth is valued presently (McPherson, 1990).

The History of Adulthood

In the past in Canada, people died at what is termed **middle age** today, and few experienced old age. The life course of women, and therefore the men they married, can be described by tracing the ages at which they married, when they

Life Expectancy at Birth				
	Both Sexes	**Males**	**Females**	**Difference**
Canada			Years	
1920–22	59	59	61	2
1930–32	61	60	62	2
1940–42	65	63	66	3
1950–52	69	66	71	5
1960–62	71	68	74	6
1970–72	73	69	76	7
1980–82	75	72	79	7
1990–92	78	75	81	6
1990–92				
Newfoundland and Labrador	77	74	80	6
Prince Edward Island	77	73	81	8
Nova Scotia	77	74	80	6
New Brunswick	78	74	81	7
Québec	77	74	81	7
Ontario	78	75	81	6
Manitoba	78	75	81	6
Saskatchewan	78	75	82	7
Alberta	78	75	81	6
British Columbia	78	75	81	6

Source: Adapted from the Statistics Canada web site
http://www.statcan.ca/english/Pgdb/People/Health/health26.htm.

gave birth to their last child, and when they died. In 1840, a woman might have married in her mid-to-late twenties, given birth to the last of four or more children at age 40, and died at age 62, so that she lived her whole adult life caring for dependent children (McDaniel, 2001). Men married when they could afford to, and spent their adult lives working to support their families. Since many women died giving birth to their last child, their husbands often remarried rather than raise children alone as widowers. Men stopped working only if declining health prevented them from doing their jobs. Because historically there has never been a tradition of the extended family in Canada, most Canadians who lived into old age continued to live in their homes, alone or with any unmarried children, until their death (Nett, 1993).

Median Age at Selected Periods of the Family Career of Canadian Women Born 1880s to 1950s									
		Period of Birth of Mother							
		1880s	1890s	1900s	1910s	1920s	1930s	1940s	1950s
		Approximate Year of First Marriage							
Period of Family Career	**80-Year Average**	1900s	1910s	1920s	1930s	1940s	1950s	1960s	1970s
Median Age at:									
1. First Marriage									
mother	22.8	24.7	23.2	22.8	23.8	23.5	21.7	20.9	21.5
father	26.1	29.1	27.2	26.2	26.8	26.5	24.8	24.3	24.1
Difference	3.3	4.4	4.0	3.4	3.0	3.0	3.1	3.4	2.6
2. Birth of first child	23.9*	(26.1)*	(24.5)	(24.0)	(24.2)	24.7	23.8	23.2	23.9
3. Birth of last child	28.1*	(28.8)	(28.0)	(27.2)	28.5	28.2	29.2	28.8	26.3
4. Marriage of last child	51.1*	(55.1)	(53.0)	(50.4)	51.1	51.0	52.0	51.6	49.1
5. Death of one spouse	67.4 68.1*	65.6	65.6	67.6	67.5	68.0	68.2	68.4	68.2
Difference Between Age at First Marriage and:									
6. Birth of first child	1.6*	(1.4)	(1.3)	(1.2)	(0.4)	1.2	2.1	2.3	2.4
7. Birth of last child	5.8*	(5.1)	(4.8)	(4.4)	4.7	4.7	7.5	7.9	4.8
8. Marriage of last child	28.8*	(30.4)	(29.8)	(27.6)	27.3	27.9	30.3	30.7	27.6
9. Death of one spouse	44.6 45.7*	40.9	42.4	44.8	43.7	44.5	46.5	47.3	46.7
Difference Between Age at:									
10. Births of first and last children	4.2*	(3.1)	(3.5)	(3.2)	(4.3)	3.5	5.4	5.6	2.4
11. Birth and marriage of last child	23.0*	(25.3)	(25.0)	(23.2)	22.6	22.8	22.8	22.8	22.8
12. Marriage of last child and death of spouse	17.0*	(10.5)	(12.6)	(17.2)	16.4	17.0	16.2	16.8	19.1

* Fifty-year average (1930–1980). Figures in parentheses are estimates.

Source: Roy H. Rogers, and Gail Witney. (1981). "The Family Cycle in Twentieth Century Canada." *Journal of Marriage and the Family* 43(3): 129. Copyrighted 2002 by the National Council on Family Relations, 3989 Central Ave. NE, Suite 550, Minneapolis, MN 55421. Reprinted by permission.

An improvement in life expectancy began in the 1850s in North America. Significant changes in the treatment of infectious diseases meant that fewer children died before reaching adulthood. The decline in mortality was not the same for men as it was for women, so a widening gap in life expectancy for men and women developed. This gender differential in mortality is explained by two health trends (Bangston & deTerre, 1991):

1. Improvements in care during childbirth resulted in a decline in maternal mortality, a major cause of death for adult women, so women lived to see their children grow up.

2. There was an increased mortality from the consequences of increased smoking, primarily a male habit until the middle of the twentieth century.

Consequently, the mortality rate of men in adulthood began to exceed that of women (Bangston & deTerre, 1991). Since the middle of the twentieth century, males outnumber females until midlife, then women increasingly outnumber men.

By 1960, men and women were marrying in their early twenties, and the average age of a woman having her last child was 28. The average family was still patriarchal, men were the earners, and there was a clear division of roles. A woman was usually a full-time mother and homemaker, but she now had technology to help her with household tasks. When the children married and left home, she was probably about 50, and she could expect to live to be 82. She and her husband could look forward to many years as an **empty-nest** couple. The adjustment to the "empty nest" was assumed to be a crisis for women, since they had lost their primary role as mother, but men and women could anticipate being grandparents and enjoying another generation of children. Additional crises in the lives of women in the patriarchal family were the adjustment to her husband's retirement, a time when he lost his primary role, and the likelihood of surviving her husband as a widow.

An increased life expectancy over the last 150 years has changed the family structure in Canada. In 1910, only 16 percent of 50-year-olds had a surviving parent. Most middle-aged adults were the senior generation in their families. By 1991, 60 percent of 50-year-olds had a surviving parent, and 25 percent of 60-year-olds (McDaniel, 2001). Since women have traditionally married men who were several years older, and because the life expectancy of men is several years less than that of women, women became the senior member of their families after they were widowed.

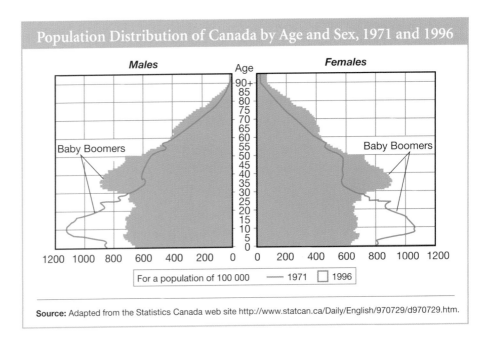

Population Distribution of Canada by Age and Sex, 1971 and 1996

Source: Adapted from the Statistics Canada web site http://www.statcan.ca/Daily/English/970729/d970729.htm.

Age Strata

There are more cohorts of Canadians alive now than at any other time. The **social clock** defines **age strata**, or layers, within a society. Each successive cohort (people born within the same time frame) follows the previous one through the socially defined ages. Each cohort faces similar challenges as it progresses through each of the transitions in adulthood, but the cohorts' needs may differ. The impact of the economic, social, and political stresses in the last century differs according to the size of the cohort; their age at the time of significant events, such as a war; and society's response to those stresses. Thus, each cohort may become a **generation** with distinctive characteristics, such as the baby boom or the echo-boom generations (McPherson, 1990; McDaniel, 1998). The different experiences of generations within a society may create conflicting needs. However, all generations co-exist within families, so the conflicting needs of different individuals in different generations are interfamily conflicts (McDaniel, 1998).

The varying experiences of different cohorts result in generations that have distinctive expectations and norms. This makes it difficult to determine whether patterns of behaviour in adulthood are developmental characteristics that apply to that stage of life, or characteristics that result from the cohort effect. For example, the anti-authoritarian behaviour of "hippies" was a

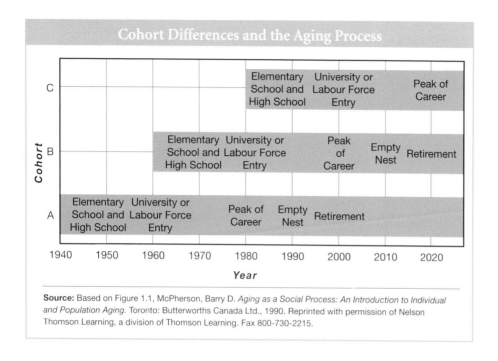

Cohort Differences and the Aging Process

Cohort									
C					Elementary School and High School	University or Labour Force Entry		Peak of Career	
B			Elementary School and High School	University or Labour Force Entry		Peak of Career	Empty Nest	Retirement	
A	Elementary School and High School	University or Labour Force Entry			Peak of Career	Empty Nest	Retirement		

1940 1950 1960 1970 1980 1990 2000 2010 2020

Year

Source: Based on Figure 1.1, McPherson, Barry D. *Aging as a Social Process: An Introduction to Individual and Population Aging.* Toronto: Butterworths Canada Ltd., 1990. Reprinted with permission of Nelson Thomson Learning, a division of Thomson Learning. Fax 800-730-2215.

cohort effect in response to social conditions of the late 1960s and early 1970s in the United States that was not repeated by successive cohorts (McPherson, 1990). Barry McPherson, a Canadian sociologist and gerontologist, suggests that socialization within the family may be more influential than the cohort effect because children acquire the values and norms of their parents. Therefore, generational units, based on social class, race, and ethnicity, differ in their expectations and social norms. For example, some baby boomers became "hippies" and were anti-government and protested the Vietnam War, but others supported the war and conscription. The children of anti-authoritarian parents may resist authority in ways more typical of the children's cohort, whereas the children of conservative parents support the status quo of their own generation. Although there may be conflicting needs between generations within a society, there is little intergenerational conflict, because social norms remain consistent from generation to generation within families (1990).

The challenge to separate cohort effects from life-course-related effects suggests that the future for today's young adults may not resemble adult life for previous or current generations (McDaniel, 2001). Myths and stereotypes persist about life in adulthood, midlife, and old age, just as they do about adolescence. In the mid-twentieth century, most research on adulthood focused on problems such as the midlife crisis, the so-called "empty-nest syndrome," and the problems of senility, or declining mental ability in old age. More

"Each generation imagines itself to be more intelligent than the one that went before it, and wiser than the one that comes after it."

—George Orwell,
Animal Farm

Baby boomers who wore high heels for decades may suffer from hip and knee problems when in their fifties.

recently, research has focused on the health problems associated with aging because of debates about the cost of health care in Canada. However, evidence suggests that many health problems result from lifestyle, which is a cohort effect, not the effects of aging. Individual choices about nutrition, exercise, smoking and drinking, and even fashion reflect the social and cultural norms of each generation and can affect health and longevity. For example, heart disease and cancer, the major causes of death for 50-year-olds, are strongly related to poor diet and lack of exercise. High-heeled shoes may not be life-threatening, but female baby boomers who wore them for decades are more likely to be disabled by knee and hip problems in their fifties and to require expensive orthopedic surgery. If successive generations are changing their diets, pursuing a more active lifestyle, and wearing more comfortable fashions, then Canadians may have fewer health problems in the future.

Adulthood in Canada

Adult individuals are expected to be financially, socially, and emotionally independent. The transition to adulthood is generally considered to be complete at about 34 years of age (Meunier, Bernard, & Boisjoly, 1998). By that age, most Canadian adults are employed, have formed intimate couple relationships, and have children. How they live their adult lives will be influenced by the success with which they made the transition to adulthood. Their lifestyles will also be affected by the changes in Canadian society. The major factors affecting family life today are the declining birth rate, employment of women outside the home, and an increased life expectancy. Dual-earner couples are negotiating marital and parental roles unlike those experienced by any other generation, as well as balancing them with the demands of workplace roles. Women in the work force contribute to an increased family income that supports a consumer lifestyle, but will face the transition of retirement in the future. Men and women can anticipate greater involvement as grandparents. Women are also more likely to acquire the financial security that should improve their independence in later life.

As the results of the 2001 Canada Census were released, the headlines in the media suggested changes in the Canadian population that were not anticipated. It is difficult to predict how people will behave in the future based on how they have acted in the past. Humans are decision makers. They have the ability to choose whether they will attend school, marry, have children, work or not work, move, or retire. Mortality is beyond people's control and remains unpredictable. Yet, foretelling the behaviour of Canadians in the future is necessary to enable governments and businesses to make policy decisions that will affect the availability of services and products that people will need. For example, underestimating the number of children that will be born could mean overcrowded or portable classrooms. In this textbook, you have examined current demographic trends related to leaving home, education, marriage and cohabitation, parenthood, dual-income families, retirement, and living arrangements. What will be the trends in these aspects of individual and family life in the future?

Predicting future trends requires a careful analysis of past behaviour and the factors that influenced it, and then speculating on how those factors might influence future behaviour. There are several important questions to consider as you complete this analysis:

- **What has been the long-term pattern?** Do not assume that a recent change will be the last change that occurs. Analyze the data over generations to determine whether short-term changes in the past resulted in long-term trends. For example, the age at which people marry has decreased and increased several times in the last century.

- **What are the cohort factors that influenced the pattern?** For example, when predicting the birth rate for Canada, the echo boom could have been predicted because of the size of the baby boom, despite the decline in the number of births per woman. However, demographers at the time did not know that effective contraception would result in baby boomers delaying parenthood. Based on fertility rates during the traditional childbearing years, demographers predicted a sharp decline in the Canadian population. A similar baby boom might occur when the echo boom begins to have children, unless other cohort factors affect their fertility.

- **What legal or policy procedures might have affected the behaviour?** For example, the passage of laws legalizing divorce changed divorce rates in Canada. Such changes reflect the opportunity to divorce, not necessarily the motivation to stay married or to divorce.

- **What social and economic changes have influenced demographic changes?** For example, the economic changes in Canada resulting from the employment of women have occurred over a long time. This change has affected demographic trends related to education, marriage, and parenthood, but the impact of this change is just beginning to affect trends for the aging years. ■

Work Versus Family Roles

The dramatic economic and social changes from 1970 to 2000 resulted in major role transformations for women and for men. The majority of young women expect to balance individual goals in a career with marriage and family (Davey,

1998), and that is exactly what adult Canadian women are doing now. Almost 80 percent of women aged 25 to 54 are now working, whether or not they have children. About 91 percent of men of that age are working. The traditional gender roles that were based on the patriarchal family no longer fit the contemporary family. Research questions that arise from this change include:

- Why have dual-earner families become the norm?
- How have husbands adjusted their roles to accommodate working wives?
- What are the stresses associated with dual-earner families?
- How do the new male and female roles affect marriage?
- What are the effects of the new roles on parenting?

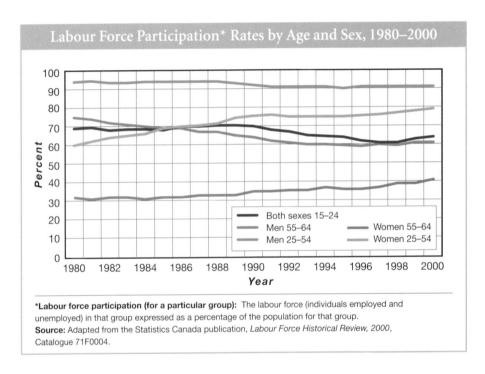

Labour Force Participation* Rates by Age and Sex, 1980–2000

*Labour force participation (for a particular group): The labour force (individuals employed and unemployed) in that group expressed as a percentage of the population for that group.
Source: Adapted from the Statistics Canada publication, *Labour Force Historical Review, 2000*, Catalogue 71F0004.

Historically, it was assumed that men would be the sole earner in a family. Generations of men experienced the economic and personal stress of supporting their families, even though this ideal proved to be unattainable for most working-class and many middle-class men in the twentieth century (Conway, 1997). Many were unable to earn enough to provide the desired standard of living, yet a working wife was an admission to this shortcoming. When the wives of middle-class men entered the work force by the mid-twentieth century, the income differential between dual-earner families and single-income families began to grow. For a time, dual-earner families could afford a higher standard of living, so a wife's income was valued because it provided some luxuries for the family. The assumption that a wife's employment merely met her individual needs and provided extras for the family supported the myth that a man was the real provider, but it *did* allow men and women to adjust gradually to the idea of women being employed (Conway, 1997). In a time period lasting about one generation, Canadians have made a dramatic transition from assuming a clear division of labour based on gender, in which men earned the sole income, to a division of labour based more on economic need.

In dual-career families, the time pressures of daily living can be reduced by the higher standard of living that the family can afford.

The traditional "breadwinner" and "housewife" roles are no longer economically viable. For several reasons, single-earner families are three times more likely than dual-earner families to be poor (Conway, 1997). In the past, married men were paid wages based on the assumption that they were supporting a family, but the "family wage" has disappeared since women began to enter the work force in the 1960s. The more education a woman has, the more likely she is to work continuously, and the higher her income is likely to be. The more education a man has, the more likely it is that his wife will work. There has been no real growth in family incomes in Canada since they peaked in 1989, and the incomes of young men have declined during that period (Morisette, 1997). As a result, having a sole earner in a family has been a major risk for poverty during the 1990s, and there is almost no chance of a young man earning enough to be the sole support of his family. John Conway, a sociologist at the University of Calgary, predicts that because there are no economic rewards for the traditional male breadwinner role in the family, it will soon disappear (1997).

Co-ordinating the demands of family and workplace roles causes stress for men and for women, resulting in **work-family conflict**, in which work responsibilities affect family roles (Aryee, 1999). Fifty percent of men and women report worry and stress related to balancing two roles. Men whose wives work take on a greater share of family and childrearing tasks than do men whose wives stay at home. An American study of dual-earner couples found that 39 percent of men and 50 percent of women reported that they have turned down transfers at work, and 22 percent of men and 30 percent of women declined promotions (Conway, 1997). Transfers and promotions can affect family roles if they require more hours at work, more travel, increased commuting time, or the family to relocate. **Family-work conflict**, in which family responsibilities affect workplace roles, does not significantly affect productivity, perhaps because workers are more focused and efficient on the job (Aryee, 1991), but 80 percent report that they cope with family problems at work or miss time for family reasons (Conway, 1997). Married women who work full time earn only 68 percent of what married men earn, perhaps because they are less likely to relocate or work longer hours to attain the better-paying jobs that single women can (Drolet, 2001). As the trends of an increasing work week, greater competition for jobs, a widening gap between highest and lowest paid, and shorter-term jobs create insecurity in the workplace, men and women in dual-earner families will experience greater stress from their conflicting roles.

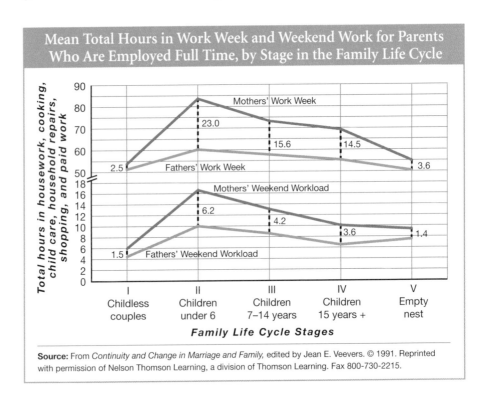

Mean Total Hours in Work Week and Weekend Work for Parents Who Are Employed Full Time, by Stage in the Family Life Cycle

Source: From *Continuity and Change in Marriage and Family*, edited by Jean E. Veevers. © 1991. Reprinted with permission of Nelson Thomson Learning, a division of Thomson Learning. Fax 800-730-2215.

The social norm of the dual-earner family has focused new attention on the work-family conflict. In the traditional patriarchal model, described by functionalists in the mid-twentieth century, a man's job was his primary role because it provided the economic support for his family. The wife's role was to support her husband's ability to do his job by managing the household and caring for the family. In the dual-earner family, both partners are likely

only the mother come home and do all the housework too. Partners in successfully balanced families appreciated what the other did around the house.

9. **They are proud.** The balanced families didn't accept negative stereotypes about themselves just because they both worked outside the home. They believed dual earning was positive for the whole family and did not feel guilty about their family arrangement. Partners in balanced families tended to achieve personal fulfillment through their children, their spouses, and their work. They recognized all these aspects of their lives provided purpose. Some took pride knowing their children would grow up sharing what happens in a home, viewing women as equal, and seeing dads do chores.

10. **They enjoy family time.** Although their lives were busy and demanding, the families enjoyed a lot of play time. They used it to relax, enjoy life, stay connected emotionally, and guard against stress. Spontaneous moments were treasured, like having a family camp-out in the living room with sleeping bags and a fire in the fireplace.

The researchers acknowledged that striking the perfect balance requires work and dedication. We believe the struggle for family-work balance will continue but, at the least, this research can allow working parents to breathe a sigh of relief. ■

Source: *Ottawa Citizen.* (2001, Dec. 29). p. H4. Dr. Jennifer Newman and Dr. Darryl Grigg are registered psychologists and directors of Newman & Grigg Psychological and Consulting Services, a Vancouver-based corporate training and development partnership. Identifying information in cases cited has been changed to protect confidentiality.

1. What criteria are used to measure the success of a dual-income parenting lifestyle?
2. What are the negative stereotypes of dual-income parenting, and what behaviour would "defy the negative clichés"?
3. What costs and benefits would you expect to face in a dual-income family?
4. From a functionalist perspective, how is Canadian society changing to support the functioning of dual-income families?
5. Suggest how symbolic interactionism would explain the satisfaction that these families feel with a dual-income lifestyle.

The new role for men who are making a commitment to family life is involved fatherhood (Gerson, 2001). Most involved fathers have working wives, and the remaining few are single fathers. Although some fathers are becoming equal partners in childrearing, 60 percent define themselves as "mother's helper." Men are more likely to choose the tasks they take on than women are, but they are performing more of the housework and child-care tasks than in the past, and are maintaining previous levels of play and nurturing duties (Galinsky, 2000). Men now face the same trade-off that women faced when they became working mothers. The new man and the new woman must choose whether to spend time with their children, at work earning money to support the family, or on leisure activities for themselves. Balancing the long-term and short-term benefits of time used for family, work, and self presents ongoing challenges (Gerson, 2001). Children raised in dual-earner families turn out well, and could make the "double shift" worthwhile for the current generation (Conway, 1997). These children have less traditional views of male and female roles, which could mean that future generations will have less difficulty adapting to the new family structure. An interesting side effect of the dual-earner family is that men are limiting the size of their families. Whether this is initiated by the wife or the husband, men agree to have fewer children because of the amount of work it takes to raise a child (Gerson, 2001).

From a social exchange perspective, the dual-earner family that has become the social norm for Canadians has costs and benefits for both men and women. The time and money required for raising children when both parents work motivates these couples to have fewer children than families in which the woman stays at home (Gerson, 2001). Men do more housework and report that they have less sex than men whose wives do not work outside the home. Both men and women have less leisure time and have less flexibility in their jobs. However, women report that they find work satisfying. The larger family income combined with the smaller family size provide economic benefits for the family, but the social prestige resulting from larger family income sometimes creates hostility and envy for men whose colleagues' wives are not employed. Men and women in dual-earner families are generally happy with their choice because it meets their needs. John Conway concludes that men do not miss the power that they had in the patriarchal family model. He speculates that, although men now have to compete with women for jobs and do more work at home, working women improve the family income and reduce the stress on men to be the sole provider (1997).

An increased life expectancy and improved health has resulted in an increase in the age of adults who assume some responsibility for their aging parents.

Middle Adulthood

The years between 40 and 65 are commonly referred to as "middle adulthood." In the mid-twentieth century, this stage was called the "launching years" and the "empty nest" because when children left home, the parenting role was complete. For couples who delayed childbearing until their late twenties or early thirties, the trend for young adults to remain at home longer means that their nest may be occupied by grown children until the parents are almost 60. Middle adulthood can be a stable period. The 45- to 54-years age group has the highest average income in Canada, the major responsibilities of raising children are complete, and marriages are over the peak divorce hurdle. The challenges of middle adulthood are the

	Number of Income Recipients				Average Income $			
Age Groups	Men		Women		Men		Women	
	1990	1995	1990	1995	1990	1995	1990	1995
Total – Age groups	9 882 395	10 516 805	9 542 490	10 399 955	33 733	31 117	19 630	19 208
15–19 years	621 205	584 530	573 065	542 675	5 370	4 350	4 561	3 813
20–24 years	930 830	916 035	898 630	891 695	16 326	12 433	12 869	9 815
25–34 years	2 346 605	2 191 875	2 173 985	2 088 455	32 464	28 435	21 404	20 161
35–44 years	2 127 875	2 370 835	1 958 430	2 239 760	43 375	38 935	24 835	24 157
45–54 years	1 461 135	1 827 570	1 275 965	1 673 415	46 199	42 787	24 215	24 772
55–64 years	1 142 500	1 211 090	1 006 030	1 113 105	39 026	35 628	18 736	18 078
65–69 years	480 570	519 640	561 520	566 180	30 686	28 540	16 544	16 157
70 years and over	771 675	895 220	1 094 875	1 284 390	25 288	25 140	17 294	17 130

Number of Income Recipients and Their Average Income in Constant (1995) Dollars by Sex and Age Groups, for Canada, 1990 and 1995

Source: Adapted from the Statistics Canada web site http://www.statcan.ca/english/census96/may12/t1.htm.

couple's adjustment in their relationship to adult children, assuming care for their parents, taking on a grandparenting role, and planning for and adjusting to retirement from the workplace.

Family Responsibilities

Relationships within families change in middle adulthood. As children are launched from the family to begin independent lives in their own households, the family contracts. However, the extended family network may actually become closer. A major role of women in midlife is that of **kin-keeper**, a cross-cultural expectation that women will organize family events and maintain contact with family members. Among middle-aged women in Canada, 57 percent report that they are responsible for organizing family life (McDaniels, 2001). However, as women take on broader roles in the workplace and the community, their traditional role as kin-keeper may be affected. Men may take on some of these responsibilities as part of the changing role they play when their wives are working. In addition, sibling relationships become closer in middle adulthood, perhaps because those who have reached midlife

Percentage of People Aged 25–54 Providing Both Unpaid Child Care and Care Assistance to a Senior, 1996

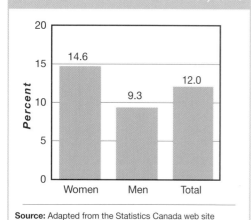

Source: Adapted from the Statistics Canada web site http://www.statcan.ca./english/kits/Family/pdf/ch3_10e.pdf.

no longer feel the need to compete (Nett, 1988). An increasing number of adults are providing some care to older family members, from performing errands and chores to providing full-time care within the extended family.

Women in midlife shoulder most of the burden of caring for older parents who become physically dependent on others. Most Canadians say that they would prefer not to be cared for by their families if physical care becomes necessary, but sometimes their financial situation leaves no other option (McDaniel, 2001). Social policies in Canada assume that the family will take care of its older members in the same way that they take care of other dependents. Reducing the length of hospital stays and sending people home to be cared for decreases the costs to the health care system but increases the costs to individuals who provide the care (McDaniel, 1998). Because of the improved health life

in focus | The Traditional Italian *Sistemazione*

Franc Sturino interviewed 92 Italian immigrants in the mid-1970s who had emigrated to Toronto between 1947 and 1967. All were from peasant family backgrounds, having originated from farming families in rural parts of Calabria. All would have worked in the agricultural sector if they had remained in Italy, but all those interviewed settled into urban Toronto and found employment in trades and businesses associated with a large urban Canadian community, usually with the help of their sponsors. The purpose of Sturino's study was to examine the organization of the family system as it was in Italy to the roles and organization of the family system as it developed in Canada.

In rural Calabria, in the middle part of the last century, the expectation was that the father's role was that of provider and the mother was expected to be

The Italian tradition of *sistemazione* ensured that young couples had the resources they needed to raise a family.

homemaker. Men worked the family holding and laboured co-operatively with their kinfolk when major tasks, such as harvesting, had to be completed. Marriage was seen as a rite of passage into adulthood. It was expected that the family assets or wealth were to be used by the parents to provide all of their children of both genders with the material resources necessary to establish their independence as adults. As such, under the traditional expectation called *sistemazione*, the family wealth was viewed as a communal asset and the father's role was to hold it in trust for the benefit of other family members. A father who allowed the family wealth to decline was, therefore, viewed as being irresponsible and unworthy by the community.

Sturino found that family roles in Canada were much the same as they were in rural Italy. The father remained the principle, if not sole, provider, and the mother was again expected to run the family home and to raise the children. Often, the Italian-Canadian woman worked outside the family home, but her earnings were always considered secondary to that of her husband. Interestingly, Sturino found that home ownership replaced the owning and working of land to ensure the status and dominance of the father in the family system. Finally, like in Italy, children were expected to show respect for their parents and to live with them until they were married. Once again, marriage was seen as the real transition into adulthood by most people in the community.

In his study, Sturino identified a system or expectation of the society that he called *sistemazione*. By this, he meant that it was the duty of the father and mother to successfully marry off each of their children and to provide them with the material resources that they needed to establish a separate household independent from their parents. Because Italians use a bilateral kinship system, the expectation was that part of the family assets would be provided to the newly married son or daughter to help them at this time. In rural Italy, *sistemazione* meant that a son would receive some land and a daughter was provided with a dowry and trousseau. In Toronto, the system continued but in a slightly different form. For the newly married man, a substantial cash gift replaced the endowment of land, whereas the newly married women received a dowry and trousseau that included modern electrical conveniences. Parents also bought furniture and major appliances for both sexes. Finally, if the family was wealthy enough, parents of either the bride or the groom or both sets of parents together would simply purchase a house for the newly married couple to discharge their obligation. Families who could not afford this would give cash or lend money to the couple so that they could afford a house, or they might have the couple live with them so that they could save the money necessary to purchase a house. This custom prevailed because the expectation of the Italian-Canadian family was that the family's wealth was held in common and that it would be transferred to family members at such time that they had most need, and not transferred at the death of the parents in the form of an inheritance. ■

Source: Franc Sturino, "Family and Kin Cohesion Among Southern Italian Immigrants in Toronto," in K. Ishwaran (ed.), *Canadian Families: Ethnic Variations*. Toronto: McGraw-Hill Ryerson Limited, 1980. Reproduced with permission of The McGraw-Hill Companies.

1. What is the meaning of *sistemazione*?
2. How is *sistemazione* different from or similar to the expectations concerning family wealth in your culture?
3. What are the costs and benefits of *sistemazione*?
4. If all Canadian families practised *sistemazione*, what changes in financial planning would be required?

expectancy of older Canadians, their physical dependency often coincides with the retirement of their caregivers. In some cases, women take early retirement to be available to care for a parent. Currently, social policies consider the effects on those who require care but not on those who provide it. Although family care can be both socially and financially beneficial for seniors, loss of employment, increase in part-time work, or early retirement can have long-term effects on the middle-aged caregiver's income and pension, which could prove costly (McDaniel, 2001).

Grandparenting

In the nineteenth century, few people had grandparents. The role of grandparent developed in the twentieth century, when couples had children while they were young, when their children married younger and had children even earlier than their parents did, and when people lived longer. Most children today have contact with at least one grandparent, and some children have great-grandparents. Grandparenting is taken on voluntarily and has no defined responsibilities. Since many Canadians now become grandparents in their forties or fifties, grandparents are younger, are probably working, and are living active, independent lives (McPherson, 1991). Although one in five children have no contact with a grandparent, 40 percent see them at least once a month (Vanier Institute of the Family, 1994). How grandparents interact with their grandchildren depends on how close they live to them, the age of the children, the extent to which the parents facilitate the relationship between their children and the grandparents, and the grandparents' lifestyle (McPherson, 1991).

Although grandparenting is a new family role, many expectations for the role have developed. Since grandparents usually do not live with their grandchildren and have intermittent contact with them, grandparents rarely have a major role in raising them, but they can serve an important role in the socialization of their grandchildren. Grandparents provide a valuable role as family historian, linking children with their family, ethnic, and cultural past. In particular, they might help adolescents who are

As parents delay having children until they are older, the role of grandparents is changing. Grandparents can be the family historians who pass on the family mythology.

forming an identity to place themselves in an ancestral context. Grandparents serve as role models for older adulthood and may counteract the stereotypical images of later life. They may act as mentors who are experienced in life transitions, and as the ultimate support person for crises or transitions within the family. Grandparents with enough money often provide gifts of luxuries (Wilcoxin, 1991). Individuals develop their own roles as grandparents since they are free of any defined roles based on gender or age.

Grandparenting is a reciprocal relationship that satisfies the needs of the older generation. Grandparents might receive more affection and recognition from their grandchildren than they did from their children because they are free of the obligation to be a disciplinarian. On the other hand, there is some potential for problems. The desire to become grandparents sometimes motivates parents to put pressure on their children to have children of their own (Wilcoxin, 1991). If grandparents and grandchildren form a cross-generational alliance when there is conflict between parent and child, they can interfere with the parent's ability to raise his or her children independently (Wilcoxin, 1991). As children get older, they generally have less contact with their grandparents, especially during adolescence. The grandparents' decreased contact with their children or grandchildren does not appear to affect feelings of loneliness or life satisfaction for them in later life, perhaps because they volunteer for the role of grandparents as much as they need to, to meet their own needs (Dulude, 1991).

Retirement

Retirement is another twentieth-century development resulting from the increase in life expectancy. **Retirement** is defined as voluntary or involuntary withdrawal from the workplace. Since the age of retirement is 65 in Canada, it has also served as an informal rite of passage into later life for people. However, the age of retirement has been declining rapidly, so that by 1995, 60 percent of men retired early (Carey, 1995). David Teffler, the author of *50+ Survival Guide*, suggests that at the beginning of the twenty-first century, there are only three phases to life: the first is spent preparing for adulthood, the second is spent working, and the third is spent in retirement (1998). As life expectancy increases and the age at retirement decreases, Canadians will spend more of their life span not working.

Retirement is promoted as the "golden years," in which working people are rewarded for years of labour by having years of leisure. For a society, mandatory retirement ensured that older workers left the workplace so that middle-aged workers could take their place and vacate entry-level positions intended for young adults. When the older generation is smaller than the successive generations, as was the case in the 1970s and 1980s, retirement eases the intergenerational conflict for job opportunities (McPherson, 1991). Also, when workers are paid more for their seniority, early retirement can reduce the labour costs for employers. Retirement as the norm for adults in their late fifties or early sixties raises some stereotypes about the productivity of older workers, and it becomes increasingly difficult for them to find jobs. However, research on the workplace roles of middle-aged adults suggests that they exhibit more productivity, less absenteeism, and greater participation (McPherson, 1990). Early-retirement plans were implemented in the 1990s to enable the large baby-boom generation to move into senior positions and give the smaller baby-bust generation some mobility. It is anticipated that, in the twenty-first century, companies will continue to encourage the baby boomers to retire early to make room at the bottom of the career ladder for the larger echo-boom generation that is entering the workplace.

At retirement, individuals experience a dramatic change in lifestyle and a reduced income. Social policies attempt to reduce the financial hardship of retirement. In 1927, the Canadian government introduced means-tested pensions for those who were 65 and who qualified as low income. This program evolved into the Guaranteed Income Supplement (GIS). The Canada and Quebec Pension Plans (CPP/QPP), formerly called Old Age Security, were introduced in 1966 and began paying full benefits to the cohort who turned 65 in 1976.

Financial planning in middle adulthood can ensure that people's retirement income is sufficient to enable them to maintain their lifestyle.

All working Canadians are required to pay CPP/QPP premiums and receive a pension based on total earnings when they reach 65 years. In addition, private occupational pension plans provide a retirement income for about 40 percent of Canadians who were employed. Individuals are also encouraged to invest money in Registered Retirement Savings Plans (RRSPs), investment funds that are tax-sheltered until they are withdrawn for income, usually in retirement. The income available for retirement depends on total employment earnings, the availability of occupational pension plans, and the success of investments.

Retirement incomes are improving. Many of today's seniors lived in a traditional patriarchal family structure. Since women were less likely to be employed, most had no occupational pensions

Quintile*	Disposable Income (minus taxes)	Employment	Private Pension	Other Market Income	OAS**/GIS	CPP/QPP	Other Transfers	Taxes
Bottom								
1980	8 805	124	233	665	6 433	666	720	35
1990	11 573	111	217	604	8 435	1 513	943	250
Change	2 768	-13	-16	-61	2 002	847	223	215
Second								
1980	12 485	436	684	1 764	7 432	1 362	856	50
1990	15 188	452	996	1 955	7 686	3 452	935	289
Change	2 703	16	312	191	254	2 090	79	239
Third								
1980	16 334	2 535	1 774	3 299	6 159	2 078	858	369
1990	19 074	2 073	2 066	3 903	6 031	4 233	1 082	1 314
Change	2 740	-462	1 292	604	-128	2 155	224	945
Fourth								
1980	23 672	7 468	3 614	6 580	5 027	2 053	744	1 814
1990	25 812	5 929	5 776	6 671	5 422	4 640	1 064	3 689
Change	2 140	-1 539	2 162	91	395	2 587	320	1 875
Top								
1980	42 389	19 990	6 939	16 104	4 668	2 325	627	8 265
1990	42 719	13 706	11 612	17 545	5 236	4 748	1 110	11238
Change	330	-6 284	4 673	1 441	568	2 423	483	2 973

Changes in Income by Source and Income Quintile, Population 65+, 1980–1990

* Quintile means 20 percent, so "bottom quintile" represents the lowest 20 percent of income earners.
** OAS is Old Age Security, which was replaced by the Canada/Quebec Pension Plan.

Note: RRSP income is included with private pensions.

Source: John Myles, *The Maturation of Canada's Retirement Income System: Income Levels, Income Inequality and Low Income Among the Elderly*, Statistics Canada and Florida State University. Adapted from the Statistics Canada publication *Analytical Studies Branch Research Paper Series*, Catalogue 11F0018MPE, No. 147.

or CPP/QPP contributions and, consequently, were dependent on their husbands. However, women who had been employed had pensions to increase the family income. The parents of the baby-boom generation had less financial hardship than previous cohorts did, because they were more likely to have had steady employment income, private pensions, and investments in RRSPs. Concerns about the size of the baby-boom generation and its impact on the Canada and Quebec Pension Plans developed in the 1980s. As a result, the CPP/QPP premiums were increased by the federal government to generate more revenue to pay the pensions. However, fewer younger men and women have occupational pension plans, perhaps because of the decline in stable,

web connection

www.mcgrawhill.ca/links/families12

To learn about changing middle and later life in Canada, go to the web site above for *Individuals and Families in a Diverse Society* to see where to go next.

unionized employment. This could affect retirement income if it is not offset by the pressure for individuals to invest independently for their retirement, using RRSPs. Preparing for retirement income is now considered to be a long-term financial responsibility that should be undertaken by individuals in early adulthood.

The Roles of Seniors in Canada

"Old age" is currently defined as beginning at age 65, the retirement age. There are more seniors in Canada than ever before (Statistics Canada, 1997). People aged 65 and older are currently 12.2 percent of the Canadian population, compared with 11.6 percent in 1991, and 8.1 percent in 1971. In 1996, Canadians aged 65 could expect to live an average of another 18.1 years, and even longer in urban areas (Statistics Canada, Health Indicators). This is longer than the average life expectancy they had at birth, because life expectancy increases as individuals age and survive the peak times of morbidity, which are infancy and adolescence. Women continue to have a longer life expectancy than men, although the gap in life expectancy is narrowing from 7.1 years in 1981 to 5.5 years in 1998 (Statistics Canada, 2001). With two decades or more to go, seniors are questioning whether the "golden years of leisure" are a full-enough life.

The lifestyles of older people in Canada reflect those they had earlier in their lives. Currently in Canada, most older families are aged patriarchal families in which most women had little work experience and therefore have little independent pension now (McPherson, 1990; Dulude, 1991). As a result, older couples continue to live on a one-pension income, while younger families are requiring two incomes. Also, economic problems are greater for widowed or divorced women than for men. Their concerns about income are greater, because there are more older women. The prospects for the baby-boom generation in old age look better because the women married men who were closer in age, had fewer children that kept them out of the workplace, entered the work force and received pensions of their own, and got improved incomes in better jobs (Dulude, 1991). Men's health is better than women's in old age, perhaps because they have someone to look after them and women don't, because they are likely to be widowed, but more recent cohorts of men and women have been healthier (Dulude, 1991). The declining gender difference in life expectancy and in the age at marriage could mean that seniors will be more likely to live as couples with two-pension incomes.

The majority of seniors are financially independent, not destitute, dependent, or lonely. They are dependent on government transfers, such as the Canada/Quebec Pension Plan and Guaranteed Income Supplement, for

"Age only matters when one is aging. Now that I have arrived at a great age, I might just as well be twenty."

—Pablo Picasso

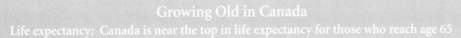

Growing Old in Canada
Life expectancy: Canada is near the top in life expectancy for those who reach age 65

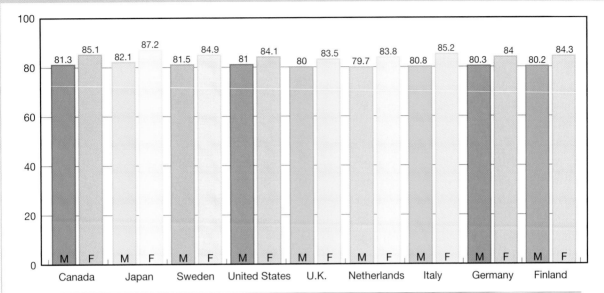

Source: *The Toronto Star*, (2001, June 16), using data from Organization for Economic Co-operation and Development; Statistics Canada; Canadian Institute of Health Information.

Growing Old in Canada
Poverty: Seniors in Canada are, on average, better off financially than those in most other countries, measured by the percentage living below the poverty line

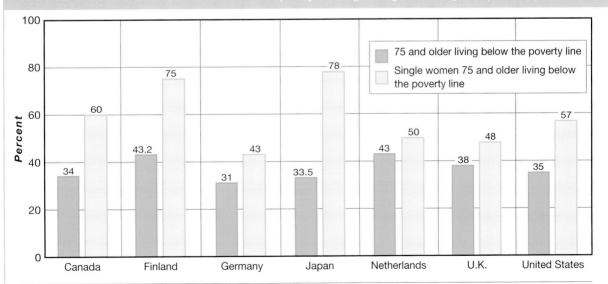

Source: *The Toronto Star*, (2001, June 16), using data from Organization for Economic Co-operation and Development; Statistics Canada; Canadian Institute of Health Information.

Susan McDaniel was born in New York City in 1946. She completed a B.A. at The University of Massachusetts, an M.A. at Cornell University in Ithaca, New York, and came to Canada to complete a Ph.D. at the University of Alberta in 1977. She has taught sociology at the University of Waterloo and the University of Alberta.

Susan McDaniel is a professor of sociology and a prominent Canadian researcher on the impact of social policy on families.

Throughout her career, Dr. McDaniel has focused on the sociology of the family and has an impressive list of over 150 publications, including research articles, essays, and scholarly books. Much of her research over the last quarter-century has examined the relationship between Canada's aging population and social policy in Canada. A common theme in her work is the ways that generations support one another and, in particular, the role of older people in the family. She has been a frequent speaker at national and international conferences on the family. She was a speaker at the United Nations Closing Conference for The International Year of the Family. In 1994, she was appointed to the Expert Task Force on Women & Social Security.

Dr. McDaniel does not subscribe to the view of an aging population being a drain on younger generations. In a 1998 essay in *Policy Options* (p. 38), she concludes:

> It does seem, however, that familial transfers tend, as they have historically, to be from elders to children for the most part, rather than from children to elders. The degree to which elders,

as a function of cohort, historical accident, or long-held values, continue to support their children well into adulthood and sometimes into the children's retirement, remains one of the gifts of families to public policy. In this sense as well as others, intergenerational sharing promotes social cohesion rather than promoting tensions, as mutual reciprocal obligations cement social solidarity and continuity from one generation to the next.

Susan McDaniel combines research with an active teaching career that earned her the Award for Teaching Excellence for the Faculty of Arts, University of Alberta, in 1994. She finds time to maintain a family life with her common-law partner, and for various leisure activities centred on the outdoors: hiking, wildlife observation, and photography. However, she lists "sociology" as her first interest. She says of herself, "Sociology is more than what I do; it defines what I am. My success as a sociologist is attributable to my boundless curiosity about the social world." ■

their income, but other sources, such as occupational pension plans and Registered Retirement Savings Plans, are increasing in value (Carey, 1999; Myles, 2000). Transfers of financial support within the family continue to flow from the older generation to the younger generation, as seniors provide

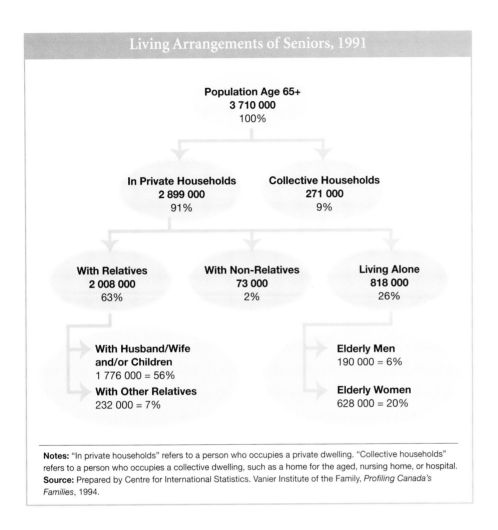

Living Arrangements of Seniors, 1991

Population Age 65+
3 710 000
100%

In Private Households
2 899 000
91%

Collective Households
271 000
9%

With Relatives
2 008 000
63%

With Non-Relatives
73 000
2%

Living Alone
818 000
26%

With Husband/Wife and/or Children
1 776 000 = 56%

With Other Relatives
232 000 = 7%

Elderly Men
190 000 = 6%

Elderly Women
628 000 = 20%

Notes: "In private households" refers to a person who occupies a private dwelling. "Collective households" refers to a person who occupies a collective dwelling, such as a home for the aged, nursing home, or hospital.
Source: Prepared by Centre for International Statistics. Vanier Institute of the Family, *Profiling Canada's Families*, 1994.

financial help with buying homes, child care, assistance with tuition costs, and eventually inheritance (Nett, 1993; McDaniel, 2001). Forty percent of seniors also provide assistance to their families in the form of household help, transportation, or health care (Vanier Institute of the Family, 1994).

Most seniors in Canada are living independently in their own homes, and the proportion is increasing (Vanier Institute of the Family, 1994). Only 3 percent of Canadian families are extended families. The majority of three-generation households are immigrant families from cultures with a tradition of extended families or result from family reunification (Che-Alford & Hamm, 1999). Seniors do not want to live with children, preferring independent homes or an institution close to their children. Older people who live with their families are those who are in the poorest health (Dulude, 1991). However, the extended

by C. F. Stuart-Russell

After some careful thought on two years of life in a seniors' building, I have found that psychologically, it is too damaging. As seniors in a new and beautiful building, we started out right. We organized and formed a residents' association. A few—too few and always the same few—ran a raft of weekly events. Some of the activities met with success, like bingo and anything to do with food—potluck dinners, Canada Day barbecues, hot lunches, and Christmas dinners. But at weekly events, attendance was disappointing. And not because people did not want to come. Human beings tend to be creatures of habit. Most seniors become more rigidly so. I noted the same few always turned out for the same weekly events. The people who came to the coffee mornings did not attend the cards-and-games evening. Those interested in crafts did not show for the dancing and social. The social people did not take in the movie. It was impossible to get the people to change. They pursued what they liked and would not try anything new. Unfortunately, with so few participants—some 15 out of close to 200 residents—it was too much to expect the volunteers to sacrifice their personal activities every week. Consequently, regular activities were virtually cancelled. Not that this was so derogatory in itself. A new approach by the residents' association committee could possibly correct the regular activities problem. But the committee cannot correct the difficulty in getting the resident seniors to come downstairs in large numbers for a particular event.

Elderly people get sick, many regularly and on a daily basis. Today they feel great. Tomorrow—a fall, arthritis, chest, leg, or arm pains—it's crisis time.

The author of this article believes that there shouldn't be seniors-only residences, but a mixture of all different age groups, to provide enduring relationships for older people.

Then often by the following week—sometimes even the next day—they are feeling fine again. And it is this "no mix" arrangement—all being seniors in one building—which is all wrong. Seniors do not want too many babies around, but a variety of age groups from the early 20s (even the odd couple with a child) and up would be more beneficial than our building's current seniors-only arrangement. And the reason it is damaging? People who are not "family" become friends. The tragedy is friends move into one's life and touch it deeply. You hear the fears and the anguish and the sorrows. And then friends die and the ache that lingers becomes as powerful as when a family member passes on. But unlike family, where deaths are hopefully spaced out over time, death in my seniors-only building strikes as many as three or five times in a single week. "The wise man seeks death all his life and therefore death is not terrible to him," Socrates wrote. But in a seniors-only building, when too many of one's new friends die so regularly and quickly, the reminder of death might not be terrible, but it is psychologically very, very depressing.

A better mix of all age groups in such residences would be more uplifting and probably quite rewarding.

Just watching young people makes even the very elderly feel much less old. ■

Source: *The Toronto Star.* (1995, January 31).

1. What living arrangements are preferred by older Canadians?
2. What are the costs and benefits of living in a seniors-only community?
3. Apply the functionalist perspective to suggest why the problems identified in this article occur.
4. What living arrangements would you like your parents or guardians to have when they are older? How should a family system be structured so that goal will be attainable?

family is twice as likely to provide health-related support not for the oldest member of the family, but for a disabled child or parent (Che-Alford & Hamm, 1999). In the last decades of the twentieth century, new institutions of care and health monitoring technology were developed that enable older people to combine independent living with the required health care support (Bangston & deTerre, 1991).

Bereavement

Marriage is much more likely to be dissolved by death in old age, not by divorce. The death of a spouse is the most stressful and disruptive event in life. Post-retirement marriages are happier, perhaps the happiest since the time of being newlyweds (Dulude, 1991) This may be because older people are better at resolving problems (Dym & Glenn, 1993). Another theory suggests that senior couples are tough marriage survivors (Dulude, 1991). Because women have traditionally married men who are several years older, and because the life expectancy of men is shorter by several years, women are more likely than men to be widowed (Dulude, 1991). Women will probably spend their final years alone, while men are likely to die with a wife and family around them. In 1988, fewer than 40 percent of older women were currently

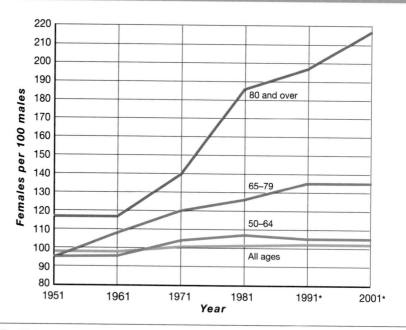

The Ratio of Females to Males in Selected Age Groups, Canada, 1951–2001

*The "High-growth" scenario here, in fact, is based on a growth rate just above replacement level. This is a much lower rate of growth than occurred in Canada during the Depression years.

Source: Reprinted with permission from McDaniel (1986, p. 109).

Original Source: Canada. 1983. *Fact Book on Aging in Canada*. Ottawa: Minister of Supply and Services Canada. p. 21. Reproduced with the permission of the Minister of Supply and Services Canada, 2002.

married. About 10 percent of women remarry, but widowers have twice the chance of remarrying (Boyd, 1988).

Men have more difficulty adjusting to the death of their spouse than women do. Men tend to have a greater dependence on their wives for meeting their needs. Traditionally, they have had fewer close friends and depend on their partners for companionship. Women, as the kin-keepers, have more actively maintained family ties and have closer relationships with their children and friends. Men may have difficulty maintaining these ties. They have performed fewer household skills in the past, so the loss of their wives has a greater impact on their lifestyles. Men are more likely to seek another marriage partner when they are widowed. However, there is a high suicide rate among recently bereaved men (Dulude, 1991).

The older a woman is when her husband dies, the more likely she is to live alone. Three-quarters of Canada's older widows are living on their own, but few of them report being lonely (Carey, 1999). Women are less likely to remarry than men, and they are usually unwilling to live with someone else, perhaps because the challenge of negotiating a domestic relationship is not worth the benefits. Most older women today left home before they were 25, married, had children, stayed married for an average of 39 years, and were widowed at an average age of 63. Many women have strong social support networks. They maintain close ties with their children and surviving siblings. Widows have friends and neighbours for company, but see less of couples and more of other women (Carey, 1999). Contrary to concerns about those who live alone, victimization declines with age (McPherson, 1990).

case study | Margaret's Lifetime of Memories

Margaret Johnson was born Margaret Lancaster in England in 1921. Her father was a grocery store manager. When Margaret's mother died in 1926, her father remarried and she was raised by a stepmother. Her childhood was a happy one, and she did all the things that English schoolgirls were able to do growing up in the 1920s and 1930s. Margaret was a good athlete and developed a life-long interest in sports. She became a very accomplished tennis player and was an excellent forward on her town's youth field hockey team. Her stepmother died when Margaret was 14, and her life took a new direction. Once again her father remarried, this time to a woman with whom Margaret had difficulty relating. Not able to get along with her father's new wife, she eventually moved in with her Aunt Beatrice and her aunt's two best friends. It was while living with them that Margaret met her husband, Ted.

Ted had enlisted in the Canadian Air Force in 1939 and had been sent to England shortly after

Margaret and her granddaughters share a close relationship.

basic training. He was stationed at a nearby air base and had been brought to Margaret's twenty-first birthday party by a mutual friend. Their romance developed quickly, but the difficulties in wartime England meant that the time they spent together was short and intermittent. Margaret knew that marrying Ted would mean she would have to move to Canada, and the thought of leaving her family and friends made the decision difficult, but eventually she agreed to do so. Soon after she and Ted were married in 1945, Margaret travelled by ship to Halifax and was one of thousands of new Canadian "war brides." Some of the other women on the ship became her lifelong friends, although they settled in communities across the country.

Margaret and Ted had two sons—John, born in 1945, and Grant, born in 1950. They bought a house in the west end of Toronto, near Ted's parents. Although they experienced some financial difficulties, especially when Ted lost his job during the recession of 1957, their life together was a happy one. Ted did not earn a high income, so Margaret worked part-time as a church secretary once her sons were in school. She and Ted had an active social life, primarily centred around his family, outdoor recreation such as hiking and camping, and the activities of raising their two sons. When Ted died of cancer in 1971, Margaret began to work full time and continued to do so until she retired at age 65. Although she was only 49 when she was widowed, Margaret never remarried. The next phase of her life centred around her job, her female friends, and her family.

As a widow, Margaret found the adjustment difficult. She missed the companionship of Ted as well as the social life that they enjoyed together as a couple. She found herself spending more and more time with single women and other widows. Since Margaret was able to manage her finances with the help of her son as she grew older, she found that she was able to indulge in some of her lifelong interests, including music, theatre, sports, and travelling. Every year she has travelled with different friends to different destinations in North America and Europe. Her social life in Toronto has been very active, since she lawn bowls every day during the summer months and goes regularly to the symphony, to the theatre, and to as many Blue Jays games as she can.

Margaret has also taken pleasure in her growing family. Both of her sons married and had children. She has enjoyed being a mother-in-law and a grandmother. Because her sons also live in Toronto, Margaret has spent a lot of time with Grant's family and has an active and warm relationship with his three children. She never said no when Grant or Pamela asked if she could babysit, especially when the children were sick. She attended their games when they were on school teams, and often took them on excursions. Today, she continues to be an important part of her adult grandchildren's lives, particularly with Emma and Colleen, whom she enjoys visiting and telling stories of her life and of their father's life when he was growing up. She has become the family archivist and has written about her life as a girl in England and the early years of her life with Ted. She e-mails Emma, Colleen, and Andy regularly now that she is an "on-line grannie."

Now in her eighties, Margaret continues to be active. She cherishes her independence and still lives in the house that she and Ted bought so many years ago, although she finds that she has become more dependent on her two sons to do some of the routine chores and maintenance that come with being a homeowner. She often gets frustrated now that her body will not allow her to do all the things that she would like it to, but she still keeps up all her activities with the "girls." As her circle of friends becomes smaller as she ages, Margaret is enjoying keeping track of her expanding family more and more. As the matriarch of the Johnson clan, she can't wait for the first great-grandchild to be born! ▪

---

1. How has Margaret's role in her family changed as she has grown older?

2. Using the perspective of symbolic interactionism, suggest how factors in Margaret's earlier life have affected her desire to live independently as an older woman.

3. What is the basis of Margaret's relationship with her grandchildren? Redraw the genogram in Chapter 2 to depict the nature of these relationships.

4. Predict the effect on the Johnson family if Margaret were to move in with them. Redraw the genogram to illustrate the possible changes in the family system.

Knowledge/Understanding Thinking/Inquiry

1. Distinguish between work-family conflict and family-work conflict, and summarize the effect that each has on dual-earner families.

2. How has women's employment affected family life at the following stages?
   - family with young children
   - midlife
   - the empty nest
   - retirement
   - later life

3. How has the increasing life expectancy of Canadians over the last 150 years changed family relationships?

4. Why are seniors less likely to be poor now than 50 years ago?

5. Why is it difficult to predict what life will be like for future generations based on the experience of earlier cohorts?

Knowledge/Understanding Thinking/Inquiry Communication

6. Have fathers benefited or suffered from their wives' working outside the home? Using the social exchange theory, write an essay supporting your opinion on the impact of dual-earner families on fathers.

7. Collect advertising images that reflect aging in later adulthood. Write a critique of the advertisers' perceptions, and speculate on the impact they have on the lives of older Canadians.

8. Examine the graph Cohort Differences and the Aging Process, on page 387. Design a graph that displays the life course of Canadians against the major social and political events of the twentieth century.

9. Using data from the table Changes in Income by Source and Income Quintile, Population 65+, 1980–1990, on page 403, design a chart to compare the percentage of income derived from each source in 1980 and 1990 for each quintile.

10. Conduct a survey to compare where older Canadians would prefer to live, with where their adult children would prefer them to live. Compare the data with the Living Arrangements of Seniors, 1991 chart on page 407, and present your data in a chart in which you predict the living arrangements of seniors in 2010.

Adult Life and Theories of Aging

CHAPTER EXPECTATIONS

While reading this chapter, you will:

- describe the development of individuals at different stages of life, drawing on a variety of developmental theories
- analyze several viewpoints on similarities and differences in male and female development and on the impact of those differences on the roles individuals play
- evaluate emerging research and theories explaining the developmental tasks of individuals at various stages of life
- summarize current research on factors influencing satisfaction within enduring couple relationships
- analyze the division of responsibility for childrearing and socialization, and the interaction of caregivers
- identify and respond to the theoretical viewpoints, thesis, and supporting arguments of materials found in a variety of secondary sources

KEY TERMS

activity theory of aging

despair

generativity

gerotranscendence

integrity

midlife transition

non-event

orderly change model

phases

psychological clock

seasons

social construction theory

stability template model

stagnation

theory of random change

wisdom

Childhood and early adulthood is Act I in life. There are several acts in the drama of life yet to be presented before the final curtain.

CHAPTER INTRODUCTION

This chapter will examine the patterns of individual development in later adulthood. Is there a midlife crisis? Are people happily married? What is the role of seniors in Canada? Using a psychological framework, the challenges of the later stages of life will be investigated using various developmental theories. The roles of occupational choices, marriage, and family life in the achievement of generativity will be explored. The changing patterns of satisfaction in marriage will be explored in light of the alterations in marriage relationships. Finally, the concept of old age as the completion of a life story will be examined from the perspective of current studies in gerontology.

The Transitional Years

L eaving home, forming enduring love relationships, and perhaps having children are important rites of passage that signify increasing maturity for individuals in most societies. Although the timing of these events may vary, they are usually assumed to occur in the first half of life, and they set the stage for mature adult life. There has been a tendency in the twentieth century to view aging in a negative light (Borysenko, 1996, p. 2):

> All human beings go through cycles in their lives, progressing from infant to child to adolescent to adult. While each stage builds upon previous biology and experience, evolving from one stage to the next sometimes requires a dying to what we have been in order to complete our metamorphosis. While the infant does not lament becoming the toddler, or the child mourn the approach of adolescence, women have been portrayed as lamenting our continued maturation into midlife and older adulthood.

However, middle age, the years from 35 to 65, and the aging years, after 65, are stages of growth and development. Because of the variations in the timing of the normative events of life, middle-aged adults are a more diverse group than people at other ages. Some are parents of young children, some are making the transition from being parents of young children to being parents of adult children, and some are becoming grandparents. In the workplace, some are at the peak of their careers, while others are preparing for early retirement. Women may be at the beginning of a career when re-entering the workforce after their childbearing years. The later years are transitional years, as men and women's children leave home, as they leave the workplace, and as they embark on the final stage of their lives (Ward, 1994). This chapter will examine the patterns of aging in the second half of life.

Early Ideas on the Life Cycle

The concept of predictable stages in life is not new. Descriptions of the stages of life have been recorded in such diverse literature as the writings of the ancient Greek philosopher and mathematician Pythagoras; in the scriptures of Hindus, Buddhists, Jews, and Christians; in the plays of Shakespeare; and in the writings of twentieth-century psychologists (Borysenko, 1996).

The ancient Chinese philosophy described seven-year stages of life for men and women that were believed to parallel the workings of the universe. Although the stages of a woman's life followed predictable biological changes, they set a pattern for social functioning based on the role of women as mothers. Not included in the cycle are the years in which a woman would be a grandmother.

In the 1930s, Charlotte Buhler, a developmental theorist, published the earliest modern study of life stages in Western society. She studied biographies and determined that there is an orderly progression of **phases**, or changes in events, attitudes, and accomplishments. She concluded that the lives of individuals parallel their biological development. According to Buhler, the first 15 years are spent in progressive growth at home. From 15 to 25 years, a period of growth and fertility occurs, and individuals focus on clarifying their individual goals. The years from 25 to 45 are the productive years, when individuals focus on stability and the culmination of their goals. From 45 to 65 years, there is a loss of reproductive ability, and individuals begin a self-assessment of the results of their goals. After age 65, there is biological decline, and individuals reflect on the fulfillment of their goals or experiences of failure (Kimmel, 1990). Buhler's early work established the foundation for the theories of human development, such as Erikson's and Levinson's, which were developed later.

"Every life is a circle. And within every life are smaller circles. A part of our life goes full circle every seven years. We speak of living in cycles of seven."

—Barbara Means Adam,
Lakota Sioux

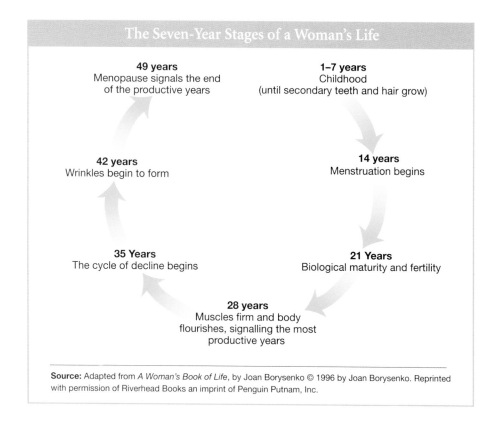

The Seven-Year Stages of a Woman's Life

49 years
Menopause signals the end of the productive years

1–7 years
Childhood
(until secondary teeth and hair grow)

14 years
Menstruation begins

42 years
Wrinkles begin to form

35 Years
The cycle of decline begins

21 Years
Biological maturity and fertility

28 years
Muscles firm and body flourishes, signalling the most productive years

Source: Adapted from *A Woman's Book of Life*, by Joan Borysenko © 1996 by Joan Borysenko. Reprinted with permission of Riverhead Books an imprint of Penguin Putnam, Inc.

Contemporary Theories of Aging

Because of the diversity of ways people live out their lives, there are various points of view on aging. The biological basis that was assumed in the past neither accounts for the cultural variations in adult behaviour in the second half of life, nor explains the historical changes in the roles of adults. Marjorie Fiske and David A. Chiriboga (1990) outlined three different models for aging that reflect the various theoretical perspectives on the impact of personality, or identity, on the behaviour of individuals:

- stability template
- orderly change
- theory of random change

The **stability template model** assumes that individuals do not change once they achieve adulthood. It is based on the belief that the basic personality is formed in childhood, as suggested by Sigmund Freud and accepted by psychoanalysts. The stability template accepts recent evidence that personality actually continues to develop into adulthood. This model explains that if an individual's identity is stable over time, he or she will respond to events and stresses in life in a consistent manner. Therefore, there will be variations in behaviour, but individual behaviour will be predictable (Fiske & Chiriboga, 1990). Erik Erikson suggests that identity formation is the focus of life and continues to be so throughout life (Erikson & Erikson, 1994). Erikson describes the central task in middle adulthood as **generativity**, which is usually interpreted as establishing and guiding the next generation. In later life, individuals seek the **integrity** that results from living out one's identity (Erikson & Erikson, 1997).

The **orderly change model** is based on the stage theories of development. It explains that an individual's identity is formed earlier in life but changes through interaction with the environment in the present (Fiske & Chiriboga, 1990). Erikson emphasized that identity formation and generativity were dependent on having opportunities to develop (Erikson, 1968). Daniel Levinson suggests that in midlife, individuals examine the life structure they have been building in early adulthood and define a new life structure for themselves in later life based on changing circumstances (Levinson, 1978). Therefore, this model suggests that identity changes according to the options

The theories that attempt to explain people's behaviour as they age differ on whether individual differences reflect an individual's unique personality, a generation's response to social change, or individual life experiences.

available in the society, and asks whether the patterns of aging will change when the timetable of the life cycle changes due to increased life expectancy (Fiske & Chiriboga, 1990).

The **theory of random change** explains that fate, or non-normative events, cause change in identity because of how individuals adapt to their new roles. This model asks whether social change affects the behaviour of a cohort, resulting in the cohort effect (Fiske & Chiriboga, 1990). American psychologist Klaus Riegel's Dialectical Analysis of Development rejects the idea of age-defined stages and suggests that individuals change over time in response to biological, cultural, psychological, and sociological factors. Patterns of behaviour exist because cohorts are exposed to the same events. Riegel believed that age was not the key factor that determined how people behaved unless it controlled opportunity, such as retirement age (Kimball, 1990). The theory of random change, therefore, suggests that although the behaviour of individuals within generations might conform to a pattern, it is not possible to predict the behaviour of future generations.

A more recent theory that accounts for the changes in aging that have been observed in Canada is the **social construction theory**. Related to symbolic interactionism, it suggests that the actions and feelings of individuals have no intrinsic meaning on their own, but are given meaning by the theoretical perspectives that are developed for their explanation (Gergen & Gergen, 2001). This theory suggests that individuals' behaviour does not necessarily differ from place to place or from generation to generation, but the meaning ascribed to the behaviour changes to reflect the expectations of the society. Therefore, individuals choose an appropriate response to life events based on how they interpret them (McPherson, 1990). The social construction theory and symbolic interactionism are useful for explaining why the empty-nest syndrome that was identified as a crisis for middle-aged women in the 1960s does not appear to exist for women in the 1990s (Borysenko, 1996).

Bernice Neugraten defined the concept of the social clock. She explained that there are common stages in life that are defined according to the expectations of society as to when certain events should occur. Daniel Levinson (1978) and John Kotre (Kotre & Hall, 1990) refer to these stages of life as **seasons**, reflecting the concept that seasons follow each other in a predictable sequence, but that each is different in nature and yet equally important for growth. The seasons are determined to some extent by a biological clock, but also by a **psychological clock**, which determines the meaning that individuals make of their own lives. The seasons of life suggest expectations about what is normal behaviour during each stage of life. Therefore, individuals choose the path of their lives in each season and live with the consequences. Fall is

"When I had journeyed half of our life's way; I found myself within a shadowed forest, for I had lost the path that does not stray."

—Dante

the season in which individuals mature and the benefits are harvested to provide for the winter. The patterns of development in later seasons of life will be explored using these research questions:

- How do individuals achieve generativity?
- Is there a midlife crisis for men and women?
- What is the effect of aging on marriage?
- What is the nature of development for older people?

research study | The Evolution of Happiness

David M. Buss has made a life study of the strategies that human beings have developed to enable them to compete in a hostile world in order to survive and to be successful in raising a family. His earlier research focused on sexual desire and mate selection. Recently, he has studied quality of life by assessing how people achieve happiness in their lives. His research suggests that happiness is more difficult to achieve in modern society despite the technological advancements that protect us from the "hostile forces of nature" and enable us to live longer. Happiness can be attained by using the following strategies that maintain the social attributes of early human societies, buffer the stress in people's lives, and reduce competition:

- **Maintain an extensive family network.** A longer life enables individuals to develop relationships with adult children and grandchildren. Communication technology allows people to keep in touch more easily.
- **Develop true friendships.** Acquaintances are useful companions, but only true friends can provide valuable social and psychological support during crises. Unfortunately, it is difficult to tell friends and acquaintances apart during good times.

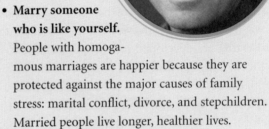

David Buss explains that all living human beings are evolutionary success stories.

- **Marry someone who is like yourself.** People with homogamous marriages are happier because they are protected against the major causes of family stress: marital conflict, divorce, and stepchildren. Married people live longer, healthier lives.
- **Become more co-operative.** Forming long-term reciprocal relationships at home, at work, and in the community, in which you expect no more than equity, establishes your reputation as a co-operative person and improves your quality of life.
- **Fulfill your desires.** The natural human desires for health, marriage, and aesthetic pleasures are fulfilled by achieving a life structure based on working to acquire and manage the resources needed. ■

Source: *American Psychologist.* (2000, January). Vol. 55, No. 1, pp. 15–23. Copyright © 2000 by the American Psychological Association. Adapted with permission.

Generativity

Erik Erikson described stages of personality development that focused on the search for identity to give meaning to life. The identity is formed in early adulthood. Having formed an identity, an individual is then able to form intimate relationships with another, and move successfully into adult life. Erikson defined the task of middle adulthood as the desire for generativity. The developmental challenge of generativity, meaning productivity, refers to the range of ways people are able to leave their mark on future generations. By investing in the future and caring for others, individuals can develop the virtue of care. However, by becoming self-indulgent, individuals can cease to develop, a state that Erikson called **stagnation**. Erikson summarized the relationship of identity to generativity in this way:

> In youth you find out what you care to do and who you care to be—even in changing roles. In young adulthood you find out who you care to be with— at work and in private life, not only exchanging intimacies, but sharing intimacy. In adulthood, however, you learn what and whom you can take care of (Erikson, 1959, p. 124).

According to Erikson, the seventh stage of life, "generativity versus stagnation," begins at 40 years of age. This age corresponds to the midlife transition identified by Daniel Levinson from his research on men and women in midlife. At this time, individuals assess their lives so far and ask several questions: "What have I done with my life? What do I really get from and give to my wife (or my husband), children, friends, work, community—and self? What is it I truly want for myself and for others?" (Levinson, 1978, p. 60)

Levinson explains that individuals build a new life structure based on their answers to these questions. They adapt to the ways that they have grown, the changing circumstances of their lives, and changes in society. Individuals continue to pursue their Dreams but look for greater meaning by giving back to their families and communities (Levinson, 1978). Adults who are generative have more meaningful relationships, have stronger attachments to their community, and have a greater sense of political agency. Generativity arises out of the formation of an identity in a desire to achieve some form of immortality of that identity (McAdams, Hart, & Maruna, 1998).

Generativity is a driving force throughout adult life. John Kotre (1996) suggests that Erikson's theory is limited by the ages he specifies for each stage. He states that because of the limits of fertility, especially for women, generativity must be defined as something more than reproduction and parenthood if it

web connection

www.mcgrawhill.ca/links/families12

To learn about Erik Erikson's theory of the stages of life or about other personality theories, go to the web site above for *Individuals and Families in a Diverse Society* to see where to go next.

is a motivation for the rest of adult life. He offers a broader interpretation of generativity than Erikson does, and identifies four different forms:

- biological generativity, which is parenthood
- parental generativity, which is the raising of children
- technical generativity, which is the passing on of knowledge
- cultural generativity, which is the sharing of culture and tradition (Kotre, 1996)

Opportunities for generativity are affected by social changes that influence the social clock and result in cohort effects. Individuals may have a need to nurture others, but society expects adults to take responsibility for themselves, care for their children, and pass on the culture to their offspring. Therefore, adults in their thirties and forties who are not ready for steady employment and a family are considered to be "out of time" with the social clock (McAdams, Hart, & Maruna, 1998). Generativity is a universal task of adulthood, but the form and the timing are defined by the society (Fiske & Chiriboga, 1990).

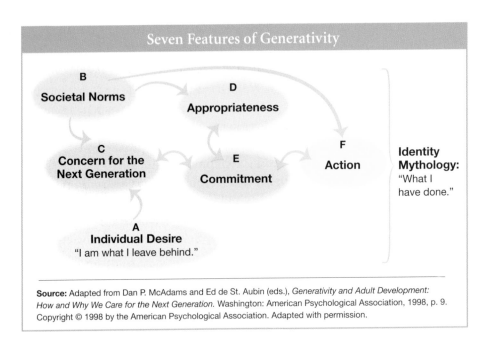

Seven Features of Generativity

B **Societal Norms**

D **Appropriateness**

C **Concern for the Next Generation**

E **Commitment**

F **Action**

Identity Mythology: "What I have done."

A **Individual Desire** "I am what I leave behind."

Source: Adapted from Dan P. McAdams and Ed de St. Aubin (eds.), *Generativity and Adult Development: How and Why We Care for the Next Generation.* Washington: American Psychological Association, 1998, p. 9. Copyright © 1998 by the American Psychological Association. Adapted with permission.

Parenthood, the biological generativity that was the focus of Erikson's original concept, is occurring later in life for most Canadians. As a result of the impact of contraception, parenthood has become a choice. The ability to choose whether or not to have children resulted in the need for individuals to rationalize the decision for themselves. Women are becoming more hesitant about having children than men are (Borysenko, 1996). John Kotre argues that parenthood declined in importance and became less valued as a role because individuals and couples found it difficult to identify reasons for having children that could be justified in a society that values individual achievement. He also suggests that individuals see less need for children when improved health enables them to live longer, healthier lives in which they can accomplish their goals. Therefore, there is less biological generativity (Kotre, 1996).

Parental generativity is attained through interaction with children, as active participants in parenting. In the past, women bore most of the responsibility for child care and parenting, so parental generativity was assumed to be the motivation for a woman's life in adulthood. Now men have gained greater opportunities for parental generativity as they share an active parenting role with their working wives (Kotre, 1996). Since this opportunity is newly acquired, it is not clear whether a father's role in parenting will be like a mother's or a separate one that reflects a masculine nature. Functionalists suggest that because men have traditionally had the role of authority in a patriarchal family, it can be argued that they are suited to providing, guiding, and supporting a family. They suggest that a role that allows men to focus on these traditional responsibilities would enable them to be better fathers (Zinsmeister, 1999).

Increased life expectancy is changing the nature of parental generativity. A longer life allows individuals to have longer connections with past and future generations within their families. Since most parents will live long enough to see their children mature into middle age, there are greater opportunities to repair and renew relationships with children as adult-adult relationships. Grandparenting provides additional parental generativity roles (Kotre, 1996). Those who did not have children achieve parental generativity by taking on the role of "guardian" and caring for others' children as teachers or child-care providers (Borysenko, 1996). Parental generativity extends the influence of individuals in providing for the future generation beyond biological parenthood.

In a complex society in which life has greater meaning than reproduction and survival, there are other ways of providing for the future and leaving one's mark on the world that extend beyond the family. Technical generativity means teaching knowledge and skills to the next generation so that they can

Having children is an expression of biological generativity. Raising children provides opportunities for parental generativity that last a lifetime.

"Evolution has made man a teaching as well as a learning animal."

—Erik Erikson

develop competence. Parents or aunts and uncles teaching children, teachers instructing students, and older men and women mentoring younger adults are some examples of the ways technical generativity is expressed. Cultural generativity means creating and sharing ideas and artifacts that will contribute to the cultural experience of society. Whether by producing beneficial products or services at work or by expressing creativity by sewing, painting, or dancing, individuals can achieve cultural generativity (Kotre, 1996). Therefore, generativity can be achieved by developing and nurturing ideas as well as children.

Social changes in the second half of the twentieth century are altering how women in Canada are achieving the life task of generativity. Prior to the 1960s, most women were homemakers. Their generativity was attained through motherhood and through the art of homemaking (Borysenko, 1996). When women are employed, they assume generativity through technical and cultural ways in addition to biological and parental ones. When levels of "mastery" and "happiness" were compared in an American study of self-esteem in women, working women scored much higher on "mastery," but stay-at-home moms scored highest on "happiness." However, the combined levels of "mastery-happiness" were highest for the busiest women in the study, the employed married women with children (Borysenko, 1996). Perhaps these results reflect the extended opportunities for generativity that individuals have when they combine working with family life.

When people are able to see positive results from their work and find their jobs meaningful, they are experiencing technical or cultural generativity.

Work provides meaningful opportunities for identity formation and for technical or cultural generativity. In Deborah Anderson and Christopher Hayes' study of gender and self-esteem, it was determined that men and women are almost identical in their assessments of the importance of work in their lives, with 88 percent of men and 91 percent of women stating it was important (1996). However, if individuals are to develop responsibility and competence, their work must be purposeful. Only 22 percent of the subjects said that the task they performed itself was important, while others identified the ability to control events on the job or to work with others as rewarding (Anderson & Hayes, 1996). In a society in which individuals believe "I am what I do," 75 percent of people will change jobs at some time, perhaps to find work that allows them to feel that they are doing something meaningful and giving something back (Kimmel, 1990).

Oral History

Oral history is a research method that uses interviewing to encourage individuals to recall and describe their life experiences. Oral history can be used in several ways in the social sciences:

- Oral histories are used by social historians to gather personal stories to add to the official records and media reports in order to understand the impact of historical events on individuals, families, and society.
- Oral history is used to gather data about earlier behaviour to determine patterns of development. These retrospective studies, in which individuals recall what they have done, can be used when longitudinal studies were not started in the past to observe behaviour.
- Oral history can also be used to enable individuals to reflect on their experiences and behaviour in the past in order to understand them from the perspective of their accumulated experience and wisdom. In this application, oral history supports the life review described by Erikson. This reflects the perspective of symbolic interactionism, because subjects relate the experiences according to the meaning they place on them.

Obtaining Oral Histories

1. Locate subjects whose experiences reflect the issues you want to study. Obtain their permission to interview them and to record the interview.

Arrange a time that is convenient and long enough to allow the subject to speak freely in answer to the questions.

2. Develop a series of open-ended questions that will prompt the subject to recall experiences and events and to describe his or her actions, observations, thoughts, and feelings at the time. Secondary questions can be used, if necessary, to encourage the subject to add details. If it is required for your study, ask the subject further questions that enable him or her to reflect on the experiences, based on what he or she now knows.

3. It is important to record the interview. The language used, the tone of voice, and the parenthetical comments all help to convey the meaning of the experiences for the subject. Transcribe the oral history word for word.

4. Artifacts, such as photographs, documents, and letters, can be used to supplement the oral history.

Oral histories can be transcribed for others to read, but the words of the subject belong to the subject, not the researcher. It is necessary to obtain the subject's permission to publish the oral history, or to include citations for any paraphrasing or quotations that are included in other work. ■

Source: Based on *Reminiscence and oral history: ...?* by Joanna Bornat. Aging and Society, March 2001, Vol. 21, Part 2, pp. 219-241. Adapted with the permission of Cambridge University Press. Copyright © 1998 by the American Psychological Association. Adapted with permission.

The Myth of the Midlife Crisis

Is there such a thing as a midlife crisis? Whether the stereotypical crisis occurs for men, for women, or for both, depends on how *crisis* is defined. The Oxford dictionary defines it firstly as "a turning point," and secondly as "a moment of danger or suspense." Developmental theories can be used to determine whether there is a turning point in individuals' lives during midlife. However, to understand individual and cultural variations, it will be more useful to use the theories of symbolic interactionism and social construction. More recent research has focused on whether some people experience midlife as a time of danger. The research questions that can be considered are:

- What are the patterns of individual development during middle age?
- How does the society in which an individual lives affect his or her development in midlife?

Midlife could be a period of stability in individuals' lives. After years of working and establishing a career, most individuals have achieved their peak. Both income and level of responsibility in the workplace usually reach their highest point between the ages of 35 and 45. Employees have developed their competencies and they know the work and their co-workers. They usually have more time for family and leisure activities. As children leave home, parents eventually have fewer financial responsibilities, so they can invest money for retirement. This should be a time of peak productivity and security (Baker, 1993). Research by developmental psychologists, however, suggests that even individuals who achieve this level of comfort and stability view it as a temporary plateau that could signal greater improvements in the future, or, more likely, the beginning of a decline. In midlife, individuals begin to notice that they will not live forever and to assess how they have been doing so far (Carter & Peters, 1996).

Daniel Levinson's research with both men and women defined a **midlife transition** that occurs between 40 and 45 years of age. This changeover marks the passage from early adulthood into middle adulthood. Levinson found that some individuals make the transition with few questions about the meaning and direction of the life structure they have established. However, he found that the majority of subjects in his studies reconsidered the life structure they had formed in light of the self they had become by midlife and the opportunities that were available at that time. Although some made no changes in their work or their family life, most experienced a refocusing of priorities in an attempt to live out their Dream. Others had to redefine their Dream and change their life structure to meet the needs of their personal identities or the circumstances of their lives (Levinson, 1978, 1996). For these individuals, midlife could be described as "a moment of danger or suspense."

web connection

www.mcgrawhill.ca/links/families12

To learn about writing oral histories, go to the web site above for *Individuals and Families in a Diverse Society* to see where to go next.

In their long-term study of adult development, Marjorie Fiske and David Chiriboga determined that individuals develop a revised sense of self during the midlife. They explained that an individual's self-concept changes to blend past experience with present circumstances into a psychological reality that reflects the greater wisdom of middle age (Fiske & Chiriboga, 1990). The slogan of midlife could be borrowed from the 1980s idiom: "Get Real!" Fiske and Chiriboga called their study "Continuity and Change in Adult Life." This title summarizes the idea that while some adults in midlife make changes in their work, family, or community lives, others continue with their lives with a new understanding of themselves and their roles. This reflects psychologist Marie Jahoda's definition of a healthy personality in adulthood, which was quoted by Erik Erikson:

> A healthy personality actively masters his environment, shows a certain unity of personality, and is able to perceive the world and himself correctly (Erikson, 1968, p. 92).

in focus | The Midlife Wake-Up Call

by Sheryl Ubelacker
Canadian Press

Tim O'Neill knew he had reached some defining moment in life when he was suddenly overwhelmed by a storm of swirling emotions. It felt like sadness. It felt like loss. It felt like panic. It felt as if some internal clock had suddenly kick-started, tick-tocking out the warning: Time . . . is . . . running . . . out. "When it hit me, I was standing somewhere and I leaned against a wall in a corridor and I just started crying," says O'Neill, still surprised at the memory. "And I thought, 'What's going on?'"

What was going on was the beginning of the midlife transition, a time when many in their mid-40s or 50s are struck by a sense of their own mortality and the knowledge there are only so many years left to realize their dreams. It may be triggered by a landmark birthday (like turning 50), the death of a parent or peer, a grown-up child leaving home, or being passed over for promotion by a younger colleague.

For many people in their mid-forties to mid-fifties, the "midlife transition" brings emotional upheaval and critical self-appraisal.

Sometimes it's the relentless signs of diminished youth that set off midlife anxiety: printed words that seem to have shrunk, hair fading to gray or relentlessly receding, laugh lines deepening into crevices, or an hour-glass figure transforming itself into a pear.

For O'Neill, who asked that his real name not be used, it struck while he was at a career placement centre after being downsized by the Montréal telecommunications company where he had worked for 20 years. Whatever the trigger, such emotional turbulence is common at the half-century watershed, psychologists say. It is even more pronounced in the boomer generation now reaching "middlescence."

"Growing up in the 1960s and 1970s led us to believe that a long, healthy, affluent, and youthful life was our birthright," say the authors of *The Healthy Boomer: A No-Nonsense Mid-life Guide For Women And Men.* "Midlife is a shock. Suddenly, the generation whose motto was 'Never trust anyone over 30' is brooding about unfulfilled dreams (and) the risk of heart attacks."

Romin Tafarodi, a social psychologist at the University of Toronto, says people are usually content as long as they perceive they're on "a certain trajectory. It's when we realize that the trajectory has taken on a slope that's not satisfactory—plateaued, if you will—or we realize that we'll never get to where we want to be before we end our lives, that things get a little dicey." People may feel demoralized, worthless, and withdrawn, he says. Other experts say this retreat into self is necessary. It's a time to "critically re-examine familiar relationships, values, and life choices," according to *The Healthy Boomer.*

O'Neill, 54, says losing his job jolted him into looking back at his life. "It was then that the soul-searching started," says O'Neill, a soft-spoken, self-described people person. He realized he'd settled for a comfortable career, but had paid for it by never feeling really happy. As he goes through midlife, O'Neill has glimpsed what he calls his true calling. He wants to become a career counsellor and life coach to help others "uncover their real needs."

While many men enter this stage concerned about unrealized dreams, for women it is often linked to the physical effects of aging, especially menopause. Lorraine O'Brien, 52, felt the first stirring of the midlife reckoning in her early 40s and she is still dealing with its many changes. While she isn't in menopause yet, the single mother of a 17-year-old son admits to feeling emotionally topsy-turvy. "I feel a bit weepy sometimes. And sometimes I feel, 'Wow, I have so much responsibility.' All of a sudden, my son is going off to university and I'm thinking, 'Okay, what's next?' For women especially, I think the separation from your children is hard because you spend so many years being a mom."

What may be O'Brien's saving grace is that she confronted "middlescence" head-on, looking inward and deciding how she wanted to spend the rest of her life. "I started reading books. I tried to understand myself and my interactions with the world around me. I changed my relationships with people. The people who came into my life were different because I changed my perspective." She is proud of her accomplishments. She has her own home west of Toronto and is in good financial shape after a varied 30-year career at a company from which she took a buyout in 1997.

Although O'Brien is job-hunting (she figures she has a good 5 to 10 years left in the workplace), she is looking forward to satisfying other dreams. She wants to eventually travel to Europe, buy a cottage, and study classical literature and music. "I think now it's my turn. I want to get on with my own life while I'm still young enough to enjoy these things and healthy enough."

Far from fighting the midlife transition, O'Brien is embracing it because it has forced her to focus on what's important. "I want to learn how to live my best life every day. Because every day presents me with choices, opportunities, challenges. And the more graceful I can become, the better quality of life I can have. I'm happy with my achievements, but I'm not finished yet."

And O'Neill is aware of Death's footsteps behind him. "That sense of mortality is with me every day. Every day, every week seems to move faster, and yet I look at what I've achieved and I think I haven't really done anything to fulfill my true purpose," he says.

"You think now's the time to do what you want to do, because there isn't that much time." ■

Source: *The Toronto Star.* (2001, Saturday April 14). pp. M6–M7.

1. What are the characteristics of the midlife transition?
2. Summarize the positive and negative aspects of midlife.
3. What coping strategies were identified by the individuals in the article?

Since work outside the home occupies so much of an individual's time, provides the income that defines the lifestyle potential, and identifies the role within society, work is a major component in an individual's identity. Career changes require adjustments in an individual's sense of what he or she does. The motivation for career changes in midlife varies. Some people, such as athletes, dancers, and other performers, know that there is an age limit on their jobs and anticipate a change. Other people experience "career plateauing" and change their expectations for what is satisfying in a job. The pyramidal shape of the workplace means that few people will be promoted to management positions (Ward, 1994). An American study showed that while those in entry-level positions valued advancement highly, those in middle age valued achievement and autonomy highest, reflecting the importance of generativity and, perhaps, the realization that all people cannot reach the top. Balancing the realities of family responsibility with career prospects can help individuals decide whether the career or the family, and what form of generativity, will have highest priority in their lives (Stevens-Long & Commons, 1992). Individuals change jobs because they lose their jobs, new opportunities arise at a time when they are ready to make changes, or they actively seek a change to reflect their revised life structure (Levinson, 1978).

"There is a proverb, 'As you have made your bed, so you must lie in it,' which is simply a lie. If I have made my bed uncomfortably, please God, I will make it again."

—G. K. Chesterton

Between Friends

Reprinted with special permission of King Features Syndicate.

When anticipated events, such as marriage, children, or a promotion, do not happen, people may feel that they have been unable to make the contribution they could have.

Because perceptions of the life cycle depend on point of view, it cannot be assumed that the male model fits the female one (Gilligan, 1993). In the past, women experienced middle age as a series of turning points in their lives. As family size declined, women faced the "empty-nest syndrome" when their last child left home, leaving them with a sense of loss and confusion about their role now that motherhood was complete. However, there was the continuity provided by her homemaking role. Now that more women share family and work roles with their partners, they experience the same challenges. The impact on women at the end of childbearing and the empty nest has declined (Baker, 1993).

Abigail Stewart and Joan Ostrove conducted a metastudy of women in the baby-boom generation by compiling the results of several longitudinal studies of American women. Their results suggest that women experience an increased sense of identity and competence in midlife, they made "midcourse corrections" based on a review of their lives, and they reported high levels of generativity (Stewart & Ostrove, 1998). Studies of future generations will be required to confirm that midlife is characterized by "turning points" not "danger," both for women and men, in a society in which they share family and work roles.

Fiske and Chiriboga examined the stress that adults experience in middle age. They determined that the effects of stress were influenced by the ability of individuals to manage them. Their study revealed that major life events were less stressful than the day-to-day frustrations of life, and much less stressful than **non-events**—those life passages that we want to happen but don't, such as not marrying or having children (Fiske & Chiriboga, 1990). Major life events, such as marriage, the birth of a child, children leaving home, or the death of a parent are stressful, but they are anticipated. There is anticipatory socialization, there are role models for coping with major life events, and because they are recognized occurrences, social support is offered. Day-to-day frustrations are more stressful because they are constant, personal, and a threat to an individual's sense of competence. The most stress results from non-events. Unemployment or early retirement also remove opportunities for living out a life according to one's Dream. For those who have delayed their generativity while they await these events, who feel they still have something to offer the world, the stresses of non-events can lead to a sense of stagnation in middle age (Kotre, 1996).

"Middle age snuffs out more talent than even wars or sudden deaths do."

—Richard Hughes

by Stephanie Whittaker

After practising law for 30 years, Jim Wright was ready to make a big career change. "I had enjoyed law, but I wanted to do something different," he said. The "something different" that Mr. Wright had in mind was a shift to the non-profit sector, where he knew he would earn less money but gratify his need to contribute to his community. With the help of a career-transition specialist, Mr. Wright landed a job two years ago as executive director of EPOC Montréal, an organization that helps unemployed young people acquire work skills and, ultimately, jobs. Mr. Wright says what makes his work most satisfying is to watch the transformation of the students who go through EPOC's program. "You have to come to one of our graduations and see the results of 21 weeks of work with the staff. [EPOC's students] undergo a vast life change here. The majority come in on welfare or unemployment insurance and leave with a job." The payoff for Jim Wright of working in a non-profit organization? "I'm helping people," he said.

That sense of community service is what drives many of the people who work in the non-profit sector. "There is a personality type that chooses this kind of work," said Clarence Bayne, Director of Concordia University's Graduate Diplomas in Administration and Sport Administration program, which offers training for careers in the non-profit sector. "They're the ones who have a great spiritual sense."

What is the non-profit sector? "It's a huge field that takes in everything from the YMCA to the Canadian Council for Refugees and the Canadian Foundation for Human Rights. Revenue Canada says there are 100 000 non-profit organizations in Canada," said Edith Katz, Co-ordinator of Marketing

People choose to work in non-profit organizations to make a difference in their community.

and Communications in the Concordia diploma program. "A non-profit organization can be as big as the University of Toronto and as small as a local community organization that helps senior citizens." Moreover, she added, career opportunities in the non-profit sector are burgeoning. "Many of these organizations are realizing it's worthwhile to have competent managers and to pay them appropriately even if they have a small budget. They need good financial management, resource management, and credibility with external funding agencies and donors. Many non-profits have good people who have professional qualifications. They may be social workers or have some other professional qualification. But they lack training in management skills."

And that, says Ms. Katz, is where the DIA/DSA program comes in. "We're training managers and administrators," she said. The program, which operates in the John Molson School of Business, teaches a raft of management courses that take in such areas as human resources and accounting. Ms. Katz says salaries in the non-profit sector tend to be lower than in the private sector but are "determined by the size of the organization, the level of the position, and the age and experience of the manager. I think people understand that salaries may not be comparable to those offered in large corporations, but those who work in the non-profit sector are there for other reasons. They're there because they want to make a difference to their communities or because they want to work toward change. They may be interested in the environment, in human rights, or in marginalized groups."

The reason Danny Lemieux chose to work in the non-profit sector was to give to others what he had received in childhood. Mr. Lemieux, Co-ordinator of Special Projects at the Point St. Charles YMCA, remembers how he frequented the Dawson Boys and Girls Club in Verdun as a child. "My father died when I was quite young," he said. "I was involved in sports and had some really great teachers who were very important in my life. They would take us places and I just assumed all teachers did that. I wanted to do for others what these wonderful teachers had done for me." Tight funding often means that people who run non-profit organizations must work as jacks of all trades. "We can't afford to have everyone doing different jobs," he said. "Sometimes, you find yourself sweeping the gym before the janitor arrives or painting your own office." Mr. Lemieux adds that he enjoys a career that creates tangible community improvements and offers flexible hours.

Jim Wright agrees. He says he didn't experience any second thoughts after deciding to leave his career as a lawyer and head into the non-profit sector. On the advice of a friend, Mr. Wright got career counselling from Robert Potvin at Murray Axmith, a career-transition firm. "I went through some testing

and at the end of it, they decided I should either be running a foundation or working in a community-based organization," he said. Wright had spent his adult life doing community work, including being a city councillor in Westmount and sitting on the board of governors at McGill University. "Robert told me to visit one or two community organizations a day. The first one I saw was Dans La Rue. EPOC Montréal was the second."

Careerists who want to obtain management skills before moving into non-profit sector jobs are enrolling in Concordia's year-long DIA program, which offers management courses specific to the non-profit field. "There is a professionalization taking place in the management of non-profit organizations," said Edith Katz. "They're increasingly being run by people with management training. Some of these people are jacks of all trades. They do accounting, marketing, fundraising, and grant proposals. The non-profit sector offers scope for people from a wide variety of academic and occupational backgrounds."

And in a larger context, said Clarence Bayne, the non-profit sector "makes democracy possible. It's the sector in which people help redistribute wealth. Our market system is efficient at producing goods and using resources. But it's not good at egalitarianism and the redistribution of resources. That's where the non-profit and volunteer sector comes in." It's also where people like Jim Wright and Danny Lemieux get to make a difference to society. ■

Source: *Ottawa Citizen*. (2001, July 28). p. K6.

1. Why did Jim Wright decide to change his career?
2. How does his new career contribute to his generativity?
3. Using a social exchange perspective, evaluate whether he has made a good choice.

Marriage Satisfaction

Couples enter marriage with great expectations, but the realities of life challenge the durability and quality of marriage. Barry Dym and Michael Glenn (1993) explained that relationships cycle through three predictable stages as they face the crises of family life. Betty Carter and Joan Peters (1996) identified predictable normative crises in life that required adjustments in families. Of these, the teenage years, children leaving home, retirement, and growing old together are the crises of later life. Research in Canada and the United States over the last fifty years suggests that the spiral of marital adjustment identified by Dym and Glenn is a downward one until the turning point at middle age.

Eugen Lupri and James Frideres published the results of a Canadian study of the quality of marriage relationships over the family life cycle in 1981. They identified a U-shaped curve of satisfaction. Both men and women reported that their marriages were very satisfying during the early years, and the level of satisfaction improved slightly in the first years of parenthood. The stresses associated with the adjustment to parenthood seemed to be temporary. However, the number of people who were very satisfied with their marriage began to decline steadily as the children got older. Marital satisfaction was lowest at midlife and bottomed out when children began to leave home. By then, those who would divorce had done so. The level of marital satisfaction improved during the empty-nest stage, reaching almost the same level of satisfaction in retirement as at the newlywed stage. Although the stages were identified with parenthood, the curve of marital satisfaction for childless couples matched the U-shaped curve, although childless couples reported a slightly higher level of satisfaction (Nett, 1993).

The patterns of marital satisfaction seem to be changing. The results of a 17-year American study of marital satisfaction challenge the U-shaped curve theory. Jody VanLaningham, David Johnson, and Paul Amato suggest that the U-shaped curve reflects the differences among generations, not the pattern for individual marriages. They found that the level of satisfaction

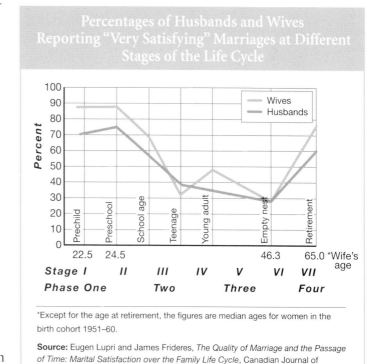

Percentages of Husbands and Wives Reporting "Very Satisfying" Marriages at Different Stages of the Life Cycle

*Except for the age at retirement, the figures are median ages for women in the birth cohort 1951–60.

Source: Eugen Lupri and James Frideres, *The Quality of Marriage and the Passage of Time: Marital Satisfaction over the Family Life Cycle*, Canadian Journal of Sociology 6 (1981): 289.

with marriage drops off dramatically after several years of marriage and continues to decline into middle age before levelling off (VanLaningham, Johnson, & Amato, 2001). The decline in marital satisfaction is reflected in divorce rates. Zheng Wu and Margaret Penning (1997) determined that divorce rates for Canadian women aged 40 to 49 more than doubled between 1971 and 1991. The increasing divorce rate might support a hypothesis that couples are less satisfied with their marriages now than previous generations were. However, VanLaningham, Johnson, and Amato concluded that there is too little evidence to determine how marital happiness will change in the later years of marriage (2001).

It is difficult to explain the decline in marital satisfaction during midlife. The functionalist perspective considers the roles and structure of the marriage. When couples are conforming to the traditional gender roles of marriage and parenthood in early parenthood, couples are more satisfied with their marriages than during the so-called "crowded years," when dual-career parents are balancing non-traditional work and family roles. However, the decline in satisfaction was first identified in the United States in 1960 when very few women worked outside the home (Nett, 1993). Recent research in the United States by Stacy Rogers and Paul Amato found that dual-income couples reported more conflict than couples in earlier generations but no less overall happiness. On the other hand, another American study found that wives' employment improved the quality of marriage because it increased the family income and buffered financial stress for the couples (Barnet & Hyde, 2001).

Social exchange perspective explains that individuals assess the costs and benefits of relationships to determine whether they are satisfied. The decline in satisfaction suggests that people assess the costs of the marriage as greater than the benefits. Various reasons have been suggested for this. The financial costs of raising children in a consumer society have resulted in dual-career families. Couples are working longer and harder, yet the real income of families has decreased and couples are experiencing financial stress. Also, the time demands of working and raising children limit the time available for the intimacy of marriage (Nett, 1993). However, couples without children have fewer demands, yet their level of satisfaction also declines. This suggests that adults' age, not children, might be the independent variable.

Family therapist Claude Guldner supports the second explanation for the decline in satisfaction with marriage using a systems perspective. He says that couples do not realize that they may be putting too much time and energy into children and work commitments and not enough into their marriage. Some couples have chosen not

Many couples have discovered that combining work and family leaves little time for their marriage.

to have sex anymore because the passion is gone (Chisholm, Atherley, Wood, & McClelland, 1999). Couples are staying together longer despite problems with their sexual relationship, but they are less satisfied with their marriages. A long-term commitment and a willingness to make the marital relationship a priority are essential for maintaining love in a marriage that includes intimacy and passion (Adams, 1996). However, lifestyle issues, such as lack of leisure time, demands of children, lack of privacy, and discrepancies in workload, might reduce the levels of passion and intimacy in marriage. Guldner argues that it is important to make the marital subsystem a priority, even when other matters interfere, because an active sex life is important for maintaining the intimacy and passion in marriage (Chisholm, Atherley, Wood, & McClelland, 1999).

Marital happiness can increase when children leave home. With fewer parenting and financial responsibilities, couples are free to indulge in spontaneous activity, such as dining out more often, and to enjoy life. The merging of gender roles in middle age results in men taking a greater interest in the home, thus reducing the conflict over household tasks (Baker, 1993). However, if couples have limited pension and investment income, the decline in income at retirement can reduce the level of satisfaction in the marriage because it increases financial stress and reduces the opportunities for activity. Couples who move away from their communities to smaller homes or who spend winters in warm places also experience more conflict (Myers & Booth, 1996). Thus, those who maintain their marriages into old age are healthier, live longer, and are happier than their widowed, divorced, or single contemporaries, so, from a social exchange perspective, marriage is a long-term investment that provides rewards in later life.

in focus | "Honey, I'm Home!"—For Good

by Kirk Bloir

"At first it was great having George around all of the time, but now he's into everything. He's rearranged my cupboards, moved the linens from one closet to the other, and has started giving me his own Hints from Heloise. When he was working, I never heard a peep about how I ran my home. If I have to hear one more time about how much he misses the 'guys' I'm going to scream. You know, I really thought it would be different, better somehow."

Retirement has its own challenges, and may not turn out to be what a couple expected.

"For the past couple of weeks, things have be great— Ginger and I were really enjoying each other's company. Now all we seem to do is fight. The other day when I helped her out by maximizing our storage space and offered a more efficient way to do the dishes, man did she hit the roof. And I really miss my pals at the shop. It seems as if my usefulness has run its course."

Retirement is one of life's milestones. However, many people view retirement as a loss of roles, income, and socially recognized productivity (Nock, 1992). Retirement itself has no predictable negative effect on physical health, self-esteem, or life satisfaction. The manner in which couples learn to adjust to retirement depends on circumstances, such as whether retirement was taken voluntarily or involuntarily, and their health (Hanks, 1990).

Adjustment Takes Time

For most couples, retirement progresses in stages (Hanson & Wapner, 1994). At first, couples experience a short-lived honeymoon in which everything seems to come together nicely. As soon as the reality of retirement hits, however, many find they're not quite as excited about the prospect of being a senior citizen or "stuck" with each other as they previously were (Smith, 1991). This is especially true when they've been "forced" to take retirement because of corporate downsizing, poor or diminished work performance, or failing health.

Men and women experience retirement differently (Hanson & Wapner, 1994). Men, many of whom have spent more than 40 years honing their identities as providers, are suddenly reliving the identity crisis of their adolescence. Women, many of whom have spent much of their lives independently keeping house and raising children, are now confronted with an intruder in their ordered world. The challenge becomes how to achieve a peaceful and successful integration of two lives into one living space. This integration depends on the couple's ability to grow, both individually and together. Adjustment is largely an individual thing;

however, the dynamics of the couple relationship vary as a function of each partner's progression. To date, no concrete evidence points to some magical time period couples can expect to spend adjusting. Most retired couples, however, report high levels of marital satisfaction (Vinick & Ekerdt, 1991).

Old Dogs and New Tricks

Initially, retired couples may find themselves invading each other's space. Wives may explore the world hidden under the hood of the car. Husbands may rearrange in attempts to maximize space. Spouses who have previously had little opportunity or desire to explore the other's domestic spheres find themselves with time on their hands and curiosity in their minds. This curiosity may cause much frustration. If one does adopt a new task, it will most likely be in an area they are more interested in and have a better aptitude for than their spouses (Szinovacz & Harpster, 1994).

Communication Is Essential

Both wives and husbands have ideas, opinions, likes, and dislikes. Attributes that attracted them to each other may now be the very things that spark frustration. Whatever the issue, couples need to talk about it in an open and honest way. If you don't like George rearranging the cupboards and linen closets, break the news to him lovingly. If you would like to do the cooking Ginger has done for years, express your interest and work out an arrangement. A few minutes of heated discussion is better than weeks of repressed anger and resentment.

Capitalize on Interests

Work typically occupies 33 percent of an average day. Without work, many find themselves wondering what's left to do. Everything's been washed, rearranged, waxed, and buffed. You've watched all the TV you can stand, and couldn't possibly read or knit anything else. After years of a regimented and regulated schedule, many are suddenly faced with a void (Cude & Jablin, 1992).

In an attempt to fill the space, brainstorm activities you would like to do as a couple, as well as things you would like to do individually. Look around your community for groups and clubs that you may want to join. Volunteer. Enroll in a college course. Start with the day, then work on the week and month, and finally plan for the years ahead. This is one of the joys of retirement—planning the rest of your life together.

Enjoy the Years Ahead

Stop and think about all the transitions you've navigated: marriage, having children, raising and launching your children, dealing with a boomerang child (one you sent out of the nest who somehow found his or her way back home), discovering the wonders of being a grandparent, coping with economic uncertainty. Now think about the happiness all of those times have brought you. Realize that there were some hurts and heartaches along the way, too. You're still together, so you must have done something right. Be proud of your accomplishments! Allow yourself and your spouse time to adjust to this new life phase—just as it took you time to get to where you are today. Remember, as a 65-year-old, you have more than 37 percent of your adult life ahead of you! Enjoy it! ■

Source: Bloir, Kirk. "Honey, "I'm Home!" – for Good: The Transition to Retirement." HYG-5159-96. Families . . . Meeting the Challenge, The Ohio State University Extension. http://ohioline.osu.edu/hyg-fact/5000/5159.html

1. What causes of marital conflict are suggested in this article?
2. Using a systems perspective, explain the adjustment that is required when one or both spouses retire.
3. From a social exchange perspective, what are the costs and benefits of retirement for each spouse?
4. Analyze the effects of retirement on generativity, and evaluate whether the activities suggested allow opportunities for generativity.

Post-Adulthood

Because aging has a negative connotation in the Western world, people tend to avoid identifying themselves as old. In North America, there is no clear sense of meaning or purpose to the last stage of life, and no clear role expectations. The development of pensions and retirement savings plans supports early retirement and the notion that old age is a reward for working hard in youth and middle age. On the other hand, media images of a lifestyle focused on leisure suggest that the senior years are a return to the simple pleasures and freedom from responsibility associated with childhood (Coleman, Ivani-Chalian, & Robinson, 1998). Another perspective suggests that death is the purpose of life, so older people focus inward to determine meaning and wholeness in life and to accept death (Kimmel, 1990). As life expectancy increases, individuals will spend a longer period of their lives in what British gerontologist Midwinter has dubbed "Post-Adulthood" (Coleman, Ivani-Chalian, & Robinson, 1998).

by Jay Ingram

We humans are similar in many ways to the great apes, a similarity that I think is sometimes exaggerated. Yes, we share more than 98 percent of our genome with chimpanzees. And yes, as far as we know, chimps are the best of the rest intellectually. But there really is not much comparison between the brain power of an adult chimp and an adult human.

But we differ from chimps and gorillas in other ways that say something about our respective evolutionary pasts. Our uniquely human attribute is a prolonged menopause. Human females live a very long time after they become infertile, which at first glance is difficult to understand. After all, the lifestyle characteristics that survived to the present are those that enhanced our ancestors' fertility and increased the numbers of offspring they had. How could living well past one's ability to have children at all qualify as such a trait?

One theory (which has been around for 40 years) is that fertility began to end earlier as ancestral human mothers needed to devote more and more of their time to their offspring. The more dependent the child, the more time the mother must invest, and continuing to give birth would simply have compromised the survival of the already born. In the evolutionary game, it's not how many you give birth to, but how many survive to reproduce.

This theory, however venerable, has its shortcomings. One is that chimps apparently contradict it. Chimpanzee females need to care for their offspring, yet many keep on giving birth, even though the later babies born to them have much lower rates of survival. It would seem that they, too, should give up fertility earlier, but they have not. A closer look reveals that, in fact, human females do not abandon fertility earlier than female chimps or gorillas. It's just that humans

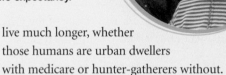

The role of grand-mothering results from a biological end to childbearing many years before the end of human life expectancy.

live much longer, whether those humans are urban dwellers with medicare or hunter-gatherers without.

The rare chimp that lives 50 years in the wild dies at about the time it would become infertile. So it appears as if menopause is not the result of an abbreviated fertility but of longevity. If so, what, then, is the evolutionary advantage involved? A team of scientists led by Kristen Hawkes at the University of Utah has come out with a new suggestion, the "grandmother hypothesis." They argue that menopausal women were of great value in our evolution because they helped gather food for their daughters and their daughters' children. The argument is based on the premise that much of the shaping of our species happened while we were hunting and gathering creatures. Among hunter-gatherers today, post-menopausal women are able to find and dig up food items like tubers that children can't cope with. So these grandmothers can actually help ensure the survival of their grandchildren, a good thing in an evolutionary sense because those grandchildren carry about 25 percent of her genes. In what must have been a difficult hand-to-mouth existence for our ancestors, having a pair of extra hands for food-gathering could have made a significant difference.

This new theory is more than just guesswork. It makes some predictions, one of which is that child-bearing women should produce babies faster than you'd expect because the grandmothers could initiate the feeding of infants, allowing them to be weaned earlier. In fact, the data show that human babies are weaned earlier than most other mammals, including primates. It is also true for mammals in general that larger mothers produce larger—but fewer—babies. Yet even humans are outliers, producing more babies for their size (by a factor of two) than the great apes. The explanation? The childbearing mother has food-gathering help.

There is scant mention in all of this of the role that the male hunters may have played. In fact, Hawkes and her colleagues argue that there simply wasn't much of a role. But I like to think that somewhere, someone is dreaming up the "grandfather hypothesis." ■

Source: *The Toronto Star.* (1998, March 1).

1. What explanation do evolutionary psychologists suggest for the fact that human women live many years after they can no longer reproduce?
2. Does a longer life provide benefits for one's children and grandchildren in our post-industrial society?
3. What would you suggest as a "grandfather hypothesis"? Give your reasoning.

Late in his life, Erik Erikson described the challenge of an eighth stage of life as "integrity versus despair." Individuals complete the formation of their identity and develop the ego's strength, **wisdom**, which to Erikson means "insight and enlightenment." Adults review their lives to assess whether they have become who they wanted to be and achieved the generativity they desired in order to achieve integrity, "the acceptance of one's one and only life cycle as something that had to be and that, by necessity, permitted no substitutions" (Erikson, 1950, p. 252). By integrating their past and present identities, individuals develop wisdom. It enables people to have an "informed and detached concern with life itself in the face of death itself" (Erikson & Erikson, 1997, p. 61). Individuals who have not achieved integrity feel **despair**, a sense that they have not done what they wanted to do with their lives and there is no time left to make changes (Erikson & Erikson, 1997). American gerontologist Dan McAdams suggests that older people who have high self-esteem frame their identities as life stories connecting the past and the present (Coleman, Ivani-Chalian, & Robinson, 1998). Integrity clarifies the meaning of life for older people who can and do maintain a grand-generative function (Erikson & Erikson, 1997).

When Erikson completed his work on development over the life span there were few who lived into very old age, so they were viewed as wise, the recipients of a divine gift, and having special obligations for living so long. In his later years, Erikson concluded that the life course as he described it was no longer accurate, and that there was probably a ninth stage. Old age in one's eighties and nineties presents new challenges. The physical decline is more noticeable, and the body begins to weaken and function less well. Erikson explained that the decline in

"The closing years of life are like the end of a masquerade party, when the masks are dropped."

—Arthur Schopenhauer

by Peter G. Coleman, Christine Ivani-Chalian, and Maureen Robinson, Department of Geriatric Medicine, University of Southampton, U.K.

RESEARCH QUESTION

What are the principal themes underlying an older individual's identity?

HYPOTHESIS

Self-esteem stays high for older individuals because they have formed an identity based on consistent themes.

METHOD

The researchers investigated the lives of older subjects using oral histories from the theoretical framework of "identity as story." This framework suggests that the development of a life story reflects the developmental tasks identified by Erik Erikson: identity, generativity, and integrity. They defined identity as "that aspect of self and personality which expresses the overall unity and purpose of the individual's life" (p. 391).

A longitudinal study was conducted in Southampton over 18 years. A sample of 339 people over the age of 65 were interviewed three times between 1977 and 1980. The survivors were re-interviewed by the same researchers in 1988 (n=101), in 1990–91 (n=70), in 1993 (n=43), and in 1995–96 (n=28), with "n=" meaning "the number of subjects." The recorded interviews were transcribed and then analyzed and compared to determine the content of the answers, using grounded theory principles, in which the researcher assumes no theoretical perspective but allows the organization to be determined by the data.

Case studies were written to summarize the changes in self-esteem over the period of the study.

RESULTS

The majority of the subjects spoke positively about their present and past lives and saw them as a connected story worth telling.

Present and past lives were connected by long-term relationships with family and friends, by paid or voluntary work, and by maintaining the same home or community.

Several identity themes were prioritized by the oldest surviving subjects:

- long-term relationships with family, including spouse, children, grandchildren, and siblings
- other interpersonal relationships
- interest activities
- health and independence

CONCLUSIONS

Family relationships were the main source of life themes for the men and women in this study. The researchers concluded that losing a family is much harder to come to terms with than leaving work. The other major theme was independence or maintaining one's home.

Life stories enable individuals to have a heightened awareness of the themes of their lives, as Erikson suggested. The researchers noted that many older people want to tell their stories but lack the resources for writing them, and suggest that initiatives to help them do this could be developed. ∎

Source: *Ageing and Society*, Vol. 18, Part 4, July 1998, pp. 389–419. Adapted with the permission of Cambridge University Press.

abilities results in individuals moving through the negative aspects of personality stages. Increasingly, individuals experience mistrust, shame, guilt, inferiority, and role confusion (Erikson & Erikson, 1997). Coping with very old age requires an acceptance of death and a willingness to set aside despair. Joan Erikson, in completing the work of Erik Erikson after his death, described the ego strength of very old age as **gerotranscendence**, a sense of rising above the difficulties of age. Individuals at what might be the ninth stage focus on the here and now. They accept that physical disabilities constrain their mobility and that time is limited. They have no sense of future. In a sense, they begin to withdraw from the world, knowing that the last step must be taken alone (Erikson & Erikson, 1997).

A longer life is a reasonable expectation for Canadians, but whether they will have satisfying ones depends on the quality of their lives in old age. The strongest direct influence on the quality of life is the opportunity for social and physical activity. This prospect is affected by an individual's cognitive ability and his or her personal perception of health. Social status, determined by levels of education and income, affects whether individuals have access to activities (Fernándes-Ballesteros, Zamarrón, & Ruíz, 2001). The **activity theory of aging** supports the value of social and physical activity as a contributor to self-esteem. It suggests that individuals are reluctant to give up roles unless they can substitute other meaningful ones (McPherson, 1990). Maintaining close relationships with friends and others is also important. If individuals are married and can remain living in the same home or in the same community, their quality of life is better. For many people, the opportunity to tell their life story in old age allows them to determine that they have lived a satisfying life (Coleman, Ivani-Chalian, & Robinson, 1998).

"To keep the heart unwrinkled, to be hopeful, kindly, cheerful, reverent— that is to triumph over old age."

—Thomas Bailey Aldrich

Significant changes in Canada and the world during the twentieth century have affected the roles that individuals play at all stages of life. Men and women have greater freedom to form an identity and to develop life structures that enable them to pursue their dreams, but they have had to develop new roles. The large numbers of Canadians who can anticipate living into old and very old age have few role models to provide the anticipatory socialization needed to prepare them. Socialization for aging is an active process as individuals anticipate the changes in their lives and make plans for the financial and social changes. Resocialization for old age is more concerned with revising existing behaviour and developing specific skills than with learning new values or traits, but can only occur with opportunities to participate with role models in appropriate activities (McPherson, 1990).

Individuals who live to a very old age achieve continuity in their lives through relationships with family, interest activities, and maintaining their residence.

web connection

www.mcgrawhill.ca/links/families12

To learn about old age in Canada, go to the web site above for *Individuals and Families in a Diverse Society* to see where to go next.

Dan McAdams suggests that individuals' identities are defined in their evolving life story, the life structure they develop and live (Coleman, Ivani-Chalian, & Robinson, 1998). Perhaps it would be beneficial to clarify what the last stage of life should be to facilitate the development of individual life stories. Erik Erikson, who outlined the developmental pattern over the span of human life, argued that "lacking a culturally viable ideal of old age, our civilization does not really harbor a concept of the whole of life" (Erikson & Erikson, p. 114). What is the role of old age in Canada and how does it reflect the lives of individuals and families in Canada?

case study | Carol's Generativity

Carol Mehisto, who has been married to her husband Steven since 1977, is a mother of two. When she graduated from Lakehead University in Thunder Bay, Carol expected to become a high school English teacher, but her year at the Faculty of Education in Toronto convinced her that she would never do that. Carol took a job as a library assistant to help cover living expenses for herself and her husband, Steven, who was a full-time student at the School of Social Work at University of Toronto. Carol did not find the job particularly challenging, but she and Steven both appreciated the income she brought into their partnership after four years of being students. When Steven took a job in Sault Ste. Marie a year later, Carol was happy to leave her job, since she was ready to move on to something else.

At first she was happy in Sault Ste. Marie, and she and Steven saw their move as a shared adventure and as the beginning of the next part of their life together. She was pleased when they could afford to buy a house, and spent a great deal of time with the real-estate agent before purchasing a small bungalow. When she was unable to find work of any kind, Carol kept herself busy painting and decorating their new home, and eventually began to pursue her interest in crafts. At this point, Carol and Steven began to talk

Carol has taken on a variety of jobs and activities throughout her life to keep herself happy, to pursue her interests, and to remain socially active.

seriously about starting a family. Although they were both in their twenties, the time seemed right, particularly to Carol, but as the months went by and she did not get pregnant, she became more and more frustrated.

When Steven received a promotion and a transfer back to Toronto, Carol saw another opportunity to make changes in her life. By this time, she felt that her future involved working with children, so she applied for a job as a library assistant again, but specified that she wanted to work in the children's division. She began to work part-time, and she enjoyed her job, especially when local elementary teachers brought their classes to the library for storytelling. She and Steven began attending services at a local church, and both of them eventually volunteered to teach Sunday-school classes, which Carol in particular found satisfying.

The next three or four years passed by quickly as

she kept house and worked part-time at the library. Still unable to get pregnant, she and Steven began to discuss the possibility of adopting children. They made several inquiries and got interviews with various agencies. They became involved with several couples, all of them in various stages of the adoption process. Along with two other couples, they formed an association that provided support and information for infertile couples, an organization that continues to operate today. Carol and Steven believed that working in the organization together and their active membership in the church enabled them to maintain a strong marriage despite their disappointment about not having children.

Eventually, their perseverance paid off and they adopted a baby boy whom they named Jeremy. Life finally seemed satisfying for Carol. She quit her job and happily became a full-time mother. She enjoyed becoming part of a stay-at-home mothers' group in her community over the next few years and made many good friends. She volunteered in the local elementary school two mornings a week and increased her activities in the local church. When she became pregnant with Kaitlyn six years later, her life seemed complete. However, like many women her age, Carol eventually found that life as a full-time mother became less rewarding as her children got older and began to attend school. She saw other mothers in the community less often, as many of them returned to work. She found it more and more difficult to fill her days and began to think about going back to work.

Family obligations delayed her return to work. Her mother had been diagnosed with Alzheimer's disease a few years earlier, and her dad was reluctant to arrange institutional care for his wife, feeling that it was his duty to care for her as long as he could. He was getting older as well, and found that some of the physical demands required were more than he could manage. As her mother's condition continued to deteriorate, her father began asking Carol to help him more and more. She helped out as best as she could, but found that she was emotionally drained. Seeing her once vibrant mother unable to care for herself physically, and more and more not even being aware of the people around her, was very stressful for Carol. Comforting her father over the loss of his life partner was equally difficult. The emotional strain on Carol and her immediate family was immense, as she sometimes felt torn between her role of wife and mother and of daughter.

When her father finally arranged for her mother to be institutionalized, Carol was both saddened and relieved, as it marked a new stage in her life. By then Kaitlyn was almost eight years old and was becoming more independent. Carol began to volunteer with a local women's group, driving older, housebound women to medical appointments and making home visits. This eventually led to a part-time job. She found her experience there very fulfilling, and it did not interfere with her family responsibilities. Recently, she began taking a night school course in gerontology at a nearby community college, and has plans to complete the diploma requirements for geriatric studies. ∎

---

1. What life structure had Carol established for herself in early adulthood and what circumstances led to the adjustment of her identity and life structure?
2. How has Carol achieved generativity in her life?
3. Evaluate whether Carol experienced a midlife crisis as a "turning point" or a "moment of danger."
4. Predict whether Carol and Steven would report a high level of satisfaction in their marriage using the functionalist, systems, and social exchange perspectives.
5. Describe the factors that are affecting the quality of life for Carol's father. How has Carol contributed to his quality of life?

chapter 13 Review and Apply

1. Create a chart in which you compare the stages of adult life and the behaviour expectations for traditional Chinese and a culture of your choice. Using a functionalist perspective, discuss whether contemporary Canadian society is organized to support the stage behaviour defined by the two descriptions.

2. Summarize the similarities and differences among Charlotte Buhler's, Erik Erikson's, and Daniel Levinson's theories of development in midlife. Identify research questions for testing the validity of the common features of the three theories.

3. Identify and explain Kotre's four forms of generativity. Give examples of how men and women could achieve each form of generativity in Canadian society. Arrange the four forms in order of the value each has in Canadian society, and provide evidence to support your ranking.

4. What are the two definitions of *crisis*? Discuss which definition is supported by the research on midlife crisis. In conclusion, what can you anticipate in midlife?

5. What factors contribute to the decline in satisfaction with marriage? Using social exchange theory, suggest why most people stay married when they are less satisfied with it after ten to twenty years.

6. Explain the meaning of integrity, despair, and wisdom in the eighth stage of life as described by Erik Erikson. Describe how he suggests the outlook on life changes when individuals enter the ninth stage.

Knowledge/Understanding   Thinking/Inquiry   Communication

7. Develop a description of the contemporary stages of adult life as they occur for Canadians. Give each stage a name that reflects the meaning of the stage, and describe the role behaviour expected.

8. Write an essay presenting and supporting an opinion on the role of employment in generativity for women in midlife.

9. Write a letter to the editor in which you respond to the article "The Midlife Wake-Up Call" on page 429, using the research presented in this chapter.

10. Investigate the activities available within your community that contribute to the quality of life for older people, and design a brochure promoting participation.

Knowledge/Understanding   Thinking/Inquiry   Communication   Application

11. Using the oral history method, conduct research to assess how individuals now in their fifties, sixties, seventies, and eighties achieved generativity in their lives. Compile the results and determine whether they are consistent. Present the results as a brief article, using quotations from the oral histories.

12. Using the oral history method, write a brief life story for an older person in your family or community. Illustrate the life story with photographs and other artifacts.

chapter 14

The Challenges of Later Life

CHAPTER EXPECTATIONS

While reading this chapter, you will:

- analyze changes in participation in the labour force, taking into consideration male and female participation rates, retirement, and the impact of work on socialization

- demonstrate an understanding of the effect of various aspects of social systems on individual development

- analyze current issues relating to intimate relationships

- summarize current research on the effects of divorce on child development and socialization

- demonstrate an understanding of the nature, prevalence, and consequences of elder abuse, and describe strategies and programs that would facilitate its prevention and remediation

- explain the impact on individual development and decision making of social changes and challenges and life events

- identify and respond to the theoretical viewpoints, the thesis, and the supporting arguments of materials found in a variety of secondary sources

The level of satisfaction that people have in their lives is affected by how they manage the various challenges that arise.

CHAPTER INTRODUCTION

This chapter will examine the changes and challenges of middle and later adult life. Current perceptions and opinions concerning the issues of unemployment and early retirement, remarriage, and elder abuse will be examined, and demographic trends will be used to determine the changes affecting dependency in old age. The normative events of dying, death, and bereavement will also be discussed. The impact of social systems and structures, economy, laws, religious beliefs, and social policy on individuals, couples, and families in later life will be considered from various theoretical perspectives.

The Second Half of Life

The second half of life presents challenges for individuals, couples, and their families. Individuals in the transition to middle adulthood often make adjustments in their lives to achieve the satisfying life they began to build in early adulthood. The focus of life is the attainment of generativity within the family, at work, or in the community. The adaptations necessary in midlife affect both partners in couple relationships and can result in stronger relationships. Those who are divorced or widowed may choose to remarry to acquire the social and emotional benefits of marriage. In later life, individuals again make adjustments in their lives as they retire from the workplace and establish new lifestyles in which their productive roles will be reduced. Challenging issues, including both normative events and unexpected crises, can affect whether middle-aged and older people are satisfied with their lives.

The most significant challenges of middle age concern the two tasks of life as identified by Freud: work and love. These are the environments in which generativity is achieved. Although some people choose to make changes in their occupation, others become unemployed. Unemployment affects an individual's identity as well as his or her marriage and family relationships because of the impact on family income, the use of time, and the division of labour. Early retirement might be planned, but it can have similar effects. Another change that individuals may choose to make in their lives is to remarry. This, too, will strongly affect the individual and his or her family. Although unemployment is usually seen as negative and marriage as positive, both are crises or turning points that require careful management by individuals and families.

Of the normative events in later adult life in Canada, aging and death are the least understood. Although life expectancy is increasing, many Canadians have little contact with older seniors. There is growing concern that they will be weak and dependent and that their numbers will strain Canada's resources in the future. This concern extends to the end of life. In a society in which death usually occurs away from home, individuals seldom anticipate their own deaths until midlife, when faced with the death of their parents. However, more people now die from extended illnesses, so individuals are more likely to be aware that they are approaching death. Individuals' social, economic, and spiritual environment determines the attitudes of aging Canadians and their families.

Remarriage

Remarriage is becoming more common in Canada, for several reasons. Although the divorce rate has been high for several decades, individuals tend to remarry when an opportunity arises (Conway, 1997). Improved health also enables widows and widowers to consider remarriage, especially after an early death of a spouse from accident or illness. Those who remarry have experienced an earlier marriage and are more familiar with the costs and benefits of marriage. They tend to marry someone they love to gain the companionship they miss from intimate relationships. Although many cynics dismiss later-life remarriages as motivated by money, the research does not support this idea.

It takes one day to marry for the second time, but much longer to balance the conflicting roles of spouse and stepparent to build a stable marriage and a blended family.

In fact, lower-income women are less likely to marry, so the possibility of remarriage for some just widens the gap between dual-income families and single-mother households. The second time around, people still marry for romance and sexual expression (Sweeney, 1997).

The adjustment to remarriage is a slow process, because it is complicated by commitments to career, children, and the extended family. John Conway quotes a Vancouver psychologist as suggesting that the adjustment can take four to seven years (Conway, 1997). Most remarriages, like first marriages, are stable, but they have a higher divorce rate (Ward, 1994). Although actual rates are difficult to measure, as many as 40 percent of remarried couples separate within four years if there are children (Conway, 1997). Emily Nett suggests that these are marriage "mistakes" (1993). The systems perspective suggests several reasons why couples may fail to establish a stable family system. If the problems from the first marriage continue in the second, the new spouse may respond in a similar way to the behaviour (Ward, 1994). Remarriage occurs later in life and coincides with greater involvement in work than during the first marriage, so there may be conflicting marital and work roles (Sweeney, 1997). Couples may have difficulty negotiating a new marital system when they have old strategies that have been established in other roles in their lives.

A successful remarriage is established in three stages. Both partners must first recover from their first marriage and get over the grief, anger, and other intense emotions that result from divorce or bereavement. Individuals who are planning to remarry should include children and other extended family members in the decision because it affects all of them. If the new family system that they establish is open, or "permeable," it will allow greater flexibility for maintaining ties to ex-spouses and in-laws for the benefit of the children (Ward, 1994). The advice to remarried couples is to focus on developing a marital subsystem with clear boundaries that emphasize the priority of their marriage, and to concentrate on solving problems as "we" (Cherlin & Furstenberg, 2001). However, spouses may discover that there is conflict between their spousal and parental roles in the family (Conway, 1997). Those with lasting remarriages often have a more practical than romantic attitude that allows them to deal with the conflict under the watchful eyes of children, in-laws, and ex-spouses (Ward, 1994).

For many, remarriage also means becoming a stepparent, a challenge that is complicated by the stereotypical roles of stepparents (Cherlin & Furstenberg, 2001). Since the parent-child relationship is older than the marriage, children may see the stepparent as an intruder in the family and resent any attempt at intimacy (Ward, 1994; Cherlin & Furstenberg, 2001). Problems also arise between stepsiblings as children adjust to changes in their birth-order status, loyalties to other parents, and new sibling rivalries. When children are older, conflict may also result from repressed sexual attraction between "sudden siblings." It is estimated that, in Canada, 47 percent of remarriages that involve children end in divorce (Ward, 1994). On the other hand, most stepfamilies surveyed in an American study in 1981 described their families as "relaxed, orderly, and close" (Cherlin & Furstenberg, 2001). There are no clear role models for stepparents, but those who tread the fine path between parent and trusted friend are more successful than those who see themselves as "healers" who hope to repair the damage done by divorce or bereavement (Cherlin & Furstenberg, 2001).

Despite the conventional wisdom concerning the benefits of improved household income, two parents supporting each other emotionally and socially in raising children, and the presence of both gender roles, remarriage does not seem to improve the well-being for children whose parents are divorced (Cherlin & Furstenberg, 2001). Many studies since the 1980s suggest a greater chance of problems for children of divorce. Behavioural problems severe enough to require a mental health professional were found in 25 to 30 percent of children of divorced or remarried parents compared with 10 percent of children living with two biological parents. Children of divorced parents are more likely to repeat a grade at school. Problems may be more severe for boys than for girls (Cherlin & Furstenberg, 2001). Stepchildren leave home earlier

by Chris Zdeb, Staff Writer

Once upon a time, there was a loving, kind, and caring stepmother, who was loved by her stepchildren. Really. Stepmoms can still be "wicked," but in today's slang it can mean they're "cool" or "excellent." They've been transformed from fairy tales by a modern society where separation and divorce are common, and where the new families that rise from them include a growing number of stepmoms. At least one in 10 Canadian families, with kids up to age 11, are stepfamilies, and at least a quarter of them have a stepmom, according to the Vanier Institute of the Family in Ottawa. The numbers have normalized being a non-biological mom or having one, at least on a societal or community level, says Bob Glossop, Vanier's executive director of programs.

The role of the stepmom has also changed. Unlike Cinderella's, Snow White's, and Hansel and Gretel's stay-at-home stepmoms, today's stepmom probably works, reducing the dependence of step-mother and stepchild to this one singular relation-ship. But blood being thicker than water, stepmoms still have issues to resolve on the home front that get in the way of living happily ever after. To start, the stepfamily's very existence is usually born of sadness. "A wife may have lost a husband, a husband may have lost a wife, children have lost all kinds of things, including their space, and their day-to-day routine," says Dilys Collier, who runs a program for the Family Centre that helps blended families succeed. "All of the relationships in this new family have been born out of loss and that means there's grieving to be done." Often, parents skip the grieving and dive into a new relation-ship and family arrangement, unaware and unprepared for the depth of the difficulties they're facing or are about to face, especially when kids are involved.

It can take up to four years for members of blended families to accept one another, or it may never happen.

The roles and responsibilities of stepparents have never been well defined, Glossop says, making it diffi-cult for stepmoms and stepdads to figure out where they stand in the family picture. Discipline is a lightning rod for clashes between stepmoms and stepkids, even for those who get along most of the time. (There are more stepdads than stepmoms, but the stepmom stereotype is big and kid-raising is still largely considered women's work.)

Craig MacNutt, 15, has a good relationship with his stepmom, but admits he responds better when he's being reined in by his biological dad, John, than when Debbie's reading him the riot act. Debbie's been his stepmom since Craig was five, but they've been living under the same roof for only three years. Craig considers Debbie a friend. Debbie considers him a son. And there's the rub. "That's where you pull and where you feel pulled," Debbie says. "You want to treat them like your own child because you love them like your own child, yet you're not allowed to do this or you feel weird doing this. It's very hard."

As the guy who sometimes referees their disputes, John wonders if Debbie and Craig occasionally clash more because Debbie is a stricter parent than he is, rather than because she's his stepmom. Craig calls Debbie "Mom," John says, unless he's unhappy with her. "Then it's Debbie." Despite the disagreements, which all three say are common to all families, they're making their blended family work. Debbie says it helped that she was already a mom when she became a stepmom, and that both her kids and John's were very young when they got together.

Corinne Robinson's kids were younger, too, when she and husband Erwin blended their families nine years ago. Robinson agrees that, and the fact her stepchildren's biological mom had bowed out of the parenting picture, made her life as stepmom easier. It also helped that her ex-husband treated Erwin's kids as if they were his own, allowing Gerald, 16, and

Jennifer, 17, to come along when his sons Chase, 16, and Shane, 14, came to stay with him in Calgary. "It was a very unique situation," Robinson says, "but the kids never felt any jealousy that they were being treated differently." Her stepchildren call her Corinne and "Mom," when they refer to her while talking to other people. "When one of the stepchildren does something that I have to discipline, right away I get the wicked stepmother type of thing," Robinson says chuckling, but it's a joke. "Being a stepmom isn't scary. Parenting four teenagers at the same time, now that's scary," she laughs. ■

Source: *Edmonton Journal*. (2002, January 15). p. E1. Reprinted with permission of the *Edmonton Journal*.

1. What point of view on stepparents does Chris Zdeb present in this article?
2. What arguments does he present to support his point of view?
3. Analyze the evidence and advice presented from the following perspectives:
   - functionalism
   - social exchange theory
   - systems theory
4. Do your observations of blended or stepfamilies support or conflict with the author's point of view?

because of tension or conflict—a solution that might be encouraged by the parents (Goldscheider & Goldscheider, 1993). However, because it is likely that parents will continue to remarry, Cherlin and Furstenberg suggest that it might be better for remarried couples to model their stepparent relationships after in-law relationships, which do not demand the intimacy associated with biological parenthood (Cherlin & Furstenberg, 2001).

Older widowed and divorced people remarry for similar reasons to those in middle age. They seek companionship, social support, health and well-being, financial standing, and sexual activity (Carleson, 1997). Widowers are twice as likely to marry than widows because there is a larger pool of eligible women (Carleson, 1997). Remarriage is less likely for widows or divorced women, often because they choose not to marry again (Davidson, 2001), but it is likely to

| abstract | Late Life Widowhood, Selfishness, and New Partnership Choices: A Gendered Perspective |

by Kate Davidson, Centre for Research on Aging and Gender, University of Surrey

Little sociological attention has been paid to the repartnering of older people after widowhood, and how age, gender, and the meaning of marriage influence choices about new cross-gender relationships. This paper reports on in-depth, semi-structured interviews with 25 widows and 26 widowers over the age of 65, widowed for at least two years, and who had not remarried. Respondents were asked about their current lifestyle and relationships and whether they had ever considered remarriage. The words "selfish" and "freedom" were often used by the widows when describing their present existence, which was associated with not having to look after someone all the time. Few of the widowers mentioned selfishness and this was more likely to be associated with feelings of anger at the loss of their spouse. None of the men associated widowhood with a sense of freedom. The paper argues that the desire for repartnering after widowhood is gender-specific. Widows are more likely to remain without a partner for intrinsic factors: the reluctance to relinquish a new-found freedom. While for widowers, extrinsic factors of older age and poor health are more salient issues in new partnership formation choices and constraints. ■

Source: *Aging and Society*. Vol. 21, Part 3, May 2001, p. 297. Reprinted with the permission of Cambridge University Press.

increase as the number of seniors increases (Carleson, 1997). A long-term stable marriage is associated with significant health benefits for men and for women of all demographic groups (Pienta, Hayward, & Jenkins, 2000). It may be that the healthiest people marry, or that married people have healthier, less risky lifestyles. Also, married couples provide social support and care for one another, which improves health and longevity. As more people who have never married or who have divorced are entering old age, they, along with those who are widowed, might consider marrying for their physical and psychological well-being during that time (Pienta, Hayward, & Jenkins, 2000).

For Better or For Worse

© Lynn Johnston Productions, Inc./Distributed by United Feature Syndicate, Inc.

When widows and widowers remarry, the approval of their adult children is crucial to the marriage's success. Children may feel that remarrying is disloyal to the memory of their deceased parent. Adult children often have difficulty accepting an older parent as an attractive and sexually desirable person, and therefore they assume that the new partner has other motives, such as "marrying for money." In some cases, children fear that the remarried parent's priorities might change and that they will lose their inheritance (Walsh, 1989). However, remarriage after widowhood usually reflects the success of the previous marriage and the desire to achieve that happy state again (Carleson, 1997). Since society expects that individuals will delay remarriage until an appropriate period of mourning has passed, there is usually a longer waiting period for remarriage after the death of a spouse than after divorce (Carleson, 1997). For those whose families cannot accept remarriage, that lonely period might last forever.

point of view | Rabbi Gives Love a Second Chance

by Zev Singer

Toward the end of the morning service on Saturday, Rabbi Reuven Bulka made an announcement he knew would surprise everyone in his synagogue, and many outside it: he is engaged to be married. Considering directness his best course, Rabbi Bulka shared with his congregants both facts and feelings—including his reasons for taking the step now, less than a year after the death of his wife of 34 years, Naomi.

The Ottawa rabbi, well known internationally as a scholar and author, but not well known for talking about himself, opened up to the members of his Alta Vista synagogue, Congregation Machzikei Hadas. At a point in the service reserved for what are usually less dramatic announcements, such as who's sponsoring the after-service refreshments, the rabbi asked the indulgence of the crowd for something that would take a few moments longer. He'd been on a trip the previous week, he explained, "to persuade a lady to change her last name." After a moment, he continued:

Rabbi Bulka surprised his congregation by announcing his engagement less than a year after the death of his first wife.

"In other words, you're looking at an engaged rabbi." Although the date has not been set, within the next few months—"probably sooner than later," he said—he will marry Leah Kalish, a 54-year-old woman from New York City, a widow of three years.

The rabbi, 57, explained why he made the bold announcement to the entire congregation, and why, by extension, he agreed to be interviewed by the *Citizen*, after the Sabbath. "I've always felt that, firstly, it's best to live a life in which you have nothing to hide. Secondly, when sharing things, it's always important to share things completely or not at all—

and to treat people respectfully and like adults and to tell everything that needs to be known that does not compromise anybody's privacy."

The decision to remarry now, he explained, was largely based on an understanding he worked out with his wife early in their marriage. "My wife and I had long ago talked about the fact that if, God forbid, either of us leaves this world that the other should as quickly, and as soon as they feel comfortable, go ahead and remarry. We never looked on this as a disloyalty to the first marriage, but on the contrary, it was a reinforcement of the fact that the marriage was good. Otherwise we wouldn't go into it again."

From the perspective of Jewish law, the official period of mourning is 30 days—the exception being the mourning period of a year after the death of a parent. From there, it's a question of personal readiness. "A number of months ago, I would not have been ready at all," he said.

Among those at Rabbi Bulka's level of religious observance, remarriage often happens in such a time frame. "It's not unusual in circumstances like this to get married what might be relatively soon, at least to an outsider," he said. He did accelerate the process a little, he said, to relieve the pressure on his five children, who live out of town, and on his congregants. Since May, when Naomi Bulka passed away, all of them, he said, have been making heroic efforts to ensure that he never spent a sabbath meal alone.

When the rabbi discreetly told a few people in New York that he was ready, they made some suggestions. Ms. Kalish was one of them. He did not know her before that, he explained. Ms. Kalish, in fact, was at one time a professional match-maker herself, arranging social events for single Jewish people to meet. Now she works for the National Conference of Synagogue Youth in New York. While

Ms. Kalish's first husband was not a rabbi, but a head hunter, her father, Rabbi Noah Rosenbloom, is a retired scholar of repute, Rabbi Bulka said. She has two sons, 20 and 19, who study in yeshiva, a Jewish seminary.

Although she will soon give up New York and move to Ottawa, Ms. Kalish has not visited Ottawa to see what the synagogue or her home will be like. She will be introduced to her new environment and the congregation after the wedding. "I guess her attitude is that either you trust or you don't," Rabbi Bulka said. "If you do, what's the difference? If a room's too big or a room's too small or the couch isn't your favourite colour, it doesn't add up to a hill of beans. When you get to this age, those things which should always be trivial become even more trivial." The wedding will likely be in New York, and it will be small, the rabbi said, out of respect for the first spouses of the couple. "But I have no doubt," he said, "that at the wedding, however small it may be, there will be tears coming out of her eyes and out of mine. You don't, when you make a step like this into the future, forget the past. You try to build upon it."

Rabbi Bulka said that while a second, later-in-life marriage will be different from one that produces children, he expects that it will be full of love. "I can tell you personally I was not looking just to have a partner that would be there just to share four walls with. That's not what it's about." The Orthodox Jewish approach to courtship and marriage is hard for some people outside the community to relate to, he said. "The Hollywood definition of love is probably more infatuation," he said, but that does not mean that the Orthodox way is unromantic. "Love is something in a sense magical, being linked in a spiritual oneness that is blissful, exhilarating," he said, "and it is something that builds through time. I consider myself fortunate that I was blessed to have such a great love in my first marriage, and I am looking forward to having that blessing in the second." ■

Source: *Ottawa Citizen.* (2002, February 4). p. D1.

1. What reasons did Rabbi Reuven Bulka give for remarrying?

2. How did he meet his fiancée?
3. What is the Orthodox Jewish custom concerning remarriage for widows and widowers?
4. How will this marriage benefit the Rabbi's children and community?
5. Do you agree with Rabbi Bulka's point of view concerning remarriage? Why or why not?

Unemployment and Early Retirement

Losing a job can be the most major psychological and social crisis for a man because it affects his identity in so many ways, and it may become a crisis for women now that they are employed at almost the same rate as men (Stevens-Long & Commons, 1992). Unemployment results from unexpected economic changes, such as plant closures, "downsizing," or the loss of a job due to age restrictions common to pilots, dancers, and athletes. Some individuals lose their jobs for personal reasons related to their competence or suitability to the job (Ward, 1990). Unemployment is more common for younger people and those with less education (Ward, 1990). However, between 1976 and 1995, there has been an increase in the rate of unemployment for men aged 55 to 64 (Conway, 1997).

Retirement is sometimes a gradual process involving several transitions in and out of the work force because those over age 50 who lose their jobs are less likely to find stable jobs (Statistics Canada, 2001). Those over 55 without the financial resources to take an early retirement face the transitional period of the "unretired retired" (Kimmel, 1990). Periods of economic crisis and rising unemployment, in which many people lose their jobs, can be devastating events for individuals (Rubin, 2001).

"We work to become, not to acquire."

—Elbert Hubbard

Work provides a framework for an individual's life structure. At work, people have clear roles to play, social contacts outside of family, meaningful activity, an identity, and status in the community (Ward, 1990). Since work provides opportunities for generativity for many men and a growing number of women, unemployment interferes with that generativity for many (Rubin, 1990). Unemployment or forced retirement can cause a deep sense of loss (Ward, 1990). Individuals respond to losing their jobs in three predictable stages:

- The first response is to deny the severity of the problem and to view unemployment as a break between jobs. People cope with the shock by getting busy with tasks that they have postponed around the home. Many unemployed Canadians do not even apply for employment insurance benefits, to which they are entitled at this stage.

- In the second stage, the increased distress leads to greater anxiety and inertia, which can hamper efforts at finding a job. Fulfilling the requirements for collecting Employment Insurance becomes an unpleasant reminder of the loss of status.

- If the individual does not find work, depression sets in. In this third stage, as individuals experience a loss of identity, they become tense, irritable, and increasingly alienated from society.

When a man is unemployed and his wife is working, it is natural for him to take on responsibility for household tasks. When the traditional roles are reversed, conflict can arise in a marriage.

When there is a widespread economic crisis within a community, such as the closing of a plant in a company town, this pattern breaks down quickly because there is nothing to support the optimism and cushion the blow (Rubin, 2001). On the other hand, similar stages can affect the transition to retirement. Some people are angry or depressed because of a failure to achieve in the workplace and feel unable to move on to other activities, even in retirement (Kimmel, 1990).

point of view | Job Insecurity Adds a "Chill Factor" to Work

by Judith Timson
Freelance Writer

There you have it—the two extremes of the current employment scene these days. The first one is characterized by an almost unbearable level of stress, and desire to get away from that stress, and the second by the fear of major layoffs taking away your job, even if you do hate it.

Headlines about rising levels of unemployment can be a handy motivational tool. In January 2002, we're at 8 percent, the highest level of unemployment in three years. With 1.3 million Canadians now out of work—and with bad news like the Ford announcement

early this month of a loss of about 1500 jobs in Oakville—people begin to genuinely obsess about whether they might even have a job, let alone what it's doing to their nervous systems.

They may even gravitate from one psychological extreme to the other. You can take this job and shove it—to me!

"How's that nasty boss of yours?" you ask a friend.

"Oh she's not that bad," she replies. "At least I have a job."

The attitude has turned to gratitude.

"Job insecurity does act as a chill factor," admits Martin Shain, a senior scientist at the Centre for

Addiction and Mental Health, and an expert on work and mental health. He likes to talk about the "biochemistry of fairness" in the workplace, which is an irresistible phrase for any workplace wonk. The fairer the workplace, says Shain, the happier and healthier the employees.

For most people, an intolerable stress level at work (which is not generated by personal issues at home) involves either working too long with too little control over one's working conditions (simply working long hours doesn't necessarily lead to burnout or stress) or working too hard for too little reward. In both cases, the result is a smouldering anger an employee feels at the unfairness of the situation.

Paula Allen of FGI, one of the largest providers of employee support, thinks that rising unemployment and the fear it generates "could shut down the anger" some people have about how they are being treated at work. But this doesn't mean that employers in a high-unemployment climate, which after all is only temporary, can forget about dealing with the issues that cause the anger in the first place, because, says Allen, the stress just doubles back even stronger. "Fear of losing your job can paralyze you to the point of inability to work at all," Allen says.

There has never been more openness than there is today about stress and burnout and breakdowns at work. Experts talk long and hard about balance in one's working life, surveys regularly warn about an epidemic of depression in the workplace and, says consultant Nora Spinks, there is about to be an explosion in stress leaves that will cost employers dearly if they don't address the root causes of psychological misery in the workplace.

Some employers are dancing as fast as they can, first to acknowledge there is a problem, and then to find ways to deal with it that won't bankrupt their companies in a vulnerable economic climate. There

High unemployment rates may influence people's attitudes toward their jobs.

are those who argue that there is too much permission to link one's mental health with one's work, and too much of a sense of entitlement in the workplace—as if it is a person's inalienable right to feel good about themselves at work. (Even the American Declaration of Independence, after all, only talks about the right to the "pursuit," not the acquisition, of such happiness.) That sense of entitlement may be tempered by the current unemployment scene. "Certainly anyone thinking of scamming the system might want to think again," says one consultant.

It's complicated to talk about how the current rising levels of unemployment—which are nowhere near the highest they've ever been—are affecting people's attitude about their jobs. We mean so many things when we talk about work. Work is financial stability, or at least viability. But it is also, for most people, synonymous with self-esteem, personal dignity, and a feeling of fulfillment or direction in life. Work also means how you're being treated—the actual conditions of employment.

So asking anyone "how's work?" these days can lead to a short, grateful outburst—"Hey, I'm still on the payroll"—or it could lead to the usual rant.

Maybe it depends on the headlines of the day. You might call it the biochemistry of the moment. ▪

Source: *The Toronto Star.* (2002, January 15).

1. What thesis does Judith Timson present in this article?
2. What evidence does she use to support her point of view?
3. Using social exchange theory, suggest how job insecurity might affect an individual's choices in the workplace.
4. Using a symbolic interactionist perspective, explain how job insecurity might affect a person's identity.
5. From a systems perspective, how might job insecurity affect a person's marriage and family?

Unemployment affects an individual's marriage and family. At first, families respond to the financial loss by the spouse increasing work hours or beginning to work (Ward, 1990). There is usually a change in the division of labour in the family as the unemployed man does the housework. These shifts in the roles of men and women are confusing for all members of the family (Rubin, 2001). The systems perspective explains that a change in the role of one member of the family requires a related change for others. Functionalism would suggest that problems arise in a traditional marriage, whether the man is unemployed or retired, when he leaves the workplace, where he was competent, and enters his wife's world (Kimmel, 1990). This alters the power balance of the family, further contributing to the sense of loss for the unemployed man (Ward, 1990). The financial crisis, identity loss, and shift in roles leads to marital problems. Fear of the future is unsettling, but then sexual problems develop as a side effect of anxiety and depression, conflict escalates, and in some marriages, alcohol abuse and sometimes violence against the spouse or children occurs. One in ten couples who experience long-term unemployment divorce (Rubin, 2001).

Couples in middle age are able to cope with unemployment more successfully because they are more likely to have developed the skills required. In midlife, couples are more financially stable if they have fewer debts, some savings, and a home that can be refinanced if necessary (Rubin, 2001). If they have been married for many years, they are more likely to have developed strategies for providing social support for each other and for resolving problems

web connection

www.mcgrawhill.ca/links/families12

To learn about unemployment and early retirement in Canada, go to the web site above for *Individuals and Families in a Diverse Society* to see where to go next.

(Dym & Glenn, 1993). However, unemployment near retirement age can have an impact on retirement income if it disrupts contributions to pensions and RRSPs (Statistics Canada, 2001). The transition to unemployment, forced retirement, or early retirement is easier when there are opportunities for anticipatory socialization for the role changes (Stevens-Long & Commons, 1992). Warnings of a downturn in industry, plant closings, or early retirement programs can allow individuals and families to prepare for the adjustments required, and for individuals to plan for career changes, a decline in work, or retirement (Stevens-Long & Commons, 1992).

Death and Mourning

"You have to learn to do everything, even to die."

—Gertrude Stein

Death is a natural life event. Critics of Western society suggest that we deny the inevitability of death, and as a result, we have difficulty in anticipating death, accepting death, and grieving. Some even suggest that we indulge in risky behaviours, such as eating foods high in fat, speeding when driving, and smoking, to defy death (McBride & Simms, 2001). Since death is separated from life as a medical event, Canadians have limited personal exposure to it and no anticipatory socialization for the appropriate attitudes or behaviours for dying or grieving (Kübler-Ross, 1969; McBride & Simms, 2001).

There is an assumption that, in old age, individuals accept death as a natural event (Howarth, 1998). As a society, we distinguish between a good and a bad death: a good death is a natural death in old age, but a bad death is "untimely" or "a waste of human life" (Howarth, 1998). As he neared his own death, Erik Erikson suggested that there might be a ninth stage of life in which individuals accept the inevitablity of their own death and become increasingly ready to die as they realize the limitations of their bodies and, sometimes, their minds (Erikson & Erikson, 1997). Earlier in the twentieth century, the **disengagement theory** suggested that as older people prepared for their own deaths, they became preoccupied with themselves and with thoughts of the past and withdrew from social activity. Recent research does not support this theory. A more current explanation is the **social death theory**, which argues that there is mutual withdrawing of older people and society (Howarth, 1998). Since death is unfamiliar, the anticipation of it is difficult. Individuals may cope by avoiding the dying and the bereaved (Kramer & Kramer, 1993).

If older people feel isolated from those around them, is it because they have become withdrawn and are reflecting on their lives and preparing for death, or is it because people are uncomfortable around those who are nearing death?

by Anne Mason, Vanier Institute of the Family

It wasn't as if his death was unexpected. The specialist had told us years before that the illness was terminal. But my father decided to live until he died, and his illness just became part of the family. When he went into hospital that Easter, it was simply another crisis to be managed. And then it wasn't. As I pulled into the parking lot at the hospital, I saw my sister standing on the sidewalk, smoking a cigarette. She had quit months before. I knew that things had changed.

The death of a parent can be a time of tremendous upheaval. The very core of the family is shaken and must be reshaped and rebuilt if it is not to fall apart. For the children, it is a loss of permanence and security. No matter what our age, we remain children as long as our parents are alive. We are protected from mortality by another generation.

As I entered my father's room, I saw the couple who were my parents. I saw a wife caring for her husband, one last time. I saw my father, frail and dying. He was already on a journey that he could only travel alone. And I knew I wasn't ready to let him go.

I felt the responsibility of a child to care for both my parents at that moment. I wanted to make those final hours or days a time for my mother to just be with him, without having to deal with all the awful but necessary mechanics of a hospital death. And I wanted more time.

It may be wishful thinking, but we tend to believe that dying is a gentle journey, with the dying person making final poignant expressions of love and reassurance. But experts tell us that dying is often filled with unmet hopes of reconciliation and completion. A dying person may not "go gently into

Clive and Vivienne Mason, the writer's parents.

that good night" and a family member—often the spouse—is usually on the receiving end of that sometimes angry struggle. Palliative care workers know that family members need tremendous support to understand that, for a dying person, the only safe place where they can direct their struggle—the one place of unconditional love—is their family. Right to the very end, a family is a place where they have to take you in, have to accept you for who you are.

Dying is no longer something we do easily within the family home. My family drew together to protect and comfort my father, to ensure that he was treated with dignity and respect in this institution called a hospital. And we discovered that those institutional people, those professional doctors and nurses, were also sons and daughters and parents. They were there for the living as well as the dying. As I lay on a cot beside my father's bed, they checked my "vital" signs too with offers of food, of a hug, of understanding and comfort through the long hours of the night.

They understood that this was a very special time for me. I had been given the gift of being with my father as he made his last journey. He had been there as I entered the world and I was able to be there as he left it. Truly the stuff of family. As my mother rested at home, I talked to my father, sang to him and, as the dawn began to break, I turned his face to the window so that we could share this one last beautiful sunrise. Father and daughter together for the last time. I said goodbye and I was ready.

My mother came and we left her alone with her love of over fifty years. My sisters and I drew close and held each other, knowing, without saying it, that our small family was no longer. We were entering a new time in our lives. A family was passing. ■

Source: *Transition Magazine*. (2001, Spring). p. 10. Published by the Vanier Institute of the Family.

1. What point of view about death does Anne Mason present in this article?
2. What reasons does she suggest for the stage of anger?
3. What evidence does she present to suggest that others experience similar stages in coming to terms with someone else's death?
4. How might the death of a parent affect a son's or a daughter's identity?

The emotional pain that results from fear of the unknown, loss of time and opportunity, guilt for things done or not done, or doubt about thoughts and feelings is greater than the physical pain endured by those with a chronic terminal illness (Kramer & Kramer, 1993). Dr. Elisabeth Kübler-Ross made it her life's work to study the process of dying to learn how to support those who are dying. She identified five stages of death, which are experienced in order, if there is time:

1. Denial of the diagnosis and attempting to find a solution or another explanation.

2. Anger at the fact of death, which might be directed at anyone, including self, family, or health-care staff.

3. Bargaining, with promises to alter who they are and what they do, to change the diagnosis.

4. Depression, arising from the certainty of death, and the resignation that there is no hope.

5. Acceptance, indicating that the individual has come to terms with his or her fate and is ready to prepare for the end of life.

A dying person goes through these stages as they come to terms with their own fate. Family, friends, and those involved in the person's care must also recognize the stages in themselves so that they are ready to enable the dying person to talk about their thoughts and prepare to die (Kübler-Ross, 1969).

Accepting the loss of a loved one is a long-term process of storing the times you shared together as memories before you are free to move on to new experiences alone.

by Glennys Howarth, Department of Behavioural Sciences, University of Sydney

RESEARCH QUESTION

What are the attitudes on death and dying of individuals over the age of 75?

HYPOTHESIS

Once an older person has completed a life review, they are freed to live in the present.

METHOD

This study was part of a larger longitudinal study of the quality of life of persons over the age of 75 who were living in their own homes. The study was conducted in London, England, between 1991 and 1993. To investigate the attitudes concerning death and dying, two interviews were conducted using 72 subjects in 55 households. Since the questions were open-ended, the answers reflect the spontaneous thoughts of the subjects and might not be representative of all older persons. Fifty-five percent of participants spoke about death.

RESULTS

Individuals distinguished between death of self and death of others:

- Although individuals desire a "good" death characterized by speed and ease, they also prefer to be able to prepare for death and have some sense of control. Those who were bereaved said that it is better for a dying person to know they are dying to be able to prepare for death.
- Older people view death as legitimate when they have completed their life goals.
- Considering funeral arrangements enables older people to prepare for death and control how others will remember them.
- Caring for a dying spouse is a natural extension of love and marriage, but it can be physically exhausting.
- Many subjects spoke of communicating with their late spouses in their minds.

CONCLUSIONS

Individuals vary in their attitudes toward death and dying for themselves and for others. If death is not "quick and easy," there appears to be a need for some control of the experience of dying. The author suggests allowing people to know when they are dying. People can be helped in dying by others providing care and relief from pain so that they are able to prepare for death through communication with those they love. ■

Source: *Ageing and Society*, Vol. 18, Part 6, Nov. 1998, pp. 673–689. Adapted with the permission of Cambridge University Press.

When individuals die, they leave **bereaved** families and friends who must cope with their emotional loss and make adjustments so that they can continue their lives without the deceased person. The **grieving process** occurs in three distinct but overlapping phases over a period of several years.

1. In the *shock phase*, bereaved individuals experience periods of numbness and crying. Daily activities will be disrupted and are completed with little thought or pleasure. At this time, others might wish to increase their closeness, but the bereaved person might prefer time alone.

web connection

www.mcgrawhill.ca/links/families12

To learn about death and mourning in Canada, go to the web site above for *Individuals and Families in a Diverse Society* to see where to go next.

2. In the *disorganization phase*, there is a need to talk about the deceased person and vent feelings of sadness, anger, anxiety, and guilt. A person might be less able to function in day-to-day life because of the necessity to make lifestyle changes. Unfortunately, other people are less available to talk after the brief period of mourning.

3. In the *reorganization phase*, new routines have been established for day-to-day life and there is less evident grief. The bereaved person has a new relationship with the deceased as someone they remember rather than someone with whom they share their life (McBride & Simms, 2001).

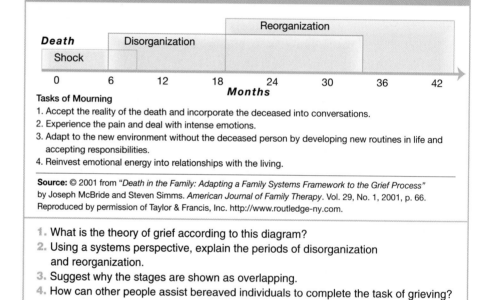

Grief Time Line

Tasks of Mourning
1. Accept the reality of the death and incorporate the deceased into conversations.
2. Experience the pain and deal with intense emotions.
3. Adapt to the new environment without the deceased person by developing new routines in life and accepting responsibilities.
4. Reinvest emotional energy into relationships with the living.

Source: © 2001 from *"Death in the Family: Adapting a Family Systems Framework to the Grief Process"* by Joseph McBride and Steven Simms. *American Journal of Family Therapy*. Vol. 29, No. 1, 2001, p. 66. Reproduced by permission of Taylor & Francis, Inc. http://www.routledge-ny.com.

1. What is the theory of grief according to this diagram?
2. Using a systems perspective, explain the periods of disorganization and reorganization.
3. Suggest why the stages are shown as overlapping.
4. How can other people assist bereaved individuals to complete the task of grieving?

"Honest listening is one of the best medicines we can offer the dying and the bereaved."

—Jean Cameron

Grieving takes time. Funerals and other social or religious rituals provide a framework for social behaviour so that others can support bereaved people (Kimmel, 1990). People can help those who are grieving by encouraging overt expressions of grief and by maintaining social contact throughout the grieving period (Walsh, 1989). To be ready to function in the future, a bereaved individual must first loosen the ties to the past by talking about the deceased person and their relationship. The more enduring the relationship, the more experiences that were shared with the deceased must be transformed into memories. A part of an individual's identity is put away with the memories

(Walsh, 1989). The systems perspective explains that others have to adjust their roles and absorb the behaviours that were the role of the deceased person (McBride & Simms, 2001). After about one year, a bereaved person will have returned to the routines of work, family, and social life. After about two years, he or she may be ready to take up new activities and interests (Walsh, 1989).

Elder Abuse

One of the recurring myths in North America is that seniors in the past and in other countries were treated with respect and compassion, but that people in contemporary times routinely confine and neglect them. The majority of older Canadians live in their own homes with their spouses or independently by their own choice (Vanier Institute of the Family, 1994). Greater concern for the well-being of all dependents, young and old, led to the new field of gerontology, revised filial responsibility laws, and increased reporting of the abuse and neglect of older people. **Elder abuse** is defined as conscious and unconscious acts involving physical, psychological, medical, material/financial, and legal harm. **Elder neglect** means failure to provide care (McPherson, 1990). Since children do not have a disciplinary role, there is no historical precedent for hitting a parent (Korbin, Anetzberger, & Eckert, 2001). Therefore, despite media headlines about "granny bashing" in the 1980s, the rate of elder abuse and neglect in Canada is fairly low (McPherson, 1990). However, unlike hitting children, there is a stigma attached to hitting older people, so victims are less likely to report the abuse (Ward, 1994).

In 1997, 2 percent of all elders in Canada reported being victims of crime. One-quarter of these crimes were perpetrated by family members, including 29 percent of all incidents for older women, and 17 percent of all incidents for older men (Ward, 1994). American figures estimate that 2.5 to 10 percent of all seniors experience some form of abuse or neglect (Ward, 1994), but recent studies suggest that only 1 in 5 or 1 in 6 report the crime (Korbin, Anetzberger, & Eckert, 2001). Victims tend to be socially isolated seniors with few social contacts and often nowhere to turn for support (Ward, 1994). Women aged 70 or older, who played the traditional spousal role and are therefore dependent, are most likely to be victims of abuse (Korbin, Anetzberger, & Eckert, 2001). Most is non-physical abuse (Ward, 1994); however, violence against elders is likely to be more severe because it is not approved and comes as a last resort when the abuser has lost control of his or her emotions. Psychological abuse is more likely to be reported than physical abuse, and severe abuse more than mild (Korbin, Anetzberger, & Eckert, 2001).

"Violence is essentially wordless, and it can begin only where thought and rational communication have broken down."

—Thomas Merton

Health care professionals can be trained to look for signs of abuse or neglect so that steps can be taken to ensure the health and well-being of older people.

In elder abuse, the elders are abused and neglected by members of the family, friends, and employees of institutions (McPherson, 1990). Elder abuse, like child abuse, occurs in situations in which victims are powerless against the middle generation (Korbin, Anetzberger, & Eckert, 2001). Most older people are abused by someone with whom they live. Twenty-five percent of abuse occurs at home and 43 percent in institutions (Ward, 1994). Canadian men and women are equally likely to be abused by their offspring, but women were twice as likely as men to be abused by their spouses (Statistics Canada, 1999). However, adult children are less likely to admit to slapping a parent than a spouse is, and the rate could be much higher (Korbin, Anetzberger, & Eckert, 2001). Sixty percent of family abusers were male, either sons or husbands. Abusers who work in institutions are more likely to be women because staff there is predominantly female (Ward, 1994).

Because elder abuse is either rare or underreported, it is difficult to explain why it occurs. Living with an elder requires a reinvestment of time and energy in a relationship that might have been distant. Often living arrangements result from a decline in the health and functioning of the older person, which will become increasingly troublesome (Korbin, Anetzberger, & Eckert, 2001). Several theoretical explanations have been suggested.

- From a social exchange perspective, caring for older seniors can be viewed as an unbalanced relationship (McPherson, 1990). Investment of time, money, and energy in parent care is seen as detrimental to an adult's own health and happiness. Difficult behaviours can be more stressful than actual physical tasks because there is no hope of the older person "growing out of it" (Korbin, Anetzberger, & Eckert, 2001).

- Symbolic interactionism suggests that individual perceptions of the older person's dependency will determine the amount of stress they feel (Korbin, Anetzberger, & Eckert, 2001). Personal factors of the abuser, such as work responsibilities, increasing age, personal health, alcohol, and financial or mental problems, determine how stressful the individual perceives the dependency to be (McPherson, 1990).

- Functionalism suggests that abuse might be the normative behaviour within a family. Some argue that individuals are socialized to accept violence as a way of acting out in a stressful situation. Roles are reversed when older people become dependent and there are fewer adult offspring to share the responsibility, and the stress can result in abuse (McPherson, 1990).

- The **theory of intergenerational transmission** suggests that people who were abused or neglected as children by their parents are likely to abuse or neglect their parents when they are very old. (McPherson, 1990).

by C. B. Dyer et al.

Older patients who have been abused or neglected have a significantly higher rate of depression and dementia, according to researchers in Houston. They studied 47 patients aged 65 and older, who were referred to a geriatric clinic for abuse or neglect, and compared them with 97 age-matched controls who were referred to the clinic for other reasons. All of the subjects underwent a comprehensive geriatric assessment. Scores on the Geriatric Depression Scale, the Mini-Mental State Examination, the Activities of Daily Living Scale, and the Instrumental Activities of Daily Living Scale were analyzed. Participants also underwent a medical history, physical exam, and an interview with a social worker.

Abuse or neglect was detected in 45 of the 47 suspected abuse cases referred to the clinic. Among abused or neglected patients, 37 had a diagnosis of self-neglect, and seven had been exposed to multiple forms of abuse and neglect. Subjects who had been abused or neglected were more likely to be white and male compared to those who were not abused or neglected. Abused or neglected patients also had significantly higher scores on the Geriatric Depression Scale than control patients. There was no difference in any of the other geriatric assessment measures. Patients who had been abused or neglected were far more likely to be diagnosed with depression (62 percent) or dementia (51 percent) than patients who were not abused or neglected (12 percent and 30 percent, respectively).

"This is the first published primary data study demonstrating that the prevalence of the clinical diagnosis of depression is increased in cases of elder neglect or abuse," conclude the authors. Depression can impair patients' decision-making abilities, rendering them unable to make good decisions about their care. It also may cause neglected patients to refuse medical care or assistance at home, the authors said. They concluded that physicians should rule out elder abuse or neglect in older patients who are depressed or demented. ■

Source: Based on Dyer, C.B., V.N. Pavlik, & K.P. Murphy, et al. (2000, February). "The high prevalence of depression and dementia in elder abuse or neglect." *Journal of the American Geriatric Society,* 48, pp. 205-208.

1. What is the authors' conclusion about this study?
2. What was the most common form of abuse or neglect detected in this study?
3. Which theoretical perspective best explains the effects of abuse and neglect on elders? Explain your choice.

Elder abuse can be prevented by teaching senior men and women how to be independent and by providing relief programs for caregivers (Ward, 1994). Social and community resources can reduce the stress for seniors and caregivers. Day programs and respite care can reduce the strain on full-time caregivers by freeing them temporarily of responsibilities for a dependent older person. The new field of gerontology is increasing people's understanding of the needs of elders so that staff at institutions can be trained in elder care. Training professionals and

web connection

www.mcgrawhill.ca/links/families12

To learn about elder abuse in Canada, go to the web site above for *Individuals and Families in a Diverse Society* to see where to go next.

police to report elder abuse and neglect can provide some assistance for the victims to move away from abusive relationships. Unlike the victims of child abuse, however, older seniors must be considered in decisions concerning their well-being. The justice system cannot provide the same protection for them as for abused children, because elders are adults who must make legal decisions and who must give permission for any actions on their behalf. However, there is no legal or social controversy—any abuse or neglect of older people is wrong (McPherson, 1990).

The Myth of the Dependency Crisis

"It is the meaning that men attribute to their life, it is their entire system of values, that defines the meaning and value of old age. The reverse applies: by the way in which a society behaves toward its old people it uncovers the naked, and often carefully hidden, truth about its real principles and aims."

—Simone de Beauvoir, *Old Age*

Some demographers have predicted that global aging presents a threat to world economies (Peterson, 1999). In Canada, there is increasing concern that the impending retirement of the large baby-boom generation, due to begin in 2010, will strain the resources of their children's generation. There is also apprehension that delayed parenthood will result in young parents also caring for their aging parents. However, Robert Glossop of the Vanier Institute of the Family counters that there is "no need for apocalyptic fears of dependency wiping out opportunity for the younger generation" because not only are people living longer and healthier lives, but they are also financing their old age through investment (Carey, 1999). The concerns of the younger generations regarding the **dependency crisis** can be summarized in these research questions:

- How is the dependency ratio in Canada changing?
- How will social security programs that support senior Canadians be funded?
- Will Canadians be able to afford health care for seniors?
- How much support will families provide for older individuals?
- How can Canadians reduce their dependency in old age?

In 1998, Canada's **dependency ratio** was 47.1. This economic ratio means that there were 47.1 children and seniors for every 100 people of working age. The dependency ratio declined from 1995 when children under 15 years were 20.4 percent of the population, seniors over 65 were 12.0 percent, and adults of working age (15 to 64 years) were 67.6 percent (Statistics Canada, 1998). The life expectancy of Canadians is rising, with men expected to live to 75.8 years and women to 81.4 years. Men can expect to be retired for 10.8 years and women for 16.1 years. More importantly, Canadian men can expect to live 93 percent of their lives in sound health, and women, 88 percent. That

by Judy Gerstel

"I'm here to apply for the position of music critic," the young woman, barely in her 20s, told the managing editor.

"What makes you think we need a music critic?" asked the surprised editor.

"I've been reading the music reviews," replied the young woman.

This happened more than 30 years ago at the *Buffalo Courier Express*, a newspaper that no longer exists. The young woman no longer exists either. But I remember her well, so well that I'm still embarrassed for her. I am also, if truth be told, a little in awe of her.

The passing of the torch from one generation to another has none of the grace of ceremony. Youth is swaddled in entitlement, intoxicated with discovery, dismissive of maturity. Youth is arrogant and greedy. It seizes what it wants like a big hungry baby. What is desired is deserved. Youth knows everything with certainty.

Maturity isn't sure about anything any more. Its grip loosens. Maturity doesn't exactly hand over the big jobs, the status, and the primacy, but grudgingly yields them, not without relief.

What youth is excited about discovering and regards as an original finding, maturity is weary of knowing and recognizes as recycled. As for cynicism, neither youth nor maturity has a monopoly. Ditto for idealism.

There's a tension between youth and maturity in the workplace that's creative if not comfortable. They may be impatient with each other, but there's solace and inspiration in sharing territory with another generation.

Youth's greatest advantage is what it lacks: the demons of awareness—of self, of limits, of consequences. Maturity is beset by those demons. They lurk and taunt and insinuate themselves into daily life and nightly rest. They resurrect the inhibitions and doubts that youth slays. The demons are notorious second guessers: "Why are you doing this? Aren't you losing your edge? Are your motives pure? Is what you're doing self-serving? Exploitive? Have you let ambition outstrip compassion? Have you done anything that matters? Do you realize how easily you can be replaced? Isn't it time to try something else, something new?"

A high-profile writer I know in his mid-50s who has easy access to superstars and celebrities for his stories in a New York daily feels he has nothing new to say and wants to leave his job to work in the non-profit sector at half the salary. An obstetrician/gynecologist, also in his mid-50s, no longer feels bonded to his patients, no longer finds the same joy or challenge in saving the lives of a hemorrhaging woman and the newborn she's delivering. He believes that his hands move infinitesimally more slowly now during surgery, although it's undetectable to anyone but himself. He wants to study history and learn something new about himself and the world. A symphony musician in his 50s finds that, after decades of bravado, his nerves occasionally overtake him, making him sweat through concerts and wonder if he can hold the bow steady, though he rarely errs. He wants to leave the city and live in nature and do volunteer work.

If youth outpaces maturity, it's not only because youth is fresher and fleeter and has more stamina, but also because maturity is no longer seduced by the road race, let alone the lure of the medal. Maturity, glimpsing the finish line and unnerved a little by the sight, wants to wander off into the forests at the side of the road and sit by the stream. Or, more likely, hike for kilometres through the mountains on the horizon and bike all day through the valleys.

I did get the job as music critic at the *Buffalo Courier Express* and the man I replaced, who had been reviewing concerts part-time and writing obituaries the rest of the time, was reassigned to obits full-time. But then, he was old, in his mid-50s. ■

Source: *The Toronto Star* (2001, January 12). p. F2. Reprinted with permission–The Toronto Star Syndicate.

1. What thesis is Judy Gerstel presenting in this essay?
2. What arguments does she present to support her point of view?
3. Gerstel refers to the tension between young and mature individuals at work. Using conflict theory, explain why that tension might extend to the entire younger and older generations.
4. Does the research on adult development and aging support the argument that "maturity is no longer seduced by the road race"?
5. What would be the economic impact if aging Canadian workers were expected to retire to make way for younger workers?

means that the **dependency-free expectancy** for Canadian men is 72 years, and for women, 73.9 years (Statistics Canada, 1999). The growth in the number of people over age 65 is balanced somewhat by a decline in the number of children under age 15 because of a declining birth rate. In fact, the peak in the dependency burden in Canada has already occurred—when baby boomers were children under 15 years (Keating & Cook, 2001).

The idea of a dependency crisis is based on concern about the social programs that the Canadian governments provide for its citizens. Education, health care, and social security are assumed to be essential services that benefit society. Social programs are funded from personal income taxes and contributions paid by the working population and are provided to all who need them. Clearly, the greater the proportion of the population that is working, the more the responsibility of paying for social programs will be shared. Children receiving education and health care are not paying income taxes and, therefore, are dependent. People over the age of 65 who receive the Canada or Quebec Pension Plan pensions and are receiving health care pay income taxes on a reduced income and are also considered to be dependents.

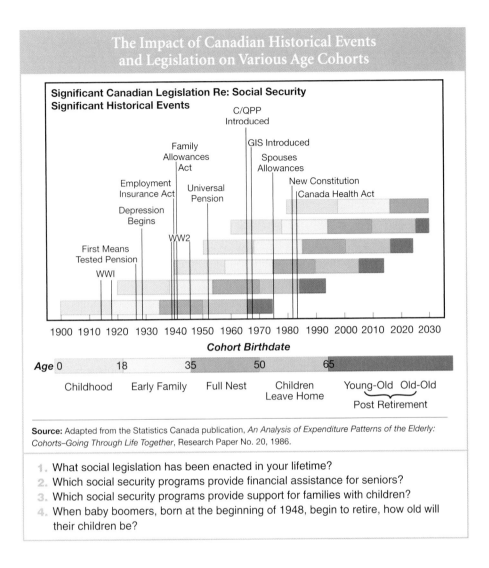

The Impact of Canadian Historical Events and Legislation on Various Age Cohorts

Significant Canadian Legislation Re: Social Security
Significant Historical Events

C/QPP Introduced

GIS Introduced

Family Allowances Act

Spouses Allowances

Employment Insurance Act

Universal Pension

New Constitution
Canada Health Act

Depression Begins

WW2

First Means Tested Pension

WWI

1900 1910 1920 1930 1940 1950 1960 1970 1980 1990 2000 2010 2020 2030

Cohort Birthdate

Age 0   18   35   50   65

Childhood   Early Family   Full Nest   Children Leave Home   Young-Old Old-Old

Post Retirement

Source: Adapted from the Statistics Canada publication, *An Analysis of Expenditure Patterns of the Elderly: Cohorts–Going Through Life Together*, Research Paper No. 20, 1986.

1. What social legislation has been enacted in your lifetime?
2. Which social security programs provide financial assistance for seniors?
3. Which social security programs provide support for families with children?
4. When baby boomers, born at the beginning of 1948, begin to retire, how old will their children be?

When Canadians retire they no longer have income from employment, and they begin to depend on retirement income. They cease paying into the Canada or Quebec Pension Plans and start to collect their pension. Many Canadians also collect company pensions and RRSPs. The availability of pension funds is influenced by the number of people contributing to the fund. As women's employment has increased, the contributions to CPP/QPP and to company pensions has increased, but so has the number of people eligible to collect a pension. Since contributions are based on earnings, unemployment and underemployment at any age could have an impact on the amount of retirement income because of reduced opportunity to contribute (Statistics Canada, 2000). Early retirement was introduced when private pension funds were earning high interest and when

A retirement income that includes government pensions, private pensions, and investment income from RRSPs allows older Canadians to enjoy their leisure time.

companies and governments wanted to reduce the number of workers. When there is a lower return on invested pension funds and a shortage of labour, early retirement no longer makes sense financially (Ambachtsheer, 2002). For those who are retiring soon, private pensions and RRSPs will provide the majority of retirement income (Carey, 1999; Myles, 2000).

The Canada Health Act ensures that all Canadians have access to medically required hospitals' and physicians' services. Since the costs of health care are paid out of "general revenues"—that is, out of personal and corporate income taxes—health care is funded by the working population. There are predictions that the aging population will strain the health care system. "Our aging population means that health-care bills will rise sharply at the same time as the proportion of workers shrinks," predicted Tom d'Aquino of the Business Council on National Issues (Walkom, 2001). This prediction is based on the assumption that, in the future, seniors will be as sick or will have as many disabilities as those in the past. However, older Canadians are healthier than they were in the past. The promotion of healthy, active lifestyles has resulted in an aging population that is more active and has a more nutritious diet (Keating & Cook, 2001). The Canada Health Act also has improved the health of aging Canadians by providing better health care (Walkom, 2001).

point of view | A Greyer Canada of the Future

In his book *Boom, Bust & Echo,* David Foot examines the changing demographic profile of Canada at the beginning of the twenty-first century and the profound implications that this change will have on the economic and social life of Canada in the next 20 to 25 years. One of the many things Foot examines is the impact of an increasing aging population in Canada.

David K. Foot, Professor of Economics at the University of Toronto, is co-author of the bestselling book *Boom, Bust & Echo.*

In contrast to what many of our politicians and some of the Canadian media have been suggesting over the past few years, Foot suggests that the greying of Canada's population over the next generation may not turn out to be as financially problematic after all.

The prevailing wisdom is that as more and more Canadians become 65 years of age and older, there will be direct conflict between a minority of working young and a majority of "greedy geezers," who will be demanding more and more government spending in areas of concern to them, particularly in health care. In addition, as Canadians live longer, they will be collecting pensions longer, which will again have to be paid for out of the pension deductions of the minority of "working young." Foot suggests a much different scenario, however.

Firstly, he argues that the research shows that older Canadians are staying healthier much longer and that seniors' health improvements will result in less economic strain on Canada's health care system than many politicians have been suggesting. Secondly, Foot debunks the claim made by many futurists that Canada is about to become a society dominated by older people. The statistics actually tell a very different story from the perceptions that many Canadians have. Far from being the most rapidly aging society in the world, Canada is actually in a much better position than most industrialized societies.

In fact, in 1998, Canada had only 12 percent of its population over the age of 65, whereas Sweden's was 17 percent in the same year. Demographic projections, according to Foot, suggest that Canada will not reach 17 percent until the year 2020, and that at its highest level, our oldest cohort will not exceed 22 percent of the total population, which is a long way from being a majority of the population. Japan, for example, has a much more rapidly aging population due to a lower birth rate and restrictive policies that prevent population growth through immigration. Therefore, even though traditionally both children and seniors have depended on working-age people to help support them, Canada will have a more favourable ratio—more than two workers per dependent—of any country in the world. This last fact, combined with the fact that Canadian seniors are now and will continue to be the wealthiest of our age cohorts, suggests that in the immediate future, older Canadians are not likely to be the financial burden to working Canadians that many have predicted they will be. ■

Source: Based on Foot, David K., *Boom, Bust & Echo: Profiting from the Demographic Shift in the 21st Century*. Toronto: Macfarlane, Walter & Ross, 1998. Adapted with permission from Footwork Consulting Inc.

1. What point of view does David Foot present concerning the dependency of older Canadians?
2. What arguments are presented to support this point of view?
3. What would be the consequences for your generation if Foot is wrong?
4. Assuming Foot is wrong, what changes would be required in Canada?

Ontario's Family Law Act and similar laws in other provinces require adult children to support their aged parents, but few claims are ever made (Bracci, 2000). Most Canadians live independently into old age, alone or with their spouses. Married people live longer, have higher incomes, are healthier, have spouses to provide care, and are therefore less likely to need support from their children. Unmarried people are less healthy and require more support from their children (Pienta, Hayward, & Jenkins, 2000). Those who care for older spouses who need support speak of their responsibilities in terms of their marriage vows, "in sickness and in health," and are reluctant to relinquish the care until it becomes too demanding for their physical abilities. Adult children also describe their role as returning the care their parents provided for them (Vanier Institute of the Family, 2001). The dementia resulting from Alzheimer's disease

by Justice Marvin Zuker

Power of attorney is based on the ability of a person to delegate authority. *The Substitute Decisions Act*, proclaimed on April 3, 1995, has enlarged the scope of potential delegation to include personal decision making and the ability to make what is popularly known as a living will.

A power of attorney is an authority given by one person (the grantor or principal) to another person (the attorney) to act on behalf of the grantor in conducting his or her financial affairs or in making personal decisions for the grantor. For example, a power of attorney dealing with

personal decision making might be limited to determining medical treatment to be administered or withheld. The attorney is legally recognized as the agent of the grantor.

A power or attorney for personal care can only be used when the grantor is incapable of making personal decisions as defined in the law. A prime motivation for signing such a document is to convey specific instructions about medical procedures the grantor does *not* wish to have performed or to provide a general statement as to the grantor's philosophy (for example, when would be an appropriate time to cease taking "heroic measures" to prolong the grantor's life when all quality of life has gone). ■

can be especially challenging for caregivers, as the person becomes increasingly unlike his or her former self and then is unable to function (Larson, Goltz & Munro, 2000). On the other hand, children of divorced parents may have unresolved issues resulting from the divorce that might affect caregiving relationships (Pienta, Hayward, & Jenkins, 2000). The stereotype of dependent elders is also challenged by recent studies in the United States explaining that in many extended families in which aging parents and adult children live together, it is the adult children who are living with and still being supported by, to some extent, their parents (Lee & Dwyre, 1996).

Sociologists Lyle E. Larson, J. Walyter Goltz, and Brenda E. Munro (2000) suggest that describing the aging population of Canada and other countries as a problem is a social construction that does not reflect the facts. They use conflict theory to suggest that the dependency crisis results from the competition between the dominant middle generations and the aging generations. The aging generations, including the large baby-boom generation, feel entitled to the benefits of a lifetime of income taxes and CPP/QPP contributions. On the other hand, the smaller middle generation, which is becoming the dominant group, seek to restrict the claims of seniors to reduce their own taxes and limit their CPP/QPP contributions. Some people have suggested that private pensions and personal RRSPs should replace government pensions and that the introduction of private health care would benefit the working generation and reduce the support available to seniors. Political journalist Thomas Walkom supports the conflict perspective and suggests that the conflict is based on a moral judgment of the baby-boom generation as "selfish, self-absorbed, and self-indulgent" (2001). The next twenty years will see the outcome of the "dependency crisis" controversy and, perhaps, ensure that the well-being of the younger generation will be secure when they inevitably reach old age.

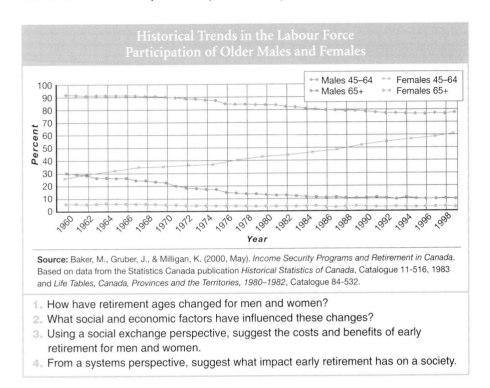

Historical Trends in the Labour Force Participation of Older Males and Females

Source: Baker, M., Gruber, J., & Milligan, K. (2000, May). *Income Security Programs and Retirement in Canada*. Based on data from the Statistics Canada publication *Historical Statistics of Canada*, Catalogue 11-516, 1983 and *Life Tables, Canada, Provinces and the Territories, 1980–1982*, Catalogue 84-532.

1. How have retirement ages changed for men and women?
2. What social and economic factors have influenced these changes?
3. Using a social exchange perspective, suggest the costs and benefits of early retirement for men and women.
4. From a systems perspective, suggest what impact early retirement has on a society.

Individuals, families, and governments can act to reduce the dependency of elders. Individuals can develop effective financial plans early in adulthood, that include investment in private pension plans, when they are available, and in contributions to RRSPs. Saving for retirement early in life will reduce the income available for lifestyle expenses, but it will ensure that individuals and families are living within their income and not accumulating debt (Chilton, 2001). Individuals can improve their dependence-free life expectancy by choosing a healthy lifestyle and limiting their exposure to harmful environments (Statistics Canada, 2001). There is convincing evidence that marrying and staying married also improves peoples' health and longevity and reduces their need for outside support (Pienta, Hayward, & Jenkins, 2000).

The Canadian government has enacted several policies and is investigating others that will reduce the dependency of seniors. Contributions to CPP/QPP were increased to raise the pension funds available. Old Age Security benefits

"The point to remember is that what the government gives it must first take away."

—John S. Coleman

web connection

www.mcgrawhill.ca/links/families12

To learn about dependency in later life in Canada, go to the web site above for *Individuals and Families in a Diverse Society* to see where to go next.

were reduced by the "clawback" of benefits from those with higher incomes. Government has shifted the pension burden to private pensions by introducing tax deductions and tax-deferred RRSPs. It is currently investigating the impact of delaying the qualifying age for CPP/QPP on retirement ages (Baker, Gruber, & Milligan, 2000). There are suggestions that the mandatory retirement age be eliminated or raised. Sweden and the Netherlands have successfully introduced partial pension provisions to encourage older people to work part-time to make a gradual transition into retirement and reduce the added costs of early retirement (Statistics Canada, 2001).

case study | Toni's Independence

When Toni Casullo was growing up on a small market farm north of Toronto, she dreamed about getting married and having children—lots of them! She was the last of seven children born to her Italian-Canadian parents who were among the first wave of immigrants to Ontario in the 1920s from Calabria, southern Italy. Unlike Toni, her first husband, Lou, was not Canadian-born. His family came to Canada during the second and much larger migration of Italians to Toronto in the late 1940s and 1950s.

Toni married Lou when she was only 16—far too young, as she constantly reminds her grandchildren. Their marriage was not a happy one, perhaps because they were both so young and because their first daughter, Gina, was born so soon after they married. Lou left Toni shortly after their fourth child, Louisa, was born, and they were divorced a few years later, a decision that shocked their Italian-Canadian families. Toni and her children lived with her widowed mother, and Toni worked to support her family.

The love of Toni's life was Ron, her second husband. She met him at a union meeting after work one day, and there was an immediate connection between them. Like Toni, Ron had been in an unhappy marriage, one of the many things that they had in common. His first wife had recently returned to England, leaving Ron with the children. When Lou left Toni and her four

After a life full of ups and downs, Toni is now enjoying being the matriarch of a large extended family.

young children and moved to Vancouver, Ron became more and more a part of her life. Eventually they moved in together. With Ron's three children and her four, Toni had the large family that she had always dreamed about. After several years and one postponed wedding, they married.

Their first few years together were sometimes rocky, however. Toni had difficulty, at times, being a stepmother to Ron's teenaged children, especially since she was only 12 years older than the oldest, Pamela. There were conflicts among the children too, because the teenagers had known each other before their parents got together. Also, Toni and Ron had to bear the entire cost of raising all the children, as well as the cost of their divorces. However, they both worked very hard toward a common goal of owning a home and, by the mid-1970s, after Ron had received a significant promotion at work, they were able to. Toni was also able to stop working, which she was glad to do because her congenital hip problem was causing her a great deal of pain by that time. She gladly took over the care of her first grandchild, Sarah, who became for her and Ron the child that they had been unable to have together.

Later, after Ron had heart surgery, he could not return to work. He received a disability pension until he retired two years later. Toni found the adjustment of having Ron at home a challenge. Although they were able to travel to Florida and establish a leisurely lifestyle, Ron found it difficult to fill his time and he missed the social contact at work. He had always shared in the cooking and housework, but when he developed an interest in making pickles and preserves for the entire family, Toni suggested that his next project should be to convert a room in the basement into a second kitchen so that she could have hers back!

Now, as Toni looks back on the life she shared with Ron, she is more inclined to remember the good times they had together. However, her life had its misfortunes as well as its rewards. Toni's oldest daughter, Gina, was a constant source of concern to her as she struggled to cope with drug addiction. For long periods of time, she would disappear from their lives only to reappear to ask for money to see her through a rough period. Also, Toni's son Joe had suffered serious head injuries in a motorcycle accident. Although he eventually recovered, he was never able to live independently and was, therefore, living in an adult group home and surviving on a government pension. When Gina, who was never able to overcome her addiction and live a more normal life, committed suicide in 1996, the rest of Toni's family came forward to share her grief and to help her get through this very difficult period.

Over the years, Toni coped with other tragedies, such as the death of her son-in-law and, more recently, the loss of one of her grandsons, but the most difficult one was Ron's sudden death from a heart attack in 1998. Even today, she misses him terribly and gets angry that he has abandoned her, since she feels that their life together should not be over yet. When her daughter Pamela complained recently about her husband's absence from home because of work, Toni talked to her about Ron and how she is constantly reminded of his absence as she performs those things that he once did for her. She misses his chatter and knowing that he is close by if she needs him, and feels that it is especially painful because she knows that he is never coming back.

Toni's income from pensions, survivor's pensions, and RRSP investments allow her to live a comfortable life in the condominium she and Ron moved to shortly before his death. However, her hip problem has become worse in the past few years and, despite a hip replacement operation, she is unable to drive and can only get around with the aid of a walker. Toni can no longer paint, which she once loved to do, so she spends her time doing needlework, which decorates the walls of her and her children's homes. Toni reminds herself that she has a wonderful family and that she has been fortunate these past few years to be surrounded by her children and grandchildren. She is proud of her grandchildren's accomplishments and looks forward to the birth of her first great-grandchild. Toni enjoys her life as the matriarch of such a large and loving family. ■

---

1. Create a genogram to analyze the relationships within Toni and Ron's blended family.
2. From a functionalist perspective, what factors have contributed to the success of Ron and Toni's second marriage?
3. Compare Toni's departure from work to Ron's. How were their transitions different?
4. Using the grief time line on page 466, explain how Toni is mourning Ron.
5. What events have contributed to Toni's satisfaction in later life?

chapter 14 Review and Apply

Knowledge/Understanding   Thinking/Inquiry

1. Remarriages are less durable than first marriages. Summarize the issues that challenge remarried couples and blended families and describe the strategies for managing each issue to enhance the chances of an enduring relationship.

2. Widowers are more likely to remarry than widows. Using the social exchange theory, assess the advantages and disadvantages of remarriage for men and for women.

3. Compare the effects of unemployment and retirement on men and their marriages in later life.

4. If there is "good death" and "bad death," what would a good death from illness be like, according to the research described in this chapter?

5. What are the similarities and differences between child abuse and elder abuse? Consider:
   - characteristics of the victim
   - characteristics of the perpetrator
   - nature of the abuse
   - theoretical explanations

6. Summarize the evidence to answer the middle generations' concerns about the dependency crisis:
   - How is the dependency ratio changing in Canada?
   - How will Canadians pay for the social security programs that support seniors?
   - Will Canadians be able to afford health care for seniors?
   - How much support will families provide for older individuals?

Knowledge/Understanding   Thinking/Inquiry   Communication

7. Write a letter from a parent to his or her adult children explaining the reasons for remarrying that reflect the results of the research presented in this chapter.

8. Investigate the community resources that are available to support unemployed workers. Design a pamphlet to promote the use of these resources.

9. Write a brief article addressed to adults suggesting how they can provide support to bereaved individuals as they complete the tasks of mourning.

10. Educating seniors can reduce the incidence of elder abuse. Design a poster to be displayed in public places to increase awareness of the nature of elder abuse and neglect.

11. Write an essay that explains the dependency issue in Canada from a functionalist perspective. Include the concepts of role, status, and socialization.

Knowledge/Understanding   Thinking/Inquiry   Communication   Application

12. Using one of the following theoretical perspectives, design and conduct a research study to compare the perceptions of married and remarried couples concerning the factors that have made their marriages successful.
- symbolic interactionism
- social exchange theory
- systems theory

Present the results as a research report.

13. Retirement, early retirement, and unemployment require adjustments in an individual's identity by challenging their financial and lifestyle security. Investigate the financial programs available in Canada and several points of view on the best strategies for providing financial security for individuals and families. Write a research essay summarizing the recommendations for long-term financial planning for young adults to enable them to weather the challenges of middle and later adulthood.

Appendix
Guide to Reading Research Reports

Reading research reports can enable you to gather information about the research that has been done by others on your research question. The format of published studies varies somewhat according to the style of the particular academic journal, but the general outline is the same. The **introduction** explains the background, the rationale, and the purpose of the study. As you read the **method**, notice how the sample group was selected and how the study was conducted. Examine the **results** to determine how many subjects completed the study (n) and the distribution of their answers. Read and summarize the **conclusions** so that you can refer to them in your own research and, perhaps, identify areas requiring further study.

Published research reports have been written by scientists and graduate students to be read by a highly qualified audience. The language and the style used in the reports are highly academic and precise, and often include the specific terminology of statistics and of the subject. You will probably encounter terminology and mathematical calculations that you have not learned yet. You could look up terms that you do not understand on the Internet if you want to learn them now. Because research reports are exposed to strict peer review, you can assume that the statistical analysis is accurate and that you can skip over any mathematical analysis that is beyond your skills at this time and still understand the results and conclusions of the study.

web connection

www.mcgrawhill.ca/links/families12

To learn about the use of statistical analysis in research go to the web site above, then to *Individuals and Families in a Diverse Society* to see where to go next.

---

research study | Young Women's Expected and Preferred Patterns of Employment and Child Care

by F. Heather Davey

There is a long-standing assumption in occupational psychology that most women plan their occupations to accommodate their plans for marriage and family because they place greater value on the latter roles (e.g., Angrist, 1969; Angrist & Almquist, 1975). More recently, researchers have found a strong commitment to both career and family roles among both college women (Baber &

Monaghan, 1988; Nevill & Super, 1988) and high school girls (Davey, 1992; Farmer, 1983). Since most young women apparently still plan to marry and to have at least one child (Baber & Monaghan, 1988; Schroeder, Blood, & Maluso, 1992), this shift from earlier findings appears to represent an increased commitment to one's career, with no reduction of commitment to family roles. However, these students had not yet faced the challenge of combining these roles. Therefore, the question of how, or even whether, they would meet this challenge remains unanswered in these studies.

There is some evidence to suggest that young women who place a high value on paid employment may still expect to curtail their career involvement because of competing family responsibilities. For example, Gaskell's (1983) study of working-class high school seniors revealed that most expected to give up their jobs upon becoming mothers because they did not anticipate earning enough to afford child care, nor did they believe that their future husbands would share child-care responsibilities. Similarly, surveys of university women have indicated that most respondents expected to interrupt their careers for significant periods of time in order to care for their children (Greenglass & Devins, 1982; Machung, 1989; Schroeder et al., 1992). Machung concluded that the career and family expectations of many of these women were incompatible and, therefore, unrealistic. She suggested that these young women failed to acknowledge the inconsistencies in their expectations because they did not know how to reconcile them. On the other hand, Granrose's (1985) sample of college women tended to expect to fit their childrearing around their careers, although she also noted that the majority lacked specific strategies for implementing this expectation.

In summary, the literature shows that by the early 1990s, the values of young women had evolved to include a high regard for both family and career involvement. Nevertheless, most young women still expected to follow the traditional pattern of discontinuous participation in the labour force in order to care for their children. While this expectation may reflect a priority for family concerns for some

women, for others it illustrates practical constraints such as lack of affordable child care (Gaskell, 1983) or social pressure (Cook, 1993).

In sharp contrast to the expectations of most young women in these studies, the census data from the past twenty years reveal a significant increase in the labour force participation rates of married women with young children. For example, the participation rate of American women who have a child less than one year old increased from 38 percent to 54 percent between 1980 and 1992; during that same period, the overall labour force participation rate for American women increased from 66 percent to 72 percent (U.S. Bureau of the Census, 1993). Clearly the participation rate for women with young children was growing more rapidly during this period than the participation of women overall. Similarly, in Canada the greatest increase in labour force participation rates since 1976 has been observed among women whose youngest child is under three years of age, from 32 percent to 62 percent (Statistics Canada, 1990).

In light of the steadily increasing participation rates of mothers of young children in the labour force over the past twenty years, it is reasonable to ask whether young women still expect to interrupt their paid employment to care for young children. Furthermore, the earlier studies did not explore the relationship between expectations and later experiences. As Schroeder et al. (1992) have noted, longitudinal studies are needed to determine the relationship between young women's earlier lifestyle preferences and their later behaviour. Therefore, the present study was designed to examine young women's values and expectations for both family and paid employment roles, and to determine the stability of these values and expectations over time.

METHOD

Participants

The sample consisted of 54 white Canadian women who had participated in a survey of occupational aspirations and expectations while in senior high school (Grades 10–12) and were willing to participate in a follow-up study (Davey, 1993). The participants' socio-economic backgrounds, determined from parents' occupations, ranged from blue collar to professional. The age range of the participants in the first study was 15 to 20 years, with a mean of 17.0 years.

In the intervening four years, all of the respondents had completed high school. Eight had entered the labour force directly after high school, 10 were in or had completed courses at a private college or a community college, 7 had left a post-secondary program without completing it, and 29 were still in or had completed university degree programs. Of this last group, 16 were employed full time or part-time at the time of the follow-up, and 3 were seeking employment. Six respondents had married during this time, and 4 of these had also become parents. Two mothers were working part time at home, 1 was at university, and 1 was in a college program.

Procedure

In the original study, participants were randomly selected to participate in a lengthy occupational survey that included questions about their preferences and expectations for combining employment and child-care responsibilities. Respondents indicated their preferences and expectations separately on a 3-point Likert-type scale on which 1–leave work before the first child is born, 2–work until the first child is born and again after the youngest child reaches a certain age (indicated by the respondent), and 3–work continuously, taking maternity leaves

as needed. Another question asked them to choose the combination of work and/or family roles they would prefer to have at age 30 from a list of all possible combinations of these variables ranging from unmarried and employed full time, to married and full-time homemaker with children (see Table 1).

Those students who expressed a willingness to participate in a follow-up to the original study received another questionnaire by mail four years later. Analyses were conducted (analysis of variance and chi-square, depending on the nature of the variables) to compare the data in the original study from the 34 respondents who participated in the follow-up, with the data from 126 respondents who participated only in the first survey. All contrasts were non-significant (p [greater than] .05), therefore, the smaller sample was deemed to be representative of the original sample.

RESULTS

The preferences and expectations of the respondents for combining career and family roles, recorded on the two occasions, are shown in Table II (not shown). Four chi-square tests were conducted to compare preferences over time, expectations over time, and preferences vs. expectations at each testing time. Because four tests were done, an alpha level of .0125 was used for each test to yield an overall alpha of .05. The respondents' preferences did not change significantly from high school to four years later ([[Chi.sup 2] = 0.99, df = 2, p [greater than] 0.125). Similarly, their expectations did not change significantly ([[Chi).sup 2] = 5.72, df = 2, p [greater than] .0125). Furthermore, their preference and expectations while still in high school were not significantly discrepant ([[Chi].sup.2 = 3.06, df = 2 p [greater than] .0125). However, their preferences and expectations after four years had become discrepant (ll Chi].sup2] = 10.00.df = 2.p [less than] .0125).

Preferences	Initial n (%)	Follow-Up n (%)
Homemaker, with children	1 (1.9)	3 (5.6)
Homemaker, no children	1 (1.9)	0 (0.0)
Unmarried career person, with children	1 (1.9)	0 (0.0)
Unmarried career person, with no children	3 (5.6)	2 (3.7)
Married career person, with children	42 (77.8)	40 (74.1)
Married career person, no children	5 (9.3)	6 (11.1)
Other	1 (1.9)	3 (5.6)

The data in Table II (not shown) reveal that, as high school students, most respondents expected to realize their preferred pattern of employment. Furthermore, for most of them, preferences did not change over time, whereas expectations did; four years later, a greater number of women expected to remain in paid employment without significant interruption, although preference for this option did not show a corresponding increase. Although this change in expectations was not statistically significant, it was a strong contributor to the emerging discrepancy between preferences and expectations. With respect to their preferred combination of roles at age thirty (Table I), the overwhelming majority preferred the option of married career woman with children, both in the first survey and at the follow-up four years later. Of the respondents who chose the final option ("Other"), one was undecided on both occasions, one hoped to be married with children and self-employed, one was unsure about marriage but determined to always work, and the last respondent, a visually impaired woman, preferred to be unmarried and working part-time. It is noteworthy that while this expanded question covered more options than did the first question, only 5 respondents chose options not covered in the first question. These options included not marrying, working part-time, being self-employed, and being unsure of preferences.

DISCUSSION

Angrist's (1969) early work documented a clear priority among the majority of college women for family roles over career roles. Later researchers have generally found that adolescent girls and young women expressed a high regard for both career and family roles (Davey, 1992; Farmer, 1981, Nevill & Super, 1988). In spite of this change in values, researchers continued to find that most young women expected significant interruptions in their careers in order to accommodate their family responsibilities (Gaskell, 1983; Greenglass & Devins, 1982; Machung, 1989; Schroeder et al., 1992). Apparently values were changing more rapidly than expectations. In contrast, the majority of the respondents in the present survey expected to work continuously. Between the first survey, when all the respondents were still in high school, and in the follow-up four years later, this expectation became even more widespread. The present findings suggest that most young women now expect to participate in career and family roles concurrently, rather than consecutively.

The majority of the young women in earlier studies (e.g., Gaskell, 1983; Machung, 1989) clearly expected that their husbands' incomes would be sufficient for the needs of their families. That the majority of the respondents in the present study expected continuous employment, a finding consistent with the employment trends among mothers of young children (Statistics Canada, 1990; U.S. Bureau of the Census, 1993), suggests that most young women no longer share this expectation. Since some of these young women would have preferred to stay home with young children, it appears that behaviour changes may now be outstripping changes in values and priorities. Perhaps the greatest impetus to this change has been the erosion of individual income (Statistics Canada, 1995). For example, the number of two-parent families living below the poverty level in Canada would nearly double if no mothers were employed (Lero, 1992). Perhaps this sample's change in employment expectations over time represents an increased awareness of economic realities.

The preference of a strong majority of young women in this sample to be a married career woman with children at age thirty is consistent with the high value for both career and family roles expressed by young women in previous studies (Davey, 1992; Farmer, 1983; Nevill & Super, 1988). Clearly, many young women are personally invested in attaining both roles. It is interesting to note that even women who wish to care full time for their children when they are young can have a strong image of themselves as career women. In other words, these women do not define career women in the narrow sense of women who place a higher priority on paid employment than on marriage and family. Instead, it would appear that they hope to strike a balance between career and family roles, or to alternate roles somewhat. If so, it would help to explain the inconsistencies noted by Machung (1989) in her sample's responses.

An important limitation of this study is the relatively short time period involved. Many respondents had not yet settled into a career when contacted the second time, and only four had become parents. It is interesting to note that, despite this limitation, a significant number of women had already revised their expectations regarding involvement in paid employment. Clearly these women have been exploring their options and adjusting their expectations accordingly. Another limitation is the small size and racial homogeneity of the sample. While the sample is representative of the area in which the study was conducted, it may not be representative of the general population, and particularly of other racial groups. A third limitation is the assumption, reflected in the response options of the questionnaire, that women assume primary responsibility for child care. While this is still the prevailing pattern in dual-career families, it is not a universal pattern.

Finally, the results of the present study suggest that profound social changes are being driven by economic exigencies. The changes in expectation of the present sample during their transition from high school to higher education and/or work suggest that at least some adolescent girls, who are at a critical decision-making stage, are unaware of these economic realities. Interestingly, of the group of students who were shortly to enter the labour market in 1989, 69 percent expected to work continuously; in 1993, 73 percent shared this expectation. In contrast, of the group who had not yet entered the labour market by 1993 because they had continued their education, only 48 percent had expected in 1989 to work continuously; this expectation was shared by 76 percent in 1993. In other words, more students expected continuous employment as they came closer to the point of being employed. This may reflect a greater awareness of the realities of the marketplace. Baber and Monaghan (1988) pointed to the need to assist young women to develop strategies for dealing with the problems that might arise from combining career and family roles. If the present sample is representative of young women, this need continues to exist.

REFERENCES

Angrist, S.S. (1969). The study of sex roles. *Journal of Social Issues, 25*, 215–232.

Angrist, S.S., & Almquist, E.M. (1975). Careers and contingencies: How college women juggle with gender. New York: Dunellen.

Baber, K.M., & Monaghan, P. (1988). College women's career and motherhood expectations: New options, old dilemmas. *Sex Roles, 19*, 189–203.

Cook, E.P. (1993). The gendered context of life: Implications for women's and men's career-life plans. *Career Development Quarterly, 41*, 227–237.

Davey, F.H. (1992, June). Career versus family or career and family? Poster session presented at the annual convention of the Canadian Psychological Association, Québec, QU.

Davey, F.H. (1993). The occupational aspirations and expectations of senior high school students. *Guidance and Counselling* 8, 16–28.

Farmer, H.S. (1983). Career and homemaking plans for high school youth. *Journal of Counseling Psychology, 30*, 40–45.

Gaskell, J. (1983). The reproduction of family life: Perspectives of male and female adolescents. *British Journal of Sociology of Education, 4*, 19–38.

Granrose, C.S. (1985). Plans for work careers among college women who expect to have families. The *Vocational Guidance Quarterly, 33*, 284–295.

Greenglass, E.R., & Devins, R. (1982). Factors related to marriage and career plans in unmarried women. *Sex Roles, 8*, 57–71.

Lero, D.S. (1992). Canadian national child care study. Guelph, ON: University of Guelph.

Machung, A. (1989). Talking career, thinking job: Gender differences in career and family expectations of Berkeley seniors. *Feminist Studies, 15*, 35–58.

Nevill, D.D., & Super, D.E. (1988). Career maturity and commitment to work in university students. *Journal of Vocational Behavior, 32*, 139–151.

Schroeder, K.A., Blood, L.L., & Maluso, D. (1992). An intergenerational analysis of expectations for women's career and family roles. *Sex Roles, 26*, 273–291.

Statistics Canada. (1990). Women in Canada: A statistical report (2nd ed.). Ottawa: Minister of Supply and Services.

Statistics Canada. (1995). Characteristics of dual-earner families, 1993. Ottawa: Minister of Supply and Services.

U.S. Bureau of the Census. (1993). Statistical abstract of the United States: 1993 (113th ed., No. 105). Washington, DC: Superintendent of Documents, U.S. Government Printing Office. ■

Source: *Sex Roles: a Journal of Research*. (1998, January). From http://www.findarticles.com. Plenum Publishing Corporation in association with The Gale Group and Looksmart, 2000. Reprinted with permission of Kluwer Academic/Plenum Publishers.

References

Abella, R. (1981). Economic adjustment on marriage breakdown: Support. *Family Law Review, 4*, 1–10.

Adams, M. (2001, July 4). Here, father doesn't know best. *The Globe and Mail*, p. A11.

Ahrons, C.R. (2001). What divorce is and is not: Transcending the myths. In S. J. Ferguson (Ed.), *Shifting the center: Understanding contemporary families*. Toronto: Mayfield Publishing Company.

Akyeampong, E., & Nadwodny, R. (2001, Winter). Evolution of the Canadian workplace: Work from home. *Perspectives*, 30–36.

Alaton, S. (1995, February 11). What is this thing called love? *The Globe and Mail*.

Allar, A.L., & Côté, J.E. (1998). *Richer and poorer: The structure of inequality in Canada*. Toronto: James Lorimer & Company Ltd.

Allen, C. (2001, Spring).To love, honor, and manipulate. *Woman's Quarterly*.

Ambachtsheer, K. (2002, March 1). Pensions need to reform as much as health care. *National Post*, p. FP11. Retrieved on April 8, 2002, from: elibrary.ca.

Ambert, A.M. (1998). Divorce: facts, figures and consequences. *Contemporary Family Trends*. Ottawa: The Vanier Institute of the Family.

Anderson, D.Y., & Hayes, C.L. (1996). *Gender, identity, and self-esteem*. New York: Springer Publishing Company.

Anderson, K. (2001). Adultery. Probe Ministries International, 2001. Retrieved January 27, 2002, from: www.probe.org.

Arkes, H. (1997).The role of nature. In A. Sullivan (Ed.), *Same-sex marriage: Pro and con*. New York: Vintage Books.

Aronson, J. (1991). Family care of the elderly: Underlying assumptions and their consequences. In J.E. Veevers (Ed.), *Continuity & change in marriage & family* (pp. 361–370). Toronto: Holt, Rinehart and Winston of Canada, Ltd.

Aryee, S. (1999, July). A cross-cultural test of a model of the work-family interface. *Journal of Management*. Retrieved February 5, 2002, from: findarticle.com.

Avard, D. (March 2000). Analysis: sex, roles and stereotypes. *Families and Health 19*, 1, 8.

Avard, D., & and Harmsen, E. (2000, October). Culture is life. *Families and Health 14*, 1, 2.

Backstein, K. (1992). *The blind men and the elephant*. Toronto: Scholastic Inc.

Baines, B. (1993). Law, gender, equality. In S. Burt, L. Code, & L. Dorney (Eds.), *Changing patterns: Women in Canada* (pp. 243–278). Toronto: McClelland and Stewart, Inc.

Baker, M. (1993). *Families in Canadian society: An introduction*. (2nd ed.). Toronto: McGraw-Hill Ryerson Limited.

Baker, M. (1996, September). Policies for reducing child and family poverty: How does Canada compare? Canadian Council on Social Development: *Perception 20* (1). Retrieved March 2002, from: www.efc-efc.ca/docs/ccsd/00000296.htm.

Baker, M., Gruber, J., & Milligan, K. (2000). *Income security programs and retirement in Canada*. Ottawa: Human Resources Development Canada.

Bala, N. (1994). The evolving Canadian definition of the family: Towards a pluralistic and functional approach. *International Journal of Law & Family 8*, 293.

Balakrishnan, T.R., Lapierre-Adamczyk, E., & Krotki, K. (1993). *Family and childbearing in Canada: A demographic analysis*. Toronto: University of Toronto Press.

Bartholet, E. *Beyond biology: The politics of adoption & reproduction*. Contemporary Women's Issues Database 2, March 1, 1995, 5–14.

Bateson, M.C. (2000). *Full circles, overlapping lives: Culture and generation in transition*. New York: The Ballantine Publishing Group.

Beaujot, R.P., & McQuillan, K. (1991). The social effects of demographic change: Canada 1851–1981 (pp. 73–82). In J.E. Veevers (Ed.), *Continuity & change in marriage & family*. Toronto: Holt, Rinehart and Winston of Canada, Limited.

Bee, H. L. (1987). *The Journey of Adulthood*. New York: Macmillan Publishing Company.

Beiser, M., Feng, Hou, Hyman, I., and Tousignant, M. (1998). *Growing up Canadian: A study of new immigrant children*. Ottawa: Human Resources Development Canada, W-98-24E.

Belanger, A., & Oikawa, C. (1999, Summer). Who has a third child? *Canadian Social Trends*, 23–26.

Bengston, V., & de Terre, E. (1991). Aging and family relations (pp. 346–360). In J.E. Veevers (Ed.), *Continuity & change in marriage & family*. Toronto: Holt, Rinehart and Winston of Canada, Limited.

Bibby, R. (2001). *Canada's teens: Today, yesterday and tomorrow*. Toronto: Stoddart, 2001.

Bodman, D.A., and Peterson, G. (1995). Parenting processes (pp. 205–228). In R. Day, K. Gilbert, B. Settles, & W. Burr (Eds.), *Research and theory in family science*. Scarborough, ON: Nelson Canada.

Boehnert, J.B. (1993). The psychology of women. In S. Burt, L. Code, & L. Dorney (Eds.), *Changing patterns: Women in Canada*. Toronto: McClelland and Stewart, Inc.

Boeree, C. G.(1997). Erik Erikson, 1902–1994. Personality theories. Retrieved October 5, 2001, from: http://www.ship.edu/~cgboeree/erikson.html

Boisvert, J., Ladouceur, R., Beaudry, M., Freeston, M.H., Turgeon L., Hardif, C., & and Roussy, A. (1995, March 3). Perception of marital problems and of their prevention by Quebec young adults. *Journal of Genetic Psychology 156* (12), 33.

Borgen, W.A., and Amundson, N.E. (1995). Models of adolescent transition. *ERIC Digest.* Retrieved October 5, 2001, from: www.ed.gov/databases/ERIC–digests/ed401502.html.

Bornat, J. (2001). Reminiscence and oral history: Parallel universes or shared endeavour? *Aging and Society*, 21, 219–241.

Borysenko, J. (1996). *A woman's book of life: The biology, psychology, and spirituality of the feminine life cycle.* New York: Riverhead Books.

Boyd, M. (1988). Changing Canadian family forms: Issues for women (pp. 85–110). In N. Mandell & A. Duffy. *Reconstructing the Canadian family: Feminist perspectives.* Toronto: Butterworth's Canada Limited.

Boyd, M., & Norris, D. (1995, Autumn). Leaving the nest? The impact of family structure. *Canadian Social Trends, 38*, 14–17.

Boyd, M., & Norris, D. (1999, Spring).The crowded nest: Young adults at home. *Canadian Social Trends, 52*, 2–5.

Boyd, S. L., & Treas, J. (2001). Family care of the frail elderly: A new look at 'women in the middle' (pp. 517–523). In S. Ferguson (Ed.), *Shifting the center: Understanding contemporary families.* Toronto: Mayfield Publishing Company.

Bracci, C. (2000). Ties that bind: Ontario's filial responsibility law. *Canadian Journal of Family Law, 17*, (2), 455–500.

Bradt, Jack O. (1989). Becoming parents: Families with young children (pp. 235–254). In B. Carter & M. McGoldrick (Eds.), *The changing family life cycle: A framework for family therapy* (2nd ed.). Toronto: Allyn and Bacon.

Brandon, P. (2000, April). An analysis of kin-provided child care in the context of intrafamily exchanges: Linking components of family support for parents raising young children. *American Journal of Ecomonics and Sociology.*

Broderick, C. B. (2002) Marriage. *World Book Encyclopedia.* Retrieved on November 10, 2001 from: findarticles.com.

Brookes, A.A. (1982). Family, youth and leaving home in late-nineteenth century rural Nova Scotia: Canning and the exodus (pp. 93–108). In J. Parr (Ed.), *Childhood and family in Canadian history.* Toronto: McClellend and Stewart.

Brown, F. H. (1989). The impact of death and serious illness on the family life cycle (pp. 457–482). In B. Carter & M. McGoldrick (Eds.), *The changing family life cycle: A framework for family therapy* (2nd ed.). Toronto: Allyn and Bacon.

Browne, A. (1997). Violence in marriage: Until death do us part? In A. P. Cardarelli (Ed.), *Violence between intimate partners: Patterns, causes, and effects.* Needham Heights, MA: Allyn & Bacon.

Bruer, J. T. (1999). *The myth of the first three years: A new understanding of early brain development and lifelong learning.* New York: The Free Press.

Bumpass, L. L., Sweet, J.A., & Cherlin, A. (2001). The role of cohabitation in declining rates of marriage (pp. 159–172). In S. Ferguson (Ed.), *Shifting the center: understanding contemporary families.* Toronto: Mayfield Publishing Company.

Burch, T. (1990). Remarriage of older Canadians: Description and interpretation. *Research on Aging 12* (4), 546–559.

Burggraf, S. P. (1997). *The feminine economy and economic man: Reviving the role of family in the post-industrial age.* Don Mills, ON: Addison Wesley Publishing Inc.

Buss, D.M. (1994). *The evolution of desire.* New York: Basic Books, Inc.

Campbell, C. (1999, April). Dads shun bimbo image and Dads: 'A culture of fatherhood.' *Families and Health 2*, 1, 5, 6.

Campbell, C. (2000, May). The joys of being a hands-on dad. *Families and Health 11*, 7.

Campbell, C. (2000, June). Help people to realize their dreams. *Families and Health 11*, 6.

Campbell, C. (2000, October). Study probes needs of immigrant fathers: Underemployment, language barriers create stress. *Families and Health 14*, 1, 3.

Cancian, F. M. (1987). *Love in America: Gender and self development.* New York: Cambridge University Press.

Carey, E. (1995, December 6). More men retiring before reaching 65. *The Toronto Star.*

Carey, E. (1996, November 18). Working adults hitting books hard, polls find. *The Toronto Star.*

Carey, E. (1999, June 9). Elderly widows not living a life of isolation: Study. *The Toronto Star.*

Carey, E. (2001, September 1). Labour crisis on horizon as boomers retire. *The Toronto Star.*

Carlson, L. (1997). Remarriage in late adulthood. *Research on Adult Development* (Psych 335-02). Retrieved March 26, 2002, from: http://www.hope.edu/academic/psychology/335/webrep2/remarry.html.

Carneiro, R. L., (1988). Indians of the Amazonian forest. (pp. 73–86). In J. S. Denslow & C. Padoch (Eds.), *People of the tropical rain forest.* Berkeley: University of California Press.

Carter, B., & Peters, J.K. (1996). *Love, honor and negotiate.* Toronto: Pocket Books.

Casavant, L. (1999, January). The growing numbers of the homeless. *Homelessness.* Parliamentary Research Branch, Library of Parliament, Retrieved November 5, 2001, from: http://www.parl.gc.ca/information/library/PRBpubs on *The challenge of suicide clusters.* (1998, June) #30. Calgary: Suicide Information & Education Centre, Retrieved October 19, 2001, from: Electric Library Canada.

Chamberlain, A. (1996, October 8). Job satisfaction. *The Toronto Star.*

Che-Alford, J., & Hamm, B. (1999, Summer). Under one roof: Three generations living together. *Canadian Social Trends, 58*, 6–9.

Cherlin, A.J., & Furstenberg, F.F. Jr. (2001). Stepfamilies in the United States: A reconsideration (pp. 405–422). In S. Ferguson (Ed.), *Shifting the center: Understanding contemporary families.* Toronto: Mayfield Publishing Company.

Chimbos, P. D. (1980). The Greek-Canadian family: Tradition and change (pp. 27–40). In K. Ishwaran (Ed.), *Canadian families: Ethnic variations.* Toronto: McGraw-Hill Ryerson Limited, 1980.

Chisholm, P., Atherley, R., Wood, C., & McClelland, S. (1999, September 8). Sex and marriage: Experts say sex is vital to healthy relationships. Why is it so difficult for couples to do what's good for them? *Maclean's*, p. 22. Retrieved on December 12, 2001, from: elibrary.ca.

Clark, A. (1998, December 28). Maclean's/CBC Poll: Sex lies and destiny: People are less tolerant of perjury than adultery. *Maclean's*, 42.

Clark, W. (1997, Spring). School leavers revisited. *Canadian Social Trends*, 44, 10–12.

Clark, W. (1999, Summer). Search for success. *Canadian Social Trends*, 53, 10–12.

Clark, W. (2000, Winter). 100 years of education. *Canadian Social Trends*, 59, 3–7.

Clarkberg, M. (1999, March). The price of partnering: The role of economic well-being in young adults' first union experiences. *Social Forces 77* (3), 945–68.

Code, L. (1993). Feminist theory (pp. 19–58). In S. Burt, L. Code, & L. Dorney (Eds.), *Changing patterns: Women in Canada.* Toronto: McClelland and Stewart, Inc.

Coleman, P., Ivani-Chalian, C., & Robinson, M. (1998, July). The story continues: persistence of life themes in old age. *Aging and Society 18* (4), pp. 389–420.

Coloroso, B. (2001). *Kids are worth it.* Toronto: Penguin Books of Canada.

Conway, J. F. (1997). T*he Canadian family in crisis* (3rd ed.). Toronto: James Lorimer & Company, Ltd.

Coontz, S. (2001). Historical perspectives on family diversity (pp. 54–76). In S. Ferguson (Ed.), *Shifting the center: Understanding contemporary families.* Toronto: Mayfield Publishing Company.

Côté, J. E., & Allahar, A. (1994). *Generation on hold: Coming of age in the late twentieth century.* Toronto: Stoddart.

Coulter, R. (1982). The working young of Edmonton (pp. 143–159). In J. Parr (Ed.), *Childhood and family in Canadian history.* Toronto: McClelland and Stewart.

Council of Ministers of Education, Canada. (1998). *Report on education in Canada.* Accessed September 16, 2001, from: http://www.cmec.ca/reports/rec98/texteng.html#learning in a changing world

Covell, K., & Howe, B. (1998, September). A policy for parent licensing. *Policy Options*, pp. 32–35.

Csikszentmihalyi, M., & Schneider, B. (2000). *Becoming an adult: How teenagers prepare for the world of work.* New York: Basic Books.

Daly, K. (1995). Reproduction in families.(pp. 229–242). In R. Day, K. Gilbert, & B. Settles (Eds.) *Research and theory in family science.* Scarborough, ON: Nelson Canada.

Davidson, K. (2001, May). Late life widowhood, selfishness and new partnership choices: A gendered perspective. *Aging and Society 21*, Part 3, 297–317.

De Cecco, J.P., and Shively, M.G. (1988). A study of perceptions and rights and needs in interpersonal conflicts in homosexual relationships. (pp. 257–272). In J.P. De Cecco (Ed.), *Gay relationships.* New York: Harrington Park Press.

Demo, D., & Cox, M. (2000, November). Families with young children: A review of research in the 1990s. *Journal of Marriage and the Family 62*, 876–895.

Dempsey, K. (2001, Autumn). Women's and men's consciousness of shortcomings in marital relations, and the need to change. *Family Matters.* Retrieved Novemeber 10, 2001, from: findarticles.com.

Devereaux, M.S. (1993, Autumn). Time use of Canadians in 1992. *Canadian Social Trends*, 13–16.

Devereaux, M.S. (Ed.) (1993, September). *Leaving school.* Ottawa: Human Resources and Labour Canada.

Deziel, S. (1999, August 23). Special report: The anguish of the street. *Maclean's, 112* (31), pp. 38–41. Retrieved November 5, 2001, from: Electric Library Canada.

Diamond, J. (1997). *Guns, germs, and steel: The fates of human societies.* New York: W.W. Norton & Company.

The disappearing family. (1995, September 9). *The Economist*, 19–20.

Drolet, M. (2001, January). T*he persistent gap: New evidence on the Canadian gender wage gap.* Ottawa: Business and Labour Market Analysis Division, Statistics Canada.

Dubin, M. (1999, November 20). Détente in the housework wars. *The Toronto Star*, pp. M1, M4.

Duffy, A., & J. Momirov. (1997). *Family violence: A Canadian introduction.* Toronto: James Lorimer & Company, Publishers.

Dugsin, R. (2001). Conflict and healing in family experience of second-generation emigrants from India living in North America. *Family Process 40*, 233–241. Retrieved October 22, 2001, from: http://www.findarticles.com.

Dulac, G. (1994, March). The changing faces of fatherhood. *Transition Magazine.* Retrieved January 3, 2002, from Child and Family Canada web site: www.efc-efc.ca/docs/vanif/00000464.htm.

Dulude, L. (1991). Getting old: Men in couples and women alone (pp. 330–341). In J. E. Veevers (Ed.), *Continuity & change in marriage & family.* Toronto: Holt, Rinehart and Winston of Canada Limited.

Durkheim, É. (1951). *Suicide: A study in sociology.* (J. Spaulding, Trans.), G. Simpson (Ed.). New York: The Free Press.

Dym, B., & Glenn, M. (1993, July/August). Forecast for couples. *Psychology Today*, 54–57, 78–79, 81–83, 86.

Eichler, M. (1997). *Family shifts: Families, policies, and gender equality.* Don Mills, ON: Oxford University Press.

Engels, F. (1972). *The origin of the family, private property, and the state.* New York: Pathfinder.

Environics Research Group (2001, May 10). Most Canadians favour gay marriage; approval of homosexuality continues to increase. Retrieved November 17, 2001, from: http://erg.environics.net/news/default.asp?aID=432)

Erikson, E.H. (1959). *Identity and the life cycle.* New York: W.W. Norton & Company Inc.

Erikson, E.H. (1968). *Identity: youth and crisis.* New York: W.W. Norton & Company Inc.

Erikson, E.H., & Erikson. J.M. (1997). *The life cycle completed.* New York: W.W. Norton & Company Inc.

Eshleman, R., & Wilson, S. (2001). *The family.* Toronto: Pearson Education Canada.

Eustace, N. (2001, Spring). The cornerstone of a copious work: Love and power in eighteenth-century courtship. *Journal of Social History.* Retrieved Novmber 10, 2001 from: findarticles.com.

Fernándes-Ballesteros, R., Zamarrón, M.D., & Ruiz, M.A. (2001, January). The contribution of socio-demographics and psychological factors to life satisfaction. *Aging and Society, 21* (1), 25–44.

Ferraro, K. J. (1997). Battered women: Strategies for survival. In A. P. Cardarelli (Ed.), *Violence between intimate partners: Patterns, causes, and effects.* Needham Heights, MA: Allyn & Bacon.

Fineman, M. (1994). *The neutered mother, the sexual family, and other twentieth century tragedies.* New York: Routledge.

Finnie, R. (2000). From school to work: The evolution of early labour market outcomes of Canadian postsecondary graduates. *Canadian Social Policy, XXVI* (2), 200–207.

Fisher, H. (1992). *Anatomy of love: The natural history of monogamy, adultery, and divorce.* New York: W. W. Norton and Company.

Fiske, M., & Chiriboga, D.A. (1990). *Change and continuity in adult life.* San Fransisco: Jossey-Bass Publishers.

Foot, D., & Stoffman, D. (2001). *Boom, bust, & echo: Profiting from the demographic shift in the 21st century.* Toronto: Macfarlane Walter and Ross.

Freeman, R. (1999, Spring). When parents part: Helping children adjust. *Transition Magazine 29* (1). Retrieved December 2001, from: www.vifamily.ca/tm/2913.htm.

Gaffield, C. (1992). Canadian families in cultural context: Hypothesis from the mid-nineteenth century (pp. 135–137). In R. Bradbury (Ed.), *Canadian Family History: Selected Readings.* Toronto: Copp Clark Pitman Ltd.

Gairdner, W. D. (1992). *The war against the family: A parent speaks out.* Toronto: Stoddart Publishing Company.

Gale Research. (1998). Erikson's theory. *Gale Encyclopedia of Childhood and Adolescence.* Retrieved February 2002, from: findarticles.com.

Galinsky, E. (2000, August). Mothers at work: Effects on children's well-being (a review). *Journal of Development & Behavioural Pediatrics.* Retrieved on February 5, 2002, from: findarticles.com.

Gaskell, Jane. (1991). Education as preparation for work in Canada: Structure, policy and student response (pp. 61–84). In D. Ashton & G. Lowe (Eds.), *Making their way: Education, training and labour market in Canada and Britain.* Toronto: University of Toronto Press.

Gaskell, Jane. (1993). Introduction (pp. xiii–xv11). In P. Anisef & P. Axelrod (Eds.), *Transitions: Schooling and employment in Canada.* Toronto: Thompson Educational Publishing, Inc.

Gee, E. M. (1995). Contemporary diversities (pp. 79–101). In N. Mandell & A. Duffy (Eds.), *Canadian families: Diversity, conflict and change.* Toronto: Harcourt Brace & Company, Canada.

Gergen, K.J., & Gergen, M.M. (2001). *The new aging: Self construction and social values.* Retrieved on March 26, 2002, from: swarthmore.edu/SocSci/kgergen1/newaging.html.

Gerson, K. (2001). Dilemmas of involved fatherhood (pp. 324–338). In S. Ferguson (Ed.), *Shifting the center: understanding contemporary families.* Mountainview, CA: Mayfield Publishing Company.

Ghalam, N. Z. (1997, Autumn). Attitudes toward women, work, and family. *Canadian Social Trends.*

Gilligan, C. (1993). *In a different voice: Psychological theory and women's development.* Cambridge, MA: Harvard University Press.

Gillis, J. R. (1996). *A world of their own making: Myth, ritual, and the quest for family values.* New York: Basic Books.

Gillis, J. R. (1974). *Youth and history.* New York: Harcourt Brace.

Glossop, R., & Theilheimer, I. (1994, March). Does society support involved fathering? *Transition Magazine.* Retrieved January 3, 2000, from Child and Family Canada web site: www.dfd-etc.ca/docs/vanif/00000003.htm.

Golden, F., & Murphy Paul, A. (1999, June 1). Making over mom and dad. *Psychology Today*, 32, 36–40.

Goldscheider, F. K., & Goldscheider, C (1993). *Leaving home before marriage: Ethnicity, familism, and generational relationships.* Madison, WI: The University of Wisconsin Press.

Goldscheider, F K., & Waite, L.J. (1991). *New families, no families? The transformation of the American home.* Berkeley, CA: University of California Press.

Goldstein, J., & Segall, A. (1991). Ethnic intermarriage and ethnic identity (pp. 165–174). In J.E. Veevers (Ed.), *Continuity & change in marriage & family.* Toronto: Holt, Rinehart and Winston of Canada Limited.

Goldstine, D., Larner, K., Zucherman, S., & Goldstine, H. (1977). *The dance away lover.* New York: William Morrow & Co. Inc.

Goode, W. (1964). *The family*. Englewood Cliffs, NJ: Prentice-Hall, Inc.

Goode, W. (1982). *The family*. (2nd ed.). Englewood Cliffs, NJ: Prentice-Hall, Inc.

Gorlick, C. (1995). Divorce: Options available, constraints forced, pathways taken (pp. 211–234). In N. Mandell & A. Duffy (Eds.), *Canadian families: Diversity, conflict, and change*. Toronto: Harcourt Brace and Company, Canada.

Gottman, J.M. (1994). *Why marriages succeed or fail*. Toronto: Simon and Schuster.

Gottman, J.M., & Silver, N. (1999). *The seven principles for making marriage work*. New York: Crown Publishers, Inc.

Gray, J. (1992). *Men are from Mars, women are from Venus: A practical guide to improving communication and getting what you want in relationships*. New York: Harper Perennial.

Greenstein, T.N. (1996, March). Gender ideology and perceptions of the fairness of the division of labour: Effects on marital quality. *Social Forces, 74* (3), 1029–1042.

Guldner, C. (1982, October). *The 6 Rs of marriage*. Lecture presented at Family Studies In-Service Workshop, Scarborough Board of Education, Scarborough, Ontario.

Haddad, T. (1998). *Custody arrangements and the development of emotional or behaviourial problems in children*. Hull, QC: Human Resources Development Canada, Applied Research Branch.

Hanvey, L., & Lock Kunz, J. (2000, June 19). *Immigrant youth in Canada*. Canadian Council on Social Development. Retrieved from: www.ccsd.ca.

Hanvey, L., & Lock Kunz, J. (2000, October). Immigrant teens face unique challenges. *Families and Health, 14*, 4.

Harevan, T. K. (2000). *Families, history and social change: Life course and cross cultural perspectives*. Boulder, CO: Westview Press.

Harmsen, E.. (2000., October). Canada grows in diversity. Vanier Institute of the *Family. Families and Health 14*, 8.

Hawking, S. (1988). *A brief history of time: From the big bang to black holes*. Toronto: Bantam Books.

Health Canada. (1999). Reproductive and genetic technologies overview paper. Government of Canada. Retrieved from: www.hc-sc.gc.ca

Helgerson, K. (1997, October 1). What makes a good marriage. *Chatelaine, 70* (10), 109–110, 113.

Herz Brown, Fredda. (1989). The impact of death and serious illness on the family life cycle. In B. Carter ; McGoldrick (Eds.), The changing family life cycle: A framework for family therapy. Toronto: Allyn and Bacon.

Hock, R. R. (1999). *Forty studies that changed psychology: Explorations into the history of psychological research*. (3rd ed.). Upper Saddle River, NJ: Prentice Hall.

Hogg, P. W., & Bushell, A.A. (1997). The charter dialogue between courts and legislatures [Charter of Rights and Freedoms]. *Osgoode Hall Law Journal, 35*, 75–124.

Holland, W. (2000). Intimate relationships in the new millennium: The assimilation of marriage and cohabitation? *Canadian Journal of Family Law 17*, 114–158.

Hollinger, P C., Offer, D., Barker, J.T., & Bell, C.C. (1994). *Suicide and homicide among adolescents*. New York: The Guilford Press.

Holubitsky, J. (2001, May 5). Belief that tuition too high hinders further education. *Edmonton Journal*. Retrieved August 21, 2001, from Electric Library Canada.

Howarth, G. (1998). 'Just live for today.' Living, caring, ageing and dying. *Ageing and Society 18*, 673–689.

Human Resources Development Canada (1999, Spring). Developments: National longitudinal survey of children and youth. *Human Resources Development Canada, 4* (1), 8–12.

Ishwaran, K. (1983). *The Canadian family*. Toronto: Gage Publishing Ltd.

Jarman, F., Howlett, S., Woods, M.J., & Crawley, T. (1992). T*he living family: A Canadian perspective*. Toronto: John Wiley & Sons.

John, J. (1997). Creation and natural law. In A. Sullivan (Ed.), *Same-sex marriage: Pro and co*n. New York: Vintage Books, 78–81.

Johnson, H., & Hotton, T. (2001). Spousal violence. In C. Trainor & K. Mihorean (Eds.), *Family violence in Canada: A statistical profile 2001*. Ottawa: Statistics Canada.

Johnson, S., & Marano, H.E. (1994, March/April). Love: The immutable longing for contact. *Psychology Today*. 32–37, 64, 67.

Jones, R. W., & Bates, J.E. (1988). Satisfaction in male homosexual couples (pp. 237–246. In J.P. De Cecco (Ed.), *Gay relationships*. New York; Harrington Park Press.

Kain, E. L. (1990). *The myth of family decline: Understanding families in a world of rapid social change*. Toronto: Lexington Books.

Kahn, Rabbi Y. H. (1997). The Kedushah of homosexual relations (pp. 237–246). In A. Sullivan (Ed.), *Same-sex marriage: Pro and con*. New York: Vintage Books.

Kantor, D., & Lehr, W. (1975). *Inside the family: Toward a theory of family process*. San Francisco: Jossey-Bass, Inc., Publishers.

Kay, L. (1994, August). 7 marriage types: Which one's yours? *Chatelaine*.

Keating, N., & Cook, L.H. (2001). Current thinking in gerontology in Canada. *Aging and Society, 21*, 131–138.

Kelman, S. (1998). *All in the family: A cultural history of family life*. Toronto: Penguin Books.

Kelman, S. (1999, Winter). Family life: Past, present, future and Lessons from history: What the past can teach us about families. *Transition Magazine, 29* (4). Retrieved December 16, 2001 from: www.vifamily.ca/tm/294/1.htm.

Kennedy, J. (2001, August 18). Uncurdling the marriage culture: Unmarried people suspect that marriage is one of life's great mysteries. Married people know it is. *Ottawa Citizen*.

Kershner, K. (1996, May 1). In vitro fertilization: Is conceiving a child worth the costs? *USA Today Magazine, 124*. Retrieved November 10, 2001, from: Electric Library Canada, www.electiclibrary.com.

Kerz, D. (2001). Old problems and new directions in the study of violence against women (pp. 427–441). In S. Ferguson (Ed.), *Shifting the center: Understanding contemporary families*. Toronto: Mayfield Publishing Company.

Kimmel, D. C. (1990). *Adulthood and aging: An interdisciplinary, developmental view*. (3rd ed.). New York: John Wiley and Sons, Inc.

Kingston, A. (1996, January) Going to the chapel: To honour? to obey? *Flare 21*, 44, 46. Retrieved on November 10, 2001, from: www.elibrary.ca

Kohn, M. L. (1980). Job complexity and adult personality (pp. 193–210). In N. J. Smelser & E. Erikson (Eds.), *Themes of work and love in adulthood. Cambridge, MA: Harvard University Press*.

Korbin, J. E., Anetzberger, G.J., & and Eckert, J.K. (2001). Elder abuse and child abuse: A consideration of similarities and differences in intergenerational family violence (pp. 466–476). In S. Ferguson (Ed.), *Shifting the center: Understanding contemporary families*. Mountainview, CA: Mayfield Publishing Company.

Kotre, J. (1996). *Outliving the self: How we live on in future generations*. New York: W. W. Norton & Company.

Kotre, J., & Hall, E. (1990). *The seasons of life: Our dramatic journey from birth to death*. Toronto: Little, Brown and Company.

Kramer, H., & Kramer, K. (1993, March). Conversations at midnight. *Psychology Today 26* (2), 26, 28.

Kübler-Ross, E. (1983). *On children and death*. New York: Macmillan Publishing.

Kübler-Ross, E. (1969). *On death and dying*. New York: Touchstone Books.

Larson, L. E., Goltz, J.W., & Munro, B.E. (2000). *Families in Canada: Social contexts, continuities, and changes*. Scarborough, ON: Prentice-Hall Canada Inc.

Larson, L. E., Goltz, W., & Munro, B.E (1994). *Families in Canada: Social context, continuities, and changes (2nd ed.)*. Scarborough, ON: Prentice-Hall Canada Inc.

Lasch, C. (1997). *Women and the common life: Love, marriage and feminism*. New York: W. W. Norton & Company.

Lawler, M.G. (2001, May 14). Time, sex, and money: The first five years of marriage. (Creighton University Study). *America*. Retrieved November 10, 2001, from: findarticles.com.

Le Bourdais, C., Neill, G., & Turcotte, P. (2000, Spring). The changing face of conjugal relationships. *Canadian Social Trends, 56*, 14–17.

Lee, G R., & Dwyer, J. W. (1996, January). Aging parent-adult child coresidence. J*ournal of Family Issues, 17* (1), pp. 46–59.

Leenars, A. A., Boldt, M., Connors, E.A., Harnisch, P., Harrington, G.G., Kiddy, K.G., Krawll, M.B., Letofsky, K., Osborg, B., Ramsay, R.F., Safinosfsky, I., & Winch, G. (1998). History: Vignettes of the development in suicide prevention (pp. 3–34). In A.A. Leenars et al (Eds.), *Suicide in Canada*. Toronto: University of Toronto Press.

Leibow, D, MD. (1995). *Love, pain, and the whole damn thing*. Toronto: Penguin Books Canada Ltd.

Levinson, D. J. (1978). *The seasons of a man's life*. New York: Ballentine Books.

Levinson, D. J.(1996). *The seasons of a woman's life*. New York: Alfred A Knopf.

Lewis, S.K., Ross, G.E., & Mirowsky, J. (1999, June). Establishing a sense of personal control in the transition to adulthood. *Social Forces, 77* (4), 1573–1599.

L'Heureaux-Dube, C. (1997). Making equality work in family law. *Canadian Journal of Family Law, 14*, 103–127.

Little, D., & Lapierre, L. (1993, December). *The class of 90: A compendium of findings from the 1992 national graduates survey of 1990 graduates*. Hull, Québec: Human Resources Development Canada.

Lublin, N. (1998). *Pandora's box: Feminism confronts reproductive technology*. Lanham, MD: Rowman & Littlefield Publishers.

Lupri, E. (1991). Fathers in transition: The case of dual-earner families in Canada (pp. 242–254). In J. E. Veevers (Ed.), *Continuity & change in marriage & family*. Toronto: Holt, Rinehart and Winston of Canada, Limited.

Lynn, M., & O'Neill, E. (1995). Families, power and violence (pp. 271–305). In N. Mandell & A. Duffy (Eds.), *Canadian families: Diversity, conflict and change*. Toronto: Harcourt, Brace & Company, Canada.

Mackie, M. (1995). Gender in the family: Changing patterns (pp. 454–76). In N. Mandell & A. Duffy (Eds.), *Canadian families: Diversity, conflict and change*. Toronto: Harcourt, Brace & Company, Canada. [page nos]

Majete, C. (1997, July 1). What you may not know about interracial marriages. *The world & I, 12*. Accessed January 13, 2002 from Electric Library Canada.

Mandell, N. (1995). Family histories (pp. 17–44). In N. Mandell & A. Duffy (Eds.), *Canadian families: Diversity, conflict and change*. Toronto: Harcourt, Brace & Company, Canada.

Mandell, N., & and Crysdale, S. (1993). Gender tracks: Male-female perceptions of home-school-work transitions (pp. 21–41). In P. Anisef & P. Axelrod (Eds.), *Schooling and employment in Canada*. Toronto: Thompson Educational Publishing, Inc.

Mann, B. (1995, Fall). New times, new fathers. *Play and Parenting Connections*. Canadian Association of Family Resource Programs.

Manning, P. (2002, April 5). Canada's test of faith. *The Globe and Mail*, p. A15.

Marcil-Gratton, N. (1998, July). *Growing up with mom and dad? The intricate family life courses of Canadian children*. Ottawa: Statistics Canada, Catalogue No. 89-566-XIE.

Marecek, J., Finn, S.E., & Cardell, M. Gender roles in the relationships of lesbians and gay men (pp. 169–176). In J. P. De Cecco (Ed.), *Gay relationships*. New York: Harrington Park Press.

Martinac, P. (1998). *The lesbian and gay book of love and marriage*. New York: Broadway Books.

Matathia, I., & Salzman, M. (1999). *Next: Trends for the near future*. New York: The Overlook Press.

Mayor's Homelessness Action Task Force. (1999, January). Retrieved November 5, 2001, from: http://www.city.toronyo.on.ca/mayor/homelessnesstf.htm

McAdams, D. P., Hart, H.M., & Maruna, S. (1998). The anatomy of generativity. In D. P. McAdams & E. de St. Aubin (Eds.), *Generativity and adult development* (pp. 2–43). Washington, DC: American Psychological Association, 7–46.

McBride, J., & Simms, S. (2001). Death in the family: Adapting a family systems framework to the grief process. *The American Journal of Family Therapy*. 29 (12), 59–74.

McCain, M. and Mustard, F. (1999, April). *Reversing the real brain drain: Early years study, the final report*. Toronto: Ontario Children's Secretariat.

McCarthy, M., & Radbord, J. L. (1998). Family law for same sex couples: Chart(er)ing the course. *Canadian Journal of Family Law 15* (2), 101–177.

McClelland, S. (2001, June 18). Life: Why dads matter: New studies show fathers' impact on child development." *Maclean's 114* (25), 34–35.

McCloskey, D. (1997, March). Canada's kids: Thriving? or just surviving? Retrieved March 24, 2002, from: http://www.cfc-efc.ca/docs/vanif/00000899.htm.

McCormick, N., & Jesser, C.J. (1991). The courtship game: Power in the sexual encounter (pp. 134–151). In J.E. Veevers (Ed) *Continuity & change in marriage & family*. Toronto: Holt, Rinehart and Winston of Canada, Limited.

McDaniel, S. A. (1993). The changing Canadian family: Women's roles and the impact of feminism (pp. 422–451). In S. Burt, L. Code, & L. Dorney (Eds.), *Changing patterns: Women in Canada*. Toronto: McClelland and Stewart, Inc.

McDaniel, S. A. (1998, September). Public policy, demographic aging and families. *Policy Options*, 36–38.

McDaniel, S. A. (2001). The family lives of the middle-aged and elderly in Canada (pp. 422–451). In M. Baker (Ed.), *Families: Changing trends in Canada*. Toronto: McGraw-Hill Ryerson, Ltd.

McGoldrick, M. (1989). The joining of families through marriage: The new couple (pp. 209–224). In B. Carter & M. McGoldrick (Eds.), *The changing family life cycle: A framework for family therapy*. Toronto: Allyn and Bacon.

McGoldrick, M., & Carter, B. (1989). Forming a remarried family (pp. 399–432). In B. Carter & M. McGoldrick (Eds.), *The changing family life cycle: A framework for family therapy*. Toronto: Allyn and Bacon.

McIntyre, L. (1988, December). Last days of Eden: Rondônia's Urueu-Wau-Wau Indians. *National Geographic*, 800–817.

McKenzie, D. (2002, February 22). Right to spank backed in poll. *The Toronto Star*. Retrieved April 2002, from: www.electriclibrary.com, www.bigchalk.com.

McLaughlin. (2001, September 22). New youth shelter opens. *Halifax Daily News*. p. 6. Retrieved November 5, 2001 from Electric Library Canada.

McLindon, J. (1987). Separate but unequal: The economic disaster of divorce for women and children. *Family Law Quarterly 21*, 351.

McPherson, B. D. (1990). *Aging as a social process: An introduction to individual and population aging*. Toronto: Butterworths Canada Ltd.

McWhirter, D. P., & Mattison, A.M. (1988). Stages in the development of gay relationships (pp. 161–168). In J.P. De Cecco (Ed.), *Gay relationships*. New York: Harrington Park Press.

Merriam, S. B., & Clark, M.C. (1991). *Lifelines: Patterns of work, love, and learning in adulthood*. San Francisco: Jossey-Bass Publishers.

Meunier, D., Bernard, P., & Boisjoly, J. (1998). Eternal youth? changes in the living arrangements of young people (pp. 157–169). In M. Corak (Ed.), *Labour markets, social institutions, and the future of Canada's children*. Ottawa: Statistics Canada.

Milan, A. (2000, Spring). One hundred years of families. *Canadian Social Trends 46*, 2–13.

Moffat, M. (1993). Youth culture and college culture (pp. 185–189). In W. A. Havilland & R.J. Gordon (Eds.), *Talking about people: Readings in contemporary cultural anthropology*. Toronto: Mayfield Publishing Company.

Morgan, C. (2001, March). The role of interest in understanding the career choices of female and male college students. *Sex roles: A journal of research*. Retrieved October 19, 2001, from: http://www.findarticles.com

Morisette, R. (1997, Autumn). Declining earnings of young men. *Canadian Social Trends*, 31–50.

Morisette, R. (1998). The declining labour market status of young men. In M. Corak (Ed.), *Labour markets, social institutions, and the future of Canada's children*. Ottawa: Statistics Canada.

Morisette, R., & Drolet, M. (2000, April). *To what extent are Canadians exposed to low-income?* Ottawa: Business and Labour Market Analysis Division, Statistics Canada.

Mortimer, J.T., Pimentel, E.E., Ryu, S., Nash, K., & Lee, C. (1996, June). Part-time work and occupational value formation in adoloescence. *Social Forces 74* (4), 1405–1418.

Morton, S. (1999). To take an orphan: Gender and family roles following the 1917 Halifax explosion (pp. 106–122). In K. McPherson, C. Morgan, & N. M Forestall (Eds.), *Gendered past: Historical essays in femininity and masculinity in Canada*. Toronto: Oxford University Press.

Mount, F. (1992). *The subversive family: An alternative history of love and marriage*. Toronto: Maxwell Macmillan Canada.

Myers, S.M.. & Booth, A. (1996, May). Men's retirement and marital quality. *Journal of Family Issues 17* (3), 336–357.

Nadeau, R. (1997, November). Brain sex and the language of love. *The World and I*. Retrieved on April 17, 2000, from: findarticles.com

National Coalition for the Homeless. (1999, April). *Homeless youth*. NCH Fact Sheet #11. Retrieved October 19, 2001, from: http://nch.ari.net/youth.html

Nannini, D. K. (2000, May). Jealousy in sexual and emotional fidelity: An alternative to the evolutionary explanation. *Journal of Sex Research*. Retrieved January 27, 2002, from: findarticles.com

Nett, E. M. (1993). *Canadian families: Past and present*. Toronto: Harcourt Brace & Company, Canada.

Peck, J. S., & Manocherian, J. (1989). Divorce in the changing life cycle (pp. 335–370). In B. Carter & M. McGoldrick (Eds.), *The changing family life cycle: A framework for family therapy* (2nd ed.). Toronto: Allyn and Bacon.

Peplau, L.A. (1988). Research on homosexual couples: An overview (pp. 142–152). In J.P. De Cecco (Ed.), *Gay relationships*. New York: Harrington Park Press.

Peplau, L.A., & Campbell, S.M. (2001). The balance of power in dating (pp. 142–152). In S. Ferguson (Ed.), *Shifting the center: Understanding contemporary families*. Mountainview, CA: Mayfield Publishing Company.

Peterson, K. (2002, January 14). Kids, parents can make the best of divorce. *USA Today*, p. 01A.

Peterson, P. G. (1999). *Gray dawn: How the coming age wave will transform America and the world*. New York: Times Books.

Phillips, P., & Phillips, E. (1993). *Women and work: Inequality in the Canadian labour market*. Toronto: James Lorimer & Company, Publishers.

Pienta, A.M., Hayward, M.D., & Jenkins, K.R. (2000, July). Health consequences of marriage for the retirement years. *Journal of Family Issues. 21* (5), 559–586.

Pole, K. (2001, May 15). Ottawa byline: Genie out of the bottle again on reproductive technologies. *Medical Post*. Retrieved January 9, 2002, from: www.electriclibrary.com.

Pole, K. (2001, May 15). Government encourages reproductive research. *Medical Post*. Retrieved January 9, 2002, from: www.electriclibrary.com.

Postman, N. (1994). *The disappearance of childhood*. New York: Vintage Books.

Queen, S., Habenstein, R., & Quadagno, J. (1985). *The family in various cultures*. New York: Harper & Row Publishers.

Report of the Pan-Canadian education indicators program 1999. (2000). Toronto: Canadian Education Statistics Council.

Rincover, A. (2001, July 14). Cultural clash hard on family. *Regina Leader Post*, p. G7.

Rogers, D., & Caputo, V. (2000, March). Growing up male, female in Canada: National survey provides insight into gender issues. Vanier Institute of the Family, *Families and Health 19*, 4.

Ross, D., Scott, K., & Kelly, M. (1996). Overview: Children in Canada in the 1990s. In *Growing up in Canada: National longitudinal survey of children and youth*. Ottawa: Ministry of Industry, 1996.

Rubin, L. B. (2001). When you get laid off, it's like losing a part of yourself (pp. 546–558). In S. J. Ferguson (Ed.), *Shifting the center: Understanding contemporary families*. Toronto: Mayfield Publishing Company.

Sakinofsky, I. (1998). The epidemiology of suicide in Canada (pp. 37–66). In A.A. Leenars, S. Wenckstern, I. Sakinofsky, R. J. Duck, M. J. Kral, & R.C. Bland (Eds.), *Suicide in Canada*. Toronto: University of Toronto Press.

Sasse, C. (2000). *Families today*. New York: Glencoe/McGraw-Hill.

Saplosky, R. (1997). T*he trouble with testosterone and other essays on the biology of the human predicament*. New York: Scribner.

Sauvé, R. (2002). *Connections—Tracking the links between jobs and family*. Ottawa: Vanier Institute of the Family, 2002. Retrieved March 2002, from: www.vifamily.com.

Sauvé, R. (2002). *The current state of Canadian family finances 2001 Report*. People Patterns Consulting. Ottawa: Vanier Institute of the Family.

Schaefer, R. T., Lamm, R.P., Biles, P., & Wilson, S.J. (1996). *Sociology: An introduction*. Toronto: McGraw-Hill Ryerson Limited.

Schlesinger, B. (1979). *Families: Canada*. Toronto: McGraw-Hill Ryerson Limited.

Schlesinger, B. (1999). *Strengths in families: Accentuating the positive*. Ottawa: The Vanier Institute of the Family.

Schlesinger, B., & Schlesinger, R.A. (1992). *Canadian families in transition*. Toronto: Canadian Scholars Press.

Schlesinger, B., & Giblon, S.T. (1984). *Lasting marriages*. Toronto: Guidance Centre, Faculty of Education, University of Toronto.

Schlossberg, N.K. (1987, May). Taking the mystery out of change. *Psychology Today*, 74–75.

Schwartz, P. (2001). Peer marriage (pp. 186–194). In S. Ferguson (Ed.), *Shifting the center: understanding contemporary families*. Mountainview, CA: Mayfield Publishing Company.

Sev'er, A. (1992). *Women and divorce in Canada*. Toronto: Canadian Scholars' Press.

Shanahan, M. J. (2000). Pathways to adulthood in changing societies: Variability and mechanisms in life course perspective. *Annual Review of Sociology 26*, 667–692.

Sheehy, G. (1995). New passages: *Mapping your life across time.* New York: Random House.

Sheehy, G. (1976). Passages: *Predictable crises of adult life.* Toronto: Bantam Books.

Sheehy, G. (1998). *Understanding men's passages: Discovering the new map of men's lives.* New York: Random House.

Small, M.F. (1995). *What's love got to do with it?: The evolution of human mating.* Toronto: Anchor Books.

Smesler, N.J., & Erikson, E.H. (1980). Themes of love and work in adulthood. Cambridge, MA: Harvard University Press.

Spong, Bishop J. S. (1997). Blessing gay and lesbian commitments (pp. 67–70). In A. Sullivan (Ed.), *Same-sex marriage: Pro and con.* New York: Vintage Books.

Stacey, J. (2001). Gay and lesbian relationships are here (pp. 195–207). In S. Ferguson (Ed.), *Shifting the center: understanding contemporary families.* Mountainview, CA: Mayfield Publishing Company.

Statistics Canada. (1997). Mortality: Summary List of Causes.

Statistics Canada. (1999). Dependency Ratio. *Health Indicators* (82-221-XIE). Retrieved on February 3, 2002, from: statcan.ca.

Statistics Canada. (1999, Winter). Health status of children. Health Reports (11) 3, pp. 25–36.

Statistics Canada. (1996, March 11). Young adults living at home. *The Daily.* Retrieved August 21, 2001, from: statcan.ca.

Statistics Canada. (1997, July 29). Age and sex: 1996 census. *The Daily.* Retrieved on February 1, 2002, from: statcan.ca

Statistics Canada. (1999, June 11). Family violence in Canada: A statistical profile. *The Daily.* Retrieved April 5, 2002, from: statcan.ca.

Statistics Canada. (1999, December 22). Report on the demographic situation in Canada. *The Daily.* Retrieved February 1, 2002, from: statcan.ca.

Statistics Canada. (1999, December 23). Labour force update: Youths and the labour force. *The Daily.* Retrieved August 21, 2001, from: statcan.ca.

Statistics Canada. (2000, September 5). Rural Youth: Stayers, leavers and return migrants. *The Daily.* Retrieved August 21, 2001, from: statcan.ca.

Statistics Canada. (2001, April 10). Survey of approaches to educational planning. *The Daily.* Retrieved August 21, 2001, from: statcan.ca.

Statistics Canada. (2002, January 23). Youth in transition survey. *The Daily.* Retrieved February 3, 2002, from: statcan.ca.

Steinberg, L. (1987, September). Bound to bicker *Psychology Today, 36,* 38–39.

Steinhauer, P. (1997, June). Windows of opportunity: Raising a healthy child depends on time—and timing. Retrieved December 2001, from Child and Family Canada web site: http://www.cfc-efc.ca/docs/vocfc/00001087.htm

Stevens-Long, J., & Commons, M.L (1992). *Adult life: Developmental processes.* Toronto: Mayfield Publishing Company.

Sturino, F. (1980). Family and kin cohesion among southern Italian immigrants in Toronto (pp. 84–104). In K. Ishwaran (Ed.), *Canadian families: Ethnic variations.* Toronto: McGraw-Hill Ryerson.

Sullivan, A., ed. (1997). *Same sex marriage: Pro and con.* New York: Vintage Books.

Sweeney, M. M. (1997, September). Remarriage of women and men after divorce: The role of socioeconomic prospects. *Journal of Family Issues 18* (5), 479–502.

Tanfer, K., & Mott, F. (1997, January 16–17). The meaning of fatherhood for men. From *Improving Data on Male Fertility and Family Formation* for the NICHD Workshop, Urban Institute, Washington, DC., January 16–17, 1997. Retrieved Februaray 24, 2002, from: http://www.fatherhood.hhs.gov/CFSForum/apenc.htm

Tannen, D. (1994, October). But what do you mean? *Redbook,* 91–93, 145–147.

Teevan, J.J., & Hewitt, W.E. (1995). *Basic sociology: A Canadian introduction.* (5th ed.) Scarborough, ON: Prentice Hall Canada Inc.

Theobald, S. (1997, November 24). University pays, research shows. *The Toronto Star.*

Torjman, S. (1994). Crests and crashes: The changing tides of family income security (pp. 69–88). In M. Baker (Ed.), *Canada's changing families: Challenges to public policy.* Ottawa: Vanier Institute of the Family.

Toronto Disaster Relief Committee. (2001). Retrieved on November 5, 2001, from: www.tdrc.net.

Trends in Canadian suicide. (1998, June) #30. Calgary: Suicide Information & Education Centre, Retrieved October 19, 2001, from: Electric Library Canada.

Trocmé, N., et al. (2001). Canadian incidence study of reported child abuse and neglect: Final report. Ottawa, Health Canada.

Tuller, N. R. (1988). Couples: The hidden segment of the gay world. In J.P. De Cecco (Ed.), *Gay relationships.* New York: Harrington Park Press.

Turcotte, P., & Bélanger, A. (1997, Winter). Moving in together. *Canadian Social Trends 47,* 7–9.

Turnbull, C. (1985). *The human cycle.* London: Triad/Paladin Books.

Ungar, T. E. (2001, February 01). Suicide prevention. *Patient Care: The Practical Journal for Canadian Primary Care Physicians,* pp. 67–70. Retrieved October 19, 2001, from: Electric Library Canada.

Vanier Institute of the Family. (2002). *From kitchen table to the boardroom table: A digest.* Retrieved on February 5, 2002, from: www.vifamily.ca/work/table/digest.htm.

Vanier Institute of the Family. (2000, November). *Child poverty 'unacceptably high': Study.* Ottawa: Vanier Institute of the Family, Families and Health 15, 5.

Vanier Institute of the Family. (2000, October). *Health of immigrant, refugee children focus of book.* Ottawa: Vanier Institute of the Family, Families and Health, 14, 5.

Vanier Institute of the Family. (2000). *Profiling Canada's families II.* Ottawa: Vanier Institute of the Family.

Van Kirk, S. (1992). The custom of the country: An examination of fur trade marriage practices (pp. 67-92). In Bradbury, B. (Ed.) *Canadian family history: Selected readings.* Toronto: Copp Clark Pitman Ltd.

VanLaningham, J., Johnson, D.R., & Amato, P. (2001, June). Marital happiness, marital duration, and the U-shaped curve: Evidence from a five-wave panel study. *Social Forces 78* (4), 1313–1339.

Vaughan, P. (1998). *The monogamy myth: a personal handbook for recovering from affairs.* New York: Newmarket Press.

Vinovskis, M. A. (2001). Historical perspectives on parent-child interactions (pp. 215–230). In S. Ferguson (Ed.), *Shifting the center: understanding contemporary families.* Toronto: Mayfield Publishing Company.

Voices for Children (1999). The new Canadian family: Fact Sheet #1." Voices for Children. Retrieved January 7, 2002, from: www.voices4children.org/factsheet/factsheet1.htm.

Waite, L.J. (1995, November). Does marriage matter? *Demography, 32* (4), 483–505.

Walker, L. (1979). *The battered woman.* New York: Harper and Row.

Walkom, T. (2001, September 8). Aging boomers not nemesis of medicare. *The Toronto Star,* pp. K1, K4.

Walsh, F. (1989). The family in later life (pp. 311–333). In B. Carter & M. McGoldrick (Eds.), *The changing family life cycle: A framework for family therapy (2nd ed.).* Toronto: Allyn and Bacon.

Ward, M. (1994). *The family dynamic: A Canadian perspective.* Scarborough, ON: Nelson Canada.

Ward, P. (1990). *Courtship, love and marriage in nineteenth-century English Canada.* Montreal & Kingston: McGill-Queen's University Press.

Ward, S. (1999, May 11). Lending a helping hand to the down and out. *Medical Post 35.* Retrieved November 5, 2001, from Electric Library Canada.

Weitzman, L. (1985). *The divorce revolution: The unexpected social and economic consequences for women and children in America.* New York: Free Press.

Wharf, B. Families in crisis (pp. 55-68). In M. Baker (Ed.), *Canada's changing families: Challenges to public policy.* Ottawa: Vanier Institute of the Family.

White, J.M., (1992). Marriage: A developing process (pp. 197–211). In K. Ishwaran (Ed.), *Family and marriage: Cross-cultural perspectives.* Toronto: Thompson Educational Publishing, Inc.

Whyte, M.K. (2001). Choosing mates—The American way (pp. 129–138). In S. Ferguson (Ed.), *Shifting the center: understanding contemporary families.* Toronto: Mayfield Publishing Company.

Whitehead, B.D. (1998). *The divorce culture: Rethinking our commitments to marriage and family.* New York: Vintage Books.

Wiederman, M.W. (1999, July). Extramarital affairs: An exaggerated myth. *USA Today.* Retrieved January 27, 2002, from findarticles.com.

Wiener, V.(1997). *The nesting syndrome: Grown children living at home.* Minneapolis: Fairview Press.

Wilcoxon, S. E. (1991). Grandparents and grandchildren: An often-neglected relationship between significant others (pp. 342–345). In J.E. Veevers (Ed.), *Continuity & change in marriage & family.* Toronto: Holt, Rinehart and Winston of Canada, Limited.

Wild, Russell. (1999). *Why men marry.* Lincolnwood (Chicago) IL: Contemporary Books.

Wilson, S. J. (2001). *Intimacy and commitment in family formation.* Toronto: McGraw-Hill Ryerson Limited.

Wilson, S. J. (1991) *Women, families, and work.* Toronto: McGraw-Hill Ryerson Limited.

Wu, Z. (1998, September). Recent trends in marriage patterns in Canada. *Policy Options,* 3–6.

Wu, Z. (1999). Premarital Cohabitation and the timeing of first marriage. *Canadaian Review of Sociology and Anthropology 36* (1), 109–127.

Wu, Z. & Balakrishnan, T.R. (1995, November). Dissolution of premarital cohabitation in Canada. *Demography 32* (4), 521–535.

Wu, Z. & Penning, M. J. (1997, September). Marital stability after midlife. *Journal of Family Issues 18* (5), 459–478.

Wu, Z. & Pollard, M. (1998, June). *Economic circumstances and the stability of nonmarital cohabitation.* Ottawa: Statistics Canada.

Yalom, M. (2001). *A history of the wife.* New York: HarperCollins Publishers Inc.

Young, A. Harvison. (1994). Joint custody as norm: Solomon revisited. *Osgoode Hall C.J. 32,* p. 785.

Zinsmeister, K. (1999, September). Fatherhood is not for wimps. *American Enterprise.* Retrieved on February 5, 2002, from findarticles.com.

Glossary

A

abstract a summary of the contents of a document, which can be used to simplify the search for pertinent research papers

activity theory of aging theory that suggests that aging individuals are reluctant to give up roles unless they can substitute other meaningful ones; supports the value of social and physical activity as a contributor to self-esteem

adolescence that period of life that follows childhood and precedes adulthood; a passage not clearly defined in Western society (from the Latin word *adolescere*, meaning to grow up)

adultery sex with a partner other than one's spouse

adulthood the period of life that follows childhood and adolescence and lasts until death

advanced industrial economy the economy in Canada in which there are fewer jobs in the traditional areas of agriculture and manufacturing, and more in the service economy

affective nurturance meeting individuals' emotional needs

age of majority the age at which you legally become an adult— in Canada, 18 years

age strata layers, or cohorts, within a society, defined by chronological age

agent of socialization a person or institution that acts to socialize an individual

androcentricity a bias that assumes male experience is human experience and therefore applies also to women

anthropology the study of humans and their culture in societies

anticipatory socialization being made aware of the expectations of a new role and practising role behaviour before taking on that new role

arranged marriage marriages that take place through negotiations between sets of parents, or their agents

artificial insemination a type of assisted reproductive technology, in which sperm is placed in the vagina or uterus by artificial means

assault in reference to violence within intimate relationships, violence against a partner is now legally defined as assault rather than abuse

assisted reproductive technologies (ART) medical technologies, such as drug therapies, artificial insemination, in vitro fertilization, and embryo implants used to help infertile people achieve the goal of having a biological child

attachment the behaviours that meet the need of an infant to maintain or attain proximity and protection with a parent or an available and responsive caregiver

authoritarian parenting a parenting style characterized by parental control and the use of reward and punishment

authoritative parenting a parenting style characterized by warmth, support, acceptance, and indirect positive control of children

autonomous self term used by Jane Loevinger to describe a self-reliant person who accepts oneself and others as being multifaceted and unique

B

baby boom the cohort born between 1947 and 1966

baby bust the cohort following the baby boomers, from 1967 to 1979

baby-boom echo the cohort born between 1980 and 1995

banns in the Christian religious marriage tradition, a public announcement three weeks prior to the marriage ceremony that a couple are to be married; may be used instead of a marriage licence

bereavement the state that families and friends are left in when a family member or close friend dies

betrothal a promise to marry

bilateral descent system a system of family lineage in which the relatives on the mother's side and the father's side are equally important for emotional ties or for transfer of property or wealth

biographical interview research method in which subjects, in interviews, are encouraged to use open-ended and wide-ranging answers to recall their life stories

biological clock the limits on behaviour determined by physical aging; commonly used to refer to the length of time that a woman's body is able to conceive and carry a child

blended family a family structure created when divorced partners with children marry

bride price the payment by a groom or his family to the bride's family

bundling an early New England courtship custom in rural families; a young unmarried couple would be tucked into bed so that they could converse privately and not get cold—a "bundling board" was placed between them for propriety

C

child abuse when a child is severely beaten or killed by a parent or guardian—the person who is responsible for loving and caring for him or her

child neglect neglect covers a wide range of parental behaviours, from failure to provide the necessities of life, to inadequate supervision, to emotional neglect, when the parent withdraws emotionally from the child, providing little love or emotional support

childhood a stage in human development that precedes adolescence; recognized as a distinct stage in the first half of the nineteenth century

clan a family grouping consisting of many related extended families

closed questions in research questionnaires, questions that require the subject to select from answers provided

cohabitation an intimate relationship in which a male and female live together as husband and wife without legally marrying; also called common-law marriage

cohort a group of individuals born in the same well-defined time period (used cautiously to understand the behaviour of individuals of the same age)

cohort effect the idea suggested by Leonard Pearlin that changes in behaviour results from socialized responses to changes in social expectations rather than from age-linked inner changes

commitment dedication to maintaining a long-term relationship

common-law marriage an intimate relationship in which a male and female live together as husband and wife without legally marrying; also called cohabitation

companionate marriage a marriage based on friendship and shared lifestyle, and that assumes the relationship is based on romantic love

conflict theory an interdisciplinary sociological and political theory that explains that power, not functional interdependence, forms the basis of social organization; conflict exists between groups in society because of inequalities in power

congenital anomalies health problems with which some children are born that lead to death

conjugal relationship a relationship based on a sexual union; includes marriage and cohabitation

consanguinity relationship based on blood

constructive conflict conflict that is managed in a non-aggressive and productive manner (contrast *destructive conflict*)

consumer family a family in which the husband was the exclusive provider and the head of the household, while the wife was the homemaker for whom products were manufactured to help create a comfortable home for the family

cottage industry an economic activity in which merchants and artisans worked in the family home, with family members helping with the work

courtship the process in mate selection that allowed for individuals to win the affection of someone to whom they are attracted

credentialism the trend in Canada for education to be valued as qualifications for jobs rather than for the knowledge and skills it provides

crisis in the family life-cycle theory, an event (such as the birth of a child) that requires a response by changing behaviour; causes development

cycle of violence the repeating pattern that both victims and perpetrators of spousal violence follow: the tension-building phase; the abusive incident or acute battering phase; the calm-and-penance phase. (See also *stages of engagement*)

D

dating a North American social invention in the twentieth century, which evolved from courtship; young men ask young women out on their own (rather than in social groups) for more of a recreational activity than for courtship

delayed parenthood when couples put off having children until they are in their thirties and forties

demographics the analysis of statistical data of a population, such as age, marital status, average income

dependency crisis the belief by some demographers that global aging presents a threat to world economies and, in Canada, the concern that the impending retirement of the large baby-boom generation, due to begin in 2010, will strain the resources of their children's generation

dependency ratio the economic ratio of dependants, that is, children and seniors, to people of working age

dependency-free expectancy the length of time individuals can expect to live before they require social, medical or financial support; the dependency-free expectancy for Canadian men is 72 years, and for women, 73.9 years

dependent variable the variable, or quality, in research that depends results from the independent variable, or the effect in a cause-and-effect situation

despair the state that individuals are in when they have not done what they wanted to do with their lives and there is no time left to make changes; according to Erikson, individuals who have not achieved integrity feel this despair

destructive conflict conflicts that are managed in a hostile and angry manner (contrast *constructive conflict*)

developmental tasks role expectations that challenge individuals to adopt new behaviours as they progress through life

developmental theories theories that use an interdisciplinary approach to describe patterns of life and to describe growth or changes in human behaviour throughout the life span

diminished parenting the lessened ability to parent for people who are suffering the stress that comes with divorce and a newly single life; parents who are facing increased emotional and financial burdens as a result of divorce cannot cope easily with the pressures of parenting

discipline specific branches of learning, such as mathematics, physics, or psychology

discrimination a difference in treatment based on classification of individuals (often in reference to gender or race)

disengagement theory a theory that suggested that as older people prepared for their own deaths, they became preoccupied with themselves and with thoughts of the past, and withdrew from social activity (contrast *social death theory*)

divorce the legal dissolution of a marriage

domestic violence violence within family relationships; in the early and mid-twentieth century, violence of the patriarch (man) of a household against his wife, children, or servants; assumed by the police (and society) to be a private matter unless the assault was witnessed

double standards biases that apply different standards for evaluating the behaviour of men and women

dower rights the rights of a wife to a share of her husband's property if he dies before her

dowry the payment, in the form of money, land, or household items, given to a bride by the bride's family so she could establish a home for her new family

Dream according to Daniel Levinson, the individual's sense of self in the adult world and the core of the life structure; most Dreams describe some combination of occupational, family, and community roles

dual-income family a family structure in which both spouses work for income

duty-based moral code a cultural value system that places a greater priority on family obligations than on personal considerations when making important decisions

E

ecofeminists feminists who believe that the domination of women is directly connected to the environmental destruction of nature, and who promote the interconnected web of life

education inflation the idea that youth today require more education to qualify for some jobs now than was required for the same jobs in the past

egalitarian marriage marriage in which the couple are equal partners in decision making

egalitarian relationships intimate relationships in which men and women share the responsibilities rather than adhere to fixed gender roles

ego the objective understanding of the self, a term introduced by Sigmund Freud

elder abuse conscious and unconscious acts against seniors involving physical, psychological, medical, material/financial, and legal harm.

elder neglect failure to provide care for seniors

embryo implants a type of assisted reproductive technology in which a human embryo is implanted in the womb

empty nest in the family life cycle theory, a term describing couples or individuals whose children have matured and left the family of origin

ethnocentrism the tendency to evaluate behaviour from the point of view of your own culture

expressive role women's emotional role of providing a supportive home for their families (contrast *instrumental role*)

extended family family consisting of all relatives (parents, children, grandparents, aunts and uncles, cousins, etc.); often used in a more limited sense to define a family structure in which a married couple and their children share a household with parents

F

family life-cycle theory a developmental perspective on the life spans of families

family studies an interdisciplinary study that integrates anthropology, sociology, psychology and other social sciences to study the behaviour of individuals and their families

family systems theory a sociological theory that explains the interactions among family members

family wage the economic concept that a man's income should provide adequate money to support a wife and children; family wage was used to justify paying women less than men for performing the same work

family-work conflict stress arising when an individual's family responsibilities affect workplace roles (contrast *work-family conflict*)

female infanticide the killing of female children immediately after birth

feminist theories conflict theories that were developed to explain the impact of sex and gender on behaviour, and to consider issues of human behaviour from the specific viewpoint of women

fertility refers to the actual reproductive performance of a person (usually a woman)

fertility rate the number of children born alive during a specified period

free-choice mate selection when individuals are attracted to each other, fall in love, and decide to marry

function in sociology, a basic and universal action or purpose of individuals or groups

functional requisites basic functions that must be carried out for societies to survive and thrive

functionalism the sociological theory that tries to explain how a society is organized to perform functions effectively (also called *structural functionalism*)

G

generation a group of people all born around the same time; each cohort may become a generation with distinctive characteristics, such as the baby boom or the echo-boom generations

generativity productivity, or the range of ways people are able to leave their mark on future generations; what Erikson describes as the basis of identity in middle adulthood

genetic diseases hereditary diseases such as diabetes, hemophilia, sickle-cell anemia

genogram a diagram that depicts the nature of the interactions within a family system

gerotranscendence a sense of rising above the difficulties of age; Erikson's term for the challenge of "old" old age

grieving process the process of mourning, and accepting the death of a loved one over time

H

heterogamy marriage between two partners who are from different racial, social, religious, ethnic, or cultural backgrounds (also called *intermarriage*; contrast *homogamy*)

homelessness having no fixed place to sleep at night

homeostasis a state of equilibrium within a system; systems theory suggests that a change in one part of a system will require other parts of the system to adjust in order to maintain this state of balance

horde a band of people, referring to the first family groupings of humans—much like the troops of primates

household a term used by Statistics Canada to mean groups of people who live together whether or not they are related by birth, adoption, or marriage

hypothesis a possible answer to a research question

I

ideal mate theory a theory of mate selection that attempts to explain attraction from a symbolic interactionist perspective; attraction is based on an individual's unconscious image of the ideal mate formed from perceptions of the meaning of certain characteristics

identity who an individual is; Erik Erikson's theory describes the formation of identity in eight stages of life

in vitro fertilization a procedure in which eggs (ova) from a woman's ovary are removed and are fertilized with sperm in a laboratory procedure, and then the fertilized egg (embryo) is returned to the woman's uterus

independent variables the variable, or quality in research that the dependent variable is based on, or the cause in a cause-and-effect situation

individualism a social philosophy that emphasizes independence and self-reliance and that favours the free action of individuals

individuation in the family life-cycle theory, the process of young adults forming an identity separate from that of the family of origin

industrial nuclear family a family structure in which there is a separation of the means of earning income (in industry or business) from the home and household tasks

infant mortality rate number of deaths of infants less than one year of age per 1000 births

infertile unable to reproduce

infidelity unfaithfulness to the intimate relationship; having extramarital affairs

insecurely attached infants babies with a limited degree of attachment to their primary caregiver (See also *attachment* and *securely attached infants*)

institutions social structures, such as the law, the economy, and the family, that by performing assigned functions enable societies to carry out the functional requisites

instrumental role men's goal-oriented role of providing for the family by working and earning an income (contrast *expressive role*)

intact family a family in which both parents are in their first marriage and have biological or adopted children

integrity completeness, uprightness, or attachment to principle; refers to Erikson's idea that, in later life, individuals seek the integrity that results from living out one's identity

intergenerational cycle of violence the evidence that individuals who experienced violence or abuse as a child, or who observed the assault or abuse of others, are more likely to become either victims or perpetrators of violence in their intimate relationships

intermarriage marriage between two partners who are from different racial, social, religious, ethnic, or cultural backgrounds (also called *heterogamy*; contrast *homogamy*)

K

kin group refers to all of a family's relatives—uncles, aunts, cousins, grandparents, in-laws, and other relatives

kin-keeper a cross-cultural expectation that women will organize family events and maintain contact with family members

L

liberal feminism a feminist theory that argues that women are unable to participate in society according to their individual abilities because discriminatory policies in society place arbitrary limits on their behaviour

life structure the pattern or design of an individual's life, according to Levinson

limerance the blissful emotional state felt when lovers fall "head over heels" in love

lineage ancestry

low income cut-off (LICO) the term that Statistics Canada uses to define families living in poverty; those who live below the low income cut-off (LICO) point have insufficient income for a minimum standard of living.

M

macro study a large-scale study of patterns of behaviour within a society

marital system the strategies for interaction and influence between the individuals in a marriage or intimate relationship

market experience perspective the idea that dating enabled individuals to learn to relate to the opposite sex and to judge character so that they would be able to determine what qualities they wanted in a marriage partner

marriage a relationship between two or more individuals based on sexual union that is recognized as legitimate and that carries specific role expectations within a society

marriage contract the mutual obligations of husband and wife

matrilineal descent system a system of family lineage in which only the relatives on the mother's side are important for emotional ties or for transfer of property or wealth

matrilocal when a family or kinship group is located near the wife's family

mentor in the world of work, a more experienced person who assists a younger person through the transition into a career path

micro study a small-scale study of individual cases

middle age the middle of the life span

midlife transition the passage from early adulthood into middle adulthood; Daniel Levinson's research defined a midlife transition that occurs between 40 and 45 years of age

monogamy having one marital partner

N

natural selection in evolution, the process by which the fittest survive because they are able to adapt to their environment mand compete successfully for limited resources

negotiation a process of conferring with others in order to reach an mutually acceptable solution to a problem

non-event life passages that we want to happen but don't, such as not marrying or having children

non-normative crises in the family life cycle, unexpected events such as unemployment, infertility, illness, or infidelity that require an adjustment in behaviour (also called non-normative events; contrast normative events)

norm the most prevalent behaviour that occurs; consistent behaviour

normative event in family life-cycle theory, the predictable events in life that require a developmental change in behaviour (also called normative crisis; contrast non-normative crisis)

nuclear family a family structure in which the husband and wife live with their children

O

open-ended questions in research questionnaires, questions that the subjects can answer freely

opinion people's thinking or judgment about something or someone (see *perception*)

orderly change model based on the stage theories of development; it explains that an individual's identity is formed earlier in life, but changes through interaction with the environment in the present

P

pair-bond the enduring relationship between a man and a woman, thought to be essential to human survival, and the trademark of humans, according to Helen Fisher

parameter in research, definitions or limits on what is being studied

parenthood the transition to parenting and rearing a child.

parenting styles the patterns of socialization of children by parents based on the balance of power among parents and their children

participant observation a type of observation in research in which the researcher is a participant in the group being studied, and the subjects are aware that they are being observed

patriarchy family organization in which men wield power and are the decision makers

patrilineal descent system a system of family lineage in which only relatives on the father's side are important for emotional ties or for transfer of property or wealth

patrilocal when a family or kinship group is located near the husband's family

pay equity equal pay for work of equal value

peer marriage a truly egalitarian companionate relationship, in which division of household and child-care roles is based on negotiation, not traditional gender roles

perception something observed or taken in through the mind or senses (see *opinion*)

perinatal referring to the period of time immediately after birth

permissive parenting a parenting style in which the children have greater power than parents in family situations

persistent poverty poverty that lasts for a long time rather than a short term result of a crisis

personality a person's characteristic patterns of motivation

phases periods of change in events, attitudes, and accomplishments; refers to life stages theory

physical abuse non-accidental physical injury to a child resulting from actions of a parent or guardian

polyandry the practice of a wife having several husbands

polygamy the practice of having several spouses

polygyny the practice of a man having more than one wife

primary caregivers the main people responsible for raising a child, usually parents

primary sources research sources that present information first-hand; results from original investigations

principle of least interest in reference to couple relationships, the principle that explains that the person with the least commitment to the relationship has the greatest power, since the person with the greater commitment is more likely to give in to maintain harmony

psychological clock referring to the life span, the pace of development of mental processes that determines the meaning that individuals make of their own lives

psychology the study of behaviour based on mental processes

Q

qualitative methods in research, those methods that are used to gather detailed information from individuals to help the researcher understand their behaviour; it assumes that each subject may behave differently and does not usually predict how others may behave

quantitative methods in research, those methods that gather information from many people, which can be analyzed to describe, explain, and predict patterns of behaviour for groups of people; the results can be analyzed using statistics to generalize from the behaviour of the sample group

questionnaires a type of survey in which the questions are written and given to the subject to answer in written form; they may contain closed questions or open-ended questions

R

radical feminism a feminist theory that argues that the difference in power between men and women result in any male-female relationship as being exploitative

reference groups in symbolic interactionism, groups of people who influence the formation of an individual's identity

research essay a type of research paper that presents and supports an argument or thesis based on research in the social sciences

research report a type of technical research paper that presents research in the social sciences; it reports the results of an original investigation, and includes a description of the method and results

resocialization the ability of an individual to discard old behaviour and to change his or her behaviour when making a transition to a new role

retirement the process of leaving the structure of the work force to live out the remainder of one's life

rites of passage societal rituals that distinguish the recognizable stages of life

role the set of behaviours that an individual is expected to demonstrate within a status

S

sample group in research, the selected group from the people being studied

Seasons used by Daniel Levinson and others to refer to the stages of life, reflecting the concept that stages follow each other in a predictable sequence, but that each is different in nature and yet equally important for growth

secondary sources research sources that analyze research; they present someone else's analysis second-hand

securely attached infants babies with a high degree of attachment to their primary caregiver (See also *attachment* and *insecurely attached infants*)

self-esteem an individual's sense of self, as part of the identity

self-fulfilling prophecy the observation that an individual's behaviour tends to conform to the expected behaviour

serial monogamy marriage to several spouses, one after the other

sexual abuse forced sexual activity within a relationship, now usually called sexual assault

shared roles the pattern of the division of labour and decision making within a relationship

significant others the people who have an important influence on a individual's development

social clock the pace of development defined by societal expectations concerning age-appropriate behaviour

social construction theory a theory of aging related to symbolic interactionism, it suggests that individuals' actions and feelings have no intrinsic meaning on their own, but are given meaning by the theoretical perspectives that are developed for their explanation; suggests that individuals' behaviour does not necessarily differ from place to place, or from generation to generation, but the meaning ascribed to the behaviour changes to reflect the expectations of the society

social death theory a theory to do with aging that says that there is mutual withdrawing of older people and society; since death is unfamiliar, the anticipation of it is difficult, and individuals may cope by avoiding the aging, the dying and the bereaved (contrast *disengagement theory*)

social exchange theory a psychological theory that attempts to explain how individuals form and interact within reciprocal relationships by analyzing the costs and benefits of the relationship

social history history of ordinary people in social relationships; it relies on existing accounts (letters, newspapers, official papers, essays, poems, etc.) from the past as its primary sources

social homogamy a theory that describes how individuals are attracted to those from a similar social background

socialist feminism a feminist theory that is based on the assumption that the status of women is a social inequality rooted in the sexual division of paid and unpaid labour; it challenges both capitalism and the patriarchal model of the family

socialization the process by which new members of a society acquire the knowledge, skills, and attitudes required to participate actively in that society

socialize teach new members, such as children or new employees, the skills, knowledge, values, and attitudes of their society

sociology the social science that explains the behaviour of individuals in social groups

spousal violence when a person uses physical force against his or her spouse

spouse a marriage partner

stability template model a theory of aging that assumes that the motivation of individuals does not change once they achieve adulthood; based on the belief that the basic personality is formed in childhood, and accepts recent evidence that personality continues to develop into adulthood.

stagnation Erik Erikson's term for a state in which individuals can cease to develop by becoming self-indulgent, rather than being in a state of generativity

stages of engagement in reference to spousal violence, two additional stages that progress after the cycle of violence is broken: the terror stage and, in some cases, the second stage of homicide

status a specific position within a social group

stereotypes preconceived and oversimplified impressions of the characteristics of people or situations; for example, expectations of people based on gender

sterilization method of causing permanent infertility by removing or disabling reproductive organs

subjects in research, the individuals being studied within a sample group

symbolic analysts people who can manipulate mathematical data and words and identify and solve problems

symbolic interactionism a psychological theory that attempts to explain how individuals choose how they will act based on their perceptions of themselves and of others

systems theory the sociological theory that attempts to explain how groups of individuals interact as a system—a set of different parts that work together and influence one another in a relatively stable way over time

T

theoretical perspective in sociological and psychological study, a point of view based on a specific theory

theory a framework for organizing and explaining observable evidence

theory of intergenerational transmission refers to elder abuse; suggests that people who were abused or neglected as children by their parents are likely to abuse or neglect their parents when they are old

theory of random change a theory of aging that explains that fate, or non-normative events, cause change in identity because of how individuals adapt to their new roles; this model asks whether social change affects the behaviour of a cohort, resulting in the cohort effect

transition a change from one stage of a life cycle to another

transitional family a family structure in which the mother temporarily leaves the work force to look after her young children

trends patterns of change in behaviour

U

universal day care licensed day care that is available and accessible for all families

V

variables in research qualities, such as gender or birth order, or behaviours, such as marrying or attending university

verbal/emotional abuse abuse in the form of insults; put-downs that can cause psychological harm

victim referring to abuse, assault or violence, the person who is mistreated

voluntary childlessness when couples deliberately decide not to become parents

W

wisdom the ego strength, meaning insight and enlightenment, that occurs when an individual completes the formation of their identity in Erik Erikson's eighth stage of life, "integrity versus despair"

work-family conflict stress arising when work responsibilities affect family roles (contrast *family-work conflict*)

Credits

Photo Credits

Collection/CORBIS/Magma; **283** Between Friends reprinted with special permission of King Features Syndicate; **289** © Bill Bachman/PhotoEdit; **296** © Ewing Galloway/Maxx Images. **Chapter 10 303** © Joe Lavine/Firstlight.ca; **307** © Ariel Skelley/CORBIS STOCK MARKET/Magma; **309** © Ed Bock/CORBIS STOCK MARKET/Magma; **310** © Michael Newman/PhotoEdit; **313** The Founders' Network; **316** © J-M Foujols/Firstlight.ca; **317** © Robert E Daemmrich/Stone Images; **319** © Elizabeth Zuckerman/Photo Edit; **321** © SW Productions/PhotoDisc; **327** © Tom McCarthy/PhotoEdit; **329** © Jim Craigmyle/Masterfile; **331** © Bill Bachmann/PhotoEdit; **334** © Michael Newman/ PhotoEdit. **Chapter 11 339** Ron Bull/Toronto Star; **341** © Mark Richards/PhotoEdit; **342** © Laura Dwight/PhotoEdit; **344** Preston Manning's office; **347** Toronto Sun (Wanda Goodwin); **349** © Bill Aron/PhotoEdit; **350** Pat McGrath/The Ottawa Citizen; **353** Rene Johnston/ Toronto Star; **356 top** Toronto Globe & Mail (Fred Lum); **bottom** © Skjold Photographs; **359** © Mark Richards/ PhotoEdit; **360** CP (Jonathan Hayward); **364** Theo Moudakis/ Toronto Star; **365** © Chad Ehlers/Maxx Images; **369** © James Shaffer/ PhotoEdit; **372** CP (Jeff McIntosh); **374** © Lucille Khornak/Firstlight.ca. **Unit 5** © S.Murphy-Larronde/ Firstlight.ca **Chapter 12 381** © Julian Hirshowitz/CORBIS/ Magma; **388** Doug Griffin/Toronto Star; **391** © Gaetano/ CORBIS/Magma; **393** © Michael Newman/PhotoEdit; **396** © Spencer Grant/PhotoEdit; **398** Rick Eglinton/Toronto Star; **400** © Dana White/PhotoEdit; **402** © David Young-Wolff/ PhotoEdit; **406** Courtesy of University of Alberta; **408** © David Young-Wolff/PhotoEdit; **411** Maureen Holloway. **Chapter 13 418** © Network Productions/Maxx Images; **421** © Image 100/Royalty-Free/CORBIS/Magma; **423** Courtesy of David M. Buss; **426** © David Young-Wolff/PhotoEdit; **427** © Bill Bachmann/PhotoEdit; **430** Colin McConnell/The Toronto Star; **432** Between Friends reprinted with special permission of King Features Syndicate; **433** © Paul Franklian/ Maxx Images; **434** © Mark Richards/PhotoEdit; **437** © Spencer Grant/PhotoEdit; **438** © Rhoda Sidney/PhotoEdit; **441** © Will Hart/PhotoEdit. **Chapter 14 457** © Michael Newman/PhotoEdit; **453** © Jack Hollingsworth/CORBIS/ Magma; **455** © Jim Skinner/Firstlight.ca; **457** For Better or For Worse © Lynn Johnston Productions, Inc./Distributed by United Feature Syndicate, Inc.; **458** Julie Oliver/The Ottawa Citizen; **461** © Felicia Martinez/PhotoEdit; **462** © Mark Richards/PhotoEdit; **464** © Billy E. Barnes/PhotoEdit; **465**

Anne Mason; **466** © Amy Etra/PhotoEdit; **470** © John A. Rizzo/Firstlight.ca; **476 top** © Dinodia/Firstlight.ca; **bottom** D'Arcy Glionna; **480** Maureen Holloway.

Text Credits

Chapter 1 4 Goode, W.J. (1964). quoted in A. Inkeles, (Ed.), *The Family: Prentice-Hall Foundations of Modern Sociology Series*. Prentice-Hall, Inc.: Englewood Cliffs, New Jersey, p. 3.; **6** *Profiling Canada's Families (1994)*. Ottawa: Vanier Institute of the Family, p. 10; **7-8** Zimmerman, S.I. (1988). *Understanding Family Policy: Theoretical Approaches*. Beverly Hills: Sage. pp.75-76. In B. Schlesinger. (1998). *Strengths in Families: Accentuating the Positive*, Ottawa: Vanier Institute of the Family Web site www.vifamily.ca/cft/strength/strength.htm; **21** Wiener, V. (1997). *The Nesting Syndrome: Grown Children Living at Home*. Minneapolis, MN: Fairview Press. p. 9. **Chapter 2 27** "Family Structures, 1994," adapted from the Statistics Canada publication, *Canadian Social Trends - Spring 1977*, Catalogue 11-008, Issue No. 44, pg. 3; **29** Reprinted with permission of the Edmonton Journal; **34** Hawking, S.W. (1988). *A Brief History of Time: From the Big Bang to Black Holes*. New York: Bantam Books. p. 9. Permission granted by Bantam Books, a division of Random House, Inc.; **46** Teevan, J.J. (Ed.) (1995). *Basic Sociology: A Canadian Introduction*, 5th ed. Scarborough, ON: Prentice-Hall Canada. p.153, reprinted with permission of Pearson Education Canada Inc. **Chapter 3 58** "Table 4.2: Expectations of Teenagers" from *Canada's Teens Today, Yesterday and Tomorrow*. Copyright © 2001 by Reginald W. Bibby. Reproduced by permission of Stoddart Publishing Co. Limited; **59-60** Justice for Children and Youth/Canadian Foundation for Children, Youth and the Law; **68** Adapted from the Statistics Canada publication, *Canadian Social Trends - Spring 1999*, Catalogue 11-008, Issue No. 52, feature "The Crowded Nest: Young Adults at Home," pg. 3; **74** Allahar, A. & Coté, J. (1998). *Richer and Poorer: The structure of inequality in Canada*. Toronto: James Lorimer & Company Ltd., Publishers, p. 134; **77** Adapted from the Statistics Canada publication *Report of the Pan-Canadian Education Indicators Program 1999*, Catalogue 81-582; **78** "Employment and Education" partially created with data from the Statistics Canada publication *Labour Force Annual Averages, 1989-1994*, Catalogue 71-529, 1995 and "Figure 3: Employment and Education" from *Boom, Bust and Echo*. Copyright © 1996,

1998 by David K. Foot and Words on Paper Inc. Reproduced by permission of Stoddart Publishing Co. Limited; **81** "University qualifications," adapted from the Statistics Canada web site www.statcan.ca/english/Pgdb/People/Health /educ21.htm, extracted September 2001; **82** "Community college diplomas," adapted from the Statistics Canada web site www.statcan.ca/english/Pgdb/People/Health/educ19.htm, extracted September 2001; **86** "How 1995 graduates found a job," adapted from the Statistics Canada publication, *Canadian Social Trends - Autumn 1997,* Catalogue 11-008, Issue No. 46, pg. 15; **86** "Median earnings of 1990 graduates" adapted from the Statistics Canada publication, *The Class of 90: A compendium of findings from the 1992 National Graduates Survey of 1990 Graduates,* December 1996, Catalogue 81-577, chart 3.2, pg. 37; **87** Abstract from Finnie, R. "School to Work: The Evolution of Early Labour Market Outcomes in Canadian Postsecondary Graduates." In *Canadian Public Policy,* Vol. xxvi, No. 2, June 2000. **Chapter 4 98-100** From *Identity: Youth and Crisis* by Erik H. Erikson. Copyright © 1968 by W. W. Norton & Company, Inc. Used by permission of W.W. Norton & Company, Inc.; **102** B. Carter, and M. McGoldrick, *The Changing Family Life Cycle.* (2nd ed.) Needham Heights, Mass: Allyn and Bacon, 1989; **103-105** "Developmental periods in the eras of early and middle adult-hood" from *The Seasons of a Man's Life* by Daniel J. Levinson, copyright © 1978 by Daniel J. Levinson. Used by permission of Alfred A. Knopf, a division of Random House, Inc. and *The Seasons of a Woman's Life* by Daniel J. Levinson, copyright © 1966 by Daniel J. Levinson. Used by Permission of Alfred A. Knopf, a division of Random House, Inc.; **119** "Table 3.2: Frequently Mentioned Occupations" from *Becoming Adult* by Mihaly Csikszentmihalyi and Barbara Schneider. Copyright © 2000 by Mihaly Csikszentmihalyi and Barbara Schneider. Reprinted by permission of Basic Books, a member of Perseus Books, L.L.C. **Chapter 5 129** Adapted from the Statistics Canada publication, *Canadian Social Trends - Autumn 1997,* Catalogue 11-008, Issue No. 46, pg. 15; **133-134** Adapted from the Statistics Canada publication, *The Daily*, May 12, 1998, Catalogue 11-001, page 13; **135** "Table 4.5: Characteristics of a 'Good Job'" from *Canada's Teens: Today, Yesterday, and Tomorrow.* Copyright © 2001 by Reginald W. Bibby. Reproduced by permission of Stoddart Publishing Co. Limited; **143** Adapted from the Statistics Canada publication, *Education Indicators in Canada,* "Report of the Pan-Canadian Education Indicators Program 1999," Catalogue 81-582, February 2000, pg. 68; **144** Adapted from the Statistics Canada publication, *Education Indicators in Canada,* "Report of the Pan-Canadian Education Indicators Program 1999," Catalogue 81-582, February 2000, pg. 68; **153** The Canadian Press; **154** Leenaars, A. A. (Ed.), *Suicide in Canada.* Toronto: University of Toronto Press, 1998, p. 17; **155** "Preventing Suicide," reprinted with permission of SIEC. **Chapter 6 163** "Marital status of Canadians" created from data published in the Statistics Canada CANSIM II database at http://cansima. statcan.ca/cgi-win/CNSMCGI.EXE, Table 051-0010; **163** Quotation from B. Carter & M. McGoldrick, *The Changing Family Life Cycle*, 2nd ed., Needham Heights, MA: Allyn and Bacon, 1989, p. 210; **164** "Forms of marriage" from *The Living Family: A Canadian Perspective,* 1st ed., by F.E. Jarman. © 1991. Reprinted with permission of Nelson Thomson Learning a division of Thomson Learning. Fax 800-730-2215; **169** "Average age at first marriage," created from data published in the Statistics Canada publications *Marriage and conjugal life in Canada,* Catalogue 91-534, April 1992 and *Canadian Social Trends,* Catalogue 11-008, Spring 2000; **170** "Life table estimates" adapted from the Statistics Canada publication *General Social Survey, 1990*; **171** "Conjugal relationships of Canadian women," adapted from the Statistics Canada publication *Canadian Social Survey,* Catalogue 11-008, Spring 2000; **173** "Why men marry" adapted from Wild, R. (1999). *Why men marry: 150 guys reveal what prompted them to pop the question.* Lincolnwood, Illinois: Contemporary Books, pp. 6-7. Reproduced with permission of The McGraw-Hill Companies; **180** "Views on how being married would change their life" adapted from Ferguson, S.J. (2001), *Shifting the center: understanding contemporary families*, (2nd ed.) Mountain View, CA: Mayfield Publishing Company. p. 166. Reproduced with permission of The McGraw-Hill Companies; **181** "Views on reasons for and against cohabitation" adapted from Ferguson, S.J. (2001), *Shifting the center: understanding contemporary families,* (2nd ed.). Mountain View, CA: Mayfield Publishing Company. p. 166. Reproduced with permission of The McGraw-Hill Companies. **Chapter 7 196** From R.J. Trotter, "The Three Faces of Love," *Psychology Today*, Sept. 1995. Reprinted with permission from Psychology Today Magazine. Copyright © (1986) Sussex Publishers, Inc.; **197** Reprinted courtesy of Helen Harris, University of California; **200** "Murstein's filter theory" from Rice, P.R. (1990). *Intimate relationships, marriages and families.* Mountain View, CA: Mayfield, p. 181. Reproduced with permission of The McGraw-Hill Companies; **201** Quotation from Ferguson, S.J. (2001), *Shifting the center: understanding contemporary families,* (2nd ed.) Mountain View, CA: Mayfield Publishing Company. p. 135; **206** "Nine psychological tasks needed for a good marriage" © 1995-1996 by the American Psychological Association. Adapted with permission. <http://helping.apa.org/family/marriage.html> and from *The Good Marriage* by Judith S. Wallerstein and Sandra Blakeslee. Copyright © 1995 by Judith S. Wallerstein and Sandra Blakeslee. Reprinted by permission of Houghton Mifflin Company. All rights reserved; **214** Table courtesy of Claude Guldner, Professor Emeritus, University of Guelph; **219** Abstract reprinted with permission of the University of North Carolina. **Chapter 8 228-229** Byfield, T. & V. "Does 'love' conquer all?" reprinted with permission of The Report Magazine; **240-241** Reprinted with permission of Norma Fitzpatrick-Bailey; **243** "Table 4.6: Types of violence in marital unions," adapted from the Statistics Canada publication, *Family Violence in Canada: A Statistical Profile 2001,* Catalogue 85-224, June 2001, pg. 39; **247** "Estranged women at greatest risk of spousal homicide, 1991-1999," adapted from the Statistics Canada publication, *Family Violence in Canada: A Statistical Profile 2001,* Catalogue 85-224, June 2001, pg. 33; **248-249** "With friends like feminists…" reprinted with permission of The Report Magazine; **250** "Divorce: Facts, figures and consequences" by Dr. Anne-Marie Ambert, York University, 1998, from the Vanier Institute of the Family web site: www.vfamily.ca/cft/divorce/divorce.htm; **254** Faller, M.B., "After divorce, who gets the friends?" reprinted with permission of The Stamford Advocate/Southern Connecticut Newspapers Inc. **Chapter 9 264** "Canadian families with children living at home," adapted from the Statistics Canada publication, *1996 Census of Population;* **277** "Low income poverty rates after transfers and income taxes for couple families with children," from Sauvé, R. (2002). *The Current State of Canadian Family Finances Report.* Okotoks, AB: People Patterns Consulting; **278** "Infant mortality rates," adapted from the Statistics Canada web site http://www.statcan.ca/english/Pgdb/People/health/health21.htm; **280** "Number of children that women and men intend to have, by age group (1995)," adapted from the Statistics Canada publication, *Canadian Social Trends,* Catalogue 11-008, Spring 1998; **282** "Women's fertility rates,

1986-1997," adapted from the Statistics Canada web site http://www.statcan.ca/english/Pgdb/People/health/health08.htm; **284-285** Adapted from Balakrishnan, T.R., Lapierre-Adamczyk, E., & Krotki,K. (1993). *Family and childbearing in Canada: A demographic analysis.* Toronto: University of Toronto Press; **286** "Proportion of births to unmarried women, 1961-1991" and "Proportion of births to unmarried women, by age of mother, 1961-1991," adapted from the Statistics Canada publication, *Canadian Social Trends,* Catalogue 11-008, Spring 1994; **287** "Percentage distribution of outcomes of teenage pregnancy, Canada, 1974-1994," adapted from the Statistics Canada publication, *Health Reports,* Catalogue 82-003, Winter 1997, Vol. 9, No. 3, pg. 12; **288** "Factors influencing fertility," adapted from the Statistics Canada publication, *Canadian Social Trends,* Catalogue 11-008, Summer 1999; **289-292** "How do parents know when their family is complete?" reprinted with permission of Ann Walmsley; **293** "Percentage of women childless at time of interview and expecting to remain childless by marital status," Table 2.7 from Balakrishnan, T.R., Lapierre-Adamczyk,E., & Krotki,K. (1993). *Family and childbearing in Canada: A demographic analysis.* Toronto: University of Toronto Press. **Chapter 10 305-306** "Cost of raising a girl to age 18" and "Cost of raising a boy to age 18" Manitoba Agriculture and Food, August 2001. http://www.gov.mb.ca/agriculture/homeec/cba28s02.html; **312** "Reversing the brain drain" reprinted with permission of Dr. J. Fraser Mustard; **317** "Who has time for the kids?" reprinted with permission by the Toronto Star Syndicate; **322** "Barbara Coloroso's parenting styles" reprinted with permission by Barbara Coloroso; **325** "Table 1.1: Distribution of Canadian children according to their age and the type of family in which they reside at the time of the survey, Cycle 1 of NLSCY, 1994-95," adapted from the Statistics Canada publication, *Growing Up with Mom and Dad? The intricate family life courses of Canadian children,* Catalogue 89-566, August 1998; **329** "Figure 3: Percentage of children in age groups by parents, usual hours of work and study, Canada, 1988," adapted from the Statistics Canada publication, *Canadian National Child Care Study: Introductory Report.* Catalogue 89-526E, February 1992, pg. 56. **Chapter 11 344-346** "Canada's test of faith," reprinted with permission of Preston Manning; **350-351** "Chretien to hear Calgary youth's divorce concerns," reprinted with permission of The Ottawa Citizen; **354** "Menu from top of Statistics Canada web site," from the Statistics Canada web site: www.statcan.ca/start. html; **358** "Table 3.7: Distribution of poor children aged 0 to 11 years by family type, 1994-1995," adapted from the Statistics Canada publication, *Growing Up in Canada (National Longitudinal Survey of Children and Youth series).* Catalogue 89-550-MPE, November 1996, pg. 34; **363** "Figure S-1: Child maltreatment investigations by level of substantiation in Canada in 1998," from Trocmé, N., et al. *Canadian Incidence Study of Reported Child Abuse and Neglect: Final Report.* Ottawa, Ontario: Minister of Public Works and Government Services Canada, 2001, Cat. H49-151/2000E; **364-365** "No looking away," reprinted with permission from The Globe and Mail; **366** "Figure S-2: Primary category of investigated maltreatment by level of substantiation in Canada in 1998," from Trocmé, N., et al. *Canadian Incidence Study of Reported Child Abuse and Neglect: Final Report.* Ottawa, Ontario: Minister of Public Works and Government Services Canada, 2001, Cat. H49-151/2000E; **367 top** "Figure S-10: Child age and sex in child maltreatment investigations by incidence of investigated maltreatment and by level of substantiation in Canada in 1998," from Trocmé, N., et al. *Canadian Incidence Study of Reported Child Abuse and Neglect: Final Report.* Ottawa, Ontario: Minister of Public Works and Government Services Canada, 2001, Cat. H49-151/2000E; **bottom** "Figure S-14: Caregiver functioning and other family stressors in child maltreatment investigations by incidence of investigated maltreatment and by level of substantiation in Canada in 1998," from Trocmé, N., et al. *Canadian Incidence Study of Reported Child Abuse and Neglect: Final Report.* Ottawa, Ontario: Minister of Public Works and Government Services Canada, 2001, Cat. H49-151/2000E; **369** "Figure S-11: Child functioning in child maltreatment investigations by incidence of investigated maltreatment and by level of substantiation in Canada in 1998," from Trocmé, N., et al. *Canadian Incidence Study of Reported Child Abuse and Neglect: Final Report.* Ottawa, Ontario: Minister of Public Works and Government Services Canada, 2001, Cat. H49-151/2000E; **370** "Spanking case an attack on family," reprinted courtesy of Rory Leishman; **373 top** "Table 3: Number of deaths by selected causes, age and sex, Canada 1997," adapted from the Statistics Canada publication, *Mortality, summary list of causes, 1997 - Shelf Tables,* Catalogue 84F0209, April 2001; **bottom** "Chart 4: Mortality rates, children aged 1 to 14 Canada, 1970-1972 to 1995-1997," adapted from the Statistics Canada

publication, *Health Reports,* Catalogue 82-003, Winter 1999, Vol. 11, No. 3. **Chapter 12 383** "Life expectancy at birth," adapted from the Statistics Canada web site http://www.statcan.ca/english /Pgdb/People/Health/health26.htm; **386** "Population distribution of Canada by age and sex, 1971 and 1996," adapted from the Statistics Canada web site http:// www.statcan.ca/Daily/English/970729/d970729.htm; **387** "Figure 1.1: Cohort differences and the aging process," adapted from McPherson, Barry D. *Aging as a Social Process: An Introduction to Individual and Population Aging.* Toronto: Butterworths Canada Ltd., 1990, p.9. Reprinted with permission of Nelson Thomson Learning, a division of Thomson Learning. Fax 800-730-2215; **390** "Labour force participation rates by age and sex, 1980-2000," adapted from the Statistics Canada publication, *Labour Force Historical Review, 2000,* Catalogue 71F0004; **392** "Mean total hours in work week and weekend work for parents who are employed full time, by stage in the family life cycle," from *Continuity and Change in Marriage & Family,* edited by Jean E. Veevers. © 1991. Reprinted with permission of Nelson Thomson Learning, a division of Thomson Learning. Fax 800-730-2215; **393-395** Reprinted with permission of Dr. Jennifer Newman; **397** "Number of income recipients and their average income in constant (1995) dollars by sex and age groups, for Canada, provinces and territories, 1990-1995," adapted from the Statistics Canada web site http://www.statcan.ca/english/census96 /may12/t1.htm; **398 top** "Percentage of people aged 25-54 providing both unpaid child care and care or assistance to a senior, 1996," adapted from the Statistics Canada web site http://www.statcan.ca/english/kits/Family/pdf/ch3_10e.pdf; **398-399** "The traditional Italian Sistemazione," adapted from *Canadian Families: Ethnic Variations,* ed. by Dr. K. Ishwaran. Toronto: McGraw-Hill Ryerson, 1980, p. 84. Reproduced with permission of The McGraw-Hill Companies; **403** "Table 4: Mean adjusted income by source and income quintile, population 65+, 1980-1990," adapted from the Statistics Canada publication *Analytical Studies Branch Research Paper Series,* Catalogue 11F0018MPE, No. 147; **405** "Growing old in Canada," reprinted with permission of the Toronto Star Syndicate; **406** Reprinted with permission by Dr. Susan McDaniel; **407** "Living arrangement of seniors, 1991," reprinted courtesy of the Vanier Institute of the Family. **Chapter 13 428** Adapted with the permission of Cambridge University Press; **430-432** The Canadian Press; **434-435**

Reprinted with permission of Stephanie Whittaker; **436** "Percentages of husbands and wives reporting 'very satisfying' marriages at difference stages of the life cycle," reprinted with permission of the Canadian Journal of Sociology; **438-439** "Honey, I'm home" – for good: The transition to retirement," reprinted with permission of the Ohio State University Extension; **441-442** Reprinted with permission of Jay Ingram; **443** Adapted with the permission of Cambridge University Press. **Chapter 14 455-456** Reprinted with permission of the Edmonton Journal; **457** Abstract reprinted with permission of Cambridge University Press; **458-460** "Rabbi gives love a second chance," reprinted with permission of the Ottawa Citizen; **461-463** "Job insecurity adds a 'chill factor' to work," reprinted with permission of Judith Timson; **465-466** Reprinted courtesy of the Vanier Institute of the Family; **467** "Just live for today," adapted with the permission of Cambridge University Press; **468** "Grief time line," reproduced by permission of Taylor &

Francis, Inc. http://www.routledge-ny.com; **473-474** Reproduced with permission of the Toronto Star Syndicate; **475** "The impact of Canadian historical events and legislation on various age cohorts," adapted from the Statistics Canada publication, *An analysis of expenditure patterns of the elderly: Cohorts – going through life together,* Research Paper No. 20, 1986; **476** "A greyer Canada of the future," adapted with permission of Footwork Consulting Inc.; **479** "Figure 1: Historical trends in the labour force participation of older males and females," based on data from the Statistics Canada publications, *Historical Statistics of Canada,* Catalogue 11-516, 1983 and *Life Tables, Canada, Provinces and the Territories, 1980-1982,* Catalogue 84-532. **Appendix 484-489** "Young women's expected and preferred patterns of employment and child care." By F. Heather Davey. *Sex Roles: A Journal of Research* (January 1998), reprinted with permission of Kluwer Academic/Plenum Publishers.

Index

A

A Brief History of Time: From the Big Bang to Black Holes, 34

A Generation on Hold, 77

Aboriginal Peoples:
    as family groups, 266–268
    as hunter-gatherers, 13
    early ancestors, 9
    suicide crisis, 153–154

Abuse:
    adult victims, 369
    child, 363, 369–372
    elder, 467–470
    emotional, 366
    granny bashing, 467
    physical, 366
    psychological, 467
    sexually, 366
    verbal, 366

Activity theory of aging, 443

Adams, Michael, 315

Addiction, 269

Adolescence, 12, 58, 62, 72

Adoption, 294–297

Adult Education Survey (1998), 81

Adultery, 173, 238, 250

Adulthood:
    a history of, 382–400
    early period, 126
    end of adolescence, 58
    transition to, 96

Advanced industrial economy, 83

Affective nurturance, 8

Age Affect Man's Belief - Job is Important to Happiness (graph), 129

Age Affect Woman's Belief - Job is Important to Happiness (graph), 129

Age of innocence, 17

Age of majority, 58

Age strata, 386

Aging:
    negative connotation, 439
    theories of, 420–422

Agricultural families, 13

Agriculture, 11, 13

Alaton, Salem, 202–204

Alberta Status of Women Action Committee (ASWAC), 248

Allahar, James, 63, 83

Alzheimer's disease, 475–476

Amato, Paul, 316, 350, 435–436

Ambert, Dr. Anne-Marie, 349

Amphetamines, 197

Anderson, Deborah, 426

Androcentricity, 43

Angus Reid survey, 116–117, 280

Anthropology (def.), 30

Anticipatory socialization, 109

Artificial insemination, 278, 340

Asch, Solomon, 32

Assisted reproductive technologies (ART), 340–345

Autonomous self, 102

Average Age at First Marriage, 1921-1998 (graph), 169

Average amount owed to student loan programs (graph), 144

Average Earnings (table), 133–134

Ayree, Samuel, 393

B

Baby boom echo, 64

Baby boom, 18, 64, 84, 401–403, 470, 477

Baby boomer, 40, 127–128, 387

Baby bust, 64

Goldstein, Daniel, 207

Goldstine, Hilary, 207

Goltz, j. Walyter, 476

Gombe, Uganda, 10

Good Marriage: How and Why Love Lasts, 206

Goodall, Jane, 9–10

Goode, William, 4, 21

Gorlick, Carolyne, 347–348

Gottainer, Greg, 326

Gottman, Dr. John, 210–211, 213, 214, 218, 239

Gould, Robert, 108

Grandparents, 333, 400–401, 425

Gray, John, 38

Greenfield, Dr. Dorothy, 342

Greenstein, Theodore N., 219

Grief Time Line (graph), 466

Grieving process, 465

Grigg, Darryl, 393

Grihastha, 96

Growing Old in Canada, Life Expectancy (graph), 405

Growing Old in Canada, Poverty (graph), 405

Guaranteed Income Supplement (GIS), 402

Guldner, Claude, 214–215, 226, 230, 436–437

H

Haddock, Shelly, 393

Halifax explosion, 5

Hall, G. Stanley, 62

Harris, Helen, 197

Harris, Peter (case study), 256–257

Harris, Steven (case study), 295–296

Harris-Vidoni family (table), 19

Hawkes, Rev. Brent, 234

Hawking, Stephen, 34

Hayes, Christopher, 426

Heterogamy,. See Intermarriage

Hetherington, Mavis, 348

Hewitt, W.E., 46

High School and Beyond, 67

Hindu society, 96

Hippie, 61

Historical Trends in the Labour Force (graph), 477

History of the Wife, 191

Hitchcock, Alfred, 190

Holloway, Garth, 136–137

Homelessness, 147–150

Homeostasis, 128

Homogamy, 193

Homosexuality, 233

Hordes, 10

House of Commons Health Committee, 343

Household (def.), 6

How 1995 Graduates Found a Job (table), 86

Howarth, Glennys, 465

Howe, Brian, 371

Hudson Bay Company, 167, 267

Human Rights Act (1977), 130

Hunter-Gatherers, 10–13, 166, 266–268

Hutterites, 139

Hyphenated Canadians, 232

Hypothesis, 46, 47

I

Identity, 98

Identity: Youth and Crisis, 101

Immigration, 21, 139, 351–353

Impact of Canadian Historical Events and Legislation on Various Ahe Cohorts (graph), 473

In a Different Voice, 100

In vitro fertilization, 278, 340